THE ROUTLEDGE HANDBOOK OF CONSUMER BEHAVIOUR IN HOSPITALITY AND TOURISM

Consumer behaviour is one of the most explored topics in tourism and hospitality marketing, interchangeably denoted by the terms 'traveller behaviour', 'tourist behaviour' or 'guest behaviour'. Consumer behaviour acts as an origin for every tourism and hospitality marketing activity. It offers an understanding of why people tend to choose certain products or services and what sort of factors influence them in making their decision. The decision process of buying tourism products or services takes time, because they are mostly intangible in nature due to which there are many risks involved in their buying process.

The Routledge Handbook of Consumer Behaviour in Hospitality and Tourism aims to explore and critically examine current debates, critical reflections of contemporary ideas, controversies and pertinent queries relating to the rapidly expanding discipline of consumer behaviour in hospitality and tourism. The *Handbook* offers a platform for dialogue across disciplinary and national boundaries and areas of study through its diverse coverage. It is divided into six parts: Part I offers an overview of consumer behaviour; Part II focuses on the service quality perspectives of consumer behaviour; Part III deliberates on customer satisfaction and consumer behaviour linkages; Part IV explores the re-patronage behaviour of consumers; Part V addresses the vital issues concerning online consumer behaviour; and Part VI elaborates upon other emerging paradigms of consumer behaviour. Although there is no dearth of empirical studies on different viewpoints of consumer behaviour, there is a scarcity of literature providing conceptual information. The present *Handbook* is organised to offer a comprehensive theoretical body of knowledge narrating consumer behaviour, especially for hospitality and tourism businesses and operations. It attempts to fill this research gap by offering a 'globalised' volume comprising chapters organised using both practical and academic approaches.

This *Handbook* is essential reading for students, researchers and academics of Hospitality as well as those of Tourism, Marketing, International Business and Consumer Behaviour.

Saurabh Kumar Dixit is an Associate Professor and Founding Head of the Department of Tourism and Hotel Management, North-Eastern Hill University, Shillong (Meghalaya), India. He holds a Bachelor's degree in Hotel Management and Catering Technology, a Master's degree in Tourism Management and a Doctorate (PhD) in Hotel Management. His research interests include Consumer Behaviour, Service Marketing, Consumer Loyalty and Guest Satisfaction in hospitality and tourism contexts. He has worked for more than 15 years in a number of Indian universities/educational institutes and has also successfully completed different research projects relating to hospitality and tourism management. He has written seven books on diverse themes of tourism in addition to many research papers. He is an editorial board member of several scientific journals, and is also an active reviewer for many international journals such as the *International Journal of Contemporary Hospitality Management*, *Tourismos* and *Anatolia*.

THE ROUTLEDGE HANDBOOK OF CONSUMER BEHAVIOUR IN HOSPITALITY AND TOURISM

Edited by Saurabh Kumar Dixit

LONDON AND NEW YORK

First published 2017 by Routledge

2 Park Square, Milton Park, Abingdon, Oxfordshire OX14 4RN

52 Vanderbilt Avenue, New York, NY 10017

Routledge is an imprint of the Taylor & Francis Group, an informa business

First issued in paperback 2020

British Library Cataloguing in Publication Data
A catalogue record for this book is available from the British Library

Library of Congress Cataloging in Publication Data
Title: The Routledge handbook of consumer behaviour in hospitality and tourism/edited by Saurabh Kumar Dixit.
Other titles: Handbook of consumer behaviour in hospitality and tourism
Description: Abingdon, Oxon; New York, NY: Routledge, 2017. |
Includes bibliographical references and index.
Identifiers: LCCN 2016044666| ISBN 9781138961678 (hardback) |
ISBN 9781315659657 (ebook)
Subjects: LCSH: Hospitality industry—Customer services—Handbooks, manuals, etc. | Tourism—Customer services—Handbooks, manuals, etc. |
Consumer behavior—Handbooks, manuals, etc. | Travelers—Psychology—
Handbooks, manuals, etc. | Tourists—Psychology—Handbooks, manuals, etc.
Classification: LCC TX911.3.C8 R68 2017 | DDC 647.94—dc23
LC record available at https://lccn.loc.gov/2016044666

ISBN: 978-1-138-96167-8 (hbk)
ISBN: 978-0-367-66006-2 (pbk)

Typeset in Bembo
by Keystroke, Neville Lodge, Tettenhall, Wolverhampton

Dedicated to my wife, Seema Dixit, without whose support the *Handbook* would not have been possible, and to the (loving) memory of my grandfather, Sant Ram Dixit

CONTENTS

Contents

Contents

FIGURES

TABLES

CONTRIBUTORS

Vedat Acar is a professional tourist guide and research assistant in the Department of Tourist Guiding at Adnan Menderes University, Turkey. Prior to joining the university in 2012, he worked as a tourist guide for three years. Mr Acar conducts research in the field of tourist guiding, leadership in tourism, rural tourism and tourist behaviour.

Samuel Adeyinka-Ojo obtained his PhD in Hospitality and Tourism from Taylor's University, Malaysia. He teaches hospitality and tourism courses in the Department of Marketing at Curtin University Sarawak, Malaysia. His research interests focus on tourism destination branding, hospitality marketing, visitor behaviour, food festivals, and sustainable rural and ecotourism destinations.

Melissa A. Baker is an Assistant Professor in the Department of Hospitality and Tourism Management in the Isenberg School of Management, University of Massachusetts Amherst, USA. She is an award-winning teacher and currently teaches courses in foodservice management and service experience management. Her research has been published in top-tier hospitality and marketing journals and focuses on service failure and recovery, customer complaining, and appearance and impression formation.

Ronnie Ballantyne is a Lecturer in Marketing, Glasgow School for Business and Society, Glasgow Caledonian University, UK; and Associate Professor of Marketing, IAE, University of Nice, France. His research interests include consumer behaviour and branding.

Ali Bavik is an Assistant Professor at the Institute for Tourism Studies (IFT), Macau. Bavik completed his PhD at the University of Otago, New Zealand, and his undergraduate studies at Eastern Mediterranean University, Northern Cyprus. His research interests are in the area of hospitality marketing and hospitality management, specifically, nepotism, organisational culture, consumer behaviour, job satisfaction and employee performance management.

John Bowen is a Professor at the University of Houston, Texas, USA. He is co-author of *Marketing for Hospitality and Tourism*, the leading hospitality marketing textbook. His publications have been recognised three times as the best article in hospitality and tourism in the year they were published. He has received the prestigious John Wiley and Sons Award, recognising lifetime research. His research interests include customer satisfaction, customer loyalty and co-creation.

Joan Carlini is a Lecturer in Marketing at Griffith University, Queensland, Australia. She has extensive experience in face-to-face and online teaching, with research interests including corporate social responsibility, branding, consumer behaviour and tourism. Her industry experience includes more than 10 years in roles such as international marketing, online marketing and hospitality.

Jennifer Kim Lian Chan is Professor and Head of the BIMP-EAGA Tourism Development Unit, Faculty of Business, Economics and Accountancy, Universiti Malaysia Sabah. She has a PhD in Tourism and Hospitality Management from University of Strathclyde, Scotland, UK. Her research interest areas include sustainable tourism, hospitality human resource development, consumer behaviour in tourism and hospitality, service experience management, and qualitative and mixed methods in tourism research. She has published more than 20 journal articles, 5 books and 12 book chapters related to tourism and hospitality management.

Valentina Della Corte is Associate Professor of Business Management at the University of Naples Federico II, Italy. Author of books, book chapters and numerous publications in national and international academic journals, her research focuses on strategic management and marketing and in particular resource-based theory, business networks and coopetition, dynamic capabilities, value creation and appropriation both intra-firm and inter-firm, and innovative marketing in tourism and heritage.

Saurabh Kumar Dixit is an Associate Professor and Founding Head of the Department of Tourism and Hotel Management, North-Eastern Hill University, Shillong (Meghalaya), India. He holds a Bachelor's degree in Hotel Management and Catering Technology, Master's degree in Tourism Management and Doctorate degree (PhD) in Hotel Management. His research interests include Consumer Behaviour, Service Marketing, Consumer Loyalty and Guest Satisfaction in hospitality and tourism contexts. He has worked for more than 15 years in a number of Indian universities/educational institutes and has also successfully completed different research projects relating to hospitality and tourism management. He has written seven books on diverse themes of tourism in addition to many research papers. He is an editorial board member of several scientific journals, and is also an active reviewer for many international journals such as the *International Journal of Contemporary Hospitality Management*, *Tourismos* and *Anatolia*.

David Drewery is a PhD student in the Department of Recreation and Leisure Studies at the University of Waterloo, Ontario, Canada. His research focuses on experience quality for leisure services. This includes a focus on experience co-creation from both management and consumer perspectives.

Erdogan Ekiz is an Associate Professor at the Tourism Institute, King Abdulaziz University, Jeddah, Kingdom of Saudi Arabia, where he serves as Head of the Travel and Tourism Department. He completed his PhD on Tourism and Hospitality Management from the School of Hotel and Tourism Management at Hong Kong Polytechnic University. He is a 'Certified Hospitality Educator', 'Qualified Learning Facilitator' and 'Advanced Trainer'.

Jörg Finsterwalder is an Associate Professor of Marketing in the Department of Management, Marketing and Entrepreneurship at the University of Canterbury, New Zealand. His research interests include co-creation of services, customer-to-customer interactions, group services, consumer tribes, value networks and service (eco)systems, customer experiences, disasters and services, film and the airline industry.

Xavier Font is Professor in Sustainability Marketing at the School of Hospitality and Tourism, University of Surrey, UK. His research focuses on understanding reasons for pro-sustainability behaviour and market-based mechanisms to encourage sustainable production and consumption.

Anestis Fotiadis is a member of the academic teaching and research staff of the College of Communication and Media Sciences of Zayed University in Abu Dhabi, UAE. He has published more than 70 research papers in international academic journals and conferences along with books and book chapters. He researches and lectures in the fields of rural tourism, sustainable development, small-scale sport event management and marketing.

Sarah Gardiner has a PhD in Marketing and is a Senior Lecturer in Tourism at Griffith University, Queensland, Australia. Prior to that, she worked for over 15 years in the private and government sectors of tourism. Her research has been published in leading tourism academic journals and she regularly undertakes consultancies for industry.

Giovanna Del Gaudio has a PhD in Tourism Business Science from University of Naples Federico II, Italy. Her research focuses on tourism destinations, value creation and value capture with applications of the resource-based view in the interconnected tourism industry. She is the author of several book chapters and articles in national and international journals.

Gaitree (Vanessa) Gowreesunkar completed her PhD in the field of tourism, marketing and communication. She is a Lecturer and researcher by profession. She is an Associate Editor of the *Journal of Media and Communication Studies* (USA) and forms part of the advisory board of the *Journal of Tourism and Leisure Studies*. She is a senior member at the International Economic Research Development Centre, Hong Kong and a research member of the Centre of Tourism Research and Development, India. She is the vice president of the African Network for Policy Research and Advocacy for Sustainability (www.anpras.org) and also serves the Women and Gender Cluster of the African Union. She has had a number of publications in international academic journals and publishes for local and international newspapers. Her research interest is not limited to tourism, marketing, communication and entrepreneurship.

Ulrike Gretzel is a Professor of Tourism in the Business School at the University of Queensland, Australia. She received her PhD in Communications from the University of Illinois at Urbana-Champaign. Her research focuses on persuasion in human–technology interaction, information search and processing, big data, adoption and use of social media, interorganisational information systems, and other issues related to the development and use of intelligent systems in tourism.

Priyanko Guchait is an Assistant Professor at the Conrad N. Hilton College of Hotel and Restaurant Management at the University of Houston, Texas, USA. His research interests include error management, learning, service failure and recovery, and team effectiveness.

Renata Fernandes Guzzo is a PhD candidate at Conrad N. Hilton College of Hotel and Restaurant Management, University of Houston, Texas, USA, and a former hospitality professor at Senac Porto Alegre College, Brazil. She has published and presented papers about lodging management and operations, strategic management, corporate social responsibility and green marketing, her main areas of research interest.

C. Michael Hall is a Professor in Marketing in the Department of Management, Marketing and Entrepreneurship at the University of Canterbury, New Zealand. He is co-editor of *Current Issues in Tourism* and has published widely in areas of tourism, gastronomy, and environmental history and change.

Robert J. Harrington is a Professor of Hospitality and Wine Business Management at Carson College of Business, Washington State University – Tri-Cities Campus, USA. His research interests include hospitality strategic management, hospitality and culinary innovation, culinary tourism, consumer behaviour, and food and wine/drink pairing.

Alana Harris holds a PhD from James Cook University, Australia in Tourism Marketing and is Manager, Academic Programs at the Hotel School Melbourne, Southern Cross University, Australia. Her research interests include communication, particularly word-of-mouth (WOM) and eWOM, social networks, mobility and destination marketing.

Azizul Hassan is a member of the Tourism Consultants Network of the UK Tourism Society, and is currently working towards a PhD at Cardiff Metropolitan University, UK. His main areas of research are technology-supported marketing in tourism, innovative marketing dynamics, destination branding in tourism, cultural heritage tourism, heritage interpretation, and sustainable management/marketing alternatives for cultural heritage industries.

Ann Hindley is a Senior Lecturer in Tourism Management at the University of Chester, UK. Her research focuses on consumer behaviour aspects of climate change and tourism and the use of projective techniques to avoid social desirability bias.

Clare Hindley is a Professor at IUBH School of Business and Management, Bad-Honnef Bonn, Germany. She has varied international experience in education and business with language, culture and communication as the guiding lights. Her research work is increasingly focused on the world of hospitality and tourism with particular interest in education, culture and sociology.

Kai Jiang is a PhD candidate in the Department of Recreation and Leisure Studies at the University of Waterloo, Ontario, Canada. Her research interests are concerned with understanding motivations of mega-sport event volunteers.

Camille Erika Kapoor is currently a PhD candidate and former Lecturer at the Conrad N. Hilton College of Hotel and Restaurant Management, University of Houston, Texas, USA. She has extensive experience in marketing and finance, including working as a consultant at PKF Consulting and a financial/marketing analyst at Gulf South Pipeline. She returned to Hilton College in 2009 to coordinate special projects for Dean John Bowen, including the 40th anniversary of Hilton College and grand reopening of the Hilton University of Houston, which was attended by alumni, industry partners and Houston Mayor Annise Parker. She is the recipient of the 2013 Donald Greenaway Teaching Excellence Award and has researched and published in the areas of generational differences/diversity and marketing consumer behaviour and loyalty. She currently advises organisations on managing generational differences in the workplace and enhancing product/service pricing. She has helped create the learning modules for the MID (Manager in Development) Program recently launched by the Club Managers Association of America (CMAA). She has taught a variety of subjects, including graduate research methods, marketing and hospitality finance, and business law.

Azilah Kasim is a Professor at the School of Tourism, Hospitality and Environmental Management, Universiti Utara Malaysia, Sintok, Kedah, Malaysia. She obtained her Bachelor's degree from Brock University, Ontario, Canada, her Master's degree from Michigan State University, USA and her Doctoral degree from the University of East Anglia, UK. She is currently a national/regional representative and board member for the Asia Pacific Tourism Association (APTA) and an associate research fellow for the Brunei Indonesia Malaysia Philippines – East ASEAN Growth Area (BIMP-EAGA) division, Universiti Malaysia Sabah. She is also on the Advisory Board of the *Asia-Pacific Journal of Innovation in Hospitality and Tourism (APJIHT)* and an active ad hoc reviewer for many international journals in her field. Her research interests include corporate social responsibility, corporate environmentalism, environmental management, hotel management and tourism marketing.

Finlay Kerr is Guest Lecturer in Marketing, Glasgow School for Business and Society, Glasgow Caledonian University, UK. His research interests include marketing strategy and branding.

Catheryn Khoo-Lattimore holds a PhD in Marketing from the University of Otago, New Zealand, was a Fulbright Scholar for the year 2013/2014, and currently teaches in the Department of Tourism, Sport and Hotel Management at Griffith University, Australia. She researches in tourist behaviour, and issues surrounding women and families as travellers.

Stella Kladou is a Senior Lecturer in Hospitality and Tourism Marketing Management at Sheffield Hallam University, UK and serves also as a Visiting Associate Professor at Boğaziçi University, Turkey. She has published in both indexed academic journals and books of prominent international publishers (e.g. Elsevier, Emerald, CABI) and presented at well-esteemed international conferences. She has also been involved in nationally – and internationally – financed marketing, cultural and tourism development projects. Her research interests include place branding, consumer behaviour, cultural tourism, and tourism and hospitality marketing.

Bonita M. Kolb has researched how marketing concepts can be used by both the tourism and creative sectors for the past 15 years. She has written six books including *Marketing for Cities and Towns: Using Branding and Events to Attract Tourists* and *Entrepreneurship for the Creative and Cultural Industries*. Having taught in both the USA and Europe, she now resides in Nashville, Tennessee as a full-time author.

Jeynakshi Ladsawut is a Lecturer in the Department of Management at Charles Telfair Institute, Moka, Mauritius. Her research is focused on tourism and hospitality marketing, with major interests in trust in social media, tourist satisfaction and tourist loyalty, consumer behaviour and marketing activities. She is undertaking her PhD at the University of Mauritius.

Kuan-Huei Lee is Assistant Professor in the Hospitality Business Programme at Singapore Institute of Technology. Her research areas include hospitality management, food tourism and food tourist behaviours. She has published papers in many academic journals including *Tourism Management*, *Annals of Tourism Research* and *Current Issues in Tourism*.

Shanshi Li is a PhD candidate in Tourism with the University of Queensland Business School, Australia. His research interests are tourism marketing and the use of psycho-physiological research methods.

Aijing Liu is an Assistant Professor at Shandong University, Weihai Campus, China. Her research interests include tourism marketing, travellers' behaviours and pro-environmental behaviour in travelling. She has published in peer-reviewed journals and international conferences.

Poh Theng, Loo holds a PhD in Hospitality and Tourism from Taylor's University, Malaysia. She is currently working as Assistant Professor in the Department of International Tourism and Hospitality in I-Shou University, Taiwan. Her research interest areas are customer complaint, service failure, service recovery, emotional labour and complaint handling.

Sandra Maria Correia Loureiro is a Professor and researcher and has published several papers in a variety of peer-reviewed journals that include *International Journal of Hospitality Management*, *Journal of Travel and Tourism Marketing*, *Current Issues in Tourism* and *Journal of Service Management*. Her work has also been presented at several international conferences (where she also acts as track chair and session chair). She has won awards for Best and Outstanding papers. Her current research interests include consumer–brand relationships and tourism marketing issues.

Emily Ma is a Senior Lecturer at Griffith University, Australia. Her research interests include hotel and restaurant management and organisational behaviour. She has published in top-tier journals such as *Cornell Hospitality Quarterly*, *International Journal of Hospitality Management* and *Journal of Hospitality and Tourism Research*.

Jianyu Ma is a Lecturer at the Shanghai Institute of Tourism, Shanghai Normal University, China. Her research interests include tourism experiences, consumer behaviour and service marketing. Her recent work uses psycho-physiological methods to better understand tourist experiences, such as using mobile eye-tracking technology to examine visitors' visual attention.

Ron McCarville is a Professor in the Department of Recreation and Leisure Studies at the University of Waterloo, Ontario, Canada. His research interests include marketing, management, consumer behaviour, persuasion and service quality. He has published in journals such as *Journal of Park and Recreation Administration*, *Leisure Sciences* and *Managing Leisure: An International Journal*. He is the author of the textbook *Improving Leisure Services through Marketing Action* and co-editor of the textbook *Leisure for Canadians*.

Keith H. Mandabach has been a Professor (since 1998) in the School of Hotel, Restaurant and Tourism Management (SHRTM) at New Mexico State University in Las Cruces, New Mexico, USA. He teaches hotel/hospitality classes and regularly speaks at academic and trade conferences in the USA and Europe. He has published 35 articles in both scholarly and trade journals concerning hotel/restaurant management.

Korstanje Maximiliano is Reader in the Department of Economics, University of Palermo, Argentina, Visiting Research Fellow at CERS, University of Leeds, UK, and Editor-in-Chief of the *International Journal of Safety and Security in Tourism* and *International Journal of Cyber-warfare and Terrorism*. He is the author of *A Difficult World: Examining the Roots of Capitalism* and editor of the book collection *How Does Terrorism Affect our Daily Lives?* He has published almost 800 papers and works and 27 books which led him to be nominated to five honorary doctorates for his contributions on the impacts of terrorism in society.

Frans Melissen is Professor of Sustainable Business Models at the Academy of Hotel and Facility Management, NHTV Breda University of Applied Sciences, the Netherlands. In his research, he focuses on the link between human behaviour and sustainable development, with a special focus on mitigating social dilemmas through developing and applying sustainable business models.

Roberta Minazzi, PhD in Marketing and Communication, is Assistant Professor of Tourism Marketing at the University of Insubria, Como, Italy. Her research interests are in social media marketing, electronic word-of-mouth, service quality management, and destination management and marketing. She is the author of papers published in national and international journals.

Luiz Moutinho is Professor of Bio Marketing and Futures Research at the DCU Business School, Dublin City University, Ireland. Previously, and for 20 years, he held the Foundation Chair of Marketing at the Adam Smith Business School, University of Glasgow, Scotland, UK. He completed his PhD at the University of Sheffield, UK in 1982. He is the Founding Editor-in-Chief of the *Journal of Modelling in Management* (*JM2*) and holds four Associate Editorships as well as being on the Editorial Boards of another 46 international academic journals. His areas of research interest encompass bio-marketing, neuroscience in marketing, EMOWEAR (a wearable tech device that detects human emotions), evolutionary algorithms, human–computer interaction, the use of artificial neural networks in marketing, modelling consumer behaviour, marketing futurecast, and tourism and marketing. Other primary areas of his academic research are related to modelling processes of consumer behaviour. He has had over 140 articles published in refereed academic journals, 29 books, more than 8,200 academic citations, an h-index of 43 and an i10-index of 137.

Christy Yen Nee Ng is a Visiting Assistant Professor at the Institute for Tourism Studies (IFT), Macau. She received her BSc in Business Administration and her MSc and PhD in Hospitality Administration at Oklahoma State University, USA. She has research interests in relationship marketing, customer satisfaction, job satisfaction and service quality.

Henrique Fátima Boyol Ngan is Lecturer in the Faculty of Business Management at the Institute for Tourism Studies (IFT), Macau. His MSc is from the University of Coimbra, Portugal. His research interests are in the area of organisational behaviour, performance judgement, psychology of advertising and neuropsychology in marketing.

Robin Nunkoo is an Associate Professor in the Department of Management, University of Mauritius, Reduit, Mauritius. He holds a PhD from the University of Waterloo, Canada and has research interests in political economy, sustainable tourism, and tourism policy and planning. He is the Associate Editor for *Journal of Hospitality Marketing and Management* and an editorial board member of several leading journals.

Ana Oliveira-Brochado holds a BS in Economics, an MS in Quantitative Methods and a PhD in Management from the University of Porto, Portugal. She is Professor of Marketing, Coordinator of the PhD in Tourism Marketing, and Vice Dean at ISCTE Business School, Lisboa, Portugal. Her main research interests are hospitality and tourism management and service quality assessment.

Michael C. Ottenbacher is a Professor in Hospitality Management and Marketing at Heilbronn University, Germany. His research interests include innovation, culinary tourism, restaurant management, strategic management and consumer behaviour.

Luke R. Potwarka is an Assistant Professor in the Department of Recreation and Leisure Studies at the University of Waterloo, Ontario, Canada. His research interests focus on consumer behaviour and sport participation legacies associated with mega-sport events.

Girish Prayag is a Senior Lecturer in Marketing in the Department of Management, Marketing and Entrepreneurship at the University of Canterbury, New Zealand. He received his PhD in Tourism Management from the University of Waikato, New Zealand. His research interests are related to emotional experiences of tourists, tourism market segmentation and destination marketing.

Bruce Prideaux is Professor of Sustainable Tourism at the Cairns campus of Central Queensland University, Australia where he heads the Centre for Tourism and Regional Opportunities. He has published over 300 journal articles, chapters and refereed conference papers. His main areas of interest include sustainability, climate change, tourism in protected areas, mobilities, innovation, remote area tourism and tourism crisis management.

Aparna Raj is Professor and former Dean, Commerce and Management, and the Head, Institute of Tourism and Hotel Management, at Bundelkhand University, Jhansi, India. Her areas of interest are tourist behaviour, organizational behaviour, human resource management, training and development, quality management and industrial relations. She has undertaken various research projects sponsored by the Indian Council for Social Sciences Research and the University Grants Commission. She has to her credit 15 books and approximately 50 published research papers in journals and books.

Shirley Rate is Associate Dean of Learning, Teaching and Quality, Glasgow School for Business and Society, Glasgow Caledonian University, UK. Her research interests include advertising and promotion.

Paulo Rita holds a PhD in Marketing from Cardiff University, UK and has a Post-Doctorate in E-Marketing from the University of Nevada Las Vegas, USA. He is Professor of Marketing at IBS–ISCTE Business School, Lisbon, Portugal, and a member of the Business Research Unit (BRU-IUL) and Magic Research Center at NOVA IMS, Universidade Nova de Lisboa. He is Director of the PhD in Marketing of ISCTE-IUL, and Director of the Master's in Hospitality and Tourism Management which is a double degree with the University of Central Florida, Orlando, USA. He is currently a member of the Executive Committee of EMAC (European Marketing Academy) and Vice President of EDAMBA (European Doctoral Programmes Association in Management and Business Administration). His areas of scientific research interest and expertise are in consumer behaviour, e-marketing/business intelligence and tourism marketing. He has published in international journals within these three areas such as *Journal of Business Ethics*, *Journal of Business Research*, *European Journal of Marketing*, *Journal of Marketing Communications*, *Decision Support Systems*, *Expert Systems with Applications*, *Neural Computing and Applications*, *Annals of Tourism Research* and *International Journal of Hospitality Management*.

Eduardo Moraes Sarmento is Associate Professor at University of Lusophone of Humanities and Technology (ULHT) and CEsA Research Unit (ISEG/University of Lisbon), and a researcher/consultant in the field of Tourism and Economy. He has published several papers in journals and international conferences. As a consultant he has conducted several market studies and studies for the international projection of Portugal as a tourism destination. His current research interests include tourism marketing and economic issues.

Noel Scott is Professor and Deputy Director of the Griffith Institute for Tourism at Griffith University, Gold Coast, Australia. His research interests include the study of tourism experiences, destination management and stakeholder organisation. His recent work has examined the design of tourism experiences in visitor attractions and how to create stronger memories through emotion, co-creation, and use of symbols, myths and legends.

Hugues Séraphin holds a PhD from the Université de Perpignan ViaDomitia, France. He joined the University of Winchester Business School, UK in 2012. He has been teaching for over 10 years, having started his career as a lecturer in French at Golden Hillock School, Birmingham, UK, and then taught Travel and Tourism at Kingston College, London, UK for six years. He also used to be a visiting lecturer at Normandy Business School, Sup de Co Larochelle, ESC Pau and Université de Perpignan ViaDomitia, France. His teaching and research interests include event management and tourism management.

Neda Shabani is a Graduate Research Assistant at the University of South Florida, Sarasota-Manatee (USFSM), USA. She is interested in conducting research in areas such as augmented reality, technology in hospitality, cybersecurity in hospitality, job burnout in hospitality, marketing technology, diffusion of innovation and job training in hospitality.

Melanie Kay Smith is an Associate Professor in the Department of Tourism, Leisure and Hospitality at the Budapest Metropolitan University of Applied Sciences, Hungary where she specialises in cultural tourism and health tourism. Some of her most recent work focuses on cross-cultural issues in hospitality and tourism, especially in a spa and wellness context.

Marios Sotiriadis is Visiting Professor at University of South Africa and University of Ningbo, China. Formerly he was Professor at TEI of Crete, Greece. He has undertaken a variety of consultancy and research projects for tourism public organisations and private businesses. He is the author of six books and six distance learning manuals. His research and writing interests include management and marketing of tourism destinations and businesses.

Abdullah Tanrisevdi is a Professor in the Department of Tourist Guiding at Adnan Menderes University, Turkey where he has been a faculty member since 1996. His research interests lie in the area of services marketing, special interest tourism and crisis management. In recent years, he has focused on quasi-experimental research designs pertaining to tourist behaviour.

Richard Tresidder is a Lecturer in Marketing at Keele Management School at the University of Keele, Staffordshire, UK. He currently lectures in subjects including retail environments and branding. He holds a PhD in Social Semiotics and a Master's degree in Socio-anthropology; his research interests surround the cultural discourses that inform tourism, hospitality and food marketing.

Anja Treuter is a former student of the University of Heilbronn, Germany. She now works for the Hotel and Restaurant Adler amSchloss in Boennigheim, Germany.

Stelios Varvaressos is Professor at TEI of Athens and tutor at the Hellenic Open University, Greece. He completed his PhD in Tourism Economy at the University of Paris VIII, France. He is the author of seven books, and his research interests include tourism economy, tourism development and tourism marketing.

Chris A. Vassiliadis is an Associate Professor of Marketing at the Department of Business Administration, University of Macedonia, Thessaloniki, Greece, where he teaches marketing courses at postgraduate and graduate levels. His research interests focus on marketing of services and the management of tourist destinations and his work has been published in various international journals and conferences including *Tourism Management*, *Journal of Travel Research*, *The Services Industries Journal*, *Journal of International Tourism Research* and *Journal of Vacation Marketing*. In addition, he is the author of two books.

Giampaolo Viglia is Senior Lecturer in the Faculty of Management at Bournemouth University, UK. His research interests lie in the areas of pricing, consumer anomalies and online reviews. Methodologically, he enjoys both quantitative studies and conducting experiments. His work has been published in a number of international journals, such as *Tourism Management*, *International Journal of Hospitality Management*, *Journal of Economic Psychology* and *The Service Industries Journal*.

Gabrielle Walters is a Senior Lecturer in Tourism at the University of Queensland Business School, Australia. Her primary research interests are in tourist behaviour and in particular tourists' psychological and behavioural responses to tourism marketing.

Adam Weaver is a Senior Lecturer in Tourism Management at Victoria University of Wellington, New Zealand. Originally from Canada, he has resided in New Zealand since 2003. His research has examined the cruise industry, particularly shipboard environments, as well as various aspects of tourism marketing. His recent articles have appeared in scholarly journals such as *Annals of Tourism Research*, *Tourism Analysis* and *Journal of Vacation Marketing*.

Brian Kee Mun Wong holds a PhD from the University of Malaya. His work has been published in top-tier journals, book chapters and international conference proceedings. His main research areas are in tourism, management, marketing and international retirement migration. He is also a reviewer for top-tier journals in these areas.

Roy C. Wood is Professor in Hospitality and Gaming Management and Associate Dean (Curriculum and Teaching) in the Faculty of Business Administration, University of Macau. He has extensive experience in public and private sector hospitality education and training and is the author, co-author, editor or co-editor of some 15 books and over 50 research papers in refereed journals.

Kyung-Hyan Yoo is an Associate Professor of Communication at William Paterson University of New Jersey, USA. Her research focuses on electronic word-of-mouth, online trust, social media communication, persuasive technology, online information search and decision-making, and other issues related to the role of information and communication technology in tourism.

ACKNOWLEDGEMENTS

The *Routledge Handbook of Consumer Behaviour in Hospitality and Tourism* would not have seen the light of day without the continued, sincere, committed, time-bound and generous support of the colleagues who contributed chapters despite their busy academic schedules. They incorporated the suggested comments and modifications with full zeal and vigour within the specified timelines. I sincerely owe a huge debt of gratitude to all the contributors to the *Handbook*. I would also like to express my sincere gratitude to many academic colleagues who strongly supported my initiative to edit the present volume. I am also grateful to different publishers for extending permissions to use their figures in this volume. I wish to express sincere thanks to Emma Travis, Commissioning Editor and Pippa Mullins, Editorial Assistant of Taylor & Francis for their heartfelt support. I would also like to express my word of appreciation for all other members of the Taylor & Francis editorial, production and marketing teams for successful execution of the *Handbook*. I would also like to thank my father and mother for their constant encouragement and motivation. Last, but not least, special thanks go to my wonderful wife, Seema, and my lovely kids, Rakshit and Rayaan, for always keeping me free from other assignments to enable me to dedicate more time for the *Handbook* – 'it is the time now to have fun and enjoyment with them'.

Saurabh Kumar Dixit

INTRODUCTION

Saurabh Kumar Dixit

The success or failure of today's highly competitive business organisations depends largely on the ability for recognising the behaviour of their consumers. This is even more noteworthy for hospitality and tourism businesses, where the products/services because of their unique intrinsic qualities are quite difficult to deal with. Tourism is a complex experiential activity, and tourists not only process cognitive information but also experience emotions which are provoked by the external environment (Lane 1994). Moreover, it is also not possible to anticipate and meet the customers' needs and requirements without accurately understanding the dogma of consumers' behaviour. The essence of the marketing concept is also that organisations achieve their objectives by satisfying customers (Houston 1986). As long ago as 1776 Adam Smith in his book *The Wealth of Nations* recognised the vital importance of consumers to market economies, famously stating that 'consumption is the sole end and purpose of all production' (Smith 1776: 719).

The tourism and hospitality industry is dominated by intangible, perishable and heterogeneous products and services with a high level of human resource interface. As the foundation of marketing in today's global business scenario it's customer satisfaction that differentiates one product from another. In order to make the customers satisfied and loyal, the hospitality and tourism organisations need to understand the needs, motivation, typology and behavioural attitudes of consumers towards the services and products. Most tourism and hospitality organisations have an unsatisfactory representation of their customers, and few study patterns of consumers at the level of detail that is necessary to market their products/services aggressively.

To analyse consumer behaviour and service performance, the services marketing literature can be organised according to a multistage approach. Therefore, consumer behaviour illustrates the significance of understanding and implementing customer desire management and customer relationship management into everyday business workflows. Tourism researchers are striving hard to uncover new-fangled dimensions of consumer behaviour in decision making. Consumer behaviour normally highlights the activities that individuals perform for making the purchase of goods or services. One of the fundamental premises of modern consumer behaviour is that individuals usually purchase products not for what they do, but for what they mean. Therefore, consumers strive to get maximum benefits from their every business transaction. Many researchers feel motivation to be a major determinant underlying their behaviour towards making any purchase decision.

1

Consumer behaviour is treated as a study of individuals, groups or organisations and the processes they use to select, secure, use and dispose of goods, services, experiences and ideas, which are associated with the satisfaction of their needs. The consumer behaviour emphasises more the consumer's experience, re-patronage or satisfaction behaviour rather than the processes involved in creating or delivering the product/service. The marketer needs to realise three related aspects of consumer behaviour: consumer motivations, consumer typologies and the consumer purchasing process. As suggested in the existing body of knowledge, most consumer behaviour models rely on three stages, i.e. pre-purchase or information search, purchase or consumption and post-consumption or evaluation of experience.

Product/service quality, satisfaction, customer loyalty and online behaviour are popular buzzwords used in modern tourism and hospitality businesses. The concept of delivering quality service for ensuring guests' satisfaction to achieve guests' loyalty and subsequent repeat business has always been a normal assumption on the part of many theorists and practitioners (Bowen and Chen 2001). Cronin et al. (2000) indicated that satisfaction is a key construct in consumer behaviour research, which influences both the decision to consume and the retention after consumption. By raising satisfaction or quality standards, companies gradually raise guests' expectation level, which then makes it more difficult and more costly to please them. Due to increasing global market competition, tourism organisations are facing challenges in retaining customers. Tourism researchers always tend to find out the reasons behind tourists' revisits and recommendations for their products/services.

The individual consumer is motivated not only by rational decisions but also by emotions and experiences. During the past few decades, marketing researchers have started to study the emotions driven by products and brands (Holbrook and Hirschman 1982). These studies have examined consumers' emotional responses to advertising (e.g. Derbaix 1995) and the role of emotions in customer satisfaction (e.g. Phillips and Baumgartner 2002); complaining (Stephens and Gwinner 1998); service failures (Zeelenberg and Pieters 1999); and attitudes (Dube et al. 2003).

With the growth of the Internet, mobile technology, e-commerce business and varied marketing models that have invaded the tourism and hospitality businesses, comprehending the nature of consumers has become an intricate task. On the one hand, in order to reduce marketing cost and improve revenue, more and more traditional service providers are beginning to establish Internet channels to sell their products or services directly to customers; on the other hand, the consumer decision-making process is assisted with information about consumers' experiences readily available from online reviews and social media.

The present *Handbook* is conceptualised, planned and organised to reflect the sundry facets of consumer behaviour. Besides elaborating the traditional know-how of the theme, the *Handbook* also illustrates the emerging areas pertaining to consumer behaviour. The first focus of the *Handbook* is on the individuals and the internal psychological processes associated with consumption. The second approach explores consumption by viewing the individual not as an isolated decision-maker, but as a social being subject to influence from others. Finally, the third outlook perceives consumers as reactive to context and consumption environments. These dimensions are deliberated separately in the present volume through different parts/chapters.

In the present *Handbook* an attempt is made to maintain objective and logical coverage of relevant illuminations of consumption behaviour. The volume is divided into 6 parts covering the different manifestations of consumer behaviour spread into 46 chapters. Seventy-six experienced researchers from diverse geographic/academic backgrounds were invited to contribute chapters to the volume on their areas of expertise. The orientation of the *Handbook* is most appropriate for undergraduate, Master's and research students besides the industry professionals dealing with consumers. The interdisciplinary organisation and content of the volume also make it of interest for even non-tourism/hospitality researchers in fields such as marketing, consumer behaviour, management, psychology, international business, sociology, etc. As editor of the *Handbook,* I strongly believe that its diverse and multidisciplinary nature will definitely enrich the existing body of knowledge of consumer behaviour in hospitality, tourism and allied disciplines.

References

Bowen, J. T. and Chen, S.-L. (2001). 'The relationship between customer loyalty and customer satisfaction', *International Journal of Contemporary Hospitality Management*, 13(5): 213–217.

Cronin Jr, J. J., Brady, M. K. and Hult, G. T. M. (2000). 'Assessing the effects of quality, value, and customer satisfaction on consumer behavioural intentions in service environments', *Journal of Retailing*, 76(2): 193–218.

Derbaix, C. (1995). 'The impact of affective reactions on attitudes toward the advertisement and the brand: A step toward ecological validity', *Journal of Marketing Research*, 32(4): 470–480.

Dube, L., Cervellon, M. C. and Han, J. (2003). 'Should consumer attitudes be reduced to their affective and cognitive bases? Validation of a hierarchical model', *International Journal of Research in Marketing*, 20(3): 259–272.

Holbrook, M. and Hirschman, E. (1982). 'The experiential aspects of consumption: Fantasies, feelings and fun', *Journal of Consumer Research*, 9(2): 132–139.

Houston, F. S. (1986). 'The marketing concept: What it is and what it is not', *Journal of Marketing*, 50(2): 81–87.

Lane, B. (1994). 'What is rural tourism?', *Journal of Sustainable Tourism*, 2(1–2): 7–21.

Phillips, D. and Baumgartner, H. (2002). 'The role of consumption emotions in the satisfaction response', *Journal of Economic Psychology*, 12(3): 243–252.

Smith, A. (1776). *The Wealth of Nations*, Harmondsworth: Penguin.

Stephens, N. and Gwinner, K. (1998). 'Why don't some people complain? A cognitive-emotive process model of consumer complaint behaviour', *Journal of the Academy of Marketing Science*, 26(3): 172–189.

Zeelenberg, M. and Pieters, R. (1999). 'Comparing service delivery to what might have been: Behavioural responses to regret and disappointment', *Journal of Services Research*, 2(1): 86–97.

PART I

Overview of consumer behaviour

Part I comprises nine chapters offering introductory insights of the behavioural expressions of consumers. Chapter 1 by Kuan-Huei Lee illustrates the theoretical background of consumer behaviour. To elaborate the concept, internal and external factors, situational and market factors influencing consumer behaviour are dealt with. The chapter further elaborates the psychographic representations of consumer requirements for effective marketing of products. It also evaluates the latest trends in consumer research to collect information for developing useful marketing strategies. In order to highlight the chapter content, a case study on local food and local life experience during the slow food movement is described.

Korstanje Maximiliano and Hugues Séraphin investigate the psychology and sociology of consumption to predict consumers' decision making in chapter 2. The chapter further analyses the changes percolating into tourism consumption from sociology by highlighting the main contributions and limitations of renowned policymakers and practitioners of the field. To underline this the main findings and limitations of the studies of three senior sociologists, who dedicated their lives to studying consumption of tourism, Dean MacCannell, John Urry and Kevin Meethan, are thrashed out.

Chapter 3, authored by Ronnie Ballantyne, Finlay Kerr, Shirley Rate and Luiz Moutinho, looks forward to illustrate the concepts of need recognition and motivation in the consumer decision-making process. Their elaborations try to explore the dynamic process of moving from a basic need and desire to a more fully formed motivation to visit a specific tourism destination or to undertake a particular tourism activity. The chapter further talks about the experience-driven consumers who are popularly called *Prosumers* and *Transumers*.

Jennifer Kim Lian Chan and Azilah Kasim illuminate the factors affecting tourist buying behaviour in chapter 4. The chapter argues that consumer experiences are a distinct offering from services and they create distinct memories and feelings through the sensory, emotional, cognitive and behavioural aspects of the tourists. Tourism and hospitality consumption has hedonic, emotional and imaginary effects of consumption and occupies a central place for influencing consumer behaviour. Other consumption factors such as the personal (buying motives, habits, tourist characteristics), psychological, environmental, situational and the quality of experience also shape the buying behaviour. Hence the chapter scrutinises the concept of experiences and tourist buying behaviour from the decision-making, experiential and behavioural perspectives.

Chapter 5, contributed by Gabrielle Walters and Shanshi Li, scans the psychological construct of tourist behaviour by highlighting the emotional engagement of tourists. It further reviews the recent trends of scientific emotion measurement by presenting the methodological techniques employed by tourism researchers to understand the role and influence of emotion on tourist behaviour. The chapter outlines psychophysiological methods to measure tourists' intuitive and unconscious emotional responses that inspect the correlations between individuals' psychological activities and corresponding physiological reactions such as an increase in heart rate and blood pressure. Psychophysiological measures of emotion can capture the unconscious emotional experiences of the consumers.

Information plays a crucial role in the decisions of consumers, therefore understanding information search behaviour is key to marketing any tourism and hospitality product more effectively. Chapter 6 by Gaitree (Vanessa) Gowreesunkar and Saurabh Kumar Dixit walks around the vital information search behaviours of consumers. Different information search models formulated by different researchers are scrutinised from the hospitality and tourism perspective. The chapter also elaborates the steps involved in the information-seeking procedure, the cost of information and the limitations of information search.

Chapter 7 by Roy C. Wood presents an alternative impression of consumer behaviour, different from its popular view in the existing body of knowledge. He starts the discussion by highlighting reflections of consumer behaviour with respect to hospitality businesses. He further outlines the decision-making process involved in dining out or availing oneself of accomodation in a hotel. To support his deliberations the author employs evidence-based information drawn from a variety of public domain sources.

Ann Hindley and Xavier Font in chapter 8 evaluate the ethical issues of consumer behaviour in travel and tourism. The chapter further throws light on ethical theory by defining ethical consumption and ethical consumerism besides outlining the nature of the ethical business and the ethical consumer. The authors also review the role of society's different actors in promoting ethically responsible consumer behaviour. Finally, the chapter summarises issues of ethical tourism and describes the ethical tourist by offering an explanation of the barriers to behaviour change hindering responsible consumer behaviour.

Chapter 9 by Clare Hindley and Melanie Kay Smith deals with the analysis of cross-cultural theory and research as applied to the tourism and hospitality industry. The chapter enables readers to understand that tourist behaviour is not only affected by motivation, demographics and lifestyle but also through culture and nationality. The case studies on halal tourism, the impact of Generation Y on the hospitality industry and guests of different nationality visiting spa hotels are used to exemplify the significance of these factors for consumer behaviour.

1

CONCEPTUAL FOUNDATION OF CONSUMER BEHAVIOUR

Kuan-Huei Lee

Introduction

The study of consumer behaviour covers the process by which each individual selects, uses and purchases a good or service to fulfil one's own interests or desires. The concept of consumer behaviour includes the marketing of products and services. The essence of marketing is to satisfy consumers' needs, create values and retain customers. Marketing strategies are formulated based on assumptions about consumer behaviour. The research to study consumer behaviour is called consumer research and is a form of market research which tries to understand the reasons why consumers acquire a specific good or service in order to formulate marketing strategies for a specific market.

Although consumers present differences in their purchasing choices, these choices are relatively stable over time, and thus predictable. Since most product and service offerings must be planned well in advance of consumer purchase, marketers need to understand why and how consumers react in any purchase situation. Therefore, the study of consumer behaviour is important to marketers to better design marketing strategies that can create higher consumer value. Consumer value can be perceived as the straightforward relationship between all the benefits a consumer derives from a product or service and all the costs of acquiring those benefits:

$$\text{Value} = \frac{\text{Benefits}}{\text{Costs}}$$

The higher the consumer value, the higher the probability that the customer is satisfied by the product or service. Marketing strategies are formulated based on assumptions about how consumers are aiming to maximize the consumer value. Providing superior consumer value requires the organization to understand, anticipate and react to the consumer's needs before its competitors.

Technology has changed how businesses sell and how consumers buy products, for example the online shop 'Taobao' of China contains over 760 million product listings and generated over US$ 1.5 trillion in 2013. Businesses do not necessarily need a physical space to display products and receive customers. Technology has helped to enhance communication with customers, and collect and analyse data with more efficiency and accuracy.

Overview of consumer behaviour

Consumer behaviour is linked with decision making of each individual by the time to make a consumption choice. Decision making is a process by which the consumer ponders different sets of options to decide upon the best alternative to fulfil his/her consumption need.

After studying a group of 25 consumers in longitudinal research about their vacation decisions, Decrop and Snelders (2005) found the decisions made by consumers are influenced primarily by personal factors, interpersonal factors and situational factors. For Decrop and Snelders, when a consumer makes a decision, it is influenced by the environmental factors (culture, social network and geo-physical environment), which are structural components that include all other factors. Then, the consumer is influenced by primary and secondary personal factors including age, family situation, occupation, personality and lifestyle. Thirdly, personal factors include many interpersonal influences that affect group decision making. Finally, situational factors are key issues when final decisions are made.

In general, there are four types of factors that influence consumer purchase decisions: internal, external, situational and marketing mix (Figure 1.1). Each of these factors is explained below.

Internal factors

Cognitive psychology deals with how people gain, process and store information. Every time that a consumer makes a purchasing decision, the consumer is influenced by his/her own perception, attitude, values and personality. This information is then transformed into knowledge and used to direct the consumer's attention towards behaviour. Fishbein's (1967) behavioural intention model suggests any purchasing action of the consumer towards a

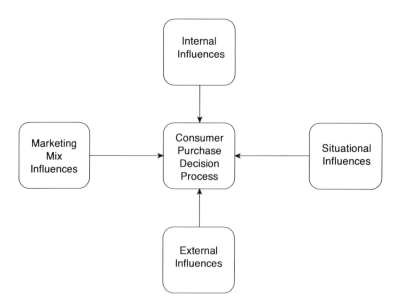

Figure 1.1 Overview of consumer behaviour

Source: Author.

product is brought by his/her own values that formed the knowledge about the product together with prior experience about the product.

External factors

Consumers are influenced by family members, reference groups, social class, cultures and subcultures when making a purchasing choice. The following is an explanation of each of the factors:

1   Family: a family is formed by two or more persons that are linked by blood, marriage or adoption residing together. Family members usually live together and might have strong influence in the decision making of any purchasing item. In a typical household with children, the decision making could exhibit the following patterns:

- Husband-dominated decisions: husband is the primary decision maker
- Wife-dominated decisions: wife has more influence than husband
- Children-dominated decisions: children are the dominant decision maker(s)
- Joint decisions: all members' influence is equal in the decision making
- Autonomic decisions: any member of the family is the primary decision maker.

There is an increasing number of different components to the members of a family; more non-traditional families and non-family households can now be found such as childless couples, unmarried couples, divorced single parents, and gay couples.

2   Reference groups: reference groups are groups that have a high degree of credibility and serve as sources of comparison, influence and norms for individuals' opinions, values and behaviours. Consumers are influenced by how these reference groups think and how they behave. Different reference groups that influence the consumption behaviour of consumers could be friendship groups, shopping groups, virtual communities and advocacy groups.

3   Social class: social class is the division of individuals of a society into a hierarchy of distinct status classes, each individual of the same class having relatively similar status. There is no common standard for how classes should be divided; factors such as life-style, consumption, patterns, hobbies and media exposure can be homogeneous within and heterogeneous among social classes. If using disposable income as the factor to divide social classes, one may distinguish affluent consumers, middle-class consumers and downscale consumers.

4   Culture and subculture: culture is the collective values, norms, customs and beliefs shared among a group of individuals. Culture is often known as the 'invisible hand' that monitors the actions and behaviours of individuals of a particular society. Culture can be expressed in different ways, for example through forms of learning, languages and symbols, rituals, and enculturation and acculturation. A subculture is a specific group that share certain values, beliefs and customs within a larger society. An individual's ethnicity, gender, religion, geographic location or age could be one stem of subculture. Most people belong to more than one subculture group which provides alternative ways to segment the market.

Situational factors

Situational factors are external to the consumer and removed from the characteristics of the product that influence consumer purchase decisions. Many contextual factors affect our choice: one's mood on the day, time pressure when the purchase is taking place and the role of the salesperson might be factors that influence the decision making. With fast access to the Internet, consumers today are much more informed and can find instant feedback from other users online.

A consumption situation that includes the seller, the buyer, a product or service is affected by other factors before, during and after the purchase transaction takes place. By understanding the relationship of these situational factors, marketers can plan accordingly through the marketing mix to reach targeted consumers.

Market factors

The four Ps of the marketing mix are marketing factors controllable by the marketer and consist of the following four elements:

1   Product: a good, service or idea to satisfy the consumer's needs
2   Price: the amount of money which is exchanged for the product
3   Place: a means of getting the product into the consumer's hands
4   Promotion: a means of communication between the seller and the buyer.

Marketers can use different strategies to present these four elements in the marketing mix. There are two different approaches that marketers can use in the product positioning, which refers to the place that the product occupies in the mind of consumers according to specific attributes different to competitors'. The first approach is head-to-head positioning, which is direct competition with competitors on similar product attributes; the second approach is differentiation positioning, presenting the product in a smaller market niche with product attributes different to those of the competitors.

Price is an indicator of value from the consumer's standpoint. The higher the price is, the higher the expectation from consumers towards the product. Pricing has a direct effect on the organization's profit since the decision influences both total revenue and total cost for the firm (Profit = Total Revenue − Total Cost).

The marketing channel is involved in the delivery of the product to consumers. The design of an effective marketing channel depends on how consumers make decisions about the product, the number and dispersion of the consumers, the amount of goods to be sold, the value perceived by consumers, the cost of various channel options, the task that must be performed and competitive practices in the market. Marketers have two main approaches to use: the direct channel or indirect channel. A direct channel means the producer sells the product directly to the consumer without any intermediaries. In an indirect channel, there are one or more intermediaries between the producer and the consumer.

An organization can use five main approaches to communicate with consumers: advertising, personal selling, public relations, sales promotion and direct marketing. Advertising is any paid format of non-personal communication about the organization, product or idea. Personal selling is the two-way flow of communication between the seller and buyer, this flow of communication being designed by the seller to influence the decision making of the buyer. Public relations is a format of communication management that tries to influence the feelings, beliefs or opinions of the buyer and other stakeholders about the organization or its product. Sales promotion refers to a short-term activity offered by the seller to awaken interest in buying the product. In direct marketing, the organization uses direct communication with consumers to generate consumers' response through face-to-face selling, direct mail, catalogues, phone, direct response advertising or online marketing.

Trends in consumer research

Consumer research refers to the process and tools utilized to study consumer behaviour. Consumer research could be considered as a form of market research which tries to link consumers to the marketer through a process to produce information for marketers to identify opportunities for marketing strategies.

One way of conducting consumer research is through psychographics. Psychographics influence an individual's everyday routine, activities, interests, opinions, values, needs and perceptions. The term 'psychographics' was introduced by Demby (1974), blending 'psychology' and 'demographics'. Consumer research is usually linked with psychographics, which through surveys and analytical studies focuses mainly on values, attitudes and market segmentation. Psychographic variables are useful to identify and segment a market. Psychographics register people's activities (what they do), interests (what they want) and opinions (what they think).

There are different formats to segment by psychographics, examples including age, gender, family structure, social class and income, race and ethnicity, geography and lifestyles.

Age

Different products are designed to target different age groups. One common categorization is Gen X, Y and Z where Gen X is the generation born after the post-World War II baby boomers, approximately from the 1960s to 1980s. Gen Y are normally called the millennials and were born between the early 1980s and early 2000s. Gen Z are the cohort born after Gen Y from the 2000s onwards. The same generation tends to share similar values, taste and experiences which are different to those of other generations.

Gender

Differentiation in marketing based on gender starts at a very early age with pink colour representing females and blue for males used in diapers, fragrances and clothes. Toy companies such as Lego and Mattel have gender-specific toys targeting kids of different gender groups.

Family structure

The family/marital status is also a relevant factor for segmentation, the status influencing consumers' spending priorities. Families with young kids have significant expenses in milk, juice and cleaning products that single adults do not.

Social class and income

People in similar social classes have equal social standing and income within the community. The basic categorization is upper, middle and lower social class according to the amount of one's income, power and status in a society.

Race and ethnicity

Different race and ethnic groups have different tastes and preferences. It is common in the United States to differentiate products and marketing plans targeting different ethnic groups: Caucasian Americans, African Americans, Hispanic Americans and Asian Americans.

Geography

Location can became an important segmentation for marketers to tailor and design different marketing plans for consumers living in the same region, state, province or country. For instance, Coca-Cola, Nike and McDonald's commercials and marketing plans are different in Asian countries and European countries.

Lifestyle

Veal (1989) suggested lifestyle is the pattern of individual and social behaviour characteristic of an individual or a group. Although consumers have similar age, gender or income, they might have very different lifestyles. In many circumstances, consumers display their lifestyle through taste and taste becomes the generative formula of lifestyle, where lifestyle can be reflected symbolically in different dimensions such as furniture, clothing, language and/or body hexis.

Big data analytics and the Internet of Things (IoT)

With the rapid development of technology and massive usage of mobile phones and computers, the collection of data has become easier and database marketing using big data analytics is the new trend for marketers, especially in the analysis of large numbers of consumers in a specific market. The enormous amount of data analysed could make predictions of behaviour much more accurate to fulfil the need of consumers.

It is anticipated that big data will transform how we live, work and think; Walmart, Amazon and Netflix are using big data to recommend products to their consumers. Twitter, LinkedIn and Facebook are mapping users' relationships into a social graph to study their preferences.

The Internet of Things (IoT) is an emerging global Internet-based information architecture that facilitates the exchange of products and services. Any object or subject can be embedded with the capability to connect and exchange information over a network. Through IoT, every object that we use daily such as a car, TV, refrigerator and lights can interact and communicate among themselves. The amount of data created through IoT can be used by marketers to assess the behavioural pattern of targeted consumers.

Segmentation by involvement in Slow Food and destination food preference

The Slow Food movement started in the small town of Bra, Italy, where the founder Carlo Petrini was born and raised. The Slow Food movement attracted global attention with the protest in response to the opening of a McDonald's restaurant in the Piazza di Spagna in Rome in 1986. On December 1989, the Slow Food movement was officially established as the International Slow Food Movement for the Defence of and the Right to Pleasure at the Opera Comique in Paris (Laudan 2004). While representatives from only 15 countries signed the initial Founding Protocol Manifesto, there are now 100,000 members in 150 countries around the world.

Arcigola, the Slow Food's first incarnation, emerged from Arci, which was the entertaining and cultural organization of the Italian Communist Party. Arcigola, which means 'arch-tester', was apprehended as an eco-gastronomical wing of Arci in 1983, and was formally established in 1986 after Petrini and Arcigola protested against the opening of the fast food restaurant McDonald's by circulating the English phrase 'slow food'. The phrase became so popular that it constitutes the name of the movement.

The philosophy of Slow Food is 'good, clean and fair'. Schneider (2008: p. 390) explained the philosophy further:

> Good food is tasty and diverse and is produced in such a way as to maximise its flavour and connections to a geographic and cultural region. Clean food is sustainable, and helps to preserve rather than destroy the environment. Fair food is produced in socially sustainable ways, with an emphasis on social justice and fair wages.

The Slow Food association is an international eco-gastronomic organization to recognize the significance of pleasure associated with food. Slow Food values the knowledge of local producers and diversity of places where food is manufactured, local recipes and flavours. It respects the rhythms of the seasons.

A group of 512 participants (Slow Food and non-Slow Food members) were asked to rank their involvement with Slow Food from 1 (strongly disagree) to 7 (strongly agree). The consumer involvement profile (CIP) scale was used in this study to measure Slow Food members' involvement. A list of 10 statements was provided:

1   I find that a lot of my life is organised around *Slow Food*.
2   Most of my friends are in some way connected with *Slow Food*.
3   *Slow Food* offers me relaxation and fun when pressures build up.
4   *Slow Food* is one of the most satisfying things I do.
5   *Slow Food* is one of the most enjoyable things I do.
6   I enjoy discussing *Slow Food* with my friends.
7   I have little or no interest in *Slow Food*.
8   *Slow Food* is very important to me.
9   You can tell a lot about a person when you see them in the *Slow Food* organisation.
10 *Slow Food* says a lot about who I am.

Participants were segmented into three groups based on their level of involvement with Slow Food. Slow Food members were divided into high involvement (HI) and low involvement (LI) groups, while the group of participants without Slow Food involvement constituted the no involvement (NI) group. A composite involvement score was calculated as the mean of the 10 involvement items; item No. 7 was reverse-scored. Participants whose mean involvement score was higher than 5.0 (5 = slightly agree, 6 = agree, 7 = strongly agree) were considered to have high Slow Food involvement (HI). A mean score of 5.0 or below was considered low Slow Food involvement (LI). Participants who were not Slow Food members had zero Slow Food involvement score; these participants were considered the no involvement (NI) group. There were 207 participants in the NI group, 125 participants in the LI group and 212 participants in the HI group.

These three different involvement groups were asked to rate their preferences towards food in the destination according to three factors: (1) engagement with local food activities; (2) eagerness to savour local food; and (3) the degree that members like to get immersed in the local community. The results suggested Slow Food members (both HI and LI) showed stronger interest towards local food than non-members (Figure 1.2). When Slow Food members in this current study arrived at a destination, they practised Slow Food values by eating local food, going to local food markets, searching for small-scale producers and interacting with the local community. Non-Slow Food participants were more averse to local food, more interested in comfortable places, were fast travellers and liked to be involved in many activities.

The results suggest Slow Food members compared with non-members were more open-minded and accept and interact with new culture to a greater degree. Those people who are more open and interact more with local people tend to be more willing to try unfamiliar local food and experience local life. These findings might assist destination managers and marketers to differentiate what kinds of activities and events are likely to attract consumers who are more

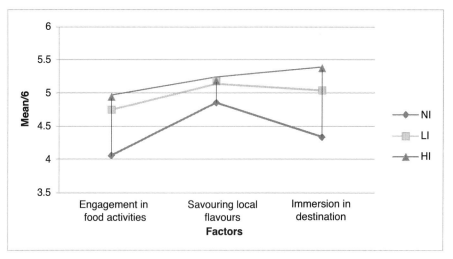

Figure 1.2 Mean comparison of factors between involvement groups

Source: Author.

engaged in traditional food. If a local food event in a destination wants to attract international tourists rather than local consumers, it might be that freelance tourists have a higher interest in attending this event than group tourists with a tour guide. Similarly, international tourists who are interested in local culture may be more eager to taste traditional local food and converse more with native people.

Bibliography

Bourdieu, P. (1990). *The Logic of Practice*, Cambridge: Polity Press.

Decrop, A. and Snelders, D. (2005). 'A grounded typology of vacation decision-making', *Tourism Management*, 26(2): 121–132.

Demby, E. (1974). 'Psychographics and from where it came', in Wells, W. D. (ed.), *Life Style and Psychographics* (pp. 9–29). Chicago, IL: American Marketing Association.

Fishbein, M. (1967). 'Attitude and the prediction of behavior', in Fishbein, M. (ed.), *Readings in Attitude Theory and Measurement* (pp. 477–492), New York: Wiley.

Flow Food Foundation and Biodiversity (2009). *Social Report 2009*, Bra, Italy: The Slow Food Foundation and Biodiversity.

Kerin, R. A., Lau, G. T., Hartley, S. and Rudelius, W. (2013). *Marketing in Asia*, 2nd edition, Maidenhead: McGraw-Hill.

Laudan, R. (2004). 'Slow Food: The French terroir strategy, and culinary modernism: An essay review', *Food, Culture and Society: An International Journal of Multidisciplinary Research*, 7(2): 133–144.

Lee, K.-H., Packer, J. and Scott, N. (2015). 'Travel lifestyle preferences and destination activity choices of Slow Food members and non-members', *Tourism Management*, 46: 1–10.

Mayer-Schönberger, V. and Cukier, K. (2013). *Big Data: A Revolution that Will Transform how We Live, Work, and Think*, New York: Houghton Mifflin Harcourt.

Schiffman, L. G. and Wisenblit, J. L. (2015). *Consumer Behavior*, 11th edition, Harlow: Pearson Education.

Schneider, S. (2008). 'Good, clean, fair: The rhetoric of the Slow Food movement', *College English*, 70(4): 384–402.

Solomon, M. R. (2015). *Consumer Behavior: Buying, Having, and Being*, 11th edition, Harlow: Pearson Education.

Veal, A. J. (1989). 'Leisure, lifestyle and status: A pluralist framework for analysis', *Leisure Studies*, 8(2): 141–153.

Weber, R. H. and Weber, R. (2010). *Internet of Things*, Dordrecht: Springer.

2

REVISITING THE SOCIOLOGY OF CONSUMPTION IN TOURISM

Korstanje Maximiliano and Hugues Séraphin

Introduction

The founding parents of sociology and anthropology have developed a pejorative meaning of market, industrialism and capitalism. As Professor Emile Durkheim puts it, the advance of the industrial ethos would inevitably result in the creation of new institutions and negative effects on the integrity of social scaffolding. Several social pathologies would have been accelerated by the erosion of social trust (Durkheim 1976, 2014). In this respect, Max Weber raised the alarm that the rational logic and its effects of depersonalization would cause irreversible changes for the style of life of Europeans. Rationality which depends on the market will somehow monopolize the culture in order to commoditize consumers (Weber 2009). Unless otherwise resolved, money will mediate between citizens in the same way as language. More recently in the literature, Zygmunt Bauman has suggested that the adoption of consumption as a main value of society paved the ways for workers to become consumed goods (Bauman 2001). Doubtless, the attention which was drawn to the theory of consumption, from the inception of sociology, led towards some conceptual limitations which were univocally accepted by sociologists of tourism. At a first glance, theorists not only developed a romantic view of evolution, where primitive cultures will disappear at the hands of modern ones, but also trivialized the role of fear in the configuration of the modern market. Secondly, consumers are not determined by rational goals, as the literature suggests; rather, they are moved by emotional bases that sometimes are impossible to forecast. This behaviour can be associated with impulsive buying decisions (Hadjali et al. 2012; Beatty and Ferrell 1998). In the first section, entitled 'From production to consumption', we discuss the reason behind the passage from a society of producers to a society of consumers. Secondly, in the 'Consuming tourism' section, three senior sociologists are placed under the lens of scrutiny in order for readers to expand their current view of consuming and tourism. This method can be to some extent compared to the Delphi method characterized by the interpretation of expert responses (Hammond and Wellington 2013). Although the original negative connotation formulated by Durkheim and Weber was carried on by modern sociologists like MacCannell and Urry but not by others like Meethan, the idea that globalized consumption was prone to commoditize cultures, landscapes and peoples nonetheless resonates in the sociology of tourism to date. The present chapter explores the ebbs and flows of the theory of consumption in tourism as well as the most relevant lines of inquiry to be investigated in the coming years. The crux of this discussion is to understand why these scholars have developed a negative connotation of tourism.

From production to consumption

Like sociologists, economists had a bad connotation of consuming theory, not only because of the chaos and social disorganization that uncontrolled consuming generates, but also because it represents a way of destroying wealth. By the upsurge of the 20th century, economists and their different waves have cast serious doubts on the problems of consumption for a productive system, instilling the widespread belief that consumption would somehow bring progress and prosperity for all members of society (Heilbroner 2011). As senior lecturer Kathleen G. Donohue acknowledges, no later than the address of Franklin D. Roosevelt where his four freedoms, which were *fear, speech, religion* and *want,* were declared, economists felt the need to conspire against the society of producers to accept that consumption was a good aspect of the economy. For this and up to the present moment, medieval and classic economies have developed a negative view of consumption. From Ricardo to Smith, scholars validated the concern that consumption would lead to bad habits that jeopardize the organization of labor as well as the rules of internal society. Looking closer, the age of consumers and liberal consumerism was introduced by the belief that the demand was more important than the offer. If the classic economy materialized how significant labour and production are, modernity issued another discourse. Now, government focused its efforts on poverty and its effects on social scaffolding:

> Even when classical liberals turned their attention to eradication of poverty, they continued to emphasize production rather than consumption. If one was entitled to consume only what one had produced, then, classical liberals reasoned, the only way that government could eliminate poverty was by increasing productivity.
>
> *(Donohue 2003: p. 4)*

Theorists of economy observed a paradoxical situation since the frenetic quest for profits pressed societies to adopt a new consumer-oriented system which was prone to produce what 'Others' needed. The idea that production was the only valid way to reach prosperity set the pace for a new paradigm, where consumption would press the supply to offer new products in plenty that otherwise would never have been yielded. Instead of stimulating economy by production, this doctrine offered a different explanation where society will progress if economists stimulate consumption. The growth of the economy undoubtedly would be helpful to prevent disastrous effects of poverty in households. The US was a proxy to face a radical change in the paradigms that ruled its economies. In doing so, the Keynesian policies fit like a glove. Strong regulatory measures as well as welfare programmes disciplined the citizenship to understand the new dilemma of the modern economy, that consumerism is the only valid way for poverty to be eradicated.

Starting from the premise that the wealth of nations was a question of equilibrium, economists thought that the only way to boost the economy of a country was at the cost of another country. In this viewpoint, a strong commercial relationship among nations should be organized in view of trade. Whenever exports supersede imports the economy rises. However, consumption was one of the main threats to well-being simply because it reduces the goods available for exporting. Here is one of the ideological pillars of modern capitalism (Donohue 2003) that explained the current disposition for globalizing trends and economies.

After 1940, *this freedom from want* was associated to one of the human basic needs and expanded to the world as an unquestionable right of citizens. Additionally, the financial crisis in 1930 paved the pathways for nations to embrace this paradigm without resistance. Liberals formulated 'the new deal of liberalism' to transform American society, even mingling the discourse of consumption with democracy. As Donohue puts it:

> This new liberal system was not without its detractors. Critics became increasingly concerned that freedom from want was being equated with a right of plenty. And they worried that material plenty was being treated as a precondition of democracy.
>
> *(Donohue 2003: p. 277)*

Ideologically, Americans have felt 'superior' to other nations because they are enthralled as the main democratic and prosperous society; although more egalitarian at the surface, American citizens are subject to more work and consumption but less leisure. Worker unions and workers not only enjoy vacation and tourism, but also are subject to a plentiful supply of products that are visually sold by television (advertising). This happens because, in a pro-consumer society, workers are bombarded with emulation and advertising creating needs to buy. This not only jeopardized their real liberty to choose, but seriously affects democracy. Detractors of capitalism, who directed their focus on the arbitrariness of producers, were involuntarily responsible or conducive to the formation of a global society of consumers. Those denunciations of an economy that protects the interests of producers as well as the need to adopt consumption to break the material asymmetries among classes, were two guiding concepts to embrace a globalized version of capitalism, prone to mass-consumption. Taking a closer look, Donohue explains that if the current system of consumption was a result of the fear some left-wing scholars faced after experiencing one of the worst financial crises of world history, this begs a more than interesting question: Is fear rooted in the logic of the market?

Consuming tourism

For reasons we have already discussed, the theory of consumption in tourism fields is multilayered but reaches some interesting places. From sociology to marketing, many voices have focused on consumption as one of the pillars of globalized tourism (Richards 1996; Hall and Williams 2013; Woodside and Dubelaar 2002; Tzanelli 2004). The recent technological breakthroughs after WWII conjoined to substantial working benefits and resulted in mass-tourism. On this complex background, the sociology of tourism draws its attention to understand the main guidelines of modern consumption, an idea inscribed in how or what people consume, and what are their preferences, hopes and fears (Woodside and King 2001; Korstanje and George 2012). Considered as an economic-centred activity, academia developed a great interest in consumption. Although many scholars have focused on this issue, in this chapter we discuss only three of them, which to our end are the most authoritative voices: Dean MacCannell, John Urry and Kevin Meethan. No less true is that other important sociologists have studied tourism but with less focus on consumption than them. If MacCannell (1976) delves into staged-authenticity and alienation as the main bulwarks of his project, Urry (2002) understands that tourism is defined by economies of sign, which are determined by symbolic allegories, while Meethan (2004) emphasizes the genealogy of tourism that mediates between self and its sense of place. Whatever the case may be, one of the greatest limitations these studies show is related to the trivialization of fear as the co-founder of the market. Here is the starting point from where this chapter will continue.

Dean MacCannell

One of the well-read scholars in the sociology of consumption (in tourism) who does not need introduction is Dean MacCannell. Basically, his original idea is related to the legacy of structuralism, with other new approaches such as interactionism and Marxism. It is important not to lose sight of the fact that tourism is for MacCannell a modern activity, resulting from the acceleration of capitalism. To some extent, he retains the same concerns as Durkheim respecting the advance of capitalism. The sociological work of MacCannell is strongly influenced by five clear-cut boundaries. From Durkheim (1976), he took not only the division between sacred and profane space, but also the role of the totem in the social cohesion of primitive minds. Goffman (1959) plays a crucial role by configuring his conception of staged-authenticity, while Karl Marx provides a much deeper discussion about the notions of class struggle, desire and alienation. With this background in mind, MacCannell proposes that tourism filled the gap left by secularization in postmodern societies. Since the totem plays a crucial role by enhancing the social cohesion of tribal societies, authenticity mediates between citizens and their institutions in industrial forms of organizations (MacCannell 1973, 1976). A much deeper symbolic matrix that forges a tourist consciousness works in a similar way to totems in the primitive minds, documented by the founding parents of ethnology. MacCannell is strongly interested in understanding the expansion of capitalism, which is based on the theory of alienation, in revitalizing the frustrated experiences of peoples. Taking a closer look, Marx was on the right side by confirming that in order that the oppression suffered by the workforce does not result in a collapse of social order, an ideological mechanism of control should be adopted. Consumption and tourism are parts of these mechanisms of control that (on the one hand) prevent the disintegration of society, but at the same time (on the other) developed a more radical interest for 'the Other' (MacCannell 1976, 1984) that Andrews and Leopold (2013) would assimilate to social capital. In sharp contrast to the thesis John Urry held, MacCannell understands that the goals of tourism are not only the leave from ordinary life as Urry concludes, but the formation of a meta-discourse towards a new consciousness. It is unfortunate that digital technologies and mass consumption are undermining the attachment of people to their cultures and traditions. This leads MacCannell to contend that tourism is reproducing 'empty meeting grounds' (MacCannell 2001, 2011, 2012). While touring, the 'Other' is not only invisibilized, but silenced. This happens because natives are exploited to fulfil the wishes of mobile consumers. This assumption places MacCannell in the line of French philosophers such as Virilio (2006) or Augé (1995). At times, the social ties among citizens is undermined by postmodernism, the 'emptied spaces' surfaced. The quest for the 'ethnic difference', which defines modern tourism today, only is valid if it reinforces one's own supremacy. The stereotypes of the West are depicted to mark the 'Others' and in so doing, the white elite is unmarked. The sense of freedom given to tourists leads us to think they are privileged citizens or take part in a selected group. With a closer look, we will realize their obsession for 'Others' is marked by egoism and individualism. Reluctant to be in contact with other tourists, modern sightseers move as cannibals, reducing the presence of 'Others' to their imagined desires (the eternal lack). The needs of discovery as well as the quest for other cultures precede a deeply profound sentiment of guilt at the extermination of the aboriginal world. Since the West never has asked for pardon for the conquest of the Americas, it was rooted in its consciousness in a pathological mode (MacCannell 2001, 2011, 2012). To correct this problem, we must adopt a new ethics that facilitates our being in this world. Instead of covering the 'Other' using our mechanisms of discipline, we ought to reconsider the current obsession for authentic experiences. Most likely, accepting the difference is the best way to get a genuine and authentic experience. The ebb and flow of individualism, or the negotiation between agents and structure, is one of the points MacCannell leaves behind but it is continued very well by other scholars such as John Urry.

John Urry

The critiques on Dean MacCannell are aimed to show that his diagnosis applies to Disneyworld alone or the consumption of mass-tourism, but it is limited when it comes to other practices. This leads John Urry to propose his diagnosis about the complexity of tourism. Rather, he adopts the Foucauldian term 'gaze' to denote the fascination of the West with vision – Oculacentrism. The term is often associated with discourses, allegories or even practices of seeing consuming contexts. The act of gazing is connecting to a much deeper cultural matrix that gives meaning to what is being watched. Studying how this matrix is formed, is a valid way of approaching different gazers and gazes. This means that tourist gaze varies across cultures and time. To wit, Urry distinguishes three types of gazes: romantic, individual and solitary (Urry 2002). As he noted, 'With what . . . I call the romantic gaze, solicitude, privacy and a personal, semi-spiritual relationship with the object of the gaze are emphasised. In such cases, tourists expect to look at the object privately or at least only with "significant others"' (Urry 2002: p. 150).

The gaze transforms areas of terror or fear into commoditized landscapes that are engaged to an 'imperial economy'. In order for the gaze to be consolidated, the distance from gazers to their object is of paramount importance. Against this backdrop, Oculacentrism is vital to accelerate the necessary conditions for the expansion of tourism. Three questions facilitate the understanding of Urry's conceptual model: Why are modern citizens prone to travel? To what extent are not only persons but cultures mobile? Is mobility the platform towards contemporary citizenry?

In theory, the current cultural values of postmodern societies confer to their citizens a certain autonomy to travel to any geographical point of the globe. The rights of mobilities are legally associated with the organization of labour. We work hard all year, in order to obtain our vacations. Far from being naïve, this idea represents the connection of labour and leisure. As a mechanism of escape, tourists get away from their home to reach new outstanding experiences, which are based on ongoing negotiations that change how people gaze. Since tourism seems to be open to the logic of escapement, leisure allows the liberalization of all social constraints. Consumption would play a crucial role by filling the gap left by the liberalization of rules. If starting from the premise that gazing represents a means of control, maintained by the West during the 19th century, to expand the imperial hegemony over the global periphery, no less true is that this process culminated in the consolidation of the tourism industry. Gazing is a way of possessing what is being gazed at but Urry said this can be done only in a hyper-mobile context, where cultures and their peoples are marked by the sign of central economies. The process of commoditization proposed by tourism can be materialized only because objects are conferred with a sign, which is exchanged in the market. We do not consume products by their features as a couple of centuries ago, but by the imposed sign over them. Coffee from Colombia, whisky from Scotland and wine from

Argentina are only some examples that validate Urry's worries. Referring to events and more particularly cultural events, Séraphin and Nolan (2014) and Andrews and Leopold (2013) explained how tourism contributes to their commodification. This exchange can be accomplished only in a context of extreme mobility. Today, airport officials recognize that almost 600 million arrivals are recorded worldwide, while this amount was 25 million in 1950. The evolution of tourism as a mass-industry reflected profitable revenue for international investors, which paradoxically were unable to promote a fairer distribution of wealth in underdeveloped countries.

In fact, Urry is convinced mobility is often based on the dominance of aesthetics over the rest of the senses. This not only explains the main reason as to why people return to mass-transport as a mechanism of evasion but also the growing importance of travel photography in recent decades. In a globalized society characterized by the predominance of spectacle, multiculturalism encourages displacement as a vehicle towards happiness, development and emotional commitment. From this angle, nation-states are reinventing their boundaries and identities constantly supported by the interchange of tourists, migrants and workers. These new forms of movements are part of social memory and broader acculturation processes which fieldworkers should explore in their studies (Urry 2007).

Though mobilities are key factors to define tourism, they are not the only ones. The eternal quest for happiness and novelty are salient factors that tourists often pursue but never reach. For Urry, MacCannell took the correct step in affirming that tourism stems from a macro-structural matrix (staged-authenticity) but he failed to give further explanation on how different gazers connect to different cultures. Rather, it is interesting not to lose sight of the micro-sociological dynamics of tourism where psychological experience is orchestrated as a mere reflection of self. To put this bluntly, each tourist seeks what they want, but this sentiment is not independent of its cognitive system. At this stage, *curiosity* (not staged-authenticity) helps in understanding how the tourist gaze is formed. Albeit modernity imposes some stereotypes and portraits, the individual attachment of self to space gives different profiles which are fulfilled with different products. There is nothing like an all-encompassing matrix of what tourism means or a tourist-consciousness but a fluid trade-off between agency and its structure. The project of structuralism where MacCannell departs puts the cart before the horse. For Urry, instead, the tourist experience not only is rooted in a mobile context, but aims at transforming the routine into a new cultural experience which cannot be obtained at home. In this respect, tourism recycles boredom into commoditized forms of entertainment.

In his seminal book, *The Tourist Gaze* (Urry 2002), Urry notes that geographies, persons and landscapes can be organized through gazing. Far from being a disorganized activity, the tourist gaze stems from the configuration of a cultural model. In order for the economy of signs to expand, mobilities connect needs with commodities. This is exactly the point of discussion shown in *The Economies and Spaces,* a project which is co-authored with Scott Lash. The current atmosphere of multiculturalism is unable to find the division between high and low mobilities (Lash and Urry 1993)

The trajectory (exchange) of goods and humans (by stimulating consumption) has created an empty space accelerating the decline of trust and social bonds among persons. Lash and Urry appeal to the Maussian development of gift theory to explain why trade seriously affects human reciprocity. They explore the role played by the tour operator, as a professional actor who is trained to mould clients' experiences. The function of travel agents consists in finding and absorbing the potential risk a traveller may face during their holidays. Today, there is a tension between experts and laypeople as to how to fix the ways these symbols should be interpreted or decoded. This explains why some tourist destinations are selected by consumers while others are surely discarded. When travelling abroad, the decisions made by consumers are influenced by a broader symbolic platform, conformed to virtualized information which is not palpable unless by the imposed sign on the consumer's mind. These allegories mould not only the personal experience but also expectancies posed on the dream destination. The personal experience and mouth-to-mouth recommendations set the pace for new ways of indoctrinating consumers' minds, that is, advertising. In the West, during the 19th and 20th centuries, a new type of re-flexibility expanded worldwide, causing an aesthetic romanticism of the 'Other'. The possibility for travellers not only to experience new sensations and landscapes, but to classify diverse geographical natures was, jointly with tourism, conducive to the assertiveness of cosmopolitanism. But this ethnical other became a mere commodity to be elaborated and exchanged by other commodities (Lash and Urry 1993).

Last but not least, the economy of signs evolves conjoined to the economies of desires, which are visually stimulated by modern tourism. In this respect, the mobile modernity cements the conditions for the monopoly of desire to be established as a mediator between citizenry and social institutions (Lash and Urry 1993: 369–371). His efforts to integrate mobilities into a coherent paradigm or clear-cut epistemology situate Urry as a leading scholar within the sociology of tourism.

Kevin Meethan

In the middle of the discussion between MacCannell and Urry we come across Senior Professor of the University of Plymouth, Kevin Meethan, who argues convincingly that modern capitalism shapes more permeable geographical boundaries and process of identities. His initial studies come from a much deeper analysis centred on the study case of York, England. In this respect, tourism and consumption should be taken seriously into consideration as something other than a mere optimization of pleasure (Meethan 1996). Through consumption, travellers remain open to new experience but retain their own identity. The concept of fluidity is vital to understanding Meethan's development. Over the years, he developed an all-encompassing model of modernization and sense of place, which introduces the legacy of John Urry. Not only have consumption and its patterns changed with the advance of tourism, but also the ways cultures are certainly decoded. In an ever-mobile and globalized world, the conformation of identities and cultures is being recycled in more fluid ways than at other times. As per the previous argument, one might speculate that consumers accept a process of production, which is previously determined by a dominant ideological discourse. Unlike other consumers, tourists should leave home to materialize their consumption. The sense given to obtained experience is previously conditioned to a cultural matrix. However, in contrast to other scholars, this matrix for Meethan seems to be replicated in the practices of tourists and their itineraries as well as the accumulated images that are later disseminated by mass media. As an ongoing negotiation with others, places, persons and goods are exchanged in order to create an imagined landscape of visited place, which does not correspond with the theory of alienation. Quite aside from what specialized literature precludes, which means that consumers are passive receptors of marketing and advertising, Meethan adds that under some conditions commodities are received or used in different manners that are externally designed. Neither Marxism nor structuralism is enough to explain the micro-sociological selectivity of consumers in a hybridized world. The concept of co-production and interpretation is one of the key factors that distinguish Kevin Meethan's development from other scholars such as MacCannell, Augé or Virilio (who are more pessimistic). The sense of place in humans is not only given in their attachment to a site or territory, but in the ways they interact with others, which lead towards the hemisphere of identity. Though conducive to the reproduction of *narratives of self*, tourism is enrooted in a specific history and territory which is elaborated from generation to generation. The experience tourists feel, after consuming, entails an 'active engagement in the memory work' (Meethan 2006: p. 9). We think often that metaphors, ideologies, imaginaries and gazes created by services consumption are not the end, but a starting point for new studies to expand the current understanding of what a narrative of place means. In this vein, Meethan gives to readers a substantial insight which merits discussion. Peoples are not passive agents that maximize their pleasure or reduce their pain, as some psychologists of consumption have stressed. The circularity of modernity is not given by a unilineal movement where subjects act as passive agents; they behave, rather, in the middle of cyclical contexts, where culture is being changed day to day. The concept of 'hybridity' in this vein should be placed under the lens of scrutiny, because it escapes to an individual understanding of things (Meethan 2003). This belief is useful for Meethan to part him from Urry. We do not live in a mobile culture, as Urry originally asserted, but in the roots of a complex intersection in what he dubbed 'the genealogy of tourism'. What type of connection is this?

One of the aspects that determine tourism consumption is the motives behind tourists making the decision to leave home, likely thousands of miles, in order to obtain some experience which is still unfamiliar for them. The *quest of otherness* plays a crucial role enabling a connection between hosts and guests. The sense of place seems not to be the site where one stands, but the idea of home that one asks for. No matter the interests, people struggle to find their home throughout their lives. This is the reason why diaspora alludes to an imagined past-time one seeks but never reaches. Travellers may very well be subject to multiple locations, identities and landscapes. For Meethan and his followers tourism is something other than a space of hedonist consumption where travellers maximize their pleasure, to the extent any travel represents a movement for self-discovery (as a rite of passage) between normality and exoticness (Meethan 2004).

Whether after MacCannell, sociologists criticized the nature of tourism as a mechanism of control conducive to commoditizing ethnicity is an open question, but Meethan goes in the opposite direction. Ethnicity and mobilities have helpfully contributed in connecting geographies with economies and peoples in a much broader allegory of the pastime (identity). As a part of human history, travels and place-making were inherently associated with conquest. Nowadays, the affordable technology allows new interpretations of the past, representing different products (allegories) for different travellers that range from migrants who are forced to abandon their families, to global tourists (Meethan 2014). If Meethan can be questioned, it is for his over-valorization of culture over other factors of analysis.

With the benefits of hindsight, Frederick Buell places the problem of mobility, culture and globalization under the lens of scrutiny. He advocates for a new theory of globalization that understands the pervasive position of culture in the threshold of time. The West colonized the peripheral world by introducing not only the idea of white superiority, but also the beliefs of 'commonalities' in a heterogeneous aboriginal landscape. As it has been formulated by colonial powers, culture serves two diverse purposes. On one hand, it appealed to forge a sentiment of 'we' against 'they', who were portrayed as 'inferior'. On the other, the process of decolonization after WWII created the inverse stage. However, the meaning of culture never was questioned. Today, culture is sold by tourism and global industries. Buell's main thesis is that culture as an invention of the colonial West expanded globalization worldwide (Buell 1994).

Conclusion

This chapter has certainly addressed the negative view of the founding parents of sociology on industrialism. These pejorative beliefs over the industrial ethos were influential for modern sociologists such as Dean MacCannell, John Urry and even Kevin Meethan, all of whom were concerned by the aftermaths of mobility and globalization in cultures. One of the aspects that conspired to form a negative view of consumption and tourism was related to the fact that sociologists (in tourism) did not pay attention to ancient history. For them, in sharp contrast to archaeologists, tourism is a modern issue which was never present in other ancient civilizations. Needless to say this is a big problem for them to see beyond the boundaries of the Middle Ages. The term *feriae* which was used for ancient Romans to give a relief to their citizens for three months still is an example illustrating that old forms of tourism preceded modernity. It even mutated into the modern terms *ferien* (German) and *feriaes* (Portuguese) which denote 'holidays'. Important archaeological evidence suggests that ancient empires such as the Assyrians, Romans, Sumerians and Babylonians developed mechanisms of escapement like 'tourism'. Imperial structures need expansion to survive. This process not only indexes another cultures and territories but also concentrates a lot of resources in its core. In order not to collapse, temporal leave should be conferred to citizens to return to their homes. That way, not only are their daily frustrations revitalized but also they renovate their trust in the imperial power. This explanation suggests that we should have to view tourism as 'the maiden of empires', a social institution older than sociologists of tourism allow. Most certainly, the role of history was trivialized by English literature because of two main reasons. One of them is the lack of interest of the Anglo-Saxons in ancient history which is useful to explain the current function of the contemporary world. Secondly, they are subject to the Middle Ages which was a period of low mobilities, and therefore no further efforts to see ancient history are made. It is safe to say that tourism in its current form resulted from the rise of the Anglo-Saxon empires (initiated by the UK and continued by the US). This does not mean that other similar forms of tourism and consumption were enrooted in the past.

References

Andrews, H. and Leopold, T. (2013). *Events and the Social Sciences*, London: Routledge.

Augé, M. (1995). *Non-lieux*, London: Verso.

Bauman, Z. (2001). 'Consuming life', *Journal of Consumer Culture*, 1(1): 9–29.

Beatty, S. E. and Ferrell, M. E. (1998). 'Impulse buying: Modeling its precursors', *Journal of Retailing*, 74(2): 169–191.

Buell, F. (1994). *National Culture and the New Global System*, Baltimore, MD: Johns Hopkins University Press.

Donohue, K. G. (2003). *Freedom from Want*, Baltimore, MD: Johns Hopkins University Press.

Durkheim, E. (1976). *The Elementary Forms of the Religious Life*, London: Allen and Unwin.

Durkheim, E. (2014). *The Division of Labor in Society*, New York: Simon and Schuster.

Goffman, E. (1959). *The Presentation of Self in Everyday Life*, New York: Anchor.

Hadjali, H. R., Salimi, M., Nazari, M. and Ardestani, M. S. (2012). 'Exploring main factors affecting on impulse buying behaviors', *Journal of American Science*, 8(1): 245–251.

Hall, C. M. and Williams, A. (eds.) (2013). *Tourism and Migration: New Relationships between Production and Consumption*, Oxford: Springer Science and Business Media.

Hammond, M. and Wellington, J. (2013). *Research Methods. The Key Concepts*, London: Routledge.

Heilbroner, R. L. (2011). *The Worldly Philosophers: The Lives, Times and Ideas of the Great Economic Thinkers*, New York: Simon and Schuster.

Korstanje, M. E. and George, B. P. (2012). Falklands/Malvinas: A re-examination of the relationship between sacralisation and tourism development, *Current Issues in Tourism*, 15(3): 153–165.

Lash, S. M. and Urry, S. L. J. (1993). *Economies of Signs and Space*, London: Sage.

MacCannell, D. (1973). 'Staged authenticity: Arrangements of social space in tourist settings', *American Journal of Sociology*, 79(3): 589–603.

MacCannell, D. (1976). *The Tourist: A New Theory of the Leisure Class*, Berkeley: University of California Press.

MacCannell, D. (1984). 'Reconstructed ethnicity tourism and cultural identity in third world communities', *Annals of Tourism Research*, 11(3): 375–391.

MacCannell, D. (2001). 'Tourist agency', *Tourist Studies*, 1(1): 23–37.

MacCannell, D. (2011). *The Ethics of Sightseeing*, Berkeley, CA: University of California Press.

MacCannell, D. (2012). 'On the ethical stake in tourism research', *Tourism Geographies*, 14(1): 183–194.

Meethan, K. (1996). 'Consuming (in) the civilized city', *Annals of Tourism Research*, 23(2): 322–340.

Meethan, K. (2003). 'Mobile cultures? Hybridity, tourism and cultural change', *Journal of Tourism and Cultural Change*, 1(1): 11–28.

Meethan, K. (2004). 'To stand in the shoes of my ancestors', in Coles, T. and Timothy, D. (eds.), *Tourism, Diasporas and Space* (pp. 139–150), London: Routledge.

Meethan, K. (2006). 'Introduction: Narratives of place and self', in Meethan, K., Anderson, A. and Miles, S. (eds.), *Tourism Consumption and Representation* (pp. 1–23), Wallingford: CABI.

Meethan, K. (2014). 'Mobilities, ethnicities and tourism', in Lew, A., Hall, M. C. and Williams, A. (eds.), *Tourism* (pp. 240–250), New York: Wiley Blackwell.

Richards, G. (1996). 'Production and consumption of European cultural tourism', *Annals of Tourism Research*, 23(2): 261–283.

Séraphin, H. and Nolan, E. (2014). 'Voodoo in Haiti: A religious ceremony at the service of the "Houngan" called "tourism"', in Frost, W. and Laing, J. (eds.), *Rituals and Traditional Events in the Modern World* (pp. 221–231), New York: Routledge.

Tzanelli, R. (2004). 'Constructing the "cinematic tourist": The "sign industry" of *The Lord of the Rings*', *Tourist Studies*, 4(1): 21–42.

Urry, J. (2002). *The Tourist Gaze*, London: Sage.

Urry, J. (2007). 'Introduction', in *Viajes y Geografías* (pp. 8–17), Buenos Aires: Prometeo.

Virilio, P. (2006). *Velocidad y política: Ensayo sobre dromología* [Speed and politics: An essay on dromology], Polizzotti, M. (trans.), Los Ángeles, CA: Semiotext(e).

Weber, M. (2009). *From Max Weber: Essays in Sociology*, London: Routledge.

Woodside, A. G. and Dubelaar, C. (2002). 'A general theory of tourism consumption systems: A conceptual framework and an empirical exploration', *Journal of Travel Research*, 41(2): 120–132.

Woodside, A. G. and King, R. I. (2001). 'An updated model of travel and tourism purchase-consumption systems', *Journal of Travel and Tourism Marketing*, 10(1): 3–27.

3

EXPLORING TOURIST TRANSFORMATION

From need to desire to experience

Ronnie Ballantyne, Finlay Kerr, Shirley Rate and Luiz Moutinho

Exploring the nature of consumer decision making

This chapter explores and illuminates the nature of consumer decision making within the tourism arena, paying particular attention to the concepts of need recognition and motivation. Importantly the chapter also traces key emergent developments in the rise of the experiential tourist or transumer, those consumers motivated and driven by a multifaceted tourism experience instead of 'fixed' traditional tourism offerings. Ultimately, in order to identify, refine and sustain robust tourism marketing strategies and tactics that promote choice and encourage loyalty the chapter explores the relationship between tourism marketing and branding initiatives and their impact on consumer decision making. This chapter is then of particular interest to those wishing to understand the nature of consumer behaviour within tourism and for those involved in the planning and execution of tourism marketing strategy.

The topic of understanding and predicting consumer behaviour is a central issue to marketing practitioners within the tourism arena. That said, the answer to 'Why do people travel?' is not easily answered – the dynamic process of moving from a basic need and desire to a more fully formed motivation to visit a specific tourism destination or to undertake a particular tourism activity is relatively complex (Holloway 1998). We have attempted to model consumer behaviour since the late 1960s (Engel et al. 1968; Howard and Sheth 1969). Although rich and mindful contribution has been made these classic models of consumer behaviour envisaged consumers as rational, information-processing beings. These classic models were then ultimately criticised for lack of goodness of fit with consumer decision making in the real world – the very nature of tourism and tourist consumer decision making tends to demonstrate underlying hedonic or emotionally driven behaviour. As such, our understanding if truth be told is still somewhat fuzzy. Nonetheless clarity regarding key elements in the consumer decision-making process and the nature of motivation, this being an understanding of why tourists behave the way they do, and general agreement about its ongoing relevance, contribution, significance and impact to the consumer decision-making process and marketing practices do indeed exist (Kay 2003).

Need recognition

There are many forms of tourism and many types of tourism consumer; that said, one defining element is consistent to all tourism consumers – the concept of need recognition. The starting point of this decision-making process is traditionally viewed as the formation of a need on the part of the consumer. Need recognition can be viewed as the consumer's perception that there is difference between their actual state of being and their desired state of being – these states of being may be physiological and/or psychological in nature. This difference or distance creates tension within the consumer and the consumer is then driven to reduce this tension through the consumption of tourism products.

Need recognition is then traditionally viewed as the first stage in consumer decision making – once activated the consumer will then engage in 'problem solving' (stages of searching for, purchasing, using, evaluating and disposing of products and services), acquiring and seeking out decision-relevant information to allow product/service evaluation, leading to choice and ultimately an evaluation as to whether or not the chosen choice alternatives satisfied the individual's need. This paradigm follows a cognitivist approach and traces a 'cycle' from stimulation, including motivation and intention formation, to actual behaviour and experience, evaluation and retention of consequences (Gnoth 1997).

It is important to recognise that this state of need recognition can be triggered by many factors. Some may be personal primers, e.g. the need to escape the mundane, or business controlled, e.g. advertising stimuli, or some may be more extraneous in nature, e.g. reference group, or indeed a combination thereof. Understanding the key primers for triggering need recognition for particular target groups is critical for the design, delivery and maintenance of tourism marketing strategy. Further scrutiny of need recognition reveals that traditionally it is believed that consumers are motivated to travel because they are 'pushed' into travelling due to internal or emotional aspects such as the desire to escape or the need for revitalisation, or because they are 'pulled' by destination attributes, e.g. cultural or natural features (Devesa et al. 2010). Although crucial, need recognition is only part of the picture. To fully appreciate the overall process of consumer decision making we must consider the concept of motivation.

The motivation construct

In general terms motivation can be described as the driving force within consumers that moves them to take particular action. Motives can be multiple in nature, e.g. to enhance one's self-esteem, to achieve, to affiliate, to avoid cognitive conflict or indeed to self-actualise. Within the context of tourism key facets within the consumer's motivational range could include the need to escape the mundane home or work environment – boredom alleviation; or the need to seek pleasurable new experiences – surprise, educational and cultural relaxation, adventure and pleasure, health and recreation, ethnic and family, social and competitive. In effect then motivation refers to the drive or push that consumers exert in order to satisfy their needs, wants, desires and dreams, it is the force that informs the nature and direction of decision making and feeds the amount of time and cognitive energy utilised. Clearly there are many variables that contribute to our overall understanding of tourist consumer behaviour; however, it is motivation that must be viewed as the critical overarching variable because it is the driving force behind all behaviour (Fodness 1994).

Traditionally the satisfaction associated with travel and tourism includes a relaxation of tension on the part of the travel consumer and a return to a state of equilibrium – where physical, social and psychological needs are met; an omnipresent core theme appears to be the desire to renew one's mental state of well-being (Moutinho et al. 2011). This is a strong underlying component with regards to the varying desires and expectations one has regarding a vacation. It is therefore reasonable and realistic to assume that the consumer will opt for a destination or type of holiday that best satisfies his/her needs and desires (Shoemaker 1994). There are two main views relating to what motivates consumers: firstly, the need for balance and harmony – the consumer is more likely to be satisfied with the expected than the unexpected. In contrast it is the unexpected that is satisfying and thus the tourist will seek complexity, not sameness. Perhaps it would be reasonable to place these two extremes at either end of a continuum and suggest that different facets of the tourism experience will address these different motives at different times. In effect consumers have a need for stability as well as novelty. In the case of travelling there are normally multiple motives, based on the tourist's expectations regarding the outcome of the tourism event. It can be argued that consumers seek situations and experiences that offer, to a degree, incongruity, uncertainty, novelty, arousal and complexity combined with a degree of familiarity (Moutinho et al. 2011). In effect, as much as global consumers continue to embrace the convenience and reliability delivered by globalised mass production, they also aspire to an alternative to the perceived homogenisation of contemporary culture, food and leisure experiences. The consumer's search for the real which we define as Authenti-seeking has a number of implications for consumer-facing sectors, from the way companies package and market their offers to how they interact with the customer base. When consumers travel in the future, it will be with more of a purpose with not only our needs in mind but also those of the destination. This new way of travelling could be described as 'deep' travel. It will be about getting under the skin of a place. We already seek authenticity – real experiences rather than fake culture packaged up for tourists – but travel in the future will go further. It will be about the appreciation of local distinctiveness, the idiosyncrasies and the detail, the things that make a place unique and special.

To this end motivation is not unidimensional in nature and must be viewed as a complex multidimensional construct changing throughout the travel process (McCabe 2000). As such we can view motivation as a meta-concept that not only functions as a key primer or trigger for travel behaviour but also illuminates (1) the underlying rationale for travelling, (2) the specific choice of destination and tourism activity and (3) overall satisfaction with the experience. This then highlights the existence of different motivation schemes at particular times for a particular destination that affect tourists' expectations and ultimately their overall satisfaction (Devesa et al. 2010).

Transumers

As we move through time consumers are becoming more motivated to participate within tourism marketing, increasingly moving from passive recipients to active participants as new travel research and planning approaches (available at the click of a mouse) are empowering consumers in unprecedented ways. Travellers are keen to take control and find/create the perfect trip, not just the cheapest trip. There has been a shift towards consumers co-creating signature tourism experiences whereby they actively contribute to the overall design and delivery of the tourism experience knowing that it is for them. These new consumers are called prosumers. Following on from the birth of prosumers a new generation of travellers is beginning to emerge – the transumers.

Transumers are consumers driven by experiences instead of the 'fixed', by entertainment, by discovery, by fighting boredom, increasingly living a transient lifestyle freeing themselves

The curious case of Mystery Makers

The rise of transumers and in turn experiential marketing has become a central focus of many marketing arenas – particularly retailing and branding, but as can be said for many marketing innovations it has been to a large degree overlooked by those involved in tourism marketing and hospitality (Williams 2006). One salient and bold example of this type of experiential tourism includes Mystery Makers of Copenhagen. Mystery Makers seek to create unique consumer experiences where participants interact with each other in creative, entertaining and 'brainteasing' situations. Mystery Makers refer to this as 'enterbrainment'.

This type of product is a world away from traditional tourism products and services; within their portfolio of enterbrainment a wide array of experiences await. These range from 'The Lab' (group play involving a minimum of four participants – here you will find yourself in a secret laboratory as part of a mysterious experiment and you have 60 minutes to crack all the codes and get out!!) to the 'Killing Room', an even more macabre situation where a serial killer is on the loose in Copenhagen. He has locked you up in his basement to test your instincts. You have to solve the puzzles to get out in time. You have 60 minutes. . . here you have to be a minimum of six to play. The Brewer's Secret offers a less scary but equally intense experience whereby one participates in a mind-blowing treasure hunt, following clues and deciphering codes across Copenhagen. To a large degree the consumer now becomes the actor in their own movie.

One of Mystery Makers' taglines is 'Life is not a problem to be solved but a mystery to be experienced'. This captures the essence of their brand and as such their philosophy is clearly aligned with these new emergent tribes of consumers such as transumers. They argue that superstition has been subdued by science and in effect we deny ourselves mysteries, myths and rituals which we need to make sense of ourselves and the world in which we live. At Mystery Makers guests will interact with each other to co-create unique signature experiences that are laden with creative, educational and entertaining value. It can be said that tourism marketing is often concerned with the transformation of the consumer's state of being – clearly this is high on the agenda at Mystery Makers and as cited previously often the consumer is driven and motivated to experience novelty and stability. Here we have the best of all possible worlds where guests can experience the rush of highly intensive out-of-the-ordinary situations but feel safe with the underlying security of knowing that it is just a game. Moreover it is working – Mystery Makers have previously won the Danish Creative Business Cup, and hold the title of Denmark's best entrepreneurs from the creative industries 2012–2013.

from the hassles of permanent ownership and possessions, moving towards generating themed immersive multidimensional tourism brand experiences that intellectually, emotionally, physically and spiritually move and stimulate them. These experiences must be unique, engaging, extraordinary, educational, environmentally appealing and memorable.

Closing remarks

In closing it is evident that understanding the variables that motivate consumers to participate in particular tourism activities is extremely important in a highly competitive context with informed and demanding tourists. We have seen that motivation is a complex multidimensional construct. In terms of developing and maintaining robust tourism marketing strategy this understanding of what motivates consumers and how this impacts their decision making is an essential condition for success and a crucial aid towards ongoing competitiveness. If one is to develop tourism marketing with magnetism – think right place, right time with right technology that allows consumers to dream, book, experience and share storytelling via the multitude of online media available – then we must isolate and understand the key touchpoints or sweet-spots that consumers desire in their journeys. The rise and influence of online recommendation from trusted 'friends' merit particular attention. To be effective in the digital world tourism marketers must transform consumers into brand ambassadors. The rise and influence of social media in consumer decision making continue to amplify, with the majority of consumers now beginning their journey online; furthermore we see more and more attention being placed on blended content whereby web domains are populated by both traditional, controlled branded content but also increasingly user-generated content such as text testimonials or stories and video. This content must inspire and help; it must be authentic and trustworthy; and of paramount importance, it must be fresh – marketers must write evergreen content – 365 days a year – to build authority so as to encourage the transformation from prospect to consumer.

Moreover a tourism brand experience platform (in terms of both online and physical artefacts) that allows for flexibility and reactivity will become a necessity – change will be necessary – as consumers get bored very quickly. As such the 'experience' must continue to evolve and change so as to allow ongoing experiences to be new – just like incremental innovation in physical product design. That is, the experience is always new and therefore desired. This move towards experiential marketing in the tourism arena is relatively new (although seminal examples such as Disneyland do exist). As cited in the opening commentary, classic models of consumer behaviour and traditional marketing frameworks view consumers as rational decision makers; in contrast to this the experiential marketing model views the consumer as a more emotional entity seeking to co-create pleasurable, memorable and meaningful experiences. This orientation is then more aligned with current and emergent trends in tourism consumer behaviour and importantly has goodness of fit with the multiple motives that consumers now have concerning their underlying rationale for a particular tourist experience and booking, experiencing and evaluation.

Finally we must consider, is the tourist consumer a novice or an expert in terms of decision making? As the marketplace becomes increasingly crowded with competing brands and organisations, consumers will not only rely on external sources of tourism brand information and reference groups to aid them in their decision making – they will simply 'fast track' their decision-making activities by consulting their prior knowledge, enabling decision-making heuristics to simplify the decision-making process and thus reducing time and cognitive effort spent on decision making (Ballantyne et al. 2006). Furthermore for the expert the decision-making process is heavily influenced by a wide array of previous experiences and prior knowledge (Parrinello 1993). In contrast the novice is more likely to be influenced initially by reference groups and controllable marketing stimuli. To this end the competitive edge within the tourism arena lies in co-creating rich, unique, value-laden memorable experiences with consumers that can easily be recalled – so much so that it becomes their aspirational state of being and thus helps to move consumers on their journey from need to desire to experience.

References

Ballantyne, R., Warren, A. and Nobbs, K. (2006). 'The evolution of brand choice', *Journal of Brand Management*, 13(April–June): 339–352.

Devesa, M., Laguna, M. and Palacios, A. (2010). 'The role of motivation in visitor satisfaction: Empirical evidence in rural tourism', *Tourism Management*, 31(4): 547–552.

Engel, J. F., Kollat, D. T. and Blackwell, R. D. (1968). *Consumer Behaviour*, New York: Holt, Rinehart and Winston.

Fodness, D. (1994). 'Measuring tourist motivation', *Annals of Tourism Research*, 21(3): 555–581.

Gnoth, J. (1997). 'Tourist motivation and expectation formation', *Annals of Tourism Research*, 24(2): 301–304.

Holloway, J. C. (1988). *The Business of Tourism*, 5th edition, Harlow: Longman.

Howard, J. A. and Sheth, J. N. (1969). *The Theory of Buyer Behaviour*, New York: Wiley.

Kay, P. (2003). 'Consumer motivation in a tourism context: Continuing the work of Maslow, Rokeach, Vroom, Haley and others', in *ANZMAC 2003: A Celebration of Ehrenberg and Bass: Marketing Discoveries, Knowledge and Contribution: Proceedings of the 2003 Australian and New Zealand Marketing Academy Conference* (pp. 600–614), Adelaide: ANZMAC.

McCabe, S. (2000). 'Tourism motivation process', *Annals of Tourism Research*, 27(4): 1049–1052.

Moutinho, L., Ballantyne, R. and Rate, S. (2011). 'Consumer behaviour in tourism', in Moutinho, L. (ed.), *Strategic Management in Tourism*, 2nd edition (pp. 83–126), Cambridge: CABI.

Parrinello, G. L. (1993). 'Motivation and anticipation in post-industrial tourism', *Annals of Tourism Research*, 20(2): 233–249.

Shoemaker, S. (1994). 'Segmenting the US travel market according to benefits realized', *Journal of Travel Research*, 33(2): 8–21.

Williams, A. (2006). 'Tourism and hospitality marketing: Fantasy, feeling and fun', *International Journal of Contemporary Hospitality Management*, 18(6): 482–495.

4

FACTORS AFFECTING TOURIST BUYING BEHAVIOUR

Jennifer Kim Lian Chan and Azilah Kasim

Introduction

The chapter presents the concept of experience within the tourism context and it relates tourist experiences to the five senses and realms of experiences. It also highlights the three-stage model of service experience consumption as well as the importance of hedonic and utilitarian factors in service experience consumption.

Tourism as service, people and experience industry

Tourism is an industry that provides a series of services and unique experiences that are created and staged by the main subsectors of tourism suppliers in their specific contexts. Tourism experiences are events or activities that engage individuals in a personal way – an intangible form of memories. Unlike goods and services, Pine and Gilmore (1999) describe the concept of experience as a form of 'stage' by the suppliers that is memorable, personal and sensational. The delivery and consumption of services and activities require the presence of both service staff and tourists during the delivery of services or activities. The outcome of tourism services largely depends on the service staff and tourists themselves at the pre-consumption, during and post-consumption stages. The service delivery or process dimensions, the human (service staff and tourists) dimensions and tourism products/service dimensions have become important elements influencing tourism experiences. These dimensions are interrelated and co-creation of service experiences happens during the delivery and consumption process.

Experience is an important factor in influencing satisfaction. In tourism experience, satisfaction results from the experiential consumption (Chan and Baum 2007a). When consuming a service, the subjective personal reactions and feelings experienced have been found to be an important part of tourists' evaluation and satisfaction with services (Otto and Ritchie 1996). Tourism suppliers have increasingly recognized the importance of the experience that led to tourist satisfaction and loyalty (Zomerdijk and Voss 2010). Simply put, an experience is part of the tourist when he or she feels, senses or acquires learning or knowledge from interacting with the elements of a context created by a service provider (Pullman and Gross 2004). Thus, more service organizations, especially tourism service organizations, are placing customer experience at the core of their service offering (Haeckel et al. 2003; Pine and Gilmore 1999; Pullman and Gross 2004; Voss et al. 2008).

Service by nature is hedonic, aesthetic and a context for emotion, whilst experience is subjective and an individualistic and intangible element. Thus, tourist experiences are a complex combination of factors from the human, technical and delivery aspects. The experiences are derived from the performance of the service and the emotion of an individual; thus the experience is made up of both cognitive and emotional components. Most companies see themselves as stagers of service providers for experiences in order to provide experiences to their customers. This suggests that tourism service providers can stage their service experiences based on the four realms of an experience by Pine and Gilmore (1999), namely, absorption, immersion, passive participation and active participation or a combination of all realms. More importantly, when designing, staging and delivering an experience within the tourism and hospitality context, one should aim at and consider the following aspects as suggested by Pine and Gilmore (1999) for the service experience consumption context: the thematic of the experience, positive cues, memorability and engage the five senses.

Definition of experience and tourist experiences

Understanding customer experience is the basis for formulating business strategy such as positioning, which is essential for a business's competitiveness, survival and success (Kasim and Dzakiria 2001). Volo (2010) records three elements that constitute the consumer experience. These are: (a) personal engagement through staged events; (b) experiences as an offering; and (c) memorability of the experiences of the consumer. The tourist experience is viewed as a complex, subjective, situational and distinctive process of consumption that is unique, special or individualistic (Mannell and Iso-Ahola 1987). Literature records a range of definitions and interpretations of tourism experience. Walls et al. (2011) propose tourist experiences to consist of individual characteristics, human interaction elements, physical experience elements and situational factors; these stimulate the experiences of an individual.

Otto and Ritchie (1996) developed six construct domains for the service experience, namely hedonic, interactive, novelty, comfort, safety and stimulation. Berry and Haeckel (2002) stated that function and emotion are the key components that determine the experience consumption. Tourist experiences are derived from a series of experiences that incorporate both physical and intangible elements, such as atmosphere/natural environment, ambience and staff (Chan 2005). It is a complex combination of factors, which shape the guest's feelings and attitudes towards his or her visit (Page and Dowling 2002). It is argued that experiences are individualistic, subjective and emotional in nature, while the service experience is inherently interpretive, subjective and affective (McCallum and Harrison 1985; Parasuraman et al. 1988). This means that key experiential aspects in tourists' experiences are influenced by service attributes provided by the suppliers (utilitarian attributes) and the attributes brought to the opportunity by the tourists (affective/personal emotive aspects). Both service attributes and the tourists' emotional state of mind contribute significantly to influence the tourists' attitude towards the nature of the service experiences consumption. The experience of leisure and tourism can be described as the 'subjective mental state that tourists feel. The affective component of the service experience has been shown to consist of subjective, emotional and highly personal responses to various aspects of the service delivery.

Several well-accepted definitions of experience and theories have been recorded in the literature with regards to the understanding of experience. Accordingly, the experience is something deeply personal, at different levels – physical, emotional, intellectual and spiritual – and 'creating memorable experience is the essence of the tourism and hospitality industry' (Pizam 2010: p. 343); consumers feel these during the consumption of the service experience or event (Pine and Gilmore 1998). Otto and Ritchie (1996: p. 166) define experience as the 'subjective felt mental state by the participants during a service encounter'; and Schänzel and McIntosh (2000: p. 37) state that experience is the 'mental, spiritual and physiological outcome resulting from on-site recreational engagement'. This implies that experience is a steady flow of multiple fantasies, feelings and fun, which may be termed the 'experiential view' (Holbrook and Hirschman 1982a: p. 132).

There are five models of consumer experiences that have been adapted to research consumer experience – hierarchical, flow, planned behaviour, typological and insider–outsider models (Prentice et al. 1998). These theories have been widely used to research and understand tourist experiences. Broadly, experiences can be conceptualized as the product or marketplace and the experiences occur in the consumers' mental places within the tourism context. Schmitt (1999) states that tourist experiences can form a framework in the five values SENSE (sensory), FEEL (emotional), THINK (cognitive), ACT (behavioural) and RELATE (relational), and these experiences provide 'sensory, emotional, cognitive, behavioural, and relational' values that are reflected in the experience sequence, as illustrated in Figure 4.1. The experience is thus formed based on the perception through the cognitive and emotive aspects of the tourist during a specific encounter or event or engagement.

Pine and Gilmore (1999: p. 11) assert that experience in the business context 'occurs whenever a company intentionally uses services as the stage and goods as props to engage an individual'. This concept can be applied to the tourism and hospitality context. The tourism and hospitality industries in nature are service- and experience-oriented. The industries provide an array of experiences and services to tourists. Within this context, tourists consume a series of experiences derived from the tangible and intangible elements using their five senses – sense, feel, think, act and relate. The result of consumption determined their behavioural reactions, and subsequently their satisfaction level. As the tourist experience has

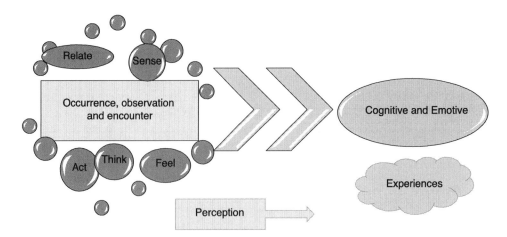

Figure 4.1 The experience sequence

Source: Developed by the authors.

multiple facets, the value of the experience is derived from the interaction involving goods and services. The experiential value can be described as extrinsic which arises from buying experiences that are utilitarian in nature, whilst intrinsic value is derived from appreciation of the experience itself. This implies that experiences are internal while goods and services are external to the tourists. This implies that the tourism businesses need to engage the tourist through experiences in order to create value.

Tourist behaviour in service experience consumption

As we are moving away from services to an experience economy, the consumer's emotive aspect has become more evident; it is pertinent in the service experience consumption and influences the way tourism suppliers operate and manage their products and services. The value or attractiveness of a tourism product or service is increasingly based on a specific experience; and creating memorable experiences is essential. Tourism suppliers increasingly become 'experience stagers' and offer an experience that engages the customers in a personal and memorable way (Pine and Gilmore 1999: pp. 3–4).

In the nature of service consumption, consumers learn and adapt their attitudinal and behavioural responses as a result of a consumption experience (Williams 2002). During and after the consumption and use of products or services, consumers develop feelings of satisfaction or dissatisfaction. Satisfaction with a consumption experience is one of two ways to measure consumer satisfaction (Otto and Ritchie 1996). It refers to the total experience, which may be influenced by a variety of factors, such as involvement, motivation, social interaction, and programme or site attributes.

In the tourism and hospitality context, tourists evaluate services based on performance and expectations, and so the assessment of services is based on consumer perceptions about service outcomes and process. Tourism and hospitality organizations provide a series of experiences that incorporate both physical and intangible elements. Two areas where tourists' opinions are critical to the success of tourism and hospitality services are: (a) the evaluation of the functionality in terms of its operation as a performance, and (b) attitude in terms of what the tourist thinks of his/her stay and the services. Tourist attitude contributes to overall feelings of satisfaction, intent to return and value (Schall 2003). The term 'quality services' in the hospitality sector often refers to the quality experienced by guests in two areas: (1) technical quality – relatively quantifiable aspects of service that consumers experience during their interactions with the accommodation; and (2) functional quality – the way the service is delivered to the guests (Kandampully et al. 2001). In order to gain an insight into how tourists perceive tourism and hospitality performance or services, it is necessary to identify and understand the way the tourists consume and their individual emotions and cognitive mind. In fact, buying behaviour in tourism differs from that in other industries. Put simply, the tourism industry is service-, experience- and people-oriented in nature. Tourist experience influences tourist buying behaviour; and tourist behaviour is diverse, multidimensional, interdisciplinary and different. The buying behaviour process in the tourism industry is very subjective, individualist and contextual.

Consumer behaviour involves the elements of mind, body, spirit, environment and feedback (Reisinger 2009). Consumer behaviour means the behaviour displayed in selecting, purchasing, using and evaluating products, services, ideas and experiences to satisfy needs and desires. Mind, body and spirit are the major aspects of human behaviour and these factors influence human needs and satisfaction. Affect (feeling, emotion and attitudes), cognition (knowing, thinking and understanding) and conation (intention, reasons, will) result from the human mind. Consumer behaviour consists of making decisions, activities, ideas or experiences that satisfy consumer needs and wants (Solomon 1996). It is different from tourist behaviour as the nature of tourism and hospitality where tourists behave in experiential contexts involves both cognitive and emotive aspects of the individual tourist, as presented in Figure 4.1, the experience sequence. This is apparent in leisure/tourism and hospitality consumption since the hedonic, emotional and imaginary outcomes of consumption seem to have a central place in the understanding of consumer buying behaviour. Experiences are a distinct offering from services and they create distinct memories and feelings through the sensory, emotional, cognitive, behavioural and relational capacities of the tourist. Thus, tourists as part of the process and their emotions and involvement affect their buying behaviour. In term of the buying process, tourist buying behaviours are influenced by environmental factors (environmental stimuli, market stimuli and marketing efforts), the tourist's factors (characteristics, psychological, decision processes) and the tourist's response factors which are related to marketing mixes – product, price, seller choice, promotional and location, as pointed out by Reisinger (2009).

From the customer's perspective, service is viewed as a phenomenon – part of the experience of life – and thus the customer's experience has elements of core needs fulfilment and emotional or hedonic content, whilst core delivery and performance are related to the provider's process. The consumption of services is distinct from that of goods, based upon the fundamental characteristics of service. These unique service characteristics stress the significance of the experiential nature of service consumption. This means that a service is consumed while it is produced and the performance of services in hospitality requires the participation of service providers and consumers, and both affect the service outcomes. The consumer's input becomes vital to the quality of service performance (Parasuraman et al. 1985).

In the service experience context, it is found that satisfaction results from the experiential nature of consumption and contains both perceptions and experiences (Otto and Ritchie 1996). The psychological environment (also called service experience) – i.e. subjective personal reactions and feelings experienced by consumers when they consume a service – has been found to be an important aspect of consumer evaluation and satisfaction with services (Ross and Iso-Ahola 1991). Arnould and Price (1993) adopt a similar approach in the context of white-water rafting and reveal that experiential themes – i.e. personal growth, self-renewal, communities and harmony with nature – are significant in explaining the underlying dimensions of satisfaction from experiential perspectives since hospitality services are more of an experience and less of a utilitarian transaction (Johns and Lee-Ross 1997). In particular, understanding experiential phenomena is crucial, as emotional reactions and decisions often prevail amongst consumers (Wakefield and Blodgett 1994). Hence, it is logical to analyse the underlying dimensions of satisfaction from the experiential perspectives. The experiences and attitudes of the consumers can be translated into future action, both economically and personally.

The three-stage model of service experience consumption – pre-consumption, consumption stage and post-consumption

The distinguishing features of services' characteristics signify the importance of the experiential nature of the service consumption process. In recognition of the importance of the experiential factor in the service consumption process, Knutson and Beck (2003) propose a model which incorporates the four major components of the consumer buying process: expectations and perception of service quality, the consumer's experience with the organization, value and satisfaction.

The experiential nature of consumption also means that customers may find it more difficult to form pre-consumption expectations about the service. Inseparability and heterogeneity lead to variability in the performance of a service. The implications of these characteristics of services mean that, even for the experienced customer, expectations are likely to change not only between successive service purchases (inter-consumption) but also within a single service journey (intra-consumption). Inter-consumption changes in expectations have received some attention from consumer behaviour researchers under the more general area of attitude change (Young 1961). In the literature, inter-consumption changes in attitudes have been predominantly attributed to the impact of communications. Other variables that influence attitude change are reference group behaviour (Kelly and Volkart 1952) and other social phenomena. The factors influencing pre-consumption include the consumer, products and situational factors. In the area of consumer satisfaction, LaBarbera and Mazursky (1983) have produced empirical evidence to support their hypothesis that satisfaction acts as a mediator between pre- and post-consumption attitudes. Satisfaction was found to influence repeat purchase intentions, but it was found that intra-consumption changes have not been examined. The principal reason for this is that general models of consumer behaviour processes are inclined to consider either the antecedents to decision-making or the consequences/evaluation of these decisions. They tend to ignore the process of consumption. Since satisfaction is a post-consumption evaluative process, consumer satisfaction researchers have also tended to disregard the potentially dynamic process of the experience during consumption. This means that, despite the importance of the experiential factor in the service experience consumption process, neither consumer behaviour nor consumer satisfaction, as they currently stand, address the post-decision stage in such a way as to incorporate the impact of experience on consumer satisfaction measurement. The environment being variable and intangible within the service itself imposes a difficulty in investigating consumer behaviour decision processes. Because, within hospitality, the duration of consumption of service is varied and also there is a wide and complex range of options available, consumer wants and needs will be varied. These will be dependent upon such factors as situation, circumstance and expenditure (Williams 2002).

The basic models of consumer behaviour categorize consumption into three components – pre-consumption, consumption and post-consumption. The parameters of experience consumption can form a framework within these three phases as follows. The pre-experience consumption phase occurs before the actual participation or consumption and includes the expectations from the tourists in terms of service quality constructs; and these expectations affect the value, level of engagement, emotion and participation of an experience.

The stages of the process that researchers have focused on are the pre-consumption and post-consumption ones. This has been driven by marketing managers' desire to: (1) influence consumers to purchase their brand during pre-consumption, and (2) predispose them favourably towards buying their product again (post-consumption). The activities of buying, using and disposing are grouped together as the 'consumption process' (Nicosia 1966). Finally, in the post-consumption stage, the individual evaluates the performance of the product. Fishbein's theory (Ajzen and Fishbein 1980) suggests that attitudes influence intentions and in turn are a predictor of behaviour. This means that intentions transform attitudes into action, but Bagozzi (1988) notes that research has found that attitudes sometimes directly affect behaviour without necessarily or fully working through intentions. This implies that evaluating the consumer's response to a consumption experience will provide the marketer with a valuable insight into the likely future performance of the products or services. Based on this, it is held that three stages of the consumption process (pre-consumption, consumption and post-consumption) are important in exploring and explaining consumer satisfaction and dissatisfaction in the service experience consumption context.

The consumption phase comprises the actual involvement or participation and real-time experience that include all encounters throughout the journey which take into account service quality dimensions. Post-experience is the last phase of experience, including the aftermath of the participation or involvement, and lays emphasis on personal perceptions of the experience, the value they place on the experience and the satisfaction with the experience (O'Sullivan and Spangler 1998: p. 28).

In the post-consumption stage, the levels of satisfaction provide the link between expectations and experience and relate directly to repurchase decisions. Satisfaction is seen to occur where consumers' expectations are met and there are limited signs of dissatisfaction, as measured against experience and norms. Satisfaction reinforces positive attitudes towards a product, leading to a greater likelihood of repeat consumption. By contrast, dissatisfaction will lead to negative attitudes and will lessen the likelihood of repetition.

The consumer behaviour literature provides an extensive framework of models and concepts aimed at identifying different processes and intervening factors that can explain consumer behaviour. Implicitly, the consumer is portrayed as a rational thinker who aims to maximize his/her utility with the purchase undertaken (Howard and Sheth 1969). Consumer choice is understood as a sequence of activities whereby information is processed to form an attitude system towards a product. Attitude is defined as an overall evaluation and portrayed as playing a major role in shaping consumer behaviour. Several factors, such as individual differences, search activity and types of involvement, are also portrayed as affecting the criteria structure of each individual. The results of the choice process, satisfaction or dissatisfaction, reinforce in turn future purchase behaviour through repeat purchase, future preferences being linked to the cognitive activity during the purchase process.

Thus, consumer behaviour is a broad and elusive area where all factors and processes are involved in the consumption process. Behaviour itself is considered to be influenced by several factors, including social, cultural and individual influence at the motivation and recognition of need stage in the consumer decision-making process (Williams 2002) and is also found in the Buyer Behaviour Model (Mill and Morrison 1998). Kotler (1996) highlights four psychological factors that influence behaviour:

- Motivation: a need that is sufficiently pressing to direct an individual to seek satisfaction
- Perception: the process by which people select, organize and interpret information to form a meaningful picture of the world
- Learning: changes observed in one's behaviour which arise from experience
- Beliefs and attitudes: the descriptive thought individuals have about something, and their evaluation, feelings and tendencies towards an object.

Realms of experiences: absorption, immersion, passive participation and active participation

Experiences have been documented in the literature as a complicated, dynamic psychological process (Chan and Baum 2007b); they fluctuate over the course of service delivery and individual engagement, and are interpreted differently by every visitor; they are subjective, intangible, continuous and highly personal phenomena (O'Dell 2007). They involve a 'transaction among environmental context, mood states, the focus of attention and perceptions of risk and competence which shapes the character and quality of the experiences' (McIntyre and Roggenbuck 1998: p. 417). Experiences can be referred to as two different states which consist of the lived experience and the evaluated experience and are subject to reflection and prescribed meaning (Highmore 2002). Larsen (2007) states that tourist experience is a past-travel-related event, which was significant enough to be stored in long-term memory. Predominantly, experiences can be studied through looking at a series of stages or events (Clawson and Knetsch 1966) and through considering the influences and personal outcomes before the trip and after the tourist returns; from the understanding of individual tourist perspectives (emotional states are integral) (Botterill and Crompton 1996); or in relation to character, or the context of the interaction, or related to modes of lived emotions – such as sensible feelings, loved body feelings, intentional value feelings and moral feelings (Lee and Crompton 1992). Cohen (1979) took a phenomenological perspective and explained that experience-seeking behaviour between people and their total world-view were dependent on the location of their countries with respect to the society to which they belonged. Wang (1999) posited that existential authenticity as tourist experiences is not based on objects, but rather on the personal feelings involved in the activities; thus the roles of authenticity and serendipitous moments should be considered (Cary 2004). Pine and Gilmore (1998) focused on the emotional, physical, spiritual and intellectual impressions felt by individuals during an event, as presented in Figure 4.2 where the experience can be divided into four quorums to determine the level of tourist involvement in terms of participation and absorption during the delivery of services.

There are four approaches to understanding visitor experiences: the satisfaction approach, benefit-based approach, experience-based approach and meanings-based approach. This

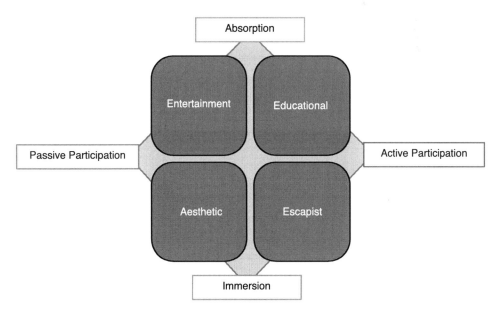

Figure 4.2 The realms of an experience

Source: Adapted from Pine and Gilmore (1999).

implies that experience is not only dynamic but can be documented at a multitude of levels and through different methodological approaches. It is therefore argued that the tourism experience comprises a strong, emotional and experiential reaction by tourists, and thus a visitor's interpretations of his/her experiences are vital to maintain quality experiences in any tourism environment. In the same vein, tourism experiences gained are likely to be derived from the service performance and the quality of experience within that particular service experience context. The quality of the experience refers to the tourists' affective responses to their desired social-psychological benefits (Chan and Baum 2007a). This implies that an array of experiences from a series of specific service transactions, such as contact with people, the physical environment or wildlife, contribute to the actual experience. The affective component of the service experience has been shown to comprise subjective, emotional and highly personal responses to various aspects of the service delivery.

Service experience dimensions

Otto and Ritchie (1996) developed six construct domains for the service experience, as shown in Table 4.1.

Elsewhere, Tung and Ritchie (2011) argue the importance of memorable experiences for service providers to deliver those experiences that are special and cherished; they also advocate the understanding of the essence of what constitutes an experience that is memorable, and confirm that memorable experiences comprise the elements of affect, expectation, consequentiality and reflection. Nevertheless, it is not certain to what extent these emotive aspects are applicable to spa providers to deliver memorable spa service experiences.

The consumer decision-making process is central to an understanding of how consumers behave and it is a complex phenomenon. A range of models of the decision process and consumer behaviour is employed in an attempt to identify, in a simplified manner, the relationships between the factors that influence behaviour. They also seek to provide a description, explanation and prediction of consumer behaviour. However, in the hospitality context, research on consumer behaviour is at a very early stage of development. Williams (2002) questions the use and relevance of these theories in exploring hospitality consumption. Still, these models can be useful and valuable in providing us with a basic understanding of consumer behaviour in hospitality consumption.

It is worthwhile reviewing the model developed by Engle and Blackwell (1982), which is a basic descriptive model of consumer decision making that encompasses four stages that involve motivation and recognition of need; information search; alternative evaluation; and

Table 4.1 The construct domains of the service experience

Domains	Service experience examples
The hedonic dimension	Enthusiastic, pleasurable, memorable activities
The interactive dimension	Getting together, being involved, making choices
The novelty dimension	Escaping, engaging in new activity
The comfort dimension	Comforting, relaxing activities
The safety dimension	Personal safety, security of belongings
The stimulation dimension	Educational, informative, challenging activities

Source: Adapted from Otto and Ritchie (1996).

consumption and outcome. Although this model has limitations in terms of its complexity and predictive capacity, it forms the basis of many future developments within decision-making research and various applications have been developed in the tourism literature.

Hedonic and utilitarian factors in service experience consumption

There has been increasing attention given to the need of examining the hedonic and affective aspects of tourist behaviour in the tourism and hospitality context – and presumably, the ways tourist behaviour differs from consumer behaviour in other contexts. Put simply, the nature of tourism and hospitality is services- and experiential-oriented, thus it is more to do with experiential context and consumption rather than product. Due to this, tourists' decision-making, satisfaction, needs and expectation within the experiential context are very much influenced by the individual emotive and hedonic aspects (Cohen et al. 2014).

In the nature of service consumption, consumers learn and adapt their attitudinal and behavioural responses as a result of a consumption experience (Williams 2002). During and after the consumption and use of products or services, consumers develop feelings of satisfaction or dissatisfaction. Satisfaction with a consumption experience is one of two ways to measure consumer satisfaction (Otto and Ritchie 1996). It refers to the total experience, which may be influenced by a variety of factors, such as involvement, motivation, social interaction, and programme or site attributes. Satisfaction with an experience is largely driven by the involvement and motivation of customers, which are more difficult to manipulate (Mannell and Iso-Ahola 1987) and also can be termed 'experienced quality' (Johns 1999).

That motives other than utilitarian can exist in the consumption of products has been noted in the consumer behaviour literature. This is apparent for leisure and tourism consumption since hedonic, emotional and imaginary outcomes of consumption seem to have a central place in the understanding of consumer behaviour. Sheth (1980) suggests that, in order to understand consumer behaviour better, other elements need to be taken into account such as habits and conditioning, situational effects, group behaviour and motivations. Levy (1959: p. 118) also notes that product evaluation could not be limited to their tangible attributes since they portray meanings to individuals beyond these tangible specificities: 'People buy things not only for what they can do, but also for what they mean.'

Following this, Holbrook and Hirschman (1982a, 1982b) produced a detailed investigation of the scope and limits of the traditional information-processing models (consumers as rational thinkers and aiming for maximization in their utility). They introduced the hedonic components of the consumption experience, as the most advanced insight into non-utilitarian consumption and to provide a framework that could relate to the analysis of leisure and tourism consumption processes. Holbrook and Hirschman (1982a: p. 92) note that consumers do not always behave as rational thinkers with careful judgemental evaluation 'but often display mental activities characterised as: primary process where their thinking is based on pleasure principles rather than rational relations'. The concept of hedonic consumption is defined as designing 'those facets of consumer behaviour that relate to the multi-sensory, fantasy and emotive aspects of one's experience with products'. Thus, utilitarian functions of products, symbolic meanings and emotions are considered as important dimensions of product evaluation. Hedonic components allow for a better understanding of products in a way that traditional consumer behaviour models have not addressed. Hedonic aspects were regarded as particularly important for products where 'the symbolic role is especially rich and salient: for example, entertainment, the arts, leisure activities encompass symbolic aspects of consumption behaviour that make them particularly fertile ground for research' (Holbrook and Hirschman 1982a: p. 134).

Holbrook and Hirschman (1982a: p. 132) also introduce the 'experiential view', which is similar to the 'phenomenological in spirit and regards consumption as a primary subjective state of consciousness with a variety of symbolic meanings, hedonic responses, and aesthetic criteria'. This implies that the evaluation of products' utilitarian functions needs to be reconsidered by adding the enjoyment and resulting feelings of pleasure that the consumption of a product might bring. The 'experiential' perspective suggests that emotional and imaginative association occurring during consumption might be equally important. These pleasurable aspects of consumption are portrayed as seeking 'fun, amusement, fantasy, arousal, sensory stimulation and enjoyment' (Holbrook and Hirschman 1982a: p. 134). This has strong implications for satisfaction formation and measurement in the service experience context and is recognized in the present research.

The hedonic perspective and experiential factors can be considered as prime determinants of behaviour and satisfaction evaluation, but whether these mediate or directly influence satisfaction or both are still matters that require clarification. This theory has highlighted two different aspects that relate to two different streams in the satisfaction literature. First, the theory suggests hedonic motives might have a strong influence on satisfaction and that the emotions and images created through actual consumption might be better predictors of satisfaction than utilitarian aspects. Second, it recognizes the importance of hedonic criteria in the consumption of some products and this could lead to a better understanding of the choice process for these products.

One stream of the satisfaction literature focuses mainly on the types of affect elicited during the consumption experience and on the importance of emotions. This approach concentrates on the antecedent of satisfaction (satisfaction as a process approach) rather than the satisfaction as an outcome. Following this, researchers have attempted to investigate the role that both hedonic and utilitarian factors might play in consumption and satisfaction processes. The hedonic perspective highlights that satisfaction might not be solely embedded in the attributes of a product. Rather, it could also be linked to the hedonic dimensions in the consumption of a product. Batra and Ahtola (1991: p. 161), who are concerned with utilitarian and hedonic dimensions of satisfaction, use the following terminology and note:

> The hedonic determinant of overall evaluation is presumed to be based on the consumer's assessment of how much pleasure he gets; his utilitarian determinant is based on this assessment about the instrumental value of the brand's functional attributes.

Their research confirms previous findings by recognizing that both utilitarian and hedonic dimensions could be present, to a greater or lesser extent, according to the type of product consumed. Similar findings from Havlena and Holbrook's work (1986: p. 394) recognize that the relative importance of each aspect might vary considerably across different products. This is also supported by Mittal (1988: p. 505) who notes the importance of both aspects:

> The functional/expressive descriptor is proposed here as a distinction, not a dichotomy. Our position is that most, perhaps all, products serve some functional needs. In addition, some service expressive needs as well.

Situations in which hedonic or expressive dimensions are more important than the utilitarian have also been termed the affective choice mode (Mittal 1988).

Functional needs are defined as 'the maximization of gains from the physical and economic environment' while the expressive needs are related to the consumer's 'consumption goals in their psycho-social worlds' (Mittal 1988: p. 505). Mano and Oliver (1993) assess the potential links between hedonic and utilitarian judgements in relation to affect and satisfaction. Their findings show that both the hedonic and utilitarian are antecedents of two affective states (pleasantness and arousal) which in turn mediate satisfaction judgements with the product consumed. Hedonic judgements appear to trigger levels of arousal that would generate higher levels of affect. Utilitarian judgements appear to mute this effect, suggesting that higher levels of utility would be expected (Krishnan and Olshavsky 1993; Mano and Oliver 1993). Satisfaction is thus posited as a consequence of affective and cognitive judgements and is affected via the positive and negative effects that these create.

References

Ajzen, I. and Fishbein, M. (1980). *Understanding Attitudes and Predicting Social Behaviour*, Englewood Cliffs, NJ: Prentice-Hall.

Arnould, E. J. and Price, L. (1993). 'River magic: Extraordinary experience and the extended service experience', *Journal of Consumer Research*, 20(1): 24-45.

Bagozzi, R. P. (1988). 'The rebirth of attitude research in marketing', *Journal of the Market Research Society*, 30(2): 163–195.

Batra, R. and Ahtola, O. T. (1991). 'Measuring the hedonic and utilitarian sources of consumer attitudes', *Marketing Letters*, 2(2): 159–170.

Berry, L. L. and Haeckel, S. H. (2002). 'Managing the total customer experience', *MIT Sloan Management Review*, 43(3): 85–89.

Botterill, D. T. and Crompton, J. L. (1996). 'Two case studies exploring the nature of the tourist's experience', *Journal of Leisure Research*, 28(1): 57–82.

Cary, S. H. (2004). 'The tourist moment', *Annals of Tourism Research*, 31(1): 61–77.

Chan, J. K. L. (2005). 'Guest Satisfaction Dimensions in the Eco Lodge Context', PhD thesis, University of Strathclyde.

Chan, J. K. L. and Baum, T. (2007a). 'Ecotourists' perception of ecotourism experience in Lower Kinabatangan, Sabah, Malaysia', *Journal of Sustainable Tourism*, 15(5): 574–590.

Chan, J. K. L. and Baum, T. (2007b). 'Motivation factors of ecotourists in ecolodge accommodation: The push and pull factors', *Asia Pacific Journal of Tourism Research*, 12(4): 349–364.

Clawson, M. and Knetsch, J. L. (1996). *Economics of Outdoor Recreation*, Baltimore, MD: Johns Hopkins University Press.

Cohen, E. (1979). 'A phenomenology of tourist experiences', *Sociology*, 13(2): 179–201.

Cohen, S. A., Prayag, G. and Moital, M. (2014). 'Consumer behaviour in tourism: Concepts, influences and opportunities', *Current Issues in Tourism*, 17(10): 872–909.

Engle, J. E. and Blackwell, R. D. (1982). *Consumer Behaviour*, 4th edition, Hinsdale, IL: Dryden.

Haeckel, S. H., Carbone, L. P. and Berry, L. L. (2003). 'How to lead the customer experience', *Marketing Management*, 12(1): 18–23.

Havlena, W. J. and Holbrook, M. B. (1986). 'The varieties of consumption experience: Comparing two typologies of emotion in consumer behaviours', *Journal of Consumer Research*, 13(3): 394–404.

Highmore, B. (2002). *Everyday Life and Cultural Theory*, London: Routledge.

Holbrook, M. B. and Hirschman, E. C. (1982a). 'The experiential aspects of consumption: Consumer fantasies, feelings and fun', *Journal of Consumer Research*, 9(2): 132–140.

Holbrook, M. B. and Hirschman, E. C. (1982b). 'Hedonic consumption: Emerging methods and proposition', *Journal of Marketing*, 46(Summer): 92–101.

Holbrook, M. B. and Hirschman, E. (1993). *The Semiotics of Consumption: Interpreting Symbolic Behaviour in Popular Culture and Works of Art*, Berlin: Mouton de Gruyter.

Howard, J. and Sheth, J. N. (1969). *The Theory of Buyer Behaviour*, New York: John Wiley and Sons.

Johns, N. (1999). 'What is this thing called service?', *European Journal of Marketing*, 33(2): 958–973.

Johns, N. and Lee-Ross, D. (1997). 'A study of service quality in small hotels and guesthouses', *Progress in Tourism and Hospitality Research*, 3(4): 351–363.

Kandampully, J., Mok, C. and Sparks, B. (2001). *Service Quality in Hospitality, Tourism and Leisure*, New York: The Haworth Press.

Kasim, A. and Dzakiria, H. (2001). 'Luring the tourists: A positioning exercise', *Asia Pacific Journal of Tourism Research*, 6(2): 40–52.

Kelly, H. H. and Volkart, E. H. (1952). 'The resistance to change of group anchored attitudes', *American Sociological Review*, 17(4): 453–465.

Knutson, B. J. and Beck, J. A. (2003). 'Identifying the dimensions of the experience constructs: Development of the model', *Journal of Quality Assurance in Hospitality and Tourism*, 4(3–4): 23–35.

Kotler, P. (1996). *Marketing Management: Analysis, Planning, Implementation and Control*, 9th edition, Englewood Cliffs, NJ: Prentice-Hall.

Krishnan, H. S. and Olshavsky, R. S. (1993). 'The dual role of emotions in consumer satisfaction/dissatisfaction', *Advances in Consumer Research*, 22(1): 454–460.

LaBarbera, P. A. and Mazursky, D. (1983). 'A longitudinal assessment of consumer satisfaction/dissatisfaction: The dynamic aspect of the cognitive process', *Journal of Marketing Research*, 20(4): 393–404.

Larsen, J. (2007). 'Aspects of a psychology of the tourist experience', *Scandinavian Journal of Hospitality and Tourism*, 7(1): 1–18.

Lee, T. H. and Crompton, J. (1992). 'Measuring novelty seeking in tourism', *Annals of Tourism Research*, 19(4): 732–751.

Levy, S. J. (1959). 'Symbols for sale', *Harvard Business Review*, 37(July): 117–124.

McCallum, J. R. and Harrison, W. (1985). 'Interdependence in the service encounter', in Czepiel, J. A. (ed.), *The Service Encounter: Managing Employee/Customer Interaction in Service Business* (pp. 35–48), Lexington, MA: Lexington Books.

McIntyre, N. and Roggenbuck, J. W. (1998). 'Nature/person transactions during an outdoor adventure experience: A multi-phasic analysis', *Journal of Leisure Research*, 30(4): 401–422.

Mannell, R. and Iso-Ahola, S. E. (1987). 'Psychological nature of leisure and tourism experience', *Annals of Tourism Research*, 14(3): 314–331.

Mano, H. and Oliver, R. (1993). 'Assessing the dimensionality and structure for the consumption experience: Evaluation, feeling, and satisfaction', *Journal of Consumer Research*, 20(3): 451–466.

Mill, R. C. and Morrison, A. M. (1998). *The Tourism System: An Introductory Text*, 3rd edition, Dubuque, IA: Prentice-Hall.

Mittal, B. (1988). 'The role of affective choice mode in the consumer purchase of expressive products', *Journal of Economic Psychology*, 9(4): 499–524.

Mittal, V., Katrichis, J. M. and Kumar, P. (2001). 'Attribute performance and customer satisfaction over time: Evidence from two field studies', *Journal of Services Marketing*, 5(5): 343–356.

Nicosia, F. M. (1966). *Consumer Decision Processes*, Englewood Cliffs, NJ: Prentice-Hall.

O'Dell, T. (2007). 'Tourist experiences and academic junctures', *Scandinavian Journal of Hospitality and Tourism*, 7(1): 34–45.

O'Sullivan, E. L. and Spangler, K. J. (1998). *Experience Marketing: Strategies for the New Millennium*, State College, PA: Venture Publishing.

Otto, J. E. and Ritchie, J. R. B. (1996). 'The service experience in tourism', *Tourism Management*, 17(3): 165–174.

Page, J. S. and Dowling, R. K. (2002). *Ecotourism: Themes in Tourism*, Harlow: Pearson Education.

Parasuraman, A., Zeithaml, V. A. and Berry, L. L. (1985). 'A conceptual model of service quality and its implications for future research', *Journal of Marketing*, 49(Fall): 41–50.

Parasuraman, A., Zeithaml, V. A. and Berry, L. L. (1988). 'SERVQUAL: A multiple-item scale for measuring consumer perception of service quality', *Journal of Retailing*, 64(1): 12–40.

Pine, B. J. and Gilmore, J. H. (1998). 'Welcome to the experience economy', *Harvard Business Review*, 76(4): 97–107.

Pine, B. J. and Gilmore, J. H. (1999). *The Experience Economy: Work is Theatre and Every Business a Stage*, Boston, MA: Harvard Business School Press.

Pizam, A. (2010). 'Creating memorable experiences', *International Journal of Hospitality Management*, 29(3): 343.

Prentice, R. C., Witt, S. F. and Hamer, C. (1998). 'Tourism as experience: The case of heritage parks', *Annals of Tourism Research*, 25(1): 1–24.

Pullman, M. E. and Gross, M. A. (2004). 'Ability of experience design elements to elicit emotions and loyalty behaviors', *Decision Sciences*, 35(3): 551–578.

Reisinger, Y. (2009). *International Tourism Cultures and Behaviours*, New York: Routledge.

Ross, E. L. D. and Iso-Ahola, S. E. (1991). 'Sightseeing tourists' motivation and satisfaction', *Annals of Tourism Research*, 18(2): 226–237.

Schall, M. (2003). 'Best practices in the assessment of hotel-guest attitudes', *Cornell Hotel and Restaurant Administration Quarterly*, 51(April): 51–65.

Schänzel, H. A. and McIntosh, A. J. (2000). 'An insight into the personal and emotive context of wildlife viewing at the penguin place, Otago Peninsula, New Zealand', *Journal of Sustainable Tourism*, 8(1): 36–52.

Schmitt, B. (1999). 'Experiential marketing', *Journal of Marketing Management*, 15(1–3): 53–67.

Sheth, J. N. (1980). 'The surpluses and shortages in consumer behaviour theory and research', *Journal of the Academy of Marketing Science*, 7(4): 414–427.

Solomon, M. R. (1996). *Consumer Behaviour*, London: Prentice-Hall.

Tung, V. W. S. and Ritchie, J. R. B. (2011). 'Exploring the essence of memorable tourism experiences', *Annals of Tourism Research*, 38(4): 1367–1386.

Volo, S. (2010). 'Conceptualizing experience: A tourist based approach', in Scott, N., Laws, E. and Boksberger, P. (eds.), *Marketing of Tourism Experiences* (pp. 13–28), New York: Routledge.

Voss, C.A., Roth, V. and Chase, R. B. (2008). 'Experience, service operations strategy and services as destinations: Foundations and exploratory investigation', *Production and Operation Management*, 17(3): 247–266.

Wakefield, K. L. and Blodgett, J. G. (1994). 'The importance of servicescapes in leisure settings', *Journal of Services Marketing*, 8(3): 66–76.

Walls, A. R., Okumus, F., Wang, Y. R. and Kwun, D. J. (2011). 'An epistemological view of consumer experiences', *International Journal of Hospitality Management*, 30(17): 10–21.

Wang, N. (1999). 'Rethinking authenticity in tourism experience', *Annals of Tourism Research*, 2(1): 349–370.

Williams, A. (2002). *Understanding the Hospitality Consumer*, Oxford: Butterworth-Heinemann.

Young, P. T. (1961). *Motivation and Emotion. A Survey of the Determinants of Human and Animal Activity*, New York: John Wiley.

Zomerdijk, L. G. and Voss, C. A. (2010). 'Service design for experience-centric services', *Journal of Service Research*, 13(1): 67–82.

5

THE ROLE AND INFLUENCE OF EMOTIONS ON TOURIST BEHAVIOUR

Gabrielle Walters and Shanshi Li

Introduction

Emotions have a significant influence on the tourism consumer's behaviour before, during and after their tourism experience. Emotion is therefore a highly relevant psychological construct to the study of tourist behaviour. How a tourist responds emotionally to marketing attempts as well as their actual tourism experience is of significant importance to tourism marketers and those responsible for the development and management of tourism products. From a research perspective, the measurement of tourist emotions provides important insight into a tourism consumer's affective response to the tourism offering. Continuing technological advancements in the methodological tools available to tourism researchers are increasing the reliability and validity of emotional data and extending its application to a wide range of tourism contexts. This chapter commences with a discussion that emphasises the important role that emotion plays in the tourist's experience from their initial decision-making process to their reactions to and satisfaction with their final choice. The chapter will then focus on the measurement of emotion, presenting a review of the current trends and advances in the methodological techniques employed by tourism researchers to better understand the role and influence of emotion on tourist behaviour.

The role and importance of emotion in tourist decision-making behaviour

Past research has positioned consumer emotions at the core of the consumer decision-making process. Tuan-Pham et al. (2001) claim that people often make evaluative judgements, whether they are positive or negative, based on their feelings and emotions or subjective responses to a target purchase decision. Graham (1995) suggests that it is one's emotions that guide the decision-making process in its entirety while motivation theorists such as Murray (1938) and McClelland (1985) propose that emotions serve as a basis for the motives behind the actual decision process. The importance of emotions to the tourism consumer's decision process in particular is emphasised by Gnoth (1997), who claims that the hedonic nature of the tourism product means that the purchase decision is driven by an emotionally driven goal. Holbrook and Hirschman (1982) and more recently, Chuang (2007) also agree that hedonic purchases such as leisure and tourism are most likely to involve an emotive as opposed to a logical motive. Hyde's (1999) research confirmed that tourism-related purchase decisions did not revolve around problem-solving activities, but rather evoked feelings and emotions related to the anticipated hedonic experience.

The unique characteristics of the tourism purchase itself provide further justification for the role of consumer emotions in the consumer decision process. For example, a holiday is rarely a spontaneous purchase and is generally preceded by planning and saving over a period of time. In addition, the tourism purchase is made with no expectations of a tangible return. In other words, the tourism consumer will invest with no expectation of material or economic return on their purchase, other than intangible satisfaction (Moutinho 1987). It is therefore not surprising that there is a consensus within the literature that tourism and leisure purchases are accompanied by considerable emotional as opposed to cognitive involvement (Crouch and Louviere 2001; Goossens 2003; Holbrook and Hirschman 1982; Hosany and Gilbert 2010; Woods 1981). The problem recognition, information search and post-purchase experience stages of the tourism consumer's decision process represent the stages within which emotions are likely to be most influential. This is discussed as follows.

Problem recognition, otherwise known as need awareness, is commonly defined as the identification of a discrepancy between the consumer's desired state and actual state (Morrison 2002; Neal et al. 2002; Sheth and Mittal 2004). This may include a state of deprivation, discomfort or need (whether physical or psychological) and consumers are made aware of their state by either internal or external stimuli (i.e. media sources) (Sheth and Mittal 2004). Internal stimuli are the physiological signals that attract the consumer's attention to their discrepant needs, for example, the physical signs of hunger or thirst. It is these signals that Izard (1977), a pre-eminent researcher in the area of emotions and consumer behaviour, views as the 'cornerstone' of the primary motivational system in human beings. They not only communicate the motivational state of one individual to another, but provide feedback to the individual to assist in the interpretation of their affective state as well as their current needs. Emotions therefore act as an important information source for this initial stage of the decision process particularly given human desire for a neutral or positive emotional state. In a tourism context, the realisation of the need for recreation and travel is an affective state usually signalling physical or mental exhaustion and/or social needs such as recognition or inclusion (Neal et al. 2002). Mathieson and Wall (1982), in their alternative decision-making model for travel purchases, refer to this phase as the felt need or travel desire.

Once the desire to travel is recognised and established, the tourism consumer then seeks relevant information in an attempt to satisfy this need. The information search phase of the decision process is defined by Fodness and Murray (1997) as 'a dynamic process wherein individuals use various amounts and types of information sources in response to internal and external contingencies to facilitate travel planning' (p. 506). It is within this stage that the tourism marketer must succeed in portraying their tourism product as one that can satisfy the tourism consumer's physiologically determined needs. The intangible nature of tourism products makes this task somewhat challenging for destination marketers and the use of emotional appeals that both capture and retain consumer interest and involvement is crucial (Cai et al. 2003). In this regard, Walters et al. (2010) emphasise the importance of marketing stimuli that encourage consumers to imagine their future tourism experience. The authors revealed a positive relationship between elaborate mental imagery and emotional response, concluding that elaborate mental images and their associated emotional responses can increase product interest and reduce purchase time. A possible explanation for this is that the tourism consumer is persuaded to bypass the alternative evaluation stage of the decision process in a bid to satisfy their ad-elicited fantasy and the subsequent emotional desire to experience the advertised destination. Further support for the importance of an imagery–emotion framework is noted in the work of del Bosque and San Martin (2008), whose findings revealed that positive images and emotions jointly participate in satisfaction formation. The authors advise on the importance of emotional appeal in tourism marketing communications should destinations aim to improve their position in the tourist's choice set.

The tourism consumer's self-assessment of their satisfaction or dissatisfaction with their purchase represents the post-purchase evaluation stage of the decision process (Sheth and Mittal 2004). During this stage the tourism consumer evaluates their overall experience in terms of its ability to deliver on the emotionally driven goals originally sought (Bagozzi et al. 1998). Post-consumption emotions, whether they are positive or negative, have a significant influence on how a tourist behaves following their tourism experience. For example, Hosany and Prayag (2013) revealed that emotional responses are powerful indicators of a tourist's propensity to recommend. In their study, tourists that experienced emotional patterns of delight and passion exhibited the highest satisfaction levels with their tourism experience. Bigné and Andreu's (2004) study also concluded that tourists with higher levels of positive emotions are more likely to show an increased satisfaction level which in turn leads to greater satisfaction intentions. Customer loyalty, a post-purchase behaviour demonstrated through repeat bookings and visitation, is also a desirable behaviour among tourism providers and one that is highly influenced by emotion. A study by Han and Back (2008) suggested that loyalty is influenced by both positive and negative emotions. Their finding that negative emotions are likely to have the greater influence on whether or not a tourism consumer remains loyal to a tourism organisation reinforces the importance of service recovery both during and following the tourist's consumption experience.

The preceding content has established the role and importance of emotion in the tourist's decision process. In particular the literature reviewed so far demonstrates the influence that emotions have on the planning, selection and evaluation of tourism experiences. Acknowledging the relationship between tourist emotion and satisfaction, recent tourism consumer research has focused on the tourist's subjective (e.g. emotional) interpretations of the physical and social environment they encounter whilst travelling. How to engage tourists emotionally during the tourism experience has become increasingly important to tourism providers and researchers, as demonstrated in the following.

Consumer emotion and the tourism experience

Emotions play an integral role in shaping tourism experiences (Kim and Fesenmaier 2015). It is argued that tourists' perceptions of their physical and social environments are grounded not only in their objective observations but also in their subjective interpretations which may be influenced by their emotional state (Arnould and Price 1993; Gibson 1986). The study of environmental psychology largely informs research that investigates the relationship between service settings, emotional states and consumer behaviour (Brunner-Sperdin et al. 2012). In tourism, Mehrabian and Russell's (1974) Pleasure–Arousal–Dominance (PAD) framework is often drawn upon to explore tourists' emotional reactions to the tourism setting. This three-dimensional framework posits that environmental perceptions stimulate different sets of emotions which influence an individual's reactions to the environment either positively or negatively (Kim and Fesenmaier 2015). The pleasure dimension serves as an indicator of valence, that is the direction of the emotion, and the arousal dimension describes the intensity of the emotion. Its relevance and use in a tourism context is justified by the multifaceted nature of the tourism setting within which the tourist is subject to a variety of different stimuli and experiences across the travel experience.

Whilst it has been established that engaging tourists emotionally during their travel experience can enhance satisfaction and incite beneficial post-purchase behaviour, the benefits of emotional engagement in a tourism setting spread beyond these two outcomes. For example, Ballantyne et al. (2007) in their research on conservation learning revealed that emotionally engaged tourists are more likely to generate public concern about the protection and survival of particular species of animals. In their study, resultant behaviours of emotionally engaged zoo visitors included donations to conservation funds, higher involvement in conservation activities and the joining of conservation membership programmes. It is important to note at this point however that tourist emotions do not have to be positive for such behaviours to take place. Learning about the mistreatment or displacement of a particular species for example is unlikely in most cases to generate positive emotions, yet such knowledge is still able to generate the level of concern needed to incite conservation behaviour. In addition, it is not only positive emotions that result in a satisfying tourism experience. For example, when visiting a dark tourism site, tourist satisfaction is often evaluated against the attraction's ability to generate negative emotional responses such as anger, fear and grief (Best 2007).

There is no question regarding the importance of consumer emotion to the tourism experience, from the initial planning stages to the experience itself. It is for this reason that capturing the essential aspects of both conscious and unconscious emotions across all phases of the travel experience is of great interest to tourism researchers. What constitutes the effective measurement of tourist emotion has surfaced as a topic of debate within recent consumer behaviour and tourism literature. The remainder of this chapter provides detailed insight into the measurement of emotion and presents a case for the use of psychophysiological-based measurement tools.

The measurement of emotion in tourism research

Traditionally, self-report methods have been widely used in tourism research to measure tourists' emotions. Such methods require respondents to rate their emotional states against a list of affective items such as joy, sadness or anger without researchers' interference (Li et al. 2014). In tourism, self-report scales are usually adapted from emotion theories in the domain of psychology to fit the specific study context (Hosany and Gilbert 2010). Two psychological approaches frequently used by tourism scholars include the basic emotion and dimensional approaches. The basic emotion approach, also known as the categorical approach, establishes a series of basic emotions (e.g. joy, disgust and fear), and the combination of these basic emotions results in other secondary emotions (Ma et al. 2013). Pearce and Coghlan (2010) examined the relationships between tourists' emotions and satisfaction levels on dynamic volunteer tourism expeditions. In particular, tourists were asked to rate both the type and intensity of emotions they feel on an 18-item affective scale (e.g. frustrated, pleased, contented, worried, depressed, sad, peaceful, etc.). To better reflect tourists' emotional experience, Hosany and Gilbert (2010) modified an existing emotional measurement scale to take into account the specific characteristics of a destination, and the validity of the Destination Emotion Scale (DES) was examined by measuring tourists' emotions in two destinations (Hosany et al. 2015). In particular, joy, love and positive surprise were identified as three salient dimensions to represent the DES. Similarly, each emotion was represented by several affective adjectives and a 7-point scale ranging from 1 = not at all to 7 = very much was used to indicate the emotion's intensity.

The dimensional approach, on the other hand, holds that all emotions can be located on a set of common dimensions such as pleasure and arousal. Pleasure refers to the pleasantness of an affective experience and is frequently measured by positive adjectives such as happy, joyful or entertained. Arousal indicates emotional intensity, ranging from 'quietness' to 'excitement'. For example, Bigné et al. (2005) compared two models that explored the influence of emotions on satisfaction, willingness to pay and loyalty. Emotion was measured using two independent dimensions (i.e. pleasure and arousal). In particular, five-point semantic differential scales with bipolar opposites such as sad–joyful and disappointed–delighted were adopted to measure the tourist's emotional experience. Other consumer studies that have utilised the dimensional approach have examined tourists' affective images of large-scale environments (Seyhmus and David 1997), and the influence of emotion on shopping values and behaviours (Yüksel 2007). Comparatively, the dimensional approach is more popular in tourism research than the basic emotional approach (Li et al. 2015). As noted by Huang (2001), it is questionable to regard emotions as discrete entities in the consumption context as they tend to be short-lived and rarely seen in their pure forms. Moreover, the dimensional approach is more parsimonious in comparison with the basic emotion approach considering that infinite types of affective words are classified into several dimensions (e.g. valence and arousal) (Mauss and Robinson 2009).

In recent years, psychophysiological methods have emerged in the tourism literature to measure tourists' intuitive and unconscious emotional responses. Psychophysiology is the branch of psychology that examines the correlations between individuals' psychological activities and corresponding physiological reactions such as an increase in heart rate and blood pressure. In the past, the use of psychophysiological measures was not common due to the costly and specialised nature of the apparatus and analysing software (Li et al. 2015). With the innovation of technology, portable and affordable equipment has been developed by several major manufacturers such as Biopac™, leading to increasing use in examining consumers' emotions in marketing, media and tourism research. Li et al. (2015) proposed five psychophysiological measures such as electro-dermal analysis, facial muscle activity, heart rate response, an eye-tracking system and vascular measures and discussed the potential for their use in tourism research. By examining the advantages and disadvantages of psychophysiological measures, they concluded that studies combining both self-report and psychophysiological measures are needed.

For the application of psychophysiological methods in tourism, Kim and Fesenmaier (2015) measured two travellers' emotional responses using the electro-dermal activities (EDA) method during a four-day visit to Philadelphia. EDA, also known as a measure of the skin conductance method, registers the activation of an individual's autonomic nervous system (ANS) and has been widely used as a reliable indicator of arousal. The EDA measure was found to be a useful tool for understanding tourists' emotional experiences in natural settings as the research revealed consistencies between the participants' EDA patterns and their self-reported tour experience. Another application of physiological measurement techniques is demonstrated by Kim et al. (2014), who by incorporating both EDA and heart rate measures were able to reveal that video is superior to high-imagery audio in evoking arousal levels among potential tourism consumers. Overall, psychophysiological methods are able to track respondents' spontaneous emotional responses that are beyond their control, which allows researchers to avoid the interference of cognitive biases and socially desirable constraints.

Self-report vs psychophysiological measures of emotion in tourism

The emergence of psychophysiological methods has challenged the use of self-report questionnaires for the measurement of emotional response. On the whole, self-report scales present a simple and inexpensive method to capture consumers' emotional reactions, especially when working with large samples (Poels and Dewitte 2006). Questionnaires are one of the most common means via which self-report emotional response scales are administered and their use is suitable for both laboratory and field-based research. However, the self-report method has been increasingly criticised in recent marketing and tourism literature (Li et al. 2015; Kim and Fesenmaier 2015). First, within self-report methods, respondents have to recall their emotional states after the experience, and entirely relying on their memories may involve a series of cognitive biases that can distort a tourist's original emotional response towards the destination (Ravaja 2004). Kyle and Lee (2012) examined the consistency of emotional memory during and after a festival. They found that attendees' recollection of their positive emotions was inconsistent with their on-site positive emotions, which suggested that respondents' retrospection of their emotions was an inaccurate account of their actual emotions. In essence, the time lag may have restricted the attendees' ability to recall exactly what their feelings were. Second, self-report measures are inadequate in terms of providing a full explanation of participants' emotional experience in real time (Micu and Plummer 2010). Emotion does not occur at just one point in time and constantly fluctuates (Fogel et al. 1992). Therefore a method that is able to capture the emotional flow patterns is required. Self-report emotion scales are only able to capture individuals' general feeling towards the experience or specific stimulus instead of tracking subjects' moment-to-moment responses. As stated by Maier (2009), it is difficult to know which elements or events embedded in a continuous stimulus are most effective in generating emotional response via a self-report scale. By measuring a tourism consumer's physical and sensory experience, one is able to capture their continuous emotions that vary across space and time (Kim and Fesenmaier 2015). Lastly, the long list of emotional items contained in a questionnaire may result in participant fatigue, particularly when traditional data collection requires tourism consumers to self-evaluate their emotions after their experience – at which time they may already be experiencing some degree of fatigue. This poses significant threats to the reliability and validity of the results obtained.

Psychophysiological methods focus on tourism consumers' physiological responses that usually occur simultaneously with their subjective emotional experience. For example, instead of asking respondents to verbally report how they feel, psychophysiological methods involve attaching sensors or electrodes to subjects and registering their physiological reactions to the external stimuli. This in turn allows the researcher to capture data that is beyond an individual's conscious control, and that is less likely to be influenced by cognitive biases. Psychophysiological methods therefore overcome the criticisms of self-report questionnaires stated earlier. First, psychophysiological measures do not depend on language, recall or cognitive thinking and thus are likely to reduce cognitive biases and respondent errors. Second, psychophysiological measures are capable of tracking individuals' moment-to-moment emotional responses, which enables the researchers to visualise the peaks and troughs of respondents' emotional flow patterns across time. This is particularly relevant to destination marketers seeking to investigate advertising effectiveness as this allows them to identify segments of their advertisement that are in need of further refinement. Finally, psychophysiological methods such as electro-dermal activity sensors offer great convenience and simplicity for the data collection. With the development of technology, wearable devices are now available to measure tourists' real-time emotions outside of a laboratory setting. Portable and non-invasive sensors attached to the wrists of participants allow researchers to measure their emotional responses for the duration of their tourism experience. The data is automatically stored for analysis after the event and avoids the risk of participant fatigue.

Recent research performed by the authors investigated the use and capabilities of facial electromyography (EMG) and skin conductance (SC) measures in registering consumers' emotional responses to destination advertisements and confirmed the effectiveness of psychophysiological measures of emotion. Thirty-three participants were exposed to three destination advertisements with differing emotional appeals while their real-time facial EMG and SC data were collected. A self-report questionnaire was also utilised to collect participants' subjective emotional responses. The results revealed that psychophysiological measures are more sensitive discriminators than those employed for self-report questionnaires when evaluating tourism advertising campaigns. While the data from the self-report questionnaire was able to distinguish the two emotional advertisements from a highly differentiated rational advertisement, it was incapable of differentiating the two emotional advertisements. Moreover, the research successfully demonstrated that both facial EMG and SC measures are more useful in tracking consumers' moment-to-moment emotional responses. The peaks identified in the traces of facial EMG and SC data were also clearly associated with specific affective frames in the advertisements. The alignment of physiological responses with the participants' subjective evaluations of the advertisements (captured via a follow-up interview) further demonstrated the reliability and validity of psychophysiological data in capturing tourism consumers' real-time emotional responses.

Conclusion

This chapter has demonstrated that tourist emotions play a pivotal role in not only their pre- and post-travel decision behaviour but also their interpretation of the travel experience itself. It is therefore essential that those responsible for experience design and the research that informs it account for the power that consumer emotions have in terms of tourist engagement and satisfaction. Favourable post-purchase behaviours, whether they entail donating to societal causes such as conservation or recommending the experience to others, are dependent on emotional engagement. The relationship between emotional engagement and satisfaction has been demonstrated across a vast array of contexts and settings. This chapter concludes by positing that a methodological shift in terms of the way emotions are measured is necessary. The authors reinforce the importance of capturing emotional responses that are beyond an individual's conscious control to avoid the influence of cognitive bias. Psychophysiological measures of emotion are recommended as a means of capturing the unconscious emotional experience.

References

Arnould, E. J. and Price, L. L. (1993). 'River magic: Extraordinary experience and the extended service encounter', *Journal of Consumer Research*, 20(1): 24–45.

Bagozzi, R. P., Baumgartner, H. and Pieters, R. (1998). 'Goal-directed emotions', *Cognition and Emotion*, 12(1): 1–26.

Ballantyne, R., Packer, J., Hughes, K. and Dierking, L. (2007). 'Conservation learning in wildlife tourism settings: Lessons from research in zoos and aquariums', *Environmental Education Research*, 13(3): 367–383.

Best, M. (2007). 'Norfolk Island: Thanatourism, history and visitor emotions', *International Journal of Research into Island Cultures*, 2(1): 30–48.

Bigne, J. E. and Andreu, L. (2004). 'Emotions in segmentation: An empirical study', *Annals of Tourism Research*, 31(3): 682–696.

Bigné, J. E., Andreu, L. and Gnoth, J. (2005). 'The theme park experience: An analysis of pleasure, arousal and satisfaction', *Tourism Management*, 26(6): 833–844.

Brunner-Sperdin, A., Peters, M. and Strobl, A. (2012). 'It is all about the emotional state: Managing tourists' experiences', *International Journal of Hospitality Management*, 31(1): 23–30.

Cai, L. A., Feng, R. and Breiter, D. (2003). 'Tourist purchase decision involvement and information preferences', *Journal of Vacation Marketing*, 10(2): 138–148.

Chuang, S. C. (2007). 'The effects of emotions on the purchase of tour commodities', *Journal of Travel and Tourism Marketing*, 22(1): 1–13.

Crouch, G. I., and Louviere, J. J. (2001). 'A review of choice modeling research in tourism, hospitality and leisure', in J. A. Mazenec, G. I. Crouch, J. R. Ritchie and A. G. Woodside (eds.), *Consumer Psychology in Tourism, Hospitality and Leisure* (pp. 67–83), Wallingford: CABI.

del Bosque, I. R. and San Martin, H. (2008). 'Tourist satisfaction: A cognitive model', *Annals of Tourism Research*, 35(2): 551–573.

Fodness, D. and Murray, B. M. (1997). 'Tourist information search', *Annals of Tourism Research*, 24(3): 503–523.

Fogel, A., Nwokah, E., Dedo, J. Y., Messinger, D., Dickson, K. L., Matusov, E. and Holt, S. A. (1992). 'Social process theory of emotion: A dynamic systems approach', *Social Development*, 1(2): 122–142.

Gibson, J. (1986). *The Ecological Approach to Visual Perception*, Hillside, NJ: Lawrence Erlbaum.

Gnoth, J. (1997). 'Tourism motivation and expectation formation', *Annals of Tourism Research*, 24(2): 283–304.

Goossens, C. F. (2003). 'Visual persuasion: Mental imagery processing and emotional experiences', in L. M. Scott and R. Batra (eds.), *Persuasive Imagery: A Consumer Response Perspective* (pp. 129–139), London: Lawrence Erlbaum Associates.

Graham, J. R. (1995). 'The customer might be cool as a cucumber but grab the emotions if you want the sale', *The American Salesman*, 40(4): 16–21.

Han, H. and Back, K.-J. (2008). 'Relationships among image congruence, consumption emotions, and customer loyalty in the lodging industry', *Journal of Hospitality and Tourism Research*, 32(4): 467–490.

Holbrook, M. B. and Hirschman, E. C. (1982). 'The experiential aspects of consumption: Consumer fantasies, feelings and fun', *Journal of Consumer Research*, 9(2): 132–140.

Hosany, S. and Gilbert, D. (2010). 'Measuring tourists' emotional experiences toward hedonic holiday destinations', *Journal of Travel Research*, 49(4): 513–526.

Hosany, S. and Prayag, G. (2013). 'Patterns of tourists' emotional responses, satisfaction, and intention to recommend', *Journal of Business Research*, 66(6): 730–737.

Hosany, S., Prayag, G., Deesilatham, S., Cauševic, S. and Odeh, K. (2015). 'Measuring tourists' emotional experiences: Further validation of the Destination Emotion Scale', *Journal of Travel Research*, 54(4): 482–495.

Huang, M. H. (2001). 'The theory of emotions in marketing', *Journal of Business and Psychology*, 16(2): 239–247.

Hyde, K. F. (1999). 'A hedonic perspective on independent vacation planning, decision-making and behavior', in A. G. Woodside, G. I. Crouch, M. Mazenec, M. Opperman and M. Y. Sakai (eds.), *Consumer Psychology of Tourism, Hospitality and Leisure (Vol. 1)* (pp. 177–209), Wallingford: CABI.

Izard, C. E. (1977). *Human Emotions*, New York: Plenum Press.

Kim, J. J. and Fesenmaier, D. R. (2015). 'Measuring emotions in real time: Implications for tourism experience design', *Journal of Travel Research*, 54(4): 1–11.

Kim, S.-B., Kim, D.-Y. and Bolls, P. (2014). 'Tourist mental-imagery processing: Attention and arousal', *Annals of Tourism Research*, 45(2): 63–76.

Kyle, G. T. and Lee, J. J. (2012). 'Recollection consistency of festival consumption emotions', *Journal of Travel Research*, 51(2): 178–190.

Li, S., Scott, N. and Walters, G. (2015). 'Current and potential methods for measuring emotion in tourism experiences: A review', *Current Issues in Tourism*, 18(9): 805–827.

McClelland, D. C. (1985). *Human Motivation*, Glenview, IL: Scott Foresman and Company.

Ma, J., Gao, J., Scott, N. and Ding, P. (2013). 'Customer delight from theme park experiences: The antecedents of delight based on cognitive appraisal theory', *Annals of Tourism Research*, 42: 359–381.

Maier, J. R. (2009). *Real-time Response Measurement in the Social Sciences: Methodological Perspectives and Applications*, Frankfurt am Main: Peter Lang.

Mathieson, A. and Wall, G. (1982). *Tourism: Economic, Physical and Social Impacts*, London: Longman.

Mauss, I. B. and Robinson, M. D. (2009). 'Measures of emotion: A review', *Cognition and Emotion*, 23(2): 209–237.

Mehrabian, A. and Russell, J. A. (1974). *An Approach to Environmental Psychology*, Cambridge, MA: Massachusetts Institute of Technology.

Micu, A. C. and Plummer, J. T. (2010). 'Measurable emotions: How television ads really work: Patterns of reactions to commercials can demonstrate advertising effectiveness', *Journal of Advertising Research*, 50(2): 137–153.

Morrison, A. M. (2002). *Hospitality and Travel Marketing*, 3rd edition, Albany, NY: Delmar Publishers.

Moutinho, L. (1987). 'Consumer behavior in tourism', *European Journal of Marketing*, 21(10): 5–44.

Murray, H. A. (1938). *Explorations in Personality*, New York: Oxford University Press.

Neal, C. M., Quester, P. and Hawkins, D. (2002). *Consumer Behaviour: Implications for Marketing Strategy*, Macquarie Park, NSW: McGraw-Hill.

Pearce, P. and Coghlan, A. (2010). 'Tracking affective components of satisfaction', *Tourism and Hospitality Research*, 10 (1): 42–58.

Poels, K. and Dewitte, S. (2006). 'How to capture the heart? Reviewing 20 years of emotion measurement in advertising', *Journal of Advertising Research*, 46(1): 18–37.

Ravaja, N. (2004). 'Contributions of psychophysiology to media research: Review and recommendations', *Media Psychology*, 6(2): 193–235.

Seyhmus, B. and David, B. (1997). 'Affective images of tourism destinations', *Journal of Travel Research*, 35(4): 11–15.

Sheth, J. N. and Mittal, B. (2004). *Consumer Behavior: A Managerial Perspective*, Mason, OH: Thomson South Western.

Tuan Pham, M., Cohen, J. B., Pracejus, J. W. and Hughes, G. D. (2001). 'Affect monitoring and the primacy of feelings in judgment', *Journal of Consumer Research*, 28(2): 167–189.

Walters, G. A., Sparks, B. and Herington, C. (2010). 'The impact of consumption vision and emotion on the tourism consumer's decision behaviour', *Journal of Hospitality and Tourism Research*, 36(3): 366–389.

Woods, W. A. (1981). *Consumer Behaviour*, New York: North Holland.

Yüksel, A. (2007). 'Tourist shopping habitat: Effects on emotions, shopping value and behaviours', *Tourism Management*, 28(1): 58–69.

6

CONSUMER INFORMATION-SEEKING BEHAVIOUR

Gaitree (Vanessa) Gowreesunkar and Saurabh Kumar Dixit

Introduction

Customers of the 21st century are busy and demanding and above all, they display unpredictable behaviour. Whenever they need information on a particular product or service, they resort to sources that are practical, convenient, less time-consuming and cost-efficient. But they can also change their decision and act otherwise at the last minute. In the tourism context, understanding the process of information search of travellers gets even more complicated. Unlike with products, the information searching in tourism does not stop once the destination is selected. Acquisition of information (e.g. choosing accommodation, transportation and tourism activities) continues after the destination selection, so that grasping an understanding of this ongoing pattern poses a considerable challenge to marketers and tourism service providers. The information-savvy tourists usually gather a variety of media and non-media types of information derived from internal and external sources in order to support their tourism decisions. However, with the emergence of travel technologies (blogs, interactive online platforms), it has become more difficult to understand the information search pattern of tourists. Research reveals that when internal sources are insufficient, tourists will usually start gathering from external sources but if the cost of external information is high, tourists might go back to internal sources or adopt other approaches of information search.

More importantly, understanding tourists' travel information-seeking behaviour helps tourism businesses to make better decisions as to where and how to allocate their limited marketing budgets, thereby ensuring marketing dollars are well spent (Gursoy and McCleary 2004; Gursoy and Terry Umbreit 2004). Destination managers, marketers and other tourism enterprises can target marketing communications more effectively because the information search represents the first step in a traveller's decision-making process (Farahani et al. 2011; Gursoy 2011).

With these notions as foundation, this chapter aims at exploring the concept of customer information-seeking behaviour. Booking.com will be used as a case study to illustrate the inform-ation search process of tourists from Mauritius planning to travel and the sources upon which they rely to make their decisions as well as the limitations and challenges they go through during the process. The chapter argues that it is fundamental to understand tourists' approach to information search and the factors that guide their search pattern. As a concluding note, the chapter will propose suggestions and recommendations for destination marketers and tourism providers so that they can craft appropriate strategies to satisfy the 21st century's super-savvy tourists.

Nature of information search

Information search has been defined as the 'motivated activity to search for information stored in memory or acquisition of decision-relevant information from the environment' (Engel et al. 1995: p. 41). In the context of tourism, the purchase of a product involves risk due to the peculiar characteristics of tourism (Zeithaml 1981). As a result, the search for tourism information is intensive. For instance, the plan for a forthcoming holiday in Mauritius cannot be tried and tested to reduce uncertainty in the consumer's mind. Searching for information becomes important to help tourists reduce the level of perceived risk. The search for tourism information is usually guided by the amount of information the tourist initially has, the ease of obtaining additional information and the willingness to dedicate effort and time to engage in search activities. Time is an important determining factor and the perceived value of time for tourists under time pressure is likely to be higher than for those with no pressure. As such, information search in tourism takes place by relying on internal sources, external sources or a combination of both.

Internal information sources

Whenever tourists realise that they need to make a decision, information search is likely to take place and almost always initially it takes place internally (Gursoy and McCleary 2004). Internal search is based on the retrieval of knowledge from memory and information derived from the immediate personal environment. Internal information sources include among others:

- Information from previous visits;
- Incidental learning and intentional learning with regard to the specific destination or a similar one;
- Information accumulated through ongoing search;
- Knowledge gathered through personal experiences;
- Advice and suggestions from family and friends;
- Information saved in online accounts of customers like Booking.com, Make-My-Trip.

All of these lead to familiarity and expertise, thus facilitating the tourists to make the purchase decision. Tourists prefer to resort to these modes of internal information search because this enables them to reduce uncertainty and serve as both opinion leaders and sources of information for their acquaintances.

External information sources

When the internal search for information does not reveal enough information, or it does not provide up-to-date information, the tourist resorts to external sources. External search is the retrieval of information from the market (Engel et al. 1995), for instance, choosing of hotels, or looking for information on transportation and recreational activities available at the destination. Basically, two types of information are observed from external sources, namely non-media information (institutional and commercial brochures, travel trade and Internet) and mass media information (advertising and reports in broadcast media). When planning their trips, tourists tend to use informative travel brochures as a key source of information as these are perceived as reliable due to the fact that operators at the destination itself produce them. Even a traveller with adequate experience may need to rely on external sources of information before a routine trip or because of some side trips or changes in route (Gursoy and Chen 2000). The external search will therefore be based on available materials from:

- Institutional sources: brochures from tourism-related organisations like travel trade, hotels and destination management organisations (DMOs);
- Commercial sources: brochures from marketplaces, metro stations, bus stands, train stations, travel guides in libraries;
- Media sources like newspapers, travel channels like 'Voyage', interactive billboards, television documentaries, or travel applications on one's mobile phone.

With the progress of technology, customers have developed an isolated culture and have become quite independent. This sophistication has altered their information search behaviour so that they are increasingly resorting to the range of tools provided by the Internet Booking Engine (IBE). An IBE is an application which helps consumers to book flights, hotels, holiday packages, insurance and other services online. Examples are Make-My-Trip, Cleartrip.com, Booking.com, Expedia.com, eBookers, Dealcheckers and the like. Because tourists of the 21st century are always busy with activities and overloaded with routine work, they often complain about lack of time. Therefore, whenever they need information on a particular destination, they often resort to sources that are practical, convenient, less time-consuming and more cost-efficient. IBEs are usually perceived as the most convenient option for most consumers. Consumers therefore search for information in the comfort of their office by working and retrieving information in parallel. Some even use their office printers to print information that needs to be discussed with family members at home. The Internet, as an external source, provides accurate and specific information that can reach its target audience with the accuracy of more personalised information sources. For instance, Booking.com even calculates cheap deals and compares travel information. The Internet satisfies the needs of consumers as it covers the entire variety of choices of travel, accommodation, transportation and leisure services, holiday packages, prices and availability (Buhalis 1998). This interactive medium not only gives information, but also provides feedback on the holiday experiences of tourists. As a result, such type of information naturally helps tourists to plan complex tourist activities and even long trips. Figure 6.1 illustrates the nature of a tourist's search prior to their purchase decision.

Information search models

In order to develop successful search user interfaces for consumers, it is imperative to understand the human information-seeking process. Tourism is an information-intensive industry and the search for its information has been guided by various models. These models are based on empirical evidence and they provide significant information on search behaviour. According to Marchionini (1989), information seeking is a special case of problem solving. It includes recognising and interpreting the information problem, establishing a plan of search, conducting the search, evaluating the results, and if necessary iterating through the

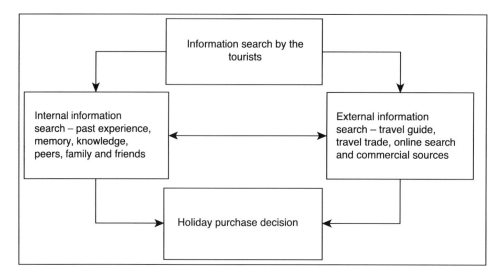

Figure 6.1 Nature of tourism information search

Source: Authors.

process again. Some of the popular models of information search that have evolved in the literature will now be explored from a tourism perspective.

Cognitive model of information seeking

When adapted to the tourism context, the 'cognitive model' of Norman (1988) suggests that a tourist goes through an intense cognitive process before indulging in tourism. Recognising a need for information is akin to formulating and becoming conscious of a goal. The tourist first identifies where they want to travel, for how long they can be away, their tourism activities preference and their budget. To achieve this goal, the tourist goes through a mental process based on both internal and external searches as elaborated in the previous section. If the mental assessment is satisfactory, the tourist executes the travel plan and, after consuming the holiday, evaluates their travel experience and relates it to their initial goal. However, the model assumes that the traveller's need is static and the information seeking proceeds gradually and successfully till all the necessary information is retrieved. In today's dynamic environment, the model might not be workable with savvy techno-tourists who keep changing their itinerary based on online information constantly fed to them through their smartphones. Figure 6.2 illustrates the cognitive model of information seeking.

The dynamic model or berry-picking model

The berry-picking model draws its analogy from berry picking. It assumes that just like farmers basically follow a given route to collect their berries, but may also proceed in cross-routes to pick the best berries, tourists also collect information in the same way; tourists seeking information will also engage in the search process using a berry-picking style. For instance, while searching hotels on Booking.com, travellers encounter a variety of options that trigger them to make new links and tourists keep following those links till they derive satisfaction from the information (Figure 6.3). The model suggests that information seeking

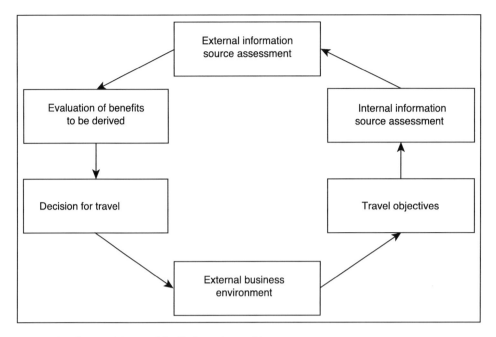

Figure 6.2   The cognitive model of information seeking

Source: Adapted from Norman (1988).

consists of a series of interconnected but diverse searches and the search result tends to trigger new goals and hence new directions are adopted by tourists. However, the drawback of this approach is that it is time-consuming and the potential traveller has to go through an intensive cognitive process that can add pressure to the tourism experience.

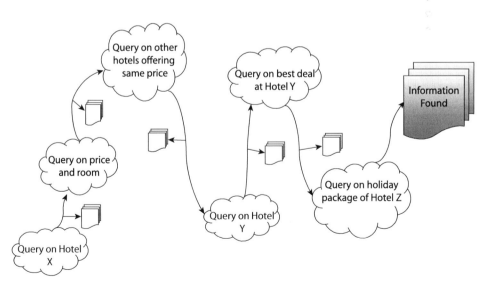

Figure 6.3   Berry-picking model

Source: Adapted from Bates (1989).

The standard model of information seeking (SMIS)

The SMIS was designed to explain that customers go through an interactive cycle whereby they first identify an information need, followed by activities of query specification, examination of retrieval results, and if needed a reformulation of the query, which takes place until a satisfactory result set is found (Broder 2002). If adapted to the tourism context, it would imply that an individual in search of a holiday will go through the following cycle:

1   Identification of a holiday resort in the Mediterranean region
2   Articulation of information need for accommodation, transportation and attractions
3   Query formulation on prices of resort, quality, facilities and support services
4   Result evaluation of the above
5   Reformulation of query if satisfaction is not derived
6   Use of result.

The SMIS model is illustrated by Figure 6.4.

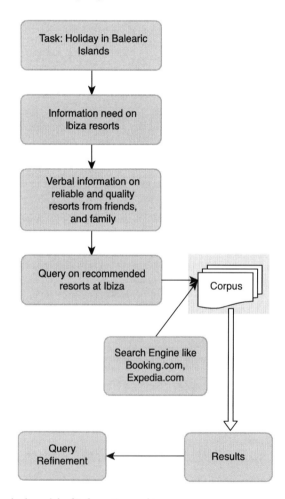

Figure 6.4   The standard model of information seeking

Source: Adapted from Broder (2002).

The Gursoy integrated model of information search

The Gursoy integrated model of information search (Figure 6.5) is based on an integrated approach. The model explains the pre-purchase information search behaviour of travellers. Pre-purchase information search represents the functional approach to explaining the nature of information sought and is defined as information search activities that are related to a recognised and immediate purchase intention. For immediate pre-purchase information needs, the visitor is likely to utilise either internal or external information sources, or both. The mode of pre-purchase information search (internal and/or external) that is likely to be utilised is influenced directly by the perceived cost of internal information search, the perceived cost of external information search and the level of travellers' involvement. The model proposes that travellers' familiarity and expertise are two important determinants in the information search process and tourists mostly start based on these two determinants whenever they start their tourism search. Familiarity and expertise are likely to be influenced by previous visits to the destination, involvement and learning, among other factors. If a traveller is highly involved with the product category, the traveller is likely to pay more attention to the incoming information and learning is more likely to be intentional. The model also suggests that if a traveller gets information through intentional learning, they are more likely to pay more attention to incoming information than a traveller who learns through incidental learning. If the traveller has been to the destination before, they are likely to have more familiarity and expertise on the destination than a traveller who has never been to the destination. Therefore, the level of involvement is likely to have a positive effect on familiarity and expertise due to the fact that if the traveller is highly involved with the product they are more likely to remember the product information. Therefore, intentional and incidental learning through previous visits and involvement are likely to influence familiarity and expertise and ultimately the search process.

Information search procedure

Tourist information search processes are one of the most widely studied areas of consumer research in tourism (Chen and Gursoy 2000). Understanding the information-seeking procedure of tourists is vital as it gives an indication of how tourists proceed to seek information and why. As elaborated in the previous sections, information searches of tourists are usually guided by familiarity with the destination, availability of time, and knowledge gathered from internal and external sources. But our present-day society is living in a wired world where information reaches people in real time. Therefore, a widening of the inform-ation search allows tourists to reach a more efficient choice, but the cost of information search from internal or external sources and facilities for online booking do influence consumers' information search patterns. Besciu (2013) suggests that, almost always, tourists go through the following pattern while engaging in the search process.

Step 1: Desire to travel

The first step of this pattern relates to the general desire to travel and this is based on considerations like availability of time and money, motivation to travel and previous experience. Tourists of the present century are unpredictable due to their intensive exposure to travel blogs and online information. As such, the information search pattern of a tourist is not an established one as at any time of the search process, the pattern can change.

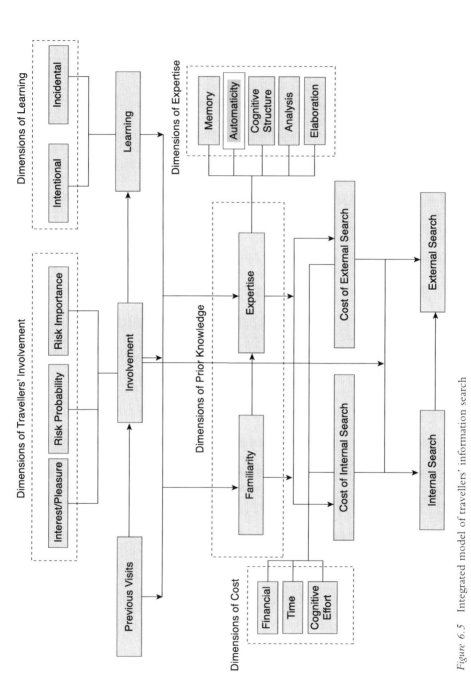

Figure 6.5 Integrated model of travellers' information search

Source: Gursoy and Chi (2008).

Step 2: Information search pattern

This phase is mainly guided by the characteristics and need of the traveller. Information searching usually takes place in the internal and external environment, but this will be influenced by socio-economic factors like available time, education background, level of exposure to online networks, familiarity with the destination or affordability. For instance, sophisticated and techno-conversant tourists will probably resort to online sources and travel blogs first, before resorting to internal sources as reported in the previous sections. The search process pattern has reversed in the present century. Because today customers are living in a wired world where information is available at the mere touch of a screen, online searches take place in parallel with internal and external searches. Working and looking for information at the same time saves time for people always short of time. The search pattern is thus guided by the perceived cost and benefit of the search process. In the case of most 21st-century customers, time is money and cost is related to time. The opportunity cost of not resorting to available online information means that more time and effort will be required to finalise the tourism decision. In tourism, the longer the delay, the lesser the possibility to enjoy a better and cheaper deal.

Step 3: Evaluation of alternatives

Once the tourist has shortlisted the destinations perceived as good value for money, they proceed with the evaluation of alternatives. Choosing an alternative is guided by various factors like price comparison, facilities provided for a similar price, cancellation policy, security, deals within the destination, online feedback from previous customers and so on. However, at this stage purchase intent may or may not lead to the purchase of the holiday, depending on how some factors can facilitate or inhibit the achievement of intent, such as the evolution of prices and tariffs, the supply situation, the financial resources of the purchaser, the pressure of time and other sociological influences.

Step 4: Purchase decision

After carefully considering the alternatives, the purchase decision takes place. This will generally be related to the booking of hotel rooms, airport transfer, and reservation of tickets for attractions among other things. However, at any moment of this pattern, the tourist may cancel their purchase decision. Tourists of the present era are highly exposed to blog reviews and online deals. For instance, if the tourist has already made a down payment, but cancelling the reservation helps the tourist enjoy a better deal like a reasonably cheaper hotel situated nearer to main attractions and with free airport transport, the tourist will cancel the booking or go for the deal. In so doing, the tourist will not only save on accommodation cost, but will also enjoy free airport transfer and save on transportation cost and time within the destination.

Step 5: Post-purchase evaluation

After consuming the holiday, the consumer will evaluate the extent to which their decision of cancelling a long pre-booked accommodation was worthwhile or not. The evaluation will be based on perceived cost and benefit in terms of time and money, level of satisfaction, tourism facilities available at the destination and so on. If the evaluation lives up to their expectations, the information accumulated is stored in the tourist's memory for future decision making and they might be more willing to purchase the product a second time and give favourable information to other potential purchasers. If they have reasons for dissatisfaction, then there is restlessness, known as cognitive dissonance. They will probably never consider another vacation at that particular destination and will certainly leave negative feedback on online platforms. Negative impacts will obviously follow.

Cost of information search

Tourists are likely to search as long as they believe that the benefits of acquiring information outweigh the costs as indicated in 'the economics of information' theory (Stigler 1961). The total cost associated with the employment of a given search strategy can be partitioned into three separate components: time spent, financial cost, and effort required (Gursoy 2001; Vogt and Fesenmaier 1998). Therefore, time spent and financial costs are likely to influence the level of external search utilised by tourists and hence determine the perceived cost. On the other hand, the effort required and the expected outcome are likely to influence the level of internal search, and determine the perceived cost.

The external information search involves the cost incurred in the external activities meant for information seeking. Time spent in these activities is considered as a most important cost of external information search (Gursoy and McCleary 2004; Stigler 1961). The cost of an external information search is not likely to be the same for different individuals. Because of the low cost and ease of retrieving information from online media, more and more travellers are utilising the Internet to find the information they need for destination selection and trip planning decisions (Gursoy and McCleary 2004).

The internal information cost includes cognitive processes such as evaluation of information, the integration of various pieces of information and the effort devoted to the retrieval of internally available information (Bettman et al. 1991). The cost–benefit framework suggests that travellers are likely to make better choices by expending cognitive effort in the selection and application of an information search strategy (Avery 1996; Payne 1982). The traveller's internal search activity is likely to be driven by both cognitive and benefit factors (Gursoy and McCleary 2004). Beach and Mitchell (1978) argued that the strategy selected by an individual would be the strategy that optimally trades off the benefits and the cognitive cost.

Limitations for conducting information search

A tourist faces various challenges in an unfamiliar environment. As a result, tourists get involved in a pre-visit process which comprises the gathering of information before travelling. Pre-visiting is an enjoyable experience as it extends the excitement of the holiday and builds anticipation. When tourists search for information, they make inferences that the inform-ation gathered has to be reliable and credible. But, many times, information derived from mass media and non-media sources does not reflect reality. As a result, one of the common problems faced when in search of information is the reliability of information and the credibility of sources. For instance, the search of information for a packaged holiday comprises risks and uncertainties, as the tourist cannot pre-test the holiday; only after reaching the destination can one confirm the reliability of the tourism information. As a result, acquiring information from either internal or external sources is not free from limitations. Basically, there are three different types of limitations associated with the process of information search.

Market uncertainty assumes that the tourist is aware of the fact that similar holidays may be sold at different prices, but those prices are unknown due to lack of information about the prices in the market where it is being sold. For instance, a tourist is planning to visit India and decides to choose an overnight accommodation in the city of Karol Bagh in Delhi. Assuming that the tourist has a Booking.com account, he looks for five-star hotels and finds out that hotels in Karol Bagh charge different prices for the same type of room advertised online. If a further assumption is drawn that hotels at Karol Bagh are guided by the same quality standard, the traveller faces a risk due to market uncertainty as he does not know which hotel offers the best deal (that is, extended facilities and more complimentary features at a cheaper price).

Technological uncertainty assumes that at the moment of purchasing a holiday, the tourist does not have information about its quality. For instance, a tourist books a deluxe room based on the photo gallery displayed by the travel site, but on arrival, discovers that the features of the room are rather nearer to those of a standard room.

Uncertainty of alternatives assumes that the tourist does not have information on the entire range of alternative possibilities and therefore chooses a holiday which is within a limited geographic area or within the boundaries of their previous tourism experience. For example, a tourist chooses to visit Disneyland Paris and is not aware that they can get a cheaper deal if they buy the entry ticket directly from Disney hotels rather than from tour operators in Paris.

For 21st-century customers, the Internet is a key information source and sophisticated customers, as part of the wired world, can access information any time in public places, at home and at their workplace via their smartphones and laptops. Therefore the limitations for information search for savvy customers are complex and interwoven with each other. These will be elaborated in the following case study.

Case study

Mauritius is a small tropical island in the Indian Ocean (Figure 6.6). It occupies an area of 720 square miles and is slightly bigger than the city of London (Gowreesunkar and Sotiriades 2015).

According to Global Finance (2015), the standard of living of Mauritians has improved due to the good economic performance of the island. This is also witnessed by the growing number of outbound tourists which means that more Mauritians travel for holidays now as compared with earlier decades. According to Statistics Mauritius (2015), approximately 326,582 Mauritians indulged in tourism in 2014 and the most popular destinations were France, the UK, the UAE, Réunion and South Africa. The Information and Communication Technology index of the country indicates Booking.com to be the preferred search engine of most outbound Mauritian tourists. Online search is convenient and provides free information on accommodation, pricing, attractions, feedback, best deals and photo galleries among others.

The present case study will consider some of the key challenges faced by a prospective Mauritian traveller. Assuming that the Mauritian has already gone through the internal and external sources of information as proposed by Gursoy and Chi's (2008) model of travellers' information search, they finally resort to Booking.com as their preferred source of information. As a first step, the Mauritian will probably follow the steps of the SMIS, comprising identification of the holiday resort (e.g. London); articulation of the information need for

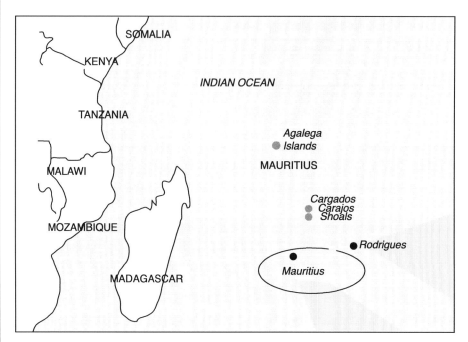

Figure 6.6   Mauritius in the Indian Ocean

Source: Adapted from Gowreesunkar et al. (2015).

accommodation, transportation and attractions; query formulation on prices of the resort, quality, facilities and support services; and result evaluation and reformulation of their query if satisfaction is not derived. In this process, the amount of search that they can undertake will depend on available time, willingness to expend effort for the search, the strength of their drive, the amount of information they initially had and the ease of obtaining additional information. The use of four to five keywords will take them to various travel search engines like Expedia.com or Make-My-Trip besides Booking.com. In a crowded and technologically advanced marketplace, the potential customer is faced with an overload of information. As a result, the Mauritian might follow the berry-picking model while searching hotels on Booking.com. They will encounter a variety of options that trigger them to more links and will further click on them till they derive satisfaction from the information. In this process, the prospective traveller will go through a cognitive pressure as elaborated by Norman's cognitive model (1988); overload of information requires mental effort and comparison of features might delay the search process. As a result, the traveller might be discouraged and switch to another holiday destination link which gives quicker and clearer indication.

The loading time is another challenge faced by online searchers. Due to the volume of online transactions taking place simultaneously, loading and response times can be time-consuming and costly. For instance, if the Mauritian selects London as the holiday trip and plans a further trip to Paris by using the Eurostar booking system, they may face the risk of losing the transaction due to long loading times which are also caused by poor connectivity. Given that the booking site allows only limited trials per day, the traveller might lose a seat if they have to wait for the next day to proceed with the booking. In other cases, if the ticket is not validated due to slow loading times, the Eurostar website prompts one to re-enter the transaction and this may lead to double payment.

Booking uncertainties are a common challenge while making online transactions. The booking of hotels, train and coach tickets usually follows a sequence. After a travel ticket is confirmed, the traveller will normally proceed with the booking of accommodation. A tourist may encounter some challenges if, for a given trip, only one part of the booking can be made online while the other part can only be done at the destination. For instance, if a Mauritian plans a pilgrimage to Vaishno Devi Shrine in Katra (India), they have the possibility of booking their flight ticket to India, but cannot book a train ticket to Katra; the Indian Railways Train Ticket Reservation does not give access to international tourists to book online. This represents a form of uncertainty as there is no guarantee that a train ticket to Katra will be available according to the planned itinerary. Moreover, if a hotel has been booked in advance at Katra, based on the initial travel plan, the Mauritian will lose their hotel booking as well as their money if no refund policy applies.

Another challenge that can affect a travel plan is that online information does not always reflect reality. Feedback left on Booking.com websites shows that tourists are often disappointed on arrival as what is displayed in the photo gallery is often not what they receive. While there is always a possibility to change accommodation, it might not be practical if the tourist is travelling with their family and has reached the hotel late at night after a long-haul travel. The booking conditions also represent an important challenge. For instance, the tourist will get no refund of their money if the cancellation policy (often written in small print at the bottom of the website) specifies that cancellation needs to be done 24 hours prior to the check-in time.

The conclusion of this small case study is that similar to Mauritians, any traveller is exposed to risks while searching for information and booking online. However, online search engines can also be an effective source of information if the user knows how to capitalise on deals and opportunities.

Conclusion

Buhalis (1998) revealed that potential tourists have become more independent and sophisticated in using a range of tools to arrange their travel needs. With its roots in consumer information-processing theory, the process-based perspective of travel information search has a long history and a prominent presence in tourism research (Um and Crompton 1992; Woodside and Lysonski 1989). The present chapter is an attempt to bring together the important facets of information seeking, to provide updated knowledge to the readers. The chapter will certainly assist researchers in uncovering the important considerations in understanding consumer information-seeking behaviour. An understanding of today's customers' behaviour while searching for information is fundamental as it will help in the crafting of appropriate marketing strategies and tailor-made quality services, and hence maintain customer satisfaction and loyalty to sustain business operations.

References

Avery, R. J. (1996). 'Determinants of search for nondurable goods: An empirical assessment of the economics of information theory', *Journal of Consumer Affairs*, 30(2): 390–420.

Bates, M. J. (1989). 'The design of browsing and berrypicking techniques for the on-line search interface', *Online Review*, 13(5): 407–431.

Beach, L. R. and Mitchell, T. R. (1978). 'A contingency model for the selection of decision strategies', *Academy of Management Review*, 3(3): 439–449.

Besciu, I. (2013). 'Behaviour of the consumer of tourism entertainment', *Cactus Tourism Journal*, 4(2): 9–19.

Bettman, J. R., Johnson, E. J. and Payne, J. W. (1991). 'Consumer decision making', in Robertson, T. S. and Kassarjian, H. H. (eds.), *Handbook of Consumer Research* (pp. 50–84), Englewood Cliffs, NJ: Prentice-Hall.

Broder, A. (2002). 'A taxonomy of web search', *SIGIR Forum*, 36(2): 3–10.

Buhalis, D. (1998). 'Strategic use of information technologies in the tourism industry', *Tourism Management*, 19(5): 409–421.

Chen, J. and Gursoy, D. (2000). 'Cross-cultural comparison of the information sources used by first-time and repeat travelers and its marketing implications', *International Journal of Hospitality Management*, 19(2): 191–203.

Engel, J. F., Blackwell, R. D. and Miniard, P. W. (1995). *Consumer Behavior*, Hillsdale, IL: The Dryden Press.

Euromonitor International (2014). *The World Travel Market Global Trends Report 2014*, London: WTM and Euromonitor.

Farahani, B. M., Mohamed, B. and Som, A. P. M. (2011). 'Photograph, information search and tourism marketing', *Asian Social Science*, 7(7): 94–101.

Global Finance (2015). 'Mauritius financial sector overview online report 2016', Available from www.globalfinance.mu [Accessed: 21 September 2015].

Gowreesunkar, V., Van der Sterren, J. and Séraphin, H. (2015). 'Social entrepreneurship as a tool for promoting global citizenship in island tourism destination management', *Ara Journal of Tourism Research*, 5(1): 7–23.

Gowreesunkar, V. and Sotiriades, M. (2015). 'Entertainment of leisure tourists in island destinations: Evidence from the island of Mauritius', *African Journal of Hospitality, Tourism and Leisure*, 4(S1): 1–19.

Gursoy, D. (2001). 'Development of Travelers' Information Search Behavior Model', Unpublished doctoral dissertation, Blacksburg, VA: Virginia Polytechnic Institute and State University.

Gursoy, D. (2011). *Modeling Tourist Information Search Behavior: A Structural Modeling Approach*, Saarbrucken, Germany: Lambert Academic Publishing.

Gursoy, D. and Chen, J. S. (2000). 'Competitive analysis of cross cultural information search behavior', *Tourism Management*, 21(6): 583–590.

Gursoy, D. and Chi, C. (2008). 'Travelers' information search behavior', in Haemoon, O. (ed.), *Handbook of Hospitality Marketing Management* (pp. 266–295), London: Routledge.

Gursoy, D. and McCleary, K. W. (2004). 'An integrative model of tourist information search behavior', *Annals of Tourism Research*, 31(2): 353–373.

Gursoy, D. and Terry Umbreit, W. (2004). 'Tourist information search behavior: Cross-cultural comparison of European Union member states', *International Journal of Hospitality Management*, 23(1): 55–70.

Marchionini, G. (1989). 'Information-seeking strategies of novices using a full-text electronic encyclopedia', *Journal of the American Society for Information Science*, 40(1): 54–66.

Norman, D. A. (1988). *The Psychology of Everyday Things*, New York: Basic Books.

Payne, J. W. (1982). 'Contingent decision behavior', *Psychological Bulletin*, 92(2): 382–402.

Statistics Mauritius (2015). *Digest of International Travel and Tourism Statistics 2014*, 41, Ministry of Finance and Economic Development, Republic of Mauritius.

Stigler, G. (1961). 'The economics of information', *Journal of Political Economy*, 69(3): 213–225.

Um, S. and Crompton, J. L. (1992). 'The role of perceived inhibitors and facilitators in pleasure travel destination decisions', *Journal of Travel Research*, 30(3): 18–25.

Vogt, C. A. and Fesenmaier, D. R. (1998). 'Expanding the functional information search', *Annals of Tourism Research*, 25(3): 551–578.

Woodside, A. G. and Lysonski, S. (1989). 'A general model of traveler destination choice', *Journal of Travel Research*, 27(4): 8–14.

Zeithaml, V. A. (1981). 'How consumer evaluation processes differ between goods and services', in Donnelly, J. H. and George, W. R. (eds.), *Marketing of Services* (pp. 186–190), Chicago, IL: American Marketing Association.

7

NOW AND WHEN

Reflecting on some realities of consumer behaviour in the hospitality industry

Roy C. Wood

Introduction

Type the words 'fast changing hospitality industry' into Google and you will elicit a large number of statements reassuring you of the sector's dynamism, characteristics that are often extended to hospitality consumers who are regularly depicted as, variously, fickle, experimental and ever-changing in their needs and wants. Such statements are also often found in 'academic' articles although they are rarely supported by any quantity or quality of research evidence that would satisfy serious researchers. The discussion in this chapter focuses on consumer behaviour in the hospitality industry, and in particular on the concept of consumer choice. It advocates a more prosaic view of these two concepts, suggesting that continuity, rather than change, is the hallmark of consumer behaviour in the sector and that changes in such behaviour are slow and incremental. The 'now' and 'when' of the chapter's title is an imperfect allusion to these suggested realities over more excitable renderings of trends in hospitality consumer behaviour.

Reflections on consumer behaviour

At its best, the subject 'consumer behaviour' seeks to systematically combine knowledge from disciplines including psychology, sociology and economics in pursuit of understanding why people choose to purchase a particular good or service from among available alternatives (Smit 2013). Consumers may have single or, more usually, multiple reasons for making such choices, and thus the analysis of reasons and choices is almost invariably multivariate in character ('consumer behaviour' should perhaps be more accurately termed 'consumer behaviours'). Because of the need to capture as precisely as possible this range of motivations to buy, an important aspect of the practice of analysing consumer behaviour is the construction of models that permit accommodation of the many variables that might be involved in decision making. As Smit (2013; see also Solomon et al. 2006) points out, a popular general model often encountered in the consumer behaviour literature conceives of the purchase process as comprising five stages: (1) awareness of a need or needs; (2) conducting information searches to generate data on how a need or needs might be met; (3) evaluation of the alternatives thus established as a result of information searching; (4) the process of decision making that leads to a purchase; and (5) post-purchase evaluation of the product or service.

Like all good models, this particular example evidences a surface simplicity which captures the essence of a process. That, however, is all it does, because each of the five stages instanced, and the model overall, embodies extensive complexities in terms of the range of concepts that may be employed to arrive at a 'solution' to any given purchase process. The consumer does not arrive at the 'need' to make a decision in a 'neutral' state. Each consumer has particular characteristics that enable and/or constrain available choice and these cover a huge range of variables of which a small number are gender; ethnicity; sexual orientation; religion; economic and social position; ethical values; and cultural and other traditions. We thus have to ask: What kind of consumer need(s) are we dealing with? In what ways is information about how needs might be met identified and processed? What criteria are invoked in evaluating between alternatives? At the root of these questions are persistent (if sometimes dilute) assumptions about the consumer as a *Homo economicus*, a rational actor who pursues rational means in achieving subjective ends, including satisfaction of needs and wants. While such forms of rationality are by no means absent from most forms of economic decision making, such processes can also be characterized by, *inter alia*, serendipity, manipulation and impulse. Choice is never wholly free: indeed a cynical view of the marketing function is that marketing processes exist to delimit and thus focus choice.

In a fortuitous example (because it occurs in a discussion of consumer behaviour when dining out in public), Warde and Martens (1998a: p. 130) note a tendency for the 'exaggeration of the scope of the freedom implied by the concept of consumer choice'. For these authors, consumers rarely encounter 'pure' states of choice, rather choice is always to some degree predetermined and pre-structured by those providing the choice. Such a view recalls Henry Ford's dictum, usually reported as 'You can have any color you like so long as it's black', alluding to the Model T Ford motor car. Accepting that those who produce goods and services do so in a manner that constrains consumer choice should theoretically simplify analysis of consumer behaviour in that such study becomes the investigation of those choices made under the constraint of pre-selected and pre-structured markets of supply. Like the magician who 'forces' his or her choice of playing card upon the audience member (who believes they are choosing freely from the pack offered), consumer behaviour in this perspective is as much about the choices of the producers of goods and services as it is about those who purchase them in their intermediate or final forms.

Alas, life and the study of consumer behaviour are not as simple as this. First, many informed commentators would maintain that real choice in markets for products and services exists, or at least that, in a capitalist system, there is at least some choice and this is better than no choice at all. One alternative to this position is to dismiss, as many Marxist scholars might, such claims and beliefs as evidence of false consciousness – the process whereby we are encouraged to delude ourselves as to the fundamentally exploitative relationships inherent in capitalism – including the degree of freedom we have in choosing what to buy. The difficulty here is that even the availability of *some* choice makes understanding of the processes underlying people's exercise of that choice worthwhile.

Secondly, even in markets where there is nominally a wide(r) range of choice, products and services, sometimes in generalized form, sometimes in the form of specific marques or brands, often, if not usually, act as close substitutes for each other. For example, in generalized form, all hotels must usually offer accommodation and some provision of, or easy access to, food and beverage. This is what strategists call a threshold competency – a competency an organization must possess in order to function in the market. But in this sense, all hotels are like any other hotel. However, products and services are normally and additionally structured hierarchically; in this way, the market comes to 'cover all the angles'. Some purveyors of goods and services operate in all parts of the hierarchy, some focus on only one. In the luxury (wrist) watch industry for example, it is perfectly usual for well-respected brands to offer 'entry level' timepieces which are substantially cheaper to buy than the brand's usual range (see, for example, Adams 2012). Similarly, many hotel companies possess brands in different hierarchical market segments and one at least, Accor, operates in all, offering simple '1 star'-type accommodation right up to '5 star' deluxe.

Finally here, and very much as a corollary of the preceding points, we can see that whatever one's view of the existence of any 'true' range of choice, producers of goods and services in a capitalist system engage in a variety of practices that usually fall under the heading of marketing and which serve at the very least to influence consumer choice behaviour through structures of value. In this sense at least, Warde and Martens (1998a) are correct. An important qualification to this, however, is that we must avoid the assumption that production imperatives simply 'act' upon consumers. Just as both academic and general understanding of consumer behaviour and corresponding marketing practices have become more sophisticated, then so have many if not most consumers, who have become more alert to, and sceptical of, the claims made for products and services. In this they are increasingly aided by the ready availability of both traditional and online sources of product and service reviews including comparison websites. Put simply, not all consumers, almost certainly not even a majority, are simple dupes but can, and do, utilize personal experience and insight and various sources of countervailing power to that of the producers of goods and services in making purchase choices.

Consumer behaviour in the food service industry

Understanding consumer behaviour in the food service industry essentially depends on the answers to three central questions – how significant is the market for dining out; what are the general influences that lead consumers to choose one restaurant over another; and what similar factors govern their choice of food? Of course, in some cases the answer to the second question yields an answer to the third – one does not choose a Chinese restaurant if one desires to eat pizza.

Significance of the market for dining out

Food is everywhere – in our newspapers, magazines, on television, online and visible on the streets of our towns and cities. However, ubiquity is not the same as significance. Consider the UK case. Warde and Martens (1998b: p. 147) noted that in 1991, only some 3.6% of total household expenditure was spent on meals out. The UK Cabinet Office (2008) noted that consumers (then) spent roughly the same proportion of their income on eating out as they did in 1968 and another UK ministry, the Department for Food, Environment and Rural Affairs (2012), observed that food eaten away from home at that point constituted around 3.3% of total household expenditure. None of this should come as a surprise: there are many demands on consumers' discretionary spending and dining out may not always be a priority for such expenditure. It is further worth noting that dining out is not an activity with which everyone engages regularly. In their sample, Warde and Martens (1999: pp. 119–120) found that 21% ate out once a week and 7% claimed to never eat out. More recent evidence suggests that 27% of adults and 19% of children eat meals out once per week or more (Adams et al. 2015).

Similarly, far from being radically experimental, the British dining public exhibits a predictable conservatism in their dining-out habits. Warde and Martens (1999: p. 120) noted that 48% of their sample had not eaten in ethnic restaurants in the year prior to their survey and 27% said they had never eaten an ethnic takeaway. The UK Cabinet Office (2008) cited 2005 data showing that 51% of dining-out sales value was accounted for by public houses (22%); hotel catering (15%); and restaurants (14%). The last category did not even include what might be thought to be more popular dining-out venues. The same data noted dining-out sales values for the following, named, kinds of outlets: burger restaurants (8%); cafes and coffee shops (7%); ethnic restaurants (7%); in-store catering (5%); pizza and pasta restaurants (5%); ethnic takeaways (6%); fish and chip shops (4%); fried chicken restaurants (4%); roadside catering (2%); and other fast food (1%). The *Horizons* (2011) marketing intelligence company suggested that the top two growth sectors in foodservice by sales in 2011 were pub restaurants and managed branded pubs (Nicholls [2013] notes that in 2012 pub restaurants accounted for 20% of all meals eaten out) and in a related report point out that whereas in the USA, fast food restaurants account for 28% of all consumer spend in the food service sector, it is half of that figure in the UK (*Horizons* 2012a).

Choosing a restaurant

Research on how consumers select restaurants has tended to focus on eliciting and ranking the role of variables in the choice of restaurant given a number of alternative scenarios (for example anniversaries – a review of key studies can be found in Stierand and Wood [2012]). In such research, the perceived quality of food, the price of food, cleanliness and quality of service emerge as most important in consumers' choice of restaurant (a further report by *Horizons* [2012b] places values of 79%, 70% and 64% respectively on the first three of these). Again this seems unexceptional, yet discussion of restaurant choice in the foodservice industry is often clouded by a focus on the concept of the 'meal experience' initially elaborated by Campbell-Smith (1967). This concept proposes the now far from radical view that when dining out, customers assess their meal experience by reference to both tangible (e.g. price and food quality) and less tangible (e.g. service, decoration, restaurant ambience) factors. Over time, theorists and practitioners alike have tended to assert the priority of the latter factors over the former but, while the less tangible elements of a meal experience are not *unimportant*, this tendency has undoubtedly led to the intangible cart being regularly placed before the tangible horse. Again, *Horizons* (2012b) found that standard of service was rated as important to dining out choices by only 55% of consumers and 'ambience' came in fifth out of 13 factors, cited as important by only 51%.

In selecting a *particular* restaurant the influence of friends and peer groups, rather than formal marketing, is more likely to be influential. In the USA, Jolson and Bushman (1978: p. 69) found that, in deciding whether to dine at a restaurant for the first time, consumers depend primarily on personal recommendations and remarks by critics in contrast to restaurant advertising. Barrows et al. (1989: p. 90) similarly identified a friend's recommendation as the most valued factor in determining whether to go to a restaurant for the first time. A Mintel survey (Anon. 1992: p. 14) pertaining to the UK found that 90% of people listed recommendation by a friend as most important in choosing a new place to eat with 25% saying they took note of reviews in newspapers or magazines. A later NOP poll found that the most influential factor in selecting where to eat out was prior experience: 84% of the sample had bought a meal from a place where they had dined before (Anon. 1998: pp. 60–62). It is worth noting that 62% of respondents in the study by Warde and Martens

(1999: pp. 128–130) had eaten out before at the venue of their most recent dining-out experience.

Choosing what to eat

There is some measure of agreement among sociologists and historians of food that in many countries, public taste in dining out changes only very slowly, as does the provision for such dining (Driver 1983; Mennell 1985; Wood 1995). In respect of the latter, Auty (1989 reported in Auty 1992: p. 325), in an often overlooked study, discovered that once a restaurant menu has been determined, changes to it are usually gradual:

> restaurateurs suited their own inclinations in running their restaurants rather than taking note of the competition in the area. If their style did not suit a regular set of diners, they went out of business rather than making dramatic changes. Changes tended to be in small increments, like adding garlic bread to the menu. Proprietors on the whole denied being competitive, though they admitted keeping an eye on what similar restaurants were doing. None could remember changing their way of doing business in response to a competitor's action, but at the same time they were quite sure that any innovative action of theirs would be copied.

Conservatism in provision is matched by conservatism in consumption. The UK *National Catering Inquiry* of the 1960s produced a number of reports exploring dining out. One such asked respondents to select their preferred dishes from a list comprising the most popular items then served by restaurants. Simultaneously, caterers were asked to estimate customer preferences for the dishes on the list. In no single case did consumer and caterer estimates coincide, although there was an overall correspondence. The most popular dishes were soup (consumers: 71%, caterers: 46%); meat (60/42); potatoes (63/78); and fruit salad (ranking, but not data, supplied) (*National Catering Inquiry* 1966: pp. 13–17). Fast forward almost 20 years: between 1983 and 1989, the UK trade magazine *Caterer and Hotelkeeper* carried an annual Gallup survey of trends in consumption. The popularity of dishes was again established by what caterers provided on their menus. For most of the period the typical lunch meal was soup of the day followed by fish and chips and then ice cream. For dinner, it was prawn cocktail, steak and chips and ice cream (Wood 1990: p. 4). In the 1990s, Warde and Martens (1999: pp. 121–122) found the most popular dinner menu when dining out to be prawn cocktail; roast meat, peas, carrots and chips; with gateau to follow. Coming right up to the present day, *Horizons* (2012b) identified the 10 dishes that appear most frequently on menus (not the same as the most popular purchases, but a reasonable surrogate). The list contained only three 'foreign' concoctions – pizza (ranked second), chicken curry (sixth) and beef lasagne (joint ninth). Beef burger and fish and chips took first and third place, respectively.

The majority of the foregoing examples are of a UK or at least Anglo-Saxon flavour. It is certainly true that there is a paucity of globally oriented research data on the topics discussed here, and no account has been taken of variations that occur within and between nation states, not least because of economic and cultural circumstances. Nevertheless, it is not unreasonable to hypothesize, especially in an era of internationalization, that similar trends might be found in other countries. The future challenge is to investigate and refute this assertion.

Consumer behaviour and hotels

Remarkably little is understood about consumer choice of hotels. As with the food service industry, voluntary participation in a hotel experience presumes a certain amount of disposable income. Many hotel guests, however, are business travellers whose hotel stays are paid for by their employers. As with restaurant food, what hotel providers think customers want does not necessarily correspond with the views of those customers. Nor, despite the huge amounts spent by hotel (and other) companies on customer loyalty schemes, is there much certain evidence that this actually encourages loyalty as the following discussion suggests.

What hotel customers want

Frequent surveys have shown that cleanliness of guest rooms comes top of travellers' list of must-have hotel attributes (e.g. Walker 2011: p. 20). Egencia® (2012), the corporate travel arm of the Expedia group of companies, in its *Business Travel by Business Travelers* (focused on the European Union) found the typical traveller to be male, aged 31–50, travelling once or twice a month in airline economy class and working in senior management, sales or technology. When asked what they wished hotels would provide as a standard, 59% wanted mobile/MP3/computer chargers; 50% toothpaste; 44% voltage converters; and 32% slippers. Hotel 'luxuries' in which travellers indulged included the use of hotel swimming pools (40%); in-room tea- and coffee-making facilities (39%); and hotel spa and fitness centres (32% and 31%, respectively). A later US survey of business travellers commissioned by Choice Hotels International (2014) indicated that 73% of business travellers valued location, 61% room value and 55% free Wi-Fi when selecting a hotel. Some 76% of travellers had made hotel reservations online and just over half had used their in-room fridge and microwave while 61% used their in-room coffee-maker.

We live in an age where the corporate hotel industry is dominated by what *The Economist* (2013a) calls the 'industrial hotel', with brands following as far as possible a standard design, and operated and managed according to standard operating procedures (SOPs):

> A manager in Dubai says he follows 2,300 rules, including the phrases used to greet guests... A 2010 Hilton manual stipulates that staff must answer phones after three rings, that guests' pets may not weigh more than 75lbs (34kg) and that scuba-diving boats must provide free pieces of fruit. A 2004 SOP book for InterContinental allows staff to wait until the fourth ring, requires drinks to be refilled when two-thirds empty and specifies that rooms must offer at least four pornographic films.

The difficulty with SOPs is that customers themselves are not standard, even though they may conform within parameters to both the explicit and implied behaviour expected of hotel guests (Wood 1994). There is a long history of hotels seeking to accommodate both simple and more complex differences beyond simple socio-economic classifications, from the *qibla* that points in the direction of Mecca, found in the rooms of hotels in Islamic countries, to periodic attempts (sometimes based on questionable assumptions) to address the presumed different needs of lone female travellers (Mazurkiewicz 1983). Beyond these 'practical' concerns there is also an occasional tendency to cast the consumption behaviour of hotel guests in more abstract, 'postmodern', terms. Waldthausen and Oehmichen (2013: p. 1) report Michael Tiedy, Senior Vice President Brand Design and Innovation at Starwood, as saying that today's hotel guests would rather 'participate than flaunt', and Sara Kearney of

Hyatt as arguing that hotel guests 'are ready to explore and crave a sense of economy and also yearn for real social interaction'. We can make of such statements what we will but in the light of the evidence sampled here, it is probably wise for hoteliers to keep in mind the old English saying 'fine words butter no parsnips'.

The problem of loyalty

We noted earlier how consumers have become more sensitive to the wiles of marketers in promoting products and services. When it comes to hotel loyalty schemes, there is growing evidence of at least mixed success. Bell et al. (2002: p. 79) argue that:

> programs to cultivate relationships with high-value customers are central to marketing management. The head of Hilton Hotels Corporation's guest rewards program calls them 'the industry's most important marketing tool.' Despite the fact that each member belongs to an average of 3.5 hotel loyalty programs, management is optimistic that they can be used to cultivate loyalty. Membership constitutes permission for the chain brand to build a customer profile for each member, to assess the potential value of each member, and to measure marketing's efforts to realize the potential value.

Bell et al. go on to argue (2002: pp. 79–80) that only 9% of guests who stay in a Hilton hotel in any one year belong to its frequent guest programme. Further, only 3% are in the elite silver, gold and diamond status yet these groups contribute disproportionately to the chain's profitability. In fact these 3% of guests contribute 11% of revenue and 46% of net profit.

According to *The Economist* (2013b) the five biggest hotel loyalty schemes lay claim to 198 million members. Citing a Deloitte survey of 4,000 US frequent travellers, the magazine's travel writer records that:

- only 8% of frequent travellers routinely stay at the same hotel brand;
- only 14% of frequent travellers routinely fly on the same airline;
- 44% of travellers had two or more loyalty cards – the schemes lacked significance for many travellers with the consequence that rather than ensuring loyalty they encouraged the 'switching' behaviour between brands they were intended to discourage; and
- the main factor in choosing a hotel or airline was value for money with loyalty schemes ranking 20th out of 26 variables for hotels and 19th out of 26 items for airlines.

The irony of all this is that not only do customers show a lack of loyalty to particular brands, they are not even particularly loyal to the loyalty schemes of which they are members! It is not as if consumer loyalty is especially unpredictable. Bhasin (2011) reported results of a US investigation of the 10 industries with most loyal customers in which none of the top 10 scorers attracted a 'loyalty rate' of more than 50%. To a small degree, these trends are also reflected in emerging evidence concerning the use of social media in the travel and hospitality sectors. For example, the Deloitte survey referred to by *The Economist* (2013b) observed that what really matters to consumers when being engaged by travel brands is a secure and easy purchase process. Furthermore, the survey results showed that:

- 80% of respondents have never downloaded a hotel or airline app to their smartphones.
- 63% of respondents never want to interact with a travel brand via social media.

- 61% use hotel and 59% use airline websites most frequently for booking.
- 49% have used flash sale sites, to follow discounts on travel.
- 44% never visit social media and review sites for travel.

Once again, if at least some of the data considered here on choice influences in hotels is correct then the sense conveyed is one of practical and pragmatic consumers with a clear focus on product and service 'essence', whose behaviour is informed by a good deal of simple economic rationality.

Conclusion

In its classic conception, marketing as a set of disciplinary practices is supposed to enable organizations to meet the needs, wants and desires of customers. As the subject has matured, however, so the suspicion has grown that more often than not, the consumers of goods and services lack centrality in the marketing analysis and planning process, perhaps more often being treated as ciphers rather than as active drivers of demand. Put another way, there is less a concern with what consumers want and more a concern with what marketers think they should want. While the concept of *Homo economicus* is deeply flawed, those interested in consumer behaviour and marketing ignore at their peril the importance of a product or service's fundamental characteristics, what might be called its 'rational appearance', comprising price, accessibility, reliability and value for money. Those interested in analysing consumer behaviour ignore at their peril both the intelligence and conservatism of consumers, as do those who seek to sell them all manner of products and services. *Caveat venditor!*

References

Adams, A. (2012). 'Entry level luxury watches', *The Watch Gallery*. Available from http://www. thewatchgallery.com/magazine/a-guide-to-entry-level-luxury-watches/ [Accessed: 24 July 2015].

Adams, J., Goffe, L., Brown, T., Lake, A., Summerbell, C., White, M., Wrieden, W. and Adamson, A. (2015). 'Frequency and socio-demographic correlates of eating meals out and take-away meals at home: Cross-sectional analysis of the UK national diet and nutrition survey, waves 1–4 (2008–12)', *International Journal of Behavioural Nutrition and Physical Activity*, 12: 51, Available from: http://www.ijbnpa.org/content/12/1/51 [Accessed: 29 November 2015].

Anon. (1992). 'Report finds word of mouth sells covers', *Caterer and Hotelkeeper*, 30 April: 14.

Anon. (1998). 'Dining by numbers', *Caterer and Hotelkeeper*, 26 March: 60–62.

Auty, S. (1992). 'Consumer choice and segmentation in the restaurant industry', *The Service Industries Journal*, 12(3): 324–339.

Barrows, C. W., Lattuca, F. P. and Busselman, R. H. (1989). 'Influence of restaurant reviews upon consumers', *FIU Hospitality Review*, 7(2): 84–92.

Bell, D., Deighton, J., Reinartz, W. J., Rust, R. T. and Swartz, G. (2002). 'Seven barriers to customer equity management', *Journal of Service Research*, 5(1): 77–85.

Bhasin, K. (2011). 'The 10 industries with the most loyal customers', Available from http://www. businessinsider.com/industries-customer-loyalty-2011-9?op=1 [Accessed: 24 May 2015].

Campbell-Smith, G. (1967). *The Marketing of the Meal Experience*, Guildford: University of Surrey Press.

Choice Hotels International (2014). 'Choice hotels survey shows hotel location, room value most important among business travelers', Available from http://media.choicehotels.com/phoenix. zhtml?c=217856&p=irol-newsArticle&ID=1924221 [Accessed: 12 August 2015].

Driver, C. (1983). *The British at Table 1940–1980*, London: Chatto and Windus.

Economist, The (2013a). 'A short history of hotels; be my guest', Available from http://www.economist. com/news/christmas-specials/21591743-be-my-guest [Accessed: 7 May 2014].

Economist, The (2013b). 'Looking for loyalty', Available from http://www.economist.com/blogs/ gulliver/2013/01/business-traveler-trends [Accessed: 29 November 2015].

Egencia (2012). 'Business travel by business travelers'.

Horizons (2011). *Market Structure and Trends: Key Highlights from 2011,* Available from http://www. hrzns.com/mint/pepper/tillkruess/downloads/tracker.php?url=http://www.hrzns.com/files/ Market_Structure_and_Trends_Key_Highlights_From_2011.pdf&force&inline [Accessed: 5 June 2014].

Horizons (2012a). *Does the US Lead?* Available from http://www.hrzns.com/mint/pepper/tillkruess/ downloads/tracker.php?url=http://www.hrzns.com/files/Does_the_US_lead.pdf&force&inline [Accessed: 5 May 2014].

Horizons (2012b). *Consumer Eating Out Trends: 10 Things You Need to Know. . .and What They Mean,* Available from http://www.hrzns.com/mint/pepper/tillkruess/downloads/tracker.php?url=http:// www.hrzns.com/files/Consumer_eating_out_trends_10_things_you_need_to_know. pdf&force&inline [Accessed: 6 June 2014].

Jolson, M. A. and Bushman, F. A. (1978). 'Third-party consumer information systems: The case of the food critic', *Journal of Retailing,* 54(4): 63–79.

Mazurkiewicz, R. (1983). 'Gender and social consumption', *The Service Industries Journal,* 3(1): 49–62.

Mennell, S. (1985). *All Manners of Food: Eating and Taste in England and France from the Middle Ages to the Present,* Oxford: Basil Blackwell.

National Catering Inquiry (1966). *The British Eating Out,* Glasgow: National Catering Inquiry.

Nicholls, L. (2013). 'The gastropub revolution: Pub-restaurants begin to dominate eating-out market', *Big Hospitality,* Available from http://www.bighospitality.co.uk/Trends-Reports/The-gastropub-revolution-Pub-restaurants-begin-to-dominate-eating-out-market [Accessed: 7 June 2013].

Smit, B. (2013). 'Consumer behaviour', in R. C. Wood (ed.), *Key Concepts in Hospitality Management* (pp. 14–18), London: Sage.

Solomon, M. R., Bamossy, G., Askegaard, S. and Hogg, M. K. (2006). *Consumer Behavior: A European Perspective,* 3rd edition, Harlow: FT Prentice-Hall.

Stierand, M. and Wood, R. C. (2012). 'Reconceptualising the commercial meal experience in the hospitality industry', *Journal of Hospitality and Tourism Management,* 19(1): 143–148.

UK Cabinet Office (2008). *Food: An Analysis of the Issues,* Available from http://webarchive.national archives.gov.uk/+/http:/www.cabinetoffice.gov.uk/media/cabinetoffice/strategy/assets/food/ food_analysis.pdf [Accessed: 11 August 2015].

UK Department for Food, Environment and Rural Affairs (2012). *Family Food,* Available from http:// webarchive.nationalarchives.gov.uk/20130103014432/http://www.defra.gov.uk/statistics/files/ defra-stats-foodfarm-food-familyfood-2009-110525.pdf [Accessed: 27 November 2015].

Waldthausen, V. and Oehmichen, A. (2013). *A New Breed of Traveler: How Consumers are Driving Change in the Hotel Industry,* London: HVS, Available from http://www.hvs.com/article/6675/a-new-breed-of-traveller-%E2%80%93-how-consumers-are-driving-change/ [Accessed: 18 June 2014].

Walker, B. (2011). 'Housekeeping, the heart of hotels', *Hospitality,* Issue 23: 18–22.

Warde, A. and Martens, L. (1998a). 'A sociological approach to food choice: The case of eating out', in A. Murcott (ed.), *The Nation's Diet: The Social Science of Food Choice* (pp. 129–144), Harlow: Addison Wesley Longman.

Warde, A. and Martens, L. (1998b). 'Eating out and the commercialization of mental life', *British Food Journal,* 100(3): 147–153.

Warde, A. and Martens, L. (1999). 'Eating out: Reflections on the experience of consumers in England', in Germov, J. and Williams, L. (eds.), *A Sociology of Food and Nutrition: The Social Appetite* (pp. 116–134), Oxford: Oxford University Press.

Wood, R. C. (1990). 'Sociology, gender, food consumption and the hospitality industry', *British Food Journal,* 92(6): 3–5.

Wood, R. C. (1994). 'Hotel culture and social control', *Annals of Tourism Research,* 21(1): 65–80.

Wood, R. C. (1995). *The Sociology of the Meal,* Edinburgh: Edinburgh University Press.

8

ETHICAL ISSUES OF CONSUMER BEHAVIOUR

Ann Hindley and Xavier Font

Introduction

This chapter considers the ethical issues of consumer behaviour, and frames them in relation to one of the key challenges of travel and tourism of our current times: that travel causes both positive and negative impacts. The first section reviews ethical theory, defining ethical consumption and ethical consumerism and outlining the nature of the ethical business and the ethical consumer. The second section reviews the role of society's different actors in ethically responsible behaviour and outlines reasons for co-operative systems failing to meet a shared responsibility. The final section provides an overview of ethical tourism and the ethical tourist and determines the barriers to change which impede responsible consumer behaviour.

Theories of ethics

Ethical theories help explain decision-making in situations where right and wrong are hard to evaluate. In this chapter we shall consider the impact that travel can have upon a tourist destination that is under threat of disappearing through climate change, aggravated through tourism. Deontological, or duty-bound, theories privilege the right and suggest the principles that we should honour and what one ought to do, whereas teleological theories privilege the good and suggest the outcomes we should promote or endeavour to bring about. Deontological theories consider that *right* is independent of *good*, meaning that if an act or intent is inherently good, then it is good, even if the consequences are bad. Thus, Ethical Formalism suggests that moral worth comes from doing one's duty.

Teleological theories are 'consequentialist' as it is the consequence of the action which is important, rather than the initial act, which could have been bad. Thus, Classical Utilitarianism maximises utility – the morally right action is to produce the greatest pleasure overall, as opposed to pain. Other teleological theories relevant to the ethical issues of travelling include Ethical Egoism (it is moral to promote one's own good or individual well-being); Enlightened Egoism (long-term welfare requires cooperative relationships); Virtue Ethics (to be good, one must be a good person); and Contemporary Consequentialism (it is irrational to make trade-offs among objectives to maximise the value of one). However, this appears to raise an ethical dilemma – to engage or not to engage in travel and tourism. Therefore, an understanding of approaches to individual or social judgements on ethical dilemmas would be useful.

Individual and social ethical dilemmas

An ethical dilemma concerns the moral conflict produced in a situation where right and wrong are hard to evaluate and this has implications for consumer behaviour. Individual ethical dilemmas include what to buy (or not), where to invest, whether to drive or to walk and whether to help or engage with issues, such as reducing carbon footprints and helping the global poor. The ethical ideology behind the differences in ethical judgements and behaviours can be explained by the Hunt–Vitell Model (Kavak et al. 2009). This model inputs background (such as cultural and personal characteristics), which feeds through to perceptions (that depend on ethical sensitivity, foresight and imagination), analysis (being affected by personal or professional duties and consequences), judgement (which evaluates the perceived problem and the alternative acts related to duty, as well as the desirability or consequences of actions) and intention (being the intention to act on the judgement), finally reaching a result (Boose and Dean 2000).

However, asking consumers how they feel about ethical dilemmas is not a good predictor of behaviour, as other considerations may prevent action taking place. Many consumers perceive that time, convenience and cost place limits on their ethical behaviour, whilst others believe that alone they cannot make a difference, thus they fail to purchase ethically. Meanwhile, social dilemmas are situations where individual interests are at odds with collective interests, with the consequences of group members acting in their own best interest impacting negatively on others. Reference Group Theory suggests that any trade-offs between the individual and the group will concern the pressure to comply to group norms with short-term individual sacrifice being required for the long-term benefit of the group (Sen et al. 2001). This therefore suggests a need to measure the ethical dilemma of tourism in the context both of the lone individual and of the individual as part of a group.

The ethical consumer

Ethical consumers are difficult to define and are not homogeneous. They do not ignore price or quality, but apply additional criteria to their purchasing decisions because of their concern about environmental issues, the poor and the impact of their choices on the world around them. Nevertheless, if they only buy ethical products based on brands they know or trust and which they can get from their usual shops at the same price, quality, performance and endurance, then the ethical consumer may be unattainable or even a myth. Further, it could be argued that there is little point in defining the 'ethical consumer' per se, given the paradox that 'consumers who care' are more likely to be ethically active than those that describe themselves as 'ethical'.

Moreover, it could be suggested that any definition of the 'ethical consumer' would have a polar opposite, but by all accounts the unethical consumer cares about the issues to some extent, although not enough to sway purchase decisions. Added complications here include the notion that not all ethical purchases are strictly ethical (a purchase made which is of primary concern to the buyer's own health, for example), whilst there are also frequent disagreements about who is right or wrong. Furthermore, ethical consumers cannot ensure that everything they purchase is ethically produced anyway. Therefore, 'ethical consumers' are not ethical all of the time and 'non-ethical consumers' are ethical some of the time. This suggests a lack of homogeneity in the ethical consumers group and a more flexible approach to decision-making by the ethical consumer. Therefore, a brief review of research on the ethical consumer is of value.

Ethical tourism

A tourism-specific consideration is of value, because it could highlight differences which are specific to the industry and its consumers. Good actions are influenced by ethics and found across the travel industry, but there is confusion as to what to call this type of tourism. Tourism ethics are rooted in a sense of social consciousness. They manifest themselves in social, environmental and economic benefits. However, across all ethical sectors, there is general confusion between terms (such as organic, Fair Trade and local produce) which is equally evident in tourism (ethical, eco, pro-poor, Fair Trade and responsible tourism).

The concept of ethical tourism was developed in response to global concerns about mass tourism with the aim of benefiting all stakeholders. It is often used interchangeably with ecotourism, responsible tourism and sustainable tourism, despite these having different meanings. Ecotourism aims for conservation and improvement in locals' well-being, through minimising negative impacts and providing positive experiences; whereas responsible tourism aims to encourage all tourism stakeholders (irrespective of their sector) to take more responsibility towards a common goal of being sustainable. Further terms include alternative tourism, which aims to be softer, small scale and low impact, through the reduction of social tensions and by providing economic benefits to the local community; and pro-poor tourism, which focuses on generating net benefits for the poor, through unlocking opportunities. Although the UK responsible tourism market has been growing, it is suggested that ethical concerns and beliefs are not penetrating further into the market. This perhaps indicates a greater interest in the perceived quality of the ethical product, rather than the moral value added to fulfil altruistic desires of the consumer. Nevertheless, a better understanding of the ethical tourist could help explain behaviour.

Who is the 'ethical tourist'?

Understanding the ethical tourist is of value, because it assists in understanding consumer behaviour towards tourism. However, as with the ethical consumer, the ethical tourist is difficult to define. Nonetheless, Speed (2007: p. 61) suggests that:

> Ethical tourists respect their hosts: by treading softly on the environment; by being educated about the culture; by ensuring their stay returns fair, economic benefits, and by ensuring all decision-making with all tourism's stakeholders is socially responsible.

Ethical tourists have a strong belief in their ability to facilitate change by sharing knowledge and experience, in the hope that others will emulate their behaviour. Despite this, ethical tourists consider the term 'ethical tourism' to be irrelevant or meaningless, because it is aspirational and difficult to achieve, while it conflicts with their own interpretations that are based upon self-interest. Ethical concerns relating to endangered species could conflict with ethical concerns relating to the Indigenous or impoverished. Which is perhaps why an ethical tourist would prefer to be called a 'responsible tourist', as it is less absolute – suggesting deontological theory is at work, as the intent is good.

Ethical holiday research provides four typologies (Mintel 2005), which enables a more rounded picture of the ethical tourist. Although the *ethical* (17%) are the most concerned, only 20% of these seek a holiday with an ethical code of practice, which suggests they are 'caring and ethical' but selectively so. The *aware* (15%) feel that companies should do more to preserve the local environment and support the locals, which suggests they are 'confused and uncertain' as to their personal role in ethical tourism. The *self-interested* (27%) are those who are more likely to be concerned about their own enjoyment, which suggests they are 'cynical and disinterested'. Finally, the *unethical* (41%) are likely to be the 'oblivious'. Overall, this suggests a continuum from ethical through to ethically oblivious, but passing through differing levels of personal responsibility and interest. But, however useful these typologies are, they seem narrow and restrictive, with the full picture likely to be less straightforward.

Ethical responsibility

The responsibilities of consumers need to be framed against those placed on government and businesses. This section first considers the roles of stakeholders in ethically responsible behaviour. A shared responsibility is then discussed, as the consequences of travel and tourism (such as carbon emissions, resource depletion and biodiversity loss) are borne by society and not just any one individual, business or government. In the middle of the section it becomes clear that the role of society in this shared responsibility is somewhat unclear, which results in inaction. Towards the end of the section, strategies to internalise negative externalities are considered, but a review of co-operative systems accepts these are vulnerable to cheats (be they consumers, businesses or governments) who enjoy collective benefits without paying their dues.

Role of individuals in responsibility

Promisingly, many consumers present pro-social behaviour, such as donating to charity, investing in socially responsible funds or giving their time, because of genuine altruism and the need to do 'good'. This suggests that tourism can help alleviate poverty and that personal ethical norms would support efforts in emissions limitations. Nevertheless, the belief in the personal right to travel is coupled with a contradictory belief that others should be denied the right to travel, for the good of the planet. Although some people want to do the right thing, consumers will often look to their government to make it easy for them to do it (Sustainable Consumption Roundtable 2006).

There is ample evidence that the most environmentally aware are unwilling to alter behaviour and the most climatically aware are the most active travellers (Gössling et al. 2013). Tourists have little vested interest in the long-term survival of any destination, as they can adapt to climate change. In progressing understanding of responsibility, there is little sense of personal responsibility with regard to climate change responses and the entrenched nature of contemporary air travel practice results in a resistance to change. Gössling et al. (2013: p. 533) conclude 'evidence of a consumer response to lessen the climate change impacts of travel suggests that there has not been a response'. This seems to suggest a low inclination towards voluntary behaviour change. Therefore, despite the 'duty-holder' being held responsible for reducing unnecessary energy consumption, the inconvenience of these reductions often requires additional legislation or other strategies to encourage the process.

Not all responsibility can be placed on the consumer, and there is a need to discuss a shared responsibility. The Triangle of Change is the relationship and shared responsibilities between government, business and the consumer in taking action for sustainable consumption (Sustainable Consumption Roundtable 2006). Although responsibility underlies the current value system and is assigned accordingly (for example a thief is punished), the issues with climate change are that harm is indirect and not readily observable; victims are not easily identifiable and responsibility is not easily assigned (Lovelock and Lovelock 2013).

Action or inaction

It would seem useful to appreciate more about why inaction occurs, rather than action. For government, doing nothing is politically safe; it avoids any unpopularity with business and allows consumers to maintain their lifestyle. Internationally, inaction could gain a short-term advantage over other nations, despite the cost of doing nothing being greater than the cost of mitigation for both undeveloped and developed countries. Nevertheless, although inaction will ultimately impact on governments, businesses and individuals, there seems to be a 'waiting for others' game at play. Consumers should not be left to agonise over complex ethical issues when in a supermarket aisle and retailers should 'choice edit', so that the consumer can choose between good products. However, there are those businesses that claim to be ready and waiting to act ethically, but which need the confidence they are not acting alone, against the grain or to no purpose. In all likelihood the individual consumer is likely to reflect this same sentiment, because industry is an influence on their knowledge and beliefs. Therefore, the short-term self-interest of industry (and the consumer) appears to outweigh responsibility and is perhaps contrary to societal (and personal) values. Further, motivation and behaviour seem only to be encouraged by inducements.

Challenges in ethical consumer behaviour

To encourage ethical behaviour there is a need to better understand consumers who face challenges which prevent ethical behaviour, or who express ethical intentions but are unable to follow through. This section reviews the structural and psychological barriers to change impeding an improvement in responsible consumer behaviour. Following this, consideration is given to ignorance, confusion and lack of motivation. In the middle of the section is a discussion on ethical claims. Towards the end, the reasons for differences between expressed ethical intentions and actual behaviour are deliberated. The final section reviews the role of cognitive dissonance, moral disengagement and diffusion of responsibility.

Barriers to change

The barriers to changing ethical consumer behaviour could be both structural and psychological. Structural barriers can restrict the ability to engage in actions and include institutional (such as split incentives that require one actor to pay the costs, while another benefits) and regulatory barriers (requiring investment). They also include cultural (such as expectations of success or car type), physical (such as heating reduction in cold climates) and economic barriers (such as low income or lack of capital). The psychological barriers of climate change behaviour are less well documented, but include habit (habitual behaviours are resistant to permanent change); perceived behavioural control (beliefs that they cannot change anything); perceived risks from behavioural change (financial, social, physical, psychological or time-lost risks); conflicting goals and aspirations; belief in solutions outside of human control (Mother Nature or religious deities will provide the solution); and mistrust and reactance (a distrust of risk messages from scientists and government, or reactance against advice as freedom is threatened) (American Psychological Association Task Force 2010).

Ignorance, confusion and lack of motivation

A better appreciation of why some tourists act ethically and responsibly, whilst others do not, would be useful. These limitations on ethical behaviour could be due to ignorance, confusion or lack of motivation to change. Tourists may be ignorant of their impacts, which range from inappropriate clothing to demonstration effect, to the undermining of locals' self-esteem, to commoditised ceremonies, cultural performances and rituals. Perhaps it is ignorance or self-serving motivations which result in tourists walking on coral or disrupting the eating and breeding patterns of wildlife. However, it is debatable whether ignorance can be applied to the non-believers on the basis that these believe climate change is a natural cycle and they therefore travel as normal.

There is confusion in tourists' ideas on tourism and climate change. The 'undecideds' are aware of possible climate change impacts, but they are also confused, indecisive and uncommitted. However, confusion can also account for some tourists taking all-inclusive holidays (because it controls their personal expenditure, despite not economically benefiting a destination) or taking illegal drugs at destinations (because of assumed legality and ready availability). Although it could be argued that the confusion arises from actions which are unintentional or not intended to cause harm to others, this surely cannot be the case for child sex tourism, which is wholly unethical. Although this goes some way to explaining some of the barriers to change, it is likely that ethical claims can add to the ignorance, confusion and lack of motivation, which impedes a change to more ethical behaviour.

Ethical intentions and behaviour

Although ethical intentions are expressed, the actual behaviour that results may be less ethical and requires consideration. The socially desirable nature of certain behaviours has led consumers to overstate their intentions to buy ethically. This has produced a gap between what consumers say and do, referred to as the attitude–behaviour gap. The behaviour emerging is 'ego-tourism', the result of wanting to get closer to threatened environments, but on one's own terms. This probably accounts for the idea that ecotourism to the Antarctic can earn 'bragging rights'. Although this seems to contradict the very nature of ecotourism, it reflects an argument that unethical eco-tourists are possible. Consumers often perceive ethical holidays as 'moralistic' and too worthy, particularly when all they want is a relaxing experience. This seems to hint (where a behaviour is known to be unethical and its ethicality is questioned) at a need to justify the behaviour undertaken.

Cognitive dissonance

In approaching the need for the individual to justify behaviour it is valuable to give brief consideration to the concept of cognitive dissonance. A state of tension and unease motivates the individual to change attitude or behaviour to achieve cognitive consistency. Behaviour has to be perceived to have an unwanted consequence if dissonance is to result (otherwise harmony is maintained), and there should be acceptance of personal responsibility for the consequences of the behaviour. This responsibility consists of freely chosen behaviour and the ability to foresee the consequences of that behaviour. Acceptance of responsibility leads to dissonance and denial of responsibility allows people to avoid the unpleasant state of dissonance. Those who are better informed about climate change feel less rather than more responsible for it, because low self-efficacy results in denial of responsibility, unless individuals feel able to do something about it. However, many challenges to ethical behaviour do not suggest a perceived awareness or acceptance by individuals of unwanted consequences of behaviour. This perhaps calls into question the use of cognitive dissonance as an explanation for unethical behaviour, and ethical theory yields alternative explanations.

Moral disengagement

Moral disengagement is similar to cognitive dissonance, but considers that harmful actions can be rationalised. It justifies conduct and allows individuals to maintain their values – separating them from their actions. Bandura (2007) suggests that individuals often find themselves in moral predicaments when they serve self-interest, because their moral standards are violated when they inflict human and environmental harm. Moral justification is a disengagement process that makes detrimental conduct both personally and socially acceptable. Selective moral disengagement can make a problem disappear through a network of participants which justify harmful practices (such as the social forces that often support environmentally detrimental activities). Nevertheless, where harmful outcomes are acknowledged, individuals can avoid self-disapproving reactions and absolve themselves of personal responsibility by shifting the responsibility to others or to situational events – 'making the planet the doer absolves consumptive lifestyles. . . of any responsibility for the earth's rising temperatures' (Bandura 2007: p. 20). Therefore, built into the social system are displacement and diffusion of responsibility, which obscure personal accountability and enable individuals to stick with behavioural practices without feeling bad about the consequences. This can explain some unethical consumer behaviour in travel and tourism.

Diffusion of responsibility

In addition, responsibility can be diffused and diminished through division because when everyone is responsible, no one individual feels responsible. Diffusion of responsibility has variously considered the bystander effect (leaving responsibility to others in group situations), moral disengagement and denial – knowledge denial ('we didn't know'), control denial ('we knew, but couldn't do anything about it') and connection denial ('whether we knew or not, it's the responsibility of someone else') (Phillips 2012). A diffusion of responsibility, at best, reduces dissonance because it enables individuals to feel less responsible, by outsourcing that responsibility to others. At worst, it rejects personal responsibility and blames others for problems. Perhaps, in the case of climate change, a diffusion of responsibility is employed because the magnitude of the message makes people feel less responsible as they lack control or have the feeling that individual actions would make no difference. What is clear is that increasing knowledge is unlikely to increase a sense of responsibility.

Conclusions

This chapter reviews ethical issues as part of travel and tourism consumer behaviour. It provides the ethical theories which can assist in understanding the individual and societal approach towards the dilemma of travel. It finds that personal or national self-interest seems to reign over collective interest. The implication of this is permanent damage or destruction of the shared resource, which impacts all of society and not just those who are self-interested. Therefore, an appreciation of the cognitive behaviour at play (which results in acceptance of responsibility, shift of responsibility or diffusion of responsibility) could assist in understanding both tourists' ethics and why ethical concerns and beliefs have not penetrated the tourism market further. Moreover, to mitigate the problem, only a better understanding of tourists' motivations, constraints, values and beliefs will allow effective strategies to be developed in order to modify or change behaviour.

References

American Psychological Association Task Force (2010). *Psychology and Global Climate Change: Addressing a Multi-faceted Phenomenon and Set of Challenges*, Washington, DC: American Psychological Association, Retrieved from http://www.apa.org/science/about/publications/climate-change.aspx [Accessed: 17 January 2016].

Bandura, A. (2007). 'Impeding ecological sustainability through selective moral disengagement', *International Journal of Innovation and Sustainable Development*, 2(1): 8–35.

Boose, M. A. and Dean, F. P. (2000). 'Analyzing ethical decision making: Applying the Hunt-Vitell Model in insurance courses', *Risk Management and Insurance Review*, 3(2): 237–249.

Gössling, S., Scott, D. and Hall, C. M. (2013). 'Challenges of tourism in a low-carbon economy', *Wiley Interdisciplinary Reviews: Climate Change*, 4(6): 525–538.

Kavak, B., Gürel, E., Eryiğit, C. and Tektaş, Ö. (2009). 'Examining the effects of moral development level, self-concept, and self-monitoring on consumers' ethical attitudes', *Journal of Business Ethics*, 88(1): 115–135.

Lovelock, B. and Lovelock, K. (2013). *The Ethics of Tourism: Critical and Applied Perspectives*, Abingdon: Routledge.

Mintel (2005). *Ethical Holidays – UK – October 2005 – Market Research Report*, Mintel Online, Available from http://academic.mintel.com.ezproxy.leedsmet.ac.uk/sinatra/oxygen_academic/search_results/showand/display/id=125548 [Accessed: 17 January 2016].

Phillips, R. (2012). 'Ethics and network organizations', *Business Ethics Quarterly*, 20(3): 533–543.

Sen, S., Gürhan-Canli, Z. and Morwitz, V. (2001). 'Withholding consumption: A social dilemma perspective on consumer boycotts', *Journal of Consumer Research*, 28(3): 399–417.

Speed, C. (2007). 'Are backpackers ethical tourists?', in K. Hannam and I. Ateljevic (eds.), *Backpacker Tourism: Concepts and Profiles* (pp. 54–81), Clevedon: Channel View Publications.

Sustainable Consumption Roundtable (2006). 'I Will if You Will: Towards Sustainable Consumption', Available from http://www.sd-commission.org.uk/data/files/publications/I_Will_If_You_Will.pdf [Accessed: 17 January 2016].

9

CROSS-CULTURAL ISSUES OF CONSUMER BEHAVIOUR IN HOSPITALITY AND TOURISM

Clare Hindley and Melanie Kay Smith

Introduction

The hospitality industry is under pressure to innovate in order to remain competitive. This innovation is steered by several trends including increasing global mobility and the need to cater for diverse guest groups and their cultures. As stated by Lin et al. (2007: p. 27), 'As the competition becomes intensively globalized, understanding and accommodating the needs of consumers from different cultural backgrounds have become increasingly important.' The following chapter outlines the need to steer away from simply seeing culture as synonymous with nationality and more closely examine what 'different cultural backgrounds' means for the hospitality industry in the 21st century. This includes religion, including the increasing importance of 'Halal tourism' and the needs of Muslim guests. The chapter also questions how far different age segments can be catered for and whether their preferences transcend national barriers.

The dominance of nationality in cultural theory and research

Some theorists view culture as a hierarchy with the national level functioning as an umbrella over many subcultures or co-cultures (Chaney and Martin 2007). This is perhaps one of the main reasons why nationality has been placed at the centre of the majority of cultural and cross-cultural studies (e.g. Hall 1959; Hofstede 1980; Haworth and Savage 1989; Gudykunst and Kim 1992; Trompenaars 1994; Sussman 2000; Davies and Fitchett 2004; Lewis 2006). A content analysis of over 3,000 journal articles related to international business (Reis et al. 2013) established that Hofstede's (1980) taxonomy is the most commonly used one despite some well-known criticisms. Following their overview of post-2000 research, Tasci and Boylu (2010) suggest that nationality is a suitable label to use when describing culture. Data on nationality is certainly the easiest to collect and it is also the case that analysis becomes more complicated when multiple variables are included.

However, several authors have argued that other factors may also be significant. Regional cultures exist, as pointed out by Lin et al. (2007: p. 33): 'More than one country can share a distinct cultural dimension (e.g. almost all Asian countries are influenced by Confucian thinking), and every country has subcultures that are uncharacteristic of the core culture.'

Jameson (2007) suggests that research has often ignored the fact that age, gender, socio-economic status, ethnicity, religion and many more issues are potentially more important than, or at least equally as important as, nationality. Poncini (2002) argued that in studies of discourse in multicultural business settings, factors such as organisational roles, business contexts and individual differences may be important. Hanek et al. (2014: p. 78) point out that '"globals" or individuals who have been exposed to multiple cultures starting at an early age, may not identify with any cultural group'. The same may be true of frequent travellers.

Cultural research in consumer behaviour

Cultural values clearly play an important role in the way consumers make purchasing decisions (Bahhouth and Ziemnowicz 2012) and nationality may be significant. In their study of consumer review behaviour, Lai et al. (2013: p. 109) use Hofstede's (1983) dimensions to look at 'two distinct cultures, American and Chinese'. However, Lim and Park (2013: p. 16) point out that the Hofstede instrument is not suitable for use at the individual consumer level. Instead, personal, psychological and social components of culture need to be considered (Manrai and Manrai 2011; Lim and Park 2013). Davies and Fitchett (2004: p. 320) point out that previous research in consumer behaviour and international marketing research has 'challenged the validity of universal models, where the content and structure of complex phenomena is seen as constant across nationality defined cultures'. Ethnicity, religious affiliation, age, gender and social group should also be considered (Briley and Aaker 2006; Bahhouth and Ziemnowicz 2012).

Cultural research in hospitality and tourism

Pantouvakis (2013) suggests that cross-cultural research is in its infancy in the fields of tourism and hospitality. However, having knowledge of the different cultural needs of guests in the hospitality and tourism sectors has become an increasingly important aspect of guest service and satisfaction (Mallinson and Weiler 2000). Employees with high cultural sensitivity often score higher than other employees in terms of their attentiveness to service, their contribution to revenue, their interpersonal skills, and their job and social satisfaction (Sizoo et al. 2005). Culture seems to influence consumer behaviour and how people behave in a service encounter (Ueltschy and Krampf 2001). Guests' cultural background can affect their preferences and expectations when experiencing service in a hotel, for example (Luk et al. 1994; Mok and Armstrong 1998). To illustrate the extent to which nationality seems to affect the preferences of guests in a hospitality and tourism context, the following case study analyses the spa preferences of guests of different nationalities in Estonia.

The preferences of different nationality guests in Estonian spas

In the context of spa hotels and resorts in the Estonian town of Pärnu, a study by Tooman et al. (2013) based on interviews with spa managers revealed differences between Finnish, Swedish, Russian and Latvian guests. For example, Finns are more price sensitive than Russians, they prefer fixed packages which are the same each time they visit and like Finnish to be spoken. Latvians are more adventurous, tend to try new treatments and are happy to speak English.

Russians socialise and party in spas more than other nationalities, whereas Swedes look for higher levels of comfort and quality.

In a later study, Tael (2015) analysed the preferences of 230 medical spa guests in the same town of Pärnu with a focus on Estonian, Finnish and Swedish visitors. Estonian and Finnish respondents had more spa-going experience than their Swedish counterparts, which is not surprising as the Estonians have a stronger tradition of using spas and the Finns often visit Estonia to use them. The Swedish expressed a higher preference for wellness rather than medical spas as they do not have a medical spa tradition. Speaking their own language was much more important for Finnish than for other visitors (similar to Tooman et al.'s [2013] study). Estonian spa-goers consider the price of the trip and treatments to be slightly more important than do Finnish and Swedish guests. However, the reasons for this are probably economic (i.e. salaries are considerably lower in Estonia). Estonian spa-goers tend to organise the spa visit themselves (or at least in their own country). Their primary motivation for visiting a medical spa is to improve health and to relax. Price is the most important attribute when choosing a spa. Finnish spa-goers tend to book through a travel agency and setting and price are the most important attributes. Swedish guests are also price sensitive but less so than Finns or Estonians. Estonian medical spa visitors place the most significance on improving health, followed by Finnish visitors, then Swedish. For example, the Finns like to see a doctor during their stay whereas it is less important for Swedish guests. Conversely, Swedish medical spa-goers placed slightly more importance on pampering than their Finnish and Estonian counterparts. Estonians and Finns are equally interested in curative treatments but the Finns are more interested in beauty services (e.g. manicure, pedicure and hairdressing).

The differences between nationalities in spas may be considered to be subtle, even negligible, but they can make quite a big difference to the packaging, promotion and management of spa visits to Estonia. However, economic and not only cultural factors may also play a role, and it is important also to consider variations between ages and genders. This study consisted of 74% women and 85% were aged 56 or above as medical spas attract older guests and spas generally attract far more women. This research also acknowledges that gender and age, amongst other things, could be equally if not more important and nationality characteristics may only be significant in groups homogeneous in other variables such as age, religion and gender.

There are still many cultural challenges in the hotel sector. For example, Heffernan and Droulers' (2008) study of the success of the Shangri-La hotel in Sydney identifies cultural problems in the initial stages of the hotel's development (e.g. differences between individualism, collectivism and humility evident in staff composition, service expectation and labour laws). On the other hand, Choi et al. (2013) found no significant differences between American and Chinese hotel managers and considered this to be potentially due to three decades having elapsed since the original studies carried out by Hofstede. They suggest that the increasingly diverse hotel industry needs more research studies to measure whether power distance is (still) a valid cultural factor differentiating China from the United States. Their study identified Americans by nationality, but recognised that the concept of nationality can have complications such as having obtained citizenship or being a second-generation immigrant.

Incorporating other components into cultural theory and consumer behaviour

The following analysis focuses on religion and age as two areas which have been neglected in some past studies or were simply seen as subordinate to nationality. The focus on religion, in particular Islam, and age, in particular Generation Y, is based on the large numbers belonging to these segments and the increasing mobility of each group and therefore their significance to the hospitality industry.

Religion

Cultural values often include religious beliefs and shape one's way of living and acting in the world (Varner and Beamer 2011; Pellerin-Carlin 2014). Lewis (2006) uses religion as an example for the distinction of cultural groups. Religion also has a considerable influence on many people's behaviour as customers (Essoo and Dibb 2004 in Battour et al. 2011). This is especially true of Muslim consumers for whom the guiding principles of religion are still of major importance (Wilson 2014). Religion and culture have often been treated as two distinct characteristics, with the hotel industry historically putting more emphasis on guests' cultural rather than religious expectations and needs. But this may be changing with the growth of Islamic or so-called 'Halal tourism' (Hamza et al. 2012). The Muslim travel index 2014 revealed that for 97% of the Muslim traveller respondents it is very important that their destination of choice can offer halal food options and for 93% the availability of praying facilities is a major issue (Halal Tourism Conference 2014). The provision of halal food, pork-free kitchens and non-alcohol mini-bars were other common responses. Females mentioned the need for female-only areas in spas and swimming pools as well as the availability of female room staff and spa therapists. Features like a bidet in the bathroom or the convenience of Arabic TV channels were also mentioned by the participants. It should be noted that non-Muslim tourists are also welcome in and are attracted to Islamic destinations. For example, at the Jawhara Hotels, an alcohol-free Arabian Gulf chain, 60% of the clientele are non-Muslims (Hamza et al. 2012).

Halal tourism in Germany

A study in 2014 (Hindley et al. 2015) with Muslim tour operators and hotel employees in Germany showed that it is nowadays absolutely necessary for hotels and their managers and employees to react to the different cultures, nationalities and religions of guests. It was pointed out that changes are not huge or cost intensive and do not risk offending existing customers.

Many people misinterpret Islam, expecting very strict regulations. However, hotels arguably do not have to change that much beyond offering halal food, the Koran and prayer mats as a minimum. Ideally the sexual channels from the TV should be removed, men and women would be offered segregated facilities and usually there is no alcoholic bar.

Hotel staff in this study were not aware of exact numbers of Muslim guests as asking about 'religion' is not part of the registration procedure. However, the interviewees saw the Muslim market as having great potential for German hotels. Muslim employees working in hotels can also be a great asset in terms of understanding the culture and fulfilling wishes. Training was stressed as vital: 'The housekeeping staff has to know that the Arabic language is written from right to left and therefore the Koran has to be put on the reverse side.' All tour operator interviewees and hotel employees agreed that Germany is not offering enough for Muslim guests and cannot yet fit into Muslim tourism company portfolios. The importance of Muslim travellers as a target market for German hotels has been recognised by hotel managers, but not many hotels proactively offer promotions, services, specified contact personnel or amenities which are directly addressed to Muslims. None of the Muslim tour operators could name hotels which would meet their criteria.

Age

As the world becomes increasingly globalised, certain traits may spread beyond borders, such as those pertaining to certain age groups or generations. Generation theory seeks to characterise and understand groups of people referred to as cohorts by classifying them into categories objectively determined by their year of birth. Thus the approach does not focus on individual characteristics and differences, but rather broadly suggests common features. Generation theory brings with it certain challenges: for example, to what extent age transcends national boundaries.

The size of Generation Y, born between 1982 and 2002 (Benckendorff et al. 2010), has been estimated at approximately 1.8 billion people worldwide (Cairncross and Buultjens 2007). Within the United States almost 80 million people belong to Generation Y which covers one third of all hotel guests within the country (TripAdvisor 2013).

The most frequently mentioned Generation Y characteristics relevant to the hospitality industry are technologically savvy, community and socially connected, socially and environmentally responsible (Mihaiu 2013; HVS 2013), price sensitive and immune to traditional advertising (Aquino 2012; Sukalakamala et al. 2013). Theorists such as Howe and Strauss (2007) and Huntley (2006) consistently describe the generation as focused on brands, friends, fun and digital culture. They are multitaskers who are networked rather than individually focused, so they are strongly influenced by friends and peers (Benckendorff et al. 2010). This young generation of travellers favours 'isolated togetherness' (Morrissey 2012: p. 6), meaning they do not mind sitting in the lounge by themselves but they like having people in their surroundings. Thus hotels established the design of 'stylish and comfortable lobbies and welcoming and convivial public gathering places' (Habeeb 2013). A study by Market Matrix illustrates that Generation Y harbours 'the least loyal, most unpredictable and least satisfied guests compared to other generations' (Travel Agent 2011). Unsatisfied Generation Y customers do not complain to the company's manager, but on review sites, resulting in a negative impact on customer loyalty or even the service purchase (Habeeb 2013). Before booking a hotel, members of Generation Y consider on average 10.2 sources, including TripAdvisor and Yelp (Lee 2013).

Generation Y is looking for 'a hotel that is part of a scene' (Drillinger 2013: p. 52). They desire a sense of belonging to the local culture, by savouring local food and getting to know indigenous people. This might include visiting friends, colleagues or acquaintances in the cities they visit (Watkins 2014). It also explains the growing popularity of couch surfing and Airbnb, which represent considerable competition for the hotel industry. Young travellers tend to be sport and fitness oriented (von Ulmenstein 2011). They highly value a healthy breakfast and see a fitness room as an essential factor (Landua 2015).

Nevertheless, one should consider that these factors are not uniform across cultures and geographical locations. A cross-cultural study by Corvi et al. (2007) pinpointed differences in the events and social circumstances between European and American members of Gen Y. The results show that such differences led to significant differences in values and characteristics between same-generation members of the two continents. For instance, even the same events may be perceived differently and have a different influence on representatives of the same generation from various cultures.

On the other hand, new generations often define themselves independently from localised cultural and political frameworks and adopt behaviours, perceptions and expectations that are borrowed from distant cultural spaces or that are born out of the expectation and mythology of freedom that the Internet and social media promote (Patil et al. 2013). Today, market researchers try to sell to 'global teens' because urban adolescents worldwide follow similar consumption patterns and have similar preferences for 'global brands' of music, videos, T-shirts, soft drinks and so on (Arnett 2002). Padgett et al.'s (2013: p. 487) study of Chinese Generation Y fast food consumption points out: 'Today, few young Chinese consumers adhere to the collectivist attitude of years past. Many Chinese individuals' personal goals are likely self-satisfaction and self-expression.'

Major hotel companies worldwide are designing concepts to attract Generation Y (Morrissey 2012; Kaspersen 2014). The different attempts all experiment with a variety of solutions, everything from smaller and more functional rooms, to community-style lobbies (Ponchione 2014). The following case study examines the Norwegian market and tries to establish whether experts in the field support the findings of the aforementioned research.

The impact of Generation Y in the Norwegian hospitality industry

Semi-structured interviews were carried out with Norwegian, Swedish and Danish hospitality experts consisting of high-ranking hotel managers, developers and CEOs with sufficient knowledge of the Norwegian hotel industry (Halvorsen et al. 2015). One of the six interviewees was involved in the creation, planning, building and operation process of the Comfort Hotel Xpress concept. The following information is based on an analysis of the first Comfort Hotel Xpress in Youngstorget, Oslo, which opened in January 2011, its website and data from the interviews (Comfort Hotel Xpress Youngstorget 2015).

The Comfort Hotel Xpress Youngstorget is described as being in 'the coolest location in Oslo'. It claims to offer rooms with 'trendy furniture' and 'cool colors'. In terms of facilities, it talks about 'smart solutions for those who don't want to waste their money on unnecessary fuss'. Examples include a 24-hour gym, roof terrace, pinball, table football, breakfast in a bag delivered directly to the room, and no mini-bar or restaurant. Instead snacks, salads and drinks are available in the lobby shop where there is space 'to mingle'. Later check-out is available, until 6 pm on Sundays. The hotel described itself as the world's first hotel with self check-in kiosks, mobile and online check-in and the option of a smartphone as a room key. There is emphasis on sustainability and green practices. In order to attract young guests, it uses such phrases as 'You won't find anything bland and boring here, we like to keep it edgy', and of course, they have a presence on Foursquare, Facebook, Twitter, YouTube, TripAdvisor and Comfort Hotels Mobile Web.

All but one interviewee considered the shift in the consumer generation to be the main reason for a change in the hotel industry. The emerging consumer books their stays online, and trusts the technology behind it. Social media was mentioned as a supplementary marketing platform, where opinions about the property may be exchanged. For example, a good TripAdvisor ranking is vital to be successful with Generation Y.

Conclusion

This chapter has shown that cross-cultural issues are of increasing importance in the hospitality and tourism industries as both mobility and competition increase. Research has shown that culture is not a static concept and includes many elements beyond the categories of nationality. Despite the fact that nationality can be a significant and therefore a vital element in analysing guest needs and expectations in the hospitality industry, other factors such as religion and age need to be taken into account.

However, further challenges may arise, such as the fact that Muslim tourists are not a homogeneous group either (Stephenson 2014) and their needs may vary according to nationality, age or gender. It is not altogether clear whether age or generation segmentation is a useful way of addressing consumer behaviour, because considerable research would need to be undertaken across several countries to be sure that age differences indeed transcend national cultural boundaries. It is also difficult to distinguish what is specific to Generation Y and what is a more general preference (e.g. sustainability, Wi-Fi access). There is also the consideration of gender, which can be even more important in some cases (e.g. far more women use spas and visit wellness hotels). Most data about guests is only provided on arrival so there is little time to prepare for very specific needs. On the other hand, it is only a matter of time before smart solutions become more widespread for providing hotel receptions with more detailed data about guests prior to check-in (i.e. language spoken, age, nationality, religion, food preferences if stated).

It would be ambitious and even unreasonable to expect the entire hospitality and tourism sector to be ready to cater for the needs of very specific segments at any time. On the other hand, as the number of Chinese or Russian guests increases, it becomes more worthwhile to provide language training for staff or some cultural pointers. The same is true of the growing number of Muslim guests. In many cases, only small changes may be required like not giving Chinese guests rooms with the number 4 in them or making sure there is a Koran and a prayer mat in a room. After all, many hotels make only small concessions to the concept of sustainability by urging guests to use their towels for several days, for example. A few cultural concessions may not require great investment and extensive training courses on the part of hotels or attractions, just an increase in knowledge, sensitivity and awareness, skills which are surely a prerequisite in a dynamic and fast-growing competitive environment anyway.

References

Aquino, J. (2012). 'Gen Y: The next generation of spenders', *CRM*, February.

Arnett, J. J. (2002). 'The psychology of globalization', *American Psychologist*, 57(10): 774–783.

Bahhouth, V. and Ziemnowicz, C. (2012). 'Effect of culture and traditions on consumer behavior in Kuwait', *International Journal of Business, Marketing, and Decision Sciences*, 5(2): 1–11.

Battour, M., Ismail, M. N. and Battor, M. (2011). 'The impact of destination attributes on Muslim tourists' choice', *International Journal of Tourism Research*, 13(6): 527–540.

Benckendorff, G., Moscardo, P. and Pendergast, D. (2010). *Tourism and Generation Y*, Wallingford: CABI.

Briley, D. A. and Aaker, J. L. (2006). 'Bridging the culture chasm: Ensuring that consumers are healthy, wealthy and wise', *Journal of Public Policy and Marketing*, 25(1): 3–66.

Cairncross, G. and Buultjens, J. (2007). 'Generation Y and work in the tourism and hospitality industry: Problem? What problem?', *Centre for Enterprise Development and Research Occasional Paper*, 9: 1–21.

Chaney, L. H. and Martin, J. S. (2007). *Intercultural Business Communication*, 4th edition, Upper Saddle River, NJ: Pearson Prentice-Hall.

Choi, D. W.-S., Stahura, K., Sammons, G. E. and Bernhard, B. (2013). 'Differences between management philosophies among American and Chinese hotel managers: A cultural comparison between Las Vegas and Shanghai', *International Journal of Hospitality and Tourism*, 14(2): 121–138.

Comfort Hotel Xpress Youngstorget (2015). Available from: https://www.nordicchoicehotels.com/comfort/comfort-hotel-xpress [Accessed: 24 September 2015].

Corvi, E., Bigi, A. and Ng, G. (2007). 'The European millennials versus the US millennials: Similarities and differences', Paper presented at the International Business Research Conference, Universita' degli Studi di Brescia, Rome, 5–6 October.

Davies, A. and Fitchett, J. A. (2004). '"Crossing culture": A multi-method enquiry into consumer behaviour and the experience of cultural transition', *Journal of Consumer Behaviour*, 3(4): 315–330.

Drillinger, M. (2013). 'Targeting millennials: Young demographic wants to have fun and stay connected – at a good value', *TravelAgent*, 342(13): 52–54.

Gudykunst, W. B. and Kim, Y. Y. (1992). *Readings on Communicating with Strangers*, Boston, MA: McGraw-Hill.

Habeeb, R. (2013). 'Accommodating influential millennial travellers', *Hotel News Now*, Available from: http://www.hotelnewsnow.com/Article/9965/Accommodating-influential-millennial-travelers [Accessed: 24 September 2015].

Halal Tourism Conference (2014). 'Europe set to benefit from the billion pound halal tourism market', Available from: https://mffcoexist.wordpress.com/2014/12/03/europe-set-to-benefit-from-the-billion-pound-halal-tourism-market/ [Accessed: 26 September 2015].

Hall, E. T. (1959). *The Silent Language,* Garden City, NY: Anchor Books/Doubleday.

Halvorsen, T., Hindley, C. N. and Wilson-Wünsch, B. (2015). 'The impact of Generation Y on the hospitality industry: A case study of a Norwegian hotel', Paper presented at the EuroCHRIE Conference 2015, Manchester, UK, 15–17 October.

Hamza, I. M., Chouhoud, R. and Tantawi, P. (2012). 'Islamic tourism: Exploring perceptions and possibilities in Egypt', *African Journal of Business and Economic Research*, 7(1): 85–98.

Hanek, K. J., Lee, F. and Brannen, M. Y. (2014). 'Individual differences among global/multicultural individuals', *International Studies of Management and Organization*, 44(2): 75–89.

Haworth, D. A. and Savage, G. T. (1989). 'A channel-ratio model of intercultural communication: The trains won't sell, fix them please', *Journal of Business Communication*, 29(3): 231–254.

Heffernan, T. and Droulers, M. (2008). 'East and West: The successful integration of cultures at Shangri-La, Sydney', *The Marketing Review*, 8(3): 297–309.

Hindley, C. N., Smith, M. K. and Winter, S. (2015). 'Creating experiences in hotels and spas: The significance of culture and religion', Paper presented at the EuroCHRIE Conference 2015, Manchester, UK, 15–17 October.

Hofstede, G. (1980). *Culture's Consequences: International Differences in Work-related Values*, Beverly Hills, CA: Sage.

Hofstede, G. (1983). 'Dimensions of national cultures in fifty countries and three regions', in J. B. Deregowski, S. Dziurawiec and R. C. Annis (eds.), *Expectations in Cross-Cultural Psychology* (pp. 333–355), Lisse, the Netherlands: Swets and Zeitlinger.

Howe, N. and Strauss, W. (2007). 'The next 20 years: How customer and workforce attitudes will evolve', *Harvard Business Review*, 85(7/8): 41–52.

Huntley, R. (2006). *The World According to Y: Inside the New Adult Generation*, Sydney: Allen and Unwin.

HVS (2013). 'Preparing for Generation Y', *HVS,* Available from: https://www.hvs.com/article/6384-canadian-monthly-lodging-outlook-april-2013 [Accessed: 10 September 2015].

Jameson, D. A. (2007). 'Reconceptualizing cultural identity and its role in intercultural business', *Journal of Business Communication*, 44(3): 199–235.

Kaspersen, L. (2014). 'Slik endrer Generasjon Y luksus-begrepet [How Generation Y changes the concept of luxury]', *DN*, 16 February, Available from: http://www.dn.no/privat/privatok onomi/2014/02/16/slik-endrer-generasjon-y-luksusbegrepet [Accessed: 12 September 2015].

Lai, J., He, P., Chou, H.-M. and Zhou, L. (2013). 'Impact of national culture on online consumer review behavior', *Global Journal of Business Research*, 7(1): 109–115.

Landua, C. (2015). 'Starwood expansion: Starwood expandiert [Starwood expansion: Starwood is expanding]', *Tophotel*, Available from: http://www.tophotel.de/20-news/4740-starwood-expand iert.html [Accessed: 24 September 2015].

Lee, T. Y. (2013). 'Top 10 trends of the next generation of travel: The millennials', *HVS*, 10 April, 1–16, Available from: http://www.hvs.com/article/6297/top-10-trends-of-the-next-generation-of-travel [Accessed: 24 September 2015].

Lewis, R. D. (2006). *When Cultures Collide*, Boston, MA: Nicholas Brealey.

Lim, H. and Park, J.-S. (2013). 'The effects of national culture and cosmopolitanism on consumers' adoption of innovation: A cross-cultural comparison', *Journal of International Consumer Marketing*, 25(1): 16–28.

Lin, C. C. J., Tu, R., Chen, K. and Tu, P. (2007). 'The changing expectations of consumers in cross-cultural service encounters', *International Management Review*, 3(3): 27–35.

Luk, S. T., de Leon, C. T., Leong, F. W. and Li, E. L. (1994). 'Value segmentation of tourists' expectations of service quality', *International Marketing Review*, 8(1): 57–70.

Mallinson, H. and Weiler, B. (2000). 'Evaluating training: A window on cross-cultural awareness of hospitality staff', in M. Ewen (ed.), *Proceedings of the Tenth Council for Australian University Tourism and Hospitality Education (CAUTHE) Conference*, Bundoora, Melbourne: La Trobe University.

Manrai, L. A. and Manrai, A. K. (2011). 'Cross-cultural and cross-national consumer research in the global economy of the twenty-first century', *Journal of International Consumer Marketing*, 23(3/4): 167–180.

Mihaiu, A. T. (2013). 'Canadian monthly lodging outlook – preparing for Generation Y', *HVS*, 7 June, 1–6, Available from: http://www.hvs.com/article/6384/canadian-monthly-lodging-outlook-april-2013 [Accessed: 16 September 2015].

Mok, C. and Armstrong, R. W. (1998). 'Expectations for hotel service quality: Do they differ from culture to culture?', *Journal of Vacation Marketing*, 4(4): 381–390.

Morrissey, J. (2012). 'The millennials check in', *The New York Times*, 12 March, Available from: http://www.nytimes.com/2012/03/13/business/young-travelers-drive-changes-in-hotel-industry.html?_r=2 [Accessed: 16 September 2015].

Padgett, B. C., Kim, H. and Huffman, B. K. G. (2013). 'The usefulness of the theory of planned behavior: Understanding. US fast food consumption of Generation Y Chinese consumers', *Journal of Foodservice Business Research*, 16(5): 486–505.

Pantouvakis, A. (2013). 'The moderating role of nationality on the satisfaction loyalty link: Evidence from the tourism industry', *Total Quality Management*, 24(10): 1174–1187.

Patil, A., Liu, J. and Gao, J. (2013). 'Predicting group stability in online social networks', 1021–1030, Available from: http://www2013.org/proceedings/p1021.pdf [Accessed: 23 September 2015].

Pellerin-Carlin, T. (2014). 'EU 10 years after its biggest enlargement: Europe's identity crisis', *University of Economics Review*, 14(3): 73–84.

Ponchione, A. (2014). 'Perspectives trends: Millennial mind – answering Gen Y', *Hospitality Design*, 36(3): 129–132.

Poncini, G. (2002). 'Investigating discourse at business meetings with multicultural participation', *International Review of Applied Linguistics*, 40(4): 345–373.

Reis, N. R., Ferreira, M. P., Carvalho Santos, J. and Ribeiro Serra, F. (2013). 'A bibliometric study of the cultural models in international business research', *BASE-Revista de Administracao e Contabilidade da Unsinos*, 10(4): 340–354.

Sizoo, S., Plank, R., Iskat, W. and Serrie, H. (2005). 'The effect of intercultural sensitivity on employee performance in cross-cultural service encounters', *Journal of Services Marketing*, 19(4): 245–255.

Stephenson, M. L. (2014). 'Deciphering "Islamic hospitality": Developments, challenges and opportunities', *Tourism Management*, 40: 155–164.

Sukalakamala, P., Sukalakamala, S. and Young, P. (2013). 'An exploratory study of the concession preferences of Generation Y consumers', *Journal of Foodservice Business Research*, 16(4): 378–390.

Sussman, N. M. (2000). 'The dynamic nature of cultural identity throughout the cultural transitions: Why home is not so sweet', *Personality and Social Psychology Review*, 4(4): 355–373.

Tael, L. (2015). 'A cross-national study of motivations and perceived benefits of visitors to medical spas in Estonia', Unpublished MA thesis, Pärnu College, University of Tartu, Estonia.

Tasci, A. D. A. and Boylu, Y. (2010). 'Cultural comparison of tourists' safety perception in relation to trip satisfaction', *International Journal of Tourism Research*, 12(2): 179–192.

Tooman, H., Tomasberg, K. and Smith, M. K. (2013). 'Cross-cultural issues in health and wellness services in Estonia', in J. Kampandully (ed.), *Health and Wellness Services* (pp. 347–361), Dubuque, IA: Kendall Hunt.

Travel Agent (2011). 'Building hotel loyalty among Gen Y'ers', *Travel Agent*, 338(5): 8.

TripAdvisor (2013). 'How to attract the Gen Y hotel guest', *TripAdvisor*, Available from: http:// www.tripadvisor.co.uk/TripAdvisorInsights/n2038/how-attract-gen-y-hotel-guest [Accessed: 20 September 2015].

Trompenaars, F. (1994). *Riding the Waves of Culture: Understanding Cultural Diversity in Business*, Chicago, IL: Irwin.

Ueltschy, L. C. and Krampf, R. F. (2001). 'Cultural sensitivity to satisfaction and service quality measures', *Journal of Marketing*, 9(3): 14–31.

Varner, I. and Beamer, L. (2011). *Intercultural Communication in the Global Workplace*, New York: McGraw-Hill.

Von Ulmenstein, C. (2011). 'Hotel guests of future want automated service with personal attention', *Whale Cottage Portfolio*, Available from: http://www.whalecottage.com/blog/accommodation/ hotel-guests-of-future-want-automated-service-with-personal-attention [Accessed: 21 September 2015].

Watkins, E. (2014). 'Millennials redefine hotel luxury', *Hotel News Now*, 13 February, Available from: http://www.hotelnewsnow.com/Article/13142/Millennials-redefine-hotel-luxury [Accessed: 12 September 2015].

Wilson, J. A. (2014). 'The halal phenomenon: An extension or a new paradigm?', *Social Business*, 4(3): 255–271.

PART II

Service quality vis-à-vis consumer behaviour

Part II of the *Handbook* has seven chapters exploring the service quality dimension of consumer behaviour. Chapter 10 by David Drewery and Ron McCarville reviews extensively the available literature on the process through which customers feel satisfied/dissatisfied at the service offered. The resulting insights help tourism and hospitality operators to enhance understanding of clients' perceptions of service quality and subsequently to improve their own offerings. The contribution therefore helps managers to offer better support and co-production of tourism experiences so that they provide value, satisfy customers and lead to a variety of positive outcomes.

Service quality research has primarily focused on customers' evaluations of service quality. However, an important shortcoming of these studies is that managers and customers might perceive service quality differently, in terms of both relevant dimensions and acceptable levels of evaluations. Ana Oliveira-Brochado and Paulo Rita in chapter 11 provide a critical analysis of management perception of service quality. Therefore, in order to deliver products/services successfully, the management must have a precise perception of the quality of the services offered to their guests, and managers are in charge of foreseeing customer demands and expectations.

Chapter 12 by Aijing Liu, Emily Ma and Christy Yen Nee Ng revisits the measurement of service quality for hospitality and tourism. The chapter analyses the different models for service quality measurement such as the Expectancy-Disconfirmation Model, SERVQUAL and its application, LODGSERV and Importance Performance Analysis. This chapter provides readers with an excellent opportunity to know how to measure service quality and to become competent to apply and design their own framework, using these tools.

Total Quality Management (TQM) is as important in tourism and hospitality as in any other field. Aparna Raj and Saurabh Kumar Dixit elaborate on the application of principles of TQM in the tourism context in chapter 13. Quality in tourism and hospitality involves consistent delivery of products and guest services according to expected standards. TQM is a participatory process that empowers all levels of employees to work in groups in order to ascertain guest service expectations and determine the best way to meet or exceed these expectations. The chapter further highlights the important factors to be considered for the successful implementation of TQM strategies in tourism organisations.

Chapter 14 authored by Michael C. Ottenbacher, Robert J. Harrington and Anja Treuter deliberates on the impact of music on restaurant consumers' perceptions of quality and consumer behaviour. The study also investigates these relationships in the casual restaurant by testing music treatments of volume and tempo in this context, and if these relationships vary during different meal periods, i.e. lunch or dinner. Findings indicate substantial differences in the effect of music based on the meal period due to implicit and explicit differences in dining duration, spending, reasons for the visit and social or business expectations/needs. The research findings provide support for the need of management to vigilantly consider the impact of music on patrons' pleasure and behaviour.

Girish Prayag, Jörg Finsterwalder and C. Michael Hall re-evaluate different ways (process vs. outcome-based) of conceptualising service experience with the concept of Service Dominant (SD) logic in chapter 15. It further outlines modern methods of measuring the service experience, including service blueprinting, service mapping and service quality. The chapter also elaborates overlooked dimensions like emotional vs. sensorial encounters, group interactions vs. individual interactions, and the influence of spirituality on customer evaluations of service experiences. Execution of the suggested measures will be helpful in improving customer experiences and offer reward to both organisations and customers.

Chapter 16 by Valentina Della Corte and Giovanna Del Gaudio focuses on the innovations in hospitality and tourism that have been achieved increasingly in order to create value for customers and that require an experience-based approach. The chapter reflects on how organisations can manage their innovative competencies and the effects of innovation on the overall customer experience. This chapter has both theoretical and practical viewpoints. From a theoretical perspective, the chapter analyses the existing contributions and models on innovations in experience by reviewing the existing body of knowledge, whereas case study of experience-based innovation explores its practical perspective.

10

SERVICE QUALITY

Customers' perspectives

David Drewery and Ron McCarville

Introduction

In service delivery, clients and providers must be ready, willing and able to undertake any tasks necessary to complete the required transactions. As each partner fulfils their required roles, they co-create value (Prebensen et al. 2015; Vargo and Lusch 2008). Clients then assess both the co-creation process and relevant outcomes as they attempt to establish service quality (Tian-Cole and Scott 2004). The goal is to determine the relative quality of the experience. Different elements of the experience are assessed and evaluations about the service are formed (Markus and Zajonc 1985). Was it good or bad? Should it be liked or disliked?

As discussed in this chapter, clients collect information from multiple aspects of the service, compare that information to their own beliefs regarding 'good' service, and use this comparison to assess the service experience. Perceptions of quality are associated with higher perceived value (Howat and Assaker 2013), higher satisfaction levels (Kyle et al. 2010; Mee et al. 2014; Theodorakis et al. 2013), greater likelihood that clients will return (Su et al. 2016), that they will spread positive word-of-mouth communications (Murray and Howat 2002; Tzetzis et al. 2014), that they will excuse the provider for mistakes (Vázquez-Casielles et al. 2007; Xie and Heung 2012), and that they will develop more willingness to pay higher levels (Zeithaml 2000). It becomes important, therefore, that providers seek to deliver good-quality services.

This chapter focuses on clients' service quality assessments. It outlines how clients judge quality and suggests how managers might improve the quality of the overall consumption experience. The goal is to help managers better support the co-production of leisure experiences so that they provide value, satisfy clients and lead to any variety of positive outcomes.

The importance of expectations in determining service quality

All service evaluations represent a comparison with some reference point (De Houwer 2009). We cannot understand whether something is good or bad unless we have a reference point for what *good* looks like. Psychologists have long argued that humans utilize internal *schemas* as they make such comparisons. Schemas represent cognitive frameworks for organizing preconceived ideas and existing information (Bartlett 1932). They automatically guide our reaction to new information, shape the way we process our interactions with the world around us, and act as reference points for understanding our experiences (Fiske and Taylor 1984; Sujan 1985). These schemas influence the ways we approach the world around us, but are also influenced by that same world. They are shaped by our ongoing interactions with the world and can be periodically updated. Updates may be necessitated, for example, by satisfying and dissatisfying experiences (van Doorn and Verhoef 2008), marketing messages (Howat et al. 1996) and word of mouth (Sweeney et al. 2014).

These schemas guide our evaluations by providing a reference point for what is good and what is bad (Fiske and Taylor 1984). Information that is consistent with previously established schemas will lead to positive feelings while discordant information creates an unfavourable state of mind (Eckblad 1981). This perspective explains why clients may experience a positive emotional response or, conversely, may become very frustrated with a service encounter. This perspective also helps to explain why clients with different life experiences can differ so greatly in their perceptions of an objectively similar service.

Historically, the importance of expectations (Parasuraman et al. 1985) was best expressed in so-called *gap* models (e.g. see Martinez and Martinez [2010] for a full review). These models suggest that clients compare the performance (P) of the provider against their expectations (E) for that performance. They assume that service quality is the mathematical difference between the E and P scores.

Dimensions of service quality

Recent conceptualizations of service quality assume that clients assess three dimensions of service delivery: interaction quality, outcome quality and environment quality (Brady and Cronin 2001). In effect, clients seek out: (1) *outcome quality*: they enter the encounter with goals they wish fulfilled; (2) *interaction quality*: they want the outcome to be achieved in a way that is consistent with their needs (i.e. speed if time is important, empathy if they require understanding, etc.); and (3) *environment quality*: they look for consistency between the space and the goals of the interaction (a spa should be luxurious, etc.).

Outcome quality

A service outcome is 'what the customer is left with when the production process is finished' (Grönroos 1984: p. 38). The client takes part hoping that valued goals will be realized (Manfredo et al. 1996). These goals may relate to anything from information gathering to problem resolution. The best outcomes are those where these goals have been attained.

Providers often think of outcomes in terms of the *core* product. The core product is why the client is making the purchase in the first place. They may welcome fast service in a fast food restaurant but the core offering is still the food itself. Without the delivery of food as an outcome, the speed of the service makes little difference. Indeed, those researchers who study food service quality continually find that the taste of food is a key determinant of overall quality (cf. Ryu and Han 2010; Zhang et al. 2010). This suggests the importance of understanding the core product sought by the client. Quality will be judged by how well that important outcome is delivered.

It is perhaps self-evident that participants assess quality by comparing perceived outcomes with their intended goals. The challenge for leisure and tourism providers, though, is uncertainty. They cannot control all service elements. Tourist providers cannot guarantee ideal travel or weather conditions. Sport providers cannot ensure that players or favourite teams always win (Greenwell et al. 2002). There are many cases in which positive (desired) outcomes may be difficult for the provider to arrange. For this reason, many providers now focus on service elements that they can control. Interaction quality offers a case in point.

Interaction quality

Services are processes, which suggests that clients evaluate the service based on *how* it was created (Surprenant and Solomon 1987). From a process perspective, the service is a series of *touchpoints* with which the client interacts (Edvardsson et al. 2011). Each touchpoint offers an opportunity to evaluate how well the service was delivered, independent of its outcome (Helkkula 2011). In many cases, these interactions involve staff members. In some settings such as fast food where the interaction with staff is minimal (Wu and Mohi 2015), interaction may refer more to interactions with a general process (e.g. the speed at which the food was delivered).

However, in many cases clients look to interactions with staff members to assess the quality of the processes they are experiencing. In such cases, staff members act as a physical representation of the service. As a result, interactions with staff are in many ways synonymous with interactions with the service. It seems fitting that Carlzon (1987) described the specific interaction between staff and client as a *moment of truth*. Ideal moments of truth are those in which staff members can represent and showcase the quality of a service.

Brady and Cronin (2001) referred to this dimension of service delivery as *interaction quality*. Clients are assessing their interactions with key staff members. These interactions happen often. A guest at a hotel is likely to interact with reception, housekeeping and restaurant staff. The actions of all these individuals will inform perceptions of service quality (Salazar et al. 2010). In making these assessments, clients look to what have been characterized as service scripts. Scripts are 'expected and appropriate behaviours which emerge between two parties in a social exchange' (Broderick 1998: p. 349). They represent the general flow of interaction that both parties expect from one another. The more closely each role follows the agreed-upon script, the more likely a service encounter will be successful (Abelson 1976, 1981). It seems ideal, therefore, that both the employee and the client have the same role expectations; that they, in effect, read from the same script.

Environment quality

Service outcomes and processes are only part of the service quality story. They are complemented by the setting in which the experience occurs. The setting provides cues that suggest the relative quality of the experience. Indeed, interviews with participants in a variety of leisure contexts suggest that physical cues offered by the setting represent about half of all the service quality factors clients think important (Brady and Cronin 2001). These cues make up what has been called the *servicescape* (Bitner 1992) or the *experiencescape* (Gentile et al. 2007).

Participants look to their surroundings to determine how well the experience meets their goals (Lin and Liang 2011). They may look for lush environments in parks, ideal conditions on playing fields, warm water, clean facilities and so forth. All physical cues signal, to the participant, the quality of the service offering (Sirgy et al. 2000). The physical environment can even influence participants' satisfaction (Alexandris et al. 2004) and behavioural loyalty (Kyle et al. 2010).

Physical cues exist along a tangibility continuum. Tangible cues, at one end of the continuum, refer to the physical aspects of the service which can be held or touched. These cues are profoundly important in helping participants understand, experience and judge a service offering. As Berry et al. (2006) suggest, clients act as detectives using these cues as if they were clues to the quality of a service. Cues that seem appropriate act as indicators of quality. We know too that clients will seek different types of cues from setting to setting. In Greek ski resorts, for example, flora and fauna were considered a critical part of the overall experience (Alexandris et al. 2006; Kyle et al. 2010). In sporting matches or other special events, the focus may be on the presentation of athletes or performers or even the mood of the crowd (Tkaczynski 2013). The goal for the provider is to provide those cues that participants think appropriate to the experience.

Intangible cues, at the other end of the continuum, cannot be touched or felt. Bitner (1992) proposed that these may include sensation-inducing sights, sounds and smells. These too help the participant judge the experience. Disney, for example, distributes fresh popcorn to guests entering their parks even in the morning. These treats are intended less to satisfy hunger but more to stimulate guests' sense of smell (Jones 2013). The distinctive popcorn smell is associated with entertainment, excitement and a sense of impending adventure. All help set the stage for the experience Disney hopes to engineer.

Together, tangible and intangible elements within the setting help create sympathetic sensory responses (Grewal et al. 2009). This in turn influences clients' emotional states (Kim and Moon 2009) that enhance the experience. The space can help evoke feelings of pleasure, enjoyment and entertainment (Puccinelli et al. 2009). These feelings then generate long-term attitudinal and behavioural responses (Baker et al. 1992; Grewal et al. 2003; Morin et al. 2007).

A small family-owned children's theme park is struggling. It offers a small pool area, mechanical rides for children under 10 years of age, and a large 20-acre wooded area intersected by hiking trails and streams. The park theme is one of environmental protection and their park mascot is an eagle named 'NaturAl'. The park has been in operation for over 50 years and has, over the years, been surrounded by urban sprawl. It now represents a green oasis in an otherwise brick and concrete environment. Its patrons are largely (70%) local with the remainder comprising passing tourists (who are primarily single-use visitors).

The original founders of the park wanted to expose urban visitors to natural settings while acting as advocates for the natural environment. Their goal was to provide a 'green' message to as many visitors as possible. As a result, admission fees were traditionally low. More than that, several valuable services (e.g. parking, access to the trails, forest and paddle boats) had always been offered free of charge. The founding family had believed that this approach was both environmentally worthwhile and good business. It exposed visitors to the wonders of nature but would also attract clients who would then pay for access to other parts of the operation.

Unfortunately, the park is struggling. Cash flow is an ongoing concern. There is never enough money in the budget to train front-line staff, to maintain trails or to create new rides. Despite the urban growth around them, visitor volume is down (especially among local users) and complaints are on the rise. The complaints tend to focus on three issues: (1) increasingly shabby visual cues in the parks, ranging from inadequate garbage collection to dated staff uniforms; (2) process problems (long lines, poor food, poor problem resolution); and (3) dated equipment and rides. Managers are pondering how best to deal with the falling attendance and complaints and have decided they need new revenue streams. In particular, they are thinking about charging for services that had traditionally been offered free of charge.

The fear is one of backlash. They understand the importance of expectations and feel they are caught between competing expectation patterns. Complaint patterns are telling them that people expect to be offered more in terms of outcomes, processes and setting-based cues but they also expect many related services to be offered free of charge. If they raise prices to increase services, they are meeting one set of expectations at the expense of the other. This is especially the case among local participants who have traditionally enjoyed these services at no cost. They will certainly notice if price levels rise and have the most to lose when they do so. What will happen if prices are applied to services that have historically been offered free?

Managers of the site have asked you to lay out the key issues, then to put forward a series of options with recommendations. How can they increase service quality in ways that don't create anger among users? They hope not to displace anyone, to minimize outcry especially from local users, and to encourage visitors to focus on quality rather than cost.

You know that, given the central role of the cognitive comparison between service and schema, the provider can manipulate either the service or clients' reference points. This could be achieved through marketing messages prior to the service encounter. How might those messages be managed?

Conclusion

Service quality represents clients' evaluations of the organization's contribution during the co-creation of an experience. These evaluations comprise many related elements which work together (Ha and Jang 2010; Ryu and Han 2010). Specifically, clients tend to react to cues from three general aspects of the service: the outcome of the service, the setting in which the service occurs, and interactions (predominantly) with staff.

By understanding these evaluations, it is possible to manage organizational resources in such a way that they create quality experiences while co-creating value with the client. Management can also change elements of the service encounter to improve service quality. These elements can be categorized in terms of outcomes, processes or the setting. Outcomes represent the end result of the encounter. Clients seek value and trust the experience will fulfil goals that they have set for it. However, the literature clearly demonstrates that many service outcomes are uncontrollable. The complexity of services and the nature of co-creation suggest that organizations must be ready to respond to services that don't go according to plan (Jaakkola and Alexander 2014).

Processes within the experience also support the creation of value. Processes, the actions, systems and activities that help with goal fulfilment, coalesce as a series of touchpoints that offer cues about the quality of the service being experienced. Organizations can therefore manage interactions with these touchpoints to improve the quality of the experience (Lemke et al. 2011; Verhoef et al. 2009). Services are so profoundly intangible, staff can best tie together the overall experience for the client. As Ellis and Rossman (2008) remind us, service quality is inevitably the responsibility of all staff members. It isn't a set of rules or policies but rather an approach that guides the way that staff members think about the task at hand.

Their role is to act with the clients' best interests in mind (Guest and Taylor 1999; Wagenheim and Rood 2010) to support the core tourism and leisure product.

Finally, services are experienced within a setting or environment. Service quality is tied inextricably to the setting in which it occurs. Providers must constantly tweak and manipulate the tangible and intangible cues within the natural and built environments. Physical spaces can be designed to enhance any leisure or tourism experience (Kaczynski and Rehman 2013; Wakefield and Blodgett 1994). The built and natural environment is a key part of any leisure encounter (Turley and Milliman 2000).

References

Abelson, R. P. (1976). 'Script processing in attitude formation and decision making', in J. S. Carroll and J. W. Payne (eds.), *Cognition and Social Behaviour* (pp. 33–46), New York: Academic Press.

Abelson, R. P. (1981). 'Psychological status of the script concept', *American Psychologist*, 36(7): 715–729.

Alexandris, K., Kouthouris, C. and Meligdis, A. (2006). 'Increasing customers' loyalty in a skiing resort: The contribution of place attachment and service quality', *International Journal of Contemporary Hospitality Management*, 18(5): 414–425.

Alexandris, K., Zahariadis, P., Tsorbatzoudis, C. and Grouios, G. (2004). 'An empirical investigation of the relationships among service quality, customer satisfaction and psychological commitment in a health club context', *European Journal of Sport Management*, 4(1): 36–52.

Baker, J., Levy, M. and Grewal, D. (1992). 'An experimental approach to making retail store environmental decisions', *Journal of Retailing*, 68(4): 445–460.

Bartlett, F. C. (1932). *Remembering*, London: Cambridge University Press.

Berry, L. L., Wall, E. A. and Carbone, L. P. (2006). 'Service clues and customer assessment of the service experience: Lessons from marketing', *The Academy of Management Perspectives*, 20(2): 43–57.

Bitner, M. J. (1992). 'Servicescapes: The impact of physical surroundings on customers and employees', *Journal of Marketing*, 56(2): 57–71.

Brady, M. K. and Cronin Jr, J. J. (2001). 'Some new thoughts on conceptualizing perceived service quality: A hierarchical approach', *Journal of Marketing*, 65(3): 34–49.

Broderick, A. (1998). 'Role theory, role management and service performance', *Journal of Services Marketing*, 12(5): 348–361.

Carlzon, J. (1987). *Moments of Truth*, New York: Ballinger.

De Houwer, J. (2009). 'The propositional approach to associative learning as an alternative for association formation models', *Learning and Behavior*, 37(1): 1–20.

Eckblad, G. (1981). *Scheme Theory: A Conceptual Framework for Cognitive-Motivational Processes*, New York: Academic Press.

Edvardsson, B., Tronvoll, B. and Gruber, T. (2011). 'Expanding understanding of service exchange and value co-creation: A social construction approach', *Journal of the Academy of Marketing Science*, 39(2): 327–339.

Ellis, G. D. and Rossman, J. R. (2008). 'Creating value for participants through experience staging: Parks, recreation, and tourism in the experience industry', *Journal of Park and Recreation Administration*, 26(4): 1–20.

Fiske, S. T. and Taylor, S. E. (1984), *Social Cognition*, 1st edition, New York: McGraw-Hill.

Gentile, C., Spiller, N. and Noci, G. (2007). 'How to sustain the customer experience: An overview of experience components that co-create value with the customer', *European Management Journal*, 25(5): 395–410.

Greenwell, T. C., Fink, J. S. and Pastore, D. L. (2002). 'Assessing the influence of the physical sports facility on customer satisfaction within the context of the service experience', *Sport Management Review*, 5(2): 129–148.

Grewal, D., Baker, J., Levy, M. and Voss, G. B. (2003). 'The effects of wait expectations and store atmosphere evaluations on patronage intentions in service-intensive retail stores', *Journal of Retailing*, 79(4): 259–268.

Grewal, D., Levy, M. and Kumar, V. (2009). 'Customer experience management in retailing: An organizing framework', *Journal of Retailing*, 85(1): 1–14.

Grönroos, C. (1984). 'A service quality model and its marketing implications', *European Journal of Marketing*, 18(4): 36–44.

Guest, C. and Taylor, P. (1999). 'Customer oriented public leisure services in the United Kingdom', *Managing Leisure*, 4(2): 94–106.

Ha, J. and Jang, S. S. (2010). 'Effects of service quality and food quality: The moderating role of atmospherics in an ethnic restaurant segment', *International Journal of Hospitality Management*, 29(3): 520–529.

Helkkula, A. (2011). 'Characterising the concept of service experience', *Journal of Service Management*, 22(3): 367–389.

Howat, G., Absher, J., Crilley, G. and Milne, I. (1996). 'Measuring customer service quality in sports and leisure centres', *Managing Leisure*, 1(2): 77–89.

Howat, G. and Assaker, G. (2013). 'The hierarchical effects of perceived quality on perceived value, satisfaction, and loyalty: Empirical results from public, outdoor aquatic centres in Australia', *Sport Management Review*, 16(3): 268–284.

Jaakkola, E. and Alexander, M. (2014). 'The role of customer engagement behavior in value co-creation: A service system perspective', *Journal of Service Research*, 17(3): 247–261.

Jones, B. (2013). '3 lessons in creating a magical customer experience', *Disney Institute*, Available from: https://disneyinstitute.com/blog/2013/05/3-lessons-in-creating-a-magical-customer-experience/168/ [Accessed 1 November 2016].

Kaczynski, A. and Rehman, L. (2013). 'The built environment and leisure behaviour', in R. E. McCarville and K. MacKay (eds.), *Leisure for Canadians* (pp. 149–154), State College, PA: Venture Publishing.

Kim, W. G. and Moon, Y. J. (2009). 'Customers' cognitive, emotional, and actionable response to the servicescape: A test of the moderating effect of the restaurant type', *International Journal of Hospitality Management*, 28(1): 144–156.

Kyle, G. T., Theodorakis, N. D., Karageorgiou, A. and Lafazani, M. (2010). 'The effect of service quality on customer loyalty within the context of ski resorts', *Journal of Park and Recreation Administration*, 28(1): 1–15.

Lemke, F., Clark, M. and Wilson, H. (2011). 'Customer experience quality: An exploration in business and consumer contexts using repertory grid technique', *Journal of the Academy of Marketing Science*, 39(6): 846–869.

Lin, J. S. C. and Liang, H. Y. (2011). 'The influence of service environments on customer emotion and service outcomes', *Managing Service Quality: An International Journal*, 21(4): 350–372.

Manfredo, M. J., Driver, B. L. and Tarrant, M. A. (1996). 'Measuring leisure motivation: A meta-analysis of the recreation experience preference scales', *Journal of Leisure Research*, 28(3): 188–213.

Markus, H. and Zajonc, R. (1985). 'The cognitive perspective in social psychology', in G. Linzey and E. Aronson (eds.), *Handbook of Social Psychology, Vol. 1*, 3rd edition (pp. 137–214), New York: Random House.

Martinez, J. A. and Martinez, L. (2010). 'Some insights on conceptualizing and measuring service quality', *Journal of Retailing and Consumer Services*, 17(1): 29–42.

Mee, L. Y., Ariffin, A. A. M. and Rahman, M. R. Z. A. (2014). 'The relationships among service quality, customer satisfaction and brand advocates in the context of fine dining restaurant services', *Advances in Natural and Applied Sciences*, 8(8): 47–52.

Morin, S., Dubé, L. and Chebat, J. C. (2007). 'The role of pleasant music in servicescapes: A test of the dual model of environmental perception', *Journal of Retailing*, 83(1): 115–130.

Murray, D. and Howat, G. (2002). 'The relationships among service quality, value, satisfaction, and future intentions of customers at an Australian sports and leisure centre', *Sport Management Review*, 5(1): 25–43.

Parasuraman, A., Zeithaml, V. A. and Berry, L. L. (1985). 'A conceptual model of service quality and its implications for future research', *Journal of Marketing*, 49(4): 41–50.

Prebensen, N. K., Kim, H. L. and Uysal, M. (2015). 'Cocreation as moderator between the experience value and satisfaction relationship', *Journal of Travel Research*, 55(7): 934–945.

Puccinelli, N. M., Goodstein, R. C., Grewal, D., Price, R., Raghubir, P. and Stewart, D. (2009). 'Customer experience management in retailing: Understanding the buying process', *Journal of Retailing*, 85(1): 15–30.

Ryu, K. and Han, H. (2010). 'Influence of the quality of food, service, and physical environment on customer satisfaction and behavioral intention in quick-casual restaurants: Moderating role of perceived price', *Journal of Hospitality and Tourism Research*, 34(3): 310–329.

Salazar, A., Costa, J. and Rita, P. (2010). 'A service quality evaluation scale for the hospitality sector: Dimensions, attributes and behavioural intentions', *Worldwide Hospitality and Tourism Themes*, 2(4): 383–397.

Sirgy, M. J., Grewal, D. and Mangleburg, T. (2000). 'Retail environment, self-congruity, and retail patronage: An integrative model and a research agenda', *Journal of Business Research*, 49(2): 127–138.

Su, L., Swanson, S. R. and Chen, X. (2016). 'The effects of perceived service quality on repurchase intentions and subjective well-being of Chinese tourists: The mediating role of relationship quality', *Tourism Management*, 52: 82–95.

Sujan, M. (1985). 'Consumer knowledge: Effects on evaluation strategies mediating consumer judgments', *Journal of Consumer Research*, 12(1): 31–46.

Surprenant, C. F. and Solomon, M. R. (1987). 'Predictability and personalization in the service encounter', *Journal of Marketing*, 51(2): 86–96.

Sweeney, J., Soutar, G. and Mazzarol, T. (2014). 'Factors enhancing word-of-mouth influence: Positive and negative service-related messages', *European Journal of Marketing*, 48(1/2): 336–359.

Theodorakis, N. D., Alexandris, K., Tsigilis, N. and Karvounis, S. (2013), 'Predicting spectators' behavioural intentions in professional football: The role of satisfaction and service quality', *Sport Management Review*, 16(1): 85–96.

Tian-Cole, S. and Scott, D. (2004). 'Examining the mediating role of experience quality in a model of tourist experiences', *Journal of Travel and Tourism Marketing*, 16(1): 79–90.

Tkaczynski, A. (2013). 'Festival performance (FESTPERF) revisited: Service quality and special events', *Advances in Hospitality and Leisure*, 9: 227–235.

Turley, L. W. and Milliman, R. E. (2000). 'Atmospheric effects on shopping behavior: A review of the experimental evidence', *Journal of Business Research*, 49(2): 193–211.

Tzetzis, G., Alexandris, K. and Kapsampeli, S. (2014). 'Predicting visitors' satisfaction and behavioral intentions from service quality in the context of a small-scale outdoor sport event', *International Journal of Event and Festival Management*, 5(1): 4–21.

Van Doorn, J. and Verhoef, P. C. (2008). 'Critical incidents and the impact of satisfaction on customer share', *Journal of Marketing*, 72(4): 123–142.

Vargo, S. L. and Lusch, R. F. (2008). 'Service-dominant logic: Continuing the evolution', *Journal of the Academy of Marketing Science*, 36(1): 1–10.

Vázquez-Casielles, R., del Río-Lanza, A. B. and Díaz-Martín, A. M. (2007). 'Quality of past performance: Impact on consumers' responses to service failure', *Marketing Letters*, 18(4): 249–264.

Verhoef, P. C., Lemon, K. N., Parasuraman, A., Roggeveen, A., Tsiros, M. and Schlesinger, L. A. (2009). 'Customer experience creation: Determinants, dynamics and management strategies', *Journal of Retailing*, 85(1): 31–41.

Wagenheim, M. and Rood, A. S. (2010). 'The relationship between employee satisfaction with organizational communication and customer orientation', *Managing Leisure*, 15(1–2): 83–95.

Wakefield, K. L. and Blodgett, J. G. (1994). 'The importance of servicescapes in leisure service settings', *Journal of Services Marketing*, 8(3): 66–76.

Wu, H. C. and Mohi, Z. (2015). 'Assessment of service quality in the fast-food restaurant', *Journal of Foodservice Business Research*, 18(4): 358–388.

Xie, D. and Heung, V. C. (2012). 'The effects of brand relationship quality on responses to service failure of hotel consumers', *International Journal of Hospitality Management*, 31(3): 735–744.

Zeithaml, V. A. (2000). 'Service quality, profitability, and the economic worth of customers: What we know and what we need to learn', *Journal of the Academy of Marketing Science*, 28(1): 67–85.

Zhang, Z., Ye, Q., Law, R. and Li, Y. (2010). 'The impact of e-word-of-mouth on the online popularity of restaurants: A comparison of consumer reviews and editor reviews', *International Journal of Hospitality Management*, 29(4): 694–700.

11

MANAGEMENT PERCEPTION OF SERVICE QUALITY

Ana Oliveira-Brochado and Paulo Rita

Introduction

In the hospitality and tourism industry, as in the service industry, the quality of services offered to guests is known to be critically important in providing a competitive advantage to businesses (Oh and Parks 1997). Service quality has many benefits, such as ensuring guests' satisfaction, intention to return, brand loyalty, positive value perceptions, positive brand associations and favourable word of mouth. Therefore, customers who are pleased with the quality of services offered will come back and recommend that business to others (e.g. Wu 2013). Previous studies in the relevant literature have most often sought to explore service quality from the perspective of guests.

In this context, several authors have developed new instruments to assess service quality in the hospitality and tourism sector (see Dortyol et al. [2014] for a review of service quality studies in the tourism and accommodation sector). Examples of scales that target the hotel business, in particular, are LODGSERV (Knutson et al. 1991), LOGQUAL (Getty and Thompson 1994), HOLSERV (Mei et al. 1999) and SSQH (Wu and Ko 2013). In addition, ECOSERV (Khan 2003) has been used to study service quality from the perspective of eco-tourists, the scale developed by Mohsin and Lockyer (2010) has been applied to luxury hotels and the scale by Brochado et al. (2015) to the hostel business. Collectively, previous studies have highlighted that the nature of service quality dimensions is directly related to the research context under analysis.

All these studies have attempted to assess service quality by mainly focusing on customers' evaluations. Although guests are the target of any service offer, Torres et al. (2013) and Dedeoğlu and Demirer (2015) stress that the differences between customers and managers' service quality expectations and perceptions have not been sufficiently researched and that this focus needs to be added to avenues of future research in hospitality and tourism. The next section explores potential service gaps in this sector.

The gap model of service quality

Parasuraman et al. (1988) developed the gap model, which defines a set of five gaps in the processes involving management perception of the service quality expected by customers.

This model also highlights the service tasks required to deliver desired services to customers. The five gaps are as follows:

- Gap 1: The difference between customer expectations and management perceptions of customer expectations
- Gap 2: The difference between management perceptions of customer expectations and service quality specifications
- Gap 3: The difference between service quality specifications and the services actually delivered
- Gap 4: The difference between service delivery and communication about services to customers
- Gap 5: The discrepancy between customer expectations of services and these customers' perceptions of service performance.

Gap 5 can be measured by means of the SERVQUAL scale, which approaches service quality through the difference between customer expectations and customer perceptions. Although measuring Gap 5 subsequently became a focus of research, this approach has been criticized on both the conceptual and operational levels (see Buttle [1996] for a review). As a result, a performance-based approach to measuring service quality called SERVPERF was introduced (Cronin and Taylor 1994). Carrillat et al. (2007) add to this debate by maintaining that, from a measurement perspective, scales should be targeted to suit specific service contexts.

In addition to the original five gaps proposed by Parasuraman et al. (1988), Lewis (1987) identifies two additional gaps:

- Gap 6: The difference between consumer perceptions of service delivery and management beliefs about the services delivered
- Gap 7: The difference between management perceptions of consumer expectations and management perceptions of service delivery.

Luk and Layton (2002) also add two new gaps to the five-gap model proposed by Parasuraman et al. (1988), identified here as Gap 8 and Gap 9. These two gaps reflect differences in managers' and front-line service providers' understanding of customer expectations and in customer expectations and service provider perceptions of these expectations:

- Gap 8: The difference between customer expectations of service providers and service providers' understanding of these expectations
- Gap 9: The difference between hotel managers' and service providers' perceptions of customer expectations of services.

Frost and Kumar (2000) further extended the five-gap model by developing an internal service quality model. The new gaps, identified in this chapter as Gaps 10 to 12, are as follows:

- Gap 10: The difference between support staff perception (i.e. internal suppliers) and front-line staff expectations (i.e. internal customers)
- Gap 11: The difference between service quality specifications and the services actually delivered, resulting in an internal service performance gap
- Gap 12: The difference between front-line staff expectations and perceptions of support staff (i.e. internal suppliers) of service quality.

Gaps 10 and 12 primarily focus on front-line staff (i.e. internal customers).

These models emphasize the importance of analysing service quality from the perspective of different stakeholders, managers, service providers and customers. In this context, there needs to be an agreement about what constitutes service quality across different stakeholders.

An analysis of these different gaps can provide insights for hotel managers seeking to evaluate and identify potential service quality shortfalls and can allow these managers to find clues to ways to close any gaps (Tsang and Qu 2000). By understanding the extent and tendency of different gaps, managers can assess whether the services offered their guests are exceeding, meeting or falling below guests' expectations. Ways to align more closely managers' and providers' perceptions of customer expectations and preferences – to ensure the consistent delivery of services at the desired level of quality – appear to be a new challenge faced by marketers.

Managers' perceptions of service quality

One of the most important stakeholders in service quality management is managers. They must have an accurate perception of the quality of the services offered their guests, and managers are in charge of anticipating customer demands and expectations. Parasuraman et al. (1988: 37) argue that 'service firm executives may not always understand what features. . . and what levels of performance of those features are necessary to deliver high quality service'. Managers who misunderstand guests' service quality expectations and perceptions might incur damages in the form of negative marketing outcomes.

According to Tsang and Qu (2000), one of the principal tasks of managers is to interact constantly with tourists in order to obtain first-hand knowledge of their expectations of services. Managers need to understand customers' desires and their experiences of service delivery to be able to design services, modify delivery processes or make further specifications to meet customer requirements properly.

Managers need to understand how customers perceive the quality of services they receive, in order to develop or change service quality standards. In this sense, how managers perceive customer expectations and preferences will directly affect managers' definitions of service quality standards.

Moreover, as managers are in charge of their staff's performance, managers must convey a correct understanding of customer expectations to their staff (Dedeoğlu and Demirer 2015). Managers, then, need to ensure that employees meet service quality standards (Tsang and Qu 2000) as they have been defined.

Since staff interact with guests more often than managers do, the latter are expected to guide their staff by examining customer expectations of service quality performance. To summarize, managers must understand guests' expectations, preferences and perceptions of performance in order to maintain consistent levels of service quality. Closing the gap between management and guest perceptions is imperative because this gap can jeopardize interactions between these two parties. Torres et al. (2013) note that managers can have different perceptions to those of guests, which might result in services needing to be delivered in ways that deviate from the specifications defined by management.

Congruity between managers' and customers' perceptions of service quality

Different hospitality and tourism stakeholders might have different perceptions of the level of service quality provided to guests. In particular, the level of expectations and perceptions of service quality by managers and customers may differ to some degree. Furthermore, researchers have found differences between customer/employee and customer/manager service quality perceptions to be statistically significant. Some examples are provided next.

Coyle and Dale's (1993) study analysed perceptions of service quality from both customer and provider viewpoints in a hotel setting. The cited authors' results reveal differences between customer expectations of hotel services and managers' understanding of these expectations. For instance, managers consider staff competence the key factor in service quality evaluations and underestimate the importance of service tangibles (e.g. decoration, facilities and cleanliness).

George and Tan (1993) investigated the congruency between food servers and managers in their perceptions of the importance of selected factors of services in a restaurant setting. The study's results reveal that the two groups have different perceptions of the importance of selected service-related factors.

Tsang and Qu (2000) analysed four gaps in service quality in the hotel industry in China: between tourists' expectations and their actual perceptions, between managers' perceptions of tourists' expectations and tourists' actual expectations, between managers' perceptions of their hotels' service delivery and tourists' actual perceptions of services, and between managers' perceptions of tourists' expectations and managers' perceptions of their hotels' service delivery. The results show that managers tend to have a reasonably good understanding of tourists' expectations. However, tourists' perceptions of the quality of the services provided are consistently lower than their expectations are, and managers overestimate service delivery as compared with tourists' perceptions of actual service quality.

Luk and Layton (2002) identified gaps between customer expectations regarding room service and managers' perceptions of these expectations and between customer expectations and service providers' understanding of these expectations. Moreover, the cited authors report that these gaps have a negative impact on overall service quality.

A study by Juwaheer and Ross (2003) revealed that managers tend to overestimate customer expectations for several service quality items: visually attractive brochures, spacious hotel rooms, good seating arrangements in restaurants and bars, and willingness of staff to help guests.

In a recent study, Dedeoğlu and Demirer (2015) concluded that both employees and managers perceive service performance to be at a higher level than customers do. The gap between managers' and employees' perceptions is not significant for all SERVQUAL dimensions, except for the empathy dimension. Moreover, the cited authors concluded that gaps between guests' expectations and managers' perceptions, guests' expectations and providers' expectations, and managers' and employees' perceptions of guest expectations have a negative impact on overall service quality evaluations.

Given that consumer and manager perceptions can differ, a closer examination of service quality gaps is needed in order to identify ways in which perceived quality can be improved. Table 11.1 provides a list of selected articles that have studied the congruity of management/guest perceptions of service quality. Both the research context and stakeholders involved, with the corresponding sample size, are provided, as well as the service quality dimensions studied and the statistical methods used by the respective authors.

Potential sources of incongruity

Incongruity between managers' and guests' service quality evaluations can have a wide range of sources. For example, it can be argued that managers do not like to mention deficiencies

Table 11.1 Selected papers on the congruity of management/guest perceptions of service quality

Reference	Research context	Stakeholders/sample size	Service quality dimensions	Statistical methods
Tsang and Qu (2000)	Hotels	90 hotel managers and 270 international tourists who visited China and stayed at hotels in Beijing, Shanghai and Guangzhou	35 service quality items	Paired sample *t*-tests
Luk and Layton (2002)	Hotel/room (four- and five-star) service in Hong Kong	21 managers, 51 room service providers and 108 guests	24 service quality items	Paired sample *t*-tests, regression analysis
Juwaheer and Ross (2003)	Mauritius	n/a	39 service quality items	Factorial analysis
Dedeoğlu and Demirer (2015)	Hotels (four- and five-star) in Antalya	Turkish, German and Russian tourists (515), hotel personnel (372) and managers (93)	22 items, organized in terms of SERVQUAL dimensions: reliability, empathy, responsiveness, assurance and tangibles	Factorial analysis, confirmatory factor analysis, multivariate analysis of variance

Source: Authors.

The objectives of this case study were twofold. First, an assessment was made of hostel managers' perceptions of the importance of different dimensions of service quality and perceived service quality. Second, a comparison was made between these managers' evaluations and their guests' expectations, thus testing whether hostel managers are aware of their customers' demands.

The research question: Do managers and hostel guests fully understand the importance of different service attributes?

The research context: The study considered hostels located in Lisbon. Lisbon hostels are quite popular, as they have received several awards based on guests' evaluations, such as those given by Hostelbookers (www.hostelbookers.com). For instance, 5 out of the 10 best medium-sized hostels in the world, according to guests' evaluations, are located in Lisbon.

The sample: This consisted of hostel managers and hostel guests drawn from hostels located in Lisbon. Twenty personal interviews with hostel managers and 200 interviews with backpackers were conducted. The sample included 106 males (53%) and 94 females (47%). In terms of age group, the majority of respondents were between 15 and 25 years old (123 guests, representing 63.1% of the sample). The remaining guests were between 26 and 29 years old (39 = 29%)

and more than 29 years old (33 = 16.9%). The guests came from a wide range of countries, from Europe (106 = 57.3%), the United States/Canada (37 = 20%), Australia (24 = 13%) and Latin America (18 = 9.7%).

The instrument: First, to get a better understanding of the most important aspects for hostel backpackers when evaluating a hostel, a content analysis was performed of the most popular hostel websites (Hostelworld.com, Hostelbookers.com, Hostels.com and Booking.com). Next, we selected the items considered by the Assured Standards defined by Hostelling International and items identified by Brochado et al. (2015). The final items were as follows: atmosphere, location, quality of staff, facilities, value for money, cleanliness, safety, a bar service, opportunities to meet other travellers, comfort, free Wi-Fi and privacy. Each participant was asked to rate the importance of each service quality attribute in their overall hostel experience on a scale ranging from 1 ('Not important') to 7 ('Extremely important').

The statistical methods: This study used descriptive statistics for each item and for both managers and guests, as well as paired *t*-tests for each item.

The results: As noted in Figure 11.1, a comparison of the importance of each service quality item for managers and for guests revealed that managers are doing a good job of understanding guest evaluations. Notably, the paired *t*-test results indicate a statistically significant difference for the attributes 'atmosphere' and 'quality of staff' (i.e. higher evaluations by guests) and 'value for money' and 'cleanliness' (i.e. higher evaluations by managers). The overall service quality gap is not statistically significant.

The theoretical implications: This study analysed the gap between guests and managers in terms of the importance they place on each service quality attribute in the hostel industry.

Figure 11.1 Managers and guests' evaluations and paired-sample *t*-tests

Source: Authors.

> **The managerial implications:** From the results, it can be concluded that gaps in importance perceptions do not seem to be a major problem area for service quality in the Lisbon hostel industry. However, as the quality of staff and atmosphere is more important for guests than it is for managers, hostel managers need to reinforce their offer in these areas.

in the quality of services and that managers, thus, may overestimate the quality of services provided to guests.

Coyle and Dale (1993) noticed that managers do not interact with guests and, therefore, do not get the opportunity to experience their first-hand expectations, preferences and service quality perceptions. According to Tsang and Qu (2000), the lack of interaction between managers and guests could be a major reason for the gap between consumer perceptions of service delivery and managers' evaluations of services delivered. According to Tsang and Qu (2000), the gap between service performance standards and actual service delivery in China can originate from several weaknesses, such as poorly qualified employees, inadequate internal systems to support contact personnel, and insufficient capacity to deliver services. Due to resource constraints, hotel staff might not perform services at levels meeting the standards required by management.

Dedeoğlu and Demirer (2015) highlight that differences between the service quality perceptions of managers, staff and guests can appear in specific dimensions of service quality. For instance, the cited authors report that a gap in the responsiveness dimension might be due to several reasons, such as unresponsive and unwilling hotel staff, low levels of staff commitment, the requirements of emotional labour, low job satisfaction, mobbing, inappropriate personality characteristics and impressions made by management characteristics.

Tsang and Qu (2000) maintain that the gap between actual service quality specifications and management perceptions of consumer expectations is due to a number of constraints, including resource constraints, a short-term profit orientation and management indifference. Because of these constraints, managers are not competent or effective in setting service quality standards and meeting tourists' expectations.

How to close these gaps?

Aligning managers, staff and guests more closely to ensure the consistent delivery of services at the desired level appears to be a challenge faced by managers in the hospitality and tourism industry. Although it could be argued that closing these gaps entirely is impossible, at least they can be narrowed by the following initiatives:

- Managers in the hotel industry need to spend more time interacting with their guests and experiencing real service delivery (Tsang and Qu 2000).
- Managers should get to know their target market and their guests better via consumer surveys, focus groups, social media (Torres et al. 2013) and market research.
- Managers need to assess whether their staff are able to meet their hotels' service quality standards (Tsang and Qu 2000).
- Managers should plan and implement training programmes with content that equips front-line employees with the required skills and knowledge to deliver good services expected by target customers.

Conclusion

Providing quality services has become an increasingly important issue in the hospitality industry. Research in this area has focused primarily on customers' perceptions or on customer and service provider interactions. The literature has highlighted the importance of managers gaining a proper understanding of their guests' expectations, service quality perceptions and importance perceptions. As a result, it is of utmost relevance for managers to understand their customers. Identifying gaps in service delivery provides managers with clear directions for how to address service quality shortfalls in their hotels. Therefore, we argue that it is imperative for managers in the hospitality industry to control and, ideally, to close any gaps in service quality perception.

References

Brochado, A., Rita, P. and Gameiro, C. (2015). 'Exploring backpackers' perceptions of the hostel service quality', *International Journal of Contemporary Hospitality Management*, 27(8): 1839–1855.

Buttle, F. (1996). 'SERVQUAL: Review, critique, research agenda', *European Journal of Marketing*, 30(1): 8–32.

Carrillat, F. A., Jaramillo, F. and Mulki, J. P. (2007). 'The validity of the SERVQUAL and SERVPERF scales: A meta-analytic view of 17 years of research across five continents', *International Journal of Service Industry Management*, 18(5): 472–490.

Coyle, M. P. and Dale, B. G. (1993). 'Quality in the hospitality industry: A study', *International Journal of Hospitality Management*, 12(2): 141–153.

Cronin, J. J. and Taylor, S. A. (1994). 'SERVPERF versus SERVQUAL: Reconciling performance based and perceptions-minus-expectations measurement of service quality', *Journal of Marketing*, 58(1): 125–131.

Dedeoğlu, B. B. and Demirer, H. (2015). 'Differences in service quality perceptions of stakeholders in the hotel industry', *International Journal of Contemporary Hospitality Management*, 27(1): 130–146.

Dortyol, I. T., Varinli, I. and Kitapci, O. (2014). 'How do international tourists perceive hotel quality?: An exploratory study of service quality in Antalya tourism region', *International Journal of Contemporary Hospitality Management*, 26(3): 470–495.

Frost, F. A. and Kumar, M. (2000). 'INTSERVQUAL: An internal adaptation of the GAP model in a large service organization', *Journal of Service Marketing*, 14(5): 358–377.

George, R. T. and Tan, Y. F. (1993). 'A comparison of the importance of selected service related factors as perceived by restaurant employees and managers', *International Journal of Hospitality Management*, 12(3): 289–298.

Getty, J. M. and Thompson, K. N. (1994). 'A procedure for scaling perceptions of lodging quality', *Hospitality Research Journal*, 18(2): 75–96.

Juwaheer, D. T. and Ross, L. D. (2003). 'A study of hotel guest perceptions in Mauritius', *International Journal of Contemporary Hospitality Management*, 15(2): 105–115.

Khan, M. (2003). 'ECOSERV: Eco-tourists' quality expectations', *Annals of Tourism Research*, 30(1): 109–124.

Knutson, B. J., Stevens, P., Wullaert, C., Patton, M. and Yokoyama, F. (1991). 'LODGSERV: A service quality index for the lodging industry', *Hospitality Research Journal*, 14(2): 277–284.

Lewis, R. C. (1987). 'The measurement of gaps in the quality of hotel service', *International Journal of Hospitality Management*, 6(2): 83–88.

Luk, T. K. and Layton, R. (2002). 'Perception gaps in customer expectations: Managers versus service providers and customers', *The Service Industries Journal*, 22(2): 109–128.

Mei, A. W. O., Dean, A. M. and White, C. J. (1999). 'Analyzing service quality in the hospitality industry', *Managing Service Quality*, 9(2): 136–143.

Mohsin, A. and Lockyer, T. (2010). 'Customer perceptions of service quality in luxury hotels in New Delhi, India: An exploratory study', *International Journal of Contemporary Hospitality Management*, 22(2): 160–173.

Oh, H. and Parks, S. C. (1997). 'Customer satisfaction and service quality: A critical review of the literature and research implications for the hospitality industry', *Hospitality Research Journal*, 20(3): 35–64.

Parasuraman, A., Zeithaml, V. A. and Berry, L. L. (1988). 'SERVQUAL: A multiple-item scale for measuring consumer perceptions of services quality', *Journal of Retailing*, 64(1): 12–40.

Torres, E. N., Adler, H., Lehto, X., Behnke, C. and Miao, L. (2013). 'One experience and multiple reviews: The case of upscale US hotels', *Tourism Review*, 68(3): 3–20.

Tsang, N. and Qu, H. (2000). 'Service quality in China's hotel industry: A perspective from tourists and hotel managers', *International Journal of Contemporary Hospitality Management*, 12(5): 316–326.

Wu, H. C. (2013). 'An empirical study of the effects of service quality, perceived value, corporate image, and customer satisfaction on behavioral intentions in the Taiwan quick service restaurant industry', *Journal of Quality Assurance in Hospitality and Tourism*, 14(4): 364–390.

Wu, H. C. and Ko, Y. J. (2013). 'Assessment of service quality in the hotel industry', *Journal of Quality Assurance in Hospitality and Tourism*, 14(3): 218–244.

12
MEASURING SERVICE QUALITY

Aijing Liu, Emily Ma and Christy Yen Nee Ng

Service quality in hospitality and tourism

Nature of service

As the world economy continues to grow, the proportions and interrelations among its basic sectors – agriculture, industry and services – are also changing (World Bank 2009). The service sector has grown in importance in the world economy and has outweighed the agriculture and industry sectors in middle-income and high-income countries (Figure 12.1). The service industry comprises businesses whose principal activity is to provide service products (Jones 2013). The service industry produces 'intangible' goods rather than products. Service itself has three unique characteristics distinguishing it from goods, including intangibility (e.g. Bateson 1977; Lovelock 1981) heterogeneity (Booms and Bitner 1981) and inseparability (Carmen and Langeard 1980) of production and consumption. Intangibility refers to services having no specific shape or weight (Bateson 1977). Heterogeneity refers to service lacking consistency because the service experience is greatly influenced by the service skills and attitude of service providers as well as the interaction between service providers and receivers (Booms and Bitner 1981). Inseparability refers to the simultaneous production and consumption process. Therefore the quality of a service experience is influenced by both service providers and customers (Carmen and Langeard 1980).

Revisit the definition of service quality

The unique features of service make it difficult to define service quality. A popular approach used is the Expectancy-Disconfirmation Model of satisfaction proposed by Oliver (1980). According to the Expectancy-Disconfirmation Model (Oliver 1980), customers have expectations before receiving services, based on previous experiences or information received from various sources (such as online review, friends or relatives). During and after the service process, customers would compare actual service performance with their expectations, leading to the following scenarios: (1) when services provided meet or exceed customers' expectations, customers feel satisfied; (2) when the services fail to meet customers' expectations, customers feel dissatisfied. Service quality is then defined as how well the

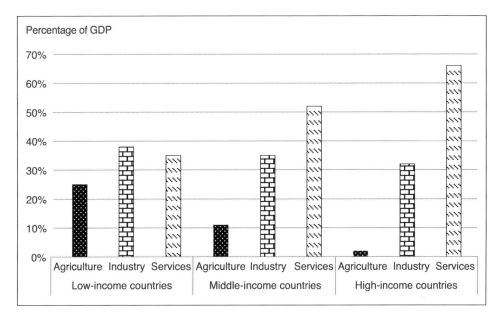

Figure 12.1 Sectorial structure of the world economy

Source: Adapted from World Bank (2009).

service level delivered matches customers' expectations (Oliver 1980; Lewis and Booms 1983).

Challenges in measuring service quality

The unique features of service also determine that we cannot measure service quality as we measure product quality. Intangibility makes it difficult to feel or touch service before actually consuming it (Lovelock 1981); and heterogeneity (Booms and Bitner 1981) makes the service processes vary from server to server and also among different customers (Carmen and Langeard 1980). These features present a challenge to measuring service quality. To effectively measure service quality, we need to identify areas that matter to the formation of a customer's quality perception. A number of pioneering researchers have made good attempts in proposing aspects of service experience that matter to the formation of service quality (e.g. Oliver 1997; Parasuraman et al. 1985). Numerous researchers contributed to the validity and reliability tests of these scales by applying them in different sectors of the service industry (Barsky and Labagh 1992) and different cultural contexts (e.g. Qu 1998). Their effort has made service quality one of the best-researched areas in the hospitality and tourism context and also made it possible for business operators to know exactly how they are performing in each aspect and what they should do to further improve their service quality. The following section will introduce a few widely applied service quality measurement approaches.

Popular models and approaches to measure service quality

The Expectancy-Disconfirmation Model

The Expectancy-Disconfirmation Model (Oliver 1997) has been widely used to explain customer satisfaction. Oliver (1997) proposed that individuals compare their actual experiences of a service with their expectations. This implies that consumers purchase services with expectations about their anticipated performance before purchase. A disconfirmation (which could be positive or negative) would occur when discrepancy appears between the expectations and the actual experiences. When the actual experience is better than an individual expected, a positive disconfirmation occurs and the customer would be satisfied, which is the starting point of customer loyalty; when the actual experience is not as good as expected, a negative disconfirmation occurs and the customer would feel dissatisfied, which may lead to complaining behaviours or switching to other service providers (Oliver 1980).

Following the Expectancy-Disconfirmation approach, an approach was developed to investigate confirmation or disconfirmation of expectations. This approach subtracts the score difference between expectations and evaluations of each aspect of service performance to reach confirmation or disconfirmation (Churchill and Surprenant 1982). It has been widely used to investigate customer satisfaction in hotel or restaurant settings (e.g. Barsky and Labagh 1992; Danaher and Haddrell 1996; Reisinger and Waryszak 1996).

SERVQUAL and its application in different contexts

Parasuraman and his colleagues are pioneers attempting to identify these essential aspects to the formation of service quality (e.g. Parasuraman et al. 1985; Parasuraman and Zeithaml 1988). They proposed a SERVQUAL measurement scale, which become the foundation of many follow-up service quality measurements across a number of hospitality and tourism contexts, including DINESERV and LOGDSERV (e.g. Knutson et al. 1991).

Parasuraman and Zeithaml (1988) proposed the SERVQUAL scale, containing 22 items. The initial scale contained 97 items and after 2 stages of data collection and item purification, the initial scale was reduced to 22 items, dividing into 5 dimensions. The 5 dimensions included Tangibles (4 items), Reliability (5 items), Responsiveness (4 items), Assurance (4 items) and Empathy (5 items). Tangibles refer to aspects such as physical facilities, equipment and appearance of employees. Reliability refers to service providers' ability to perform the promised service dependably and accurately. Responsiveness refers to employees' willingness to serve customers in a prompt manner. Assurance refers to employees' ability to inspire trust and confidence using their knowledge and courtesy. Empathy is the amount of caring and individualized attention the service provider delivers to its customers. Detailed measurements are listed in Table 12.1.

SERVQUAL was one of the first multiple-dimensional measurement scales to measure service quality via a comparison between customers' expectations and perceptions over a number of statements (Parasuramann and Zeithamal 1988), making significant contributions to the operationalization of service quality. However, it was proposed and applied for general service organizations, such as banks, credit card companies, repair and maintenance companies and telephone companies (Parsuramann and Zeithaml 1988), and therefore might not be suitable for hospitality and tourism contexts. Therefore, many researchers started to develop specific measurement scales for the hospitality and tourism industry (e.g. Knutson et al. 1991; Stevens et al. 1995).

Table 12.1 The SERVQUAL measurements of service quality

Criteria	Sub-criteria (SC)
Tangible	1. Excellent telephone companies will have modern-looking equipment.
	2. The physical facilities at excellent telephone companies will be visually appealing.
	3. Employees of excellent telephone companies will be neat-appearing.
	4. Materials associated with the service (such as pamphlets or statements) will be visually appealing in an excellent telephone company.
Reliability	5. When excellent telephone companies promise to do something by a certain time, they will do so.
	6. When customers have a problem, excellent telephone companies will show a sincere interest in solving it.
	7. Excellent telephone companies will perform the service right the first time.
	8. Excellent telephone companies will provide their services at the time they promise to do so.
	9. Excellent telephone companies will insist on error-free records.
Responsiveness	10. Employees of excellent telephone companies will tell customers exactly when services will be performed.
	11. Employees of excellent telephone companies will give prompt service to customers.
	12. Employees of excellent telephone companies will always be willing to help customers.
	13. Employees of excellent telephone companies will never be too busy to respond to customer requests.
Assurance	14. The behaviour of employees of excellent telephone companies will instil confidence in customers.
	15. Customers of excellent telephone companies will feel safe in their transactions.
	16. Employees of excellent telephone companies will be consistently courteous with customers.
	17. Employees of excellent telephone companies will have the knowledge to answer customer questions.
Empathy	18. Excellent telephone companies will give customers individual attention.
	19. Excellent telephone companies will have operating hours convenient to all their customers.
	20. Excellent telephone companies will have employees who give customers personal attention.
	21. Excellent telephone companies will have the customers' best interests at heart.
	22. The employees of excellent telephone companies will understand the specific needs of their customers.

Source: Adapted from Parasuraman and Zeithaml (1988: p. 25).

LODGSERV

In the hotel and accommodation sector, Knutson et al. (1991) developed the LODGSERV measurement scale. LODGSERV contains 26 items and was specifically designed to measure customers' expectations in relation to hotel service experience (Table 12.2). Knutson and his colleagues made two significant contributions by proposing and validating the LODGSERV measurement. First of all, the LODGSERV scale also returned a consistent five dimensions just like the SERVQUAL scale, which further validated the reliability of Parasuraman and Zeithaml's (1988) work. Second, at the end of Knutson et al.'s (1991) study, they suggested that the process in developing LODGSERV can be replicated for other segments of the hospitality industry, such as CLUBSERV for private clubs and DINESERV for fine dining restaurants. This inspired researchers to make various attempts in developing specific measurement scales for particular contexts of the industry (e.g. Barber and Scarcelli 2010; Stevens et al. 1995).

Researchers also made attempts in validating the LODGSERV scale in different contexts. For example, Lockyer (2003) enhanced the LODGSERV model by adding specific items on cleanliness of the hotel guest room, bathroom and lobby. Akbaba (2006) adapted the

Table 12.2 The LODGSERV measurement

Dimension	*Items*
Reliability	Equipment works
	Dependable/consistent
	Quickly correct problems
	Services on time
Assurance	Trained/experienced employees
	You feel comfortable
	Company supports employees
	Knowledgeable staff
	Reservationists are knowledgeable
Responsiveness	Prompt service
	Staff shift where needed
	Do special requests
Tangibles	Neat personnel
	Quality food/beverage
	Attractive room
	Decor reflects concept
	Attractive public areas
	Up-to-date equipment
Empathy	You feel special/valued
	No red tape
	Sympathetic employees
	Sensitive employees
	Convenient hours
	Anticipates your needs
	Complimentary services
	Has healthful menus

Source: Adapted from Knutson et al. (1991: p. 281).

Table 12.3 Hotel service quality measurement in Turkey

Attributes	Items
Tangibles	The equipment of the hotel works properly
	Atmosphere and equipment comfortable and appropriate
	Modern-looking equipment
	Materials associated with the services are adequate and sufficient
	Adequate capacity
	Food and beverages served
Adequacy in service supply	Providing prompt service
	Providing the services at promised times
	Performing the services right the first time
	Providing the services as they were promised
	Employees are always available when needed
	Consistency in services
	Employees are always willing to serve
Understanding and caring	Treating guests in a friendly manner
	Flexibility in services
	Understanding the specific needs of guests
	Individualized attention
	Providing assistance in other required areas
Assurance	Convenient operating hours
	Providing a safe and secure place
	Instilling confidence in guests
	Occupational knowledge of employees
Convenience	Ease of access to the hotel
	Reaching information
	Resolving guest complaints

Source: Adapted from Akbaba (2006: pp. 180–181).

SERVQUAL measurements to Turkey's hotel industry. The results also returned five dimensions with slight variations. The five dimensions are Tangibles, Adequacy in service supply, Understanding and caring, Assurance and Convenience. Detailed measures are summarized in Table 12.3.

Wilkins et al. (2007) applied the SERVQUAL measurements in the context of Australian hotels. Their study revealed seven dimensions, namely Stylish comfort, Quality staff, Personalization, Room quality, Speedy service, Added extras and Quality food and beverage. Details are summarized in Table 12.4. Mei et al. (1999) developed a new scale called HOLSERV based on the SERVQUAL instrument to measure service quality in hotel settings. They had three dimensions of service quality in the hotel industry, which are 'employees', 'tangibles' and 'reliability', and claimed that 'employees' accounted for most of the variance among the three dimensions. A study conducted by Saleh and Ryan (1992) identified five dimensions of service quality in the hotel industry, which differed from those in the SERVQUAL instrument. These five dimensions are 'conviviality', 'tangibles', 'reassurance', 'avoid sarcasm' and 'empathy'. 'Conviviality' is the best predictor of overall service quality. Albacete-Saez et al. (2007) developed a service quality measurement scale for rural accommodation with five dimensions, including Personnel response, Complementary offer, Tourist relations, Basic demands and Tangible elements.

Table 12.4 Hotel service quality measurement in Australia

Criteria	Sub-criteria
Stylish comfort	The hotel atmosphere is stylish
	The hotel is first class
	The hotel lobby is grand
	The artefacts and paintings added to the image of the hotel
	The ambience of the hotel is relaxing
Quality staff	Respectful and polite staff
	Staff who are quick to respond to requests
	High-quality staff who are well trained
	People are nice to you at checkout
	Unobtrusive staff
Personalization	VIP treatment, being the focus of attention
	The staff remember your name
	Being recognized in the lobby
	Staff remembering your requirements
Room quality	Range of toiletries available in the bathroom
	Luxurious branded toiletries
	Lots of large, fluffy towels
	Deluxe appliances
Speedy service	Not being kept waiting for more than a minute
	Immediate service
	Not having to queue for more than one minute
	Every need is anticipated
Added extras	Floor concierge
	Timesaving services such as valet parking
	Regular shuttle buses to the airport
	Provision of gym and other recreational facilities
Quality food and beverage	Exquisite food presentation
	Provision of fine dining restaurant
	Good range of bars to buy a drink
	Provision of a sumptuous buffet breakfast

Source: Adapted from Wilkins et al. (2007).

Importance performance analysis

Importance performance analysis (IPA) is a simple and effective technique to measure service quality, which was first introduced by Martilla and James (1977). IPA measures customers' perceptions of the importance of various service quality attributes and the performance of these attributes. The scores are then plotted to a scatter plot (Figure 12.2). The overall means of the importance and performance of attributes were used as the basis to divide the scatter plot into four quadrants. Quadrant I is high in importance and performance and is named 'Keep up the good work'. Quadrant II is high in importance but low in performance and is named 'Concentrate here'. Quadrant III is low in importance and performance and is named 'Low priority' and Quadrant IV is low in importance but high in performance and is named 'Possible overkill' (Martilla and James 1977).

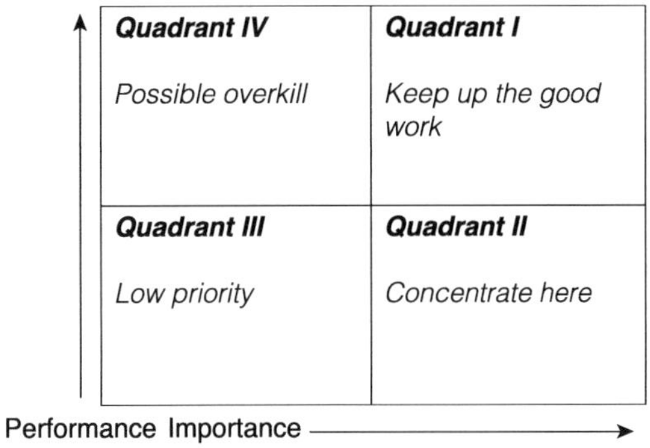

Quadrant IV	Quadrant I
Possible overkill	Keep up the good work
Quadrant III	Quadrant II
Low priority	Concentrate here

Performance Importance ⟶

Figure 12.2   The importance/performance plot

Source: Adapted from Ma et al. (2011).

Consequently, adding the locations of service quality attributes into the plot can help managers formulate different strategies to enhance service quality performance (Lambert and Sharma 1990). For example, attributes with high importance scores but low performance scores require the highest level of attention and managers need to 'Concentrate here'. Attributes with low importance scores and low performance scores need less attention, so managers can treat these aspects as 'Low priority'. Aspects with low importance scores but high performance scores probably have used too much resources and attributes with high importance and performance scores need to 'Keep up the good work' (Figure 12.2).

IPA is often used together with established service quality measurements, such as SERVQUAL and DINESERV (Cronin and Taylor 1992). IPA has been used by many researchers in various contexts and is a proven effective tool in understanding service quality importance and performance as well as identifying directions for improvements (e.g. Hansen and Bush 1999; Chu and Choi 2000; Enright and Newton 2004; Huana et al. 2002; Mak et al. 2011).

Although IPA is popular in service quality and marketing research and management, there are some critics of this method. Matzler et al. (2004) noted that IPA contained two assumptions. First, that the two attributes (performance and importance) are independent variables; second, that there is a linear and symmetrical relationship between attribute performance and overall performance. However, researchers have found that the relationship between attribute performance and customer satisfaction is not symmetrical (Matzler et al. 2004) and there is a causal relationship between attribute importance and attribute performance (Ryan and Huyton 2002).

Applications in hospitality and tourism research

This section will introduce a case study using a service quality measurement scale and the IPA approach to investigate customers' perception about a fine dining restaurant. As mentioned before, combining service quality measures with the IPA technique is a popular approach used by researchers and this case study is a good example utilizing this method.

Fine dining restaurants are restaurants offering full table services using an upscale food and beverage menu. Attracting and maintaining customers are challenging tasks for fine dining restaurants due to increasing competition (Mealey 2016). Therefore, fine dining restaurants need to offer customers not only the finest in food, but also the finest in service and atmosphere. In an introductory-level research class, we designed a research activity for students to use IPA, measuring customers' perceptions about fine dining restaurant service. A questionnaire was designed (see Appendix 12.1 at the end of the chapter) and data were collected from a local fine dining restaurant in Australia. As this was only an activity, the sample was only 100, while in actual applications a sample size of at least 200 is preferred.

The questionnaire asked customers to rate perceived importance and actual performance of eight restaurant service quality attributes, including location, image, relaxing atmosphere of the restaurant, cleanliness of the restaurant, whether the restaurant has a famous chef, taste and presentation of food and friendliness of employees.

The IPA results showed that three attributes fell into the 'Keep up the good work' quadrant, namely 'Cleanliness of the restaurant', 'Friendly employees' and 'Famous chef'. One attribute, 'Image', fell into the 'Low priority' quadrant. One attribute, 'Food presentation', fell into the 'Possible overkill' quadrant and two attributes fell into the 'Concentrate here' quadrant, including 'Food taste' and 'Restaurant location'.

The IPA tool is a simple but very effective way to assess customers' perceptions on service quality. It can also be used to assess employees' perceptions on job satisfaction and other aspects of the work environment, such as organizational culture and leadership support.

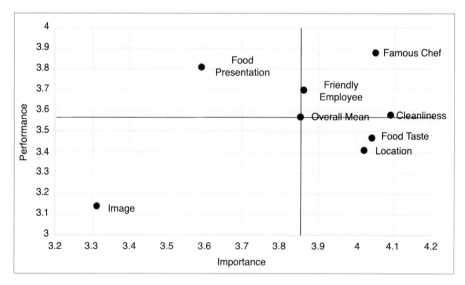

Figure 12.3   The IPA of a restaurant

Source: Adapted from Ma et al. (2011).

Conclusions

This chapter started by outlining the scope and importance of the service industry. It then introduced three unique characteristics of service as compared to products. The nature of services makes it difficult to measure service quality and Oliver (1980) and Parasuraman and Zeithaml (1988) were among the first group of researchers who attempted to measure service quality by identifying unique features that matter. The chapter then introduced a few popular measurement scales for service quality in general service settings, such as banking and retailing, and also in particular in hospitality and tourism contexts. Hopefully it can help readers to form a good understanding of service quality measurements.

References

Akbaba, A. (2006). 'Measuring service quality in the hotel industry: A study in a business hotel in Turkey', *Hospitality Management*, 25(2): 170–192.

Albacete-Saez, C. A., Fuentes-Fuentes, M. M. and Llorens-Montes, F. J. (2007). 'Service quality measurement in rural accommodation', *Annals of Tourism Research*, 34(1): 45–65.

Barber, N. and Scarcelli, J. (2010). 'Enhancing the assessment of tangible service quality through the creation of a cleanliness measurement scale', *Measuring Service Quality*, 20(1): 46–69.

Barsky, J. D. and Labagh, R. (1992). 'A strategy for customer satisfaction', *Cornell Hotel and Restaurant Administration Quarterly*, 33(5): 32–40.

Bateson, J. E. (1977). 'Do we need service marketing?' *Marketing Consumer Services: New Insights*, Marketing Science Institute, Report #77-115 (December), Cambridge, MA: Marketing Science Institute.

Booms, B. and Bitner, M. (1981). 'Marketing strategies and organisation structures for service firms', in J. Donnelly and W. George (eds.), *Marketing of Services: 1981 Special Educators' Conference Proceedings* (pp. 46–51), Chicago, IL: American Marketing Association.

Carmen, J. M. and Langeard, E. (1980). 'Growth strategies for service firms', *Strategic Management Journal*, 1(1): 7–22.

Chu, R. K. S. and Choi, T. (2000). 'An importance-performance analysis of hotel selection factors in the Hong Kong hotel industry: A comparison of business and leisure travellers', *Tourism Management*, 21(4): 363–377.

Churchill, G. R. and Surprenant, C. (1982). 'An investigation into determinants of customer satisfaction', *Journal of Marketing Research*, 19(4): 491–504.

Cronin, J. and Taylor, S. A. (1992). 'Measuring service quality: A reexamination and extension', *Journal of Marketing*, 56(3): 55–68.

Danaher, P. J. and Haddrell, V. (1996). 'A comparison of question scales used for measuring customer satisfaction', *International Journal of Service Industry Management*, 17(4): 4–26.

Enright, M. and Newton, J. (2004). 'Tourism destination competitiveness: A quantitative approach', *Tourism Management*, 25(6): 777–788.

Hansen, E. and Bush, R. J. (1999). 'Understanding customer quality requirements: Model and application', *Industrial Marketing Management*, 28(2): 119–130.

Huan, T. C., Beaman, J. and Shelby, L. B. (2002). 'Using action-grids in tourism management', *Tourism Management*, 23(3): 255–264.

Jones, J. (2013). 'UK service industries: Definition, classification and evolution', Available from http://webarchive.nationalarchives.gov.uk/20160105160709/http://www.ons.gov.uk/ons/rel/naa1-rd/national-accounts-articles/uk-service-industries--definition--classification-and-evolution/index.html

Knutson, B., Stevens, P., Wullaert, C., Patton, M. and Yokoyama, F. (1991). 'Lodgserv: A service quality index for the lodging industry', *Hospitality Research Journal*, 14(3): 277–284.

Lambert, D. M. and Sharma, A. (1990). 'A customer-based competitive analysis for logistics decisions', *International Journal of Physical Distribution and Logistics Management*, 20(1): 17–24.

Lewis, R. C. and Booms, B. H. (1983). 'The marketing aspects of service quality', in L. Berry, G. Shostack and G. Upah (eds.), *Emerging Perspectives on Services Marketing* (pp. 99–104), Chicago, IL: American Marketing Association.

Lockyer, T. (2003). 'Hotel cleanliness: How do guests view it? Let us get specific: A New Zealand study', *Hospitality Management*, 22(3): 297–305.

Lovelock, C. H. (1981). 'Why marketing management needs to be different for services', in J. Donnelly and W. George (eds.), *Marketing of Sciences* (pp. 5–9), Chicago, IL: American Marketing Association.

Ma, E., Qu, H., Njite, D. and Chen, S. (2011). 'Western and Asian customers' perception towards Chinese restaurants in the United States', *Journal of Quality Assurance in Hospitality and Tourism*, 12(2): 121–139.

Mak, A. H. N., Wong, K. K. F. and Chang, R. C. Y. (2011). 'Critical issues affecting the service quality and professionalism of the tour guides in Hong Kong and Macau', *Tourism Management*, 32(6): 1442–1452.

Martilla, J. A. and James, J. C. (1977). 'Importance–performance analysis', *Journal of Marketing*, 41(1): 77–79.

Matzler, K., Bailom, F., Hinterhuber, H. H., Renzl, B. and Pichler, J. (2004). 'The asymmetric relationship between attribute-level performance and overall customer satisfaction: A reconsideration of the importance–performance analysis', *Industrial Marketing Management*, 33(4): 271–277.

Mealey, L. (2016). 'Things you should know about restaurant fine dining', *The Balance*, 2 September, Available from https://www.thebalance.com/restaurant-fine-dining-2888686 [Accessed 14 November 2016].

Mei, A. W. O., Dean, A. M. and White, C. J. (1999). 'Analyzing service quality in the hospitality industry', *Managing Service Quality*, 9(2): 136–143.

Oliver, R. L. (1980). 'A cognitive model of the antecedents of satisfaction decisions', *Journal of Marketing Research*, 17(1): 46–49.

Oliver, R. L. (1997). *Satisfaction: A Behavioural Perspective on the Consumer*, New York: McGraw-Hill.

Parasuraman, A. and Zeithaml, V. A. (1988). 'SERVQUAL: A multiple-item scale for measuring consumer perceptions of service quality', *Journal of Retailing*, 64(Spring): 12–40.

Parasuraman, A., Zeithaml, V. A. and Berry, L. L. (1985). 'A conceptual model of service quality and its implications for future research', *Journal of Marketing*, 49(Fall): 41–50.

Qu, H. (1998). 'Determinant factors and choice intention for Chinese restaurant dining: A multivariate approach', *Journal of Restaurant and Foodservice Marketing*, 2(2): 35–49.

Reisinger, Y. and Waryszak, R. (1996). 'Catering to Japanese tourists: What service do they expect from food and drinking establishments in Australia?', *Journal of Restaurant and Foodservice Marketing*, 1(3/4): 53–71.

Ryan, C. and Huyton, J. (2002). 'Tourists and aboriginal people', *Annals of Tourism Research*, 29(3): 631–647.

Saleh, F. and Ryan, C. (1992). 'Analyzing service quality in the hospitality industry using the SERVQUAL model', *The Service Industries Journal*, 11(3): 324–343.

Stevens, P., Knutson, B. and Patton, M. (1995). 'DINESERV: A tool for measuring service quality in restaurants', *Cornell Hotel and Restaurant Administration Quarterly*, 36(2): 56–60.

Wilkins, H., Merrilees, B. and Herington, C. (2007). 'Towards an understanding of total service quality in hotels', *Hospitality Management*, 26(4): 840–853.

World Bank (2009). *Growth of the Service Factor*, Washington, DC: World Bank.

Appendix 12.1

Importance Performance Survey Response Sheet

The survey has two parts. In Part A, please rate how important the listed aspects of restaurant service are. In Part B, please rate how satisfied are you with these features.

1. What is your gender (Please circle one)?

    Male   Female

2. Please circle the appropriate number for the following service aspects based on:

How **Important** they are to you and how **Satisfied** you are with the following aspects.

1 = Not Important (NI)   1 = Not Satisfied (NS)
2 = Somewhat Important (SI)   2 = Somewhat Satisfied (SS)
3 = Fairly Important (FI)   3 = Fairly Satisfied (FS)
4 = Very Important (VI)   4 = Very Satisfied (VS)
5 = Extremely Important (EI)   5 = Extremely Satisfied (ES)

	Part A					**Part B**				
Service aspects	*Importance ratings*					*Satisfaction ratings*				
A. The location of the restaurant.	1	2	3	4	5	1	2	3	4	5
B. The image of the restaurant.	1	2	3	4	5	1	2	3	4	5
C. The atmosphere of the restaurant is relaxing.	1	2	3	4	5	1	2	3	4	5
D. Whether the restaurant has a famous chef.	1	2	3	4	5	1	2	3	4	5
E. The cleanliness of the restaurant.	1	2	3	4	5	1	2	3	4	5
F. The presentation of the food.	1	2	3	4	5	1	2	3	4	5
G. The taste of the food.	1	2	3	4	5	1	2	3	4	5
H. The friendliness of employees.	1	2	3	4	5	1	2	3	4	5

Thank you for your participation!

13

APPLICATION OF TOTAL QUALITY MANAGEMENT IN THE TOURISM SECTOR

Aparna Raj and Saurabh Kumar Dixit

Introduction

'Tourism is the world's largest industry and makes a major contribution to the economies of most developed and developing countries' (Jones and Haven-Tang 2005: p. 1). This smokeless industry has to face various challenges, prominent among them being quality management, and the importance of this challenge is growing with ever-increasing customer expectations.

Each tourist, being a unique individual, has their own set of wishes and expectations, and tourism is a complex product that incorporates a number of services, the quality of which is influenced by a great many factors (such as infrastructural facilities, safety, sanitation and hygiene, attitude of the host community, etc.).

What is quality?

Quality can be interpreted as the 'customer's expressed and implied requirements which are met fully'. This is a core statement from which some eminent definitions of quality have been derived. They include: the totality of features and characteristics of a product or service that bears on its ability to meet a stated or implied need, 'fitness for use' (Juran 1988) and 'conformance to requirement' (Crosby 1979). The International Organization for Standardization (ISO) defines quality standards as: 'A document that provides requirements, specifications, guidelines or characteristics that can be used consistently to ensure that materials, products, processes and services are fit for their purpose' (ISO 2015).

Crosby refined his definition of quality to 'getting everyone to do what they have agreed to do and to do it right the first time' (1979: p. 3). There are no second chances when we have a dissatisfied customer at hand.

Quality in service industries has both static and dynamic dimensions (Day and Peters 1994). The former represent the expectation of the customers that always changes over time and the latter occur during service delivery and offer opportunities for the customer to be delighted by the extra efforts of staff, but dynamic quality is not achieved easily. By definition, spontaneous acts of dynamic quality cannot be prearranged or scripted, but are nevertheless an important means of customer satisfaction (Ingram et al. 1997).

For success in a highly competitive tourism market, a tourism enterprise/destination has to make sure that it is providing the goods or services that the customer wants; that it gets its quality right; and that it delivers on time. This leads to customer satisfaction and achieving a suitable level of profits. Quality in service delivery leads to more repeated visits and greater sales revenue. This enables serving staff on performance-related pay to earn more and enhance the quality of their service to the customer. In addition, the extra profit generated enables tourism enterprise/destination management to invest in upgrading facilities for the customer and in training schemes besides creating an innovative business environment for tourism services improvement.

Quality in tourism is:

> the result of a process which implies the satisfaction of all the legitimate product and service needs, requirements and expectations of the consumer, at an acceptable price, in conformity with mutually accepted contractual conditions and the underlying quality determinants such as safety and security, hygiene, accessibility, transparency, authenticity and harmony of the tourism activity concerned with its human and natural environment.
>
> *(UNWTO 2003)*

What is Total Quality Management?

Total Quality is a description of the culture, attitude and organisation of a company that strives to provide customers with products and services that satisfy their needs. The culture requires quality in all aspects of the company's operations, with processes being done right the first time and defects and waste eradicated from operations.

The simple objective of Total Quality Management (TQM) is 'do the right things, right the first time, every time'. TQM is infinitely variable and adaptable. Although originally applied to manufacturing operations, and for a number of years only used in that area, TQM is now becoming recognised as a generic management tool, just as applicable in service and public sector organisations. There are a number of evolutionary strands, with different sectors creating their own versions from the common ancestor. TQM is the foundation for activities which include:

- Commitment by senior management and all employees
- Meeting customer requirements
- Reducing development cycle times
- Just In Time/Demand Flow Manufacturing
- Improvement teams
- Reducing product and service costs
- Systems to facilitate improvement
- Line management ownership
- Employee involvement and empowerment
- Recognition and celebration
- Challenging quantified goals and benchmarking
- Focus on processes/improvement plans
- Specific incorporation in strategic planning.

This shows that TQM must be practised in all activities, by all personnel, in manufacturing, marketing, engineering, R&D, sales, purchasing, HR, etc.

TQM can be seen as a mixture of:

- *Quality culture*: ensuring people understand and act to build quality in, to 'get it right first time', to take responsibility for fixing problems at source rather than passing them on, etc.
- *Quality strategy*: a clear direction for quality improvement and sustainability, accompanied by measures and effective policy deployment
- *Quality improvement*: effectively making use of all the capabilities within the organisation to review and strive for continuous improvement in quality
- *Quality tools*: which help support the aforementioned activities.

Components of TQM

TQM includes seven broad components:

1 A focus on the customer or user of a product so that the customer's needs and expectations are satisfied consistently
2 Active leadership from top executives to establish quality as a fundamental value to be incorporated into a company's management philosophy
3 Quality concepts (e.g. statistical process control or computer-assisted design, engineering and manufacturing) that are thoroughly integrated throughout all activities of a company
4 A corporate culture established and reinforced by top executives, that involves all employees in contributing to quality improvements
5 A focus on employee involvement, teamwork and training at all levels in order to strengthen employee commitment to continuous quality improvement
6 An approach to problem solving that is based on continuously gathering, evaluating and acting on facts and data in a systematic manner
7 Recognition of suppliers as full partners in the quality management process.

Tourism quality standards

The World Tourism Organization (WTO 2003) has designed six standards for tourist products or services that have to be brought into consideration when taking decisions on tourism services quality related to tourism product design and marketing. These standards are:

1 *Safety and security*: A tourism product or service cannot represent danger to life, damage to health and other vital interests and integrity of the consumer. Safety and security standards are normally established by law and should be considered as quality standards per se.
2 *Hygiene*: Hygiene standards should be maintained in all standards of accommodation facilities and food outlets. An accommodation facility just has to be safe and clean, one cannot pretend that such requirements are more important to high–class establishments. Food safety standards must be met and be common to all types of food outlets, from street vendors to luxury gourmet restaurants to airline catering.
3 *Accessibility*: Accessibility means making a destination accessible, for which the required infrastructural facilities should be available. This determinant requires that physical, communication and service barriers must be done away with to allow, without discrimination,

the use of mainstream tourism products and services by all people irrespective of their natural and acquired differences, including people with disabilities.

4   *Transparency*: This is a key element to provide for legitimacy of expectations and consumer protection. It relates to providing and effectively communicating truthful information on the characteristics and coverage of the product and its total price. It includes what is covered by the price and what is not in the product being supplied.

5   *Authenticity*: In a commercial world, authenticity is the hardest and most subjective quality determinant to attain. It also has marketing and competition dimensions. Authenticity is culturally determined and one of its results is making the product markedly distinct from other similar products. Authenticity must meet consumer expectations. It diminishes and eventually terminates when the product loses its links with its cultural and natural background.

6   *Harmony*: Harmony with the human and natural environment pertains to sustainability which is a medium- and long-term concept. 'Maintaining the sustainability of tourism requires managing environmental and socio-economic impacts, establishing environmental indicators and maintaining the quality of the tourism products and tourist markets' (WTO 2003). There can be no sustainability without quality. Quality should be implemented through a comprehensive system under conditions of consistency and harmony for the quality system components or its subsystems (value chain components).

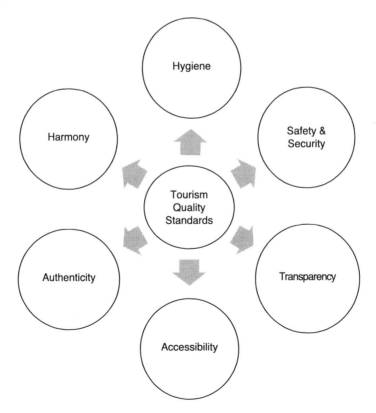

Figure 13.1   Tourism quality standards

Source: Adapted from WTO (2003).

Difficulties in the tourism sector

The management of tourism organisations fully comprehends that a high quality of service has to be ensured in order for the business to grow in the long-term perspective. However, there are a specific set of challenges and difficulties that are associated with the provision of a high-quality service in the tourism sector.

Some of these difficulties are associated with the nature of the service industry in particular. The main differences of the service industry from the manufacturing industry are summarised by Laws (2004) as intangibility, inseparability, heterogeneity and perishability of services. These differences make the perception of quality ambiguous and highly subjective in the service industry in general, and the tourism sector in particular.

The task of ensuring the high quality of services is complicated for tourism organisations since the quality is highly subjective and dependent upon individual perceptions, as well as a wide range of other factors.

The levels of qualifications of service providers in tourism organisations present challenges in ensuring high quality of services. Many of the staff in the tourism sector enter without much formal education, which may have a negative impact on quality management issues within tourism organisations, caused by the lack of formal education of staff in higher educational establishments where the value and benefits of high-quality provision are taught.

Another aspect of challenges of ensuring high-quality standards in tourism organisations relates to the specifications of the industry. Specifically, 'the tourism industry comprises a mix of small numbers of large, often multinational, businesses and large numbers of often family-run SMEs [small and medium enterprises] and micro businesses' (Dudovskiy 2012). This division creates a situation where the large, multinational tourism organisations are able to provide quality in their services by investing a significant amount of money whereas the large numbers of SMEs face challenges in meeting quality standards as set by the large organisations.

Tourism is a service which is highly affected by external factors beyond the control of tour operators like weather, infrastructure facilities, transportation, etc. These factors are to a great extent responsible for the tourists' perception of the quality of service provided to them. The problem becomes even more complicated in view of the fact that tourists consume other elements of the total tourism product during their overall tourism experience, mainly in the destination area. With the large number of destinations that tour operators deal with, and offer to the customers, an individual tour-operating company is not in a position to control the quality of all the elements of the total tourism product offered by the providers operating in the host area. Furthermore, many of these elements are offered by the public sector (e.g. infrastructure, security, police, urban transport, education). Moreover, the human aspect of the product is of utmost importance for total tourist satisfaction, and this can be confronted only at the time of tourism product consumption. This lack of control results in customer dissatisfaction, since the standards promised or implied in advertisements are not matched by the reality of the visitors' experience during their stay.

Moreover, it has to be stated that the tourism industry is highly sensitive to a wide range of external shocks such as economic crisis, any threats associated with the spread of various viruses and illnesses, threats of terrorist attacks, etc. Any such or similar types of external shocks are going to negatively affect all tourism organisations covering relevant geographical areas regardless of the level of effectiveness of their quality management programmes.

It is due to these factors which are beyond the control of the tourism operators that there emerges a tourism quality control gap. This gap relates to the discrepancy between the need

for quality control at every stage of delivery of the total tourism product and the feasibility of the individual tourism company exerting actual control over this process. The existence
of this gap accounts for an inability of individual tourism companies to offer the total quality
tourism product that the customer expects at the beginning of the tourist purchase
consumption process. The tourism quality control gap is also responsible for the increasing
number of tourists dissatisfied with their total tourism experience.

Factors that lead to successful TQM implementation in the tourism sector

Quality in tourism is a complex phenomenon, affected by three broad phenomena: factors
in the environment, factors related to software and factors related to hardware. It is the
positive feedback from all these factors which would lead to a satisfied customer, but as can
be observed, many of these factors are beyond the control of the tour operator and hence
lead to gaps in quality control.

The success or failure of TQM in service systems largely depends on the initiatives and
enthusiasm of members constituting the service organisation. Organisations that want to
implement TQM effectively must have patience, because TQM is a long-term process and
requires major changes in cultural aspects as well as employee mindset in an organisation.
Therefore, to make the TQM movement a success, a new initiative has to be generated
across the globe and the following initiatives need to be taken:

*   identify the key areas of service
*   identify the key practices for successful implementation of TQM
*   commitment by the top management in implementing TQM for continuous
    improvement

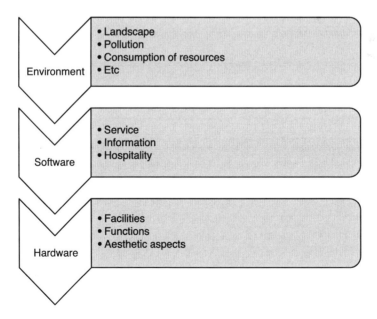

Figure 13.2   Factors that lead to successful TQM implementation in the tourism sector

Source: Adapted from Romeiss-Stracke (1995).

133

- a vision for the change
- customer focus and orientation should always be there
- management structure issue
- human resource focus
- environmental focus
- innovation focus.

With such initiatives, TQM can be successfully applied to service industries to achieve better results.

Kumar (2010) proposes a five-step process for improving quality and customer satisfaction levels for hotels and tourism organisations. The stages consist of:

- defining the standards of the quality service with measurable indicators
- assessment of the current situation
- developing the strategies for service improvement
- initiating the proposed solutions
- providing feedback, recognition and awards.

For TQM to be successful in the tourism sector, Sethi (2006) identifies the main principles of the concept for the service industry to include:

- putting customers first
- focusing on quality
- obtaining profit through service
- increased attention to customer care
- prioritising the quality of the service
- achieving excellence in service, etc.

TQM in the Ritz-Carlton hotel company

At The Ritz-Carlton Hotel Company, our Ladies and Gentlemen are the heart of our company. They are proud to share their skills and knowledge to lift up the communities around them, inspire our customers to join us in our efforts, and create new opportunities to help the global community achieve the Sustainable Development Goals. The Ritz-Carlton is proud to be the first Founding Partner of IMPACT 2030 and to promote the ability of our employees to make a real and sustainable impact. (Hervé Humler, President and COO, The Ritz-Carlton Hotel Company, LLC)

In the United States, the Ritz-Carlton Investing Company was established by Albert Keller who bought and franchised the name in the early 1900s. The hotels embody the finest luxury experience, American ingenuity and social sensibilities. Ritz-Carlton revolutionised hospitality in America by creating luxury in a hotel setting.

In 1983, the Ritz-Carlton Hotel Company, LLC was formed. In 1998, the success of the Ritz-Carlton Hotel Company had attracted the attention of the hospitality industry, and the brand was purchased by Marriott International. Since this purchase, the Ritz-Carlton has continued to grow, providing exceptional service and genuine care to their guests across the globe. At present the hotel company operates with 91 hotels worldwide in 30 countries and territories: Aruba, Austria, Bahrain, Canada, Cayman Islands, Chile, China, Egypt, Germany, India, Indonesia, Israel, Japan, Kazakhstan, Malaysia, Mexico, Oman, Portugal, Puerto Rico, Qatar, Russia, Saudi Arabia, Singapore, South Korea, Spain, Thailand, Turkey, the United Arab Emirates, US Virgin Islands, and the United States (Ritz-Carlton 2016).

The gold standards are the foundation of the TQM of Ritz-Carlton. The values and philosophies of the gold standards (Ritz-Carlton 2016) include six quality management standards: *The Credo, Motto, Three Steps of Service, Service Values, The 6th Diamond* and *The Employee Promise* to serve the guests (Ritz-Carlton 2016).

The Credo: The Ritz-Carlton Hotel is a place where the genuine care and comfort of guests is the highest mission. Hotels pledge to provide the finest personal service and facilities to guests who will always enjoy a warm, relaxed, yet refined ambience.

Motto: At the Ritz-Carlton Hotel Company, the motto, 'We are Ladies and Gentlemen serving Ladies and Gentlemen' exemplifies the anticipatory service provided by all staff members.

Three Steps of Service:

1   A warm and sincere greeting.
2   Use the guest's name. Anticipation and fulfilment of each guest's needs.
3   Fond farewell. Give a warm goodbye and use the guest's name.

Service Values of the Ritz-Carlton:

1   Build strong relationships and create Ritz-Carlton guests for life.
2   Always be responsive to the expressed and unexpressed wishes and needs of guests.
3   Be empowered to create unique, memorable and personal experiences for guests.
4   Understand one's role in achieving the Key Success Factors, embracing Community Footprints and creating The Ritz-Carlton Mystique.
5   Continuously seek opportunities to innovate and improve The Ritz-Carlton experience.
6   Own and immediately resolve guest problems.
7   Create a work environment of teamwork and lateral service so that the needs of guests and each other are met.
8   One has the opportunity to continuously learn and grow.
9   Be involved in the planning of the work.
10 Be proud of one's professional appearance, language and behaviour.
11 Protect the privacy and security of the guests, one's fellow employees and the company's confidential information and assets.
12 Be responsible for uncompromising levels of cleanliness and creating a safe and accident-free environment.

The 6th Diamond: Stresses the emotional engagement of the staff.

The Employee Promise:

At The Ritz-Carlton, hotel Ladies and Gentlemen are the most important resource in service commitment to the guests. By applying the principles of trust, honesty, respect, integrity and commitment, hotels nurture and maximise talent to the benefit of each individual and the company. The Ritz-Carlton fosters a work environment where diversity is valued, quality of life is enhanced, individual aspirations are fulfilled and The Ritz-Carlton Mystique is strengthened.

Conclusion

The senior-level managers of tourism organisations need to understand that 'quality assurance is a persistent problem and needs to be better understood, measured and managed' (Cooper 2003: p. 97). Therefore, tourism organisation managers should not approach quality issues as one-time problems and they should devise appropriate programmes and initiatives to address quality management issues in a constant and systematic way.

Devising effective employee training and development programmes also needs to be mentioned as an integral part of the recommendations formulated for tourism organisations for the simple fact that customer quality perception is formed primarily on the basis of service offered by the workforce. The training and development programmes need to be organised in a constant and systematic manner and should aim at increasing the knowledge of the workforce regarding the importance of quality management and equip them with specific knowledge, skills and competencies required to contribute to the quality of the service.

The TQM model implemented at Ritz-Carlton emphasises employee education and training, employee participation and customer focus, and the organisation has so far been successful in implementing these strategies in its daily operation to attain TQM. But it fails to realise the importance of inculcating leadership in employees, since supervision of management is crucial to ensure that the service quality is not faltering at any point in time (Hashmi 2007).

References

Cooper, C. P. (2003). *Classic Reviews in Tourism*, Clevedon, UK: Channel View Publications.

Crosby, P. (1979). *Quality is Free: The Art of Making Quality Certain*, New York: New American Library.

Day, A. and Peters, J. (1994). 'Rediscovering standards: Static and dynamic quality', *International Journal of Contemporary Hospitality Management*, 1(2): 81–84.

Dudovskiy, J. (2012). 'Issues of quality in managing a tourism organisation', *Research Methodology*, 25 July, http://research-methodology.net/issues-of-quality-in-managing-a-tourism-organisation/ [Accessed 18 October 2015].

Hashmi, K. M. (2007). 'Introduction and implementation of Total Quality Management', *iSix Sigma*, 52–59.

Ingram, H., Tear, R., Ridley, S. and Ferrone, L. (1997). 'Strategic competitive advantage through structure, quality and teamwork', in Teare, R., Farber Canziani, B. and Brown, G. (eds.), *Global Directions: New Strategies for Hospitality and Tourism* (pp. 133–164), London: Cassell.

ISO (2015). 'Standards', Available from: http://www.iso.org/iso/home/standards.htm [Accessed 20 April 2016].

Jones, E. and Haven-Tang, C. (2005). *Tourism SMEs, Service Quality and Destination Competitiveness*, Wallingford: CABI.

Juran, J. M. (1988). *Juran on Planning for Quality*, New York: The Free Press.

Kumar, R. (2010). *Marketing of Hospitality and Tourism Services*, New Delhi: Tata McGraw-Hill Education.

Laws, E. (2004). *Improving Tourism and Hospitality Services*, Wallingford: CABI.

Ritz-Carlton (2016). Website, Available from: https://www.ritzcarlton.com [Accessed 8 April 2016].

Romeiss-Stracke, F. (1995). *Service-Qualität im Tourismus: Grundsätze und Gebrauchsanweisungen für die touristische Praxi*, Munich: Allg. Deutscher Automobil-Club.

Sethi, P. (2006). *Handbook of Leisure and Tourism*, New Delhi: Anmol Publications.

UNWTO (2003). Quality Support Committee at its sixth meeting, Varadero, Cuba, 9–10 May.

WTO (2003). 'WTO guide for local authorities on developing sustainable tourism', Available from: http://www.e-unwto.org/doi/pdf/10.18111/9789284402809 [Accessed 14 November 2016].

14

THE IMPACT OF MUSIC'S VOLUME AND TEMPO ON DINING CONSUMERS' BEHAVIOURS AND PERCEPTIONS OF QUALITY

Michael C. Ottenbacher, Robert J. Harrington and Anja Treuter

Introduction

Several recent studies have considered restaurant consumers' holistic interpretation of the dining experience based on the physical environment (Ryu and Han 2011), atmospherics (Liu and Jang 2009) and servicescape (Kim and Moon 2009). Generally, the dining atmosphere or environment has been divided into several key components: facility aesthetics, ambience, lighting and layout. These elements add to the attractiveness of a dining environment and can influence consumer traffic to a restaurant (Ryu and Han 2010). Of particular interest in the current study is the ambience element and its impact on consumer responses. Ambience comprises several intangible background characteristics for the consumer, which are generally non–visual in nature. Earlier study has shown a strong connection between ambient conditions and perceptions of service quality (Kim and Moon 2009). Examples of ambience elements include sounds, music, scents and temperature.

Ambience and sensory aspects of the dining experience have been of growing interest for both practitioners and researchers over the past few years (Ryu et al. 2012). It could be argued that the trend of bringing together food science and culinary arts in what has been termed molecular gastronomy is based on addressing the role of additional sensory excitement to the dining experience. For instance, scientific research related to molecular gastronomy considers the role of colour, sounds, taste compounds, aroma compounds and other sensory-derived 'out of context' states (Edwards-Stuart 2012). In this vein, the current study considers the role of sound in the dining experience. Specifically, the authors consider the impact of music on restaurant consumers' perceptions of quality and consumer behaviours in the casual restaurant sector. This study extends earlier studies by testing these relationships in the casual restaurant sector, testing music treatments of volume and tempo in this context and determining whether these relationships vary based on meal period.

Literature review

The literature on the relationship between music and a dining experience encompasses several areas: (1) those considering the restaurant servicescape (Ryu and Han 2010, 2011), (2) the relationship between music and food or beverage (Crisinel et al. 2012), (3) the impact of music characteristics in various foodservice situations (Caldwell and Hibbert 2002), and (4) the role of music in other retail or service settings (Oakes 2000).

While earlier studies found that the dominant servicescape factor connected to these pleasurable feelings was facility aesthetics, ambience had the second strongest connection to dining pleasure and the strongest connection to perceptions of service quality (Kim and Moon 2009). Ambience is a holistic term for a number of intangible sensory characteristics impacting consumer responses. Examples include sounds (music, room noise, sounds of food cooking, etc.), scents or aromas, textural elements (fabric, table coverings, napkins, etc.) and temperature. Thus, ambient conditions relate to the five human senses; these sensory aspects of the dining atmosphere are proposed to impact on several facets of consumer behaviours such as arousal, dining pleasure and satisfaction (Bitner 1992).

Research in the restaurant servicescape supports the notion that the situation in which the dining consumption occurs significantly affects consumer inclinations for types of products and services (Ryu and Han 2011). While this proposition is generally believed to be true, little research has been performed considering situational variables such as the impact of meal period, purpose of visit and type of patron.

Several studies have considered the impact of music characteristics in various foodservice situations. These studies demonstrate the potential for music with have multiple effects on patron perceptions and behaviours. The research to date in foodservice settings has assessed four compositional attributes of music: music tempo (Caldwell and Hibbert 2002), music type (Magnini and Thelen 2008), music complexity (North and Hargreaves 1996) and music volume (Guéguen et al. 2004). These studies provide several interesting relationships as well as point out some of the weaknesses of this research stream.

For instance, an early study by Milliman (1986) analysed the impact of slow and fast instrumental music on restaurant patrons. Compared with fast instrumental music, slow instrumental music increased duration of stay and beverage sales. This study did not have a control treatment of no music to test any differential effects between music treatments vs. no music in the restaurant. Caldwell and Hibbert (2002) also looked at music tempo and its impact on consumer behaviour. In an Italian restaurant in Glasgow, findings indicated slow–tempo music increased food and beverage spending compared with fast-tempo music. The authors also found that personal preference levels of music impacted on duration of stay, total spending, enjoyment, intent to return and likely recommendations to a friend.

North and Hargreaves (1996) and North et al. (2003) considered the impact of music type or genre on consumer behaviours. Similar to the findings by Caldwell and Hibbert (2002), North and Hargreaves (1996) found that the more patrons enjoyed or liked the type of music, the higher the intent to return in this lab setting. In a field setting, North et al. (2003) found a correlation between music type and purchase behaviour. Specifically, classical music increased food sales compared with pop music in this British restaurant setting. In a mock fine dining experience for 66 US students, Magnini and Thelen (2008) found that music type (classical vs. no music) influenced cognition of brand identity and atmosphere but there was no relationship with perceived service quality. A weakness of this study is the lab setting, which may have impacted perceived service element perceptions.

Guéguen et al. (2004, 2008) analysed the impact of music volume on beverage consumption in bars. Findings indicate that louder music in bars (88 to 91 dB[A]) resulted in greater beverage consumption. While interesting, these relationships may not hold in most restaurant settings as the volume treatments used are not generally acceptable for dining atmosphere norms.

Oakes (2000) used a synthesis of existing literature to create a framework of music and consumer behaviour relationships in retail settings. Based on the servicescape model (Bitner 1992), Oakes' (2000) framework was called 'musicscape'. The musicscape model highlighted the interdependence of key musical attributes, valence moderators and resulting cognitive, behavioural and emotional effects. While very little testing has been done using the musicscape model, chefs and restaurateurs are experimenting with sound and other sensory elements of the dining experience to influence emotional perceptions of food (Edwards-Stuart 2012).

While sensory testing is not a new phenomenon, most research on specific sound elements in food and beverage environments has been done in artificial lab settings (e.g. Crisinel et al. 2012). While lab research provides greater control, many times it lacks realism (particularly) given the more holistic nature of the restaurant experience. Field research in an actual restaurant setting appears more relevant when the objective of the research is to increase external validity and when trying to determine parameter estimates of a population (Dobbins et al. 1988).

For the current study, objectives of generalizability and population parameter assessment on the effect of music in the dining experience were deemed important by the authors. Further, studies completed to date in foodservice settings provide only equivocal findings given numerous situational factors, context issues and weaknesses in the research design. Therefore, the current study extends earlier research in several areas. First, no study to date has assessed for differences of the impact of music attributes based on meal period. Given differences in length of stay, spending and purpose of visit due to meal period, it seems likely to be an important situational variable to consider. Second, this study considers direct effects of music tempo and music volume as well as the 2×2 treatment effects (volume and tempo combinations). Third, the study includes a no-music control treatment, which has not been the case in several of the earlier studies (Caldwell and Hibbert 2002; Guéguen et al. 2004). Finally, the current study analyses the impact of music on quality perceptions (product, service and atmosphere), actual behaviours (duration of stay and spending) and intention to return. Based on these objectives and prior research, the following hypotheses emerge:

H1a: Music volume level will impact consumer behaviours of restaurant patrons in the casual dining sector.

H1b: Music volume level will impact quality perceptions of restaurant patrons in the casual dining sector.

H2a: Music tempo will impact consumer behaviours of restaurant patrons in the casual dining sector.

H2b: Music tempo will impact quality perceptions of restaurant patrons in the casual dining sector.

H3: Music treatments (tempo × volume) will impact consumer behaviours of restaurant patrons in the casual dining sector.

H4: The impact of music volume, tempo and 2×2 music treatments will vary by meal period.

Methods

This study was conducted during lunch and dinner meal periods at a casual restaurant in Germany. The selected restaurant had a broad range of customers and offered a wide range of food and beverages. The experiment took place over a period of 25 meal periods.

The influence of music was based on treatments to music tempo and volume. A Mix Meister BPM Analyzer was used to determine the tempo of songs (bpm) selected for the study. This selection resulted in 20 slow- and 20 fast-tempo songs; all songs were recent chart hits featuring pop and rock music of the past few years. The music service platform 'Napster' was used to choose songs and create two playlists. In consultation with management, music genre and volume were selected to ensure an appropriate fit between the music and the restaurant (Magnini and Thelen 2008). Playlist 1 (defined as slow music) contained titles that were under 100 bpm; these ranged from 83 to 99 bpm. Playlist 2 included fast-tempo songs of over 110 bpm, ranging from 111 to 172 bpm.

To ensure consistency in music volume, a sound-measuring instrument was placed in the middle of the room where data was collected. The measurements of the soft music treatment (background music) ranged from 55 to 65 dB(A). The decibel range used for the loud music treatment was 70 to 80 dB(A). The intent of this treatment was clearly noticeable music in the dining space.

All guests entering the defined area in the restaurant were observed. The status of the food and drink orders was tracked via a mobile phone connected to the cash register system. The length of stay was recorded in minutes and the printed sales slip enabled verification of total spending. After the guests finished their meals and 30 minutes after they ordered their drinks, the observer approached each table and asked them to complete a survey. Some guests declined to participate in the study; the resulting respondents totalled 340 out of 411 total guests (82.7% response rate). The survey instrument was developed synthesizing earlier research on the role of music in food and beverage or restaurant settings (Caldwell and Hibbert 2002; Magnini and Thelen 2008; Guéguen et al. 2004).

The survey included a short introduction and general questions regarding frequency of visits and the reason for visiting the restaurant. The total instrument contained 29 items. The Cronbach's alpha for the instrument was .94, providing evidence of good reliability. Participants received a small thank-you in the form of sweets to take with them following the meal.

Participants in the study ranged in age from 17 to 77 years old; the mean was 38.56 years and median was 37 years. In terms of gender, about half the participants in the study were women and about half men, with 48.7% female and 51.3% male.

Measures

The survey instrument and observation were used to collect data on demographic information, cognitive effects on quality perceptions (food, drink, service and atmosphere) and to quantify behavioural variables (intent to return, duration of stay, total food and drink spending). Music volume and tempo were manipulated to test the effects of these variables independently as well as to create five treatments as described in the following section.

Music volume and music tempo

In this study, two main compositional variables (volume and tempo) were manipulated to assess the direct impact of music volume (soft vs. loud) and music tempo (slow vs. fast) as well as to create five total treatments: soft/slow music, slow/loud music, soft/fast music, loud/fast music and no music. These represented the groups of interest (IVs) for the tests in this study. The restaurant patrons at each meal period represent intact groups or cases. Therefore, music treatments were randomly assigned to minimize threats to internal validity. Of course, unequal cell sizes for each treatment are due to variations in participation rates at each meal period.

Quality ratings

Participants were asked to assess their perception of the quality level for nine items of the restaurant. This response was on a 6-point scale with 1 = very good and 6 = very bad. This assessment of perceived quality included service, food, beverage, overall atmosphere, lighting, temperature, furnishings, layout, and noise level.

Consumer behaviours

Five items were used to assess behaviours by restaurant consumers based on music variables. These included intent to return, duration of stay, total spending, food spending and drink spending. To assess the likelihood of the participants' intent to return to the restaurant, the participants were given three possible options: yes, no and maybe. The responses were coded as 3 = yes, 2 = maybe and 1 = no. The duration of stay was determined in minutes based on observation by the researchers. The mean duration of stay was 67.75 minutes and the median was 54 minutes. Duration of stay ranged from 17 to 219 minutes with a standard deviation of 38.57 minutes.

Total spending was calculated in Euros based on the actual guest cheque per person and included both food and beverages. The mean was 10.97 Euros and median spending was 10.50 Euros. Per person spending ranged from 2.40 to 26.50 Euros with a standard deviation of 4.27 Euros. Food spending was calculated as food per person in Euros and drink spending was calculated as alcoholic beverage spending per person (in Euros).

Lunch vs. dinner meal periods

Data and surveys were collected from restaurant patrons during both lunch and dinner meal periods. This resulted in 126 participants during the dinner meal period and 214 participants during the lunch meal period. Separate tests were conducted based on meal period. This separation allowed the researchers to assess the situational impact of meal period on quality perceptions and consumer behaviours in the casual restaurant context.

Data analysis

Multivariate analysis of variance (MANOVA) was used to determine whether significant differences existed between the treatment groups (music volume levels, music tempo levels and combined music treatments) for the (1) eight quality ratings and (2) five consumer behaviours. Because MANOVA allows simultaneous testing of all interrelated variables of interest (i.e. when moderately correlated), we determined it was appropriate to use for this analysis (Hair et al. 1998). In addition, post hoc tests were run using Tukey's honestly significant difference method to provide complete control over the familywise error rate with an alpha of .05.

Results

The results of the global MANOVA measures and post hoc tests are presented for the quality levels and consumer behaviours. Tables 14.1 and 14.2 provide results of the impact of music treatments on consumer behaviours for lunch (Table 14.1) and dinner (Table 14.2). Within each table, sections are devoted to the impact of music volume, music tempo and the five music combinations using no music and each 2×2 (high/low or fast/slow) combination.

The top portion of each table section provides results of the global MANOVA and the bottom portion of each table section provides results of the post hoc tests. For all global tests, Roy's largest root was used as the multivariate test. Roy's uses the variance from the

Table 14.1 The impact of music treatments on consumer behaviours during lunch

Section 1:

Music volume on dining behaviours (no music [n] = 39, soft [n] = 62, loud [n] = 74)

Effect: Roy's largest root	Value	F	Hypothesis df	Error df	Sig.
Intercept	21.85	735.13	5	168	.000
Music soft/ loud	.08	2.72	5	169	.02
DV	Comparisons		Mean diff.	SE	Sig.
Time in minutes	Soft (56.61)	Loud (46.80)	9.82	3.87	.03

Music volume on quality perceptions (no music [n] = 45, soft [n] = 80, loud [n] = 89)

Effect: Roy's largest root	Value	F	Hypothesis df	Error df	Sig.
Intercept	3.26	73.60	9	203	.000
Music soft/ loud	.10	2.30	9	204	.02
DV	Comparisons		Mean diff.	SE	Sig.
Service quality	Soft (1.53)	Loud (1.89)	−.36	.17	.08

Section 2:

Music tempo on dining behaviours (no music [n] = 39, soft [n] = 62, loud [n] = 74)

Effect: Roy's largest root	Value	F	Hypothesis df	Error df	Sig.
Intercept	21.87	734.89	5	168	.000
Music slow/ fast	.09	3.03	5	169	.01

Music tempo on quality perceptions (no music [n] = 45, soft [n] = 80, loud [n] = 89)

Effect: Roy's largest root	Value	F	Hypothesis df	Error df	Sig.
Intercept	3.33	75.02	9	203	.000
Music slow/ fast	.08	1.75	9	204	.08
DV	Comparisons		Mean diff.	SE	Sig.
Temperature	Slow (1.88)	Fast (1.47)	.41	.17	.05

(Continued)

Table 14.1 The impact of music treatments on consumer behaviours during lunch *(continued)*

Section 3:
Music treatments on dining behaviours (no music [n] = 39, loud/fast [n] = 36, loud/ slow [n] = 38, soft/fast [n] = 34, soft/slow [n] = 28)

Effect: Roy's largest root	Value	F	Hypothesis df	Error df	Sig.
Intercept	23.32	774.26	5	166	.000
Music treatments	.12	3.88	5	169	.002
DV	Comparisons		Mean diff.	SE	Sig.
Time in minutes	Loud/fast (42.86)	Soft/slow (59.00)	−16.14	5.66	.04

Source: Authors.

dimension that separates the groups most and is usually more powerful than other global MANOVA tests (Hair et al. 1998). Post hoc results shown are only those relationships that were significant.

Lunch: music volume

In Table 14.1, the findings of the global MANOVA and post hoc tests for differences between treatments on dining behaviours and quality perceptions are presented. For each test in section 1, three treatments or groups were tested: no music, soft music and loud music. The global MANOVA indicated a significant difference between music volume treatments.

Using Roy's, differences in dining behaviours were significant (F = 2.72, p = .02) across the three music volume treatments. Post hoc tests indicated that significant differences existed between soft music and loud music in the duration of stay by restaurant patrons. During the lunch period, diners in the soft music treatment stayed 56.61 minutes on average compared with 46.80 minutes for diners in the loud music treatment (p < .03). There were no significant differences with the no music treatment.

Using Roy's, differences in quality perceptions were also significant (F = 2.30, p = .02) across the three music volume treatments. Post hoc tests indicated that (marginally) significant differences existed between the soft music and loud music treatments in diner perceptions of service quality but only at the p = .08 level. During the lunch period, diners in the soft music treatment rated the service quality higher (1.53 average) than the loud music treatment diners (1.89 average). Here again, there were no significant differences with the no music treatment.

Lunch: music tempo

In section 2 of Table 14.1, the findings of the global MANOVA and post hoc tests for differences between music tempo treatments on dining behaviours and quality perceptions are presented. The global MANOVA indicated a significant difference between music tempo treatments.

Using Roy's, differences in dining behaviours were significant (F = 3.03, p = .01) across the three music tempo treatments. Post hoc tests indicated no significant differences existed between no music, slow music and fast music for individual dependent variables (DVs) of dining behaviours.

Using Roy's, differences in quality perceptions were marginally significant (F = 1.75, $p = .08$) across the three music tempo treatments. Post hoc tests indicated that one significant difference existed between slow music and fast music treatments in diner perceptions of temperature quality ($p = .05$). In this case, the restaurant temperature was viewed as more appropriate by diners in the fast music treatment (1.47 vs. 1.88 for the slow treatment rating). There were no significant differences with the no music treatment.

Lunch: music 2×2 treatments

In section 3 of Table 14.1, the findings of the global MANOVA and post hoc tests for differences between the four 2×2 music treatments and no music on dining behaviours are presented. For each test, five treatments or groups were tested: no music, soft/slow music, soft/fast music, loud/slow music and loud/fast music.

The global MANOVA indicated a significant difference between music treatments. Using Roy's, differences in dining behaviours were significant (F = 3.88, $p = .002$) across the five music treatments. Post hoc tests indicated a significant difference between soft/slow music and loud/fast music in the duration of stay by restaurant patrons. During the lunch period, diners in the soft/slow music treatment stayed 59.00 minutes on average compared with 42.86 minutes for diners in the loud/fast music treatment ($p = .04$). There were no significant differences with the no music treatment.

Dinner: music volume

In Table 14.2, the findings of the global MANOVA and post hoc tests for differences between treatments on dining behaviours and quality perceptions are presented. For each test in section 1 of this table, three treatments or groups were tested: no music, soft music and loud music. The global MANOVA indicated a significant difference between music volume treatments. Using Roy's, differences in dining behaviours were significant (F = 3.10, $p = .01$) across the three music volume treatments.

Post hoc tests indicated that six significant differences existed between music volume treatments during the dinner meal period. Two differences were significant for the DV intent to return; diners in the loud music treatment were more likely to return to the restaurant than those in the no music treatment ($p = .05$) or soft music treatment ($p = .01$). Compared with the no music situation, average total spending was significantly higher for diners in the loud treatment (+2.91 Euros) and the soft music treatment (+3.47). The spending patterns were similar for food spending, with the loud treatment at +3.36 Euros ($p = .01$) and the soft music treatment at +3.22 ($p = .01$) compared with the no music situation.

Using Roy's, differences in quality perceptions were also significant (F = 2.99, $p = .02$) across the three music volume treatments. Post hoc tests indicated a marginally significant difference between soft music and loud music treatments in diner perceptions of overall atmosphere quality but only at the $p = .09$ level. During the dinner period, diners in the loud music treatment rated the overall atmosphere quality higher (1.00 average) than the soft music treatment diners (1.49 average). There were no significant differences with the no music treatment.

Table 14.2 The impact of music treatments on consumer behaviours during dinner

Section 1:
Dinner: the impact of music treatments on consumer behaviours

Effect: Roy's largest root	Value	F	Hypothesis df	Error df	Sig.
Intercept	19.27	381.57	5	99	.000
Music soft/ loud	.16	3.10	5	100	.01

DV	Comparisons		Mean diff.	SE	Sig.
Intent to return	No music (2.39)	Loud (2.90)	−.51	.21	.05
Intent to return	Soft (2.38)	Loud (2.90)	−.52	.18	.01
Total spending	No music (9.18)	Loud (12.09)	−2.91	1.20	.05
Total spending	No music (9.18)	Soft (12.65)	−3.47	1.17	.01
Food spending	No music (3.91)	Loud (7.27)	−3.36	1.07	.01
Food spending	No music (3.91)	Soft (7.13)	−3.22	1.04	.01

Music volume on quality perceptions (no music [n] = 45, soft [n] = 80, loud [n] = 89)

Effect: Roy's largest root	Value	F	Hypothesis df	Error df	Sig.
Intercept	5.04	151.27	4	120	.000
Music soft/ loud	.10	2.99	4	121	.02

DV	Comparisons		Mean diff.	SE	Sig.
Overall atmosphere quality	Soft (1.49)	Loud (1.00)	.49	.23	.09

Section 2:
Music tempo on dining behaviours (no music [n] = 39, soft [n] = 62, loud [n] = 74)

Effect: Roy's largest root	Value	F	Hypothesis df	Error df	Sig.
Intercept	19.24	380.99	5	99	.000
Music slow/ fast	.13	2.56	5	100	.03

DV	Comparisons		Mean diff.	SE	Sig.
Intent to return	Slow (2.39)	Fast (2.81)	−.39	.18	.07
Total spending	No music (9.18)	Slow (12.95)	−3.77	1.18	.01
Total spending	No music (9.18)	Fast (11.85)	−2.67	1.18	.06

Food spending	No music (3.91)	Slow (7.51)	−3.60	1.05	.003
Food spending	No music (3.91)	Fast (6.88)	−2.97	1.05	.02

Music tempo on quality perceptions (no music [n] = 45, soft [n] = 80, loud [n] = 89)

Effect: Roy's largest root	Value	F	Hypothesis df	Error df	Sig.
Intercept	5.04	151.10	4	120	.000
Music slow/ fast	.06	1.82	4	121	.13

Section 3:

Music treatments on dining behaviours (no music [n] = 39, loud/fast [n] = 36, loud/ slow [n] = 38, soft/fast [n] = 34, soft/slow [n] = 28)

Effect: Roy's largest root	Value	F	Hypothesis df	Error df	Sig.
Intercept	22.80	433.12	5	95	.000
Music treatments	.23	4.58	5	98	.001
DV	Comparisons		Mean diff.	SE	Sig.
Intent to return	Loud/fast (2.90)	Soft/slow (2.14)	.76	.24	.02
Intent to return	Loud/slow (2.89)	Soft/slow (2.14)	.75	.25	.03
Total spending	No music (9.18)	Loud/slow (13.91)	−4.73	1.41	.01
Total spending	No music (9.18)	Soft/fast (13.12)	−3.94	1.34	.03
Food spending	No music (3.91)	Loud/slow (8.59)	−4.68	1.26	.003
Food spending	No music (3.91)	Soft/fast (7.62)	−3.70	1.19	.02

Source: Authors.

Dinner: music tempo

In section 2 of Table 14.2, the findings of the global MANOVA and post hoc tests for differences between music tempo treatments on dining behaviours and quality perceptions are presented. The global MANOVA indicated a significant difference between music tempo treatments. Using Roy's, differences in dining behaviours were significant (F = 2.56, $p = .03$) across the three music tempo treatments.

Post hoc tests indicated that five significant differences existed between music tempo treatments during the dinner meal period. One difference was significant for the DV intent to return; diners in the slow music treatment were more likely to return to the restaurant than those in the fast music treatment ($p = .07$). Compared with the no music situation, average total spending was significantly higher for diners in the slow treatment (+3.77 Euros, $p = .01$) and the fast music treatment (+2.67, $p = .06$). The spending patterns were similar for food spending, with the slow treatment at +3.60 Euros ($p = .003$) and the fast music treatment at +2.97 ($p = .02$) compared with the no music situation.

147

Using Roy's, differences in quality perceptions were non-significant (F = 1.82, *p* = .13) across the three music tempo treatments during the dinner meal period.

Dinner: music 2×2 treatments

In section 3 of Table 14.2, the findings of the global MANOVA and post hoc tests for differences between the four 2×2 music treatments and no music on dining behaviours are presented. As with the lunch test, five treatments or groups were tested: no music, soft/slow music, soft/fast music, loud/slow music and loud/fast music. The global MANOVA indicated a significant difference between music treatments. Using Roy's, differences in dining behaviours were significant (F = 4.58, *p* = .001) across the five music treatments. Post hoc tests indicated six significant differences between music treatments.

Two differences were significant for the DV intent to return; diners in the loud/fast and loud/slow treatments were more likely to return than diners in the soft/slow treatment (*p* = .02 and *p* = .03, respectively). Compared with the no music situation, average total spending was significantly higher for diners in the loud/slow treatment (+4.73 Euros, *p* = .01) and the soft/fast music treatment (+3.94, *p* = .03). The spending patterns were similar for food spending, with the loud/slow treatment at +4.68 Euros (*p* = .003) and the soft/fast music treatment at +3.70 (*p* = .02) compared with the no music situation.

Discussion

Earlier studies have shown relationships among music and other elements of the dining ambience with consumer perceptions, emotional responses and consumer behaviours. The current study considered these relationships in the context of a casual dining experience in Germany. While earlier studies in the hospitality literature, generally, considered the more holistic term of ambience, this study focused on the impact of volume and tempo music treatments in an actual field setting.

The stated hypotheses received support but the strength of this support varied by meal period and whether the multivariate dependent variables were related to quality perceptions or consumer dining behaviours.

In terms of music volume as a treatment, hypothesis 1a received strong support but relationships varied between lunch and dinner. For lunch diners, duration of stay increased when soft music was played compared with loud music. In this treatment, soft music represented background music and loud music represented music that was identifiable and in the foreground of the dining experience. This finding may indicate a greater need for accurate communication without distractions due to business meetings and less time to achieve business or social dining objectives.

During the dinner meal period, music volume impacted diners' intent to return and spending behaviours. Dinner patrons in the loud treatment indicated a greater intention to return than those in the soft treatment or no music treatment. This finding implies that, during dinner meal periods in casual dining situations, music identifiable in the foreground creates a more pleasurable ambience and enjoyable experience (Caldwell and Hibbert 2002). Regardless of volume level (background or foreground), casual restaurant diners during the dinner meal period increased food spending and total spending when music was part of the ambience. In the casual dining setting, beverage spending and consumption was not significantly increased for the higher-volume music treatment. This finding was in contrast to Guéguen et al. (2004) who found that music volume significantly increased beverage consumption in bars. One explanation for the discrepancy is that (in contrast to a bar) the main product in a casual dining restaurant is food rather than beverage. Thus, these findings may suggest that higher volume increases product sales during the evening hours but the type of product may depend on the sector (restaurant or bar).

Only one quality perception variable was significantly related with the music volume treatment and then only marginally significantly. During the lunch period, soft music increased perceived service quality compared with loud music. Clearly, the connection between music volume and quality perceptions requires additional study to provide unequivocal relationships. Therefore, hypothesis 1b was only marginally supported.

The tests of the effects of music tempo on consumer behaviours of restaurant patrons in the casual dining sector provided support for hypothesis 2a but only during the dinner meal period. Compared with no music, slow and fast music treatments significantly increased diners' food spending and total spending. This finding both supports and contradicts earlier studies on the effects of music tempo (Caldwell and Hibbert 2002; Milliman 1986). While slow-tempo music had the highest total and food spending, the difference was not significantly higher than for fast music tempo. But, compared with no music, slow and fast music tempos increased spending overall.

Hypothesis 2b received marginal support. During the lunch period, diners in the fast-tempo treatment perceived the restaurant temperature to be more appropriate than did their slow-music counterparts. Here again, this marginal finding indicates a need for additional research to assess the impact of music tempo on various consumer behaviours and the impact on arousal, dining pleasure and physiological perceptions (Bitner 1992).

Tests of hypothesis 3 found support for a connection among music treatments (tempo × volume) and consumer behaviours of restaurant patrons in the casual dining sector. For the lunch period, loud/fast music decreased duration of stay compared with soft/slow music. For the dinner period, loud/fast and loud/slow music styles increased intent to return compared with soft/slow music. Finally, compared with no music, loud/slow and soft/fast music situations increased total spending and food spending. The loud/slow situation had the highest spending overall but it was not statistically significantly different from other music treatments.

These findings indicate the importance of music and styles in creating a pleasurable dining ambience in the casual dining sector. Management's selection of an appropriate and effective music treatment depends on an understanding of the purpose of diners' visit to the establishment, target customers, and understanding potential meal period effects. The meal period effects shown in this study support hypothesis 4 and highlight a weakness in the literature when it comes to testing or establishing this effect.

Conclusion

Key findings indicate substantial differences in the effect of music based on meal period due to implicit and explicit differences in dining duration, spending, reasons for the visit and differences in social or business expectations/needs. In this study, lunch and dinner meal periods provided substantially different effects of music treatments on duration of stay, intent to return, total spending, food spending and (but to a lesser extent) quality perceptions.

Implications

Findings provide support for the need of management to carefully consider the impact of music on patrons' enjoyment and behaviours. In terms of music volume, its impact varied between lunch and dinner. For lunch diners, duration of stay increased when soft, background music was played. Additionally, loud/fast music appears to decrease duration of stay and soft/slow music appears to increase duration of stay. Management should consider the relationship between seat turnover and the potential for additional revenue as part of the music volume and tempo decision. As part of this decision, management should also consider the need for accurate communication without distractions at a particular meal period. For instance: Are patrons conducting business or important social conversations? How much time is normally spent at the given meal period and is the time sufficient to achieve business or social dining objectives with foreground music distractions? These are some of the questions casual dining managers should ask to create an acceptable ambience for guests. These questions need to be balanced against findings for dinner patrons. During dinner, patrons in the foreground music situation indicated a greater intention to return than those in the soft treatment or no music treatment. This finding implies that music identifiable in the foreground can create a more pleasurable ambience and enjoyable experience.

Second, music is an important part of the casual dining ambience for the dinner meal period. Regardless of volume (at least within the range in this study), music increased both food spending and total spending. When combining volume and tempo, patron spending appears to be impacted by both volume and tempo (loud/slow and soft/fast music combinations). Thus, a quality music program or soundtrack system is likely to pay good dividends for casual dining restaurants, particularly during the dinner meal period.

Music tempo is an important consideration for ambience during the dinner meal in the casual dining sector. Regardless of tempo, slow or fast, music is likely to increase spending overall. While music's effects on quality perceptions were marginal in this study, a relationship cannot be ruled out. This relationship may be affected by the target market such as age or gender rather than a one-size-fits-all approach. Therefore, an implication is that managers in the casual dining sector should consider music likeability issues for the primary target markets of the firm to maximize the benefits of a pleasurable ambience.

Limitations and future research

This study looked at the role of music in the casual dining sector in Germany. While this represents an under-researched segment and geographic location, it limits the generalizability of the results and findings may not be applicable to the broad range of foodservice sectors and geographic locations. Earlier studies have shown relationships among music and other elements of the dining ambience with consumer perceptions, emotional responses and consumer behaviours. But, as shown in the current study, situational variables are crucial to understanding the relationship between music, ambience and consumer responses. Future research should continue on the path to sorting out more situational variable relationships with practical implications for industry. While much of the earlier and ongoing research is based in lab settings or haute cuisine situations, the study of a variety of sensory effects in actual field settings of a variety of restaurant segments is likely to be fruitful for understanding consumer responses and strategies for maximizing pleasurable responses of targeted patrons. Additionally, future research should substantiate the current findings in other geographic locations of the casual dining sector.

References

Bitner, M. J. (1992). 'Servicescapes: The impact of physical surroundings on customers and employees', *Journal of Marketing*, 56(2): 57–71.

Caldwell, C. and Hibbert, S. A. (2002). 'The influence of music tempo and musical preference on restaurant patrons' behavior', *Psychology and Marketing*, 19(11): 895–917.

Crisinel, A. S., Cosser, S., King, S., Jones, R., Petrie, J. and Spence, C. (2012). 'A bittersweet symphony: Systematically modulating the taste of food by changing the sonic properties of the sound track playing in the background', *Food Quality and Preference*, 24(1): 201–204.

Dobbins, G. H., Lane, I. M. and Steiner, D. D. (1988). 'A note on the role of laboratory methodologies in applied behavioral research: Don't throw the baby out with the bath water', *Journal of Organizational Behavior*, 9(3): 281–286.

Edwards-Stuart, R. (2012). 'Molecular gastronomy in the UK', *Journal of Culinary Science and Technology*, 10(2): 97–105.

Guéguen, N., Le Guellec, H. and Jacob, C. (2004). 'Sound level of background music and alcohol consumption: An empirical evaluation', *Perceptual and Motor Skills*, 99(1): 34–38.

Guéguen, N., Le Guellec, H., Jacob, C., Morineau, T. and Lourel, M. (2008). 'Sound level of environmental music and drinking behavior: A field experiment with beer drinkers', *Alcoholism: Clinical & Experimental Research*, 32(10): 1795–1798.

Hair, J. F., Anderson, R. E., Tatham, R. L. and Black, W. C. (1998). *Multivariate Data Analysis*, 5th edition, Upper Saddle River, NJ: Prentice-Hall.

Kim, W. G. and Moon, Y. J. (2009). 'Customers' cognitive, emotional, and actionable response to the servicescape: A test of the moderating effect of restaurant type', *International Journal of Hospitality Management*, 28(1): 144–156.

Liu, Y. H. and Jang, S. (2009). 'The effects of dining atmospherics: An extended Mehrabian-Russell model', *International Journal of Hospitality Management*, 28(4): 494–503.

Magnini, V. P. and Thelen, S. T. (2008). 'The influence of music on perceptions of brand personality, décor, and service quality: The case of classical music in a fine-dining restaurant', *Journal of Hospitality and Leisure Marketing*, 16(3): 286–300.

Milliman, R. E. (1986). 'The influence of background music on the behavior of restaurant patrons', *Journal of Consumer Research*, 13(2): 286–289.

North, A. C. and Hargreaves, D. J. (1996). 'The effects of music on responses to a dining area', *Journal of Environmental Psychology*, 16(1): 55–64.

North, A. C., Shilock, A. and Hargreaves, D. J. (2003). 'The effect of musical style on restaurant customers' spending', *Environment and Behavior*, 35(5): 712–718.

Oakes, S. (2000). 'The influence of the musicscape within service environments', *Journal of Services Marketing*, 14(7): 539–556.

Ryu, K. and Han, H. (2010). 'Influence of the quality of food, service, and physical environment on customer satisfaction and behavioral intention in quick-casual restaurants: Moderating role of perceived price', *Journal of Hospitality and Tourism Research*, 34(3): 310–329.

Ryu, K. and Han, H. (2011). 'New or repeat customers: How does physical environment influence their experience?', *International Journal of Hospitality Management*, 30(3): 599–611.

Ryu, K., Lee, H. R. and Kim, W. G. (2012). 'The influence of the quality of the physical environment, food, and service on restaurant image, customer perceived value, customer satisfaction, and behavioral intentions', *International Journal of Contemporary Hospitality Management*, 30(3): 200–223.

15

SERVICE EXPERIENCES IN THE TOURISM AND HOSPITALITY INDUSTRY

Conceptualization and measurement

Girish Prayag, Jörg Finsterwalder and C. Michael Hall

Introduction

This chapter critically evaluates existing ways of conceptualizing and measuring service experiences in the tourism and hospitality industry. The chapter starts with an overview of different ways (process vs. outcome-based) of conceptualizing service experience and progresses to review the concept of service-dominant (SD) logic. This is followed by a review of current methods of measuring the service experience, including service blueprinting, service mapping and service quality. The chapter thereafter discusses the 'overlooked' dimensions of the service experience such as group interactions, religious criteria and spiritual dimensions amongst others. A case study on halal and service experiences is also provided. The chapter concludes with several suggestions on how to progress the service experience research agenda in the tourism and hospitality industry.

The concept of service experience(s)

Although there is widespread agreement on the importance of the concept of service experience in marketing, there are divergent views on how it should be characterized (Helkkula 2011). Traditionally, service experience has been conceptualized as an experience that is unique to an individual at a specific point in time, in a specific location, in the context of a specific event. Also, service experiences often occur as a series of events that influence customer satisfaction (Laws 1998). More recent conceptualizations of the term suggest that service experiences are simultaneously individual and social (Goulding 2005) but increasingly experiential (Mathwick et al. 2001). The latter dimension is the foundation for service excellence (Mathwick et al. 2001). Service experiences incorporate what are commonly referred to as service encounters and these encounters happen at different stages of the consumption process such as pre-purchase, onsite and post-purchase (Klaus 2014; Vitterso et al. 2001). This view of service experiences has been described as the 'process view' that implicitly suggests various stages or phases over time, thereby involving a transformation or change in customer behaviour and evaluations of the encounter (Helkkula 2011). Indeed, service experience, according to this view, is not a state but a dynamic process that evolves from the pre-purchase to post-purchase stages of the consumption process. Organizations need to understand the totality of the service experience, including customer experiences and its meaning, to be able to deliver superior encounters with customers (Meyer and Schwager 2007).

There is also the view of outcome-based service experiences, where the latter is often linked to outcomes such as service quality, perceived value and satisfaction (Klaus and Maklan 2011; Parasuraman et al. 1985). According to this view, service experiences are associated with customers' evaluations of the service, preferences, moods and emotions (Fiske and Taylor 1991). The consumer mainly assesses two components of service quality: technical and functional. The former refers to what the customer is actually receiving from the service while the latter refers to the manner in which the service is delivered (Parasuraman et al. 1985). Hence, management of the service experience is primarily concerned with quality issues and productivity. Far too often companies focus on the 'technical quality', leaving untapped a crucial resource – the ability to understand and manage the true nature of customer satisfaction (Otto and Ritchie 1996). Perhaps more than any other service industry, tourism has the potential to elicit strong emotional and experiential reactions by consumers (Otto and Ritchie 1996). In fact, tourism and hospitality experiences can elicit extraordinary experiences (Arnould and Price 1993) through interactions with the physical (natural and built) environments, called servicescapes (Bitner 1992), as well as through interactions with others (employees and other customers) (Finsterwalder and Kuppelwieser 2011). Industry managers using only service quality or attribute-based measures of service may therefore not fully understand the impact of the service experience on consumers (Otto and Ritchie 1996).

The multifaceted nature of the service experience and the complex service environment facing many industries such as airlines, healthcare and tourism are increasingly characterized by interconnection of services and performance management, requiring service managers to develop service management strategies from customers' point of view (Gustafsson et al. 2003; Obenour et al. 2006). Management of the physical setting, service design and resourcing decisions are crucial management responsibilities that facilitate or hamper the delivery of service excellence. Increasingly, service organizations are using service (re)design for radical changes in service delivery (Faché 2000). Also, by focusing on customer touchpoints (i.e. encounters between the customer and the organization), organizations are able to understand how service experiences are constructed and remembered while customers actively participate in service design. This is perhaps why the concept of service experience is described as the core of the service offering and service design (Zomerdijk and Voss 2010). It is a key concept of the service-dominant logic (SD-logic), which views the service experience as the basis of all business (Vargo and Lusch 2004).

The SD-logic

A central tenet of the SD-logic is the co-creation of service experiences (Vargo and Lusch 2004). On the supplier side, co-creation can be driven by service design innovation that enables the organization to remain competitive (Shaw et al. 2011). In the past, service providers adopted a service orientation to remain competitive. Service orientation has been conceptualized in two different ways. First, service orientation occurs at the individual level whereby service employees are either service oriented or not. Second, the extent to which an organization is service oriented determines its service orientation (Homburg et al. 2002).

The latter specifically considers internal service design characteristics and how the marketing strategy supports the organization to become service oriented. In recent years, this concept of service orientation has evolved alongside the SD-logic (Vargo and Lusch 2004). One major criticism of service orientation is that companies tend to be management driven as opposed to customer driven in service design. To the contrary, SD-logic is philosophically grounded in a commitment to collaborative processes with customers, service partners and employees. It is based on an interwoven fabric of actors, viewed as employees, customers, organizations and other business partners, rather than the often fragmentary approach of service orientation that focuses mainly on service industries, thereby making the SD-logic a more holistic approach to managing service and product experiences (Lusch et al. 2007).

SD-logic encourages an organization to be customer centric, market driven and learning oriented (Li and Petrick 2008). The tourism industry in particular relies on building relationships with customers, building networks among service providers to deliver experiential value, and service excellence to remain competitive. These facets of the tourism industry suggest that SD-logic should be a given for businesses (Li and Petrick 2008) and support for its adoption can be found in several tourism and hospitality studies (Fitz Patrick et al. 2013; Shaw et al. 2011). For example, Fitz Patrick et al. (2013) used SD-logic to examine hotel intellectual capital (IC) disclosures of 20 publicly listed European and US hotels and found that these hotels typically disclose information related to brand value, guest experience and employees but are overlooking the capacity for value creation from such intellectual capital.

The concept of co-creation is relatively well advanced in some of the elements of the tourism industry, even if research on this phenomenon is still in its infancy (Shaw et al. 2011). In tourism, multiple actors, such as travel agencies, booking offices, tour operators, their employees as well as their customers, and other resources such as the destination itself, including its infrastructure and features, are involved in co-creating service experiences. Such service experiences are fluid and transcend traditional boundaries across service businesses and customers. These boundaries are often defined in economic terms but also include cultural and geographical components that must be managed. In this way, the tourist is not only a (co-)creator of the service experience (i.e. adopting producer and consumer roles interchangeably) but also a creator of experiences for other consumers and producers at the destination. For example, an important issue in the attractiveness of some destinations, events or locations is the presence of other visitors who are part of a shared experience without which the experience would be much less enjoyable (Reicher 2011).

Although SD-logic captures the interactions of the different dynamic actors and structures through systems thinking and by delineating different systems levels (micro, meso and macro) (Chandler and Vargo 2011; Vargo and Akaka 2012), stronger emphasis needs to be placed on tourism-specific elements in SD-logic and 'the larger constellations within which actors become joined by service over time and space' (Chandler and Lusch 2015: p. 6). For example, the experience of tourists often includes landscapes that require an understanding of the interactions between space, place and time or 'sense of place' to fully appreciate their effects on 'own' and 'other' tourist behaviour. A major weakness of SD-logic in a complex multiscale product environment, such as tourism, is the capacity for different actors to collaborate together as part of the tourism value chain given different sets of orientations towards consumers (Cooper and Hall 2013). As noted already, non-human, or non-controllable, elements of the tourism system that may be extremely important with respect to destination and tourist experiences, and may even be dominant drivers for customer satisfaction in some markets (Hall et al. 2011), do not sit easily within the governance and metagovernance structures required for the implementation of SD-logic at a destination scale. Given the perceived limitations of SD-logic to deal with the role and participation of non-humans in tourism systems it is therefore not surprising that a number of scholars interested in the visitor experience have engaged in actor-network theory as a way of explaining successful attractions and experiences (Van der Duim and Caalders 2008; Zapata et al. 2011).

Measurement of service experiences

The design of services to create memorable experiences is not new (Zehrer 2009). Traditionally, the service blueprint technique has been used to create and enhance customer service experiences. The service blueprint is essentially a method by which the service production and delivery process is described including chains of activities, the use of facilitating goods and equipment, and time and cost effects (Gummesson 1990). It records and maps the events and processes which the customer experiences (Laws 1998). The service blueprint is based on the identification of 'moments-of-truth' and 'fail points' that enable organizations to maximize customer satisfaction or activate service recovery strategies (Zeithaml et al. 1990). It remains a favoured approach in service design that enables service providers to understand critical incidents and shape customers' emotional experiences accordingly (Zehrer 2009).

In general, a service blueprint has three main mechanisms: (1) it should incorporate a time dimension within the service design, thereby allowing managers to follow the progression of the service delivery system which the customer experiences; (2) it should show the core and ancillary services as well as their interconnectedness; and (3) it should incorporate service performance standards for each stage of the process (Shostack 1985). More recently, the concept of service experience blueprint (SEB) has emerged to reflect the shift from managing services to managing experiences (Patrício et al. 2008). Modern technology has revolutionized service delivery and service offerings have evolved to multi-interface systems where technology plays a central role for both front stage interactions and back stage support processes (Patrício et al. 2008). SD-logic emphasizes the role of service providers offering value propositions, which customers accept or renegotiate and then transform into value through usage in a particular context (Chandler and Vargo 2011; Vargo and Lusch 2004). In this new context, differentiating the service experience and adding value to the firm's offerings (Pine and Gilmore 1998) require a multidisciplinary method for service experience design (Patrício et al. 2008). Accordingly, SEB has been proposed as a new multidisciplinary method of service design for technology-enabled multi-interface service experiences.

A related technique, service mapping, emerged alongside the initial service blueprint. Service mapping visually defines a service system, displaying each sub-process within the sequence. The service map shows five components: (1) the explicit actions the customer takes, (2) the visible specific contact points and interactions between the customer and front-line staff, (3) invisible contact employee actions, (4) support processes and (5) physical evidence (Berry 1995; Bitner et al. 2008; Laws 1998). Equally popular are the drama production principles in service design. This approach is based on a theatre metaphor, suggesting that the service experience needs to be orchestrated during the service encounter where actors, directors, supporting cast, the set, the audience and the script must be cohesively aligned to provide the best customer experience (Grove et al. 1998). However, this approach has been criticized given that many service encounters today are more participatory than spectator based (Pine and Gilmore 1999).

Within the tourism and hospitality industry, measurement of service experiences has prioritized service quality dimensions using the SERVQUAL (Parasuraman et al. 1985) and SERVPERF (Cronin and Taylor 1992) methods or adapted versions thereof. SERVQUAL was originally designed with 10 dimensions and later refined to 5 (reliability, tangibility, responsiveness, assurance and empathy). The five dimensions pertain to the evaluation of the human interaction element in service delivery (Bitner et al. 1990; Parasuraman et al. 1988). The model has been criticized for several deficiencies in its conceptualization (Cronin and Taylor 1992) and operationalization (Babakus and Boller 1992). The main criticism with regards to dimensionality centres on the disconfirmation paradigm used by SERVQUAL. Also, the applicability of the SERVQUAL instrument to tourism services has been questioned (e.g. Saleh and Ryan 1991). The tourism experience is different from other experiences (e.g. retail) in the sense that tourists have the opportunity of creating satisfaction by upgrading or downgrading experiences. They will engage in value displacement, which is the downgrading of an unsatisfactory experience in terms of its contribution to an overall holiday experience (Ryan 1995). Others have sought to develop industry-specific service quality measures such as DINESERV (Stevens et al. 1995) for restaurants, LODGSERV (Knutson et al. 1990) for the lodging industry and HOLSERV (Wong et al. 1999) for mid-luxury hotels, but these measures are still embedded in the original SERVQUAL dimensions. One fundamental flaw with SERVQUAL and its adapted versions is that the model focuses on individual components of the service encounter, which are judged as good or bad quality, but this does not imply that the overall service experience is also of high or low quality (Maklan and Klaus 2011). These models are outcome focused and ignore that the service experience may be sensorial, emotional, physical and spiritual (Gentile et al. 2007), thus failing to capture the true essence of service encounters or moments of truth as described in the services marketing literature (Bitner et al. 1994).

'Overlooked' dimensions of service experiences in tourism and hospitality
Emotional and sensorial encounters

Despite the increasing number of studies evaluating emotional aspects of both tourism (e.g. Bigné et al. 2005; Prayag et al. 2013) and hospitality experiences (Jang and Namkung 2009; Prayag et al. 2015a), emotional aspects have been captured mainly using recall techniques in the post-consumption stage which are problematic (Hosany et al. 2015; Li et al. 2015). With a few exceptions (Kim and Fesenmaier 2015; Nawijn et al. 2013), capturing emotion *in situ* or real time can offer better insights into the tourist experience. To this effect, the use of neuroscience techniques is necessary to understand emotional encounters of tourists as they happen but these remain rarely used (Li et al. 2015). Likewise, tourism and hospitality studies have systematically prioritized the visual aspects of the tourism experience over other senses (Pan and Ryan 2009). Several authors argue the need to incorporate other senses in evaluations of the servicescapes such as smellscapes, soundscapes, tastescapes or geographies of touch (Agapito et al. 2013; Urry 2002). The combination of traditional psychology models of the influence of the senses on behaviour with, for example, the ecological model (Gibson 1979) which highlights the environment as a crucial determinant of what is perceived, will strengthen research in capturing and understanding of the tourist experience. Apart from the five human senses (exteroceptive senses), which provide information on how we react to the external environment, neuroscience suggests that sensory signals received by the brain can also derive from the internal body (interoceptive senses), pertaining to body awareness (Agapito et al. 2013; Damasio 2003). Thus, using a paradigm of embodiment may also expand our comprehension of tourist encounters with, for example, food (Everett 2008) and destinations (Scarles 2010). In this way new insights into service experiences based on the role of human senses in consumer behaviour can be achieved as well as their influence on perception, judgement and behaviour (Krishna 2012).

Group interactions and encounters in service experiences

While existing service quality measures incorporate a strong service interaction dimension, this dimension is far too often evaluated at the individual level. This is important to customize service delivery but there is also the need to include evaluations of group interactions as the evaluation of group service encounters to improve quality. Service encounters in the tourism industry tend to involve a high level of human interaction, requiring managers to understand these dynamics as they influence customers' assessment of their experiences (Stauss and Mang 1999). The majority of tourism and hospitality experiences happen in contexts where multiple customers are present, often in group interactions and encounters. In the services marketing literature, a group has been defined as 'the assemblage of two or more people who share common interests or goals, perceive or may develop some form of cohesiveness and who interact with one another' (Finsterwalder and Tuzovic 2010: p. 111). The involvement of multiple customers in the service experience can be differentiated through the way they cooperate with each other to create the experience (Finsterwalder and Tuzovic 2010). For example, white-water rafting experiences require participants to cooperate with each other in delivering the experience (Arnould and Price 1993; Finsterwalder and Kuppelwieser 2011; Hall and McArthur 1991), highlighting the importance of understanding group interactions in the service encounter.

Spirituality and service encounters

While several studies suggest that the tourism experience can be spiritual (Prayag et al. 2015b), including the travel experience itself (Willson et al. 2013), and despite the influence of spirituality on consumer behaviour being well acknowledged (Ulvoas-Moal 2010), spiritual and religious aspects of the service experience have been largely ignored in the tourism and hospitality industries, with the possible exception of wilderness and climbing experience in which transcendental experiences have long been recognized (Hall 1992; Tsaur et al. 2013). However, a rich body of research exists on workplace spirituality (WPS) (Lips-Wiersma and Mills 2014) and how it facilitates emotional labour. Religious support, for example, positively buffers the negative effects of emotional labour (Byrne et al. 2011). WPS can therefore contribute meaningfully to improve service quality, customer satisfaction and loyalty (Lee et al. 2014). For example, the spiritual climate at work has a positive impact on customer experiences due to pleasant employee service (Pandey et al. 2009). Also, consumer religiosity and spirituality have a strong effect on forgiveness as a response to service failure (Tsarenko and Tojib 2012). Hence, understanding spiritual and religious aspects of service experiences, including service response, may offer alternative ways of conceptualizing service encounters and the management of service delivery.

Halal requirements of consumers and service encounters

One of the most significant areas of service experience that includes a religious dimension is the basic requirement of meeting the needs of travellers who follow different sets of religious beliefs and possible interaction between members of different religions (Poria et al. 2003). However, from a service marketing perspective far too much framing of the religion and travel relationship is undertaken in the context of pilgrimage and other spiritual journeys (Eid 2012). As a result, the more mundane, yet arguably essential elements of the everyday tourism and hospitality service experience for believers such as religious food requirements, room requirements and other religious strictures are often ignored (Du Rand and Heath 2006; Wan Hassan and Hall 2003). Everyday actions are as important to religious identity as specific acts of pilgrimage are, and it is important that the tourism and hospitality industry seek to understand and work with customers who consume within a religious context in order to be able to provide positive experiences (Syed Marzuki et al. 2012, 2013). This necessity is also becoming increasingly important as international tourism continues to grow, leading tourism and hospitality providers to have to supply services outside of the cultural and religious norms of their own country.

A good example of the need to be aware of the religious context of service in tourism and hospitality is the case of halal. Halal is the term that is applied to what is permissible in Islam. Although it is often thought of by many non-Muslims as only referring to certain types of meat and how it has been slaughtered and prepared, it in fact refers to the total set of what is permissible to consume and how to consume in everyday life (Syed Marzuki et al. 2012). Awareness of halal is extremely important when providing services to Muslim customers as there is evidence to suggest that Muslim customers tend to be more committed to their beliefs and practices than those of other faiths, including with respect to the acceptance of taboos on certain types of foods (Muhamad and Mizerski 2013). A clear starting point for hospitality services with respect to halal is clearly the importance of making halal foods available and ensuring that they are prepared in such a way as to not come into contact with foods that are 'haram' (prohibited). However, for accommodation providers the provision of services to the Islamic tourism market is much wider in terms of the need to provide environments that reinforce guest modesty and even segregated areas for swimming and spa use (Nassar et al. 2015). In predominantly Muslim countries the demand for halal services will not be regarded as unusual; however, in Western countries the growth in Islamic travel provides new challenges in terms of service practices as well as employee education.

Conclusion

Although a focus on service experiences in general and in the tourism and hospitality industry in particular is not entirely new, it marks an important shift in perspective towards integrating the customer in the creation of meaningful sensory and emotional encounters. The shift signifies a move from a company- and product-oriented view via a relationship-focused understanding towards a more customer-centric approach. This necessitates a different approach in regard to the design and marketing of customer experiences (Schmitt 2014) in tourism and hospitality. Customers as the supposed co-creators of their own experiences should be more closely integrated in service experience design processes, after service experiences have been mapped or blueprinted and fail points identified. To this effect integrating the 'overlooked' dimensions may not only improve both researchers' and practitioners' understanding of tourism and hospitality service experiences but also provide creative and innovative ways for the industry to differentiate and compete more effectively to serve an increasingly heterogeneous customer base.

Service experiences should appeal to all customer senses, and not only the visual, to create memorable encounters. Also, customers' service experiences do not occur in a vacuum but increasingly in the vicinity of 'others' that impact both production and consumption. Taking this aspect of service encounters, including customers' willingness and ability to collaborate and to socially interact with fellow customers, into account will be necessary to progress the service research agenda in tourism. Additionally, new facets of experiences such as spiritual service encounters and the religious context of consumption require more investigation and research as well as implementation in staff training and education programmes. It is suggested that pursuing these avenues should improve customer experiences of service encounters in a way that benefits all actors, companies and customers alike.

References

Agapito, D., Mendes, J. and Valle, P. (2013). 'Exploring the conceptualization of the sensory dimension of tourist experiences', *Journal of Destination Marketing and Management*, 2(2): 62–73.

Arnould, E. J. and Price, L. L. (1993). 'River magic: Extraordinary experience and the extended service encounter', *Journal of Consumer Research*, 20(1): 24–45.

Babakus, E. and Boller, G. W. (1992). 'An empirical assessment of the SERVQUAL scale', *Journal of Business Research*, 24(3): 253–268.

Berry, L. L. (1995). 'Relationship marketing of services – growing interest, emerging perspectives', *Journal of the Academy of Marketing Science*, 23(4): 236–245.

Bigné, J. E., Andreu, L. and Gnoth, J. (2005). 'The theme park experience: An analysis of pleasure, arousal and satisfaction', *Tourism Management*, 26(6): 833–844.

Bitner, M. J. (1992). 'Servicescapes: The impact of physical surroundings on customers and employees', *Journal of Marketing*, 56(2): 57–71.

Bitner, M. J., Booms, B. H. and Mohr, L. A. (1994). 'Critical service encounters: The employee's viewpoint', *Journal of Marketing*, 58(4): 95–106.

Bitner, M. J., Booms, B. H. and Tetreault, M. S. (1990). 'The service encounter: Diagnosing favourable and unfavourable incidents', *Journal of Marketing*, 54(2): 71–84.

Bitner, M. J., Ostrom, A. L. and Morgan, F. N. (2008). 'Service blueprinting: A practical technique for service innovation', *California Management Review*, 50(3): 66–94.

Byrne, C. J., Morton, D. M. and Dahling, J. J. (2011). 'Spirituality, religion, and emotional labour in the workplace', *Journal of Management, Spirituality and Religion*, 8(4): 299–315.

Chandler, J. D. and Lusch, R. F. (2015). 'Service systems: A broadened framework and research agenda on value propositions, engagement, and service experience', *Journal of Service Research*, 18(1): 6–22.

Chandler, J. D. and Vargo, S. L. (2011). 'Contextualization and value-in-context: How context frames exchange', *Marketing Theory*, 11(1): 35–49.

Cooper, C. and Hall, C. M. (2013). *Contemporary Tourism: An International Approach*, Oxford: Goodfellows.

Cronin Jr, J. J. and Taylor, S. A. (1992). 'Measuring service quality: A re-examination and extension', *Journal of Marketing*, 56(3): 55–68.

Damasio, A. (2003). 'Feelings of emotion and the self', *Annals of the New York Academy of Sciences*, 1001: 253–261.

Du Rand, G. E. and Heath, E. (2006). 'Towards a framework for food tourism as an element of destination marketing', *Current Issues in Tourism*, 9(3): 206–234.

Eid, R. (2012). 'Towards a high-quality religious tourism marketing: The case of Hajj service in Saudi Arabia', *Tourism Analysis*, 17(4): 509–522.

Everett, S. (2008). 'Beyond the visual gaze? The pursuit of an embodied experience through food tourism', *Tourist Studies*, 8(3): 337–358.

Faché, W. (2000). 'Methodologies for innovation and improvement of services in tourism', *Managing Service Quality: An International Journal*, 10(6): 356–366.

Finsterwalder, J. and Kuppelwieser, V. G. (2011). 'Co-creation by engaging beyond oneself: The influence of task contribution on perceived customer-to-customer social interaction during a group service encounter', *Journal of Strategic Marketing*, 19(7): 607–618.

Finsterwalder, J. and Tuzovic, S. (2010). 'Quality in group service encounters: A theoretical exploration of the concept of a simultaneous multi-customer co-creation process', *Managing Service Quality: An International Journal*, 20(2): 109–122.

Fiske, S. T. and Taylor, S. E. (1991). *Social Cognition*, 2nd edition, New York: McGraw-Hill.

Fitz Patrick, M., Davey, J., Muller, L. and Davey, H. (2013). 'Value-creating assets in tourism management: Applying marketing's service-dominant logic in the hotel industry', *Tourism Management*, 36(1): 86–98.

Gentile, C., Spiller, N. and Noci, G. (2007). 'How to sustain the customer experience: An overview of experience components that co-create value with the customer', *European Management Journal*, 25(5): 395–410.

Gibson, J. J. (1979). *The Ecological Approach to Visual Perception*, Boston, MA: Houghton-Mifflin.

Goulding, C. (2005). 'Grounded theory, ethnography and phenomenology: A comparative analysis of three qualitative strategies for marketing research', *European Journal of Marketing*, 39(3): 294–308.

Grove, S. J., Fisk, R. P. and Dorsch, M. J. (1998). 'Assessing the theatrical components of the service encounter: A cluster analysis examination', *The Service Industries Journal*, 18(3): 116–134.

Gummesson, E. (1990). 'Marketing organization in service businesses: The role of the part-time marketer', in R. Teare, L. Moutinho and N. Morgan (eds.), *Managing Marketing Services in the 1990s* (pp. 35–48), London: Cassell Educational.

Gustafsson, A., Nilsson, L. and Johnson, M. D. (2003). 'The role of quality practices in service organizations', *International Journal of Service Industry Management*, 14(2): 232–244.

Hall, C. M. (1992). *Wasteland to World Heritage: Wilderness Preservation in Australia*, Carlton, VIC: Melbourne University Press.

Hall, C. M., James, M. and Baird, T. (2011). 'Forests and trees as charismatic mega-flora: Implications for heritage tourism and conservation', *Journal of Heritage Tourism*, 6(4): 309–323.

Hall, C. M. and McArthur, S. (1991). 'Commercial white water rafting in Australia: Motivations and expectations of the participant and the relevance of group size for the rafting experience', *Leisure Options: Australian Journal of Leisure and Recreation*, 1(4): 25–31.

Helkkula, A. (2011). 'Characterizing the concept of service experience', *Journal of Service Management*, 22(3): 367–389.

Homburg, C., Hoyer, W. D. and Fassnacht, M. (2002). 'Service orientation of a retailer's business strategy: Dimensions, antecedents, and performance outcomes', *Journal of Marketing*, 66(4): 86–101.

Hosany, S., Prayag, G., Deesilatham, S., Causevic, S. and Odeh, K. (2015). 'Measuring tourists' emotional experiences: Further validation of the destination emotion scale', *Journal of Travel Research*, 54(4): 482–495.

Jang, S. S. and Namkung, Y. (2009). 'Perceived quality, emotions, and behavioral intentions: Application of an extended Mehrabian–Russell model to restaurants', *Journal of Business Research*, 62(4): 451–460.

Kim, J. J. and Fesenmaier, D. R. (2015). 'Measuring emotions in real time: Implications for tourism experience design', *Journal of Travel Research*, 54(4): 419–429.

Klaus, P. (2014). *Measuring Customer Experience. How to Develop and Execute the Most Profitable Customer Experience*, New York: Palgrave Macmillan.

Klaus, P. and Maklan, S. (2011). 'Bridging the gap for destination extreme sports: A model of sports tourism customer experience', *Journal of Marketing Management*, 27(13–14): 1341–1365.

Knutson, B., Stevens, P., Wullaert, C., Patton, M. and Yokoyama, F. (1990). 'LODGSERV: A service quality index for the lodging industry', *Journal of Hospitality and Tourism Research*, 14(2): 277–284.

Krishna, A. (2012). 'An integrative review of sensory marketing: Engaging the senses to affect perception, judgment and behaviour', *Journal of Consumer Psychology*, 22(3): 332–351.

Laws, E. (1998). 'Conceptualizing visitor satisfaction management in heritage settings: An exploratory blueprinting analysis of Leeds Castle, Kent', *Tourism Management*, 19(6): 545–554.

Lee, S., Lovelace, K. J. and Manz, C. C. (2014). 'Serving with spirit: An integrative model of workplace spirituality within service organizations', *Journal of Management, Spirituality and Religion*, 11(1): 45–64.

Li, S., Scott, N. and Walters, G. (2015). 'Current and potential methods for measuring emotion in tourism experiences: A review', *Current Issues in Tourism*, 18(9): 805–827.

Li, X. R. and Petrick, J. F. (2008). 'Examining the antecedents of brand loyalty from an investment model perspective', *Journal of Travel Research*, 47(1): 25–34.

Lips-Wiersma, M. S. and Mills, A. (2014). 'Understanding the basic assumptions about human nature in workplace spirituality: Beyond the critical versus positive divide', *Journal of Management Inquiry*, 23(2): 137–147.

Lusch, R. F., Vargo, S. L. and O'Brien, M. (2007). 'Competing through service: Insights from service-dominant logic', *Journal of Retailing*, 83(1): 5–18.

Maklan, S. and Klaus, P. (2011). 'Customer experience: Are we measuring the right things?', *International Journal of Market Research*, 53(6): 771–792.

Mathwick, C., Malhotra, N. and Rigdon, E. (2001). 'Experiential value: Conceptualization, measurement and application in the catalogue and Internet shopping environment', *Journal of Retailing*, 77(1): 39–56.

Meyer, C. and Schwager, A. (2007). 'Understanding customer experience', *Harvard Business Review*, 85(2): 117–126.

Muhamad, N. and Mizerski, D. (2013). 'The effects of following Islam in decisions about taboo products', *Psychology and Marketing*, 30(4): 357–371.

Nassar, M. A., Mostafa, M. and Reisinger, Y. (2015). 'Factors influencing travel to Islamic destinations: An empirical analysis of Kuwaiti nationals', *International Journal of Culture, Tourism and Hospitality Research*, 9(1): 36–53.

Nawijn, J., Mitas, O., Lin, Y. and Kerstetter, D. (2013). 'How do we feel on vacation? A closer look at how emotions change over the course of a trip', *Journal of Travel Research*, 52(2): 265–274.

Obenour, W., Patterson, M., Pedersen, P. and Pearson, L. (2006). 'Conceptualization of a meaning-based research approach for tourism service experiences', *Tourism Management*, 27(1): 34–41.

Otto, J. E. and Ritchie, J. B. (1996). 'The service experience in tourism', *Tourism Management*, 17(3): 165–174.

Pan, S. and Ryan, C. (2009). 'Tourism sense-making: The role of the senses and travel journalism', *Journal of Travel and Tourism Marketing*, 26(7): 625–639.

Pandey, A., Gupta, R. K. and Arora, A. P. (2009). 'Spiritual climate of business organizations and its impact on customers' experience', *Journal of Business Ethics*, 88(2): 313–332.

Parasuraman, A., Zeithaml, V. A. and Berry, L. L. (1985). 'A conceptual model of service quality and its implications for future research', *Journal of Marketing*, 49(4): 41–50.

Parasuraman, A., Zeithaml, V. A. and Berry, L. L. (1988). 'SERVQUAL', *Journal of Retailing*, 64(1): 12–40.

Patrício, L., Fisk, R. P. and Falcãoe Cunha, J. F. (2008). 'Designing multi-interface service experiences: The service experience blueprint', *Journal of Service Research*, 10(4): 318–334.

Pine, B. J. and Gilmore, J. H. (1998). 'Welcome to the experience economy', *Harvard Business Review*, 76(4): 97–105.

Pine, B. J. and Gilmore, J. H. (1999). *The Experience Economy: Work is Theatre and Every Business a Stage*, Boston, MA: Harvard Business Press.

Poria, Y., Butler, R. and Airey, D. (2003). 'Tourism, religion and religiosity: A holy mess', *Current Issues in Tourism*, 6(4): 340–363.

Prayag, G., Hosany, S. and Odeh, K. (2013). 'The role of tourists' emotional experiences and satisfaction in understanding behavioural intentions', *Journal of Destination Marketing and Management*, 2(2): 118–127.

Prayag, G., Khoo-Lattimore, C. and Sitruk, J. (2015a). 'Casual dining on the French Riviera: Examining the relationship between visitors' perceived quality, positive emotions, and behavioral intentions', *Journal of Hospitality Marketing and Management*, 24(1): 24–46.

Prayag, G., Mura, P., Hall, M. and Fontaine, J. (2015b). 'Drug or spirituality seekers? Consuming ayahuasca', *Annals of Tourism Research*, 52(May): 175–177.

Reicher, S. (2011). 'Mass action and mundane reality: An argument for putting crowd analysis at the centre of the social sciences', *Contemporary Social Science*, 6(3): 433–449.

Ryan, C. (1995). *Researching Tourist Satisfaction: Issues, Concepts, Problems*, London: Routledge.

Saleh, F. and Ryan, C. (1991). 'Analysing service quality in the hospitality industry using the SERVQUAL model', *The Service Industries Journal*, 11(3): 324–345.

Scarles, C. (2010). 'Where words fail, visuals ignite: Opportunities for visual auto ethnography in tourism research', *Annals of Tourism Research*, 37(4): 905–926.

Schmitt, B. (2014). 'Experiential marketing: A new framework for design and communications', *Design Management Review*, 25(4): 19–26.

Shaw, G., Bailey, A. and Williams, A. (2011). 'Aspects of service-dominant logic and its implications for tourism management: Examples from the hotel industry', *Tourism Management*, 32(2): 207–214.

Shostack, G. L. (1985). *Planning the Service Encounter*, Lexington, MA: Lexington Books.

Stauss, B. and Mang, P. (1999). 'Culture shocks in inter-cultural service encounters?', *Journal of Services Marketing*, 13(4/5): 329–346.

Stevens, P., Knutson, B. and Patton, M. (1995). 'DINESERV: A tool for measuring service quality in restaurants', *Cornell Hotel and Restaurant Administration Quarterly*, 36(2): 5–60.

Syed Marzuki, S. Z., Hall, C. M. and Ballantine, P. (2012). 'Restaurant manager and halal certification in Malaysia', *Journal of Foodservice Business Research*, 15(2): 195–214.

Syed Marzuki, S. Z., Hall, C. M. and Ballantine, P. W. (2013). 'Sustaining halal certification at restaurants in Malaysia', in C. M. Hall and S. Gössling (eds.), *Sustainable Culinary Systems: Local Foods, Innovation, and Tourism and Hospitality* (pp. 256–274). Abingdon: Routledge.

Tsarenko, Y. and Tojib, D. (2012). 'The role of personality characteristics and service failure severity in consumer forgiveness and service outcomes', *Journal of Marketing Management*, 28(9–10): 1217–1239.

Tsaur, S. H., Yen, C. H. and Hsiao, S. L. (2013). 'Transcendent experience, flow and happiness for mountain climbers', *International Journal of Tourism Research*, 15(4): 360–374.

Ulvoas-Moal, G. (2010). 'Exploring the influence of spirituality: A new perspective on senior consumers' behavior', *Advances in Consumer Research*, 37: 917–919.

Urry, J. (2002). *The Tourist Gaze*, 2nd edition, London: Sage.

Van der Duim, R. and Caalders, J. (2008). 'Tourism chains and pro-poor tourism development: An actor-network analysis of a pilot project in Costa Rica', *Current Issues in Tourism*, 11(2): 109–125.

Vargo, S. L. and Akaka, M. A. (2012). 'Value co-creation and service systems (re)formation: A service ecosystems view', *INFORMS Service Science*, 4(3): 207–217.

Vargo, S. L. and Lusch, R. F. (2004). 'Evolving to a new dominant logic for marketing', *Journal of Marketing*, 68(1): 1–17.

Vitterso, J., Vorkinn, M. and Vistad, O. I. (2001). 'Congruence between recreational and actual behavior – a prerequisite for optimal experiences?', *Journal of Leisure Research*, 33(2): 137–159.

Wan Hassan, M. and Hall, C. M. (2003). 'The demand for halal food among Muslim travelers in New Zealand', in C. M. Hall, E. Sharples, R. Mitchell, B. Cambourne and N. Macionis (eds.), *Food Tourism Around the World: Development, Management and Markets* (pp. 81–101), Oxford: Butterworth-Heinemann.

Willson, G. B., McIntosh, A. J. and Zahra, A. L. (2013). 'Tourism and spirituality: A phenomenological analysis', *Annals of Tourism Research*, 42(July): 150–168.

Wong, O. M. A., Dean, A. M. and White, C. J. (1999). 'Analysing service quality in the hospitality industry', *Managing Service Quality: An International Journal*, 9(2): 136–143.

Zapata, M. J., Hall, C. M., Lindo, P. and Vanderschaeghe, M. (2011). 'Can community-based tourism contribute to development and poverty alleviation? Lessons from Nicaragua', *Current Issues in Tourism*, 14(8): 725–749.

Zehrer, A. (2009). 'Service experience and service design: Concepts and application in tourism SMEs', *Managing Service Quality: An International Journal*, 19(3): 332–349.

Zeithaml, V. A., Parasuraman, A. and Berry, L. L. (1990). *Delivering Quality Service: Balancing Customer Perceptions and Expectations*, New York: The Free Press.

Zomerdijk, L. G. and Voss, C. A. (2010). 'Service design for experience-centric services', *Journal of Service Research*, 13(1): 67–82.

16

INNOVATIONS IN EXPERIENCE

Valentina Della Corte and Giovanna Del Gaudio

Introduction

The tourism industry is a hypercompetitive sector where abrupt and radical changes occur, the demand is identified through its variety and vulnerability, there is a growing process of globalization as well as there being continuous changes in inter-firm relationships (D'Aveni 1994), thus imposing dynamic strategic rules of the game. These peculiarities help us to understand in what a volatile context tourist firms operate nowadays and their consequent challenge in creating attractive products and offers to sustain their competitive advantage.

Furthermore, in this scenario witnessing the increase of dynamic tourist configurations (i.e. the dynamic packages of tour operators or of airline companies, etc.), customer satisfaction is more and more difficult to gain and the creation of an 'experiential product' becomes the mandatory path to go through for the achievement of a competitive position on the global market.

For tourist firms, the choice of concentrating their attention on the experiential component is due to the fact that this approach reveals a series of benefits (Buchmann et al. 2010) that concern the perception of the main strengths of tourist products, the creation of emotions, the sense of belonging and the social support on the demand side, while on the supply side, tourist firms can obtain empowerment and control if they adopt this kind of perspective.

The most important question is 'How can tourist firms achieve an experiential product?', or better, 'What do they need for the creation of experiential offers?'

The answer is the implementation of 'innovation' and, hence, the deployment of dynamic capabilities (Teece et al. 1997) that allow the adoption and management of such innovation, in the fruition phase.

The role of innovation has been studied for years in both economic and social fields (Schumpeter 1939). The relationship between innovation and positive outcomes has been demonstrated by several studies (Tavassoli and Karlsson 2015), although its ideation, introduction, implementation and management can be risky and uncertain (Mattsson and Orfila-Sintes 2014).

However, the creation of an experiential product through the use of innovation still represents a clear gap existing in the literature. Innovation and experience in the tourism industry have been analysed as distinct research streams. The possible interconnections have been underestimated, being analysed as separate rather than in their eventual cause–effect relationship.

Starting from this gap, the aim of this chapter is to demonstrate, through both the theoretical and the practical sections, that innovation and experience have to be conceived as connected since innovation can influence the generation of an experiential product and can represent itself as a cross-component in the experiential approach.

For this purpose, the chapter is structured in two main parts. The first one reviews the literature on the topics of innovation and experience. For the completion of the theoretical framework, the resource-based theory (RBT – Barney 1991), the service-dominant logic (SDL – Vargo and Lusch 2004), and the dynamic capability view (Teece et al. 1997) are analysed.

The second part refers to the analysis of a case study that facilitates the understanding not only of how innovation influences the creation of an experience approach but also of what are the real and concrete benefits obtained by the firm from the adoption of this vision and by the customer who lives the tourist experience. Finally, some conclusions underline the main theoretical and managerial insights and the further directions for the growth of research on these topics in the tourism industry.

Literature review and theoretical framework

The topics of innovation and experience in tourism have received considerable attention during the past two decades (Volo 2010; Buchmann et al. 2010; Dwyer et al. 2014). Although these themes constitute a pillar within both the tourism literature and the practical tourism world, their study as well as their application conceive them as separate issues rather than strictly interconnected. This chapter shows that the adoption of innovation and the creation of experience must be studied and applied simultaneously because innovation can both generate and support the tourist experience. In this sense, innovation is not only a determinant of experience but also an inseparable completion of experience. According to some authors (Volo 2010), innovation has a great impact on experience while for others the boundary between innovation and experience is not so clear since they have been studied separately. Hence, innovation as antecedent can provide an experience-based approach. On the other hand, the classic vision that views innovation and experience as two different topics has to be overcome, since innovation goes hand in hand with experience.

Right from these first reflections, it is possible to point out that both innovation and experience require an overlapping perspective between demand and offer. Indeed, on one side there is the managerial perspective since innovation has to be adopted/implemented and the tourism offer must be ideated in the light of experience. On the other, innovation must be used or drive use, and experience must be perceived in order to produce tourists' satisfaction.

At this point, it is appropriate to question why innovation and experience are so important in the tourism field. This strong overlap and dyad between innovation and experience can be explained through the comprehension of what the tourist product is and why it needs these two fundamental components.

The tourist product, also conceived according to an overlapping perspective (Casarin 1996; Pencarelli and Forlani 2002; Della Corte 2000, 2013), from a demand side:

> represents the global experience lived by the tourist while, from the offer side, is a
> complex product, made of local resources and firms' competencies, linked to the

actions of several actors in the market, which provide the different services, more or less integrated, according to different forms and configurations.

(Della Corte 2009: p. 1)

The strength of the cohesion between different perspectives (demand and offer) should ensure 'the creation of involving and unforgettable experiences' (Pencarelli and Forlani 2002) for the tourists. Indeed, tourist firms have become experience providers nowadays (Dwyer et al. 2014).

By definition, a tourist product is an 'experience product' shaped by multidimensional aspects (Cerquetti 2007). To foster innovation is considered an important facilitator or driver of strategic flexibility (Dwyer et al. 2014). In this way, tourist firms acquire advantage from the implementation of innovation (Zhou and Wu 2010). First of all, it is important to define what innovation is. Table 16.1 shows a series of definitions.

From Table 16.1, it emerges that innovation is conceived of as synonymous with 'new' in its delineation of new products or processes (Fagerberg and Godinho 2005; Tavassoli and Karlsson 2015), new knowledge and organizational designs (Tavassoli and Karlsson 2015). Several authors follow the classification made by Schumpeter (1939) who conceived of four different kinds of innovation: product, process, marketing and organizational.

Indeed, etymologically 'innovation' comes from the Latin words *novus* (new) and *innovatio* (something new). Both words express a change due to the ability of the firm (Tavassoli and Karlsson 2015), of the entrepreneur (Schumpeter 1939; Tidd and Bessant 2009) or of the managers. Innovation, indeed, results from the ability of entrepreneurs and top managers to

Table 16.1 Definitions of innovation

Author/s	Year	Definition
Schumpeter	1939	'New combination' of existing resources
Fagerberg et al.	2005	'Invention is the first occurrence of an idea for a new product or process, while innovation is the first attempt to carry it out into practice' (p. 4)
		'single innovation is often the result of a lengthy process involving many interrelated innovations'
Damanpour and Aravind	2012	It has generally been defined as the generation (development) or adoption (use) of new ideas or behaviours
Tavassoli and Karlsson	2015	Innovation is here seen as the purposeful result of the ability of firms to generate new knowledge and their decisions to apply it to new products and product varieties, processes, organizational designs, and combinations of inputs and markets
Zanello et al.	2016	Innovation includes not only the adoption of new products or processes, or new organizational and marketing practices (where 'new' means new to the world, new to the country or new to the firm), but, in line with Schumpeter (1934), also new business models and new sources of supply

Source: Authors.

understand the dynamics of market development and to recognize opportunities (Hamel and Prahalad 1990) through intense activity of scanning and monitoring of changes. These capabilities are the so-called 'dynamic capabilities' that can be bound to quick learning about external context and anticipation strategies, change in business models, ICT (information and communication technology) engagement and new product development. The deployment of dynamic capabilities allows radical innovations/changes and changes in existing ones, through new strategic concepts (Teece 2007).

Beyond this classification, innovation in the tourism industry is shaped by numerous factors (e.g. customer service, effective strategic plans and marketing campaigns, use of new technologies; Della Corte 2013). Hence, innovation can be analysed at different levels (Della Corte et al. 2009):

- Organizational level
- Network level
- Experiential level
- Technological level.

Although, at a first glimpse, the experiential and technological levels of innovation can respectively appear as synonymous with experience-based tourist product and innovation, this chapter will clarify the differences between these concepts. Indeed, for example, innovation seems to frequently be synonymous with ICT (Huang and Zhang 2015).

On the other hand, tourist experience, as a whole and not as a level of innovation, is 'a collusion between objects, places, others and a tourist's embodied interaction with this' (Buchmann et al. 2010: p. 230). The implementation of innovation also must be applied in both open and user innovation perspectives (Chesbrough 2003). Open innovation focuses on the role of the interactions between external and internal ideas in creating value (Chesbrough 2003), while 'user innovation' emphasizes the role of users leading innovators for their skills and competences.

The theoretical framework is also completed through the overlapping between RBT and SDL. RBT helps in the understanding of the bundle of strategic resources and competences, both at firm level and at systemic level, that are necessary for the creation of an experiential tourist product in order to sustain competitive advantage. In the competitive arena, firms and the tourist system sustain a competitive advantage if these resources are valuable, rare, not easy to imitate and exploited by the organization (the so-called VRIO resources – Barney 1991), as RBT claims.

The opportunity for the firms located within a specific destination is connected with the interaction with other tangible (cultural, natural, historical, gastronomic, etc.) and intangible (destination identity, brand image, shared values resources, local culture of offer, etc.) resources.

On the other hand, SDL outlines the importance that value is created when the consumer really encounters the service and, hence, the tourist product shaped by all its components. In the SDL approach, the tourist is conceived of as an operant resource (Vargo and Lusch 2004) since he/she can be a value co-producer and co-creator.

The overlapping between RBT and SDL is explained through the vision that the tourist can potentially be a value-creating resource that should make 'changes or a reorientation of the strategic policies' (Della Corte 2013). In this case, the consumer becomes a strategic resource, according to the RBT perspective, only if the firm can implement and manage the process that views the tourist and the company as leading actors of the value creation process.

The levels of innovation

The concept of innovation has to be inflected considering its different levels (organizational, experiential, network and technological) as well as the marketing and strategic politics that can be activated at both induced (these aim at attracting the tourist towards the destination before travel) and organic levels (this kind of strategy acts when the tourist experiences the destination).

Rather than 'real innovators', tourist firms are characterized by 'imitators and adapters' (Krizaj et al. 2014) that implement incremental innovations (Krizaj et al. 2014; Hjalager 2010). Innovations in this kind of industry differ from those in manufacturing sectors, since innovation changes do not depend on 'market research, design, R&D' (Krizaj et al. 2014), but rather on 'hidden' (Krizaj et al. 2014) and different dynamics.

Furthermore, innovation in the tourism industry must be considered not only at firm level (Camisón and Monfort-Mir 2012) but also at systemic level (Della Corte et al. 2009), trying to capture all the elements that shape tourist satisfaction (i.e. single services, attractiveness of tourist products, destination image; see Della Corte 2009, 2013).

Therefore, the identified dimensions of innovation refer, on one side, to firm level (organizational innovation), while on the other, to the network level (systemic innovation). This multilevel analysis becomes more complex if technological and experiential innovations support the firms and the system in the creation of unique and unforgettable tourist experiences.

Starting from the analysis of the firm level, the *organizational dimension* refers to the organizational structure, human resources competences, organizational culture, leadership style (García-Morales et al. 2011), collective processes (García-Morales et al. 2011) and administrative practices able to increase competitiveness. Novelties in internal organizational or, more generally, in organizational behaviours shape the organizational level of innovation.

The prevailing presence of SMEs (small and medium enterprises) in some geographic contexts (e.g. Italy, Bulgaria, Finland) makes it difficult to find this kind of innovation. Instead, big companies show a high degree of innovative capabilities for organizational changes.

Resources and competences, contemplated within RBT, need to be owned, exploited and combined but also organized (Barney 1991) in order to achieve a sustainable advantage. Hence, not only the organizational routines but also innovation in organization support the resources in being organizationally used in strategic terms.

This innovation is often deployed through the implementation of a competitive organizational model. In this direction, the organizational innovativeness can be implemented at different stages of the company life cycle, as the case study will demonstrate.

Organizational changes can reinforce the market position as well as affect a firm's performance. Indeed, organizational innovation is the key ingredient for better performance (García-Morales et al. 2011). If a firm is the first mover in the generation of innovation at organization level, this allows it to create so-called 'isolation mechanisms' (Lieberman and Montgomery 1998). These isolation mechanisms are inaccessible to competitors because they depend on the knowledge used for the creation and implementation of organizational innovation. In this way, a firm can obtain important benefits.

This kind of innovation requires an overall view that recalls other organizational aspects (e.g. leadership style, collective processes and human resources competences), since, first of all, managers must act as 'agents of changes' (García-Morales et al. 2011), to afterwards spread and disseminate the knowledge of this innovation to the other interested members (Senge et al. 1994; Nonaka and Takeuchi 1995).

While for the companies of other sectors, organizational innovation can be measured in terms of new patents, new products or the total amount that the organization has spent on R&D (García-Morales et al. 2011), in the tourist firms we can consider new systems referring to the 'structure of tasks and units, [that] modify the organization's management processes and administrative systems, motivate and reward organizational members, and enable organizational adaptation and change' (Damanpour and Aravind 2012: p. 423) as the output of organizational innovation.

Systemic innovation is the result of the cooperation between different actors coming from the same sector or from different areas. More precisely, this innovation arises from the activation of coopetition (cooperation + competition; see Dagnino and Padula 2007; Luo 2007) strategies where actors compete and cooperate at the same time for knowledge and resource sharing. In the optic of the tourism product, the coopetition mechanisms are necessary in order to create a systemic vision and to avoid the informative asymmetries that can occur between the demand and offer sides. If tourists require a more integrated product, an orchestration and coordination among products and services of the destination, tourist firms have to adopt systemic innovation. This enables them to guarantee a systematic synergy between the different elements of the destination, generating then the related tourist satisfaction.

The strategic factor of systemic innovation is the coopetition between policymakers, tourist operators, public and private actors, research institutes, regional agencies and associations, etc. The synergic involvement of the main stakeholders represents the will, by both pivotal and other actors, of local development.

This process must have elements of novelties in order to produce the systemic innovation, to create value and to strategically plan the local development, managing resources, competences, activities and dynamic capabilities in a systemic way. In SDL terms, the systemic innovation becomes more and more important since:

> tourism innovation systems have challenged the structure of service network toward a new one, and representation that captures new conceptualisations such as value line as a thinking logic, a mental model that views actors as facilitators of experiences and consumers/tourists as active contributors that are included in managing services.
>
> *(Sfandla and Björk 2013: p. 496)*

The single actors that shape the network and the system as a whole can be considered 'experience facilitators' (Sfandla and Björk 2013: p. 496).

This kind of innovation becomes the competitive factor of differentiation since it allows for strategic coordination in a new manner.

Technological innovation refers to the ideation and implementation of new tools and technologies that facilitate and enable processes, activities and content sharing. This level of innovation encompasses the other dimensions, acting as a transversal component that supports organizational, systemic and experiential innovation. Tourist firms that undertake the decision to implement technological innovation show proactive behaviour rather than 'wait and see' tactics.

Technological innovation has not only changed the rules of the tourism industry but also the way in which the tourist product is perceived and consumed (Huang and Zhang 2015).

The contribution of this innovation is fundamental in the induced phase in order to address the travel intentions and in the organic phase since it supports and increases the *in situ* tourist experience.

During the induced phase, technological innovation can support the tourist's decision process. Marketing strategies should use non-conventional techniques to promote and commercialize the destination and the single firms. In the organic phase, technology should be in support of resource valorization and fruition.

With reference to *experiential innovation*, the cultural and territorial identities assume a primary role since the promotion and valorization of the tourist experience must be the mirror of local resources. This vision is linked with the concept of the experiential tourist product: nowadays tourists like not only simply visiting the territorial attractions but also living real experiences within the destination. The concept of experiential innovation implies the necessity of creating an involvement with the places/resources in terms of sensorial pleasure, offering variety and cognitive stimulation (Park et al. 1986). The experience-based holiday emphasizes action, adventure and imagination.

The *experiential innovation* covers different aspects that contribute to the creation of a destination identity in the tourist's mind. The challenge of local actors and governance entities is to direct their strategic plans and marketing policies towards new horizons in the tourist experience (Vir Singh 2004). Hence, experiential innovation has to be applied at both systemic and firm levels, through the implementation of activities focused on the creation of highly experiential tourist products.

This innovation acts on the more symbolic or emotional aspects of consumption. It has a central role in the overall innovation process, since it acts both during the service provision and in terms of the immediate word-of-mouth (click-of-mouse) process, that also invests in the induced level (that is, the level aimed at capturing the interest of the consumer; Della Corte 2013) of the marketing process. It is in fact a transversal factor that greatly influences the whole process.

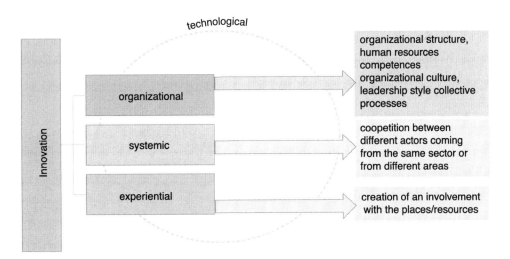

Figure 16.1   The levels of innovation

Source: Authors' own elaboration.

Innovation in experiences: the case study of Butterfield and Robinson

This section focuses particularly on the experiential dimension of innovation to explore how and to what extent experiential innovation influences and/or exploits the other kinds of innovation.

In particular, the case study helps in understanding the real existence of emotional engagement with the visited place or attraction. The subject of the case study is Butterfield and Robinson (B&R) for two main reasons. It is a tour operator and this kind of tourist actor demonstrates its complexity for the numerous and different offered services. This multiplicity allows one to examine if innovation can exist at different levels. Secondly, B&R has won 'awards (PURE Award for Experiential Travel) at the world's leading trade show for high end experiential travel' (PRWEB 2014).

B&R specializes in biking and walking routes. It was born in 1966, creating a unique concept that combines adventure in bike trips and various experiential elements.

In order to verify if the product of B&R can be defined as experiential, it is useful to analyse the different elements according to Smith's (1994) model (transportation and accommodation, restaurant, tours, cultural activities and entertainment, security and comfort, involvement in the product creation).

Transportation and accommodation are essential components for tour operators since they shape the classic configuration of the package. Starting from the transportation, this tour operator uses cycling as the main concept. The bike tours as well as the walking tours allow tourists to appreciate different landscapes, unexplored paths, to discover the local culture, to visit different places and attractors. For example, the 'Atlantic France Biking' starts from the pine forest of Ile de Orléon and finally arrives at Charentes Maritimes. In this case, the transportation becomes experiential because it is an unusual vehicle with which to visit so many distant places and it represents the starting point for an immersive tour. Bike tourism encompasses recreational, leisure and sporting activity and is embraced under slow tourism (Lamont 2009). In this kind of tourism, the travel is the key element (Dickinson and Lumsdon 2010) since the tourist can enjoy and experience various accommodations, different local foods, etc. The use of the bike is a slow alternative where 'there is a conscious trade-off between time and the quality of the experience' (Weerawardena and O'Cass 2004: p. 120).

Secondly, the accommodations are chosen according to the philosophy of living and experiencing the local culture. B&R does not propose classical hotels but rather castles, riads (traditional Moroccan houses), ryokans (traditional Japanese inns), etc. The basic idea is that they 'find properties that are unique expressions of the region. Often that means they've had a previous life as a monastery or a castle' (www.butterfield.com). These types of overnight accommodations go beyond the standard hotels and allow one to know an important aspect of the local lifestyle and culture. Indeed, they have the characteristics of being of 'unique character, personalized, homely, quality, and value added', making them highly experiential (Mcintosh and Siggs 2005).

As regards the restaurant component, B&R uses the expression 'food + wine' to propose a range from exclusive restaurants to traditional tastes of destinations and quiet picnics. Experiential innovation is deployed through, for example, mozzarella-making and pasta-making in Puglia, lessons on French wine with an international expert or a local market of fresh fish in Vancouver. The experience resides in the fact that food and food making belong also to the 'sensory level, and not just an intellectual one' (Long 1998: p. 195).

With reference to cultural activities and entertainment, B&R defines its offer with the term 'multiactive'. Biking or walking, it is possible to see the cultural attractions of the cities and UNESCO sites with a slow and peaceful rhythm. The true innovation resides in the fact that these components are thought through for the different targets. Indeed, also children can horseback-ride in the Dolomites or participate in sandcastle building, painting and artisanal chocolate lessons in Belgium. The integration within the local culture and history as well as the entertainment activities contribute to an experiential approach.

The best equipment for the different activities ensures the components 'security and comfort' and they are organized according to three pillars: bikes, walking/sticks and family equipment. Although these elements cannot be classified as experiential, it is also true that the partnerships between B&R and the world's leading bike manufacturers allow bike lovers to have custom-made vehicles (i.e. a Bianchi hybrid bike or a Scott e-venture electric-assisted bike). This represents the base for the experiential tours.

Finally, the involvement of the customer in the product creation is highlighted by the CEO, Norman Howe (Shankman 2015): 'People's understanding of how they perceive and experience the world has evolved into a more sophisticated, more mature sense of where the real magic lies. . . We see a lot of demand for emerging destinations that our customers like to get to first.' In this way, B&R creates a process of 'listening, action and co-creation' with the customer through social media marketing tools such as Facebook and a blog.

In this sense, technological innovation helps the strengthening and building up of new activities, products, etc. The technological support is used not only in the induced and organic phases but also in the post-travel stage.

The organizational innovation is perceived through a model that views not only the perfect work of executives and other staff within the organization but also the people directly involved in the service encounter. For example, the guides are teachers, painters, architects, botanists and biologists with the characteristics of consummate hosts, mind-readers and raconteurs.

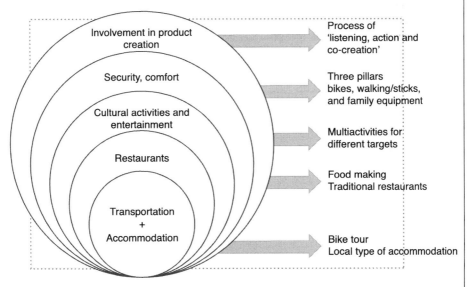

Figure 16.2   Butterfield and Robinson: innovations in experience

Source: Authors' own elaboration.

The systemic innovation is shown through the numerous partnerships in each served destination.

All these components help, support and complete the experiential product of Butterfield and Robinson.

This case study shows how innovation and experience are strictly interconnected in the tourism industry for the creation of high-quality experiential products that support and increase tourists' satisfaction. Moreover, the dynamic capabilities view highlighted the importance of the founders in creating this kind of offer in the tourism sector, in implementing a successful business model, and so anticipating/provoking changes. Indeed, RBT helped in understanding the importance of strategic resources such as the entrepreneurial capabilities or the brand identity of the company both in the niche market of bike lovers and for amateurs. Finally, SDL outlined the real willingness of B&R in creating and modifying the product according to the customers' needs and suggestions.

References

Barney, J. (1991). 'Firm resources and sustained competitive advantage', *Journal of Management*, 17(1): 99–120.

Buchmann, A., Moore, K. and Fisher, D. (2010). 'Experiencing film tourism: Authenticity and fellowship', *Annals of Tourism Research*, 37(1): 229–248.

Camisón, C. and Monfort-Mir, V. M. (2012). 'Measuring innovation in tourism from the Schumpeterian and the dynamic-capabilities perspectives', *Tourism Management*, 33(4): 776–789.

Casarin, F. (1996). *Il marketing dei prodotti turistici: specificità e varietà*, Turin: Giappichelli.

Cerquetti, M. (2007). 'La componente culturale del prodotto turistico integrato: la creazione di valore per il territorio attraverso i musei locali', *Sinergie*, 7(73–74): 421–438.

Chesbrough, H. (2003). 'The logic of open innovation: Managing intellectual property', *California Management Review*, 45(3): 33–58.

D'Aveni, R. (1994). *Hypercompetition: Managing the Dynamics of Strategic Management*, New York: Free Press.

Dagnino, G. B. and Padula, G. (2007). 'Untangling the rise of coopetition', *International Studies of Management and Organization*, 37(2): 32–52.

Damanpour, F. and Aravind, D. (2012). 'Managerial innovation: Conceptions, processes, and antecedents', *Management and Organization Review*, 8(2): 423–454.

Della Corte, V. (2000). *La gestione dei sistemi locali di offerta turistica*, Padua: Cedam.

Della Corte, V. (2009). *Imprese e sistemi turistici. Il management*, Milan: Egea.

Della Corte, V. (2013). *Imprese e sistemi turistici. Il management. II Edizione*, Milan: Egea.

Della Corte, V., Savastano, I. and Storlazzi, A. (2009). 'Service innovation in cultural heritages management and valorization', *International Journal of Quality and Service Sciences*, 1(3): 225–240.

Dickinson, J. E. and Lumsdon, L. (2010). *Slow Travel and Tourism*, London: Earthscan.

Dwyer, L. M., Cvelbar, L. K., Edwards, D. J. and Mihalič, T. A. (2014). 'Tourism firms' strategic flexibility: The case of Slovenia', *International Journal of Tourism Research*, 16(4): 377–387.

Fagerberg, J. and Godinho, M. M. (2005). 'Innovation and catching-up', in J. Fagenberg, D. C. Mowery and R. R. Nelson (eds.), *The Oxford Handbook of Innovation* (pp. 514–542), New York: Oxford University Press.

García-Morales, V. J., Matías-Reche, F. and Verdú-Jover, A. J. (2011). 'Influence of internal communication on technological proactivity, organizational learning, and organizational innovation in the pharmaceutical sector', *Journal of Communication*, 61(1): 150–177.

Hamel, G. and Prahalad, C. K. (1990). 'The core competence of the corporation', *Harvard Business Review*, 68(3): 79–91.

Hjalager, A. M. (2010). 'A review of innovation research in tourism', *Tourism Management*, 31(1): 1–12.

Huang, Y. and Zhang, M. (2015). 'Spatial analysis of regional distribution of tourism industry and tourism-related disciplines: A case study of Guangdong Province', *Journal of Tourism, Hospitality and Sports*, 6: 45–57.

Krizaj, D., Brodnik, A. and Bukovec, B. (2014). 'A tool for measurement of innovation newness and adoption in tourism firms', *International Journal of Tourism Research*, 16(2): 113–125.

Lamont, M. (2009). 'Reinventing the wheel: A definitional discussion of bicycle tourism', *Journal of Sport and Tourism*, 14(1): 5–23.

Lieberman, M. B. and Montgomery, D. B. (1998). *First-mover (Dis) Advantages: Retrospective and Link with the Resource-Based View*, Stanford, CA: Graduate School of Business, Stanford University.

Long, L. M. (1998). 'Culinary tourism: A folkloristic perspective on eating and otherness', *Southern Folklore*, 55(3): 181–204.

Luo, Y. (2007). 'A coopetition perspective of global competition', *Journal of World Business*, 42(2): 129–144.

Mcintosh, A. J. and Siggs, A. (2005). 'An exploration of the experiential nature of boutique accommodation', *Journal of Travel Research*, 44(1): 74–81.

Mattsson, J. and Orfila-Sintes, F. (2014). 'Hotel innovation and its effect on business performance', *International Journal of Tourism Research*, 16(4): 388–398.

Nonaka, I. and Takeuchi, H. (1995). *The Knowledge-Creating Company: How Japanese Companies Create the Dynamics of Innovation*, New York: Oxford University Press.

Park, C. W., Jaworski, B. J. and MacInnis, D. J. (1986). 'Strategic brand concept-image management', *Journal of Marketing*, 50(4): 135–145.

Pencarelli, T. and Forlani, F. (2002). 'Il marketing dei distretti turistici-sistemi vitali nell'economia delle esperienze', *Sinergie*, 58(2): 231–277.

PRWEB (2014). 'Butterfield and Robinson awarded for experiential travel and innovative blog', *PRWEB*, 25 November.

Schumpeter, J. A. (1934). *The Theory of Economic Development: An Inquiry into Profits, Capital, Credit, Interest, and the Business Cycle,* New Brunswick, NJ: Transaction.

Schumpeter, J. A. (1939). *Business Cycles*, New York: McGraw-Hill.

Senge, P., Roberts, C., Ross, R. B., Smith, B. J. and Kleiner, A. (1994). *The Fifth Discipline Fieldbook*, New York: Doubleday.

Sfandla, C. and Björk, P. (2013). 'Tourism experience network: Co-creation of experiences in interactive processes', *International Journal of Tourism Research*, 15(5): 495–506.

Shankman, S. (2015). 'Interview: Butterfield and Robinson CEO on the evolution of active travel', *Skift*, 29 January.

Smith, S. L. (1994). 'The tourism product', *Annals of Tourism Research*, 21(3): 582–595.

Tavassoli, S. and Karlsson, C. (2015). 'Persistence of various types of innovation analyzed and explained', *Research Policy*, 44(10): 1887–1901.

Teece, D. J. (2007). 'Explicating dynamic capabilities: The nature and microfoundations of (sustainable) enterprise performance', *Strategic Management Journal*, 28(13): 1319–1350.

Teece, D. J., Pisano, G. and Shuen, A. (1997). 'Dynamic capabilities and strategic management', *Strategic Management Journal*, 18(7): 509–533.

Tidd, J. and Bessant, J. (2009). *Inovação e empreendedorismo: administração*, Porto Alegre: Bookman.

Vargo, S. L. and Lusch, R. F. (2004). 'Evolving to a new dominant logic for marketing', *Journal of Marketing*, 68(1): 1–17.

Vir Singh T. (2004). *New Horizons in Tourism: Strange Experiences and Stranger Practices*, Wallingford, UK: CABI.

Volo, S. (2010). 'Bloggers' reported tourist experiences: Their utility as a tourism data source and their effect on prospective tourists', *Journal of Vacation Marketing*, 16(4): 297–311.

Weerawardena, J. and O'Cass, A. (2004). 'Exploring the characteristics of the market-driven firms and antecedents to sustained competitive advantage', *Industrial Marketing Management*, 33(5): 419–428.

Zanello, G., Fu, X., Mohnen, P. and Ventresca, M. (2016). 'The creation and diffusion of innovation in developing countries: A systematic literature review', *Journal of Economic Surveys*, 30(5): 884–912.

Zhou, K. Z. and Wu, F. (2010). 'Technological capability, strategic flexibility, and product innovation', *Strategic Management Journal*, 31(5): 547–561.

PART III

Customer satisfaction perspective

Part III comprises eight chapters covering the diverse dimensions of customer satisfaction and explores its linkages with consumer behaviour. Chapter 17 authored by David Drewery and Ron McCarville highlights the relation among service delivery, emotional constructs and behaviour. The service delivery, fulfilling the needs and desires of customers, creates positive emotional responses. Such clients become more likely to share stories of their positive experience with other clients and remain loyal to service providers in the future. In this way, satisfaction leads to positive outcomes for both the customer and the service provider.

Gaitree (Vanessa) Gowreesunkar and Stelios Varvaressos deal with the prime attributes influencing consumer behaviour besides offering an insight on the role of customer satisfaction in tourism in chapter 18. Customer satisfaction is considered a complex experience and influenced by different emotional constructs, behaviours and attributes. Understanding of elements causing satisfaction or dissatisfaction among tourists is vital for the success or failure of any business venture. Tourism destinations offer a combination of products and services and satisfaction/dissatisfaction usually occurs as a result of customer interactions with these elements. To explain the relationship between customer satisfaction and product/service attributes the chapter elaborates the Kano and HOLSAT models.

Pricing is considered to be a vital constituent in the consumer decision-making process, with implications in terms of customer satisfaction. Chapter 19 by Giampaolo Viglia outlines the relation between customer satisfaction and product pricing. The introduction of dynamic pricing strategies in several industries including hospitality and tourism has increased consumers' sensitivity towards price acceptance. The incorporated case study on hospitality also effectively endorses the chapter content and linkage between customer satisfaction and pricing.

Anestis Fotiadis, Marios Sotiriadis and Chris A. Vassiliadis explore visitor perceptions of destination image, satisfaction with their tourism consumption experience and the resulting behavioural intentions in chapter 20. The first section of the chapter deals with the review of historical and current literature by taking into account the main elements and attributes of tourism destination image (TDI) explored by academic tourism research, whereas the second section illustrates the application of the concept of TDI through a practical tourism problem by presenting a relevant case study.

Jianyu Ma and Noel Scott examine the concept of customer delight and causes of its stimulation in hospitality and tourism organizations in chapter 21. This chapter uses cognitive appraisal theory to explain a number of cognitive paths by which delight and other emotions are elicited. Delight is defined as an emotional response coexisting with customer satisfaction and is a specific emotion acquired by a consumption experience that impacts on attitudes, perceptions and behaviours. The chapter further discusses the antecedents and consequences of delight, the relationship between delight and satisfaction, and simultaneously provides a brief review of previous studies examining delight.

During recent years, scientific and technological advancements have had significant influence on the cruise industry, and thus considerable progress has been made in the design, power supply, accommodation and catering facilities of passenger ships. Chapter 22, authored by Abdullah Tanrisevdi and Vedat Acar, explores travel patterns, behavioural intentions and motivations of cruise passengers visiting Kuşadası Port, Turkey. The rapid changes in the international cruise business are the major motivating factor to conduct this study en route for understanding cruise tourists' behaviour.

Chapter 23 by Poh Theng, Loo deals with customer complaint behaviour, considered as one of the most important elements in consumer behaviour. The illumination of customer complaint behaviour enables service industry practitioners to recognise better ways to handle customer complaints and also to minimise them. Customer complaining behaviour is also influenced by cultural, demographic and other companion factors. Hospitality and tourism organisations can develop effective customer complaint management systems to maximise the level of customer satisfaction, customer loyalty and, ultimately, their profits.

Chapter 24 by Priyanko Guchait focuses on service errors/failures and service recovery performance in hospitality organisations. The topic is considered critical for practitioners and researchers in the field of hospitality management because of its impact on company revenues, profitability and the customer base. The chapter explores organisational error management culture which can lead to effective service recovery performance. This chapter also explains the underlying mechanism (mediators) linking error management culture and service recovery performance besides making recommendations to hospitality managers to facilitate them to establish error management cultures.

17

SERVICE, EMOTIONAL SATISFACTION AND BEHAVIOUR PATTERNS

David Drewery and Ron McCarville

Introduction

The goal of any service is to satisfy clients' wants and needs. With such satisfaction come positive feelings and with positive feelings come behavioural responses. The service provider is particularly interested in two types of responses. These responses are repeat behaviour and the spreading of positive word of mouth. In this chapter, we consider how positive emotions generated by successful service delivery can encourage both such behaviours. We explore how providers can encourage clients to (1) return to the provider and (2) say nice things to others about the service and the service provider. We view client satisfaction as the key to this process.

There are many situational elements that can influence client satisfaction. They range from the actions of other users to the weather. These elements are largely outside service providers' control. We focus here on the importance of service delivery creating positive emotional outcomes. Under the right conditions, excellent service shapes clients' emotions and eventually their behaviours. This chapter outlines the process through which service quality shapes subsequent client responses.

Perceived service quality

Services represent a set of tangible and intangible elements used by providers to fulfil clients' goals and expectations. Perceptions of *service quality* emerge when clients assess the inferiority or superiority of these elements. This assessment represents a comparison between pre-conceived notions about those various elements and the service as experienced by the client (Bitner and Hubbert 1994; Zeithaml et al. 1996). Whether the service is judged as good or bad is dependent on some objective criteria (such as the speed of delivery) in relation to clients' expectations about those characteristics (Parasuraman et al. 1988). Services that meet and exceed such expectations are deemed superior, while those that fail to meet expectations are considered lacking.

Several models have emerged to help providers organize service delivery to best meet clients' preferences (e.g. Dabholkar et al. 1996; Grönroos 1984; Parasuraman et al. 1988; Rust and Oliver 1994). Each lays out principles for understanding how and why clients separate good service from bad. They then seek to guide providers' actions towards good service. By way of example, a hierarchical model by Brady and Cronin (2001) suggests that clients tend to evaluate: (1) outcome – whether they received the service they were promised;

(2) interaction with others – primarily the human element regarding staff involvement in the process; and (3) the setting – the environment, place and space in which the service was delivered. Service quality is improved when the outcome is satisfying for the client, interactions with staff are helpful, and the setting is consistent with the intended nature of the service (Alexandris et al. 2006; Kyle et al. 2010).

Emotions and emotional satisfaction

Emotions emerge as clients assess what is happening around them. According to Scherer (1987, 2005), emotions are short episodes of changes that occur within our bodies as a result of evaluations of relevant internal or external stimuli. Therefore, emotions may result from an interaction between the service and clients' senses (Holbrook and Hirschman 1982; Shaw 2007). The nature and strength of emotional responses differ between individuals because each individual's experience is unique (Meyer and Schwager 2007).

Leisure services may be particularly emotional in nature. Clients in leisure contexts can be very much involved in the experience and its potential outcomes. Everything from performance on a field of play, to interpersonal dynamics with other participants can be deeply emotional for spectators at a sporting event (Funk et al. 2009). Disgruntled staff can ruin a great day while happy and helpful staff can create cherished memories (Slåtten 2009). Fellow participants, leisure settings and the nature of the activities themselves all build emotional buy-in on the part of participants (Chhetri et al. 2004; Lin et al. 2014; Nawijn et al. 2013).

The emotional response to service experiences (and the strength of those emotions) depends on (1) perception and (2) comparisons between what is perceived and what is expected. Consider each in turn. *Perception* is a process through which a stimulus is sensed and recognized by the brain (see Goldstein and Brockmole 2016). Perception is a first step in any emotional response chain. A jogger may be passing through a serene garden but its serenity will only be realized if he or she becomes aware of the garden and its attributes. Failure to attend to the garden in this case would not create the positive emotional response the garden's designers had intended.

Second, emotional responses depend very much on the comparison of new information with existing mental models. Early psychologists such as Piaget (1928) and Bartlett (1932) called these models *schemata* (*schema* if singular). Our mental models help us to organize everything about the world, including our identity, preferences, memories and expectations. It is the interaction between sensory perception and recollection of various information from our mental models that helps to make sense of an experience, and to respond to it accordingly. So, the sight of well-kept gardens and ponds may elicit positive emotional responses for those clients who enjoy such scenes but may be lost on those who seek more active spaces (perhaps for sport or family activities). If the service is able to align with clients' existing schemata and expectations, it is likely to encourage positive emotional responses.

Emotion is then linked to satisfaction levels (see Bigné et al. 2005; Enrique Bigné et al. 2008; Slåtten et al. 2009). Satisfaction has both cognitive and emotional components (Oliver 1980). These components are closely linked but are conceptually distinct (Cronin et al. 2000). It is perhaps easiest to view the cognitive component as a comparison between perceptions of the service and expectations for the service (Oliver 1993). Cognitive satisfaction emerges when perceptions of service are *greater than* expectations of service (Parasuraman et al. 1988).

Conversely, *emotional satisfaction* emerges from a cognitive evaluation of emotional states (see Ladhari 2009; Wong 2004). When the assessment reveals that one's emotions are positive (e.g. I feel happy, I am hopeful, joyous, delighted, pleased, etc.), *emotional satisfaction* is high (Liljander and Strandvik 1997). Assessments that suggest negative emotional states (e.g. anger, frustration, shame, grief) mean emotional satisfaction is low. The connection between service and emotional satisfaction does not necessarily involve clients' expectations. Many emotions may emerge in the absence of expectations. Clients standing in line to enter a swim complex may not expect an emotional response while in the queue. They may be delighted, though, with the antics of a toddler in the line with them. Expectations were absent but the delight would be very much present. Similarly, clients may not expect to see another client become irate, but may experience shock and fear as a result. This is why forward-thinking service providers design services to facilitate positive emotional responses and minimize negative ones. For example, they may arrange queues in plain sight of fun centres (slides in pools and so on). While waiting in the queue, clients are entertained by the sights and sounds arranged by the provider. In this way, the provider doesn't leave emotional satisfaction to chance (Bagozzi et al. 1999; Yüksel and Yüksel 2007; Zeelenberg and Pieters 2004).

Emotional satisfaction and behavioural response

We know that these emotional responses can influence clients' subsequent behavioural responses. *Behavioural responses* are the patterns of observable action clients demonstrate following an experience. Behavioural responses typically begin as attitudes or intentions (i.e. subjective assessment of the likelihood a behaviour will be seen at a later point) but more importantly manifest later as observable actions. There are two general behavioural responses with which we are concerned in this chapter: (1) re-patronage behaviours and (2) communication behaviours (Jani and Han 2011).

Re-patronage behaviours occur when the client returns to either a provider or a service. Re-patronage is the fundamental basis for the long-term sustainability of any service (Reichheld and Teal 2001). Services that rely on revenue generated through purchase are unlikely to survive unless clients use the service. Services that are evaluated based on popularity, such as in some public recreation agencies, are also unlikely to continue if participation levels falter (Wakefield and Blodgett 1994). While the choice to re-patronize the service is influenced by many factors, it is largely influenced by previous experience with the provider (Jones et al. 2007).

Positive emotions like comfort, stimulation and sentimentality (Han and Jeong 2013) are excellent predictors of re-patronage (Ali and Amin 2014; Kim and Perdue 2013; Yu and Dean 2001) and may lead to long-term behavioural loyalty (Curtis et al. 2011). Negative emotions, conversely, tend to deter clients from returning to use the service (Gelbrich 2010; Han and Jeong 2013; Harrison-Walker 2001; Howat et al. 1996; Murray and Howat 2002; Tiet et al. 2006). Instead, negative emotions can cause clients to *defect* or *switch* to other services.

The connection between clients' emotional satisfaction and behavioural responses may be explained by a number of theoretical connections. One brief explanation is that our emotions promote learning (i.e. how we *perceive* and *code* our experiences into our existing schema; Sharot and Phelps 2004) and that learning guides future action (Baumeister et al. 2007). Essentially, clients can learn that participation with a given service is emotionally satisfying, and this may guide future decisions to return. Essentially clients seek value (Vargo et al. 2008) and are more likely to return to providers that offer this value.

A second explanation is that emotional satisfaction is important in building relationships between client and provider (Hennig-Thurau et al. 2002) and that strong emotional bonds facilitate loyalty (Han et al. 2008; Harrison-Walker 2001; Sierra and McQuitty 2005). Service experiences that are capable of generating positive emotions create lasting ties between clients and the organization. Those clients with emotional ties feel compelled to re-patronize the service at subsequent opportunities.

Communication behaviours are those actions that involve sharing information about the experience with others. There are two general types of communication behaviours. The first is *word of mouth* (WOM; Richins 1980), which involves information shared with those other than the provider. Clients might share information with their friends, family or other potential clients in the community at large. They use a number of channels to spread WOM, including posting on social media (Drewery 2014). These posts could share how wonderful the experience was, or could warn others against participating. WOM is important to consider because it can spread quickly – for better or for worse (Wetzer et al. 2007) – and because it shapes others' opinions of the service (Gremler et al. 2001; Lee et al. 2008).

The second type of communication behaviour is often called *voice* behaviour. Voice comes in different forms, and can be either positive or negative. For example, clients can provide feedback directly to staff which could come in the form of praise or complaints. Praise is very much a success story. Not only does it suggest that clients are happy with services, the literature suggests that happy clients both inspire and satisfy staff in turn. Conversely, complaints can be particularly problematic. Complaints can decrease staff commitment to delivering excellent service (Bell and Luddington 2006) and can influence other clients' emotions (Tombs and McColl-Kennedy 2005).

Both WOM and voice are shaped by clients' emotional states (Gelbrich 2010; Lee et al. 2007; Murray and Howat 2002). Clients who feel happy, content and satisfied are more likely to say nice things to other clients (Brown et al. 2005; Howat et al. 1999; Madrigal 1995). Clients who are frustrated, angry or feel regret may share an array of negative information with staff, friends, family and other potential clients (Drewery 2014; Gelbrich 2010). Positive feedback, such as saying 'thank you', likely occurs when clients feel gratitude or joy. Complaints to the provider instead emerge when negative emotions are present. This is the case because negative emotions such as anger tend to activate expressive and aggressive coping tendencies (Han and Jeong 2013; Lazarus 1991) which may manifest in harmful comments to the provider (Bonifield and Cole 2007; Strizhakova et al. 2012).

Forward-thinking providers try to use voice to their advantage. They try to design systems that track and learn from clients' communication. Clients who share honest feedback offer the provider an opportunity to learn about what went well and what did not. Both WOM and various forms of voice can help to identify and solve problems (Bove and Robertson 2005). Frustrated clients are often happy to tell the provider not only what went wrong, but also what they want done about it. This means that providers can respond with an appropriate service recovery initiative. More than that, the provider can redesign future offerings to avoid moments that prompt dissatisfaction.

Gremler, D. D., Gwinner, K. P. and Brown, S. W. (2001). 'Generating positive word-of-mouth com-munication through customer-employee relationships', *International Journal of Service Industry Management*, 12(1): 44–59.

Grönroos, C. (1984). 'A service quality model and its marketing implications', *European Journal of Marketing*, 18(4): 36–44.

Han, H. and Jeong, C. (2013). 'Multi-dimensions of patrons' emotional experiences in upscale restaurants and their role in loyalty formation: Emotion scale improvement', *International Journal of Hospitality Management*, 32: 59–70.

Han, X., Kwortnik, R. and Wang, C. (2008). 'Service loyalty: An integrative model and examination across service contexts', *Journal of Service Research*, 11(1): 22–42.

Harrison-Walker, L. J. (2001). 'The measurement of word-of-mouth communication and an investigation of service quality and customer commitment as potential antecedents', *Journal of Service Research*, 4(1): 60–75.

Hennig-Thurau, T., Gwinner, K. P. and Gremler, D. D. (2002). 'Understanding relationship marketing outcomes: An integration of relational benefits and relationship quality', *Journal of Service Research*, 4(3): 230–247.

Holbrook, M. B. and Hirschman, E. C. (1982). 'The experiential aspects of consumption: Consumer fantasies, feelings, and fun', *Journal of Consumer Research*, 9(2): 132–140.

Howat, G., Absher, J., Crilley, G. and Milne, I. (1996). 'Measuring customer service quality in sports and leisure centres', *Managing Leisure*, 1(2): 77–89.

Howat, G., Murray, D. and Crilley, G. (1999). 'The relationships between service problems and perceptions of service quality, satisfaction, and behavioral intentions of Australian public sports and leisure center customers', *Journal of Park and Recreation Administration*, 17(2): 42–64.

Jani, D. and Han, H. (2011). 'Investigating the key factors affecting behavioral intentions: Evidence from a full-service restaurant setting', *International Journal of Contemporary Hospitality Management*, 23(7): 1000–1018.

Jones, M. A., Reynolds, K. E., Mothersbaugh, D. L. and Beatty, S. E. (2007). 'The positive and negative effects of switching costs on relational outcomes', *Journal of Service Research*, 9(4): 335–355.

Kim, D. and Perdue, R. R. (2013). 'The effects of cognitive, affective, and sensory attributes on hotel choice', *International Journal of Hospitality Management*, 35: 246–257.

Kyle, G. T., Theodorakis, N. D., Karageorgiou, A. and Lafazani, M. (2010). 'The effect of service quality on customer loyalty within the context of ski resorts', *Journal of Park and Recreation Administration*, 28(1): 1–15.

Ladhari, R. (2009). 'Service quality, emotional satisfaction, and behavioural intentions: A study in the hotel industry', *Managing Service Quality: An International Journal*, 19(3): 308–331.

Lazarus, R. S. (1991). 'Cognition and motivation in emotion', *American Psychologist*, 46(4): 352–367.

Lee, J., Park, D. H. and Han, I. (2008). 'The effect of negative online consumer reviews on product attitude: An information processing view', *Electronic Commerce Research and Applications*, 7(3): 341–352.

Lee, S. Y., Petrick, J. F. and Crompton, J. (2007). 'The roles of quality and intermediary constructs in determining festival attendees' behavioral intention', *Journal of Travel Research*, 45(4): 402–412.

Liljander, V. and Strandvik, T. (1997). 'Emotions in service satisfaction', *International Journal of Service Industry Management*, 8(2): 148–169.

Lin, Y., Kerstetter, D., Nawijn, J. and Mitas, O. (2014). 'Changes in emotions and their interactions with personality in a vacation context', *Tourism Management*, 40: 416–424.

Madrigal, R. (1995). 'Cognitive and affective determinants of fan satisfaction', *Journal of Leisure Research*, 27(3): 205–227.

Meyer, C. and Schwager, A. (2007). 'Understanding customer experience', *Harvard Business Review*, 85(2): 116–126.

Murray, D. and Howat, G. (2002). 'The relationships among service quality, value, satisfaction, and future intentions of customers at an Australian sports and leisure centre', *Sport Management Review*, 5(1): 25–43.

Nawijn, J., Mitas, O., Lin, Y. and Kerstetter, D. (2013). 'How do we feel on vacation? A closer look at how emotions change over the course of a trip', *Journal of Travel Research*, 52(2): 265–274.

Oliver, R. L. (1980). 'A cognitive model of the antecedents and consequences of satisfaction decisions', *Journal of Marketing Research*, 17(4): 460–469.

Oliver, R. L. (1993). 'Cognitive, affective, and attribute bases of the satisfaction response', *Journal of Consumer Research*, 20(3): 418–430.

Parasuraman, A., Zeithaml, V. A. and Berry, L. L. (1988). 'SERVQUAL', *Journal of Retailing*, 64(1): 12–40.

Piaget, J. (1928). *The Child's Conception of the World*, London: Routledge.

Reichheld, F. F. and Teal, T. (2001). *The Loyalty Effect: The Hidden Force behind Growth, Profits, and Lasting Value*, Cambridge, MA: Harvard Business Press.

Richins, M. L. (1980). 'Consumer perceptions of costs and benefits associated with complaining', in H. K. Hunt and R. L. Day (eds.), *Refining Concepts and Measures of Consumer Satisfaction and Complaining Behavior* (pp. 50–53), Bloomington: Indiana University Press.

Rust, R. T. and Oliver, R. W. (1994). 'The death of advertising', *Journal of Advertising*, 23(4): 71–77.

Scherer, K. R. (1987). 'Toward a dynamic theory of emotion: The component process model of affective states', *Geneva Studies in Emotion and Communication*, 1: 1–98.

Scherer, K. R. (2005). 'What are emotions? And how can they be measured?', *Social Science Information*, 44(4): 695–729.

Sharot, T. and Phelps, E. A. (2004). 'How arousal modulates memory: Disentangling the effects of attention and retention', *Cognitive, Affective, and Behavioral Neuroscience*, 4(3): 294–306.

Shaw, C. (2007). *The DNA of Customer Experience*, New York: Palgrave Macmillan.

Sierra, J. J. and McQuitty, S. (2005). 'Service providers and customers: Social exchange theory and service loyalty', *Journal of Services Marketing*, 19(6): 392–400.

Slåtten, T. (2009). 'The effect of managerial practice on employee-perceived service quality: The role of emotional satisfaction', *Managing Service Quality: An International Journal*, 19(4): 431–455.

Slåtten, T., Mehmetoglu, M., Svensson, G. and Sværi, S. (2009). 'Atmospheric experiences that emotionally touch customers: A case study from a winter park', *Managing Service Quality: An International Journal*, 19(6): 721–746.

Strizhakova, Y., Tsarenko, Y. and Ruth, J. A. (2012). '"I'm mad and I can't get that service failure off my mind": Coping and rumination as mediators of anger effects on customer intentions', *Journal of Service Research*, 15(4): 414–429.

Tiet, Q. Q., Rosen, C., Cavella, S., Moos, R. H., Finney, J. W. and Yesavage, J. (2006). 'Coping, symptoms, and functioning outcomes of patients with posttraumatic stress disorder', *Journal of Traumatic Stress*, 19(6): 799–811.

Tombs, A. G. and McColl-Kennedy, J. R. (2005). 'The impact of social density, purchase occasion and displayed emotions of others on customer affect and behavioural intentions', in European Marketing Academy (ed.), *34th European Marketing Academy Conference*, Universita Bocconi, Milan, 24–27 May, EMAC.

Vargo, S. L., Maglio, P. P. and Akaka, M. A. (2008). 'On value and value co-creation: A service systems and service logic perspective', *European Management Journal*, 26(3): 145–152.

Wakefield, K. L. and Blodgett, J. G. (1994). 'The importance of servicescapes in leisure service settings', *Journal of Services Marketing*, 8(3): 66–76.

Wetzer, I. M., Zeelenberg, M. and Pieters, R. (2007). 'Consequences of socially sharing emotions: Testing the emotion-response congruency hypothesis', *European Journal of Social Psychology*, 37(6): 1310–1324.

Wong, A. (2004). 'The role of emotional satisfaction in service encounters', *Managing Service Quality: An International Journal*, 14(5): 365–376.

Yu, Y. T. and Dean, A. (2001). 'The contribution of emotional satisfaction to consumer loyalty', *International Journal of Service Industry Management*, 12(3): 234–250.

Yüksel, A. and Yüksel, F. (2007). 'Shopping risk perceptions: Effects on tourists' emotions, satisfaction and expressed loyalty intentions', *Tourism Management*, 28(3): 703–713.

Zeelenberg, M. and Pieters, R. (2004). 'Beyond valence in customer dissatisfaction: A review and new findings on behavioral responses to regret and disappointment in failed services', *Journal of Business Research*, 57(4): 445–455.

Zeithaml, V. A., Berry, L. L. and Parasuraman, A. (1996). 'The behavioral consequences of service quality', *The Journal of Marketing*, 60(2): 31–46.

18

ATTRIBUTES INFLUENCING CUSTOMER SATISFACTION IN TOURISM

Gaitree (Vanessa) Gowreesunkar and Stelios Varvaressos

Introduction

Customer satisfaction is of paramount importance since it constitutes the foundation of successful tourism businesses (Kotler and Armstrong 2010). Studies show that high-quality experiences usually lead to better overall perceived service quality, customer satisfaction and post-consumption behavioural intentions (Zeithaml et al. 1996; Kim 2014). However, in tourism, customer satisfaction is a complex topic; a tourist destination is an amalgam of tourist products, services and public goods consumed under the same brand name, thus offering the consumer an integrated experience (Buhalis 2000; Leiper 1995). Consequently, several attributes of the destination contribute to and affect tourist satisfaction, namely destination services, recreational facilities, cultural tours, hotel services, restaurant services and host culture, destination's natural environment, local culture and climate, among others (Yuksel 2001; Pizam et al. 1978). The various positive and negative experiences therefore occur as a result of customer interactions with these attributes, and it is the cumulative effects that ultimately determine the tourists' overall evaluation of the experience. Applying this point to the 21st-century context, it would be reasonable to suggest that the understanding of customer satisfaction has become even more complicated. This is because, in tourism, not only do tourists travel, but information also travels. Tourists of the present era live in a wired world and they are sophisticated, savvy and above all, have a permanent online presence through social networks. As such, information on products and services of several destinations, perceptions of a holiday destination, and comparisons of different facilities, the best deals and level of service are constantly fed online. This implies that tourists are updated permanently on tourism products and in real time. To keep pace with this trend, it becomes important for destination managers and marketers to understand the virtual interactions of tourists in order to evaluate customer perceptions of their experiences and their interpretation of attributes leading to their satisfaction.

With this as foundation, the aim of this chapter is to analyse attributes that influence customer satisfaction within the context of a tourism destination. The introductory part of the chapter situates the chapter by offering an insight on the role of customer satisfaction in tourism. A few definitions are proposed while the discussion is extended to a tourism destination context. The chapter thereafter offers an insight on major attributes influencing customer satisfaction at a destination. These are substantiated by a few models of customer satisfaction adapted to the tourism field. The final part of the chapter addresses the attributes of customer satisfaction in tourism. To contextualise the theoretical underpinnings guiding customer satisfaction attributes in tourism, a case study on dolphin watching in Mauritius is proposed. Customer satisfaction attributes of tourists involved in dolphin-watching activities are analysed and implications are discussed. The chapter is concluded with a discussion on attributes that influence customer satisfaction within a tourism destination. The strong and weak points are highlighted and recommendations directed towards the improvement of destination attributes and hence the satisfaction of the discerning tourists are proposed.

Customer satisfaction in tourism

Although there are several different conceptual approaches in defining customer satisfaction, it is generally viewed as an affective (e.g. liking/pleasure) and cognitive (e.g. thinking/ judging) evaluation of a pleasurable level of consumption-related fulfilment from a product and/or service (Gregory et al. 2015: p. 54). In the context of tourism, customer satisfaction gets more complex; a tourism experience comprises a combination of products and services (accommodation, attractions, transportation and ancillary services) and evaluating which part of the experience generates satisfaction or dissatisfaction is quite complicated. As a result, the UNWTO (1985) defines tourism customer satisfaction as a psychological concept that involves the feeling of well-being and pleasure that results from obtaining what one hopes for and expects from an appealing product and/or service. It is a response, an emotional or cognitive judgement linked to a particular moment (prior to purchase, after purchase or after consumption). The concept of customer satisfaction in tourism can also be explained by the disconfirmation paradigm of Neal and Gursoy (2008). The model suggests that consumers are likely to have positive confirmation if the performance is superior to their expectations, implying that consumers are highly satisfied and will be more willing to purchase the same service in the future. On the other hand, if the actual performance is worse than expectations, consumers are likely to have a negative disconfirmation, where consumers will be dissatisfied. Within a tourism destination, customer satisfaction is often judged by two questions: what is required and what is desired? For instance, a man travelling with his family requires a connecting room at a resort, but upon arrival, he discovers that his booking was made on two separate rooms. Because what was required was not provided, the tourist will experience dissatisfaction and might evaluate the whole experience as a negative one, despite satisfactory food and services provided at the hotel. In another case, a tourist books an online ticket in an economy class, but being upgraded to business class free of charge will be judged as satisfactory given that what was provided exceeded the expectation of the tourist and she has the possibility to enjoy business-class facilities, something desired by most economy-class passengers.

Attributes determining customer satisfaction in tourism

Satisfaction is a complex phenomenon encompassing various dimensions, aspects, elements and attributes (Zeithaml and Bitner 2003). Attributes are those 'must be' or 'value added' qualities of the tourism product that are considered important by tourist customers. An attribute is hence a subjective element and it is determined by the perception of the customers. In tourism, consumers make their quality and satisfaction judgements via holiday experiences related to all components of a complicated tourism system (Weiermair 2000). Satisfaction and dissatisfaction may occur as a result of customer interactions with these components, and it is the cumulative effect that will ultimately determine the tourists' overall evaluation of the experience. For instance, a beach tourist might consider boat house services as a 'must be' quality whereas another beach tourist might perceive this facility as 'value added' given that for him, a clean and safe beach is a far more important attribute than a boat house. Therefore, not all attributes are equal in terms of their effect on overall customer satisfaction (Gregory et al. 2015; Crick and Spencer 2011) and different customer segments may value product attributes differently. According to Tonge and Moore (2007), attributes may be categorised into the following.

Desirable attribute: If these attributes are present, it results in satisfaction but if not present, there is no dissatisfaction.
Essential attribute: Without these attributes dissatisfaction increases, yet their existence does not necessarily improve satisfaction.

To provide a deeper understanding of attributes in tourism, Cadotte and Turgeon (1988) propose the following categories of attributes.

Satisfiers: Factors that generate satisfaction when present yet which do not generate dissatisfaction when not present;
Dissatisfiers: Factors that can generate dissatisfaction if they do not work properly, yet which do not generate praise when they work properly or above a certain standard level;
Critical attributes: Factors which generate both complaints and praise; and
Neutral attributes: Factors that generate neither many complaints nor much praise.

To be successful in the tourism business, one must therefore understand how customers perceive the product or service attributes, their importance and performance when compared with those of competitors (Lilien et al. 1993). Assessing attributes that influence customer satisfaction will help detect areas of strengths or shortfalls within a tourism destination. There is an exhaustive list of attributes that affect customer satisfaction in tourism. The most important ones are expanded next.

Service quality

Studies indicate that service quality and customer satisfaction are closely related (Cronin and Taylor 1994; Oliver 1993; Babakus and Inhofe 1991). Conceptually, service quality is defined as a global judgement or attitude relating to the overall excellence or superiority of a service (Parasuraman et al. 1988). It is determined by how well customers' needs are met. In the context of tourism, service quality is not limited to external customers (tourists) but rather extends to internal customers (service providers). Internal customers' satisfaction is important as satisfied employees are committed to continuous improvement and delivering quality service (Zeithaml and Bitner 2003). For example, if after a massage, a hotel customer feels that her skin was irritated by Ayurveda oil, a satisfied service provider will offer an extra massage or any other service free of charge in order to correct the perception of the customer on the overall service quality of the hotel; ultimately this act might presumably convert the feeling of dissatisfaction into that of satisfaction. Service quality is also interpreted by the gap model; tourists have expectations when they purchase a tourism product. If the expectation is met, the perceived service quality of tourists is positive and if the expectation is exceeded, the tourists will be ready to spread positive word of mouth (WOM) and recommend the destination and will probably post their perception of the service online. The converse is also true. Therefore, service quality is an important attribute that tourists will always look into while purchasing a holiday.

Destination entertainment

At the tourism destination, the mere existence of resources is insufficient to generate satisfaction and future visitation. Entertainment is an important pull factor and tourist satisfaction with a destination's performance is often viewed as a key indicator as it can stimulate behaviour and motivate visitors to recommend and revisit a place (Pritchard and Morgan 2001). Whenever tourists select their holiday destinations, they search for the entertainment and attractions available at the destination. For instance, a family travelling with kids to Europe will usually search for destinations that offer entertainment for the kids. As a result, Paris may be the preferred choice of the family due to the presence of Disneyland Paris. Studies show that the quality and types of entertainment offered at the destination do influence tourism satisfaction and are significant in the formation of tourists' destination experience (Beerli and Martin 2004; Smith 1994). This implies that entertainment can be considered as both an essential and a desirable attribute for the tourist. In a study conducted by Gowreesunkar and Sotiriades (2015), the presence of entertainment was found to be an important attribute contributing to customer satisfaction in the Mauritian tourism experience. The study revealed that, if appropriately exploited, this could contribute significantly to customer satisfaction.

Service encounters

Service encounters are those moments when customers interact with service providers to consume the tourism product. A service encounter may give rise to two outcomes, namely satisfaction with the service offered or service failures. It is therefore an important attribute that can significantly impact on customer satisfaction. For instance, after a holiday trip, a tourist is about to check in his luggage, but due to his excess luggage, airport officers force him to open the luggage and retain the passenger till further notice. This type of encounter might result in disappointment with the entire tourism experience even if the stay within the destination was judged as satisfactory. From a pro-tourism perspective, airport officers could have advised the passenger how to deal with excess luggage and allowed the passenger to check in. Service encounters are therefore moments of truth when unexpected incidents take place and service providers are called upon to use their talent and expertise to handle the critical incidents to the satisfaction of the tourists. In another extreme case, if during a family holiday, one of the members meets with an accident, things further complicate; cancellation of attraction visits and hotel rooms or changing of return tickets to get back home cumulate into other critical incidents which might be judged as positive or negative depending on the quality of the encounters with service providers.

Destination facilities

Tourists are on holiday and whenever they travel, they look for a hassle-free trip. When prospective tourists plan a holiday, they usually look for destinations that will facilitate the travel process and provide a value-for-money experience. Facilities available at the destination therefore play an important role in the level of satisfaction of the tourists and are thus treated as an essential attribute. For instance, infrastructure, superstructure, road signs, visitor facilities, variety and quality of accommodation, eating and drinking facilities, food, credit card acceptance, public toilets, rapid customer clearance, cleanliness and hygiene, international call facilities, quality/price ratio, reliable tour operators and travel agents, receptive locals, language interpretation, police services, medical care, exchange bureaus, tourism offices and inland transportation *inter alia* contribute towards the satisfaction of the tourism experience.

Price

Price is not only a determinant in the purchase of a tourism product but an important source of satisfaction for tourists. Tourists are generally price sensitive, and given that conversion of their money into foreign currencies can either increase or decrease its value, they search for price information from both online and offline sources to generate a feeling of satisfaction if they have been able to enjoy a deal, a promotion or a discount. Given the fact that tourism is one of the most price non-transparent industries due to fluctuation such as in the pricing of airlines, car rentals and hotels (Maxwell 2008), tourists derive satisfaction if they perceive that the price they paid for a tourism product is within the range of acceptability of prices; this is defined as the maximum and minimum acceptable price thresholds (Pedraja and Yagüe 2000). They therefore accept prices within their price range but reject prices outside this range. The sophisticated tourists have a permanent online presence, and comparison of prices and deals becomes an important source of customer satisfaction if a value-for-money transaction is perceived. For instance, there is a feeling of satisfaction if tourists perceive that the rack rate of a hotel room within the destination is similar or has minimum discrepancy to what is being offered online. Moreover, perceived opportunity cost can also affect customer satisfaction. For example, if after booking a hotel, a tourist discovers that the price charged by another travel site is cheaper, there is a feeling of dissatisfaction. Ultimately, price also represents an important attribute in tourism satisfaction.

Exposure to online sources

Customers of the present century live in a wired world and due to their permanent presence in the online environment they are constantly exposed to feedback from potential travellers. Information on cleanliness, comfort, location, facilities and staff *inter alia* already gives an indication to future tourists where they can book their next vacation if they want to enjoy a value-for-money trip and derive maximum satisfaction. Alongside the personal recommendations of friends, online reviews are the most important factor influencing the booking of accommodations. As a result, it may be argued that exposure to online sources may be considered as an essential attribute while planning a holiday trip. The work of Zhao and Dholakia (2009) shows that in an online environment, customer satisfaction is guided by the following.

Customer feedback

These are reviews and feedback from actual travellers. Furthermore, some web sites allow customers to interact with web site representatives in real time. For instance, if when logging into an online travel account, a prospective tourist discovers that visitors are often the prey of locals, potential travellers might shift their choice to other destinations as they would recognise that visiting the destination will bring no satisfaction to them. This gives an indication of the quickness with which information travels between online users.

Customer to customer communication

Many web sites allow their customers to communicate with each other in order to show credibility for the quality of their services. These online sources guide the choice of travellers, who, if satisfied, proceed with the booking of the tourism product. Satisfied customers will therefore obviously spread positive WOM recommendations about the destination to friends and relatives. This in turn impacts on the behavioural intention of tourists.

Information search

Travellers of the present century are always busy and sources of information which give quick and reliable information are preferred as compared to travel sites which offer billions of pieces of information that further complicate the search process and consume more time. At Travelocity.com, last minute customers often pay a higher price for their tickets compared to those who book in advance.

Online ordering system

Travellers are engaged in online transactions for their convenience and practical purpose. As such, they derive satisfaction whenever online transactions are not complicated and are quickly processed. For instance, busy travellers will experience a feeling of satisfaction with travelocity.com; when ordering an airline ticket online, buyers can pick the flight and pay for it online right away. In contrast, on flychina.com, the process is complicated; once a flight is selected, the customer is urged to fill out and send an online order form, then wait for an e-mail confirmation, and then fax the confirmed order form with credit card information.

Customer satisfaction and product/service attributes

Various models have been developed to explain the relationship between customer satisfaction and product and service attributes. Some of them are briefly explained next.

The Kano model

The Kano model of customer satisfaction proposes that the relationship between an attribute's performance and satisfaction is non-linear (Kano et al. 1984; Yang 2005). In this model, a distinction is made for those attributes that have a one-dimensional effect, that is, if they work properly, they generate satisfaction and if they are absent or do not work properly they generate dissatisfaction. Some of the factors, referred to as 'basics' or 'musts', can generate dissatisfaction if they are not present, yet their presence does not generate additional satisfaction. Others, referred to as 'excitement factors', do not generate dissatisfaction if they are absent, however, their presence or correct operation produces greater satisfaction. According to the model, product and service attributes can be classified into three categories:

1   *Basic attributes.* These attributes fulfil the basic functions of a product and customers see them as prerequisites. If they are not present or their performance is insufficient, customers will be extremely dissatisfied. On the other hand, if they are present or have sufficient performance, they do not bring satisfaction.

2   *Performance attributes.* For these attributes, satisfaction is proportional to the performance level – the higher the performance, the higher will be the customer's satisfaction and vice versa. Usually, customers explicitly demand performance attributes.

3   *Excitement attributes.* These attributes are key factors for customer satisfaction. If they are present or have sufficient performance, they will bring superior satisfaction. On the other hand, if they are not present or their performance is insufficient, customers will not get dissatisfied. These attributes are neither demanded nor expected by customers.

The initial Kano model was developed for manufacturing industries. Revision of the model was deemed necessary to make it more applicable to services in general. The revised Kano model utilises a pair of statements to assess the level of satisfaction related to the presence and absence of attributes in the service performance, namely:

The presence of the attribute: How would you feel if the product had the attribute?
The absence of the attribute: How would you feel if the product did not have the attribute?

The comparison of responses to the two statements allows researchers to categorise the attributes within one of the four quadrants of the model or the zone of indifference:

Desirable attribute: If these attributes are present, it results in satisfaction but if not present, there is no dissatisfaction.
Essential attribute: Without these attributes dissatisfaction increases, yet their existence does not necessarily improve satisfaction.
Positive attribute: The presence of positive attributes during the purchase process is positively related to overall satisfaction.
Zone of indifference: Budget and fund availability.

The revised Kano model suggests that the above attributes have varying effects on customers' overall satisfaction and at different levels, and offers two primary areas of focus for tourism as follows:

The purchase process

Financial ability: Due to the relatively high initial cash outlay, vacation ownership developers offer financing options to consumers to assist in the purchase process.

The usage/experience process

Personalisation: The opportunity to speak to someone directly to help with reservations and product usage.
Fun: Variety of attractions and activities to do at the destination or near the resort.
Quality: Overall resort quality including furnishings, in-room amenities and services offered.

Traditional customer satisfaction models suggest that higher satisfaction on all attributes is better. But Kano et al. (1984) challenged this notion and proposed that focusing on improvement of all product attributes is unproductive, as the effect on customer satisfaction may diminish as attribute performance improves, or have no effect if performance declines. In essence, there are asymmetric effects on customer satisfaction. Therefore, it is important for destination managers to understand and to identify the product (or service) attributes perceived by customers as important, and to examine how customers perceive these product (or service) attributes.

The HOLSAT model

The HOLSAT model was developed by Tribe and Snaith (1998) as a research instrument for measuring holiday satisfaction. The design of the HOLSAT survey builds on previous work (the SERVQUAL instrument) to develop indicators of service quality from the consumer perspective. The model seeks to clarify some uncertainty which exists between the terms 'expectations', 'perceived importance' and 'rating of the performance of a service' on the one hand and 'satisfaction' and 'service quality' on the other hand (Sukiman et al. 2013). One of the important characteristics of the HOLSAT instrument is its ability to consider positive as well as negative attributes when attempting to describe the key characteristics of a holiday destination. HOLSAT differs from many models by measuring satisfaction as the relationship between performance and prior expectation rather than performance alone as is the case with SERVPERF (Cronin and Taylor 1994), or performance relative to importance as in Importance-Performance Assessment (Martilla and James 1997) or performance related to best quality (an absolute measure of what consumers think an excellent service would provide) as is the case with SERVQUAL (Parasuraman et al. 1988). The key attributes chosen by Truong and Foster (2006) were based on Cooper et al.'s (1993) five As:

1   *Accessibility*: relates to transportation and access to and within the destination like roads, flight connections, possibility of booking a trip to the destination, cars, scenic buses and other transportation facilities.
2   *Attractions*: designates both natural and man-made attractions, e.g. beach, waterfalls, museums, amusement parks.
3   *Accommodation*: refers to overnight facilities, camp sites, guesthouses, hotels, holiday centres, private B&Bs, holiday homes and the like.
4   *Amenities*: Refers to the physical infrastructure supporting the destination and various facilities provided at the destination.
5   *Ancillary services*: Relates to the provision of catering, entertainment, information and transportation at the destination.

Assessing customer satisfaction

Tourism businesses use a combination of direct and indirect methods to measure, monitor and assess customer satisfaction. Indirect methods mainly aim at tracking actual sales and profit figures compared with forecast and previous period performances. Direct methods include customer research and customer feedback. Research can be conducted into current customers, potential customers and competitors' customers. Normally, both quantitative and qualitative research methods are used to collect data from customers. The main methods used in evaluating customer satisfaction include the following.

Customer feedback (complaint capture and analysis): A management system is required to capture and analyse the volume and characteristics of complaints, the main aim being to identify and correct service failure points that are causing customer dissatisfaction. Various techniques are implemented, such as customer questionnaires, complaint letters or comments cards. An effective complaint capture system will employ many channels (sources), such as questionnaires, emails, telephone calls and websites and social media. It will also include a channel to facilitate employee feedback on customer complaints.

Customer surveys include post-transaction surveys (email questionnaires), key account customers and frequent guests, employee surveys (to provide feedback) and focus groups of customers and employees (to explore customer satisfaction issues in depth).

Mystery shopping (or secret shopper) is a key tool in auditing the service process in tourism-related services. It is used to measure quality of service, or compliance with regulations, or to gather specific information about products and services. Tourism providers are using the tool to assess and improve service delivery. Therefore, it constitutes an auditing tool to measure and assess service quality, just like SERVQUAL. Mystery shoppers perform specific tasks and then provide detailed reports or feedback about their experiences.

Benchmarking is a method that enables companies to compare their own business performance on a wide range of indicators against their competitor set and best practice in the industry. The benchmarking process enables the marketing team to identify and correct important weaknesses compared with the competitor set, and ultimately to improve customer satisfaction.

Difficulties in assessing customer satisfaction in tourism

Because a holiday comprises a combination of various products and services, assessing satisfaction through the characteristics of a tourism offer involves several problems. First, due to their subjective perceptions, tourists are unable to assess the characteristics of product offerings objectively and they often add their own interpretations (Johnston and Heineke 1998). Second, consumers normally do not evaluate each component of the offer in the same way as products and services have different features and the feeling of satisfaction can be weighted using the same assumptions. For instance, food and massage do not give the same type of satisfaction. Third, when the measurement of customer satisfaction is based on a general destination's attributes, the calculated score of satisfaction will be limited by the choice of tourists; for instance, a tourist will not evaluate the heritage attribute of a destination if it was not part of their trip. Satisfaction should therefore be measured separately from the elements of tourism offers.

Dolphin watching on the island of Mauritius

Mauritius is a small tropical island in the Indian Ocean. Famous for its sea, sun and sand tourism, it occupies an area of 720 square kilometres and is slightly bigger than the city of London (Gowreesunkar and Sotiriades 2015). Over the past ten years, dolphin watching has become a popular and lucrative tourist attraction as well as one of the key tourism activities in Mauritius. As a result, the western coast of Mauritius is now internationally known as a sanctuary for dolphins daily visited by those mammals which can be seen in the morning socialising and relaxing in its calm bays (Figure 18.1). A study conducted by Gowreesunkar and Rycha (2015) reveals that there is a growing number of leisure tourists involved in dolphin watching in Mauritius.

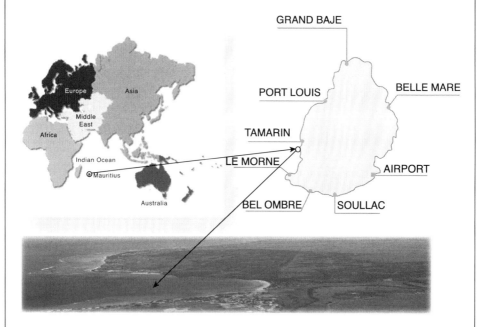

Figure 18.1   Dolphin watching at Tamarin Bay, Mauritius

Source: Gowreesunkar and Rycha (2015).

In the present case study, the concept of satisfaction is defined as the degree to which leisure tourists evaluate the dolphin-watching product attributes as meeting and exceeding expectations. Attributes that are attached to the dolphin-watching activity are those positive features of the destination that explained why the leisure tourists chose it. Customer satisfaction will therefore be influenced by the performance of these attributes: the timely arrangement of taxis; the journey from the hotel to the dolphin-watching embarkation point; the boat experience; the waiting time to see the dolphins; and finally the dolphin-watching activity. In the present case, the presence of those mentioned attributes is essential as failure in any one of them may negatively affect the whole experience. For instance, if the taxi picks up the tourists after the scheduled time, the tourists might miss the boat taking them to the dolphin watching and a further arrangement would be needed. But, more importantly, they might miss the dolphin watching as dolphins visit the lagoon at a specific time. Ultimately, the first dissatisfaction caused by the taxi cumulates into other dissatisfactions.

Application of the HOLSAT model to dolphin-watching tourists

Within the context of the study, the important features of the model are that it enables the tourists to express satisfaction/dissatisfaction by evaluating both positive and negative attributes. Positive attributes are features that convey good impressions of the dolphin-watching activity, whereas negative attributes are those that transmit unfavourable impressions. Attributes that are attached to the dolphin-watching activity are those features that are associated with the very reason for the tourists to choose Mauritius as their holiday destination. As suggested by the Kano model, the presence of essential and desired attributes influences customer satisfaction. As a result, Table 18.1 combines some of the features of the Kano model while applying the HOLSAT model.

Implications

As explained throughout this chapter, a tourist destination is usually perceived as a single entity, and satisfaction is often evaluated through the characteristics of the tourism offer. In the context of the present case study, it is plausible to suggest that customer satisfaction has been influenced by the various attributes present in the process of dolphin watching: for instance, those attributes like timely taxi pick–up, safety and security features on the boat and hassle-free dolphin watching with the possibility of diving and taking pictures. While reverting to the Kano model, these attributes would fulfil the basic functions of the tourism activity and tourists perceive them as prerequisites. If they are not present, the leisure tourists will be extremely dissatisfied. The performance attributes suggest that the higher the possibility to see the dolphins up close, the higher will be the customer satisfaction and vice versa. The excitement attributes are neither demanded nor expected by customers. For instance, if food and beverages are provided during the boat trip while these were not included in the package, this will bring superior satisfaction to the leisure tourists.

However, not all of the factors mentioned in Table 18.1 affect overall satisfaction in the same way. For instance, food and beverages might be a source of satisfaction for some tourists while others might derive satisfaction only if they succeed in diving with the dolphins. In other cases, a repeat visitor might experience satisfaction just with the idea of the sea trip and being on the sea, as during their previous visit, they already dived with the dolphins. Thus, it is unlikely that the same occurrences or generic behaviour can be considered as the underlying causes of all pleasing or displeasing encounters. The same conclusion is shared by Bleuel (1990), who argues that there is no one-to-one correspondence between satisfaction and dissatisfaction, suggesting that the attributes or sources that generate satisfaction are not the same as those that generate dissatisfaction. The overall conclusion reached in the survey is that the sources of dissatisfaction are not necessarily the reverse of the causes of satisfaction.

Table 18.1 Attributes causing tourist satisfaction/dissatisfaction in dolphin watching

Positive attributes	Negative attributes
Timely arrangement of taxi pick-up to embarkation point – essential attribute	Unfavorable weather
Aesthetic feature of boat – essential attribute	Poor condition of boat without facilities for elderly, children and physically challenged tourists
Safety and security at sea – essential attribute	No safety kits provided (life jacket)
Facilities for elderly, physically challenged and children – essential attribute	Dirty and polluted environment
Guided tour by professionals – desired attribute	Unprofessional guide or no guide
Less waiting time to see the dolphin – desired attribute	Erroneous information by skippers during dolphin-visiting time
Food and beverage served on board – desired attribute	Lack of control over unlicensed operators offering the same trip at cheaper cost
Diving with dolphin – desired attribute	Limited possibility to dive with dolphin
Diving accessories provided – desired attribute	Long waiting time to see dolphins due to the presence of other boats
Ease of taking picture – desired attribute	Difficulty to take pictures of dolphin
Beach hawkers selling souvenirs at cheaper price – desired attribute	Unauthorized operators intimidating dolphins to give better view to clients

Source: Authors.

Conclusion

This chapter aimed at exploring the concept of customer satisfaction in the context of a tourism destination. The various factors affecting tourism satisfaction were explored. It was found that the services and facilities offered by a destination and the various attributes attached to them are those features that lead consumers to choose one product over others. Those attributes directly influenced choice, aroused consumers' purchase intentions and differentiated them from competitors' offerings. The case study on dolphin watching was particularly helpful in establishing the sources of satisfaction and dissatisfaction of tourists involved in dolphin watching in Mauritius. These were further illustrated by the HOLSAT and the Kano models. Based on the case study, it was clear that not all attributes have the same role in satisfying customer needs, and it becomes important to find out how their performance impacts on customer satisfaction. Understanding customer satisfaction through the performance of essential attributes or desirable attributes (Kano model) or positive and negative attributes (HOLSAT model) allows destination managers to provide facilities and services that match visitor expectations, while also validating that visitors are satisfied with their experiences. In order to maintain a competitive edge and continue to attract visitors, there is an increasing urgency for the destination to ensure that tourists are satisfied with the overall holiday experience as well as attributes attached to the tourism product in the form of services, events and activities. A satisfied tourist provides positive WOM promotion at no cost, and with online facilities, tourists provide more instantaneous feedback which is captured by online users in real time. Social networks and online blogs both provide ample avenues for consumers to publicly share their views, preferences and experiences with others as well as opportunities for hotels to take advantage of WOM marketing via web services. Taken together, the chapter has contributed to a broader and more comprehensive understanding of attributes influencing customer satisfaction at a tourism destination.

Bibliography

Alexandris, K., Dimitriadis, N. and Markata, D. (2002). 'Can perceptions of service quality predict behavioural intentions? An exploratory study in the hotel sector in Greece', *Managing Service Quality*, 12(4): 224–231.

Asadi, A., Pool, J. and Jalil, M. R. (2014). 'The effect of perceived price fairness through satisfaction and loyalty on international tourists' price acceptance of Islamic-Iranian art products', *Education, Business and Society: Contemporary Middle Eastern Issues*, 7(4): 201–215.

Azzopardi, E. and Nash, R. (2013). 'A critical evaluation of importance-performance analysis', *Tourism Management*, 35(1): 222–233.

Babakus, E. and Inhofe, M. (1991). 'The role of expectations and attribute importance in the measurement of service quality', in M. C. Gilly (ed.), *Proceedings of the Summer Educators' Conference* (pp. 142–144), Chicago, IL: American Marketing Association.

Babin, B. J., Lee, Y.-K., Kim, E.-J. and Griffin, M. (2005). 'Modeling customer satisfaction and word-of-mouth: Restaurant patronage in Korea', *Journal of Service Marketing*, 19(3): 133–139.

Baker, D. A. and Crompton, J. L. (2000). 'Quality, satisfaction and behavioural intentions', *Annals of Tourism Research*, 27(3): 785–804.

Bayraktar, E., Tatoglu, E., Turkyilmaz, A., Delen, D. and Zaim, S. (2012). 'Measuring the efficiency of customer satisfaction and loyalty for mobile phone brands with DEA', *Expert Systems with Applications*, 39(1): 99–106.

Beerli, A. and Martin, J. D. (2004). 'Factors influencing destination image', *Annals of Tourism Research*, 31(3): 657–681.

Beldona, S. and Cobanoglu, C. (2007). 'Importance–performance analysis of guest technologies in the lodging industry', *Cornell Hotel and Restaurant Administration Quarterly*, 48(3): 299–312.

Beldona, S. and Kwansa, F. (2008). 'The impact of cultural orientation on perceived fairness over demand-based pricing', *International Journal of Hospitality Management*, 27(4): 594–603.

Bleuel, B. (1990). 'Customer dissatisfaction and the zone of uncertainty', *Journal of Services Marketing*, 4(1): 49–52.

Breiter, D. and Milman, A. (2006). 'Attendees' needs and service priorities in a large convention centre: Application of the importance–performance theory', *Tourism Management*, 27(6): 1364–1370.

Buhalis, D. (2000). 'Marketing the competitive destination in the future', *Tourism Management*, 21(1): 97–116.

Cadotte, E. R. and Turgeon, N. (1988). 'Key factors in guest satisfaction', *Cornell Hotel and Restaurant Administration Quarterly*, 2(4): 45–51.

Campo, S. (2009). 'Exploring non-linear effects of determinants on tourists' satisfaction', *International Journal of Culture, Tourism and Hospitality Research*, 3(2): 127–138.

Chen, C. F. and Tsai, D. (2007). 'How destination image and evaluative factors affect behavioural intentions?', *Tourism Management*, 28(5): 1115–1122.

Chen, S.-C. (2015). 'Customer value and customer loyalty: Is competition a missing link?', *Journal of Retailing and Consumer Services*, 22: 107–116.

Chu, R. and Choi, C. (2000). 'An importance-performance analysis of hotel selection factors in the Hong Kong hotel industry: A comparison of business and leisure travelers', *Tourism Management*, 21(4): 363–377.

Cooper, C., Fletcher, J., Gilbert, D. and Wanhill, S. (1993). *Tourism: Principles and Practice*, Harlow: Longman Scientific and Technical.

Crick, A. and Spencer, A. (2011). 'Hospitality quality: New directions and new challenges', *International Journal of Contemporary Hospitality Management*, 23(4): 463–478.

Cronin, J. and Taylor, S. (1994). 'SERVPERF versus SERQUAL: Reconciling performance-based and perception-minus-expectations measurement of service quality', *Journal of Marketing*, 58(1): 125–131.

Deng, W. (2007). 'Using a revised importance-performance analysis approach: The case of Taiwanese hot springs tourism', *Tourism Management*, 28(5): 1274–1284.

Deng, W., Kuo, Y. and Chen, W. (2008). 'Revised importance–performance analysis: Three-factor theory and benchmarking', *The Service Industries Journal*, 28(1): 37–51.

Dmitrovi, T., Kneževi Cvelbar, L., Kolar, T., Makovec Brenčič, M., Ograjenšek, I. and Žabkar, V. (2009). 'Conceptualizing tourist satisfaction at the destination level', *International Journal of Culture, Tourism and Hospitality Research*, 3(2): 116–126.

Duke, C. R. and Persia, M. A. (1996). 'Performance-importance analysis of escorted tour evaluations', *Journal of Travel and Tourism Marketing*, 5(3): 207–223.

Gowreesunkar, G. B. and Rycha, I. (2015). 'A study on the impacts of dolphin watching as a tourism activity: Western Mauritius as a case study', *International Journal of Trade, Economic and Finance*, 6(1): 67–72.

Gowreesunkar, G. B. and Sotiriades, M. (2015). 'Entertainment of leisure tourists in island destinations: Evidence from the island of Mauritius', *African Journal of Hospitality, Tourism and Leisure*, 4(S1): 1–19.

Gregory, A. M., Parsa, H. G., Nusair, K., Kwun, D. J. and Putrevu, S. (2015). 'Examining the effects of vacation ownership product attributes on customer satisfaction', *International Journal of Contemporary Hospitality Management*, 27(1): 52–70.

Haahti, A. and Yavas, U. (2004). 'A multi-attribute approach to understanding image of a theme park. The case of Santa Park in Lapland', *European Business Review*, 16(4): 390–397.

Hornback, K., and Eagles, P. (eds.) (1999). *Guidelines for Public Use Measurement and Reporting at Parks and Protected Areas*, Gland, Switzerland and Cambridge, UK: IUCN.

Hosany, S. and Witham, M. (2010). 'Dimensions of cruisers' experiences, satisfaction, and intention to recommend', *Journal of Travel Research*, 49(3): 351–364.

Huan, T. C., Beaman, J. and Shelby, L. B. (2002). 'Using action-grids in tourism management', *Tourism Management*, 23(3): 255–264.

Hudson, S., Hudson, P. and Miller, G. A. (2004). 'The measurement of service quality in the tour operating sector: A methodological comparison', *Journal of Travel Research*, 42(3): 305–312.

Hudson, S. and Shephard G. W. H. (1998). 'Measuring service quality at tourist destinations: An application of importance–performance analysis to an alpine ski resort', *Journal of Travel and Tourism Marketing*, 7(3): 61–77.

Hui, T. K., Wan, D. and Ho, A. (2007). 'Tourists' satisfaction, recommendation and revisiting Singapore', *Tourism Management*, 28(4): 965–975.

Ibrahim, T. D., Inci, V. and Olgun, K. (2014). 'How do international tourists perceive hotel quality? An exploratory study of service quality in Antalya tourism region', *International Journal of Contemporary Hospitality Management*, 26(3): 470–495.

Johnston, R. and Heineke, J. (1998). 'Exploring the relationship between perception and performance: Priorities for action', *The Service Industries Journal*, 18(1): 101–112.

Kano, N., Nobuhiku, S., Fumio, T. and Shinichi, T. (1984). 'Attractive quality and must-be quality', *Journal of the Japanese Society for Quality Control*, 14(2): 39–48.

Kim, J.-H. (2014). 'The antecedents of memorable tourism experiences: The development of a scale to measure the destination attributes associated with memorable experience', *Tourism Management*, 44(1): 34–45.

Kim, M. K., Park, M. C. and Jeong, D. H. (2004). 'The effects of customer satisfaction and switching barrier on customer loyalty in Korean mobile telecommunication services', *Telecommunications Policy*, 28(2): 145–159.

Kotler, P. and Armstrong, G. (2010). *Principles of Marketing*, 13th Global edition, Upper Saddle River, NJ: Pearson Education.

Ladhari, R. (2009). 'Service quality, emotional satisfaction, and behavioural intentions: A study in the hotel industry', *Managing Service Quality*, 19(3): 308–331.

Leiper, N. (1995). *Tourism Management*, Melbourne: RMIT Press.

Lilien, G. L., Kotler, P. and Moorthy, K. S. (1993). *Marketing Models*, New York: Prentice-Hall.

Litvin, W. S., Goldsmith, E. R. and Pan, B. (2008). 'Electronic word-of-mouth in hospitality and tourism management', *Tourism Management*, 29(3): 458–468.

Loureiro, S. M. C. and González, F. J. M. (2008). 'The importance of quality, satisfaction, trust, and image in relation to rural tourist loyalty', *Journal of Travel and Tourism Marketing*, 25(2): 117–136.

McCool, S. F. (2002). 'Tourism in protected areas: Continuing challenges and emerging issues for sustaining visitor experiences', Paper presented at the *Celebrating Mountains Conference*, 24–27 November, Jindabyne, NSW, Australia.

Martilla, J. A. and James, J. C. (1997). 'Importance-performance analysis', *Journal of Marketing*, 41(1): 77–79.

Maxwell, S. (2008). *The Price is Wrong: Understanding What Makes a Price Seem Fair and the True Cost of Unfair Pricing*, Hoboken, NJ: John Wiley and Sons.

Mohsin, A. (2007). 'Assessing lodging service down under: A case of Hamilton, New Zealand', *International Journal of Contemporary Hospitality Management*, 19(4): 296–308.

Neal, J. D. and Gursoy, D. (2008). 'A multifaceted analysis of tourism satisfaction', *Journal of Travel Research*, 47(1): 53–62.

Oh, H. (2001). 'Revisiting importance-performance analysis', *Tourism Management*, 22(6): 617–627.

Oliver, R. L. (1993). 'A conceptual model of service quality and service satisfaction: Compatible goals, different concepts', in T. A. Swartz, D. E. Bowen and S. W. Brown (eds.), *Advances in Services Marketing and Management: Research and Practice*, 2nd edition (pp. 65–85), Greenwich, CT: JAI Press.

Oliver, R. L. (1997). *Satisfaction: A Behavioural Perspective on the Consumer*, New York: McGraw Hill.

Palmer, A. and McCole, P. (2000). 'The role of electronic commerce in creating virtual tourism destination marketing organisations', *International Journal of Contemporary Hospitality Management*, 12(3): 198–204.

Parasuraman, A., Zeithaml, A. V. and Berry, L. L. (1988). 'SERVQUAL: A multiple-item scale for measuring consumer perception of service quality', *Journal of Marketing*, 64(1): 12–40.

Pedraja, M. and Yagüe, M. J. (2000). 'Perceived quality and price: Their impact on the satisfaction of restaurant customers', *International Journal of Contemporary Hospitality Management*, 16(6): 373–379.

Pizam, A., Neumann, Y. and Reichel, A. (1978). 'Dimensions of tourist satisfaction with a destination area', *Annals of Tourism Research*, 5(3): 314–322.

Pritchard, A. and Morgan, N. J. (2001). 'Culture, identity and tourism representation: Marketing Cymru or Wales?', *Tourism Management*, 22(2): 167–179.

Quadri-Felitti, D. and Fiore, A. M. (2013). 'Destination loyalty: Effects of wine tourists' experiences, memories, and satisfaction on intentions', *Tourism and Hospitality Research*, 13(1): 47–62.

Radojevic, T., Tanisic, N. and Statnic, N. (2015). 'Ensuring positive feedback: Factors that influence customer satisfaction in the contemporary hospitality industry', *Tourism Management*, 51: 13–21.

Rust, R. T. and Oliver, R. L. (1994). 'Service quality, insights, and managerial implications from the frontier', in R. T. Rust and R. L. Oliver (eds.), *Service Quality: New Directions in Theory and Practice* (pp. 72–94), Thousand Oaks, CA: Sage.

Ryan, C. and Huimin, G. (2007). 'Perceptions of Chinese hotels', *Cornell Hospitality Quarterly*, 48(4): 380–391.

Saha, G. C. and Theingi (2009). 'Service quality, satisfaction, and behavioural intentions: A study of low-cost airline carriers in Thailand', *Managing Service Quality*, 19(3): 350–372.

Slack, N. (1994). 'The importance–performance matrix as a determinant of improvement priority', *International Journal of Operations and Production Management*, 14(5): 59–75.

Smith, S. (1994). 'The tourism product', *Annals of Tourism Research*, 21(3): 582–595.

Solnet, D. (2008). 'Supporting the contemporary tourism product: Service management', in C. Cooper and C. M. Hall (eds.), *Contemporary Tourism: An International Approach* (pp. 307–343), Oxford: Elsevier Butterworth-Heinemann.

Sukiman, M. F., Omar, S. I., Muhibudin, M., Yussof, I. and Mohammed, B. (2013). 'Tourist satisfaction as a key to destination survival in Pahang', *Procedia – Social and Behavioural Science*, 91: 78–87.

Tarrant, A. and Smith, E. K. (2002). 'The use of a modified importance–performance framework to examine visitor satisfaction with attributes of outdoor recreation settings', *Managing Leisure*, 7(2): 69–82.

Tonge, J. and Moore, S. (2007). 'Importance-satisfaction analysis for marine parks hinterlands: A Western Australia case study', *Tourism Management*, 20(3): 768–776.

Tribe, J. and Snaith, T. (1998). 'From SERVQUAL to HOLSAT: Holiday satisfaction in Varadero, Cuba', *Tourism Management*, 19(1): 25–34.

Truong, T. H. and Foster, D. (2006). 'Using HOLSAT to evaluate tourist satisfaction at destinations: The case of Australian holidaymakers in Vietnam', *Tourism Management*, 27(5): 842–855.

UNWTO (1985). *Identification and Evaluation of Those Components of Tourism Services Which Have a Bearing on Tourist Satisfaction and Which Can Be Regulated, and State Measures to Ensure Adequate Quality of Tourism Services*, Madrid: World Tourism Organization.

Wade, D. J. and Eagle, P. F. J. (2003). 'Use of importance-performance analysis and market segmentation for tourism management in parks and protected areas: An application to Tanzania's national parks', *Journal of Ecotourism*, 2(3): 196–212.

Weiermair, K. (2000). 'Tourists' perceptions toward and satisfaction with service quality in the cross-cultural service encounter: Implications for hospitality and tourism management', *Managing Service Quality*, 10(6): 397–409.

Xiao, H. and Huyton, J. (1996). 'Tourism and leisure: An integrative case in China', *International Journal of Contemporary Hospitality Management*, 8(6): 18–24.

Yang, C.-C. (2005). 'The refined Kano's model and its application', *Total Quality Management and Business Excellence*, 16(10): 1127–1137.

Yoon, Y. and Uysal, M. (2005). 'An examination of the effects of motivation and satisfaction on destination loyalty: A structural model', *Tourism Management*, 26(1): 45–56.

Yüksel, A. and Yüksel, F. (2001). 'Comparative performance analysis: Tourists' perceptions of Turkey relative to other tourist destinations', *Journal of Vacation Marketing*, 7(4): 333–355.

Zehrer, A. (2009). 'Service experience and service design: Concepts and application in tourism SMEs', *Managing Service Quality*, 19(3): 332–349.

Zeithaml, V. A., Berry, L. L. and Parasuraman, A. (1996). 'The behavioural consequences of service quality', *Journal of Marketing*, 60(2): 31–46.

Zeithaml, V. A. and Bitner, M. J. (2003). *Services Marketing*, New York: McGraw-Hill.

Zhang, H. Q. and Chow, I. (2004). 'Application of importance-performance model in tour guides' performance: Evidence from mainland Chinese outbound visitors in Hong Kong', *Tourism Management*, 25(1): 81–89.

Zhao, M. and Dholakia, R. (2009). 'A multi-attribute model of web site interactivity and customer satisfaction: An application of the Kano model', *Managing Service Quality: An International Journal*, 19(3): 286–307.

19

CUSTOMER SATISFACTION AND PRICING DECISIONS

Giampaolo Viglia

Introduction

Pricing is very important in marketing decisions. We judge the price of a product according to an expectation that we have in mind. This expectation regarding a price has been theorized by previous literature as the reference price (Briesch et al. 1997).

Price expectation is driven by consumers' prior experience and it is influenced by the current price. People become accustomed to a certain price level and they judge external evidence according to the expected reference. A crucial relevant factor is also given by social comparison: customers judge what they have to pay according also to what other customers, especially in the same social group, had to pay for the same or a similar product (Mezias et al. 2002). When driven by social forces and not by prior expectations, the proper conceptualization of the reference price is price fairness (Xia et al. 2004).

The adaptation to a new level of prices may depend on the type of consumer, whether they are loyal or switchers: consumers who are loyal to few brands generally integrate only these pieces of evidence while switchers tend to integrate all the prices of promoted products, unwittingly integrating incidental and irrelevant price information for a particular good or service.

Wrong pricing is an element of customers being or feeling ripped off. Therefore it is necessary to investigate the way prices are stored in the mind of the customer. People are more accurate in recalling price ranks than in estimating numerical prices. Remembering only price ranks means that customers don't remember the precise price but only the position of one product with respect to the other (e.g. Holiday Inn is usually cheaper than Hilton).

In making a purchase decision, consumers consider store specific reference prices of what they are interested in as a basis for price comparison. This way of doing this is biased on average, as consumers consider predominantly the prices of the products they have familiarity with. For instance, one might consider the company Easyjet to be cheaper than the company Ryanair just because of a specific personal experience where Easyjet was cheaper than Ryanair. Nonetheless, this does not mean that Easyjet is cheaper than Ryanair on average.

When the task is not so relevant (i.e. the value of the item is low), consumers use price memory implicitly, invoking heuristics. Imagine, for example, the purchase of a touristic postcard. In this case, consumers have a price in mind and they tend to recall that price, adapting to the current conditions. This last point appears to be particularly interesting, as consumers were shown to be willing to pay much more for the same product depending on the location (e.g. purchase of a beer in a small kiosk close to the seaside or in a supermarket).

Common pricing practices and recent pricing trends

Recent attention has been paid towards the integration of dynamic pricing mechanisms directly into online review websites to favour an immediate online booking. There are plenty of these examples in the hospitality industry with big giants such as TripAdvisor and Google already using this approach.

The traditional maximization of the Revenue Per Available Room (RevPar) is now obtained through algorithms that account for both the pricing and occupancy components. Nonetheless, due to the sharing economy boom, there is a contemporary spread of new participative pricing mechanisms where the consumer is involved in the price-setting process. Some of these mechanisms, such as price negotiations between buyer and seller, were already in place and simply had a new renaissance. Other mechanisms, like Name Your Own Price (NYOP) and Pay What You Want (PWYW), are completely new. In NYOP the buyer sets the price they would like to pay for a product and the seller can accept the offer or not (Voigt and Hinz 2014). In PWYW the decision is completely delegated to the consumer, in that the seller has to accept whatever amount the consumer offers, even zero (Kim et al. 2009). It is quite evident how these mechanisms can be quite risky for the seller as, economically speaking, individuals would maximize their utility by paying zero. However, some hotel chains such as IBIS are already implementing PWYW, with the goal of increasing the awareness of the product being offered and, in turn, the quantities of rooms sold.

Price and customer satisfaction

Customer satisfaction can be defined as the creation of value for consumers, by demonstrating the ability and responsibility to meet customers' expectations and satisfy customers' needs (Dominici and Guzzo 2010). The price of a stay in a particular location was shown to be related to customer satisfaction (Radojevic et al. 2015). This suggests that hotel guests are more demanding in terms of their requirements and expectations when paying more for a certain service. Price plays a highly significant role in perceptions held by guests with regards to the quality and value of the consumed product, as the general expectation is that higher price means higher service (Matzler et al. 2006). Nonetheless, higher prices have also been shown to be associated with lower customer value. Recent research has investigated the relation between pricing and customer satisfaction in online environments (Ye et al. 2014). Post-purchase perceptions, which are a proxy for customer satisfaction, have been shown to be mediated by the price level.

The relation between price and satisfaction judgements appears to be linked to the concept of price fairness (Herrmann et al. 2007). Not to break this equilibrium, the hospitality or tourism company has two options. A first option is billing a premium price. This will increase the customer expectations. In this case the company has to handle the higher customer expectations, delivering the service in a timely manner and with a greater quality. A way to do this effectively is allocating more resources to enhance customer satisfaction. The second option is to keep the price low, thus maintaining relatively low expectations in the mind of the customer.

To explore the nature of customer satisfaction and pricing, the study presents a case study design in a hospitality context. The case study presented next will deal with this second scenario. The goal of the case study is also to disentangle the concept of price expectation from the concept of price fairness.

Not breaking the rule. The Premier Inn promise

Premier Inn, a subsidiary of Whitbread PLC, is the UK's largest hotel chain, with over 670 hotels in the UK, equalling over 55,000 rooms. They are positioning themselves in the budget hotel market.

Budget hotels are defined as branded chain hotels below four-star level, with generally a standardized appearance and a no-frills service, often with limited food and beverage facilities (Clarke and Chen 2009).

This research focuses on Premier Inn hotels in the Poole and Bournemouth area. The case study consisted of consumer opinions of two Premier Inn hotels in order to draw relations between price and customer satisfaction. We conducted focused interviews with a selection of guests. Moreover, since customer satisfaction is strongly influenced by the interaction between customers and employers, this case also examines employee behaviour.

More precisely, the three groups of stakeholders investigated are presented in Table 19.1.

Table 19.1 Stakeholder group composition of face-to-face semi-structured interviews

Stakeholder group	Male	Female	Total informants
1. Leisure customers	6	5	11
2. Business customers	8	5	13
3. Employees	7	6	13
Total informants	21	16	37

Source: Author.

The fieldwork was carried out over a one-month period.

Two investigators analysed the data to increase the study's internal validity and reliability. The three key research questions of this research were adapted to the group of stakeholders interviewed and generally formulated as 'did the price paid match your expectations?', 'do you think that the price charged is fair?' and 'are you satisfied with the service received?'/'has the training received been beneficial to the provision of guest service?'

A general analytic framework (Yin 2009) was used to analyse and interpret the data. This analytic framework comprises three stages: (1) analysis of individual interviews and transcripts, (2) identification of shared themes and (3) analysis of the shared themes.

Research findings

Drawing from the illustrative case and the review of the literature, we identify the underlying dynamics in the relation between pricing and customer satisfaction.

For 'did the price paid match your expectations?' and 'do you think that the price charged is fair?', the findings show that on average customers were satisfied, thus showing concerns towards the adoption of dynamic pricing and overbooking practices.

1 *Dynamic pricing*: The most common stakeholders' triggers are related to adoption of dynamic pricing practices, which are common in the hospitality industry. For Sarah, a leisure traveller, 'I am very happy with the value for money provided by Premier Inn. What I find more difficult to accept is to pay a different price for the exact same service.' This rip-off appeared to be particularly salient when generated by comparison with others: 'I'm used to paying a different price depending on the booking time. But when I discovered that I paid almost double that of my neighbour I could not believe it' (Brian, business traveller).

2 *Overbooking*: Consumers generally book a hotel to reduce the uncertainty with respect to other cheaper solutions (e.g. hostels). When this uncertainty is not efficiently reduced, like in the case of hotels informing the guest that his or her room was overbooked, there is a perception of a broken promise. For example, a leisure traveller reported: 'when we arrived at midnight after six hours of flight we found out that there was no room available for us. We paid a reasonable fare for the reservation, and I understand that this might happen, but it was really difficult to cope with.'

As for the satisfaction with the service received and the training for the provision of service, both customers and employees were very happy on average. The only two criticisms that emerged were related to the technology factor, on the consumer side, and to the motivation of employees, on the employees' side.

3 *Technology factor*: Many travellers book hotels online with the use of mobile devices (Okazaki et al. 2015). For this reason, a fast and efficient app to book and manage the reservation is essential. Looking forward, the use of wearable devices will increase the need of integrating the various steps of the hotel experience with smart applications. Harry, a leisure traveller, exemplified this concisely: 'Staff is very friendly at Premier Inn, but for me the customer experience starts before, when I open the mobile app. In the latter aspect many improvements are needed. I hope one day to check-in with a barcode and to open my room with my watch.'

4 *Motivation of employees*: Despite being a budget hotel, Premier Inn claims to be a customer-focused business. Empowerment levels were determined to be very high. This is significant as it shows a level of work which allows employees increased self-efficacy and pride in Premier Inn. Motivation of employees regarding the provision of exceptional guest service was the only factor to have a mixed response, suggesting that although employees feel they can and are allowed to offer a good service, their motivation could be improved through ad hoc staff training. This is worrying for Premier Inn, as there is a risk that customers could be coming away from an experience satisfied but not 'wowed'. As an anonymous employee suggested: 'We suffer from a lack of team engagement. The training is perceived as needed and not as an opportunity to offer a great service.'

The results show that for effective customer satisfaction to take place in low-priced hotels the relationship between the company and the consumer has to go beyond the usual forms of service experience, such as staff friendliness. A deep technological integration is required, and clear reasons for paying a different price for the same service have to be offered to the consumer. The findings give evidence of how overbooking is a significant factor affecting customer satisfaction, and this negative effect remains vivid even after having paid a low price for the reservation. For this reason, in the remaining part of the chapter, we explore the overbooking concept and how to increase the acceptance of this policy.

Reservation, cancellation and consequences

A great element of dissatisfaction related to pricing is the application of the overbooking practice by tourism and hospitality operators.

When booking, travel consumers are generally required to buy a reservation. The reservation is a forward contract between the firm and the customer that gives the consumer two types of rights:

1   A 'reservation right', which is the guarantee to benefit from the purchased service in the future at a fixed price;
2   A 'cancellation right', which is the option for the customer to cancel (in some cases with a penalty) before the date of the use of the service.

Customers value both reservation and cancellation. They value reservation as they are buying beforehand the guarantee to use the service they require. This becomes particularly salient when the prices of the chosen product are cheaper if bought in advance (e.g. an air travel ticket). They also value the cancellation option for the flexibility to make amendments if they wish or they need to do so. The firm has two types of duties: honouring the reservation when customers show up (or providing high compensation if it cannot honour the reservation) and in the cases where customers cancel or do not show up, bearing the wasted capacity. Recently, companies operating in the tourism and hospitality sectors have been offering discounts to customers who are willing to buy non-amendable fares. The underlying idea is that they protect themselves from the uncertainty related to last-minute cancellations. Moreover, firms use overbooking.

Overbooking involves denied service costs but, most importantly, has an effect on customer satisfaction. In what follows we discuss the implications of denied service and how to reduce negative effects on customer satisfaction.

Denied service and effects on customer satisfaction

The legal compensation involved here often requires payment of the monetary damages. Nonetheless, the consumer generally views this as inadequate. For instance, a hotel customer who planned to take a vacation would not find particularly rewarding a full compensation for the denied hotel service plus an additional percentage of the contracted service for the ruined vacation. The effective solution in this case is offering to consumers a substitute hotel with ancillary benefits, such as an upgrade. This behaviour tends to be less expensive for the company and more rewarding than pure monetary compensation for the consumer. The possible negative effects on customer satisfaction of a denied service require a strategic selection of the customers who will be offered an alternative solution. From a legal point of view, such selection must not be discriminatory. For example the US Department of Transportation (DOT) states that every airline carrier has to establish priority rules for determining which passengers holding confirmed reserved space shall be denied boarding on an oversold flight in the event that an insufficient number of volunteers come forward; such rules shall not cause any advantage or disadvantage to any particular person. The default option is usually on a first come first served basis, so that late customers are generally offered the alternative solution. Nonetheless, there are many business situations where this allocation is undesirable. In the case of hotel overbooking, the application of a first come first served basis would create important difficulties for customers who arrive very late in the evening.

This segment of consumers would be the most affected by this strategy, and it would be difficult to relocate them during the night, when they are often irritable and tired. Most importantly, customers who arrive late are typically business travellers who pay the highest rates and represent the most profitable segment for most hotels. A possible solution adopted by hotels is to use alternative criteria: monitoring arrival rates during the day to anticipate oversold conditions and, if at some point the probability of reaching an over-sale increases, finding alternative arrangements for early-arriving customers.

In many tourism and hospitality situations, it is possible to require in the first instance a pool of volunteers during the allocation of services. For example in budget hotels, operators can select specific guests (such as young, student travellers, etc.) for denied-reservation offers. The goal is to select a target segment of customers that is happy to receive a nicer hotel room in exchange for keeping their initial reserved room available.

Customers need time to accept overbooking practices, and providers have to learn how to develop painless strategies. Overbooking remains a primary source of dissatisfaction for customers. Customers' satisfaction occurs when expectations are met (Baker 2013). Therefore operators should offer services that are capable of delivering. In the specific case of over-booking, in order to avoid customer dissatisfaction, a warning about the risk of potential overbooking should be clearly outlined in the reservation phase.

Conclusions

While customer satisfaction through good service experience remains a solid pillar, a new discussion clarifies new threats to consumer satisfaction. Firstly, dynamic pricing strategies undermine the price perceived to be fair to be charged, especially when another known individual pays a substantially different price. Despite the concept of reference price including both the expectation and fairness constructs, the results from the case study show that the fairness construct is the most affected by dynamic pricing strategies. This result is consistent with the recent findings of Viglia et al. (2016). Secondly, technological improvements are the new frontier of customer satisfaction. Consumers are looking for independence, and expect technology that is able to increase their autonomy. Finally, the case study research and the subsequent discussion investigate the possible drawbacks of overbooking, a practice used by hoteliers to benefit from all their available capacity. Even in the context of low prices, this practice appears to be breaking the rules of a promise, and should be used with the discussed approaches, and in general with extreme caution.

References

Baker, D. M. A. (2013). 'Service quality and customer satisfaction in the airline industry: A comparison between legacy airlines and low-cost airlines', *American Journal of Tourism Research*, 2(1): 67–77.

Briesch, R. A., Krishnamurthi, L., Mazumdar, T. and Raj, S. P. (1997). 'A comparative analysis of reference price models', *Journal of Consumer Research*, 24(2): 202–214.

Clarke, A. and Chen, W. (2009). *International Hospitality Management*, 2nd edition, Oxford: Elsevier.

Dominici, G. and Guzzo, R. (2010). 'Customer satisfaction in the hotel industry: A case study from Sicily', *International Journal of Marketing Studies*, 2(2): 3–12.

Herrmann, A., Xia, L., Monroe, K. B. and Huber, F. (2007). 'The influence of price fairness on customer satisfaction: An empirical test in the context of automobile purchases', *Journal of Product and Brand Management*, 16(1): 49–58.

Kim, J. Y., Natter, M. and Spann, M. (2009). 'Pay what you want: A new participative pricing mechanism', *Journal of Marketing*, 73(1): 44–58.

Matzler, K., Renzl, B. and Rothenberger, S. (2006). 'Measuring the relative importance of service dimensions in the formation of price satisfaction and service satisfaction: A case study in the hotel industry', *Scandinavian Journal of Hospitality and Tourism*, 6(3): 179–196.

Mezias, S. J., Chen, Y. R. and Murphy, P. R. (2002). 'Aspiration-level adaptation in an American financial services organization: A field study', *Management Science*, 48(10): 1285–1300.

Okazaki, S., Campo, S., Andreu, L. and Romero, J. (2015). 'A latent class analysis of Spanish travelers' mobile internet usage in travel planning and execution', *Cornell Hospitality Quarterly*, 56(2): 191–201.

Radojevic, T., Stanisic, N. and Stanic, N. (2015). 'Ensuring positive feedback: Factors that influence customer satisfaction in the contemporary hospitality industry', *Tourism Management*, 51: 13–21.

Viglia, G., Mauri, A. and Carricano, M. (2016). 'The exploration of hotel reference prices under dynamic pricing scenarios and different forms of competition', *International Journal of Hospitality Management*, 52: 46–55.

Voigt, S. and Hinz, O. (2014). 'Assessing strategic behavior in name-your-own-price markets', *International Journal of Electronic Commerce*, 18(3): 103–124.

Xia, L., Monroe, K. B. and Cox, J. L. (2004). 'The price is unfair! A conceptual framework of price fairness perceptions', *Journal of Marketing*, 68(4): 1–15.

Ye, Q., Li, H., Wang, Z. and Law, R. (2014). 'The influence of hotel price on perceived service quality and value in e-tourism: An empirical investigation based on online traveler reviews', *Journal of Hospitality and Tourism Research*, 38(1): 23–39.

Yin, R. K. (2009). *Case Study Research: Design and Methods*, Thousand Oaks, CA: Sage.

20

DESTINATION IMAGE, CUSTOMER SATISFACTION AND BEHAVIOURAL INTENTIONS

The state-of-the-art and a new research agenda

Anestis Fotiadis, Marios Sotiriadis and Chris A. Vassiliadis

Introduction

The global tourism market is by its very nature fiercely competitive; no other marketplace has as many 'brands' all competing for attention and selection by the potential tourist. This is the main reason that destination marketers, at city, state and national levels, arguably have a far more challenging role than other consumer services or goods marketers (Pike 2008). It is not surprising therefore that tourism destination image (TDI) is of crucial importance and has demanded the attention of tourism academia and researchers. There is now a substantial body of research that documents and highlights how influential destination images are in the selection of vacation places by the potential visitor. These consumers use their perceptions about destinations in their decision making and the destination as a 'brand' is always a factor in their final choice.

An understanding of destination image and its attributes has important implications for strategic image management and may aid in designing and implementing tourism marketing programmes that create or enhance the image of countries, regions and places. Researchers have considered and analysed the topic of destination image from three main perspectives: (1) consumer behaviour/segmentation, (2) competition and (3) image formation and its components (Gallarza et al. 2002; Bigné Alcañiz et al. 2009). This chapter gives an integrated review of these three issues and summarizes and critiques the literature on the broad topic, then suggests a revised research agenda for the field. This is shown in two sections. The first deals with a view of historical and current literature taking into account the main elements and attributes of TDI explored by academic tourism research. The second presents a case study that illustrates the application of the concept of TDI to a practical tourism problem.

Review of literature: research on tourism destination image, customer satisfaction and behavioural intentions

Image is a broad construct that is widely applied in marketing and behavioural sciences to represent a person's perceptions of products, objects, behaviours and events where such perceptions are driven by beliefs, feelings and impressions (Crompton 1979). In the area of tourism destination marketing, image has been given many different definitions; however, most agree that TDI is a 'set of impressions, ideas, expectations and emotional thoughts' an individual has about a specific place (Beerli and Martin 2004; Kim and Richardson 2003).

Today it is essential for a tourism business to measure the satisfaction level of its customers. This is addressed at the global level by institutions such as the Hong Kong Polytechnic University which publishes an overall 'Tourist Satisfaction Index' (TSI) that includes in the measurement model consideration of the potential fluctuations in tourist satisfaction, namely satisfaction measures for tourist attractions, for hotels, for immigration services, for restaurants, for retail shops and for transportation, using sectoral-level models constructed by sophisticated programming using the Smart PLS software program (Ringle et al. 2005). The survey is conducted annually. The analysis of the survey data (with sample sizes of more than 2,500 cases) is based on the estimation procedure of partial least squares structural equation modelling with a weighting scheme determined by confirmatory factor analysis. This type of modelling with multiple satisfaction determinants is a more effective approach for tourist satisfaction assessment based on the complexity of the problem revealed in the related literature (Yoon and Uysal 2005). The theoretical basis for the TSI model is the proposition that tourists develop expectations of a tourism product from marketing communications, advertising, promotions and word of mouth before they decide to buy and then associate or contrast the last or actual performance after the product experience with their initial expectations for the elements of the tourism product that were delivered.

A number of authors have suggested that satisfaction is the consumer's evaluation of the perceived discrepancy between his or her prior expectation and perceived performance of the received product or service after consumption (Kozak 2001). Focusing on tourism in particular, Baker and Crompton (2000) defined satisfaction holistically as the tourist's emotional state after experiencing a trip, thereby confirming that evaluating satisfaction must be seen as a post-consumption process. Knowledge of the factors that increase tourists' satisfaction level can assist tourism managers in everyday business practice because they can improve the most critical services provided (Ross and Iso-Ahola 1991; Noe and Uysal 1997; Schofield 2000) and simultaneously become more competitive based on a higher performance in delivery (Kotler 1994). This approach creates tourism-product loyal tourists whose repeat visitation is a critical goal in any tourism business plan (Um et al. 2006; Yoon and Uysal 2005).

It is important for forecasting reasons to measure and analyse actual behaviour in the tourism market and specifically to assess the intention to visit or revisit a tourist destination, or the willingness to buy. Here, revisitation can be described as the level of tourist loyalty related to a tourist destination. Behavioural intention to visit or to revisit a tourism destination has been defined as an individual's readiness or willingness to make a visit or repeat visit to a destination. It is the most accurate prediction of the action to visit or revisit (Han and Kim 2010; Cole and Scott 2004). This is important because a number of authors have argued that it is better to attract active visitors to come back than to search for new visitors and persuade them to visit (Um et al. 2006). Petrick et al. (2001) pointed out that intention to revisit a destination is affected by the tourist's level of satisfaction, the perceived value, and past tourist behaviour, but high levels of intention should not lead to complacency and rejuvenating the tourism offering with innovation and differentiation strategies is likely to attract many actual active tourists (Assaker and Hallak 2013; Bigné et al. 2009).

Measuring perceived quality at the destination level

We now turn to an investigation of the importance of quality as perceived by customers of service industries, which has spurred extensive research into understanding the whole field of quality issues. As Grönroos (1984) suggests, services have two quality dimensions: technical quality, which refers to the outcomes (i.e. what the customer gets); and functional quality, which refers to the actual service processes (i.e. how the customer gets it). According to further thinking by Grönroos (2004), technical quality refers to the combination of end results the service provides, whereas functional quality refers to the perceptions of how the service consumers evaluate their interactions with the service provider during the actual delivery process, for example the personal interactions with staff in the theme park who deliver the services. Perceived quality and customer satisfaction are crucial for providers in order to attract, retain or create tourist loyalty (Kayat and Hai 2013). As Homer (2008) mentions, quality and image do affect attitudes and importantly low image is much more damaging than low quality. This implies that tourists favour destinations in which they are 'delighted' because the resulting perception of quality of services and products is higher than their prior expectations (Fotiadis and Vassiliadis 2010; Fotiadis 2016). When this occurs one can easily transform the image one has had for a destination in the past. This is why continuous quality improvement is a strategy that several destinations have used to improve their ongoing competitiveness (López-Toro et al. 2010).

Analysis of destination image and customer satisfaction

Understanding of images held of a destination by consumers (the TDI) is important to determine whether there is congruence between the desired brand image and that which resides in the minds of consumers. Diachronically, the multi-attribute conceptualization of TDI serves as common ground for most destination image researchers (Gallarza et al. 2002; Zhang et al. 2014).

The two main approaches are those developed by Echtner and Ritchie (1991) and Gartner (1993), with the latter being more popular among recent researchers (Zhang et al. 2014). Gartner's (1993) approach postulates that TDI consists of cognitive, affective and conative components. More specifically, the cognitive image is expressed through the sum of beliefs and knowledge which are part of the valuations of the perceived attributes of the destination (Bigné Alcañiz et al. 2009; Stylos and Andronikidis 2013). In addition, Pike (2008) contends that it is the sum of what is known or believed by the individual about a tourism destination, as well as the associated knowledge that may or may not have been derived from a previous visit that are important. The affective component refers to the emotional responses or appraisals of the individual, echoing tourists' deeper feelings towards the destination (Bigné et al. 2005). People may develop affective evaluations for a place (i) before entering that environment, (ii) during their presence there and (iii) after leaving that place to move somewhere else. Before tourists make their travel decision, they formulate a more positive affective TDI when the destination-related emotions match their motives and the benefits they pursue. Although conative TDI has been considered by many scholars as synonymous with intention (Prayag 2009), and simply representing the how and why knowledge about the way feelings of new or repeat visitors contribute to the selection or not of a specific destination for vacations (Pike and Ryan 2004; Tasci et al. 2007), there is alternative evidence that conative destination images and behavioural intentions to visit are distinct constructs (Perugini and Bagozzi 2004; Prestwich et al. 2008). Hence, TDI theory suggests that cognitive and affective images represent individuals' subjective associations or perceptions related to a destination's characteristics (Chen and Uysal 2002; Kim and Richardson 2003) and conative image outlines the idealized and desired future situation the individual wants to experience for himself/herself (Dann 1996). Table 20.1 summarizes some authors and their various definitions and related views regarding the concept of TDI and its contributing constructs.

Table 20.1 Tourism Destination Image (TDI): definitions and related views

Authors and studies	*Definitions and statements*
Kim and Richardson (2003), Beerli and Martin (2004)	It is a set of impressions, ideas, expectations and emotional thoughts an individual has of a specific place
Echtner and Ritchie (1993), Dann (1996), Pike and Ryan (2004), Tasci et al. (2007)	It is a multi-attribute concept; TDI consists of cognitive, affective and conative components. TDI is a complex combination of various features and their associated attributes
Baloglu and McCleary (1999), Beerli and Martin (2004)	The three TDI components or dimensions contribute to the formation of a global image that is considered to be greater than the sum of its parts, and that is used by the consumer to simplify the task of decision making
Kim and Yoon (2003), Li and Wang (2010)	The three dimensions of TDI can be studied separately in order to understand the complexity of the whole
Tasci et al. (2007)	The essence of TDI is to find out how tourism destinations are seen and felt
Sönmez and Sirakaya (2002)	For the development of successful marketing strategies and to create a positive destination positional impact it is important to have a clear understanding of the TDI because image is based on the tourist's expected benefits, psychological characteristics, and meanings
Agapito et al. (2013)	TDI consists of a subjective interpretation of a destination made by individuals which influences tourist behaviour
Woodside and Lysonski (1989)	There is an evident relationship between positive perceptions of destinations and positive purchase decisions. Negative images, even if unjustified, will influence potential tourists and result in a decision not to purchase
Gallarza et al. (2002), Agapito et al. (2013)	In the literature, there continues to be a lack of useful practical applications and conceptual frameworks for TDI. There is also a lack of empirical validation of the relationships among the dimensions that are believed to constitute a TDI

Source: Authors.

Customer satisfaction is crucially interrelated with TDI. As Yuksel et al. (2010) indicated, when tourists visit a destination an attachment is created based on the image they had and the specific goals they finally achieved. This attachment can make tourists loyal to a destination. Ranjbarian and Pool (2015) say that satisfaction is a behavioural phenomenon formed based on customer expectation for a destination's features and it significantly affects revisiting intentions. Cheng and Lu (2013) on their research about TDI for island tourism proved that image affects perceptions of novelty, hedonics and perceived value.

Destination image and consumer behaviour: influence of TDI on consumer behaviour

Cheng and Lu (2013) believe that TDI is the main element that affects tourists' destination choices. For that reason an assessment of the TDI could enhance strategic managerial decisions related to the perceived strengths and weaknesses of a destination and even help in improving destination development and rejuvenation (Beerli and Martin 2004). Several studies have associated destination image directly with a behavioural component that encompasses the actions of individuals by showing the link to the probability of visiting/revisiting a destination or actually recommending it to others (Pike and Ryan 2004; Konecnik and Gartner 2007; Bigné et al. 2009).

To understand the relationship between TDI and consumer behaviour, researchers have examined three of these links in some depth: (1) TDI and perceived value as described in the 'quality satisfaction behavioural intentions' paradigm, (2) effects of various constructs (e.g. novelty seeking, familiarity, overall satisfaction, destination loyalty) on consumer behaviour, and (3) relationship/linkage between TDI, tourist satisfaction and post-consumption behavioural intentions (future intentions) of tourists covering loyalty/intention to revisit and word-of-mouth activities.

How these issues have been addressed in academic studies is shown next in a synoptic manner:

1   The *first issue* covering the quality satisfaction behavioural intentions dimensions is investigated in Chen and Tsai's (2007) research where they examine how destination image and evaluative factors affect behavioural intentions mention. Their results delineate that destination image is the most important factor for behavioural intentions which can be affected directly and indirectly.

2   The *second issue*, detailed analysis of destination image constructs, was explored by several researchers. In their research Chen and Lin (2012) verify that destination familiarity affects destination image and travelling intentions. Loyalty is another very important construct of destination image followed by affective image and cognitive image (Zhang et al. 2014). Future intentions to travel to a destination and immediate ones are positively affected by destination image as it affects novelty seeking and satisfaction (Assaker et al. 2011).

3   The *third issue*, the relationship of TDI to future intentions, has been examined by the following studies. Destination image is a direct predecessor for how tourists perceive quality, their level of satisfaction, and their willingness to return to and recommend a destination (Bigné et al. 2001, 2009). Chen and Tsai (2007: p. 1115) developed a path related to future intentions and TDI: 'destination image→trip quality→perceived value→satisfaction→behavioral intentions'. Another important factor for future intentions is word of mouth as it affects destination image, tourist attitude and intention to travel (Reza Jalilvand et al. 2012).

These studies have attempted to link the theoretical models to the practice of defining and managing TDI in the conceptual tourism environment. However, they lack practical inputs from those working in the day-to-day world of tourism. Consequently the following case study is used to illustrate the related issues and aspects of TDI strategy, i.e. tourist satisfaction and post-consumption behaviour.

The island of Mauritius: segmentation of visitors based on destination image and loyalty

This case study presents the main elements of some excellent research on the practical understanding and application of TDI. It demonstrates that useful information for industry can be provided in an academic journal article and indicates the pathways that academic research in tourism is following in the present decade.

Background and knowledge gaps

The island of Mauritius is located off the east coast of Africa, in the Indian Ocean, and is positioned as a resort-based destination with its sun, sea and sand (3S) offering. Its leading visitor markets are France, Germany, the UK, South Africa, India and China. The destination has long held some exotic appeal and visitors' expectations have been partly formed by the 'organic and induced images' of a tropical destination described by friends or promoted in travel guides and travel programmes. An organic image is one that develops based on what is learned of a country from non-commercial sources, for example friends, acquaintances and social media. Induced image refers to the effects of the destination's marketing and promotion efforts. Once at a destination, visitors develop a more complex and personal image (referred to as the TDI), based on a re-evaluation of the destination attributes, both those previously expected and those currently experienced (Echtner and Ritchie 1991).

Purpose

Prayag's (2009) research paper attempted to address these knowledge gaps. Primarily the study's purpose was to assess the influence of socio-demographic characteristics on destination image, satisfaction and loyalty, or more specifically: (1) to assess differences in satisfaction levels with image attributes among visitors, thereby offering a segmentation perspective on the visitors to Mauritius; and (2) to identify whether satisfaction with image attributes is a predictor of visitors' loyalty levels.

Literature review

The author performed an extensive literature review, essentially on the components of TDI (e.g. deconstruction of island-specific image attributes, destination image components, cognitive image and visitors' socio-demographics) and the relationship between TDI's cognitive component and visitor loyalty. In this research the relationship between revisit intentions and intention to recommend was assessed using satisfaction with the cognitive attributes of the location.

Methodology

The primary data collection approach was a self-administered survey of hotel guests visiting for vacation purposes. This resulted in a sample of 705 respondents with valid and useable data which was analysed using a *k*-means clustering algorithm and discriminant analysis, from which three clusters of visitors were identified. More specifically, the following methodological steps were undertaken.

Questionnaire design

A combination of unstructured (in-depth interviews) and structured methods was used to identify pertinent destination attributes. A final list of 29 attributes was retained, containing more cognitive images, which was measured on a 7-point Likert scale. A pre-test of the questionnaire on 50 international visitors was undertaken prior to final data collection.

Sampling and data collection

For the identification of meaningful segments, the sample was designed using nationality as the key investigative variable. Data were collected from visitors from five main countries only: France, Germany, the UK, India and South Africa. Visitors were approached on selected beaches around hotels in Mauritius. The data collection method was self-completion of the questionnaire in the presence of the interviewer.

Data analysis

This research used the method of post hoc segmentation. A two-step approach was used to analyse the data. Initially, cluster analysis was used to identify homogeneous subsets of visitors based on levels of satisfaction with image attributes. Thereafter, these clusters were profiled using chi-square tests and analysis of variance (ANOVA) to understand the differences among segments. Finally, two regression models were estimated to identify the image attributes that were the most important predictors of behavioural loyalty using the proxies of revisit and recommendation intentions as the dependent variables.

Findings

- The results indicated that characteristics of the traveller were responsible for the main differences between the three clusters. Useful segmentation variables were: main purpose of visit, length of stay, holiday's arrangement (package or not), nationality and marital status.
- Predictors of behavioural loyalty: Different image attributes predict visitors' revisit and recommendation intentions. The results indicated that a group of 13 image satisfaction items were significant predictors of revisit intentions with 'satisfaction with the reputation of Mauritius' being the strongest predictor of the group.
- The most interesting cluster comprised holidaymakers of various nationalities, travelling on a holiday package and staying less than 16 days.

In conclusion TDI is seen to play a critical role and Mauritius remains a popular holiday destination, an 'island paradise', due to satisfactory experiences with its attractions based on the 3Ss for most holidaymakers from traditional markets, travelling on a packaged tour and staying for less than 16 days.

A research agenda: suggestions for future research

As we are living in a dynamic global environment where travel for tourism purposes is becoming a fundamental social requirement, this research on a topic of such importance as destination image, customer satisfaction and tourist behaviour must continue. The area is also dynamic and a new generation of tourists will have images of potential destinations directly affected by new technological trends. New tourism markets will be seen to arise (for example, Iran) and new customers from generation Y will enthusiastically enter the tourist market where the images they form and the images they perceive will be very interesting topics for future investigation. Many of the world's problems such as income inequality, climate change, refugee immigration, economic disturbances and local instabilities will mean that sustainability and environmental issues must be further investigated, especially where these concern destination image and tourism impact perceptions.

References

Agapito, D., Mendes, J. and Valle, P. (2013). 'Conceptualizing the sensory dimension of tourist experiences', *Journal of Destination Marketing and Management*, 2(2): 62–73.

Assaker, G. and Hallak, R. (2013). 'Moderating effects of tourists' novelty-seeking tendencies on destination image, visitor satisfaction, and short- and long-term revisit intentions', *Journal of Travel Research*, 52(5): 600–613.

Assaker, G., Vinzi, V. E. and O'Connor, P. (2011). 'Examining the effect of novelty seeking, satisfaction, and destination image on tourists' return pattern: A two factor, non-linear latent growth model', *Tourism Management*, 32(4): 890–901.

Baker, D. A. and Crompton, J. L. (2000). 'Quality, satisfaction and behavioural intentions', *Annals of Tourism Research*, 27(3): 785–804.

Beerli, A. and Martin, J. (2004). 'Factors influencing destination image', *Annals of Tourism Research*, 31(3): 657–681.

Bigné, J. E., Andreu, L. and Gnoth, J. (2005). 'The theme park experience: An analysis of pleasure, arousal and satisfaction', *Tourism Management*, 26(6): 833–844.

Bigné, J. E., Sánchez, I. and Andreu, L. (2009). 'The role of variety seeking in short and long run revisit intentions in holiday destinations', *International Journal of Culture, Tourism and Hospitality Research*, 3(2): 103–115.

Bigné, J. E., Sánchez, M. I. and Sánchez, J. (2001). 'Tourism image, evaluation variables and after purchase behaviour: Inter-relationship', *Tourism Management*, 22(6): 607–616.

Bigné Alcañiz, E., Garcia, I. S. and Sanz Blas, S. (2009). 'The functional-psychological continuum in the cognitive image of a destination: A confirmatory analysis', *Tourism Management*, 30(5): 715–723.

Chen, C.-C. and Lin, Y.-H. (2012). 'Segmenting mainland Chinese tourists to Taiwan by destination familiarity: A factor cluster approach', *International Journal of Tourism Research*, 14(4): 339–352.

Chen, C.-F. and Tsai, D. (2007). 'How destination image and evaluative factors affect behavioral intentions?', *Tourism Management*, 28(4): 1115–1122.

Chen, J. S. and Uysal, M. (2002). 'Market positioning analysis: A hybrid approach', *Annals of Tourism Research*, 29(4): 987–1003.

Cheng, T.-M. and Lu, C.-C. (2013). 'Destination image, novelty, hedonics, perceived value, and revisiting behavioral intention for island tourism', *Asia Pacific Journal of Tourism Research*, 18(7): 766–783.

Cole, S. T. and Scott, D. (2004). 'Examining the mediating role of experience quality in a model of tourist experiences', *Journal of Travel and Tourism Marketing*, 16(1): 79–90.

Crompton, J. L. (1979). 'Motivations for pleasure vacation', *Annals of Tourism Research*, 6(4): 408–424.

Dann, G. M. S. (1996). 'Tourists' images of a destination – An alternative analysis', *Journal of Travel and Tourism Marketing*, 5(1/2): 41–55.

Echtner, C. M. and Ritchie, J. P. (1991). 'The meaning and measurement of destination image', *Journal of Tourism Studies*, 2(2): 2–12.

Fotiadis, A. K. (2016). 'Modifying and applying time and cost blocks: The case of E-Da theme park, Kaohsiung, Taiwan', *Tourism Management*, 54(June): 34–42.

Fotiadis, A. and Vassiliadis, C. (2010). 'Rural tourism service quality in Greece', *e-Review of Tourism Research (eRTR)*, 8(4): 69–84.

Gallarza, M. G., Saura, I. G. and García, H. C. (2002). 'Destination image: Towards a conceptual framework', *Annals of Tourism Research*, 29(1): 56–78.

Gartner, W. C. (1993). 'Image information process', *Journal of Travel and Tourism Marketing*, 2(2/3): 191–215.

Grönroos, C. (1984). 'A service quality model and its marketing implications', *European Journal of Marketing*, 18(4): 36–44.

Grönroos, C. (2004). 'The relationship marketing process: Communication, interaction, dialogue, value', *Journal of Business and Industrial Marketing*, 19(2): 99–113.

Han, H. and Kim, Y. (2010). 'An investigation of green hotel customers' decision formation: Developing an extended model of the theory of planned behavior', *International Journal of Hospitality Management*, 29(4): 659–668.

Homer, P. M. (2008). 'Perceived quality and image: When all is not "rosy"', *Journal of Business Research*, 61(7): 715–723.

Kayat, K. and Hai, M. A. (2013). 'Perceived service quality and tourists' cognitive image of a destination', *Anatolia: An International Journal of Tourism and Hospitality Research*, 25(1): 1–12.

Kim, H. and Richardson, S. L. (2003). 'Motion picture impacts on destination images', *Annals of Tourism Research*, 30(1): 216–237.

Kim, S. and Yoon, Y. (2003). 'The hierarchical effects of affective and cognitive components on tourism image', *Journal of Travel and Tourism Marketing*, 14(2): 1–22.

Konecnik, M. and Gartner, W. C. (2007). 'Customer-based brand equity for a destination', *Annals of Tourism Research*, 34(2): 400–421.

Kotler, P. (1994). *Marketing Management: Analysis, Planning, Implementation and Control*, 8th edition, Englewood Cliffs, NJ: Prentice-Hall International.

Kozak, M. (2001). 'Repeaters' behaviour at two distinct destinations', *Annals of Tourism Research*, 28(3): 784–807.

Li, X. and Wang, Y. (2010). 'Evaluating the effectiveness of destination marketing organizations' websites: Evidence from China', *International Journal of Tourism Research*, 12(5): 536–549.

López-Toro, A. A., Díaz-Muñoz, R. and Pérez-Moreno, S. (2010). 'An assessment of the quality of a tourist destination: The case of Nerja, Spain', *Total Quality Management and Business Excellence*, 21(3): 269–289.

Noe, F. P. and Uysal, M. (1997). 'Evaluation of outdoor recreational settings. A problem of measuring user satisfaction', *Journal of Retailing and Consumer Services*, 4(4): 223–230.

Perugini, M. and Bagozzi, R. P. (2004). 'The distinction between desires and intentions', *European Journal of Social Psychology*, 34(1): 69–84.

Petrick, J. F., Morais, D. D. and Norman, W. C. (2001). 'An examination of the determinants of entertainment vacationers' intentions to revisit', *Journal of Travel Research*, 40(1): 41–48.

Pike, S. (2008). *Destination Marketing*, Burlington, MA: Butterworth-Heinemann.

Pike, S. and Ryan, C. (2004). 'Destination positioning analysis through a comparison of cognitive, affective and conative perceptions', *Journal of Travel Research*, 42(4): 333–342.

Prayag, G. (2009). 'Tourists' evaluation of destination image, satisfaction and future behavioral intentions – The case of Mauritius', *Journal of Travel and Tourism Marketing*, 26(8): 836–853.

Prestwich, A., Perugini, M. and Hurling, R. (2008). 'Goal desires moderate intention – behavior relations', *British Journal of Social Psychology*, 47(1): 49–71.

Ranjbarian, B. and Pool, J. K. (2015). 'The impact of perceived quality and value on tourists' satisfaction and intention to revisit Nowshahr City of Iran', *Journal of Quality Assurance in Hospitality and Tourism*, 16(1): 103–117.

Reza Jalilvand, M., Samiei, N., Dini, B. and Yaghoubi Manzari, P. (2012). 'Examining the structural relationships of electronic word of mouth, destination image, tourist attitude toward destination and travel intention: An integrated approach', *Journal of Destination Marketing and Management*, 1(1–2): 134–143.

Ringle, C., Wende, S. and Will, A. (2005). *Smart PLS 2.0 (Beta)*, Hamburg: http://www.smartpls.de.

Ross, R. L. and Iso-Ahola, S. E. (1991). 'Sightseeing tourists' motivation and satisfaction', *Annals of Tourism Research*, 18(2): 226–237.

Schofield, P. (2000). 'Evaluating Castlefield urban heritage park from the consumer perspective: Destination attribute importance, visitor perception, and satisfaction', *Tourism Analysis*, 5(2–4): 183–189.

Sönmez, S. and Sirakaya, E. (2002). 'A distorted destination image? The case of Turkey', *Journal of Travel Research*, 41(2): 185–196.

Stylos, N. and Andronikidis, A. (2013). 'Exploring the cognitive image of a tourism destination', *TOURISMOS: An International Multidisciplinary Journal of Tourism*, 8(3): 77–97.

Tasci, A. D. A., Gartner, W. C. and Cavusgil, S. T. (2007). 'Conceptualization and operationalization of destination image', *Journal of Hospitality and Tourism Research*, 31(2): 194–223.

Um, S., Chon, K. and Ro, Y. (2006). 'Antecedents of revisit intention', *Annals of Tourism Research*, 33(4): 1141–1158.

Woodside, A. G. and Lysonski, S. (1989). 'A general model of traveler destination choice', *Journal of Travel Research*, 27(2): 8–14.

Yoon, Y. and Uysal, M. (2005). 'An examination of the effects of motivation and satisfaction on destination loyalty: A structural model', *Tourism Management*, 26(1): 45–56.

Yuksel, A., Yuksel, F. and Bilim, Y. (2010). 'Destination attachment: Effects of customer satisfaction and cognitive, affective and conative loyalty', *Tourism Management*, 31(2): 274–284.

Zhang, H., Fu, X., Cai, L. A. and Lu, L. (2014). 'Destination image and tourist loyalty: A meta-analysis', *Tourism Management*, 40(February): 213–223.

21

CUSTOMER DELIGHT FROM HOSPITALITY AND TOURISM EXPERIENCE

Jianyu Ma and Noel Scott

Introduction

The study of delight is an emerging research area in marketing and tourism that is both practically and theoretically important (Crotts et al. 2008). In the 1980s, academics and practitioners began to find that customers wanted more than to be satisfied (Cadotte et al. 1987; Churchill and Surprenant 1982; Deming 1986; Rollins and Bradley 1986). In the 1990s, services research found that higher levels of satisfaction and/or service quality may produce exceptional behavioural results, such as greater loyalty (Parasuraman et al. 1993; Schlossberg 1990). Customer delight was thought to be the key to the more elusive goals of loyalty and loyalty-driven profit. Since these beginnings, research into delight has grown substantially in the consumer behaviour, marketing and tourism literatures.

The standard model of customer delight (abbreviated as the ORV model after its authors: Oliver et al. 1997) examines the effects of delight on word of mouth (WOM) and repurchase intentions (Figure 21.1). Customer delight is conceptualised as an emotional response which results from a surprising and positive level of performance (Chitturi et al. 2008; Finn 2005; Oliver et al. 1997), and is considered to provide an explanation for the observed variation in the intentions of consumers reporting the same level of satisfaction. The concept of customer delight builds on a history of the study of affective (Westbrook 1987) and experiential (Holbrook and Hirschman 1982) emotional responses to consumption, and has received significant attention from academia and practitioners since the 1990s. Later, by using cognitive appraisal theory, multiple paths leading to customer delight were identified, thereby explaining how delight can be generated without surprising stimuli.

In this chapter, we discuss the antecedents and consequences of delight, and the relationship between delight and satisfaction, and provide a brief review of studies examining delight. The elicitation of delight is presented firstly through a discussion of delight and satisfaction, which are considered as two overlapping concepts. The impact of delight on behavioural intentions is then examined, followed by a review of the concept of delight in tourism.

The psychology of delight

Customer delight as an emotional outcome from a post-consumption experience has been studied as a blend of positive affect, arousal and surprise (Oliver 1993; Oliver et al. 1997;

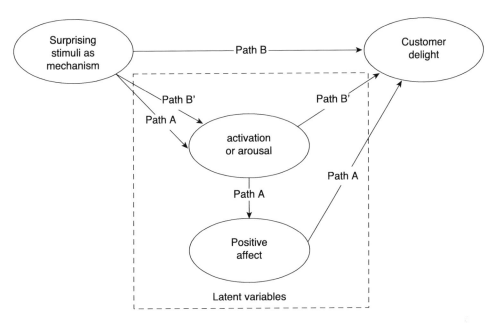

Figure 21.1 The psychology of customer delight

Source: Authors.

Westbrook and Oliver 1991). These authors identified delight using the category or dimensions approaches to emotions such as Izard's (1977, 2008) Differential Emotions Scale (DES), Plutchik's basic emotions typology and Russell's PAD typology. These researchers concluded that delight is a second-level emotion (rather than a basic emotion), characterised by a combination of high pleasure (elation, high arousal and positive affect) and high activation or surprise (Mehrabian and Russell 1974; Watson et al. 1988). In the ORV model, surprise is proposed as the mechanism by which arousal or activation is achieved, and delight occurs on the condition that surprising consumption activates a highly aroused positive affect (Path A in Figure 21.1), when the outcome is unanticipated (Path B in Figure 21.1) or as a function of the activated latent arousal level (Path B' in Figure 21.1). The formation of delight as a sequence of 'surprise to arousal to positive affect to delight' (Path A) has been empirically supported in studies of theme park visitors and symphony-goers (Oliver et al. 1997). These results indicate that, as predicted by the ORV model, delight is generated as a function of arousal and affect, with surprise as an initiator of the affect–arousal sequence. The ORV model indicates that customer delight is related to other outcomes such as pleasure, happiness and joy, but is distinguished from these positive emotions by the arousal level.

However, other researchers have investigated whether surprise is necessary for formation of delight (Kumar et al. 2001). In the ORV model, the more unexpected the level of positive surprise, the greater the consumer's delight. However, the ORV model does not claim that surprise is the only activation mechanism to elicit delight from a consumption experience. Kumar et al.'s (2001) study found that the existence of perceived surprise is independent of feeling delighted for respondents attending a live Irish dance performance. Respondents felt delight, regardless of their expressed levels of surprise. Also, the extent of delight experienced by non-surprised spectators was not significantly different to the extent of delight experienced by those who were very surprised. Although Kumar et al.'s (2001) study adopted Plutchik's (1980) approach to understand delight as a combination of joy and surprise, it also introduced two types of joy: 'magic joy' and 'real joy' (Schactel 1959):

> 'Magic joy' is a short-lived experience when a person feels that the unexpected fulfilment of a wish or need can (or will) change his/her situation; while 'real joy' results from any ongoing activity which brings an individual into contact, physically and/or mentally, with some aspect of the world around him/her.
>
> *(Kumar et al. 2001: p. 18)*

Kumar et al. (2001) proposed that there are two kinds of delight depending on the type of joy felt by individuals. Therefore consumers experience delight from joy and surprise, or when they are captivated by an experience which evokes feelings of real joy. Consumers experiencing real joy are more likely to return to repeat the experience, since real joy is believed to sustain ongoing loyalty (Schactel 1959).

The concept of real joy is similar to the consumption emotion 'joy and interest' discussed by Westbrook and Oliver (1991: p. 89). In a study of the emotions experienced by automobile owners, two groups experiencing positive emotions were identified and labelled 'happy/contented' and 'delighted' based on their emotional responses (Westbrook and Oliver 1991: p. 89). Both groups report positive affect and a high level of satisfaction from the consumption experience. The distinction between them is that the delighted group reports feeling surprise, while the happy/content group reports feelings of interest instead. Westbrook and Oliver (1991) noted that the two groups differ, in that for one the antecedents of positive affect are joy and surprise, while for the other the antecedents are joy and interest. Interest is considered a measure of consumers' response to a retailer and found to have a significant interaction with satisfaction in predicting positive WOM and re-patronage intentions, as well as having a direct effect on loyalty intentions (Jones and Reynolds 2006). Therefore, positive emotions co-existing with satisfaction are considered to have more than a single dimension of valence, and to include arousal derived from either surprise or interest. Westbrook and Oliver (1991) also proposed that in the formation of positive affect the dimension of interest is related to enduring involvement. This indicates that surprise might not be the only mechanism to elicit highly aroused positive affect; rather, joy and interest are coincident with the concept of real joy, as noted by Kumar et al. (2001).

Following this line, an alternative path to delight other than via pleasant surprise has been noted (St-James and Taylor 2004). These authors propose that individuals might derive personal emotional arousal from consumption experiences they imbue with a subjective, symbolic meaning associated with themes of interpersonal warmth, aesthetic experiences or leisure experiences. Named 'delight-as-magic' by the authors (St-James and Taylor 2004: p. 756), this kind of delight does not necessitate the presence of surprise and novelty, and may be repeated over time as individuals continue to engage in activities that entail a strong hedonic motivation.

In order to reconcile these arguments on the paths leading to delight, Ma et al. (2013) adopted cognitive appraisal theory (CAT) to propose multiple paths to delight (with or without surprise) among theme park-goers. CAT predicts the antecedents of emotions, unlike the category and dimensions approaches to emotions which only describe emotional outcomes. CAT considers emotions are the result of an individual's evaluation of an experience on combinations of appraisal dimensions (Roseman and Smith 2001). The particular appraisal dimensions used, and the individual's subjective judgement of the experience on them, lead to a specific emotional response (Scherer et al. 2001). Consideration of the appraisal dimensions related to high aroused positive emotion and indicates that 'delight can be elicited when respondents appraise their theme park experience *either* as unexpected, *or* as important to their personal well-being or special needs, *or* as in their interest, *or* as highly goal congruent' (Ma et al. 2013: p. 373). The elicitation of delight is then linked to an individual's motivation or goal for an experience, which suggests people with specific motivations such as being interested in the activities, or who associate personal importance with the experience, may be delighted without surprise.

In summary, previous research has suggested that it is more concise and useful to consider customer delight as a multidimensional construct rather than to use the simple surprise–pleasure–delight (ORV) model. Customer delight is thus a more complex construct than proposed by extant conceptualisations in the marketing literature.

The relationship between delight and satisfaction

The ORV model suggests that delight is a mixture of arousal activated by surprising consumption and positive affect, while satisfaction is the result of disconfirmation and positive affect (see Figure 21.2). In this approach, the different antecedents lead to distinctive experiential outcomes. However, the distinction between delight and satisfaction, as well as their independent antecedents, has been questioned in a number of studies. Nyer (1997) failed to distinguish joy from satisfaction in a discriminant validity test when intending to

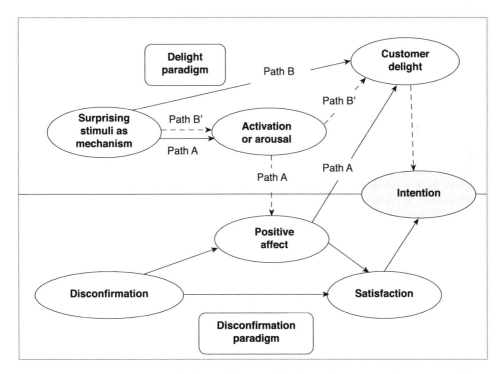

Figure 21.2   Model of customer delight, satisfaction and behavioural intention (the ORV model)

Note: The dashed lines indicate that no significant correlations were found as hypothesised in the context of either the theme park or the symphony performance

Source: Oliver et al. (1997).

examine joy, satisfaction, sadness and respondents' WOM and complaining intentions using an experimental research design which used constructed consumption experience scenarios. Nyer (1997) explained this by arguing that constructed scenarios do not have the same involvement level as found when experiencing a real consumption event. In real consumption contexts such as upscale restaurants and rural lodgings, the two concepts are discriminated (Bowden and Dagger 2011; Loureiro 2010).

Surprise is suggested as a shared antecedent of both satisfaction and joy. Surprise is found to have a direct effect on satisfaction measured as a result of positive disconfirmation, as well as on the feeling of joy measured as aroused positive affect (Vanhamme and Snelders 2003). The role of surprise in satisfaction judgement is established as an affective contribution to the formation of satisfaction based on a consumer's product use experience (Vanhamme 2001). In the context of front-line services provided by financial advisors, surprise has a significant impact on customers' satisfaction as an evaluation, and trust as an emotion, towards the advisor (Bergeron et al. 2008). Therefore, the proposal of the ORV model to use surprising consumption as the antecedent to separate delight and satisfaction is challenged.

In the tourism literature, however, there is no discussion of the difference between delight and satisfaction in terms of their antecedents. Instead, emotions are seen as determined by the attributes of the experiences (Barnes et al. 2011; Berman 2005; Evans and Burns 2007; Loureiro et al. 2014; Yang 2011). Some authors have investigated the relationship between hedonic/utilitarian benefits and delight/satisfaction outcomes (Chitturi et al. 2008; Füller and Matzler 2008; Torres and Kline 2006). The results indicate that products meeting or exceeding consumers' hedonic wants enhance delight, while products meeting or exceeding utilitarian needs enhance satisfaction (Chitturi et al. 2008).

In summary, most previous studies have identified delight and satisfaction as two distinct emotional outcomes of consumption experiences. However, surprise is not the only antecedent to distinguish between them nor is it sufficient to elaborate subtle nuances in consumption outcomes. Indeed, Souca (2014) has questioned whether delight impacts on intentions directly, in parallel with the effect of satisfaction, or delight only accounts for an upper zone of the impact of satisfaction on intentions.

The consequences of customer delight and satisfaction

In the ORV model, customer delight is distinct from customer satisfaction, and a parallel antecedent of desired behavioural outcome. Therefore, the emotional responses to a consumption experience have been separated from customer satisfaction by their distinctive effect on intentions as emotional consequences. An integrative model of the behavioural basis for customer delight, including its hypothesised antecedents and consequences, is shown in Figure 21.2. Customer delight and satisfaction are identified as distinct concepts that influence intention.

Oliver et al. (1997: p. 319) argue that: 'The experience of delight creates a desire for future recurrences of this sensation.' This argument is fundamental to the nature of hedonic consumption, in that 'emotional arousal' such as joy is seen as generated by consumption (Hirschman and Holbrook 1982: p. 95). The repeated pursuit of such emotions is regarded as continuously pleasure seeking, and differences in repeated consumption are due to subtle variations in the variety and intensity of the positive affect (Oliver et al. 1997). The broaden-and-build theory of emotional consequence states that, 'certain discrete positive emotions – including joy, interest, contentment, pride and love – . . . all share the ability to broaden people's momentary thought-action repertoires and build their enduring personal resources, ranging from physical and intellectual resources to social and psychological resources' (Fredrickson 2001: p. 219). Thus, delight as a positive emotion reinforces a link to behavioural intentions to undertake further pleasurable performance in parallel with satisfaction.

However, there is inconsistency between the hypothesised direct impact of delight on intentions and the results in the two hedonic consumption settings: theme parks and symphony performances. One effect of delight on intentions was not empirically supported in the theme park context, although it was significant for the symphony attendees (Oliver et al. 1997). Also, no significant relationship between delight and intentions was found among upscale restaurants' diners (Bowden and Dagger 2011). To account for these inconsistent effects, studies consider that consumption contexts or experiences might be moderating variables in the impact of delight on behavioural intentions (Bowden and Dagger 2011; Oliver et al. 1997). For example, delightful moments that occur at the theme park or high-end restaurant because of surprising consumption might be viewed just as 'normal' and inconsequential to the primary purpose of an experience such as a family outing, while delight might be more central to experiencing an orchestral performance. This claim reflects the limitation of the ORV model in defining the antecedents of delight. It is also suggested that 'the meaning of delight in contexts is central to its role in more critical consumer response [and] discussion now turns to the likelihood of consumers expressing delight in a service context' (Oliver et al. 1997: p. 329). This argument suggests that it would be worthwhile to examine the motivational factors related to delight.

Despite the lack of significant impact of delight on intentions in some contexts, the ORV model was later retested using a much larger sample size (Alexander 2012; Finn 2005, 2006, 2012; Loureiro 2010; Loureiro and Ribeiro 2014), and the direct effect of delight on intentions was found in other contexts and using different analysis methods. This replication of the ORV model found a significant impact of delight on intentions in the contexts of business-to-consumer (B2C) websites (Finn 2005) and online retailers (Finn 2006), and by the use of transformed satisfaction data and non-linear structural equation modelling (Finn 2012). The ORV model is also supported in the study of visitors to rural lodgings using partial least squares path analysis to maximise variances (Loureiro 2010). Delighting customers was found to improve loyalty intentions as measured by positive WOM and repurchase intentions, rather than merely satisfy them (Chitturi et al. 2008).

The inconsistencies in the effects of delight and satisfaction on intentions are also a result of the ambiguous relationship between the two concepts. Some studies regard delight as the extreme end in the effect of satisfaction on behavioural intentions (Fullerton and Taylor 2002; Ngobo 1999). Taking the non-linear effect of satisfaction on intentions into consideration, Keiningham and Vavra (2001) and Rust and Oliver (2000) viewed delight as an upper zone of a dual-threshold cubic effect of satisfaction on behavioural intentions. However, Finn (2012) argued that their findings are context specific, and delight can be distinguished as a direct effect on intentions in parallel with the linear or non-linear effect of satisfaction on intentions. Therefore, the assumption of delight as an extreme example of satisfaction is questionable (Alexander 2010).

In summary, the consequences of delight and satisfaction need further examination. The issue calls for understanding how delight and satisfaction impact on intentions, as well as how the two responses are subjectively elicited based on personal motivations. By integrating problems of the ORV model relating to the antecedents and consequences of delight and its relationship with satisfaction, the weaknesses of the ORV model can then be identified. The insufficient explanation of the antecedents of delight leads to the ambiguous relationship between delight and satisfaction, and impacts on the respective behavioural consequences of the two outcomes. The next part examines studies on the ORV model, in order to see how the model has been extended or optimised in the past 15 years.

Studies of customer delight

The ORV model has attracted considerable attention with over 100 citations so far. Of those studies that used the model, many have a managerial perspective and address the economic implications of a need to delight the customer (Keiningham and Vavra 2001; Mascarenhas et al. 2004; Ngobo 1999; Rust and Oliver 2000), as well as designing ways to delight the customer (Berman 2005; Evans and Burns 2007; McNeilly and Feldman 2006). For example, the attributes that led to delightful and terrible shopping experiences for retail shoppers were explored such as interpersonal interaction and effective problem resolution (Arnold et al. 2005).

Similarly, in the tourism and hospitality literature, research on delight has focused on managerial outcomes, including the drivers of guest delight in the hotel industry (Crotts et al. 2008) and a conceptual model of creating customer delight in the management of a hotel (Torres and Kline 2006). In one study, excitement within the three-factor structure of satisfaction (in this model, satisfiers, dissatisfiers and hybrid factors) contributed differently to overall satisfaction that was found to lead to customer delight (Füller and Matzler 2008). However, this study does not identify what distinguishes delight from satisfaction, thereby limiting understanding of the differences between the consequences of these concepts. In recent years, a number of studies have replicated the ORV model in tourism contexts such as vocational holidays (Magnini et al. 2011), rural lodgings (Loureiro 2010) and restaurants (Bowden and Dagger 2011).

Table 21.1 provides a summary of previous research on customer delight in the marketing, tourism and hospitality literature (except those mentioned in the first part of the chapter on alternative antecedents of delight). Ordered by date, the evolution of studies on delight may be summarised as: (1) a change from conceptualisation studies to empirical tests; and (2) a shift in focus from exploring objective attributes of delight to understanding the causes of delight as due to a personal interpretation of a consumption experience. However, Table 21.1 illustrates a lack of theoretical studies of both the causes and effects of delight. There has also been little work carried out to elaborate on the concepts of delight and satisfaction from the perspective of emotional responses, and limited extension of the ORV model in terms of addressing the weaknesses of the model as a whole.

Oliver et al. (1997: p. 332) make the following suggestion:

> Considering some inconsistencies of the ORV model among studies, it is recommended that future studies of delight address both measurement of the concept and new theoretical insights into the psychology of delight. It would be worthwhile to study the elicitation of customer delight in an alternative theoretical way in order to answer questions such as; 'what are the conditions conducive to the expression of delight in consumption? What are the variables which mediate whether or not delight has an impact on behaviour, or behavioural intentions? Is surprising stimuli or performance the only approach to producing delight?'

Surprise in a consumption experience is considered one of the external triggers to generate delight; however, the internal motives determine whether delight is regarded as a consequential result of the consumption experience, and therefore whether it encourages intentions (Irabatti 2011).

Table 21.1 Previous studies on customer delight

Sources	Research themes	Research methods	Conclusions	Limitations and future research
Schneider and Bowen (1999)	Delight and outrage to retain customers	Conceptual framework	Linking delight and outrage to consumers' needs spectrum from self-esteem, justice and security. Meeting consumers' need of self-esteem will likely elicit delight, while failing to meet consumers' need of security will likely lead to responses of outrage	Lack of empirical test to support the conceptual correlations between the emotions and needs
Rust and Oliver (2000)	Economy to delight customer under competition	Model formulation	Delighting the customer heightens purchase expectations and makes satisfaction more difficult in the future; delighting firm suffered by raising expectations, but the non-delighting competition is hurt more through customer attrition to the delighting firm. Delight as a result of high level of surprisingly positive disconfirmation is not sustained	Further examinations on how delight is memorised and institutionalised through the mechanism of raised expectations
Arnold et al. (2005)	Sources of delightful and terrible shopping experience	Critical incident analysis of in-depth interviews	Delightful experiences are derived by interpersonal incidents such as helpful salesperson, friendly salesperson; non-interpersonal incidents like unanticipated acquisition and value; the outcome of delightful experience is positive WOM	Lack of examination of the nature of affective responses to delightful retail experience

(Continued)

Table 21.1 Previous studies on customer delight *(continued)*

Sources	Research themes	Research methods	Conclusions	Limitations and future research
Berman (2005)	Design of delightful experience	Conceptual framework	Managerial design to delight customer, such as recognising the importance of courtesy, empathy and efforts in understanding customer needs; finding the right product/delivering anticipated value; making sure that novelty and entertainment are provided	Restricted the antecedents of delight in unanticipated events or surprise stimuli
Torres and Kline (2006)	Managerial model for hotels to achieve delight	Conceptual framework	The model presents the basic consumer, employee and organisational influences that lead to satisfaction and delight by better processes of managing customer relations and outcomes of delighting customers	Lack of study on the subjective antecedents of customer delight
Crotts et al. (2008)	Key drivers of delight and attributes related to delight	A survey of festival visitors	The four-question survey is a practical tool for gauging guest satisfaction and delight, as well as identifying the key drivers of guests' overall satisfaction and repeat visit intention	No statistical test was conducted to test the significance between drivers and outcomes
Chitturi et al. (2008)	Role of utilitarian and hedonic benefits in eliciting delight and satisfaction	Experimental scenarios of 3 products and 240 respondents	Utilitarian benefits enhance satisfaction while hedonic benefits promote delight; the antecedent feelings of satisfaction are prevention emotions of confidence and security, while those of delight are promotion emotions of cheerfulness and excitement; delighting customers improves loyalty	Services experience rather than products are needed to further test; hedonic benefits leading to delight rather than surprise

Sources	Research themes	Research methods	Conclusions	Limitations and future research
Valenzuela et al. (2008)	Cross–culture differences in delight	Experiments with East Asians and Westerners	By defining delight as surprisingly pleasant, Westerners are found to be more surprised and delighted than Easterners by unexpected positive events; Easterners derive greater pleasure from an unexpected event associated with luck than do Westerners	Different responses to 'unexpectedness' between Westerners and Easterners, without understanding the meaning of delight in different cultures
Bowden (2009)	Customer engagement and customer delight	Conceptual framework	Delighted consumers are more likely to generate affective commitment to the specific brand and hence are more likely to be loyal to the brand	Lack of empirical test of delight and affective commitment to loyalty
Loureiro (2010)	Replicate ORV model in rural tourism lodgings	Path analysis using partial least squares	Delight and satisfaction as distinct constructs are supported; disconfirmation is a predictor of both delight and satisfaction; satisfaction is a more significant determinant of loyalty than delight	The sample is restricted to tourists in the northern region of Portugal
Alexander (2010)		Literature review	It is concluded: delight as the extreme ends of satisfaction is dubious; a theoretical model of delight and anger/outrage as its opposite is needed; the expectancy disconfirmation model is inappropriate to explain delight/anger and their consequences; if surprise is a part of delight, is it possible for a supplier to continuously surprise customers?	The study does not measure delight or anger/outrage and (dis)satisfaction directly

(Continued)

Table 21.1 Previous studies on customer delight *(continued)*

Sources	Research themes	Research methods	Conclusions	Limitations and future research
Crotts and Magnini (2011)	Surprise as essential to elicit delight	Narrative analysis of blogs	Surprise is an essential component of delight for travellers	The results are specific to the context of hotel staying experiences
Magnini et al. (2011)	Hotel attributes leading to delight	Content analysis and text mining of travel blogs	The most important cause of delight in the hotel is customer service; the triggers of delight of domestic and international travel, as well as travellers from developed versus developing countries, are different	The results are culturally bound. It is suggested to elaborate the amount of joy from surprise and joy from high disconfirmations
Bowden and Dagger (2011)	Replicate ORV model in high-end restaurant settings	Path analysis	Delight is not found to lead to loyalty. Although delighting customers may add value to their experiences, it does not translate into loyalty bonds for new and repeat purchase customers. Surprise is not significantly related to delight	Findings are context specific. It is suggested to understand personal meanings of delight

Source: Authors.

References

Alexander, M. W. (2010). 'Customer delight: A review', *Academy of Marketing Studies Journal*, 14(1): 39–53.

Alexander, M. W. (2012). 'Delight the customer: A predictive model for repeat purchase behaviour', *Journal of Relationship Marketing*, 11(2): 116–123.

Arnold, M. J., Reynolds, K. E., Ponder, N. and Lueg, J. E. (2005). 'Customer delight in a retail context: Investigating delightful and terrible shopping experiences', *Journal of Business Research*, 58(8): 1132–1145.

Barnes, D. C., Ponder, N. and Dugar, K. (2011). 'Investigating the key routes to customer delight', *Journal of Marketing Theory and Practice*, 19(4): 359–375.

Bergeron, J., Roy, J. and Fallu, J. M. (2008). 'Pleasantly surprising clients: A tactic in relationship marketing for building competitive advantage in the financial services sector', *Canadian Journal of Administrative Sciences*, 25(3): 171–184.

Berman, B. (2005). 'How to delight your customers', *California Management Review*, 48(1): 129–151.

Bowden, J. L.-H. (2009). 'The process of customer engagement: A conceptual framework', *Journal of Marketing Theory and Practice*, 17(1): 63–74.

Bowden, J. L. H. and Dagger, T. S. (2011). 'To delight or not to delight? An investigation of loyalty formation in the restaurant industry', *Journal of Hospitality Marketing and Management*, 20(5): 501–524.

Cadotte, E. R., Woodruff, R. B. and Jenkins, R. L. (1987). 'Expectations and norms in models of consumer satisfaction', *Journal of Marketing Research*, 24(3): 305–314.

Chitturi, R., Raghunathan, R. and Mahajan, V. (2008). 'Delight by design: The role of hedonic versus utilitarian benefits', *Journal of Marketing*, 72(3): 48–63.

Churchill, J. G. A. and Surprenant, C. (1982). 'An investigation into the determinants of customer satisfaction', *Journal of Marketing Research*, 19(4): 491–504.

Crotts, J. C. and Magnini, V. P. (2011). 'The customer delight construct: Is surprise essential?', *Annals of Tourism Research*, 38(2): 719–722.

Crotts, J. C., Pan, B. and Raschid, A. E. (2008). 'A survey method for identifying key drivers of guest delight', *International Journal of Contemporary Hospitality Management*, 20(4): 462–470.

Deming, W. E. (1986). *Out of the Crisis*, Cambridge, MA: Massachusetts Institute of Technology, Center for Advanced Engineering Study.

Evans, S. and Burns, A. D. (2007). 'An investigation of customer delight during product evaluation: Implications for the development of desirable products', *Proceedings of the Institution of Mechanical Engineers – Part B – Engineering Manufacture*, 221(11): 1625–1638.

Finn, A. (2005). 'Reassessing the foundations of customer delight', *Journal of Service Research*, 8(2): 103–116.

Finn, A. (2006). 'Generalizability modeling of the foundations of customer delight', *Journal of Modeling in Management*, 1(1): 18–32.

Finn, A. (2012). 'Customer delight: Distinct construct or zone of nonlinear response to customer satisfaction?', *Journal of Service Research*, 15(1): 99–110.

Fredrickson, B. L. (2001). 'The role of positive emotions in positive psychology: The broaden-and-build theory of positive emotions', *American Psychologist*, 56(3): 218–226.

Füller, J. and Matzler, K. (2008). 'Customer delight and market segmentation: An application of the three-factor theory of customer satisfaction on life style groups', *Tourism Management*, 29(1): 116–126.

Fullerton, G. and Taylor, S. (2002). 'Mediating, interactive, and non-linear effects in service quality and satisfaction with services research', *Canadian Journal of Administrative Sciences/Revue Canadienne des Sciences de l'Administration*, 19(2): 124–136.

Hirschman, E. C. and Holbrook, M. B. (1982). 'Hedonic consumption: Emerging concepts, methods and propositions', *Journal of Marketing*, 46(2): 92–101.

Holbrook, M. B. and Hirschman, E. C. (1982). 'The experiential aspects of consumption: Consumer fantasies, feelings, and fun', *Journal of Consumer Research*, 9(2): 132–140.

Irabatti, P. (2011). 'Customer delight: An effective weapon at retailers to fight against global recession', *Journal of Contemporary Research in Management*, 6(1): 39–50.

Izard, C. E. (1977). *Human Emotions*, New York: Plenum Press.

Izard, C. E. (2008). 'Emotion theory and research: Highlights, unanswered questions, and emerging issues', *Annual Review of Psychology*, 60: 1–25.

Jones, M. A. and Reynolds, K. E. (2006). 'The role of retailer interest on shopping behaviour', *Journal of Retailing*, 82(2): 115–126.

Keiningham, T. and Vavra, T. (2001). *The Customer Delight Principle: Exceeding Customers' Expectations for Bottom-Line Success*, Chicago, IL: McGraw-Hill.

Kumar, A., Olshavsky, R. and King, M. F. (2001). 'Exploring alternative antecedents of customer delight', *Journal of Consumer Satisfaction, Dissatisfaction and Complaining Behaviour*, 14: 14–26.

Loureiro, S. M. C. (2010). 'Satisfying and delighting the rural tourists', *Journal of Travel and Tourism Marketing*, 27(4): 396–408.

Loureiro, S. M. C., Miranda, F. J. and Breazeale, M. (2014). 'Who needs delight?: The greater impact of value, trust and satisfaction in utilitarian, frequent-use retail', *Journal of Service Management*, 25(1): 101–124.

Loureiro, S. M. C. and Ribeiro, L. (2014). 'Virtual atmosphere: The effect of pleasure, arousal, and delight on word-of-mouth', *Journal of Promotion Management*, 20(4): 452–469.

Ma, J., Gao, J., Scott, N. and Ding, P. (2013). 'Customer delight from theme park experiences: The antecedents of delight based on cognitive appraisal theory', *Annals of Tourism Research*, 42: 359–381.

McNeilly, K. M. and Feldman, T. B. (2006). 'I love my accountants – they're wonderful: Understanding customer delight in the professional services arena', *Journal of Services Marketing*, 20(3): 152–159.

Magnini, V. P., Crotts, J. C. and Zehrer, A. (2011). 'Understanding customer delight: An application of travel blog analysis', *Journal of Travel Research*, 50(5): 535–545.

Mascarenhas, O. A., Kesavan, R. and Bernacchi, M. (2004). 'Customer value-chain involvement for co-creating customer delight', *Journal of Consumer Marketing*, 21(7): 486–496.

Mehrabian, A. and Russell, J. A. (1974). *An Approach to Environmental Psychology*, Cambridge, MA: MIT Press.

Ngobo, P.-V. (1999). 'Decreasing returns in customer loyalty: Does it really matter to delight the customers?', *Advances in Consumer Research*, 26: 469–476.

Nyer, P. U. (1997). 'A study of the relationships between cognitive appraisals and consumption emotions', *Journal of the Academy of Marketing Science*, 25(4): 296–304.

Oliver, R. L. (1993). 'Cognitive, affective, and attribute bases of the satisfaction response', *Journal of Consumer Research*, 20(3): 418–430.

Oliver, R. L., Rust, R. T. and Varki, S. (1997). 'Customer delight: Foundations, findings, and managerial insight', *Journal of Retailing*, 73(3): 311–336.

Parasuraman, A., Berry, L. L. and Zeithaml, V. A. (1993). 'More on improving service quality measurement', *Journal of Retailing*, 69(1): 140–147.

Plutchik, R. (1980). *Emotion: A Psychoevolutionary Synthesis*, New York: Harper and Row.

Rollins, R. and Bradley, G. (1986). 'Measuring recreation satisfaction with leisure settings', *Recreation Research Review*, 13(1): 23–27.

Roseman, I. J. and Smith, C. A. (2001). 'Appraisal theory: Overview, assumptions, varieties, controversies', in K. R. Scherer, A. Schorr and T. Johnstone (eds.), *Appraisal Processes in Emotion: Theory, Methods, Research* (pp. 3–19), New York: Oxford University Press.

Rust, R. T. and Oliver, R. L. (2000). 'Should we delight the customer?', *Journal of the Academy of Marketing Science*, 28(1): 86–94.

Schactel, E. G. (1959). *Metamorphosis: On the Development of Affect, Perception, Attention and Memory*, New York: Basic Books.

Scherer, K. R., Schorr, A. and Johnstone, T. (eds.) (2001). *Appraisal Processes in Emotion: Theory, Methods, Research*, Oxford: Oxford University Press.

Schlossberg, H. (1990). 'Satisfying customers is a minimum: You really have to "delight" them', *Marketing News*, 24(May 28): 10–11.

Schneider, B. and Bowen, D. E. (1999). 'Understanding customer delight and outrage', *MIT Sloan Management Review*, 41(1): 35–45.

Souca, M. L. (2014). 'Customer dissatisfaction and delight: Completely different concepts, or part of a satisfaction continuum?', *Management and Marketing*, 9(1): 75–90.

St-James, Y. and Taylor, S. (2004). 'Delight-as-magic: Refining the conceptual domain of customer delight', *Advances for Consumer Research*, 31(1): 753–758.

Torres, E. N. and Kline, S. (2006). 'From satisfaction to delight: A model for the hotel industry', *International Journal of Contemporary Hospitality Management*, 18(4): 290–301.

Valenzuela, A., Mellers, B. and Strebel, J. (2007). 'Cross-cultural differences in delight', in S. Borghini, M. A. McGrath and C. C. Otnes (eds.), *European Advances in Consumer Research, Volume 8* (pp. 243–244), Duluth, MN: Association for Consumer Research.

Vanhamme, J. (2001). 'The role of surprise in satisfaction judgements', *Journal of Consumer Satisfaction, Dissatisfaction and Complaining Behaviour*, 14: 27–45.

Vanhamme, J. and Snelders, D. (2003). 'What if you surprise your customers. . . Will they be more satisfied? Findings from a pilot experiment', *Advances for Consumer Research*, 30(1): 48–55.

Watson, D., Clark, L. A. and Tellegen, A. (1988). 'Development and validation of brief measures of positive and negative affect: The PANAS scales', *Journal of Personality and Social Psychology*, 54(6): 1063–1070.

Westbrook, R. A. (1987). 'Product consumption-based affective responses and postpurchase processes', *Journal of Marketing Research*, 24(3): 258–270.

Westbrook, R. A. and Oliver, R. L. (1991). 'The dimensionality of consumption emotion patterns and consumer satisfaction', *Journal of Consumer Research*, 18(1): 84–91.

Yang, C.-C. (2011). 'Identification of customer delight for quality attributes and its applications', *Total Quality Management and Business Excellence*, 22(1): 83–98.

22

CRUISE PASSENGERS' TRAVEL PATTERNS, BEHAVIOURAL INTENTIONS AND MOTIVATIONS

Abdullah Tanrisevdi and Vedat Acar

Introduction

It is crucial to gain new customers when customers are lost. However, gaining new customers is an expensive process involving advertising, promotion, sales costs as well as start-up operating expenses. In addition to this, it is difficult for businesses to earn profit for a period of time after gaining new customers (Zeithaml et al. 1996). Research suggests that retention of the current customer is cheaper than finding new ones. When taking into account that the cruise industry has a large proportion of new customers in its customer profile, it is important to better understand variables associated with visitor retention (Petrick et al. 2006). Teye and Leclerc (2003) emphasized that cruises gave an opportunity for initial discovery of a destination allowing passengers to return for a longer visit and further, more in-depth cultural discovery.

When looking back at the history of cruise tourism, especially since the end of World War II, it is seen that a number of renowned passenger ships have gone into service. During recent years, scientific and technological advances have had significant influence on the cruise industry, and thus considerable progress has been made in the design, power supply, accommodation and catering facilities of passenger ships. Thanks to those ships, efficiency in the cruise industry has started to increase and make it possible for ships to compete with land-based holidays, including hotels (Lois et al. 2004). İnan et al. (2011) emphasized that cruise tourism may be evaluated as a 'niche market' in this sense when compared with 3S (sun, sea and sand) tourism.

According to the 2011 report of CLIA (Cruise Lines International Association) it has been suggested that the number of passengers taking part in cruise tourism has increased 7.6% on average per annum since 1980, that over 191 million passengers have taken a cruise (2+ days) from 1980 to 2010, that 67% of the total passengers have been generated between 2000 and 2010 and that 39% of total passengers have been generated between 2005 and 2010 (CLIA 2011). In addition to this, it has also been suggested that 82% of cruise passengers were of the same opinion, that 'a cruise vacation is a good way to sample destinations that they may wish to visit again on a land-based vacation', and that 40% of cruise vacationers stated that 'they returned to vacation at a destination first visited by cruise'. According to the report, it may be said that cruise tourism plays a fundamental role within general tourism activities with regards to 'customer retention'. From this point of view, travel patterns, behavioural intentions and motivations of cruise passengers visiting Ege Port, located in Kuşadası, a province of Aydın, Turkey, have been investigated in this study.

Behavioural intention

Behavioural intentions play the role of a key determinant in implementing behaviours and subjective norms (Lee 2005: p. 63). There have been a lot of studies aimed at explaining effects of attitudes and actions on behaviours. The study of Fishbein and Ajzen (1975: p. 302) may be ranked among this research. They handled the subject of the influence of social environment on behaviour, and indicated that the subjective norm was the individual's perception that most people having importance for the individual think one should or should not perform the aforementioned behaviour. According to Lee (2005: p. 63), attitudes play significant roles in determining future intentions. Perceived service quality and visitor satisfaction may be ranked among the factors directly influencing visitors' future behavioural intentions about a tourist service and their intent relating to future visitations. Thus, high level of perceived service quality or overall satisfaction is supposed to generate positive word of mouth and repeat visitations whereas low level of perceived service quality or overall satisfaction is supposed to result in negative word of mouth and no future visitations (Lee 2005: p. 63).

Taylor et al. (1997) suggested that quality attitudes and satisfaction judgements had important roles in the formation of purchase intentions of Mexican consumers. Furthermore, satisfaction judgements are more important in predicting purchase intentions as compared with quality attitudes. According to Boulding et al. (1993), strategically, customers were more likely to perform useful behaviours towards business when overall service quality perceptions of customers increased. Similarly, Dabholkar and Thorpe (1994) found that there was a strong, positive relationship between overall satisfaction and post-purchase intentions. According to the authors, although it is important to ensure customers do not develop negative feelings about a company, it does not necessarily mean that customers would feel positive about the company. Research has underlined that there was a relationship between satisfaction and risk and that satisfied tourists may have been in search of new destinations, although risk-averse tourists may have preferred staying with familiar destinations even if they were dissatisfied (McKercher and Wong 2004). Tam (2000) defended the idea that service quality had a positive effect on determining behavioural intentions but suggested that this impact depended upon satisfying customers. Zeithaml et al. (1996) emphasized that higher service quality assessments would have a positive effect on customers' behavioural intentions whereas lower service quality assessments would result in lower behavioural intentions. Within this context, it is possible to say that behavioural intentions are important determinants of whether customers remain loyal to a business or not (Zeithaml et al. 1996).

İnan et al. (2011) defended that recommendation had an importance in determining tourists' repurchase intentions as well as individual experiences. As is seen in the literature, the number of studies aiming at investigating a direct relationship between quality, satisfaction and behavioural intentions are considerably limited (Cronin et al. 2000). Zeithaml et al. (1996), investigating the relationship between those concepts, categorized behavioural intentions as 'favorable behavioural intentions' and 'unfavorable behavioural intentions'. Customers praising the company, preferring the company over others, increasing the volume of their purchases or agreeably paying a price premium may be ranked among the favourable behavioural intentions, while complaining to friends or external agencies, contemplation of switching to competitors and decreasing the amount of business a customer does with the company may be ranked among unfavourable behavioural intentions (Zeithaml et al. 1996; Lee 2005: p. 65). To sum up, the effects of quality, value and satisfaction variables on behavioural intentions cannot be ignored. Therefore, quality affects not only value and satisfaction perceptions, but also behavioural intentions (Cronin et al. 2000). Tam (2000) suggested that managers should not seek to change customers' expectations when they want to increase customers' satisfaction judgements. Instead of this, changing customers' service performance perceptions may be of utility.

Motivation

Ryan and Deci (2000a) stated that 'to be motivated' means to be 'moved to do something' and emphasized that an individual feeling no impetus or inspiration to act is characterized as unmotivated and that an individual being energized and activated to win through is characterized as motivated. According to the researchers, people have not only different amounts, but also different kinds, of motivation. Thus, it is hard to say that there is a unitary motivation phenomenon. According to Goossens (2000), carrying out effective tourism marketing depends upon understanding consumers' motivation influentially. Crompton and McKay (1997) stated that motives were key components in the decision-making process. When assessed within this context, tourism motivation would be conceptualized as a dynamic process of internal psychological factors (needs and desires) creating a state of tension or disequilibrium within individuals (Crompton and McKay 1997).

Fondness (1994) cited in Goossens (2000) developed a scale known as the 'easy to administer self report scale' resembling the taxonomy of Crompton (1979), identifying nine motives which are: escape from a perceived mundane environment, exploration and evaluation of self, relaxation, prestige, regression, enhancement of kinship relationships, facilitation of social interaction, novelty and education. According to this scale, by associating the individual with motivation, needs and personal objectives, five reasons for travel have been defined on understanding, predicting and influencing the relationship between tourist motivation and behaviours. The knowledge function (or cultural and educational motives), the utilitarian function 'punishment minimization' (or the need to escape or stimulus avoidance), reward maximization (or pleasure and sensation seeking) and the value expressive functions relating to self-esteem and ego enhancement (or social prestige) are ranked among those reasons for travel (Goossens 2000; Teye and Leclerc 2003).

There has been significant research done about the relationship between human needs and job attitudes and work motivation since McGregor (1966) applied Maslow's (1943) needs hierarchy theory to the field of management (Baard et al. 2004). However, the studies on travel motivation have been limited as compared with the research conducted in the field of marketing or destination choice (Meng et al. 2008). According to Yoon and Uysal (2005), factors pushing people into travel are internal factors, psychological forces and external factors depending upon destination attributes. In a similar way, Uysal et al. identified five motivation domains consisting of escape, excitement/thrills, event novelty, socialization and family togetherness (Crompton and McKay 1997 citing Uysal et al. 1993). Undoubtedly, understanding why people select and visit a destination has a vital importance for tourism marketers. Meng et al. (2008) emphasized that tourists were more likely to choose destinations believed to best satisfy their internal needs or push factors. Thus, destination managers and marketers are allowed to better understand what motives push people to travel and what destination-specific factors influence the selection of a specific destination (Gursoy et al.

2010). In addition to this, investigation of travel motivations makes it possible for them to predict travel patterns in the future. Yuan et al. (2005) explained that travellers' choosing the destination or type of vacation in order to satisfy optimally their internal needs was the underlying assumption in travel motivation research.

Crompton and McKay (1997) indicated that there was a relationship between the escape–seeking dichotomy of Iso-Ahola and push–pull factors. Iso-Ahola's Model of Tourism Motivation comprises two motivational factors (seeking and escaping). According to the model, escaping is defined as the desire to leave the everyday environment behind oneself while seeking is defined as the desire to gain psychological (intrinsic) rewards by travelling in contrasting new or old environments (Crompton and McKay 1997 citing Iso-Ahola 1982: p. 261). When handled in a traditional way, push factors may be said to be influential in explaining the desire to go on vacation whereas pull factors explain the choice of the destination (Goossens 2000; Yuan et al. 2005). According to Yoon and Uysal (2005), intrinsic motivation is correlated with feelings, drives and instincts whereas external motives are mental representations such as knowledge or beliefs. In other words, Ryan and Deci (2000a) emphasized that intrinsic motivation may have only occurred in the activities holding intrinsic interest for an individual (those having the appeal of novelty, challenge or aesthetic value for individuals). Goossens (2000) suggested that not only feelings of pleasure, excitement and relaxation (push factors) but also tourist attractions such as sunshine, friendly people and culture (pull factors) were ranked among important sources of tourist information. According to the author, a combination of push and pull factors and hedonic responses had significant influence on motivating tourists to plan a trip. On the other hand, some supportive conditions are required to maintain and enhance one's inherent propensity in spite of the human being liberally endowed with intrinsic motivational tendencies. Not only tangible rewards but also threats, deadlines, directives, pressured evaluations and imposed goals were suggested to affect motivation in a negative way (Ryan and Deci 2000b).

Although most researchers have not handled push and pull factors as a single integrated concept in their theoretical models and empirical studies, it is possible to say that this is not a new idea. More clearly, push and pull factors of tourist behaviour would be two sides of the same motivational coin and the concept of 'emotion' would be the psychological factor connecting these two sides. In this sense, consumers, especially tourists, are pushed by their emotional needs and pulled by the emotional benefits of leisure services and destinations (Goossens 2000). Gursoy et al. (2010) found that interest in historic sites and culture had a positive impact whereas relaxation had a negative impact in their research aiming at determining destination-specific and non-destination-specific factors for four key cultural heritage attractions in Tampa, Florida. In addition to this, it was found that both push and pull factors were more likely to have an effect on travellers' destination and attraction selection process. On the other hand, such motivating factors as climate, shopping, fun and sand, outdoor and leisure activities were found not to have significant effects on the cultural heritage site visitation patterns of travellers. Ryan and Deci (2000a) emphasized that quality of experience and performance may be different when one acts for intrinsic versus extrinsic reasons. The authors also characterized intrinsic motivation as activities done for their inherent satisfaction rather than for some separable consequences. Therefore, it is possible to say that an intrinsically motivated person has a tendency to act for the fun or challenge entailed rather than on account of external prods, pressures or rewards (Ryan and Deci 2000a).

Yuan et al. (2005) emphasized that wine tasting, experiencing local wineries, enjoying a day out and special events were ranked among the push motives in their study about tourists' motivations for attending wine festivals. In a similar way, Uysal et al. (1993) identified five motivation domains consisting of escape, excitement/thrills, event novelty, socialization and family togetherness (Crompton and McKay 1997). According to other research about cruise travellers' motivation factors and satisfaction in Hong Kong, escaping from normal life, socialization, seeing a beautiful environment and scenery were found to be among the major travelling motivation factors. On the other hand, cultural understanding, social status, business purpose and self-discovery were found to be less important compared with other motivation factors. Hung and Petrick (2011) stated that people having higher cruising motivation were more likely to attend cruise tours in the future. According to the research, the escape/relaxation dimension was seen as the strongest motivation factor and people prefer cruise tourism for freedom, escaping and relaxation (Hung and Petrick 2011). In their research on backpackers' motivations, Paris and Teye (2010) emphasized that novelty, self-development and relationship aspects of travel motivations such as exploring other cultures, increasing knowledge, having once-in-a-lifetime experiences, experiencing excitement, being free, independent and open minded and organizing one's own journey were ranked among the most important travel motivations. Cultural knowledge (exploring other cultures, increasing knowledge, interacting with the local people) and relaxation would be at the core of backpackers' travel motivations in that research. As for Gitelson and Crompton (1984) there were differences between first-time and repeat visitors in terms of motivation. According to the authors, there were five reasons why people return to destinations. Those were risk reduction, meeting the same kind of people, emotional childhood attachment, a chance to explore the destination more widely and a chance to expose it to others. Thereby, first-time visitors were in search of new cultural experiences and novelty whereas repeat visitors were in search of relaxation or spending time with friends or relatives (Gitelson and Crompton 1984; McKercher and Wong 2004). In their research on the subject of white Caucasians and ethnic minorities, Teye and Leclerc (2003) stated that ethnic minorities had much larger party sizes and were in search of uninhibited activities and thus, they were more motivated.

Kuşadası Port was the first cruise port in Turkey, became the busiest cruise port in Turkey and one is of the busiest ports of call in Europe and seventh in the Mediterranean region according to UMA (Under-Secretariat of Maritime Affairs of Turkey) (www.medcruise.com; www.globalports.com.tr). The port's popularity mostly stems from its being close to such archaeological and historical sites as Ephesus, The House of Virgin Mary, Priene, Miletos and Didyma. So those factors were taken into consideration when choosing the port for study.

Method

Data collection

The study was conducted on cruise passengers visiting Egeport, located in Kuşadası, a province of Aydın, Turkey. The study is of a descriptive nature with regards to its objectives. Constructing the profile of cruise passengers visiting Kuşadası has formed the descriptive approach of the study. The data was collected through a questionnaire in the spring of 2012. Within the scope of the descriptive research objective, a questionnaire consisting of two pages was prepared to measure demographic characteristics, travel patterns, behavioural intentions and motivations of cruise passengers. We benefit from question structures and scales used in previous studies (Hung and Petrick 2011; Duman 2002; Naylor 1996; Cronin et al. 2000), prepared the questionnaire in English and got an English teacher to check its language proficiency. After the emendations, the draft questionnaire was examined by three faculty members, checking whether there were any statements that were complicated or causing misunderstanding. In the light of the received feedback, the questionnaire was revised. Before data collection, a pilot study was conducted with ten cruise passengers who had visited the port. As a result of the pilot study, it was determined that the participants had difficulty in understanding some statements, so they were amended. After some corrections the questionnaire was prepared for data collection. The questionnaire was divided into two sections. Section 1 consisted of questions aimed at determining demographic characteristics and travel patterns of the participants. Section 2 involved items related to behavioural intentions (16 items) and motivation (13 items). All items were measured on a 7-point Likert scale (1 = strongly disagree, 7 = strongly agree).

Research sampling

The target population of the study comprised cruise passengers visiting Kuşadası. The convenience sampling method, a type of non-probability sampling method, was used for data collection. That sampling method is often used when categorical data or lists of participants are difficult to obtain. By permission of the executives of Global Ports Holding Kuşadası, 500 questionnaires were distributed and filled out by cruise passengers when they got to the port and while coming back on to the ship after their visit. In accordance with this purpose, a help desk was provided by the researchers and the researchers invited cruise visitors to the table and carried out face-to-face questionnaires. 407 of the 500 questionnaires distributed were filled out by the visitors.

Findings

Demographic characteristics and travel patterns

The majority of the participants were male (62.4%), 56 years and older (57.9%) and married (76.3%). 40.8% of the cruise passengers had a graduate degree while 23.3% had a college degree and more than half of the participants were retired (52.8%). With regards to nationality, the great majority of the participants were American (38.7%) and British (20.2%). In terms of household income before taxes, more than half of the participants stated that their household incomes approximately were between $80,000 and $119,999 (32.9%) and $40,000 and $79,999 (31%) and 67% described their income level as 'average'. With regards to the total price of their most recent cruise vacation, 27.2% stated that it was between '$3,000 and $5,000', while another 21.4% stated it was 'less than $3,000' and 20.9% between '$6,000 and $8,999'. In terms of the approximate amount spent or expected to spend on shopping in Turkey, 41.2% stated that they spent or expected to spend '$0–250' for shopping. These findings show that the participants did not want or expect to spend very much. About half of the participants (44.2%) stated that they had taken a cruise vacation five or more times and 50.8% stated that their most recent cruise vacation had lasted '8–14 days'. 73.5% travelled with someone else on their most recent cruise vacation and 63.2% described the composition of the group travelling with them as 'couple'. Pertaining to their past experience with Turkey as a vacation destination, 58.7% were 'first-time visitors' and 41.3% 'repeat visitors' and the great majority of the repeat visitors (62.4%) had been in Turkey twice before. 52.5% made their decision to travel to Turkey 'between a month and six months' before their actual trip, 58.1% purchased their cruise vacation through a 'travel agency office' and 58.8% purchased their vacation by paying at the travel agency. According to those demographic characteristics and travel patterns, the participants taking part in this study were predominantly retired, experienced cruisers, exhibited repurchase behaviour and took their vacations with their spouses. In addition to this, it is possible to suggest that travel agents had an important place for cruise tourists while making their vacation decision.

Behavioural intention

In the study, 16 items were used to measure 'plans for future cruise vacations' of the participants. Mean scores of 7 out of the 16 were found to be above '5'. Three of these were 'I will say positive things about cruising to other people' ($\overline{X}$ = 5.96, SD = 1.31), 'I will recommend cruising to others' ($\overline{X}$ = 5.84, SD = 1.29) and 'I will encourage my friends and relatives to go on a cruise experience' ($\overline{X}$ = 5.60, SD = 1.48), showing the highest mean scores. According to the two items of 'I intend to participate in this experience more frequently in the future' ($\overline{X}$ = 5.23, SD = 1.56) and 'In the future, this cruise experience will be my first choice among alternative vacation experiences' ($\overline{X}$ = 5.02, SD = 1.59), it was found that the participants were enthusiastic about repurchasing cruise tours in the future. According to another two out of seven items about the increasing monetary costs ($\overline{X}$ = 5.04, SD = 1.67; $\overline{X}$ = 5.26, SD = 1.64), they showed a tendency to continue participating in this experience in the future even if the monetary costs increased. On the other hand, mean scores of three items were found to be the lowest about the future cruise vacation dimension. Those were about whether, if the participants came across any problem about their cruise experiences, they would share with other participants ($\overline{X}$ = 2.76, SD = 1.61) and their friends ($\overline{X}$ = 2.90, SD = 1.67) and complain about the related staff to authorities ($\overline{X}$ = 2.88, SD = 1.73). Overall, participants of the study seemed to harbour positive intentions towards cruise tours in the future.

Motivation

Thirteen items were used to measure the motivations associated with the participants' most recent cruise vacation. Mean scores of 2 out of the 13 were found to be above '5'. According to these items, the participants had a tendency to cruise to experience other cultures ($\overline{X}$ = 5.65, SD = 1.54) and gain knowledge ($\overline{X}$ = 5.52, SD = 1.58). On the other hand, the three items 'I cruise to do something that impresses others' ($\overline{X}$ = 2.37, SD = 1.68), 'I cruise to increase my feelings of self worth' ($\overline{X}$ = 2.97, SD = 1.94) and 'I cruise to help me feel like a better person' ($\overline{X}$ = 3.02, SD = 1.91) showed the lowest mean scores. It is possible to state that gaining knowledge and experiencing other cultures had significant influence on cruise participants' motivations as compared with escape, relaxation, entertainment and interaction with friends and family.

Conclusion

It is well understood that the international cruise tourism market has achieved growth and the market continues to progress in destinations apart from North America. Turkey mostly takes part in this market with such destinations as Kuşadası (2010: 517 calls, 493.911 pax; 2011: 568 calls, 662.456 pax; 2012: 464 calls, 564.317 pax; 2013: 428 calls, 577.685 pax) (www.ubak.gov.tr), İstanbul Salı Pazarı (2010: 342 calls, 508.246 pax; 2011: 420 calls, 627.897 pax, 2013: 404 calls, 677.390 pax; 2014: 331 calls, 589.353 pax) (Deniz Ticareti 2015, www.turizmdebusabah.com), İzmir Alsancak (2010: 141 calls, 355.899 pax; 2011: 272 calls, 504.921 pax; 2012: 286 calls, 552.764 pax; 2013: 191 calls, 486.493 pax; 2014: 137 calls, 335.891 pax) (www.izto.org.tr), Bodrum (2010: 92 calls, 31.691 pax; 2011: 82 calls, 45.914 pax; 2012: 136 calls, 53.480 pax; 2013: 136 calls, 29.551 pax), Marmaris (2010: 84 calls, 146.531 pax; 2011: 84 calls, 170.021 pax; 2012: 88 calls, 110.279 pax; 2013: 112 calls, 152.685 pax) (www.turizmdebusabah.com, www.ubakgov.tr) and Antalya (2010: 61 calls, 138.827 pax; 2011: 77 calls, 139.795 pax; 2012: 60 calls, 159.756 pax; 2013: 70 calls, 167.794 pax) (www.globalports.com.tr). It will be useful for managers of food and beverage establishments, gift shops, travel agents and other tourism establishments in those destinations hosting international cruise tourists to develop marketing strategies by taking advantage of demographic characteristics, vacation decision-making processes, vacation behaviours and market segment characteristics of the consumers taking part in those tours. Therefore, in Turkey's market, providing service as a destination with the ports of Kuşadası, İstanbul, İzmir and Marmaris in the international cruise market, the demand increase in the domestic market is considered important by cruise tourism managers and travel agents whose speciality is cruise tourism. However, there is insufficient data about consumer behaviours in the domestic market. For this reason, studies need to be carried out about both the domestic market growing day by day and international cruise tourists visiting Turkey, which will make a great contribution to developing effective marketing strategies by improving the wealth of knowledge about the domestic and foreign markets. In accordance with this purpose, the vacation decision-making process, vacation behaviours, evaluation of service quality of cruise tours, market segments, motivation types, satisfaction levels and repurchase behaviour intentions of cruise passengers are suggested as research subjects in the future.

References

Baard, P. P., Deci, E. L. and Ryan, R. M. (2004). 'Intrinsic need satisfaction: A motivational basis of performance and well-being in two work settings', *Journal of Applied Social Psychology*, 34(10): 2045–2068.

Boulding, W., Kalra, A., Staelin, R. and Zeithaml, V. A. (1993). 'A dynamic process model of service quality: From expectations to behavioral intentions', *Journal of Marketing Research*, 30(1): 7–27.

CLIA (2011). 'Cruise market overview, statistical cruise industry data through 2010', Available from http://cruising.org/sites/default/files/misc/2011FINALOV.pdf [Accessed 1 October 2014].

Crompton, J. L. (1979). 'Motivations for pleasure vacation', *Annals of Tourism Research*, 6(4): 408–424.

Crompton, J. L. and McKay, S. L. (1997). 'Motives of visitors attending festival events', *Annals of Tourism Research*, 24(2): 425–439.

Cronin, J. J., Brady, M. K. and Hult, G. T. M. (2000). 'Assessing the effects of quality, value and customer satisfaction on consumer behavioral intentions in service environments', *Journal of Retailing*, 76(2): 193–218.

Dabholkar, P. A. and Thorpe, D. I. (1994). 'Does customer satisfaction predict shopper intentions?', *Journal of Consumer Satisfaction, Dissatisfaction and Complaining Behavior*, 7(1): 161–171.

Deniz Ticareti (2015). 'İstanbul Salıpazarı kruvaziyer limanı 2013-2014 yılı 12 aylık gemi ve yolcu istatistik bilgisi', July 2015.

Duman, T. (2002). 'A Model of Perceived Value for Leisure Travel Products', Unpublished Doctoral Dissertation, Pennsylvania State University, State College, PA, USA.

Fishbein, M. and Ajzen, I. (1975). *Belief, Attitude, Intention and Behavior: An Introduction to Theory and Research*, Reading, MA: Addison-Wesley.

Gitelson, R. J. and Crompton, J. L. (1984). 'Insights into the repeat vacation phenomenon', *Annals of Tourism Research*, 11(2): 199–217.

Goossens, C. (2000). 'Tourism information and pleasure motivation', *Annals of Tourism Research*, 27(2): 301–321.

Gursoy, D., Bonn, M. A. and Chi, C. G. (2010). 'An examination of general, nondestination-specific versus destination-specific motivational factors', *Journal of Hospitality Marketing and Management*, 19(4): 340–357.

Hung, K. and Petrick, J. F. (2011). 'Why do you cruise? Exploring the motivations for taking cruise holidays, and the construction of a cruising motivation scale', *Tourism Management*, 32(2): 386–393.

İnan, E. A., Akıncı, S., Kıymalıoğlu, A. and Akyürek, M. S. (2011). 'Kruvaziyer turizminde turistlerin tavsiye niyetlerinde destinasyon imajına etkisi', *Ege Akademik Bakış*, 11(3): 487–497.

Lee, S. Y. (2005). 'A Conceptual Model of the Roles of Price, Quality and Intermediary Constructs in Determining Behavioral Intention to Visit a Festival', Doctor of Philosophy dissertation, Texas A&M University.

Lois, P., Wang, J., Wall, A. and Ruxton, T. (2004). 'Formal safety assessment of cruise ships', *Tourism Management*, 25(1): 93–109.

McGregor, D. (1966). 'The human side of enterprise', *Reflections*, 2(1): 6–15.

McKercher, B. and Wong, D. Y. Y. (2004). 'Understanding tourism behavior: Examining the combined effects of prior visitation history and destination status', *Journal of Travel Research*, 43(2): 171–179.

Maslow, A. H. (1943). 'A theory of human motivation', *Psychological Review*, 50(4): 370–396.

Meng, F., Tepanon, Y. and Uysal, M. (2008). 'Measuring tourist satisfaction by attribute and motivation: The case of a nature-based resort', *Journal of Vacation Marketing*, 14(1): 41–56.

Naylor, G. (1996). 'How Consumers Determine Value: A New Look at Inputs and Process', Unpublished Doctoral Dissertation, The University of Arizona, Tucson, AZ.

Paris, C. M. and Teye, V. (2010). 'Backpacker motivations: A travel career approach', *Journal of Hospitality Marketing and Management*, 19(3): 244–259.

Petrick, J. F., Tonner, C. and Quinn, C. (2006). 'The utilization of critical incident technique to examine cruise passengers' repurchase intentions', *Journal of Travel Research*, 44(February): 273–280.

Ryan, R. M. and Deci, E. L. (2000a). 'Intrinsic and extrinsic motivations: Classic definitions and new directions', *Contemporary Educational Psychology*, 25(1): 54–67.

Ryan, R. M. and Deci, E. L. (2000b). 'Self-determination theory and the facilitation of intrinsic motivation, social development and well-being', *American Psychologist*, 55(1): 68–78.

Tam, J. L. M. (2000). 'The effects of service quality, perceived value and customer satisfaction on behavioral intentions', *Journal of Hospitality and Leisure Marketing*, 6(4): 31–43.

Taylor, S. A., Nicholson, J. D., Milan, J. and Martinez, R. V. (1997). 'Assessing the roles of service quality and customer satisfaction in the formation of the purchase intentions of Mexican consumers', *Journal of Marketing Theory and Practice*, 5(1): 78–90.

Teye, V. and Leclerc, D. (2003). 'The white Caucasian and ethnic minority cruise markets: Some motivational perspectives', *Journal of Vacation Marketing*, 9(3): 227–242.

turizmdebusabah.com, 'İstanbul Salıpazarı kruvaziyer limanı özelleştirmesi kısa tanıtım dökümanı', Available from http://www.turizmdebusabah.com/images/01642013_istabul_sali_pazari_Tanitim_Dokumani.pdf [Accessed 20 April 2016].

www.globalports.com.tr, 'Statistics', Available from http://www.globalports.com.tr/tr/liman-operasyonlari/kruvaziyer-operasyonlari/ege-ports/istatistikler.aspx [Accessed 20 April 2016].

www.izto.org.tr, 'İzmirde kruvaziyer turizmi', Available from http://www.izto.org.tr/tr/izmirde-kruvaziyer-turizmi [Accessed 20 April 2016].

www.medcruise.com, 'Ege ports – The port of Kusadasi', Available from http://www.medcruise.com/port/495/kusadasi-bodrum-antalya [Accessed 20 April 2016].

www.ubak.gov.tr, 'Deniz Ticareti 2013 istatistikleri', Available from http://www.ubak.gov.tr/BLSM_WIYS/DTGM/tr/Kitaplar/20140613_162122_64032_1_64480.pdf [Accessed 20 April 2016].

Yoon, Y. and Uysal, M. (2005). 'An examination of the effects of motivation and satisfaction on destination loyalty: A structural model', *Tourism Management*, 26(1): 45–56.

Yuan, J. J., Cai, L. A., Morrison, A. M. and Linton, S. (2005). 'An analysis of wine festival attendees' motivations: A synergy of wine, travel and special events?', *Journal of Vacation Marketing*, 11(1): 41–58.

Zeithaml, V. A., Berry, L. L. and Parasuraman, A. (1996). 'The behavioral consequences of service quality', *Journal of Marketing*, 60(2): 31–46.

23

CUSTOMER COMPLAINT BEHAVIOUR

Poh Theng, Loo

Customer complaint behaviour (CCB) and its importance

There are many studies that have defined customer complaint behaviour (CCB) over the past few decades (Sharma et al. 2010). The earliest definition of CCB was introduced by Jacoby and Jaccard (1981), as being the action taken by an individual to communicate negative comments about a product or service towards a company or a third-party organizational entity. Later, Singh (1988) proposed CCB as behavioural (public or private action) and non-behavioural responses (no action) triggered by perceived dissatisfaction with a purchase and consumption experience. The dissatisfaction was caused by the negative disconfirmation of purchase expectations that led to complaint behaviour (Keng et al. 1995). Overall, CCB can be defined as behavioural and non-behavioural actions taken by a dissatisfied customer for his or her below-expected purchase or consumption experience.

Understanding CCB is critical for the services industry, including the hospitality and tourism industry. This is especially so as Goodman (1999) reveals that it is five times more expensive to win a new customer than to keep a current customer. Understanding CCB can enable industry practitioners to be aware of their areas for improvement, such as effective complaint remedies and service recovery to restore customer satisfaction and customer loyalty; these are, undoubtedly, imperative. Previous studies have proved that customer satisfaction in complaint remedies affects customer re-patronage intentions (Conlon and Murray 1996; Davidow 2000; Susskind 2005). Furthermore, a better understanding of CCB can help hospitality and tourism organizations to be proactive in handling complaints (Wildes and Seo 2001). Services organizations should view understanding CCB as an opportunity to strengthen relationships with customers (Blodgett et al. 1995; Kim and Boo 2011) and to learn about problems in order to provide better-quality products and services (Ngai et al. 2007). By doing so, services organizations in hospitality and tourism can develop effective customer complaint management systems for maximization of customer satisfaction, customer loyalty and, ultimately, profits. The importance of understanding CCB is further supported by a study of Blodgett et al. (1995) which revealed that 77% of all customers who had a bad experience did not complain but they engaged in negative word-of-mouth (WOM). However, only 48% of the complaining customers engaged in negative WOM before seeking redress. According to past statistics, on average, 50% of the customers tend to complain about a

Table 23.1 Types of CCB responses

Hirschman (1970)	Exit is an active and destructive response to dissatisfaction which is related to the break of relationship with the service provider. Voice is a verbal and constructive response with an expectation of change in the organization's practices, policies and responses which is usually addressed with friends and other organizations. Loyalty has two aspects which are constructive and passive, whereby customers hope that things will evolve in a positive way
Singh (1988)	Voice responses (seeking redress from the seller or no action). Private responses (WOM communication). Third-party responses (implementing legal action)
Broadbridge and Marshall (1995)	Do nothing. Take private action by switching brands, boycotting the product or service or warning family and friends Take public action by seeking direct redress from the services organizations, bringing legal action, complaining to the media or registering a complaint with a consumer association

Source: Author.

problem to a front-line employee but only 1–5% of customers will launch their complaints to a manager or headquarters (Goodman 1999). These statistics show the importance of understanding CCB by the organizations and service employees so that they are able to respond and handle customer complaints effectively.

CCB is generally divided into three categories including: (a) exit, (b) voice or complaining to service provider, and (c) negative WOM to friends and associates (Singh 1990). There are earlier studies that introduced different types of CCB responses as shown in Table 23.1.

Among the three categories, negative WOM is the most devastating category which could affect the organization's image and profits tremendously because on average, there are double the numbers of people being told about a bad experience than about a good experience (Goodman 1999). Moreover, one angry customer would tell an average of 12 people about one bad experience and those 12 people will tell 6 each, and the 6 will then tell 3 each. The impact of this estimation needs to be multiplied by 100 for customers who have Internet access (Sullivan 2001). In short, knowing and understanding CCB is essential and it brings greater benefits to companies such as customer satisfaction, employee satisfaction and profits. There are three fundamental theories explaining CCB which are equity theory, attribution theory and justice theory. The theories are presented in the next section.

Justice theory and attribution theory

Customer dissatisfaction towards products and services is initiated when customers experience either social resources loss (e.g. losing face when a front desk officer was rude while processing check-in), economic resources loss (e.g. waste of money and time for poor food quality), or both throughout the service experience process (Smith et al. 1999). On top of that, customer dissatisfaction can be due to perceived inequity in a service failure encounter (McCollough et al. 2000). When customers perceive inequity or injustice towards the service recovery process, they will be dissatisfied and angry which affects customer re-patronage and negative WOM behaviour (Blodgett et al. 1997). According to Clemmer and Schneider (1996) as cited in the study of Blodgett and his colleagues (1997), Clemmer and Schneider have concluded upon three dimensions of justice including distributive justice (perceived fairness of negotiation outcomes), procedural justice (perceived fairness of policies and procedures of negotiation by which the outcome is produced) and interactional justice (interpersonal treatment experienced during the service encounter process). Complaining customers who experience greater distributive justice (e.g. monetary compensation offered like refunds or discounts) and interactional justice (polite and friendly employee in handling the problems) are inclined to engage in re-patronage and less likely to engage in negative WOM (Blodgett et al. 1997). Nevertheless, for complaining customers who are treated rudely, even a good compensation is not sufficient to stop them from warning others not to visit the companies and they vow never to purchase any product or service in the future from that company. Regarding procedural justice (e.g. waiting time and efficiency of the complaint handling process), this has no effect on both customers' re-patronage behaviour and negative WOM behaviour.

CCB can also be further explained in relation to attribution theory. When service failures happen, customers assess the failures according to: (a) controllability (if it could be avoided), (b) stability (likelihood to recur), and (c) locus (who is to blame) (Eberly et al. 2011). Complaining customers who perceive that a problem is likely to recur and could be controlled are more likely to engage in negative WOM behaviour and less likely to re-patronize the companies (Blodgett et al. 1995). Indeed, stability and controllability are two imperative elements that determine CCB. Therefore, if a customer perceives the failure as his or her fault, or is less likely to recur or is unavoidable, then the customer tends to be satisfied and loyal to the companies (Hess et al. 2003). Overall, service providers, especially in tourism and hospitality, are required to know and understand the topic on CCB well, including factors affecting CCB.

Factors affecting CCB

There are several factors affecting CCB which have been studied by many researchers in the past; amongst these are cultural factors, demographic factors, other companion factors and attitude towards complaining factors. Each factor is elaborated in the following sections.

Cultural factors

Customers with different cultural backgrounds evaluate service quality differently and demonstrate different types of complaint behaviours (Huang et al. 1996; Lee and Sparks 2007; Loo et al. 2013). Asian consumers – Korean, Malaysian, Chinese and Japanese – are more likely to avoid voice actions and third-party actions. They tend to express their unpleasant experience only to their friends and relatives (Kim and Lynn 2007; Liu and McClure 2001). Studies conducted in the hotel and restaurant industry supported that hotel guests from a higher power distance who are collectivist guests tend to take no actions but engage in private action such as warning family and friends (Huang et al. 1996;

Heung and Lam 2003). Among three countries of complainers (Japanese, Chinese and Korean), the Japanese are more likely to take a voice response than other actions, more than the Chinese (Kim and Lynn 2007). Asian customers tend to stop patronizing a company (Heung and Lam 2003) and switch to other companies or brands after they have voiced their complaints. A study in the hotel industry found that Asian guests are less likely to complain to the hotel because they fear 'losing face' and they are also less familiar with channels for launching complaints (Ngai et al. 2007). Another reason is that Asian customers perceive that taking public action by voicing their dissatisfaction is considered as extreme behaviour (Hui and Au 2001).

Meanwhile, American customers tend to voice their dissatisfaction to service providers but this is also to show affection towards the company (Liu and McClure 2001). Asian customers are more likely to engage with third-party action (writing a letter to a local newspaper or taking legal action) than Western customers (Liu and McClure 2001). The reason Asian customers tend to engage in a third-party response is that this action is viewed as an indirect way to deal with the problems (Kim and Lynn 2007). Indeed, Asian customers do not want to confront front-line employees face-to-face. Thus, they are more likely to choose this approach compared with Western customers. Nevertheless, Asian customers might become public complainers when there is no deep commitment towards a restaurant and when they are paying a high price for the service (Kim et al. 2014).

Demographic factors

Demographic factors such as age, gender and educational level play a critical role in CCB (Keng et al. 1995). The majority of previous studies in the areas of hotels and restaurants have highlighted that customers with a higher level of education tend to launch a complaint more frequently as they know the alternatives by which to launch complaints (Heung and Lam 2003; Keng et al. 1995; Lam and Tang 2003). Jones et al. (2002) state that a high propensity to complain only via WOM is likely among those who are younger, who have children and who are still working. Younger customers file more complaints than older customers (Day and Landon 1977; Heung and Lam 2003; Lam and Tang 2003). However, another study contradicts other earlier findings, in that it reported that older complaining customers tend to lodge complaints publicly but customers with a higher education tend not to complain publicly (Ngai et al. 2007). Older complainants tend to resort to public actions but people with a higher level of education tend not to complain publicly (Ngai et al. 2007).

In terms of gender, male customers are more likely to file complaints than female customers (Cornwell et al. 1991; Huang et al. 1996). This is due to the fact that males want to get things straight; therefore, there are more complaints to management and to third parties from male customers (Huang et al. 1996; Ngai et al. 2007). However, this is different from another study which reported that females are more likely to lodge complaints than males (Heung and Lam 2003). In a nutshell, young and well-educated female customers are more likely to complain more frequently.

Other companion factors

When a customer encounters service failure in company and with customers of the same sex, they tend to disclose more about their emotions and attitudes, which could lead to the customers being more likely to engage in complaining behaviour (Dindia and Allen 1992;

Huang et al. 2014). In other words, customers who encounter service failures when they are with others will have a higher probability to complain compared with when they are alone. Different levels of closeness between the two persons lead to different complaint intentions (Huang et al. 2014).

Attitude towards complaining (ATC) factors

Attitude towards complaining (ATC) refers to the individual needing to seek redress when he or she is dissatisfied with a product or service (Richins 1982). ATC is an important factor of CCB. In fact, research conducted in a franchise restaurant found that ATC is the most influential factor that affects a customer's propensity to complain (Kim and Boo 2011). Customers who have a positive ATC show greater propensity to complain in terms of seeking redress (Blodgett et al. 1995; Bodey and Grace 2007; Voorhees and Brady 2005), as they do not feel uncomfortable complaining (Bodey and Grace 2007). ATC also affects WOM behaviour, affecting the tendency of future complaining and repurchase intentions (Halstead and Droge 1991). On the other hand, there are some customers who have a positive ATC but they are reluctant to seek redress; they will usually silently exit and/or engage in negative WOM behaviour (Blodgett et al. 1995).

Summary

Knowing the factors affecting CCB, hospitality and tourism companies such as hotels and restaurants should have a better idea about customer relationship management and customer handling strategies. With customers who have a positive ATC, as well as customers (especially Asian customers) who tend to avoid voice action and third-party action, companies can provide comment cards or online feedback forms for them, and in return companies should show appreciation for those who are willing to fill out the forms (Heung and Lam 2003; Kim and Lynn 2007). Furthermore, both Asian and non-Asian customers view the action to 'apologize and follow up the problem immediately' as the most effective complaint handling method compared with any kind of compensation (Ngai et al. 2007). Thus, face-to-face communication with customers is necessary and is a more effective way to build customer confidence and trust (Heung and Lam 2003). By doing so, companies can enhance customer satisfaction and minimize dissatisfied customers engaging in private actions after service consumption. For young, educated, female customers, as well as different customer dining groups (dining with peer groups and companions of the same gender), there should be different handling strategies where service employees should be proactive in approaching such customers to collect feedback before the customers start complaining. Companies and employees should work together to promote better service experience regardless of whether this comes before, during or after the service consumption process. Continuous discussion, and reviewing of corrective or preventive actions to be taken in order to enhance the customer service experience need to be conducted, which at the same time minimizes negative CCB. Of utmost importance is that the service team, from top to bottom, should promote unity by having the same love of loving each other within the service team as well as loving the customers, and being one in spirit and purpose, in serving customers. The following case study demonstrates a well-known chain café management's response towards a customer who encountered poor service. The customer engaged with private action via WOM by posting comments on his Facebook wall and the company's Facebook page too.

Jacob wanted to order a cup of coffee but he was not sure which type of coffee to choose. So, he asked the staff member, Peter, some questions before deciding. It was a busy day as it was Christmas Eve; Peter had been working continuously for about 12 hours without a break. Therefore, Peter was exhausted mentally and physically. While he was taking Jacob's order, he started to feel impatient and shouted at Jacob, 'There are many customers queuing behind you. Can you be quick and make up your mind or else just leave?' Jacob felt so embarrassed and frustrated and confronted Peter. After that, Jacob demanded to speak to the manager or owner but the owner was not around. He felt so frustrated and mad with Peter's behaviour and left the café together with his wife, Ruth. His wife had video-recorded the whole conversation. After leaving the café, they immediately posted the video and typed their stories on their Facebook page as well as the café's Facebook page. The video went viral and was shared by Jacob and Ruth's friends to warn their family and friends about the café's poor service. The chain café's district manager, named Chen, contacted Jacob and apologized to him and promised that the terrible customer service would not happen in the future. Chen offered a $100 voucher and told Jacob that Peter was going to be fired. Jacob was surprised by this; he was upset and felt guilty at the company's decision of terminating Peter. In fact, Jacob thought that as the company is a well-known chain café its management should take responsibility to ensure that their employees are well-trained.

This case study gives a scenario where common results and reactions happen, what with the advancement of technology. Nowadays, a bad experience can be shared easily in a few seconds and it can spread rapidly, and globally. This case study also reflects the importance of knowing and understanding CCB which helps service providers to better understand about customers' complaining behaviour. They should then train their employees not only about service skills but also on emotion management. Terminating employees who make mistakes is not always a good solution; customers do not necessarily view the incident as solely the fault of the employee but also the company's management who should be responsible for the quality of service provided. In this case study, the company should not have allowed Peter to work for such long hours without rest or a break. In fact, the company's management should review their operations manpower management.

References

Blodgett, J. G., Hill, D. J. and Tax, S. S. (1997). 'The effects of distributive, procedural, and interactional justice on post complaint behaviour', *Journal of Retailing*, 73(2): 185–210.

Blodgett, J. G., Wakefield, K. L. and Barnes, J. H. (1995). 'The effects of customer service on consumer complaining behaviour', *Journal of Services Marketing*, 9(4): 31–42.

Bodey, K. and Grace, D. (2007). 'Contrasting "complainers" with "non-complainers" on attitude toward complaining, propensity to complain, and key personality characteristics: A nomological look', *Psychology and Marketing*, 24(7): 579–594.

Conlon, D. E. and Murray, N. M. (1996). 'Customer perceptions of corporate responses to product complaints: The role of explanations', *Academy of Management Journal*, 39(4): 1040–1056.

Cornwell, T. B., Bligh, A. D. and Babakus, E. (1991). 'Complaint behaviour of Mexican-American consumers to a third-party agency', *Journal of Consumer Affairs*, 25(1): 1–18.

Davidow, M. (2000). 'The bottom line impact of organizational responses to customer complaints', *Journal of Hospitality and Tourism Research*, 24(4): 473–490.

Day, R. L. and Landon, E. L. (1977). 'Toward a theory of consumer complaint behaviour', in A. G. Woodside, J. N. Sheth and P. D. Bennett (eds.), *Consumer and Industrial Buying Behaviour* (pp. 425–437), Amsterdam: North Holland Publishing.

Dindia, K. and Allen, M. (1992). 'Sex differences in self-disclosure: A meta-analysis', *Psychological Bulletin*, 112(1): 106–124.

Eberly, M. B., Holley, E. C., Johnson, M. D. and Mitchell, T. R. (2011). 'Beyond internal and external: A dyadic theory of relational attributions', *Academy of Management Review*, 36(4): 731–753.

Goodman, J. (1999). 'Basic facts on customer complaint behaviour and the impact of service on the bottom line', *Competitive Advantage*, 9(1): 1–5.

Halstead, D. and Droge, C. (1991). 'Consumer attitudes toward complaining and the prediction of multiple complaint responses', *Advances in Consumer Research*, 18(1): 210–216.

Hess, R. L., Ganesan, S. and Klein, N. M. (2003). 'Service failure and recovery: The impact of relationship factors on customer satisfaction', *Journal of the Academy of Marketing Science*, 31(2): 127–145.

Heung, V. C. and Lam, T. (2003). 'Customer complaint behaviour towards hotel restaurant services', *International Journal of Contemporary Hospitality Management*, 15(5): 283–289.

Huang, J.-H., Huang, C.-T. and Wu, S. (1996). 'National character and response to unsatisfactory hotel service', *International Journal of Hospitality Management*, 15(3): 229–243.

Huang, M. C.-J., Wu, H. C., Chuang, S.-C. and Lin, W. H. (2014). 'Who gets to decide your complaint intentions? The influence of other companions on reaction to service failures', *International Journal of Hospitality Management*, 37: 180–189.

Hui, M. K. and Au, K. (2001). 'Justice perceptions of complaint-handling: A cross-cultural comparison between PRC and Canadian customers', *Journal of Business Research*, 52(2): 161–173.

Jacoby, J. and Jaccard, J. J. (1981). 'The sources, meaning, and validity of consumer complaint behaviour: A psychological analysis', *Journal of Retailing*, 57(3): 4–24.

Jones, D. L., McCleary, K. W. and Lepisto, L. R. (2002). 'Consumer complaint behaviour manifestations for table service restaurants: Identifying sociodemographic characteristics, personality, and behavioural factors', *Journal of Hospitality and Tourism Research*, 26(2): 105–123.

Keng, K. A., Richmond, D. and Han, S. (1995). 'Determinants of consumer complaint behaviour: A study of Singapore consumers', *Journal of International Consumer Marketing*, 8(2): 59–76.

Kim, J. and Boo, S. (2011). 'Influencing factors on customers' intention to complain in a franchise restaurant', *Journal of Hospitality Marketing and Management*, 20(2): 217–237.

Kim, J.-H. and Lynn, J. (2007). 'Classification of Asian complainers in restaurant services', *Asia Pacific Journal of Tourism Research*, 12(4): 365–375.

Kim, M. G., Lee, C. H. and Mattila, A. S. (2014). 'Determinants of customer complaint behaviour in a restaurant context: The role of culture, price level, and customer loyalty', *Journal of Hospitality Marketing and Management*, 23(8): 885–906.

Lam, T. and Tang, V. (2003). 'Recognizing customer complaint behaviour: The case of Hong Kong hotel restaurants', *Journal of Travel and Tourism Marketing*, 14(1): 69–86.

Lee, Y.-L. and Sparks, B. (2007). 'Appraising tourism and hospitality service failure events: A Chinese perspective', *Journal of Hospitality and Tourism Research*, 31(4): 504–529.

Liu, R. R. and McClure, P. (2001). 'Recognizing cross-cultural differences in consumer complaint behaviour and intentions: An empirical examination', *Journal of Consumer Marketing*, 18(1): 54–75.

Loo, P. T., Boo, H. C. and Khoo-Lattimore, C. (2013). 'Profiling service failure and customer online complaint motives in the case of single failure and double deviation', *Journal of Hospitality Marketing and Management*, 22(7): 728–751.

McCollough, M. A., Berry, L. L. and Yadav, M. S. (2000). 'An empirical investigation of customer satisfaction after service failure and recovery', *Journal of Service Research*, 3(2): 121–137.

Richins, M. L. (1982). 'An investigation of consumers' attitudes toward complaining', *Advances in Consumer Research*, 9(1): 502–506.

Sharma, P., Marshall, R., Alan Reday, P. and Na, W. (2010). 'Complainers versus non-complainers: A multi-national investigation of individual and situational influences on customer complaint behaviour', *Journal of Marketing Management*, 26(1–2): 163–180.

Singh, J. (1988). 'Consumer complaint intentions and behaviour: Definitional and taxonomical issues', *The Journal of Marketing*, 53(1): 93–107.

Singh, J. (1990). 'Voice, exit, and negative word-of-mouth behaviours: An investigation across three service categories', *Journal of the Academy of Marketing Science*, 18(1): 1–15.

Smith, A. K., Bolton, R. N. and Wagner, J. (1999). 'A model of customer satisfaction with service encounters involving failure and recovery', *Journal of Marketing Research*, 36(3): 356–372.

Sullivan, D. (2001). *Document Warehousing and Text Mining: Techniques for Improving Business Operations, Marketing, and Sales*, New York: John Wiley and Sons.

Susskind, A. M. (2005). 'A content analysis of consumer complaints, remedies, and repatronage intentions regarding dissatisfying service experiences', *Journal of Hospitality and Tourism Research*, 29(2): 150–169.

Voorhees, C. M. and Brady, M. K. (2005). 'A service perspective on the drivers of complaint intentions', *Journal of Service Research*, 8(2): 192–204.

Wildes, V. J. and Seo, W. (2001). 'Customers vote with their forks: Consumer complaining behaviour in the restaurant industry', *International Journal of Hospitality and Tourism Administration*, 2(2): 21–34.

24

ENHANCING SERVICE RECOVERY PERFORMANCE THROUGH ERROR MANAGEMENT CULTURE

Priyanko Guchait

Introduction

Errors occur in every hospitality organization. Errors have been defined as unintended deviation from plans, goals or adequate feedback processing as well as incorrect action that results from lack of knowledge (Van Dyck et al. 2005). Employees make errors as they speak, as they interact with others and as they pursue their everyday work activities. Errors can occur at any level and department in a hospitality organization: external errors involving customers – front-of-house (servers placing wrong orders, missing reservations) or back-of-house (cooks overcooking meat) – and internal errors involving employees, managers and departments (errors in accounts, finance and HR departments) (Guchait et al. 2016b). Hospitality researchers have concentrated on one type of errors: service failures. Service failures refer to service performance that falls below a customer's expectations. Service failures include product defects, wrong orders, lost orders, missed reservations, food not cooked to order, mischarging and others. Service failure occurs because of several reasons such as time pressure, high workload and fatigue (Karatepe 2012a). Several negative consequences of service failures are possible including customer dissatisfaction, customer defection, negative word-of-mouth, loss of revenue, loss of time, increased costs, endangering employees and customers, and employee stress and poor performance (Swanson and Hsu 2011; Guchait et al. 2012).

As a result, hospitality organizations make attempts to prevent service failures by using sophisticated technologies, rigid systems and strict policies focused on controlling employee behaviour (Hart et al. 1990). However, complete prevention of service failures is impossible (Karatepe 2006). Therefore, along with error prevention, it is necessary for hospitality organizations to ask the question of what can be done after a service failure has occurred. This makes service recoveries crucial for hospitality organizations (Michel et al. 2009). Service recovery refers to actions taken by a hospitality organization to resolve problems that caused a service failure, alter negative attitudes of dissatisfied customers and to ultimately retain these customers (Tsai et al. 2014). Moreover, since front-line employees play a critical role in the service recovery process, the service recovery performance of employees is important for organizational success (Karatepe 2006).

Purpose

First, this chapter reviews the literature on service recovery performance and identifies all the predictors that have been examined. Second, this chapter proposes organizational error management culture as an important predictor of employee service recovery performance. Third, this chapter proposes mediators to explain the underlying mechanism linking error management culture and service recovery performance. Fourth, the chapter provides a theoretical model of service recovery performance, including predictors and mediators that have been empirically tested in prior studies and the ones highlighted in this chapter. This theoretical framework will help hospitality scholars to build on this line of research. Finally, this chapter provides recommendations to managers on how error management cultures can be developed in hospitality organizations to improve service recovery performance.

Background of service recovery and service recovery performance research

Customer-focused

To date, much of the research on service recoveries has focused on the impact of service recovery strategies (e.g. adequately resolving customer complaints) on customer-related outcomes (e.g. Tsai et al. 2014). Specifically, empirical research has linked improved service recovery with increased customer satisfaction (Chuang et al. 2012), trust, loyalty (Dewitt et al. 2008), word-of-mouth (Hocutt et al. 2006), repurchase intentions (Swanson and Hsu 2011), behavioural intentions to return (Guchait et al. 2012) and commitment (Vazquez-Casielles et al. 2010). Research in service recovery has been grounded within a justice theory framework as a basis for explaining customers' perceptions and behaviours associated with various service recovery strategies (Vazquez-Casielles et al. 2010). In general, the results have shown that service recovery responses such as offering refunds and upgrades, apologies and speed of recovery (Roschk and Gelbrich 2014) can have a positive influence on customers' perceptions of fairness (Wirtz and Mattila 2004) and subsequent emotional and behavioural responses (Guchait et al. 2012). Other factors that have been found to influence customers' service recovery evaluations are relationship quality (Vazquez-Casielles et al. 2010), service failure types (Chuang et al. 2012) and demographic differences (Chung-Herrera et al. 2010).

Employee-focused

Recently, attention has moved beyond a customer focus and has settled on the roles and influences of front-line staff and managers in the service recovery process. In doing so, hospitality scholars have focused on service recovery performance. Service recovery performance refers to employee actions and abilities to resolve a service failure to the satisfaction of the customer (Babakus et al. 2003). Several antecedents of service recovery performance have been identified. Boshoff and Allen (2000) proposed two categories of antecedents: managerial attitudes and employee perceptions of the work environment. Managerial attitudes involved three factors: top management commitment to customer service, customer service orientation of the firm, and rewarding customer service excellence. Employee perceptions of the work environment consisted of six variables: teamwork, empowerment, customer service training, role ambiguity, role conflict and organizational commitment. Empirical support was found for role ambiguity, training, empowerment and rewards (Babakus et al. 2003; Yavas et al. 2003; Ashill et al. 2005). Furthermore, perceived organizational support was found to be a significant predictor of service recovery performance

(Karatepe 2012a). In essence, scholars have demonstrated and proposed that availability of *organizational resources and support* results in improved service recovery performance. *Leadership* has also been identified as a critical antecedent of employees' service recovery performance. Supportive management, servant leadership, authoritative leadership and supervisor support for error management have been linked with service recovery performance (Ashill et al. 2008; Lin 2010; Guchait et al. 2014). Furthermore, mediating effects of organizational commitment, job satisfaction and job embeddedness have been found between organizational/leadership support and service recovery performance (Babakus et al. 2003; Karatepe and Karadas 2012). Scholars have also noted the value of *co-worker/team support* for service recovery performance (Karatepe 2012b). Guchait et al. (2014) demonstrated that co-worker support for error management leads to effective service recovery performance. De Jong and Ruyter (2004) outlined the influence of intra-team support on adaptive and proactive behaviour in service recovery. Finally, *individual employee characteristics* have been identified as antecedents of service recovery performance. Trait competitiveness, intrinsic motivation, emotional exhaustion, depersonalization and self-efficacy were found to impact service recovery performance (Karatepe 2006; Ashill et al. 2009; Karatepe et al. 2009; Lin 2010).

Although extensive research has been done in the area of service recovery performance, scholars have noted gaps in the research (Choi et al. 2014; Guchait et al. 2014). Previous research on service recovery performance mostly focused on generic antecedents (e.g. perceived organizational support, role ambiguity). However, in more recent research, there has been a growing interest in specific predictors that fit the context, fit the problem and the criterion factor being investigated – rather than focusing on broad and general predictors. For example, Susskind et al. (2003) extended the research on perceived organizational support (Eisenberger et al. 2002) into service-focused contexts and focused on employees' perceptions of support for service-related duties – rather than their general perceptions of the organization's concern for their well-being – in order to examine the impact on employees' service-related performance. Similarly, in order to examine impact on patient safety, Leroy et al. (2012) examined leader behavioural integrity for safety instead of examining general leader behavioural integrity. The current chapter builds on recent research and makes a contribution to the service recovery performance research by identifying an antecedent that is context specific and relevant to the criterion factor. This chapter proposes organizational error management culture as a crucial antecedent of service recovery performance. Moreover, recent research has highlighted the need to investigate this relationship (Guchait et al. 2014). Error management has been defined as a strategy that focuses on minimizing the negative consequences of errors/service failures by early detection and error correction, and on preventing similar errors in the future by analysing the causes of and learning from errors (Van Dyck et al. 2013). Recent service recovery research has noted that successful service recoveries involve efforts by the hospitality organization not only to return aggrieved customers to a state of satisfaction following a service failure, but also to learn from such incidences to improve service processes, and to provide support to employees through training and rewarding for this purpose (Michel et al. 2009). This makes error management culture crucial for effective service recoveries.

Error management culture and service recovery performance

Error management culture has been defined as shared organizational practices and procedures related to communication about errors, sharing error knowledge, helping in error situations and quickly detecting and handling errors (Van Dyck et al. 2005). Service recoveries are likely to be effective in organizations strong in error management culture because such organizations pursue two goals simultaneously. The first goal is to *control* the potential damage resulting from the service error/failure by quickly detecting the service error and resolving/correcting it. As a result, the negative consequences of service failures (e.g. customer dissatisfaction) are minimized. The second goal is to *learn* from the service failure incidents. Such cultures encourage open communication of service errors/failures, which results in learning from such service failure incidents. Employees learn from not only their own errors but others' errors as well. Such organizations consider errors as important sources of information and encourage employees to use such incidents as learning opportunities. Availability of such information allows organizations to analyse the causes of errors. As a result, learning from errors and analysing causes of errors help organizations prevent similar service failures in the future.

Error management culture is likely to improve employees' service recovery performance. Organizations strong in error management culture encourage communication about service errors/failures, which leads to shared knowledge about service errors/failures (i.e. service failure types, trends, high-risk situations) and effective service recovery strategies (Cannon and Edmondson 2001). When service employees are aware of various failure types they are quick to detect the problem (Reason 1990). Additionally, their knowledge of various service recovery strategies results in quick and efficient service recoveries (Helmreich and Merritt 2000). Shared knowledge and mutual understanding of service problems also help employees better understand their work environment. Employees can improve their anticipation accuracy of each other's behaviours and needs and adapt their own behaviours to suit the needs of others in the work unit. Thus, open communication about errors makes it possible for employees to help others in service failure and recovery situations (Guchait et al. 2015).

Since employees talk freely about errors in strong error management cultures, they develop a mutual understanding of high-risk situations. In other words, they can anticipate situations when a service failure is more likely to occur and catch the error before its negative consequences can unfold (error trapping) (Helmreich and Merritt 2000). Open error communication in the work unit helps with quick error detection, which leads to proactive and efficient handling of errors (i.e. service recoveries), thereby reducing negative consequences of errors (e.g. customer dissatisfaction). For example, an expeditor who notices that a wrong food order is about to be delivered or the food was not cooked properly, and corrects it (quickly stops the delivery and ensures that the food is quickly recooked to perfection) even before the food reaches the customer. In this case, the employee is able to anticipate/identify service problems before customers identify and complain about the service problem. When customers notice that employees took the initiative to report the service problem, and also took actions to resolve the problem, the customers are likely to be pleasantly satisfied.

Finally, strong error management cultures that discourage blame and punishment set the stage for effective error handling because employees need not be preoccupied with defensively ruminating on the error they made (Keith and Frese 2009). Instead of using their resources to deal emotionally with negative feelings such as guilt, shame and fear, they can use all their resources to quickly correct the error. Therefore, an error management culture is likely to result in effective and coordinated error handling (Van Dyck et al. 2005), leading to improved service recovery performance. Next, this chapter explains the underlying mechanisms linking error management culture and service recovery performance.

Mediators

Errors/service failures contribute to learning in individuals and groups (Frese 1995). Because errors are a form of negative feedback that indicates things did not go as planned or certain goals have not been achieved (Van Dyck et al. 2005), they provide valuable information about how to improve and adapt one's course of action ultimately to achieve those goals. Learning from errors takes place when people freely communicate about errors (Carmeli and Gittell 2009). *Learning behaviour* has been defined as a continuous process of reflection and action characterized by activities such as reflecting on results, asking questions, experimenting, seeking feedback, sharing information, asking for help and discussing errors or unexpected outcomes. Through these activities, individuals acquire, share and combine knowledge (Edmondson 1999).

It is easy to say 'learn from your errors, mistakes and failures'. However, hospitality employees are in a dilemma. Leaders and organizations tend to advocate strict adherence to company protocols, consequently leading to a focus on avoiding service errors, while at the same time expecting timely reports of service errors (Leroy et al. 2012). As a result, employees find themselves in a double-bind situation, struggling to decide whether to hide or reveal service errors. Such a situation could be crucial in the services/hospitality industry, because the industry focuses on service quality. It is critical to provide error-free service to guests by introducing sophisticated technologies, developing rigid systems and enacting strict policies and procedures to control employee behaviour (Hart et al. 1990). Yet, the industry relies on people reporting failures and errors to improve operating processes, learn from errors and enhance error recovery strategies to increase guest satisfaction, which tend to dramatically impact company revenue (Tax and Brown 1998). Therefore, engagement in learning behaviour is crucial for effective service recoveries. The questions that need to be asked are: what enables learning behaviour in organizations, groups and individuals? How do you resolve the employee dilemma of whether to avoid or learn from errors? Previous studies have indicated that organizations' error management culture can address this issue (Van Dyck et al. 2005; Guchait et al. 2014).

Error management culture is likely to promote *psychological safety*. Psychological safety refers to one's beliefs about how others will respond when he/she would ask questions, seek feedback or report an error (Carmeli and Gittell 2009). Error management culture promotes a safe learning environment where organizational members feel safe taking interpersonal risks by discussing errors (Edmondson 1999). Strong error management cultures harbour interpersonal trust, mutual respect, and a sense of confidence that employees will not be embarrassed, rejected or punished for speaking up about errors (i.e. communicating about service errors, admitting mistakes) (Guchait et al. 2016a). Therefore, employees are more likely to engage in learning behaviours in strong error management cultures as employees are more likely to perceive psychological safety. Moreover, the nature of relationships between members facilitates or impedes learning behaviours in organizations (Carmeli and Gittell 2009). High-quality relationships conceptualized as shared knowledge, shared goals and mutual respect increased employees' perceptions of psychological safety which consequently increased learning behaviours (Carmeli and Gittell 2009). In strong error management cultures, people have: (a) shared goals about handling errors, (b) shared knowledge about errors and error management strategies and how their individual roles are interlinked, and (c) mutual respect for each other that enables them to work in an atmosphere of openness and learning. In turn, increased learning behaviour is likely to improve service recovery performance. Therefore, building on previous research, this chapter proposes the mediating effects of *psychological safety* and *learning behaviour* between error management culture and service recovery performance.

Another potential mediator explaining the relationship between error management culture and service recovery performance is *trust*. Trust has been defined as a willingness to accept vulnerability to another person, regardless of the ability to monitor their performance, based on positive expectations of their behaviour (Rousseau et al. 1998). Trust has been well demonstrated as a driver of employee (a) attitudes such as satisfaction, commitment and intention to leave, and (b) behaviours such as increased risk-taking, performance, organizational citizenship behaviours, and reduced counter-productive behaviours (Dirks and Ferrin 2002). Proposed mechanisms for these various positive impacts included reciprocity, equity, positive interpersonal relationships, social exchange relationships and availability of job resources (DeConinck 2010). For example, scholars noted that organizational support increased employees' organizational and leader trust, which resulted in employees' reciprocating with positive attitudes and behaviours (Dirks and Ferrin 2002). Along similar lines and using the same mechanisms it can be expected that strong error management culture will increase employee perceptions of trust (in the organization, leader/supervisor, and group/co-workers), and increased trust will result in effective service recovery performance. Therefore, building on previous research, this chapter proposes the mediating effects of trust between error management culture and service recovery performance.

Finally, this chapter proposes organizational *fairness* as a potential mediator. Organizational justice/fairness theory asserts that employees are concerned with how fair the procedures and outcomes are at their organization, particularly by attending to the formal rules and policies, and the interactions employees have at work (Colquitt et al. 2001). Historically, organizational justice has been understood and researched as three types: (1) distributive (the perceived fairness of outcomes), (2) procedural (the perceived fairness of processes and procedures used to make decisions) and (3) interactional justice (the treatment employees experience at work). Especially with procedural and interactional justice, organizational justice encourages social exchange relationships to be formed (Roch and Shanock 2006). When employees perceive they have been treated fairly, they feel obligated to repay the organization through positive attitudes and behaviours (Colquitt et al. 2001). Organizations strong in error management cultures are likely to increase employee perceptions of organizational fairness, which in turn is likely to improve service recovery performance. Service employees prefer to work for an organization that is fair. Fairness is reflected in an organization strong in error management culture because such organizations understand that errors/service failures occasionally occur at the workplace and take a learning and forgiving approach instead of blaming and punishing. Therefore, this chapter proposes the mediating effect of organizational fairness between error management culture and service recovery performance.

Summary

Service failures occur in every hospitality organization. Thus, it is essential to develop shared practices of dealing with service failures. An error management culture is characterized by open communication about service errors/failures, sharing error knowledge, helping in error situations, quick error detection and damage control, analysing errors, and coordinated and effective error handling (Van Dyck et al. 2005). Research that explicitly deals with the concept of error management culture is still in its infancy (Keith and Frese 2009). However, available research demonstrates error management culture to be related to favourable organizational outcomes (e.g. firm profitability) (Van Dyck et al. 2005). Error management culture (perceived by employees) has also been linked with individual employee outcomes (i.e. employee helping behaviours during service failure and recovery situations) (Guchait et al. 2015). These studies suggest that adopting an error management approach is worthwhile for organizations. To extend this line of research the current chapter proposed the influence of error management culture on service recovery performance. Moreover, the underlying mechanisms linking error management culture and service recovery performance were explained. Overall, the study provides directions for future research in the area of error management and service recovery performance (see Figure 24.1).

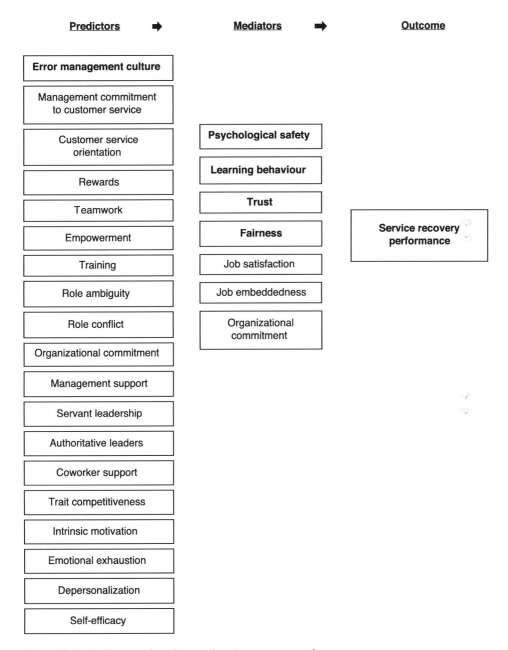

Figure 24.1 Predictors and mediators of service recovery performance

Source: Author.

Practical implications

Adopting an error management approach involves making a deliberate choice that requires active pursuit (Keith and Frese 2009). Otherwise, the natural default seems to be using the failure-avoidance approach, and reluctance to openly communicate about errors (Homsma et al. 2009). A failure-avoidance (error-prevention) approach focuses on making attempts to reduce the number of errors. The major reason why hospitality organizations need to deal with error management is because service errors/failures will occur in every hospitality organization – and it helps to be able to control the negative consequences of service errors/failures (e.g. customer dissatisfaction) and maybe enhance the positive consequences (e.g. customer satisfaction, learning) after the service failure has occurred – in other words, after the error prevention has failed. Hospitality organizations often have a negative view of errors because of biases. The hindsight bias makes people think that the employee responsible for the service error/failure should have known better. The attribution error makes people think that the service error/failure occurred due to some negative characteristics of the service employee (e.g. incompetence) rather than due to unfavourable working conditions. Hospitality organizations that want to establish strong error management cultures need to make explicit and repeated efforts to reduce the tendency of negative reactions towards errors (Keith and Frese 2009).

Implementation of an error management culture in hospitality organizations is not easy considering the inherent difficulty in changing culture. A first step could be to make observations and explicitly reflect on shared practices and procedures for dealing with service errors/failures in the organization. Most hospitality organizations seem to have a vision of service quality and providing error-free service but not about handling errors. Second, organizations should consider incorporating error management principles in training. That is, employees should learn how to detect errors and how to handle errors when they do occur. For example, departments should provide employees with a list of potential problems and detailed, step-by-step instructions on how to fix an error. Hospitality organizations can also focus on error recovery training. For example, simulations can be used to train employees on predicting errors, or detecting errors quickly, and resolving errors before they result in a major problem. Third, organizations should consider ways in which error management can be integrated in their performance appraisal and reward systems. For employees in hospitality

---

John is a newly appointed manager at Hotshot restaurant which emphasizes service quality. Employees are expected to provide error-free service and products to customers. People in the organization discuss providing high service quality, and how to prevent service errors, on a daily basis. However, John observed that people never discuss service failure incidents and effective ways of handling errors, nor do they report errors or share information about errors. Based on his observations of customer complaints and comment cards, John noticed that service errors occasionally occur. Customers also expressed dissatisfaction with the way errors were handled. John also noted that employees tended to blame others when service errors occurred.

Why do people at Hotshot restaurant avoid communication about service errors?

What can John do to encourage employees to communicate about service errors and discuss effective service recovery strategies?

What kind of long-term problems may the company face if this problem is not resolved?

organizations to discuss their errors openly, it is important they do not fear negative consequences such as reduced career opportunities or the possibility of being fired. On the contrary, rewards should be allocated for quickly detecting, reporting and effectively handling errors, and helping others in error situations. Finally, leadership behaviour is critical to develop strong error management cultures. Managers in hospitality organizations should be role models in communicating openly about errors, thereby encouraging front-line employees to do the same. In doing so, managers can set clear expectations that occasional errors may be inevitable, but the goal is to minimize their occurrence and to manage and recover errors efficiently and effectively, instead of ignoring the problem or blaming others.

References

Ashill, N. J., Carruthers, J. and Krisjanous, J. (2005). 'Antecedents and outcomes of service recovery performance in a public health-care environment', *Journal of Services Marketing*, 19(5): 293–308.

Ashill, N. J., Rod, M. and Carruthers, J. (2008). 'The effect of management commitment to service quality on frontline employees' job attitudes, turnover intentions and service recovery performance in a new public management context', *Journal of Strategic Marketing*, 16(5): 437–462.

Ashill, N. J., Rod, M., Thirkell, P. and Carruthers, J. (2009). 'Job resourcefulness, symptoms of burnout and service recovery performance: An examination of call centre employees', *Journal of Services Marketing*, 23(5): 338–350.

Babakus, E., Yavas, U., Karatepe, O. M. and Avci, T. (2003). 'The effect of management commitment to service quality on employees' affective and performance outcomes', *Journal of the Academy of Marketing Science*, 31(3): 272–286.

Boshoff, C. and Allen, J. (2000). 'The influence of selected antecedents on frontline staff's perceptions of service recovery performance', *International Journal of Service Industry Management*, 11(1): 63–90.

Cannon, M. D. and Edmondson, A. C. (2001). 'Confronting failure: Antecedents and consequences of shared beliefs about failure in organizational work groups', *Journal of Organizational Behavior*, 22(2): 161–177.

Carmeli, A. and Gittell, J. H. (2009). 'High-quality relationships, psychological safety, and learning from failures in work organizations', *Journal of Organizational Behavior*, 30(6): 709–729.

Choi, C. H., Kim, T., Lee, G. and Lee, S. K. (2014). 'Testing the stressor-strain-outcome model of customer-related social stressors in predicting emotional exhaustion, customer orientation and service recovery performance', *International Journal of Hospitality Management*, 36: 272–285.

Chuang, S., Cheng, Y., Chang, C. and Yang, S. (2012). 'The effect of service failure types and service recovery on customer satisfaction: A mental accounting perspective', *The Service Industries Journal*, 32(2): 257–271.

Chung-Herrera, B. G., Gonzalez, G. R. and Hoffman, K. D. (2010). 'When demographic differences exist: An analysis of service failure and recovery among diverse participants', *Journal of Services Marketing*, 24(2): 128–141.

Colquitt, J. A., Conlon, D. E., Wesson, M. J., Porter, O. L. H. and Ng, K. Y. (2001). 'Justice at the millennium: A meta-analytic review of 25 years of organizational justice research', *Journal of Applied Psychology*, 86(3): 425–445.

DeConinck, J. B. (2010). 'The effect of organizational justice, perceived organizational support, and perceived supervisor support on marketing employees' level of trust', *Journal of Business Research*, 63(12): 1349–1355.

De Jong, A. and De Ruyter, K. (2004). 'Adaptive versus proactive behavior in service recovery: The role of self-managing teams', *Decision Sciences*, 35(3): 457–491.

Dewitt, T., Nguyen, D. T. and Marshall, R. (2008). 'Exploring customer loyalty: Following service recovery', *Journal of Service Research*, 10(3): 269–281.

Dirks, K. T. and Ferrin, D. L. (2002). 'Trust in leadership: Meta-analytic findings and implications for research and practice', *Journal of Applied Psychology*, 87(4): 611–628.

Edmondson, A. C. (1999). 'Psychological safety and learning behavior in work teams', *Administrative Science Quarterly*, 44(2): 350–383.

Eisenberger, R., Stinglhamber, F., Vandenberghe, C., Sucharski, I. L. and Rhoades, L. (2002). 'Perceived supervisor support: Contributions to perceived organizational support and employee retention', *Journal of Applied Psychology*, 87(3): 565–573.

Frese, M. (1995). 'Error management in training: Conceptual and empirical results', in C. Zucchermaglio, S. Bagnara and S. Stucky (eds.), *Organizational Learning and Technological Change* (pp. 112–124), Berlin: Springer-Verlag.

Guchait, P., Kim, M. G. and Namasivayam, K. (2012). 'Error management at different organizational levels: Frontline, manager, and company', *International Journal of Hospitality Management*, 31(1): 12–22.

Guchait, P., Lee, C., Wang, C. and Abbott, J. L. (2016a). 'Impact of error management practices on service recovery performance and helping behaviors in the hospitality industry: The mediating effects of psychological safety and learning behaviors', *Journal of Human Resources in Hospitality and Tourism*, 15(1): 1–28.

Guchait, P., Pasamehmetoglu, A. and Abbott, J. L. (2015). 'The importance of error management culture in organizations: The impact on employee helping behaviors during service failures and recoveries in restaurants', *Journal of Human Resources in Hospitality and Tourism*, 14(1): 45–67.

Guchait, P., Pasamehmetoglu, A. and Dawson, M. (2014). 'Perceived supervisor and co-worker support for error management: Impact on perceived psychological safety and service recovery performance', *International Journal of Hospitality Management*, 41: 28–37.

Guchait, P., Simons, T. and Pasamehmetoglu, A. (2016b). 'Error recovery performance: The impact of leader behavioral integrity and job satisfaction', *Cornell Hospitality Quarterly*, 57(2): 150–161.

Hart, C., Heskett, J. L. and Sasser, W. E. (1990). 'The profitable art of service recovery', *Harvard Business Review*, 68(4): 148–156.

Helmreich, R. L. and Merritt, A. (2000). 'Safety and error management: The role of crew resource management', in B. J. Hayward and A. R. Lowe (eds.), *Aviation Resource Management* (pp. 107–119), Aldershot, UK: Ashgate.

Hocutt, M. A., Bowers, M. R. and Donavan, D. T. (2006). 'The art of service recovery: Fact or fiction?', *Journal of Services Marketing*, 20(3): 199–207.

Homsma, G. J., Van Dyck, C., De Gilder, D., Koopman, P. L. and Elfring, T. (2009). 'Learning from error: The influence of error incident characteristics', *Journal of Business Research*, 62(1): 115–122.

Karatepe, O. M. (2006). 'The effects of selected antecedents on the service recovery performance of frontline employees', *The Service Industries Journal*, 26(1): 39–57.

Karatepe, O. M. (2012a). 'Perceived organizational support, career satisfaction, and performance outcomes: A study of hotel employees in Cameroon', *International Journal of Contemporary Hospitality Management*, 24(5): 735–752.

Karatepe, O. M. (2012b). 'The effects of coworker and perceived organizational support on hotel employee outcomes: The moderating role of job embeddedness', *Journal of Hospitality and Tourism Research*, 36(4): 495–516.

Karatepe, O. M. and Karadas, G. (2012). 'The effect of management commitment to service quality on job embeddedness and performance outcomes', *Journal of Business Economics and Management*, 13(4): 614–636.

Karatepe, O. M., Yorganci, I. and Haktanir, M. (2009). 'Outcomes of customer verbal aggression among hotel employees', *International Journal of Contemporary Hospitality Management*, 21(6): 713–733.

Keith, N. and Frese, M. (2009). 'Enhancing firm performance and innovativeness through error management culture', in N. M. Ashkanasy, C. P. M. Wilderom and M. F. Peterson (eds.), *Organizational Culture and Climate* (pp. 137–157), New Delhi: Sage.

Leroy, H., Dierynck, B., Anseel, F., Simons, T., Halbesleben, J. R. B., McCaughey, D., Savage, G. T. and Sels, L. (2012). 'Behavioral integrity for safety, priority of safety, psychological safety, and patient safety: A team-level study', *Journal of Applied Psychology*, 97(6): 1273–1281.

Lin, W. (2010). 'Relevant factors that affect service recovery performance', *The Service Industries Journal*, 30(6): 891–910.

Michel, S., Bowen, D. and Johnston, R. (2009). 'Why service recovery fails: Tensions among customer, employee, and process perspectives', *Journal of Service Management*, 20(3): 253–273.

Reason, J. (1990). *Human Error*, Cambridge, UK: Cambridge University Press.

Roch, S. G. and Shanock, L. R. (2006). 'Organizational justice in an exchange framework: Clarifying organizational justice distinctions', *Journal of Management*, 32(2): 299–322.

Roschk, H. and Gelbrich, K. (2014). 'Identifying appropriate compensation types for service failures: A meta-analytic and experimental analysis', *Journal of Service Research*, 17(2): 195–211.

Rousseau, D. M., Sitkin, S. B., Burt, R. S. and Camerer, C. (1998). 'Not so different after all: A cross-discipline view of trust', *Academy of Management Review*, 23(3): 393–404.

Susskind, A. M., Kacmar, K. M. and Borchgrevink, C. P. (2003). 'Customer service providers' attitudes relating to customer service and customer satisfaction in the customer-server exchange', *Journal of Applied Psychology*, 88(1): 179–187.

Swanson, S. R. and Hsu, M. K. (2011). 'The effect of recovery locus attributions and service failure severity on word-of-mouth and repurchase behaviors in the hospitality industry', *Journal of Hospitality and Tourism Research*, 35(4): 511–529.

Tax, S. S. and Brown, S. W. (1998). 'Recovering and learning from service failure', *Sloan Management Review*, 40(1): 75–88.

Tsai, C., Yang, Y. and Cheng, Y. (2014). 'Does relationship matter? – customers' response to service failure', *Managing Service Quality*, 24(2): 139–159.

Van Dyck, C., Dimitrova, N. G., de Korne, D. F. and Hiddema, F. (2013). 'Walk the talk: Leaders' enacted priority of safety, incident reporting, and error management', in T. Simons, H. Leroy and G. T. Savage (eds.), *Leading in Health Care Organizations: Improving Safety, Satisfaction and Financial Performance* (pp. 95–117), Bingley, UK: Emerald Group.

Van Dyck, C., Frese, M., Baer, M. and Sonnentag, S. (2005). 'Organizational error management culture and its impact on performance: A two-study replication', *Journal of Applied Psychology*, 90(6): 1228–1240.

Vazquez-Casielles, R., Alvarez, L. S. and Martin, A. M. D. (2010). 'Perceived justice of service recovery strategies: Impact on customer satisfaction and quality relationship', *Psychology and Marketing*, 27(5): 487–509.

Wirtz, J. and Mattila, A. S. (2004). 'Consumer responses to compensation, speed of recovery, and apology after a service failure', *International Journal of Service Industry Management*, 15(2): 150–166.

Yavas, U., Karatepe, O. M., Avci, T. and Tekinkus, M. (2003). 'Antecedents and outcomes of service recovery performance: An empirical study of frontline employees in Turkish banks', *International Journal of Bank Marketing*, 21(5): 255–265.

PART IV

Consumer loyalty outlook

Part IV of the *Handbook* covers the contributions elaborating loyalty and re-patronage behaviour of hospitality and tourism consumers. The part consists of seven chapters. Chapter 25 by Christy Yen Nee Ng, Brian Kee Mun Wong and Emily Ma summarizes the antecedents of customer loyalty. The chapter looks at a number of antecedents of customer loyalty, in particular customer-related factors (satisfaction, trust, commitment and identification) and product-related factors (service quality, perceived value, corporate reputation/image and switching costs). The chapter also highlights the different dimensions and stages of loyalty building. The chapter enables the reader to appreciate the precursors of loyalty in order to use it for the overall growth of an organisation.

Chapter 26 by Jeynakshi Ladsawut and Robin Nunkoo extends discussion on customer loyalty and proposes a reorganized loyalty development model for tourism organisations. The chapter further talks about the factors influencing the loyalty behaviour of customers besides the impact of new technological advancements on consumer loyalty. Finally, this chapter depicts new constructs that revamp a loyalty integrated model. Service providers need to understand the importance of customer loyalty and more importantly the diverse factors that have impacts on the tourist loyalty construct for the competitiveness of their businesses.

Keith H. Mandabach defines the concept of customer engagement from a marketing perspective and clarifies how it differs from simple relationship marketing in chapter 27. The chapter further details the engagement strategies used in hospitality and tourism businesses to increase the participation of customers as part of the process of building customer loyalty. Engagement strategies adopted by the organisation, employees, management and customers are also explained as the engagement process. The chapter further emphasises that the customer engagement process works best when rooted in the organisational culture and should not be compartmentalised.

In chapter 28, John Bowen highlights four prominent trends affecting the customer loyalty of hotel guests and this is revealed through his extensive literature review. The chapter begins with a brief discussion on customer loyalty and hotel loyalty programmes and focuses on environmental factors that affect hotel loyalty programmes. The chapter further analyses the current environmental trends to outline how to manage the effects of these trends to increase or maintain behavioural and attitudinal loyalty. He affirms that most present hospitality and travel loyalty programmes are still based on only the behavioural component. The chapter also outlines the implications of social media, online travel agencies and millennials for customer loyalty.

Camille Erika Kapoor and Renata Fernandes Guzzo in chapter 29 analyse the brand experience and consumer loyalty. The brand experience is the sum of different interactions between consumers and a brand; it is especially relevant to understand how those interactions happen to increase consumer loyalty. The chapter suggests that brand experience does not just explain general judgements about a brand; rather this concept aggregates specific sensations and behavioural responses triggered by actually experiencing a brand. The chapter further summarizes the contribution of brand communities in promoting brand loyalty.

Chapter 30 by Sandra Maria Correia Loureiro and Eduardo Moraes Sarmento looks at relationship marketing, which is regarded as a process of exchange and mutual cooperation for generating strong customer relationships, that in turn influence customer loyalty and firms' profits. The chapter analyses the use of social software platforms as a tool to enhance hospitality relationship experiences. The authors further outline the development of a hospitality relationship experiences framework for drivers of guest–hotel engagement besides providing managerial implications and suggestions for further research in this context.

Chapter 31 by Stella Kladou provides an insight on customers' behavioural intentions with regards to destination brands. Destination brand equity is considered to be a concept where practitioners seek to understand how to develop successful brand strategies from the customer's perspective. Most such studies focus on four dimensions (i.e. awareness, image, quality and loyalty) of customer-based brand equity; a few recent studies have debated the incorporation of the assets dimension into it, resulting in the operationalization of a five-dimensional model. Finally, the author argues that awareness, association, quality and loyalty are dimensions that are not independent from one another; rather, they are closely interrelated.

25

ANTECEDENTS OF CONSUMER LOYALTY

Christy Yen Nee Ng, Brian Kee Mun Wong and Emily Ma

Concept and dimensions of customer loyalty

A critical issue for the continued success of a company is its capacity to build customer loyalty. The concept of customer loyalty has been researched extensively in business and service contexts and is believed to be a company's most enduring asset (Bolton et al. 2004). Oliver (1997: p. 392) defines customer loyalty as 'a deeply held commitment to rebuy or repatronize a preferred product/service consistently in the future, thereby causing repetitive same brand set purchasing, despite situational influences and marketing efforts having the potential to cause switching behaviour'. There are two dimensions of customer loyalty: behavioural loyalty and attitudinal loyalty (Dekimpe et al. 1997; Dick and Basu 1994; Jacoby and Chestnut 1978; Yi and La 2004). According to Hammond et al. (1996), behavioural loyalty is the consumer's tendency to repurchase. Attitudinal loyalty, on the other hand, as defined by Jacoby and Chestnut (1978), refers to the customer's predisposition towards a brand, which is a function of psychological processes. Attitudinal loyalty is often measured by the degree of customers' revisit intentions and their recommendations to others (Li and Petrick 2008; Oppermann 2000; Yoon and Uysal 2005).

Further, Oliver (1999) suggested that there are three stages of attitudinal loyalty formation, including cognitive, affective and conative stages. Cognitive loyalty derives from previous knowledge or recent information based on experience (Oliver 1999). According to Back and Parks (2003), Evanschitzky and Wunderlich (2006), and Oliver (1999), individuals in this stage develop loyalty through comparison between their preferred product and alternatives based on earlier or indirect knowledge related to the offering, and its performance. According to Oliver (1999), loyalty at this stage is very weak and shallow, and therefore, service providers yearn for a greater level of customer loyalty. The second stage of loyalty is affective loyalty. Affective loyalty represents consumers' feelings of linking to the product or service provider, developed through acquisitively satisfying usage occasions. Most researchers agree that the affective loyalty stage involves emotions and satisfaction, which are critical in attitudinal loyalty formation (Bandyopadhyay and Martell 2007; Han et al. 2009; Oliver 1999). Lee et al. (2010) found that cognitive components, such as value and quality, positively influence affect in a green hotel context. In a comprehensive manner, Yuksel et al. (2010) found that travellers' cognitive loyalty about a specific destination significantly increases their affective loyalty level.

Nevertheless, customer loyalty is not adequately assured at the affective stage. The third loyalty stage is conative loyalty. In the conative loyalty stage, consumers form behavioural intentions to repurchase as indicated in the loyalty definition (Oliver 1999). Consumers build a deeper level of loyalty than in the previous stage, the affective stage. A study conducted by Han and Back (2008) showed that the emotional components of affect encourage a considerable increase of behavioural intentions, in a hotel setting. According to Oliver (1999), true loyalty can only be accomplished at the action loyalty stage, which is also the last stage of loyalty. In this stage, consumers show patterns of repurchase and positive word-of-mouth behaviour (Kandampully et al. 2011; Oliver 1999). Bandyopadhyay and Martell (2007) indicated that a positive attitude towards a particular brand or product could lead consumers to continue patronage and enhanced frequency of patronage. The study of Evanschitzky and Wunderlich (2006) found that conative loyalty, resulting from cognitive and affective loyalty, encourages action loyalty (behavioural loyalty). Also, Back and Parks (2003) found that hotel guests' behavioural loyalty is a positive function of conative brand loyalty built through the cognitive and affective stages.

Antecedents of loyalty

Seeing customer loyalty as the most enduring asset of a company (Bolton et al. 2004), identifying key antecedents of loyalty is important. Therefore, this section identifies and summarizes a number of antecedents of customer loyalty. Based on characteristics of antecedents, we further categorize these antecedents into customer-related factors and product/service-related factors.

Customer-related antecedents

Satisfaction

Customer satisfaction has been an intensively discussed subject area of consumer and marketing research for more than two decades (Hennig-Thurau and Klee 1997). It has been defined as one of the objectives of marketing activity, linking the processes of purchasing and consumption with post-purchase phenomena (Churchill and Surprenant 1982). According to Oliver's expectancy disconfirmation theory (1980), customer satisfaction is understood as the customer's emotional or feeling reaction to the perceived difference between performance evaluation and expectation. Many researchers have suggested that customer satisfaction influences customer loyalty, which in turn affects profitability (e.g. Anderson and Fornell 1994; Gummesson 1993; Schneider and Bowen 1995; Zeithaml et al. 1990). In hospitality contexts, Kim et al. (2001) confirmed that satisfaction was an important predictor for commitment and behavioural intentions. Han and Ryu (2006) found that in a restaurant context, customer satisfaction is highly correlated with customers' behavioural intentions. In the tourism context, studies found that the tourist's satisfaction has a direct influence on destination loyalty (Chi and Qu 2008; Kim and Brown 2012; Yoon and Uysal 2005; Yuksel et al. 2010). For example, the study of Yuksel et al. (2010) indicated that the strong relationship between customer satisfaction and customer loyalty has led the maximization of visitor satisfaction to become one of the primary objectives of destination managers. Kotler (1994: p. 20) also mentioned that, 'The key to customer retention is customer satisfaction.' Satisfied customers do not guarantee a returning business but dissatisfied customers will definitely not be coming back.

Trust

Trust has been defined as the willingness to rely on exchange partners that one has confidence in (Moorman et al. 1993). Morgan and Hunt (1994) suggested that trust is an individual's confidence in the exchange partner's reliability and integrity. Researchers generally agree that confidence and reliability are two key components of trust (e.g. Moorman et al. 1993; Morgan and Hunt 1994). Trust has been recognized as a requirement for customer relationship building and as a prior state for the development of commitment (Garbarino and Johnson 1999; Morgan and Hunt 1994). Doney and Cannon (1997) found that trust can reduce uncertainty because people know they can rely on a trusted firm.

Previous literature recognized trust as a primary indicator of customer exchange relationships and consequently facilitating customer loyalty (Narteh et al. 2013; Vlachos et al. 2009; Wilkins et al. 2009). Leaniz and Rodríguez (2014) conducted a study on how Corporate Social Responsibility (CSR) influences hotel customer loyalty. Their research confirms that hotel companies that carry out CSR initiatives benefit from building customer trust, identification and commitment, and consumer trust positively influences customer loyalty. Similarly, Kassim and Abdullah (2010) confirmed the link between trust and customer loyalty in two cultural contexts, Malaysia and Qatar.

Commitment

Commitment, similar to trust, is viewed as an essential ingredient for successful long-term relationships (Dwyer et al. 1987; Hennig-Thurau et al. 2002; Moorman et al. 1992; Morgan and Hunt 1994). Moorman et al. (1992: p. 316) define commitment as 'an enduring desire to maintain a valued relationship'. In other words, committed customers are motivated to maintain the relationship because they feel it is worth it. Commitment can be divided into three dimensions: affective commitment, continuance commitment and normative commitment (Allen and Meyer 1990). Affective commitment refers to feelings of emotional attachment to the identification with exchange partners (Fullerton 2003), which is based on the customer's desire in maintaining the relationship. In contrast, continuance commitment is based on the need to maintain it (Bendapudi and Berry 1997). Normative commitment is a commitment based on a sense of obligation to a group or organization (Allen and Meyer 1990). Normative and continuance commitment are less applicable in marketing (Fullerton 2005; Mattila 2006) as compared with affective commitment, which is obtained through an emotional bond with the service provider. Affective commitment is believed to be the major driver of customer loyalty in the hotel industry (Narteh et al. 2013).

Identification

Researchers also suggest that customer loyalty is influenced by customer and organizational identification (Choo et al. 2011; Marin et al. 2009; Sen and Bhattacharya 2001). Organizational identification can be defined as the sense of oneness individuals have with an organization (Mael and Ashforth 1992). Rooted in social identity theory (Tajfel and Turner 1979), Bhattacharya and Sen (2003: p. 77) propose that 'some of the strongest customer–company relationships are based on customers' identification with the companies that help satisfy one or more key self-definition needs'. Bhattacharya and Sen (2003) also mentioned that customer company identification originates a physiological attachment in customers leading them to care about the company, increasing a sense of loyalty.

Organizational identification can also be defined as the degree to which individuals define themselves as organization members (Mael and Ashforth 1992: p. 104). Because individuals tend to identify with organizations that share similar characteristics to themselves, organizations can increase employee organizational identification by emphasizing similarities between the organization and employees, and enhancing the organization's reputation. Bergami and Bagozzi (2000) defined organizational identification as the degree of overlap between employees' self-definition and perceived organizational identity. Ashforth and Mael (1989) and Bhattacharya and Sen (2003) suggested that organizational identification can occur without formal membership, opening up the possibility to apply organizational identification to consumer identification without membership status. For instance, a frequent customer identifies with a particular hotel without any formal membership. It is possible that a customer can become committed and develop loyalty to an organization without membership but through identification. Within the hospitality industry, a recent study conducted by So et al. (2013) determines that customer identification is a critical predictor of hotel loyalty.

Service-related antecedents

Service quality

The relationship between service quality and customer loyalty is well established across the services industries, from banking, telecommunications and insurance (Lee and Cunningham 2001; Rasheed and Abadi 2014) to retail (Das 2014; Wong and Sohal 2003), tourism, hospitality, and casino services (Lee and Cunningham 2001; Lee et al. 2004; Prentice 2013; Shi et al. 2014). Service quality refers to the organization's capability to deliver services in accordance with the customer's level of expectation (Parasuraman et al. 1985): in other words, the perceived quality derived from the assessment of differences between the actual service performed and customers' expectations (Baker and Crompton 2000; Cronin 1990; Zeithaml 1988). Past studies have indicated a positive direct effect of quality on customer loyalty (e.g. Aydin and Ozer 2005; Bitner 1990; Cronin and Taylor 1992; Lee and Cunningham 2001; Lee et al. 2004; Parasuraman et al. 1985; Prentice 2013).

Wong and Sohal (2003) assessed the impact of service quality dimensions on customer loyalty at two levels of retail relationships (i.e. interpersonal level and store level) and found a positive association between service quality and customer loyalty, with the relationship being stronger at store level. Tangibles were reported as the most significant predictor of loyalty at store level and empathy at the interpersonal level. Similarly, Lee et al. (2004) in their study of visitors to Umpqua National Forest in Oregon show the direct effect of service quality on visitors' loyalty.

While Shi et al. (2014) confirmed that service quality has a direct effect on customer loyalty in the Macau gaming industry, Das (2014) also found that retailer perceived quality has positive impacts on retailer loyalty in the context of food service.

The other school of thought believes that service quality needs a mediator to influence customer loyalty, thus indicating an indirect effect (Caruana 2002; Spreng and Mackoy 1996; Yu et al. 2005). Olsen (2002) evaluated the relationship between perceived quality performance, customer satisfaction and repurchase loyalty, using four different 'generic' product categories of seafood. Satisfaction plays a mediating role between perceived quality and repurchase loyalty. Lee et al. (2004) explored the relationships between service quality and satisfaction, and their effects on behavioural loyalty among forest visitors. Results show that service quality has a direct relationship with both visitors' satisfaction and loyalty. Satisfaction also played a mediating role in this study.

Despite satisfied customers being more likely to stay loyal to a brand or an establishment (Anderson and Sullivan 1993; Hallowell 1996), satisfaction does not necessarily precede customer loyalty in all circumstances (Bitner 1990; Heskett et al. 1994; Shoemaker and Lewis 1999), but product or service quality may instead (Prentice 2013; Zeithaml et al. 1996). For example, studies have also found that customer satisfaction may not necessarily guarantee loyalty (Kale 2005; Shi et al. 2014). Shi et al. (2014) found that only casino members' satisfaction acts as a mediator between service quality and customer loyalty. Besides customer satisfaction, several other variables, such as trust perceived value (Rasheed and Abadi 2014) and brand reputation (Selnes 1993), mediate the relationship between satisfaction and brand loyalty.

Perceived value

Perceived value has been characterized as a key component in explaining consumer behaviour in the marketing literature (Petrick 2004; Ravald and Gronroos 1996). Customers often compare benefits received with the cost involved, and pick the product that offers the best perceived value compared with the next best alternatives (Lovelock 2000; Zeithaml 1988). A purchase is considered worthy when the perceived value meets or exceeds customers' expectation. On the contrary, customers may switch to competing brands when the perceived value is low, thus resulting in a loyalty decline (Anderson and Srinivasan 2003). This theoretical understanding between perceived value and customer loyalty is well established. However, the relationship is divided into three different schools of thought.

Although proposed as a cognitive construct, as it developed, researchers started to consider perceived value as a multidimensional construct. Researchers generally agree that in addition to the cognitive component, there should be an affective component in perceived value (e.g. Bolton and Drew 1991; Floh et al. 2014; Vogel et al. 2008). Later, Floh et al. (2014) proposed a four-dimensional conceptualization of perceived value, including functional, economic, emotional and social value.

The first school of thought believes in the direct relationship between perceived value and loyalty (e.g. Agustin and Singh 2005; Bolton and Drew 1991; Brodie et al. 2009; Floh et al. 2014; Parasuraman and Grewal 2000; Rasheed and Abadi 2014). For example, Bolton and Drew (1991) in their study on the telephone services industry rated perceived value as an important determinant of consumers' loyalty. Rasheed and Abadi (2014) examined the three factors of service quality, trust and perceived value of customer loyalty within the banking, insurance and telecommunications industries in Malaysia. A direct positive relationship between perceived value and customer loyalty was indicated. A similar significant relationship between the two variables was also evident in the restaurant service industry (Kwun and Oh 2004).

The next group of researchers suggested an indirect influence of perceived value on loyalty through a mediator. Satisfaction was often found to be an effective mediator. Chiou's (2004) empirical study confirms a positive effect between perceived value and overall satisfaction, which then leads to loyalty. Lam et al. (2004) reported satisfaction as a full mediator when loyalty was measured as word of mouth, but when loyalty was measured as repeat patronage, satisfaction appeared to be a partial mediator. Similar results were reported in the online market (e.g. Yang and Peterson 2004) and in the tourism field (Pandža Bajs 2015).

Lastly, researchers have also proposed that perceived value moderates the relationship between satisfaction and loyalty. Anderson and Srinivasan (2003) examined the effect of e-satisfaction on e-loyalty in an online environment. They found that 'the relationship between e-satisfaction and e-loyalty appears strongest when the customers feel that their current e-business vendor provides higher overall value than that offered by competitors' (p. 128).

Corporate reputation/image

Aaker (1996: p. 113) described 'image' as 'the net result of all the experiences, impressions, beliefs, feelings and knowledge that people have about a company'. Corporate reputation refers to the customer's overall evaluation of an organization's offerings, communication effectiveness, interactions with the organizations, and involvement in their corporate activities (Walsh and Beatty 2007). A well-reputed brand is perceived as trustworthy compared with the one with a poor reputation. Besides, corporate reputation often links to product quality when intrinsic attributes are difficult to distinguish (Kirmani and Rao 2000; Polo Pena et al. 2013) or when customers are having difficulty in processing heavy information loads in making a purchase decision (Bromley 2001; Hardaker and Fill 2005). In other words, a good reputation is seen as a mechanism to reduce the perceived risk and lead to favourable purchase and repurchase intent (Andreassen 1999; Pan et al. 2012; Yoon et al. 1993).

In the context of the service industry, corporate reputation or image is significant because the quality of service is more difficult for the customer to examine as compared with product quality (Kim and Choi 2003). A good reputation no doubt provides a competitive advantage to the organization by attracting and keeping loyal customers. The direct relationship between corporate reputation and customer loyalty has been repeatedly observed (e.g. Caruana and Ewing 2010; Hall 1992; Hu et al. 2009). Johnson et al. (2001) propose that reputation, as an attitude, should directly influence intentional loyalty. Similar direct relationships were reported in the retail market (Sirgy and Samli 1989), the broadband service market (Giovani et al. 2014) and airport services (Nesset and Helgesen 2014).

The importance of reputation in the tourism industry has also been highlighted by several researchers (Bigné et al. 2001; Cai et al. 2004; Chen and Tsai 2007; Kandampully and Suhartanto 2000; Yoon and Uysal 2005). In the tourism field, scholars generally agree that the reputation of a destination influences tourists' behaviour. Tourists highly rely on destination reputation in deciding their travel plan, particularly in terms of risk level (Bigné et al. 2001). Loureiro and Kastenholz (2011) also indicated that rural lodging units' reputation has proved to be the most important factor determining visitors' loyalty.

Caruana and Ewing's (2010) study confirmed the positive relationship between corporate reputation and online loyalty and it also discovered 'reputation' as a mediator between perceived value and loyalty. Reputation has also been reported to have an indirect effect on loyalty through satisfaction (Chen and Tsai 2007; Chi and Qu 2008), service quality (Bloemer et al. 1998; Giovani et al. 2014) and trust (Ball et al. 2004). However, despite the majority of the studies supporting the relationship between reputation and loyalty, the recent study by Ramseook-Munhurrun et al. (2015) on tourist loyalty in Mauritius found no significant relationship. The finding opens another chapter of understanding the restrictions on the interaction between corporate reputation and customer loyalty in different locations or industries.

Switching costs

Beerli et al. (2004: p. 258) define switching costs as 'the technical, financial or psychological factors which make it difficult or expensive for a customer to change brand'. Switching costs are multidimensional and they vary across different industries (Fornell 1992). Some of the switching costs identified are artificial or contractual costs, learning costs, transaction costs (Barroso and Picón 2012; Klemperer 1987; Yang and Peterson 2004), financial costs, performance, psychological and behavioural costs, safety costs, social costs, time losses (Barroso and Picón 2012; Murray 1991; Yang and Peterson 2004), benefits loss costs and personal relationships loss costs (Barroso and Picón 2012). They comprise procedural, economic or financial and psychological or relational elements (Burnham et al. 2003; Fornell 1992). Switching cost is one switching barrier (Colgate and Lang 2001; Han et al. 2009) and thus can be used as a mechanism to keep customers (Colgate and Lang 2001), regardless of their satisfaction level. Referring to the resource investment model for loyalty formation developed by Morais et al. (2003, 2005), there are potentially six types of resources which the customers may invest in their relational exchanges with the provider: love, status, information, services, goods, and money. Customers are expected to invest in the relationship if the provider is making an investment in them. These investments eventually will lead to loyalty.

Barroso and Picón (2012) in their insurance market study in Spain suggested that switching costs basically reflect the customer's perception of efforts, money and/or time involved in the switching activity. High switching costs are often theorized to cause better customer loyalty. Thus, switching costs are used as a marketing strategy to garner customer loyalty (Dick and Basu 1994). Pan et al. (2012) in their meta-analysis of 139 empirical research studies found that switching cost has a significant positive relationship with customer loyalty; similar findings were also observed with other researchers (e.g. Beerli et al. 2004; Fornell 1992; Lam et al. 2004; Ping 1997; Selnes 1993). In fact, Bateson and Hoffman (1999) stressed that switching costs are among the most significant predictors of loyalty. Through a meta-analytic review of the previous literature, Blut et al. (2014) found a stronger effect of external switching costs (e.g. potential financial losses, potential discomfort with breaking relationships with the brand and its employees) than internal switching costs (e.g. learning, risk and search costs) on customer loyalty. The findings indicate different binding effects of the two types of switching costs on customer loyalty as customers have a tendency to avoid certain losses. In the context of Chinese hotels, Qiu et al. (2015) found that switching costs have a positive effect on loyalty among the high-tariff hotels but no significant effects on customer loyalty among the low-tariff hotels.

While most studies found a positive relationship between switching costs and customer loyalty, some reports revealed a negative association (e.g. Han et al. 2011; Jones et al. 2000). When the switching costs are high, customers simply feel uncomfortable and may quit the relationship with the seller. Similar to service quality, perceived value and corporate reputation, the role of switching costs in determining loyalty is still debatable. All other factors being equal, a customer will generally stay with their existing provider in order to economize switching costs (Dwyer et al. 1987; Heide and Weiss 1995). However, Fornell (1992) and Beerli et al. (2004) suggested that satisfaction would probably have a higher weight as an antecedent of loyalty compared with switching costs. Customer satisfaction has also been found to mediate the association of switching costs and customer loyalty (e.g. Jones et al. 2000; Oliva et al. 1992).

In addition, researchers have also hypothesized switching costs as a moderator, influencing the customer satisfaction–loyalty link (Anderson and Sullivan 1993; Lee et al. 2001; Qiu et al. 2015; Yang and Peterson 2004), perceived quality–loyalty link (Wang 2010), perceived value–loyalty link (Yang and Peterson 2004) and trust–loyalty link (Aydin et al. 2005). Besides, the moderating effect on customer loyalty is contingent on the situational variables (i.e. types of businesses, customers, market structure and products). It is worth noting that the significant moderating effect is inconsistent on different occasions (Lee et al. 2001; Yang and Peterson 2004).

The Shangri-La customer loyalty efforts

Inspired by James Hilton's novel, *Lost Horizon*, the Shangri-La Hotels and Resorts group was founded in 1971 in Singapore (Shangri-la.com 2015). Over the years, Shangri-La has been recognized as the leading luxury hotel group in the Asia Pacific region as well as one of the world's finest hotel companies, receiving numerous awards. The company now manages and/or owns more than 90 hotels worldwide with a room inventory of over 38,000 (Shangri-la.com 2015).

Shangri-La distinguishes itself from other luxury hotel groups with its 'Shangri-La Hospitality from a caring family', which has embedded in it unique cultures of Asian hospitality. The group strives to maintain the highest service standards at its properties to ensure customer satisfaction and foster customer loyalty. Shangri-La believes that customer loyalty is a key driver of business (Shangri-la.com 2015) and aims to delight guests every time by creating engaging experiences straight from the service providers' heart. This clearly indicates that the Shangri-La group recognizes service quality and customer satisfaction as essential antecedents of customer loyalty (Anderson and Fornell 1994; Lee et al. 2001; Schneider and Bowen 1995).

Shangri-La also developed the Golden Circle frequent guests programme to expand its loyal customer base. The Golden Circle programme has three levels of membership, Gold, Jade and Diamond, with increased benefits and higher requirements to qualify. Being a member of the programme makes every stay in the hotel, or purchase of services provided in the hotel, a value-added activity (measured by points). Hotel guests can redeem awards in the formats of hotel stay, dining experience or gifts. Shangri-La started the programme as part of its uncompromising commitment to recognizing customers' loyalty (Shangri-la.com 2015). Looking from the theory on customer loyalty, however, Shangri-La actually applied the 'switching cost' concept here. By staying in Shangri-La and becoming a member, points are accumulated each time a guest stays or spends in the hotel. These points can only be redeemed/consumed in Shangri-La, creating switching costs for guests who joined the membership programme. Switching cost is one switching barrier (Colgate and Lang 2001) and can be used as a mechanism to keep customers. Using membership and creating a potential switching cost thus has become a popular technique for business operators. For example, airlines were among the earliest sectors to adopt this, with mileage awards programmes. Banks also have home loans packaged with credit cards with award points and no annual fees. However, switching costs (e.g. in the format of lost benefits and convenience) will occur if customers want to switch to other banks offering lower interest rates.

In addition, Shangri-La recognizes image and reputation's impact on customer loyalty and started its corporate social responsibility programmes early. It has developed a number of projects focusing on the environment, health and safety, employees, supply chain, and stakeholder relations under the theme of sustainability. Many projects are children focused. For example, Shangri-La's Rasa Sentosa Resort and Spa developed a project called 'Letting Hope Shine' with Delta Senior School in China to help families with children who suffer from life-threatening illnesses (Shangri-la.com 2015). The importance of image/reputation has been well recognized in the hospitality and tourism literature (Hong and Yang 2011; Hu et al. 2009). A good reputation provides a competitive advantage to the organization and will directly influence customer loyalty by attracting and keeping loyal customers (Johnson et al. 2001).

Conclusion

This chapter introduced the concepts and antecedents of customer loyalty. A number of antecedents were covered, such as customer satisfaction, service quality, image/reputation and switching cost. A case study on the Shangri-La group was introduced which worked on various aspects that may influence customer loyalty. Customer loyalty is an important concept in the hospitality and tourism disciplines and we hope this chapter has helped you understand customer loyalty better.

References

Aaker, D. A. (1996). *Building Strong Brands*, New York: Free Press.

Agustin, C. and Singh, J. (2005). 'Curvilinear effects of consumer loyalty determinants in relational exchanges', *Journal of Marketing Research*, 42(1): 96–108.

Allen, M. J. and Meyer, J. P. (1990). 'The measurement and antecedents of affective, continuance and normative commitment to the organization', *Journal of Occupational Psychology*, 63(1): 1–18.

Anderson, E. W. and Fornell, C. (1994). 'A customer satisfaction research prospectus', *Service Quality: New Directions in Service and Practice*, 14(1): 239–266.

Anderson, E. W. and Sullivan, M. W. (1993). 'The antecedents and consequences of customer satisfaction for firms', *Marketing Science*, 12(2): 125–143.

Anderson, R. E. and Srinivasan, S. S. (2003). 'E-satisfaction and e-loyalty: A contingency framework', *Psychology and Marketing*, 20(2): 123–138.

Andreassen, T. W. (1999). 'What drives customer loyalty with complaint resolution?', *Journal of Service Research*, 1(4): 324–332.

Ashforth, B. E. and Mael, F. A. (1989). 'Social identity theory and the organization', *Academy of Management Review*, 14(1): 20–39.

Aydin, S. and Özer, G. (2005). 'The analysis of antecedents of customer loyalty in the Turkish mobile telecommunication market', *European Journal of Marketing*, 39(7/8): 910–925.

Aydin, S., Özer, G. and Arasil, O. (2005). 'Customer loyalty and the effect of switching costs as a moderator variable: A case in the Turkish mobile phone market', *Marketing Intelligence and Planning*, 23(1): 89–103.

Back, K. J. and Parks, S. C. (2003). 'A brand loyalty involving cognitive, affective, and conative brand loyalty and customer satisfaction', *Journal of Hospitality and Tourism Research*, 27(4): 419–435.

Baker, D. A. and Crompton, J. L. (2000). 'Quality, satisfaction and behavioral intentions', *Annals of Tourism Research*, 27(3): 785–804.

Ball, D., Coelho, P. S. and Machas, A. (2004). 'The role of communication and trust in explaining customer loyalty: An extension to the ECSI model', *European Journal of Marketing*, 38(9/10): 1272–1293.

Bandyopadhyay, S. and Martell, M. (2007). 'Does attitudinal loyalty influence behavioral loyalty? A theoretical and empirical study', *Journal of Retailing and Consumer Science*, 14(1): 35–44.

Barroso, C. and Picón, A. (2012). 'Multi-dimensional analysis of perceived switching costs', *Industrial Marketing Management*, 41(3): 531–543.

Bateson, J. E. G. and Hoffman, D. K. (1999). *Managing Services Marketing: Text and Readings*, New York: The Dryden Press.

Beerli, A., Martin, J. D. and Quintana, A. (2004). 'A model of customer loyalty in the retail banking market', *European Journal of Marketing*, 38(1/2): 253–275.

Bendapudi, N. and Berry, L. L. (1997). 'Customers' motivations for maintaining relationships with service providers', *Journal of Retailing*, 73(1): 15–37.

Bergami, M. and Bagozzi, R. P. (2000). 'Self-categorization, affective commitment and group self-esteem as distinct aspects of social identity in the organization', *British Journal of Social Psychology*, 39(4): 555–577.

Bhattacharya, C. B. and Sen, S. (2003). 'Consumer-company identification: A framework for understanding consumers' relationships with companies', *Journal of Marketing*, 67(2): 76–88.

Bigné, J. E., Sánchez, M. I. and Sánchez, J. (2001). 'Tourism image, evaluation variables and after purchase behaviour: Inter-relationship', *Tourism Management*, 22(6): 607–617.

Bitner, M. J. (1990). 'Evaluating service encounters: The effects of physical surroundings and employee responses', *Journal of Marketing*, 54(2): 69–82.

Bloemer, J., Ruyter, K. and Peeters, P. (1998). 'Investigating drivers of bank loyalty: The complex relationship between image, service quality and satisfaction', *International Journal of Bank Marketing*, 16(7): 276–286.

Blut, M., Beatty, S. E., Evanschitzky, H. and Brock, C. (2014). 'The impact of service characteristics on the switching costs–customer loyalty link', *Journal of Retailing*, 90(2): 275–290.

Bolton, R. N. and Drew, J. H. (1991). 'A longitudinal analysis of the impact of service changes on customer attitudes', *Journal of Marketing*, 55(1): 1–9.

Bolton, R. N., Lemon, K. N. and Verhoef, P. C. (2004). 'The theoretical underpinnings of customer asset management: A framework and propositions for future research', *Journal of the Academy of Marketing Science*, 32(3): 271–292.

Brodie, R. J., Whittome, J. and Brush, G. J. (2009). 'Investigating the service brand: A customer value perspective', *Journal of Business Research*, 62(3): 345–355.

Bromley, D. B. (2001). 'Relationships between personal and corporate reputation', *European Journal of Marketing*, 35(3/4): 316–334.

Burnham, T. A., Frels, J. K. and Mahajan, V. (2003). 'Consumer switching costs: A typology, antecedents and consequences', *Journal of the Academy of Marketing Science*, 31(2): 109–126.

Cai, L. A., Wu, B. and Bai, B. (2004). 'Destination image and loyalty', *Tourism Review International*, 7(3–4): 153–162.

Caruana, A. (2002). 'Service loyalty: The effects of service quality and the mediating role of customer satisfaction', *European Journal of Marketing*, 36(7/8): 811–828.

Caruana, A. and Ewing, M. T. (2010). 'How corporate reputation, quality, and value influence online loyalty', *Journal of Business Research*, 63(9–10): 1103–1110.

Chen, C.-F. and Tsai, D. (2007). 'How destination image and evaluative factors affect behavioural intentions?', *Tourism Management*, 28(4): 1115–1122.

Chi, C. G.-Q. and Qu, H. (2008). 'Examining the structural relationships of destination image, tourist satisfaction and destination loyalty: An integrated approach', *Tourism Management*, 29(4): 624–636.

Chiou, J. (2004). 'The antecedents of consumers' loyalty toward internet service providers', *Information and Management*, 41(6): 685–695.

Choo, H., Park, S. Y. and Petrick, J. F. (2011). 'The influence of resident's identification with a tourism destination brand on their behavior', *Journal of Hospitality Marketing and Management*, 2(2): 198–216.

Churchill, G. A. and Surprenant, C. (1982). 'An investigation into the determinants of customer satisfaction', *Journal of Marketing Research*, 19(4): 491–504.

Colgate, M. and Lang, B. (2001). 'Switching barriers in consumer markets: An investigation of the financial services industry', *Journal of Consumer Marketing*, 18(4/5): 332–347.

Cronin, L. (1990). 'A strategy for tourism and sustainable developments', *World Leisure and Recreation*, 32(3): 12–18.

Cronin, J. J. and Taylor, S. A. (1992). 'Measuring service quality: A reexamination and extension', *Journal of Marketing*, 56(3): 55–68.

Das, G. (2014). 'Linkages of retailer awareness, retailer association, retailer perceived quality and retailer loyalty with purchase intention: A study of Indian food retail brands', *Journal of Retailing and Consumer Services*, 21(3): 284–292.

Dekimpe, M. G., Steenkamp, J. E. M. and Vanden, A. P. (1997). 'Decline and variability in brand loyalty', *International Journal of Research in Marketing*, 14(5): 405–420.

Dick, A. S. and Basu, K. (1994). 'Customer loyalty: Toward an integrated conceptual framework', *Journal of the Academy of Marketing Science*, 22(2): 99–113.

Doney, P. M. and Cannon, J. P. (1997). 'An examination of the nature of trust in buyer–seller relationships', *Journal of Marketing*, 61(2): 35–51.

Dwyer, F. R., Schurr, P. H. and Oh, S. (1987). 'Developing buyer-seller relationships', *Journal of Marketing*, 51(4): 6–21.

Evanschitzky, H. and Wunderlich, M. (2006). 'An examination of moderator effects in the four-stage loyalty model', *Journal of Service Research*, 8(4): 330–345.

Floh, A., Zauner, A., Koller, M. and Rusch, T. (2014). 'Customer segmentation using unobserved heterogeneity in the perceived-value–loyalty–intentions link', *Journal of Business Research*, 67(5): 974–982.

Fornell, C. (1992). 'A national customer satisfaction barometer: The Swedish experience', *Journal of Marketing*, 56(1): 6–21.

Fullerton, G. (2003). 'When does commitment lead to loyalty?', *Journal of Service Research*, 5(4): 333–344.

Fullerton, G. (2005). 'The service quality-loyalty relationship in retail services: Does commitment matter?', *Journal of Retailing and Consumer Services*, 12(2): 99–111.

Garbarino, E. and Johnson, M. S. (1999). 'The different roles of satisfaction, trust, and commitment in customer relationships', *Journal of Marketing*, 63(2): 70–87.

Giovani, A. N., Zondiros, D. and Tomaras, P. (2014). 'The antecedents of customer loyalty for broadband services: The role of service quality, emotional satisfaction and corporate image', *Procedia – Social and Behavioral Sciences*, 148: 236–244.

Gummesson, E. (1993). *Quality Management in Service Organizations*, New York: St John's University and the International Service Quality Association.

Hall, R. (1992). 'The strategic analysis of intangible resources', *Strategic Management Journal*, 13(2): 135–144.

Hallowell, R. (1996). 'The relationships of customer satisfaction, customer loyalty, and profitability: An empirical study', *International Journal of Service Industry Management*, 7(4): 27–42.

Hammond, K., East, R. L. and Ehrenberg, A. (1996). *Buying More and Buying Longer: Concepts and Measures of Consumer Loyalty*, working paper, London: London Business School.

Han, H. and Back, K. (2008). 'Relationships among image congruence, consumption emotions, and customer loyalty in the lodging industry', *Journal of Hospitality and Tourism Research*, 32(4): 467–490.

Han, H., Back, K. and Barrett, B. (2009). 'Influencing factors on restaurant customers' revisit intention: The roles of emotions and switching barriers', *International Journal of Hospitality Management*, 28(4): 563–572.

Han, H., Back, K. J. and Kim, Y. H. (2011). 'A multidimensional scale of switching barriers in the full-service restaurant industry', *Cornell Hospitality Quarterly*, 52(1): 54–63.

Han, H. and Ryu, K. (2006). 'Moderating role of personal characteristics in forming restaurant customers' behavioral intentions: An upscale restaurant setting', *Journal of Hospitality and Leisure Marketing*, 15(4): 25–53.

Hardaker, S. and Fill, C. (2005). 'Corporate service brands: The intellectual and emotional engagement of employees', *Corporate Reputation Review*, 7(4): 365–376.

Heide, J. B. and Weiss, A. M. (1995). 'Vendor consideration and switching behavior for buyers in high-technology markets', *Journal of Marketing*, 59(7): 30–43.

Hennig-Thurau, T., Gwinner, K. P. and Gremler, D. D. (2002). 'Understanding relationship marketing outcomes', *Journal of Service Research*, 4(3): 230–247.

Hennig-Thurau, T. and Klee, A. (1997). 'The impact of customer satisfaction and relationship quality on consumer retention: A critical reassessment and model development', *Psychology and Marketing*, 14(8): 737–764.

Heskett, J. L., Jones, T. O., Loveman, G. W., Sasser, W. E. and Schlesinger, L. A. (1994). 'Putting the service-profit chain to work', *Harvard Business Review*, 72(2): 164–174.

Hong, S. and Yang, S.-U. (2011). 'Public engagement in supportive communication behaviors toward an organization: Effects of relational satisfaction and organizational reputation in public relations management', *Journal of Public Relations Research*, 23(2): 191–217.

Hu, H. H. S., Kandampully, J. and Juwaheer, T. D. (2009). 'Relationships and impacts of service quality, perceived value, customer satisfaction, and image: An empirical study', *The Service Industries Journal*, 29(2): 111–125.

Jacoby, J. and Chestnut, R. W. (1978). *Brand Loyalty Measurement and Management*, New York: Wiley.

Johnson, M. D., Anders, G., Tor Wallin, A., Line, L. and Cha, J. (2001). 'The evolution and future of national customer satisfaction index models', *Journal of Economic Psychology*, 22(2): 217–245.

Jones, M., Mothersbaugh, D. and Beatty, S. (2000). 'Switching barriers and repurchase intentions in services', *Journal of Retailing*, 76(2): 259–274.

Kale, S. H. (2005). 'Change management: Antecedents and consequences in casino CRM', *UNLV Gaming Research and Review Journal*, 9(2): 55–67.

Kandampully, J., Juwaheer, T. D. and Hu, H. H. S. (2011). 'The influence of a hotel firm's quality of service and image and its effect on tourism customer loyalty', *International Journal of Hospitality and Tourism*, 12(1): 21–42.

Kandampully, J. and Suhartanto, D. (2000). 'Customer loyalty in the hotel industry: The role of customer satisfaction and image', *International Journal of Contemporary Hospitality Management*, 12(6): 346–351.

Kassim, N. and Abdullah, M. A. (2010). 'The effect of perceived service quality dimensions on customer satisfaction, trust, and loyalty in e-commerce settings: A cross-cultural analysis', *Asia Pacific Journal of Marketing and Logistics*, 22(3): 351–371.

Kim, A. K. and Brown, G. (2012). 'Understanding the relationship between perceived travel experiences, overall satisfaction, and destination loyalty', *Anatolia – An International Journal of Tourism and Hospitality Research*, 23(3): 328–347.

Kim, J. B. and Choi, C. J. (2003). 'Reputation and product tampering in service industries', *The Service Industries Journal*, 23(4): 3–11.

Kim, W. G., Han, J. S. and Lee, E. (2001). 'Effects of relationship marketing on repeat purchase and word of mouth', *Journal of Hospitality and Tourism Research*, 25(3): 272–288.

Kirmani, A. and Rao, A. R. (2000). 'No pain, no gain: A critical review of the literature on signaling unobservable product quality', *Journal of Marketing*, 64(2): 66–79.

Klemperer, P. (1987). 'Markets with consumer switching costs', *Quarterly Journal of Economics*, 102(2): 375–394.

Kotler, P. (1994). *Marketing Management: Analysis, Planning, Implementation and Control*, New Delhi: Prentice-Hall.

Kwun, J. and Oh, H. (2004). 'Effects of brand, price, and risk on customers' value perceptions and behavioral intentions in the restaurant industry', *Journal of Hospitality and Leisure Marketing*, 11(1): 31–49.

Lam, S. Y., Shankar, V., Erramilli, M. K. and Murthy, B. (2004). 'Customer value, satisfaction, loyalty, and switching costs: An illustration from a business-to-business service context', *Journal of the Academy of Marketing Science*, 32(3): 293–311.

Leaniz, P. M. G. and Rodríguez, I. R. D. B. (2014). 'Exploring the antecedents of hotel customer loyalty: A social identity perspective', *Journal of Hospitality Marketing and Management*, 24(1): 1–23.

Lee, J., Graefe, A. R. and Burns, R. C. (2004). 'Service quality, satisfaction, and behavioural intention among forest visitors', *Journal of Travel and Tourism Marketing*, 17(1): 73–82.

Lee, J., Hsu, L., Han, H. and Kim, Y. (2010). 'Understanding how consumers view green hotels: How a hotel's green image can influence behavioral intentions', *Journal of Sustainable Tourism*, 18(7): 901–914.

Lee, J., Lee, J. and Feick, L. (2001). 'The impact of switching costs on the customer satisfaction-loyalty link: Mobile phone service in France', *Journal of Services Marketing*, 15(1): 35–48.

Lee, M. and Cunningham, L. F. (2001). 'A cost/benefit approach to understanding service loyalty', *Journal of Services Marketing*, 15(2): 113–130.

Li, X. and Petrick, J. F. (2008). 'Examining the antecedents of brand loyalty from an investment model perspective', *Journal of Travel Research*, 47(1): 25–34.

Loureiro, S. M. C. and Kastenholz, E. (2011). 'Corporate reputation, satisfaction, delight, and loyalty towards rural lodging units in Portugal', *International Journal of Hospitality Management*, 30(3): 575–583.

Lovelock, C. H. (2000). *Service marketing*, 4th edition, Upper Saddle River, NJ: Prentice-Hall International.

Mael, F. and Ashforth, B. E. (1992). 'Alumni and their alma mater: A partial test of the reformulated model of organizational identification', *Journal of Organizational Behavior*, 13(2): 103–123.

Marin, L., Ruiz, S. and Rubio, A. (2009). 'The role of identity salience in the effects of corporate social responsibility on consumer behavior', *Journal of Business Ethics*, 84(1): 65–78.

Mattila, A. S. (2006). 'How affective commitment boosts guest loyalty (and promotes frequent-guest programs)', *Cornell Hotel and Restaurant Administration Quarterly*, 47(2): 174–181.

Moorman, C., Deshpandé, R. and Zaltman, G. (1993). *Relationship between Providers and Users of Market Research: The Role of Personal Trust*, Cambridge, MA: Marketing Science Institute.

Moorman, C., Zaltman, G. and Deshpande, R. (1992). 'Relationships between providers and users of market research: The dynamics of trust within and between organizations', *Journal of Marketing Research*, 24(1): 314–328.

Morais, D. B., Backman, S. J. and Dorsch, M. J. (2003). 'Toward the operationalization of resource investments made between customers and providers of a tourism service', *Journal of Travel Research*, 41(4): 362–374.

Morais, D. B., Dorsch, M. J. and Backman, S. J. (2005). 'Building loyal relationships between customers and providers: A focus on resource investments', *Journal of Travel and Tourism Marketing*, 18(1): 49–57.

Morgan, R. M. and Hunt, S. D. (1994). 'The commitment-trust theory of relationship marketing', *Journal of Marketing*, 58(3): 20–38.

Murray, K. (1991). 'A test of services marketing theory: Consumer information acquisition activities', *Journal of Marketing*, 55(1): 10–25.

Narteh, B., Agbemabiese, G. C., Kodua, P. and Braimah, M. (2013). 'Relationship marketing and customer loyalty: Evidence from the Ghanaian luxury hotel industry', *Journal of Hospitality Marketing and Management*, 22(4): 407–436.

Nesset, E. and Helgesen, O. (2014). 'Effects of switching costs on customer attitude loyalty to an airport in a multi-airport region', *Transportation Research Part A: Policy and Practice*, 67: 240–253.

Oliva, T. A., Oliver, R. L. and MacMillan, I. C. (1992). 'A catastrophe model for developing service satisfaction strategies', *Journal of Marketing*, 56(3): 83–95.

Oliver, R. L. (1980). 'A cognitive model of the antecedents and consequences of satisfaction decisions', *Journal of Marketing Research*, 17(4): 460–469.

Oliver, R. L. (1997). *Satisfaction: A Behavioral Perspective on the Consumer*, New York: McGraw-Hill.

Oliver, R. L. (1999). 'Whence customer loyalty?', *Journal of Marketing*, 63(4): 33–44.

Olsen, S. O. (2002). 'Comparative evaluation and the relationship between quality, satisfaction, and repurchase loyalty', *Journal of the Academy of Marketing Science*, 30(3): 240–249.

Oppermann, M. (2000). 'Tourism destination loyalty', *Journal of Travel Research*, 39(1): 78–84.

Pan, Y., Sheng, S. and Xie, F. T. (2012). 'Antecedents of customer loyalty: An empirical synthesis and reexamination', *Journal of Retailing and Consumer Services*, 19(1): 150–158.

Pandža Bajs, I. (2015). 'Tourist perceived value, relationship to satisfaction, and behavioural intentions: The example of the Croatian tourist destination Dubrovnik', *Journal of Travel Research*, 54(1): 122–134.

Parasuraman, A. and Grewal, D. (2000). 'The impact of technology on the quality-value-loyalty chain: A research agenda', *Journal of the Academy of Marketing Science*, 28(1): 168–174.

Parasuraman, A., Zeithaml, V. A. and Berry, L. L. (1985). 'A conceptual model of service quality and its implications for future research', *Journal of Marketing*, 49(4): 41–50.

Petrick, J. F. (2004). 'Are loyal visitors desired visitors?', *Tourism Management*, 25(4): 463–470.

Ping, R. A. (1997). 'Voice in business to business relationships: Cost of exit and demographic antecedents', *Journal of Retailing*, 73(2): 261–281.

Polo Pena, A. I., Frías Jamilena, D. M. and Rodríguez Molina, M. A. (2013). 'Antecedents of loyalty toward rural hospitality enterprises: The moderating effect of the customer's previous experience', *International Journal of Hospitality Management*, 34: 127–137.

Prentice, C. (2013). 'Service quality perceptions and customer loyalty in casinos', *International Journal of Contemporary Hospitality Management*, 25(3): 49–64.

Qiu, H., Yeb, B. H., Baic, B. and Wang, W. H. (2015). 'Do the roles of switching barriers on customer loyalty vary for different types of hotels?', *International Journal of Hospitality Management*, 46: 89–98.

Ramseook-Munhurrun, P., Seebaluck, V. N. and Naidoo, P. (2015). 'Examining the structural relationships of destination image, perceived value, tourist satisfaction and loyalty: Case of Mauritius', *Procedia – Social and Behavioral Sciences*, 175: 252–259.

Rasheed, F. A. and Abadi, M. F. (2014). 'Impact of service quality, trust and perceived value on customer loyalty in Malaysia services industries', *Procedia – Social and Behavioral Sciences*, 164: 298–304.

Ravald, A. and Gronroos, C. (1996). 'The value concept and relationship', *European Journal of Marketing*, 30(2): 19–30.

Schneider, B. and Bowen, D. E. (1995). *Winning the Service Game*, Boston, MA: HBS Press.

Selnes, F. (1993). 'An examination of the effect of product performance on brand reputation, satisfaction and loyalty', *European Journal of Marketing*, 27(9): 19–35.

Sen, S. and Bhattacharya, C. B. (2001). 'Does doing good always lead to doing better? Consumer reactions to corporate social responsibility', *Journal of Marketing Research*, 38(2): 225–243.

Shangri-la.com (2015). 'Awards', Available from http://www.shangri-la.com/corporate/about-us/awards/ [Accessed: 12 November 2016].

Shi, Y., Prentice, C. and He, W. (2014). 'Linking service quality, customer satisfaction and loyalty in casinos, does membership matter?', *International Journal of Hospitality Management*, 40: 81–91.

Shoemaker, S. and Lewis, R. C. (1999). 'Customer loyalty: The future of hospitality marketing', *International Journal of Hospitality Management*, 18(4): 345–370.

Sirgy, M. J. and Samli, A. C. (1989). 'A path analytic model of store loyalty involving self-concept, store image, geographic loyalty, and socioeconomic status', *Journal of the Academy of Marketing Science*, 13(3): 265–291.

So, K. K. F., King, C., Sparks, B. A. and Wang, Y. (2013). 'The influence of customer brand identification on hotel brand evaluation and loyalty development', *International Journal of Hospitality Management*, 34: 31–41.

Spreng, R. A. and Mackoy, R. D. (1996). 'An empirical examination of a model of perceived service quality and satisfaction', *Journal of Retailing*, 72(2): 201–214.

Tajfel, H. and Turner, J. C. (1979). 'An integrative theory of intergroup conflict', in W. Austin and S. Worchel (eds.), *The Social Psychology of Intergroup Relations* (pp. 33–52), Monterrey, CA: BrooksCole.

Vlachos, P. A., Tsamakos, A., Vrechopoulos, A. P. and Avramadis, P. K. (2009). 'Corporate social responsibility: Attributions, loyalty and mediating role of trust', *Journal of the Academy of Marketing Science*, 37(2): 170–180.

Vogel, V., Evanschitzky, H. and Ramaseshan, B. (2008). 'Customer equity drivers and future sales', *Journal of Marketing*, 72(1): 98–108.

Walsh, G. and Beatty, S. E. (2007). 'Customer-based corporate reputation of a service firm: Scale development and validation', *Journal of the Academy of Marketing Science*, 35(1): 127–143.

Wang, C. (2010). 'Service quality, perceived value, corporate image, and customer loyalty in the context of varying levels of switching costs', *Psychology and Marketing*, 27(3): 252–262.

Wilkins, H., Merrilees, B. and Herington, C. (2009). 'The determinants of loyalty in hotels', *Journal of Hospitality and Management*, 19(1): 1–21.

Wong, A. and Sohal, A. (2003). 'Service quality and customer loyalty perspectives on two levels of retail relationships', *Journal of Services Marketing*, 17(5): 495–513.

Yang, Z. and Peterson, R. T. (2004). 'Customer perceived value, satisfaction, and loyalty: The role of switching costs', *Psychology and Marketing*, 21(10): 799–822.

Yi, L. and La, S. (2004). 'What influences the relationship between customer satisfaction and repurchase intention? Investigating the effects of adjusted expectations and customer loyalty', *Psychology and Marketing*, 21(5): 351–374.

Yoon, E., Guffey, H. J. and Kijewski, V. (1993). 'The effects of information and company reputation on intentions to buy a business service', *Journal of Business Research*, 27(3): 215–228.

Yoon, Y. and Uysal, M. (2005). 'An examination of the effects of motivation and satisfaction on destination loyalty: A structural model', *Tourism Management*, 26(1): 45–56.

Yu, C.-M. J., Wu, L.-Y., Chiao, Y.-C. and Tai H.-S. (2005). 'Perceived quality, customer satisfaction, and customer loyalty: The case of Lexus in Taiwan', *Total Quality Management and Business Excellence*, 16(6): 707–719.

Yuksel, A., Yuksel, F. and Bilim, Y. (2010). 'Destination attachment: Effects on customer satisfaction and cognitive, affective and conative loyalty', *Tourism Management*, 31(2): 274–284.

Zeithaml, V. A. (1988). 'Consumer perceptions of price, quality and value: A means–end model and synthesis of evidence', *Journal of Marketing*, 52(7): 2–22.

Zeithaml, V. A., Parasuraman, A. and Berry, L. L. (1990). *Delivering Quality Service*, New York: The Free Press.

Zeithaml, V. A., Berry, L. L. and Parasuraman, A. (1996). 'The behavioral consequences of service quality', *Journal of Marketing*, 60(2): 31–46.

26

DEVELOPING A CONSUMER LOYALTY MODEL

Jeynakshi Ladsawut and Robin Nunkoo

Introduction

Repeat tourists are viewed as a less risky target market and are more profitable for tourism and hospitality businesses (Petrick 2004). Whilst there are different typologies of tourists such as repeaters and continuous switchers, it is important for destination marketers to attract new customers while retaining existing ones. Destination marketers usually assess the degree of loyalty to determine the effectiveness of their marketing strategies (Flavian et al. 2001). Loyalty is an important factor influencing the competitiveness of destinations. The concept of loyalty, originated in the 1920s (Copeland 1923), is defined as a 'deeply held commitment to re-buy or re-patronize a preferred product/service consistently in the future, thereby causing repetitive same brand or same brand set purchasing, despite situational influences and marketing efforts having the potential to cause switching behaviour' (Oliver 1999: p. 34). Loyalty in the tourism literature is borrowed from the consumer behaviour literature, but adapted to the specific characteristics of the tourism and hospitality industry (Baloglu 2001). It is widely accepted that tourists who are satisfied with their destination visit would revisit that destination. However, a range of factors influence tourists' loyalty towards a destination and an understanding of such antecedents is important to developing and improving marketing strategies. The purpose of this study is to identify key constructs that relate to loyalty behaviours in the tourism industry. Whilst research in the tourism literature focuses on antecedents of tourist loyalty such as satisfaction, value, motivation and service quality, there is a dearth of research on the impacts of new-fangled technologies such as social media and their impacts on the loyalty model. This chapter therefore considers a new loyalty integrated model with antecedents of tourist loyalty such as trust in social media, destination image, consumption emotion and satisfaction (see Figure 26.1).

Specifically, precursors of tourist loyalty such as the relationship between trust in social media and destination image are reviewed. Constructs such as consumption emotion and tourist satisfaction are also central to this research in an attempt to further clarify their relationships with tourist behavioural intentions.

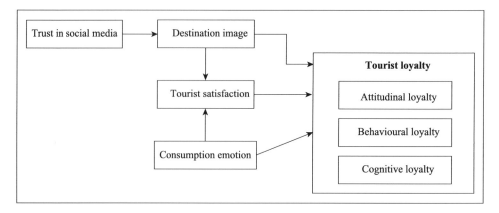

Figure 26.1 A consumer loyalty model

Source: Authors.

Tourist loyalty

Tourist loyalty can be conceptualized into behavioural loyalty, attitudinal loyalty and composite loyalty (Jacoby and Chestnut 1978). The authors view behavioural loyalty as the intention to visit while attitudinal loyalty is the intention to recommend the destination to others and composite loyalty is a combination of both behavioural and attitudinal loyalty. Behavioural loyalty illustrates the probability, frequency and volume of purchase among loyal tourists (Dick and Basu 1994). Attitudinal loyalty projects the understanding of tourist destination preferences, the rationale behind the intention to purchase and their commitment to such destinations (Yoon and Uysal 2005). Composite loyalty shows the behaviour of tourists who would regularly purchase the same destination and in parallel recommend the destination. These characteristics of loyalty are usually present in repeat visitors who tend to increase their duration of stay at a destination and spread positive word of mouth to other prospective tourists. Such behaviours are viewed as a free marketing tool amongst destination marketers. Destination marketers devote considerable attention to tourist loyalty as it is a desired target which significantly contributes to their profitability (Petrick 2004).

Tourist satisfaction

Other than repeat visits and recommendations that display loyalty behaviours, tourist satisfaction is also a precursor to tourist loyalty. Tourist satisfaction is a topic that is consistently found in the literature and is a crucial determinant in consumer behaviour (Oliver 1980). Tourist satisfaction is defined as:

> the goodness of fit between his/her expectation about the destination and the perceived evaluative outcome of the experience at the destination area, which is simply the result of a comparison between his/her previous images of the destination and what he/she actually sees, feels, and achieves at the destination.
>
> *(Chon 1989: p. 5)*

Generally, satisfaction is considered as an outcome of an experience, even though tourists do not travel to achieve satisfaction, but to gain experiences that fulfil their needs and wants (Quinlan and Carmichael 2010). Schofield (2000) posits that the performance of a destination is evaluated using tourist satisfaction as a parameter. The expectation disconfirmation model (Oliver 1980) reveals that tourists usually have expectations before and during travel and expect these to be fulfilled. The outcomes of their purchase and consumption can be either positive or negative; that is, there may be positive disconfirmation if their purchases were better than expected. The outcome of being dissatisfied usually generates churn behaviours amongst tourists whereby repeat patronage is not observed (Soscia 2007). Yoon and Uysal (2005) support that there is a positive relationship between tourist satisfaction and tourist loyalty. The more tourists are satisfied the more they are likely to recommend and revisit the destination (Sun et al. 2013). Service providers should therefore differentiate between satisfied and dissatisfied tourists as the element of satisfaction leads to the spread of positive word of mouth. It also generates more repeat intentions, hence tourist loyalty behaviours can be depicted. Westbrook (1987) establishes that when consumers are satisfied with products purchased they will display positive emotions as opposed to exhibiting negative emotions if they are dissatisfied with their consumption purchases.

Proposition 1: There is a direct positive relationship between tourist satisfaction and tourist loyalty.

Consumption emotion

Emotion is a subject that is rarely seen in the tourism literature (Buda et al. 2014) and therefore researchers need further understanding and insights. It is highlighted that affect connotes an alternative expression for emotions (Schwarz and Clore 1996) or feelings. Consumption emotions are emotions generated as a result of specific consumption experiences (Westbrook and Oliver 1991). Havlena and Halbrook (1986) and Han et al. (2009) define consumption emotions as affective emotions that are generated immediately as a consequence of consumed experiences. Since emotions differ in various contexts and are usually broad (Hosany and Gilbert 2009), scholars use the term consumption emotion. The rationale is that emotions are felt as a result of products or services consumed and the consequences can be of positive or negative nature (Richins 1997). Post-purchase of marketed offerings, customers experience customer satisfaction which is an immediate emotional response to their purchase (Han and Back 2008). Researchers demonstrate that consumption emotion is a concept closely linked to satisfaction (Liljander and Strandvik 1997). Consumption emotions occur after consumption but before satisfaction judgements are felt (Mano and Oliver 1993). Consumption emotion can be felt as a mixture of several consumption emotions simultaneously and can be studied on its own as an isolated concept or with multiple variables such as attitudes, loyalty (Ruth et al. 2002) and satisfaction. When tourists positively evaluate a destination it is likely that they will be emotionally involved and because of an overall good impression they are more prone to revisit the destination (Zhang et al. 2014). It is thus important to study the relationship between consumption emotion and tourist loyalty which will help in bridging the gap in identifying antecedents of tourist loyalty. Consumption emotions have not only been found to be an important antecedent to customer loyalty (Han and Back 2008), but they also contribute to building customer loyalty (Barsky and Nash 2002). Although the relationship between consumption emotions and loyalty is well conceived in the literature, its direction can be both positive as well as negative (Ladhari et al. 2007).

Proposition 2: There is a direct positive relationship between consumption emotion and tourist loyalty.

Proposition 3: There is a direct positive relationship between consumption emotion and tourist satisfaction.

Destination image

Although some researchers have considered the relationship between consumption emotion and satisfaction on tourist loyalty, the popularity of destination image as an antecedent to tourist loyalty is also observed in the literature. 'Destination images are simplifications of the complex beliefs, attitudes, impressions and ideas a person has about a place' (Çakmak and Isaac 2012: p. 124). The term destination image originates from Gunn (1972) who distinguishes between induced images being images that are used for marketing purposes and organic ones which are impressions that are communicated unintentionally. Thus, destination image relates to the preconceived idea of a destination that tourists develop in their mind before being physically present at the location. It is observed that travel behaviour largely depends on image and destination image plays the key role of facilitating behavioural intentions. If the destination emits a combination of positive induced and organic images, this encourages tourists to repeatedly purchase the same destination over time. Repeat patronage due to destination image thus leads to tourist loyalty.

Chon (1989) used destination image as a differentiating factor to satisfaction, whereby a goodness of fit is used between the expected destination image and the experienced image. Studies show a relationship between destination image and tourist satisfaction (Kim et al. 2011; Chi and Qu 2008). This is further supported by Bigné et al. (2001) who ascertain that tourist satisfaction is positively influenced by destination image. In view that destination image formation occurs before the actual purchase, it is essential to determine if expectations of tourists are met after purchase and if the outcome of the disconfirmation process is positive. Olson and Dover (1979) define expectations as preconceived concepts about a particular product or service. Expectation is viewed as an important precursor to customer satisfaction (Boulding et al. 1993). A positive destination image produces favoured preconceived images of the destination in the minds of tourists (Nicoletta and Servidio 2012) and hence influences tourist satisfaction which triggers repeat patronage. In line with this perspective, the information search process in the tourist decision-making process allows the creation of destination images. Tourists' online information search process is highly rewarding as service providers tend to personalize their services online to have more effective marketing campaigns (Ho et al. 2012). The dynamism of Web 2.0 is triggering an increased amount of tourism experiences through online information search. Tourists find it beneficial to use social media for travel information search as these pages are regularly updated, hence real-time information is obtained. Electronic word of mouth (eWOM) is thus generated and this connotes that marketers need to understand the drivers of online search behaviours. Since tourists are using a combination of online and offline platforms for their information search, trustworthiness of information sources becomes an important factor to consider. Marketers should therefore understand the influences of trust of social media amongst tourists.

Proposition 4: There is a direct positive relationship between destination image and tourist loyalty.

Proposition 5: There is a direct positive relationship between destination image and tourist satisfaction.

Trust in social media

Social media is seen as a representation of Web 2.0, taking in numerous forms of consumer-generated contents such as blogs, virtual communities, social networks and collaborative tagging which are gaining popularity amongst online travellers (Xiang and Gretzel 2010). Drury (2008: p. 274) describes social media as 'online resources that people use to share "content", videos, photos, images, texts, ideas, insights, humor, opinion, gossip, news and the list goes on'. The 21st century has shown an increased use of social media as an information search tool (Huang et al. 2010). Tourists are more independent of travel agencies and are searching for information online principally from social media (Jacobsen and Munar 2012). Ramkissoon and Nunkoo (2012) posit that understanding tourist search behaviours is crucial as they generate major implications for destination marketers. A primary reason for this shift in behaviour is because of its risk reduction component where feedback obtained from third parties makes the information trustworthy (Xiang and Gretzel 2010). Recognizing the importance of social media, destination marketers need to create and curate content online to trigger destination images which shape behavioural intentions inducing loyalty. Ho et al. (2012) suggest that personalizing marketing campaigns online can be beneficial to tourism marketers as their content will be customized to suit tourists' needs during the online information search process. At a destination level, marketers need to understand the antecedents of the adoption of social media by tourists for their information search (Parra-Lopez et al. 2011). Such understanding will lead to more tailor-made induced images for tourists which will positively influence destination image and hence encourage repeat purchase intentions to the destination. However, for this technique to work marketers need to determine if tourists trust content delivered through social networks.

Trust

According to Nunkoo (2012: p. 39), trust 'is defined as a psychological state or orientation of an actor (the truster) toward a specific partner (the trustee) with whom the actor is in some way interdependent to attain valued outcomes or resources'. In this study, the truster would be any tourist willing to use social media as an information search tool and the trustee would be any destination marketing organizer who is creating online content. The importance of trust is relevant here as tourists are searching for information online more, hence the need for them to trust the medium used. Tourist adoption of social media as a trustworthy tool has various implications for service providers. Morgan and Hunt (1994) view trust as a mediator between the seller and buyer that reduces uncertainty in business transactions. In the literature, it was found that there is a strong relationship between trust and intention to purchase (Lumsden and MacKay 2006). Thus, trust eases customer satisfaction and encourages patronage intentions (Pentina et al. 2013). Trust in social media amongst tourists influences positive destination image which leads to purchase intentions. There are two important factors to be considered related to destination image formation: the suppliers' side promoting an image to attract tourists to the destination; and secondly, potential tourists who perceive the image of a destination before purchase (Castro et al. 2007). It is believed that destination image leads to the choice of destination for purchase (Baloglu and McCleary 1999). In view that customers tend to share their experiences on social media platforms, eWOM is continuously generated. This reinforces trust in social media which continuously updates customers on their destination preferences. Authors view trust as an important element which is linked to expectancy (Chen 2014). The latter reveals that if customers have a high level of trust towards a brand, therefore the expectancy will be positive, hence, evaluation of the brand will be positive. This can also be mirrored in the tourism industry. If tourists have high trusting beliefs in social media, there will be a high probability that they will process the positive information and have positive expectancy of the destination image. Hence their evaluations of the destination will be positive.

Proposition 6: There is a direct positive relationship between trust in social media and tourist loyalty through destination image.

Conclusion

In view that tourist loyalty is a key determinant of a destination's competitiveness, service providers need to continuously monitor tourist loyalty. Overall, this chapter depicts new constructs that revamp a new loyalty integrated model. Since loyalty is beneficial to both tourists and service providers, monitoring its evolution is important. A common precursor to loyalty that is widely studied in the literature is tourist satisfaction. If tourists are satisfied with a destination, they are more willing to revisit over time, which demonstrates their loyalty behaviour. Therefore, destination marketers must use the relevant strategies to encourage tourists to revisit their destinations and avoid switching behaviours. The interrelationship between tourist satisfaction and consumption emotion is highlighted in this study where tourists' emotional involvement drives their satisfaction with a destination. As a result of satisfaction, consumption emotion also leads to tourist loyalty. Additionally, this study also links tourist loyalty to destination image. If destination marketers project a positive destination image it is more likely that tourists will be satisfied with the destination. Positive destination image will also encourage repeat patronage which drives tourist loyalty. It is important to highlight that marketers can influence positive destination image through the use of social media. Given that social media are commonly used amongst tourists for information search purposes, information provided by marketers may be appealing and encourage tourists to revisit a destination instead of looking for new destinations. Therefore trust in social media is crucial for service providers to observe. Presumably, the more tourists trust social media, the more positive destination images will be formed. This triggers positive consumption emotions amongst tourists and leads to tourist satisfaction. Moreover, as tourists are satisfied they tend to be more loyal to such destinations.

Mauritius is an island destination which relies on tourism acting as a catalyst for its economy. Its tourism industry is currently faced with fierce competition. Situated in the Indian Ocean, Mauritius faces direct competition from other island destinations such as the Seychelles, Comoros and Maldives. Tourism started in the 1950s with 1,803 tourists in 1954; the island was then in a pristine state. In 1973, the total international tourist arrival amounted to 67,994 while in 2014, the average number of tourists visiting the island was 86,581 just per month. Data collected in 2014 (Statistics Mauritius 2014) showed that tourists flying to Mauritius in 2014 originated from Europe (54%), Africa (26%), Asia (15%), Australia (1.7%) and America (1.6%). The tourism sector contributed US$1 billion to the Mauritian earnings in 2014. Tourists stayed on average 11 days in 2014 and the average expenditure per tourist amounted to MUR 42,642 rupees (US$1,212). Ivanov and Webster (2013) support that the competitiveness of a destination is judged by drivers such as globalization. The Travel and Tourism Competitiveness Index 2015 filed an index of 141

---

economies across the world. The top ranked was Spain with a value of 5.31 and the last one was Chad with a value of 2.43. Mauritius was globally ranked 56th with a value of 3.90 and ranked third in Eastern and Southern Africa with enabling environment pillars and values such as good business environment, safety and security, health and hygiene, human resources and labour market and ICT readiness. Since tourism is an asset to Mauritius, it is in the interest of the island to encourage tourist loyalty. The main challenge would be to create a lasting destination image for tourists that is appealing and will motivate the latter to revisit Mauritius rather than choosing another tourist destination. Marketers should capitalize on tourists' shift of consumer behaviour where information search is mostly done online as opposed to offline. This shift in the use of information search tools such as social media shows that destination marketing organizations should concentrate their promotional efforts online. Although Mauritius is highly visible on social media, search engine optimization (SEO) is encouraged. Doing so provides updated information to tourists who have Mauritius in their evoked set. If destination marketers in Mauritius use social media as a marketing tool, they would be able to increase the level of trust in social media amongst tourists. This would increase the level of tourists' online engagement towards the destination. In parallel the interest towards Mauritius will grow. Hence, Mauritius will be more present in the evoked set of tourists. As such, tourists' online engagement with Mauritius will be favoured as this continuously revives the positive consumption emotions accumulated from their previous visits such as satisfaction towards the destination. Therefore, encouraging future behaviours through online engagement allows tourists to curate content about Mauritius online and recommend the destination to other prospective tourists. Rethinking tourist loyalty through the Internet could become a core component of Mauritian destination marketing organizations and could gain competitive advantage over other destinations. The destination marketers should therefore have a framework to track the loyalty level in relation to the destination and find ways to encourage tourist patronage to Mauritius.

References

Baloglu, S. (2001). 'Image variations of Turkey by familiarity index: Informational and experiential dimensions', *Tourism Management*, 22(2): 127–134.

Baloglu, S. and McCleary, K. (1999). 'A model of destination image formation', *Annals of Tourism Research*, 26(4): 868–897.

Barsky, J. D. and Nash, L. (2002). 'Evoking emotion: Affective keys to hotel loyalty', *Cornell Hotel and Restaurant Administration Quarterly*, 43(1): 39–46.

Bigné, J. E., Sánchez, M. I. and Sánchez, J. (2001). 'Tourism image, evaluation variables and after purchase behaviour: Inter-relationship', *Tourism Management*, 22(6): 607–616.

Boulding, W., Kalra, A., Staelin, R. and Zeithaml, V. A. (1993). 'A dynamic process model of service quality: From expectations to behavioural intentions', *Journal of Marketing Research*, 30(1): 7–27.

Buda, D. M., d'Hauteserre, A.-M. and Johnston, L. (2014). 'Feeling and tourism studies', *Annals of Tourism Research*, 46: 102–114.

Çakmak, E. and Isaac, R. K. (2012). 'What destination marketers can learn from their visitors' blogs: An image analysis of Bethlehem, Palestine', *Journal of Destination Marketing and Management*, 1(1–2): 124–133.

Castro, C. B., Armario, E. M. and Ruiz, D. M. (2007). 'The influence of market heterogeneity on the relationship between a destination's image and tourists' future behaviour', *Tourism Management*, 28(1): 175–187.

Chen, Y. (2014). 'The drivers of green brand equity: Green brand image, green satisfaction, and green trust', *Journal of Business Ethics*, 93(2): 307–319.

Chi, C. G. and Qu, H. (2008). 'Examining the structural relationships of destination image, tourist satisfaction and destination loyalty: An integrated approach', *Tourism Management*, 29(4): 624–636.

Chon, K. (1989). 'Understanding recreational travelers' motivation, attitude and satisfaction', *The Tourist Review*, 44(1): 3–7.

Copeland, M. T. (1923). 'Relation of consumers' buying habits to marketing methods', *Harvard Business Review*, 1(3): 282–289.

Dick, A. S. and Basu, K. (1994). 'Customer loyalty: Toward an integrated conceptual framework', *Journal of the Academy of Marketing Science*, 22(2): 99–113.

Drury, G. (2008). 'Opinion piece: Social media: Should marketers engage and how can it be done effectively?', *Journal of Direct Data and Digital Marketing Practice*, 9(3): 274–277.

Flavian, C., Martinez, E. and Polo, Y. (2001). 'Loyalty to grocery stores in the Spanish market of the 1990s', *Journal of Retailing and Consumer Services*, 8(2): 85–93.

Gunn, C. (1972). *Vacationscape: Designing Tourist Regions*, Austin: Bureau of Business Research, University of Texas.

Han, H. and Back, K. (2008). 'Assessing customers' emotional experiences influencing their satisfaction in the lodging industry', *Journal of Travel and Tourism Marketing*, 23(1): 43–56.

Han, H., Back, K. and Barrett, B. (2009). 'Influencing factors on restaurant customers' revisit intention: The roles of emotions and switching barriers', *International Journal of Hospitality Management*, 28(4): 563–572.

Havlena, W. J. and Holbrook, M. B. (1986). 'The varieties of consumption experience: Comparing two typologies of emotion in consumer behaviour', *Journal of Consumer Research*, 13(3): 394–404.

Ho, C.-I., Lin, M.-H. and Chen, H.-M. (2012). 'Web users' behavioural patterns of tourism information search: From online to offline', *Tourism Management*, 33(6): 1468–1482.

Hosany, S. and Gilbert, D. (2009). 'Measuring tourists' emotional experiences toward hedonic holiday destinations', *Journal of Travel Research*, 49(4): 513–526.

Huang, C., Chou, C. and Lin, P. (2010). 'Involvement theory in constructing bloggers' intention to purchase travel products', *Tourism Management*, 31(4): 513–526.

Ivanov, S. and Webster, C. (2013). 'Globalisation as a driver of destination competitiveness', *Annals of Tourism Research*, 43: 628–633.

Jacobsen, J. K. S. and Munar, A. M. (2012). 'Tourist information search and destination choice in a digital age', *Tourism Management Perspectives*, 1: 39–47.

Jacoby, J. and Chestnut, R. W. (1978). *Brand Loyalty: Measurement and Management*, New York: John Wiley and Sons.

Kim, S.-H., Holland, S. and Han, H.-S. (2011). 'A structural model for examining how destination image, perceived value, and service quality affect destination loyalty: A case study of Orlando', *International Journal of Tourism Research*, 15(4): 313–328.

Ladhari, R., Brun, I. and Morales, M. (2007). 'Determinants of dining satisfaction and post-dining behavioural intentions', *International Journal of Hospitality Management*, 27(4): 563–573.

Liljander, V. and Strandvik, T. (1997). 'Emotions in service satisfaction', *International Journal of Service Industry Management*, 8(2): 148–169.

Lumsden, J. and MacKay, L. (2006). 'How does personality affect trust in B2C e-commerce?', in *Proceedings of 8th International Conference on Electronic Commerce* (pp. 471–481), 14–16 August, Fredericton, NB, Canada.

Mano, H. and Oliver, R. L. (1993). 'Assessing the dimensionality and structure of the consumption experience: Evaluation, feeling, and satisfaction', *Journal of Consumer Research*, 20(3): 451–466.

Morgan, R. M. and Hunt, S. D. (1994). 'The commitment-trust theory of relationship marketing', *Journal of Marketing*, 58(3): 20–38.

Nicoletta, R. and Servidio, R. (2012). 'Tourists' opinions and their selection of tourism destination images: An affective and motivational evaluation', *Tourism Management Perspectives*, 4: 19–27.

Nunkoo, R. (2012). 'Political Economy of Tourism: Residents' Power, Trust in Government, and Political Support for Development', PhD thesis, University of Waterloo, Ontario, Canada.

Oliver, R. L. (1980). 'A cognitive model of the antecedents and consequences of satisfaction decisions', *Journal of Marketing Research*, 17(4): 460–469.

Oliver, R. L. (1999). 'Whence customer loyalty?', *Journal of Marketing*, 63: 33–44.

Olson, J. C. and Dover, P. (1979). 'Disconfirmation of consumer expectations through product trial', *Journal of Applied Psychology*, 64(4): 179–189.

Parra-López, E., Bulchand-Gidumal, J., Gutiérrez-Taño, D. and Díaz-Armas, R. (2011). 'Intentions to use social media in organizing and taking vacation trips', *Computers in Human Behavior*, 27(2): 640–654.

Pentina, I., Zhang, L. and Basmanova, O. (2013). 'Antecedents and consequences of trust in a social media brand: A cross-cultural study of Twitter', *Computers in Human Behaviour*, 29(4): 1546–1555.

Petrick, J. F. (2004). 'Are loyal visitors desired visitors?', *Tourism Management*, 25(4): 463–470.

Quinlan, C. S. and Carmichael, B. A. (2010). 'The dimensions of the tourist experience', in Morgan, M., Logosi, P. and Ritchie, B. J. R. (eds.), *The Tourism and Leisure Experience: Consumer and Managerial Perspectives* (pp. 3–26), Bristol: Channel View Publications.

Ramkissoon, H. and Nunkoo, R. (2012). 'More than just biological sex differences: Examining the structural relationship between gender identity and information search behaviour', *Journal of Hospitality and Tourism Research*, 36(2): 191–215.

Richins, M. L. (1997). 'Measuring emotions in the consumption experience', *Journal of Consumer Research*, 24(2): 127–146.

Ruth, J. A., Brunel, F. F. and Otnes, C. C. (2002). 'Linking thoughts to feelings: Investigating cognitive appraisals and consumption emotions in a mixed-emotions context', *Journal of the Academy of Marketing Science*, 30(1): 44–58.

Schofield, P. (2000). 'Evaluating Castlefield urban heritage park from the consumer perspective: Destination attribute importance, visitor perception, and satisfaction', *Tourism Analysis*, 5(2/4): 183–189.

Schwarz, N. and Clore, G. L. (1996). 'Feelings and phenomenal experience', in Higgins, E. T. and Kruglanski, A. W. (eds.), *Social Psychology: Handbook of Basic Principles* (pp. 433–465), New York: Guilford Press.

Soscia, I. (2007). 'Gratitude, delight, or guilt: The role of consumers' emotions in predicting postconsumption behaviours', *Psychology and Marketing*, 24(10): 871–894.

Statistics Mauritius (2014). 'Tourist arrivals by country of residence. January–December (2013–2014), monthly tourist arrival', Statistics Mauritius.

Sun, X., Chi, C. G.-Q. and Xu, H. (2013). 'Developing destination loyalty: The case of Hainan Island', *Annals of Tourism Research*, 43: 547–577.

Westbrook, R. A. (1987). 'Product/consumption-based affective responses and postpurchase processes', *Journal of Marketing Research*, 24(3): 258–270.

Westbrook, R. A. and Oliver, R. L. (1991). 'The dimensionality of consumption emotion patterns and consumer satisfaction', *Journal of Consumer Research*, 18(1): 84–91.

Xiang, Z. and Gretzel, U. (2010). 'Role of social media in online travel information search', *Tourism Management*, 31(2): 179–188.

Yoon, Y. and Uysal, M. (2005). 'An examination of the effects of motivation and satisfaction on destination loyalty: A structural model', *Tourism Management*, 26(1): 45–56.

Zhang, H., Fu, X., Cai, A. and Lin, L. (2014). 'Destination image and tourist loyalty: A meta-analysis', *Tourism Management*, 40: 213–223.

27

CUSTOMER ENGAGEMENT IN BUILDING CONSUMER LOYALTY

Keith H. Mandabach

Introduction

The focus of this chapter is on the marketing concept of building customer engagement (CE) by utilizing relationship marketing to build loyalty, CE and customer loyalty. These methods are used by hospitality and tourism businesses to integrate customers' participation into the process of building loyalty, and cognitive, social, emotional and behavioural approaches to the process are examined. The chapter discusses the multiple levels of customer experience as well as the impact of digital and social media on customer perceptions in today's market. Engagement strategies used by the organization, employees, management and customers are explained to understand the engagement process. Three specific case studies for the application of these strategies are provided.

Marketing concept of CE

Building customer loyalty through CE and interaction is a theoretical construct that is part of the research agenda for tourism/hospitality issues. CE is the engagement of customers with one another, with a company or a brand. The initiative for engagement can come from either the consumer or company (Anderson 2006). The concept of CE is an extension of relationship marketing. Relationship marketing is the approach most hotel, restaurant and tourism businesses have historically used for a major focus for their marketing strategies. At the centre of the relationship marketing perspective is the idea that customers have continuing value over the period they frequent a specific business or company (Berry 1983). Instead of concentrating on a single sale, one is thinking of getting the customer to return or possibly interest others in frequenting the business. The focus is, therefore, on the relationships created rather than transactions (Shiri et al. 2012).

Relationship marketing relies on the concept that customers who are really engaged and connected with a tourism destination, hotel or restaurant through their engagement demonstrate a positive attitude that draws in new customers. This is not just relying on customers recommending the business to their friends, but using the impact of their experience to do the talking. When the marketing researchers first defined CE in 2005, it was defined as turning on a prospect to a brand idea enhanced by the surrounding context of the business (ARC 2006).

The industry has always employed simple approaches to building customer loyalty and engaging customers. A lodging property, restaurant or any other tourist business must be well maintained, and have the proper ambience that patrons expect. The first visual impression is crucial, but the first human interaction is also just as important. This is the moment of truth for the customer. A business's associates must be knowledgeable while approachable to be able to create emotional and social connections with the guests. They also must interact on multiple levels with, and utilize effectively, the property's technology system(s) and device(s) used by the tourism business and the customers.

This is taken to include simple human touches, for instance addressing the patron by name, a smile and appropriate eye contact with good voice tone might provide a warm welcome for the patron. In today's market this process might include an introductory text, a social media post or electronic information that will make the guest experience streamlined and connected. Most importantly we must listen to the patron (in real time and in virtual time), meet the patron's need and deliver on their requests. Ensuring you have met the needs of your guests is essential to customer satisfaction and consequently better CE. It is also important to set standards and goals for employees on CE so that performance might be measured. The engagement process is truly effective if there is a system to estimate the degree and depth of visitor interaction against a clearly defined set of goals (Hollebeek 2011).

CE is a psychological state that occurs by virtue of interactive, co-creative customer experiences with a particular agent/object/brand or business. This occurs under a specific set of context-dependent conditions generating differing CE levels and exists as a dynamic, multidimensional repetitive process that co-creates value. It is subject to stakeholder-specific expression of relevant cognitive, emotional and/or behavioural dimensions that one hopes results in profound attitude responses and patron satisfaction (Brodie et al. 2011).

This has been studied in the tourism industry, most notably in the hotel industry (Barsky 1992; Oh and Parks 1997; Pizam and Ellis 1999; Skogland and Siguaw 2004). Customer satisfaction coupled with the service experience appears to create customer loyalty (Denove and Power 2007). This is a form of cognitive learned behaviour (CBL). The CBL model also recognizes external structural causes of behaviour. The external or situational structures primarily provide the consumer with information which can be broken into discriminative stimulus cues and reinforcing stimulus cues.

Customer loyalty is the continued and regular patronage of a business in the face of alternative economic activities and competitive attempts to disrupt the relationship. Building customer loyalty through CE and interaction is a theoretical construct that is part of the research agenda for tourism/hospitality issues (Toporek 2011). Loyal customers are probably likely to repeat their purchases of a hotel's products (Bowen and Shoemaker 1998; Mattila 2006) and are more likely to recommend the hotel (Getty and Thompson 1995). Loyalty has traditionally been described as having two dimensions: behavioural and emotional (Dick and Basu 1994; Kandampully and Suhartanto 2000; Oliver 1997, 1999). Behavioural loyalty is often measured through repeat purchases (Bowen and Chen 2001; Bowen and Shoemaker 1998; Getty and Thompson 1995). Emotional loyalty is measured through a customer's intention to recommend or repeat a purchase (Hayes 2008). Loyalty research in marketing once focused on purchase behaviour but is now more focused on attitudinal behaviour (Baloglu 2002; Dube and Renaghan 1999). Loyalty, both behavioural and emotional, is a method to evaluate the success of a CE process in a tourism business.

When one evaluates success in developing loyalty through CE it is important to measure the level of a customer's cognitive, emotional and behavioural investment in specific brand interactions. One might want to examine three CE dimensions which are immersion (cognitive), passion (emotional) and activation (behavioural). To do this effectively one must be aware of the multiple levels of the customer experience and link the engagement process to this experience while focusing on key performance indicators which first effect cognitive engagement, then lead your customers to passion for your business and activate their loyalty (Brodie et al. 2011). Everyone develops an opinion of a business and the reviews that are the result of their experience most often are related to performance issues. In the hospitality and tourism business we hope they are positive. But sometimes they are not.

Alex and Mary own an 18-room hotel/restaurant in a small coastal city in Mexico. Alex enjoyed a very successful career as an Executive Chef in luxury hotels around the world and he fell in love with Mary when he worked as an Executive Chef in Cancun. He opened a restaurant of his own but it was destroyed by a hurricane five years ago and after the insurance issues were finally resolved, they searched for and found this pleasant little hotel to operate. During renovation they resolved to stay in every room in the hotel and also developed menus for the restaurant. They also hired the couple who had served as maid and maintenance man for the previous owner. Alex also was able to convince a former cook to join him in the new venture. The plan was to open slowly, a few rooms at a time and for the couple, Mary and Alex, to work together to provide impeccable service. Mary developed a fantastic web page and social media site for the venture and they opened to rave reviews. But they also had spent more money on renovation than expected and thus quickly needed to fill all the rooms and open the restaurant to the public. They hired additional wait associates, cooks, maids and dishwashers. They attempted to train the new associates quickly to provide quality service. Mary really tried to instil the idea that all employees needed to provide gracious service, as well as provide a detailed operations manual that addressed what she thought was every contingency. Alex was busy all the time cooking for all of the customers who adored his gourmet food.

This worked well for the first month. On the fourth Sunday after opening two customers with reservations did not arrive as scheduled. Mary was furious because these customers had booked the best room for two weeks and guaranteed it with a credit card. On Monday, Mary charged the customers for the first two days of the seven days of their reservation on the credit card as per the stated policy and opened the rooms to the public for rental on TripAdvisor and Expedia. Before noon the rooms were rented and Mary and Alex took the night off, leaving the couple that had worked for the previous owner in charge. When they returned they discovered the missing guests had arrived and been turned away because they had rented out the rooms. Their flight had been delayed from Australia. The couple told them the people were very angry and the couple had called the police to get the irate Australians out of the hotel. Mary discovered that they had taken pictures and videos of the experience and posted on Facebook as well as posted reviews on TripAdvisor, Expedia and Yelp. Immediately cancellations came in and the hotel that had been totally booked had no reservations.

1   What steps might have been taken to prevent this problem?
2   How might Mary and Alex change the current public perception of their hotel?
3   If you were Mary and Alex, what would you say to the couple you left in charge?

Understanding multiple levels of customer experience

Prior to a customer visiting a restaurant, hotel or tourist business a customer first becomes aware of the business and forms an impression. One needs to remember that people have preconceptions as a result of their previous experience with different types of tourism businesses. Prior to the Internet, sources of the initial impression were the business itself and its signage, advertising, newspaper articles or reviews or word of mouth from a friend or associate. Today it is most often an online interaction but the opinions of others are still one of the most important factors. Of course it is important that the initial impression tells the truth about one's business. Sometimes online content does not match the actual business. Many of us have seen 'mouth-watering' pictures of a menu entrée and been disappointed when it was delivered. The same happens with hotel rooms where the ocean view is only available if one stands on a chair in the washroom. While one might manage to get people to your establishment this way, it is more important to have an honest website with products one can deliver. Because false premises cause more harm than good.

The initial experience is where a business may demonstrate that the actual experience will surpass the customer's prior perceptions. Most consumers are a touch apprehensive about their first experience with a tourism business. It is important that the exterior of the premises be in top form and that the interior have the appropriate ambience. The initial greeting should be warm and clear. It also provides the associate with the opportunity to learn about the customer (have you dined with us before?) as well as providing the new guest with a choice of some sort. Customers relish being in control and it is important to engage the guests in the initial contact. When speaking the associate should understand the proper volume, pitch, tone and pace of speech and use short sentences so that the customers will be able to understand what is said. It is also very important to focus on the customer and listen for a response or a question. It is a good idea to make eye contact (if appropriate for the culture), stand with proper posture and avoid intruding on customer body space while making welcoming gestures and careful body movements.

The actual experience is where the engagement by the organization, the associates (employees) and management and connection to the business happen as the quality product the customer desires is delivered. Customers want to have a great experience but there are a large number of factors that impact on their impressions and most of them can be answered if one asks the right questions. Is the temperature of the room comfortable? Is the lighting easy on the eyes but bright enough to read a menu? Are the associates dressed in clean clothes and is the restaurant free of offensive odours? Is the music pleasant and at the right volume? If a restaurant, are the establishment, the menu, the china, the flatware, the glassware, linen, windows and parking clean? Does the customer get prompt service and do they get the quality they expect? There are many more questions because in the tourism business one is always trying to meet the high standards all customers expect. People do not visit our businesses to have an OK tour, meal or hotel experience, they want it to be great/fantastic/wonderful/awesome! The intangible which is service is what makes our business wonderful and by connecting to the customer one must demand or at least encourage the customer to please visit us again! It is very important that your tourism business document any positive/negative quality or service issues as they occur so that a record of what happened is available. If one has a record it is much easier to engage the customer when issues come up.

The digital experience is when our customers use their phones (although sometimes they use cameras) to document their experience. While the selfie might be a requisite photo for many of our customers, one of the most successful ways to improve the experience is to encourage everyone working in the operation to help customers as they document their experience in your business. Engaging the customer and asking about the actual experience often makes the actual experience better for the customers and should also be an integral part of customer service in every operation. Many operations maintain a digital record of what occurs in the business through the use of cameras in appropriate places, which can be helpful when responding to customer interactions. Others simply keep a written diary that may be supplemented with digital photos/videos.

The social media experience occurs when the customer posts their experience on a social media site. Most people want to have had an excellent experience and vigilant monitoring of the social media is a requisite for CE. This chapter is not focused on social media but utilizing and encouraging the use of social media is imperative to build loyalty and use your customers to build your business. Some businesses encourage customers to 'like' their business. Others reward customers for positive reviews but the key is to make it easy for customers to mention your business by having your own actively monitored site on multiple platforms. So, when they type in their location your business address is listed, or when they mention the business it automatically links the customer to the business. The other key is to work to prevent negative posts because if you are engaging the customer effectively you may be able to react to the issue and turn the situation around. Engagement means anticipating issues. If a comment surfaces on social media, it is important to mount a timely and effective response whether the comment is positive or negative.

The post experience has two facets: one based on customer reflection or review of the experience and the other is the business's approach to make that review as positive as it can be. Hopefully by the end of the actual experience the customer is engaged with our business and there are simple ways to reach out to the customer. Usually reviews and comments from customers are either about the performance or attitudinal behaviour. I know a restaurant owner who calls his customers and another who friends his customers on Facebook with a message the day after they dine. There are numerous digital approaches to determine customer identity and contact information utilizing credit card transactions, phone numbers, email and social media. If the customers are already engaged, if the experience was not up to par, they often let the business know about whatever the problem was. A nice touch to CE at this level is tracking performance and creating meaningful dialogue with the customers. The savvy operator is aware of what has happened in the tourism business and is prepared for the dialogue.

Susmita Patel is the front office manager of the 105-room Western Hotel in Los Angeles in the USA and a recent graduate of State University's well-respected hotel management training pro-gramme. She is very happy in her position and believes she received excellent training from the general manager when she started at the hotel. The owners have managed to acquire seven properties of about the same size by purchasing ageing properties and renovating the entire properties until they are first-rate three-star hotels. The top priority of the owners is to maintain the hotels in top shape.

Ms Patel is very pleased that her front office is so efficient and well run. She spends most of her time interacting with the guests. But she also makes a point of walking around the hotel and inspecting rooms with the Executive Housekeeper. She also asked her General Manager if she might set up sites on Facebook, Yahoo, Yelp and TripAdvisor. She is surprised to see a post on the Yahoo site one day where a guest claimed the hotel has bedbugs. She does not recall any complaints about bedbugs. A call to housekeeping confirms the same. The hotel General Manager is also unaware but orders a top-rated exterminator to examine the hotel the following day. As Ms Patel checks the other social media sites, she sees a number of posts that claim that her hotel is infested with bedbugs. The next day she tours the property with the exterminator who reports signs of bedbugs in two rooms. Her General Manager is furious with her for suggesting the social media experiment.

1   What should Susmita do?
2   What do you think happened?
3   How could this situation have been prevented?

Understanding the engagement process

The CE process works best when rooted in the organizational culture of a tourism business and one must take care not to compartmentalize the process. Whatever your business consists of, it is important that your management and associates are educated about the business. It is best to first analyse the business, communicate to everyone what your business is and what makes it unique, and ensure that everyone in the operation knows their role in the business. It is important that the associates and management also know and understand why your customers value your service/product and believe in your business. Basically it is important to know and understand what the customers believe makes the operation special. An example is the Ritz-Carlton, the luxury hotel brand owned by Marriott which in corporate communications describes what makes the company special as the 'Ritz-Carlton Mystique' and it is this kind of understanding of the intangible that makes a hospitality business great. After one understands what the special product is that your business delivers, the business must endeavour to continue providing excellence in every product or service offered. Management must be confident and provide the associates with the tools needed to deliver excellence in every way and believe in their teams' capabilities to consistently deliver (Robison 2008).

Communicate results and use associates to their full potential

In the hospitality business we measure quality in terms of financial results, customer counts, customer surveys, check averages, average daily rates, occupancy and a myriad other statistics, all of which are often compared with competition and industry norms. The more management shares this information with associates, the easier it usually is to communicate the importance of quality and engage the employees in the CE process. It demonstrates owners and managers are encouraging open two-way communication. Associates have knowledge of their jobs and customers and might be able to suggest strategies to improve the operation. Thus now that associates are engaged, it will be easier to engage them with the customers and build customer loyalty. Empowered associates are able to interact decisively with customers and build trust (Peoplemetrics 2010). Customers are usually already in the pre-contact experience because they have searched and learned about your business already and their perceptions of the actual experience can be impacted dramatically by your employees being knowledgeable and welcoming.

Thus when customers meet the associates and the business for the first time, engagement will occur. It takes a certain agility to discover the needs of each customer and communicate the intangibles they are seeking. Often these are subtle signals of their needs and provide the opening for success. The hospitality industry has a history of remembering patrons' favourites, be they drinks, pillows, slippers, teas or chocolate. Engagement is personalizing the experience and allowing the customer a feeling that they are a valued part of your business. Educate the associates to cue these special needs and engagement is an easier process. The business also must have a method of tracking the customers and their characteristics. This can be done manually or digitally. Customers today expect to connect and the most common connections are via Facebook, Instagram or Twitter. They also expect dialogue from a business they are engaged in.

Building dialogue

Dialogue means communication. A tourism business operator should understand customer needs and find a way to regularly communicate with them. This is more effective if customers believe you are personally accessible and they feel connected. Sometimes this is easier to accomplish if you focus your efforts on what the key competencies of your business are and if, when messaging, you focus on performance not behaviour. Communications from customers usually focus on either performance or behaviour. Performance issues usually relate to what the customer actually experienced and it is best to first respond to these comments because they can be addressed. Behaviour comments are usually but not always judgemental, for example 'the food is not seasoned enough' or 'the servers should not have tattoos'. It is very difficult to address these comments because others may feel differently. There will be times when it may be unclear why the customers are upset or what they are upset about.

One trains staff to discuss and to message target audiences with a focused approach that communicates your business's key competencies. Smaller businesses have an advantage because they may be able to respond more rapidly than larger businesses and should focus on personalizing their interactions with customers as much as possible to build customer loyalty. Whatever kind of business, utilize your customers to build a dialogue that makes your business positive. Instead of having to respond to customer posts, one might focus on building the level of positive posts from your loyal customers and build business that way. By tracking the customers in a variety of ways, you and your employees build accessibility to the business and improve the dialogue which improves customer loyalty. Knowing your customers is essential to your success and tracking who they are is important.

Customer tracking may include the use of a credit card charge analysis system, Wi-Fi passwords that require an email address to access or the use of a reservation management system that captures and tracks customers using various identifying methodologies. Security is very important and it may be illegal in your country or province to keep credit card numbers and identifying information in the same place. Because of the nature of social media and digital customer tracking, a tourism business might seek help with its homepage or with the customer tracking or listening part of CE. An example of an outside firm that can provide help with engagement is Constant Contact (© 2016), located in the USA. The company started as an email marketing service and has followed the digital trends so that it now provides coaching and services including event management, social media marketing and survey tools that provide interactive support. They offer a sample service for free and do not be surprised if within minutes of signing up you receive a follow-up phone call from a coach ready to help you learn more about building customer loyalty through engagement. Another firm that assists is the National Business Research Institute (NBRI 2016), also located in the USA. For your specific business and location in the world there are numerous companies offering this service and it would be wise to investigate through an online search. There are undoubtedly firms in your area that specialize in these services and a Web search is the easiest way to discover a local firm to help your business build loyalty through engagement.

Miranda Lapides grew up in the catering/restaurant business in a city of 75,000 in the southwest USA. Her family owned and operated an out-of-the-way mildly successful BBQ restaurant, smokehouse, special event and catering event business. By the time she started university (graduating with honours from the College of Business with a speciality in marketing), this business was the largest catering company in the area and Miranda had met almost every customer that the business had served. This was the personal way to do business. Miranda was encouraged by her associates, customers and friends to expand the restaurant business and she borrowed money to remodel the restaurant. When the remodel was complete she was disappointed with the restaurant business volume but the catering business grew exponentially. She found an excellent manager with great customer relations skills for the restaurant and focused on the catering operation. When she completed her master's degree with a focus on finance, she felt confident that she was ready to become a restaurant mogul.

By 2000, she and her manager had developed a spreadsheet list of customers that included phones, emails and addresses. There were a few other caterers in the area but Miranda was doing almost 80% of the catering business with an annual volume of slightly less than $2 million. One of her clients, who was a prominent banker, told her about a project he was involved in to remodel a tired southwestern café near the local college campus and transform it into a vibrant sports bar. The banker client called a few months later and asked Miranda if she was interested in taking over the project to open the sports bar. Her focus was to provide interesting, simple, high-quality food coupled with a wide variety of craft brews. Twenty flat-screen TVs combined with a state-of-the-art music system provided entertainment. She designed daily events to promote the operation, an extensive patio where she had live music on weekends and had over 120 seats total in the restaurant area. The associates wore sport referees' shirts and shorts. Miranda encouraged the associates to customize the shirts and shorts. Management associates included Miranda, a general manager and two assistant managers. Miranda stressed management by walking around and also installed a video surveillance system. The renovations and training were expensive but Miranda was able to borrow over half a million dollars (which she used for capital expenses) because of her successful catering business cash flow.

Prior to opening she offered every client on her customer list the opportunity to attend a grand opening event that would raise money for breast cancer research. She then announced that all attendees who signed up for her client list would receive a 10% discount on purchases. The grand opening raised $20,000 for charity and business was very good after that. Miranda trained her associates effectively and made certain that everyone had a big smile on their faces all the time. She also established interesting rules for all employees:

- All employees must have their name prominently displayed in at least two places on their uniforms. Every employee's customization of their uniforms is rated weekly and a prize given for the best effort.

- Each employee is encouraged to create their own script for customer interaction which must include a method to learn the customer's name, what they usually drink or eat, what they liked or disliked about their experience, and one other unique fact about the customer.
- All employees were asked to encourage customers to take photos of food, drink and more.
- Hosts were asked to find out customers' first and last names and check in the Point of Sale system whether the customer was on the master client/customer list.

Managers were required to spend their time in the restaurant and bar supporting the associates and interacting with the guests. Every guest, every day would be asked by a manager (or the owner) how their experience was and if they had any suggestions for improvement. Managers and employees were given full authority to remedy any issues in the quality of the food or experience. Even though the business grew, Miranda stressed to everyone that everyone needed to have a personal approach to every customer. She said that her biggest challenge was keeping it fresh and engaging her customers because if you engage the customers, they will help you build your business.

1   What do you think is the biggest weakness in Miranda's business strategy?
2   What suggestions would you have to improve the business?
3   Do you think it is possible for Miranda to 'keep it fresh' for a long period of time?
4   So how do you build that kind of customer loyalty?

Summary

CE in building consumer loyalty requires a holistic marketing perspective. Cognitive, social, emotional and behavioural approaches all must be part of the process. By involving the customers in the business one hopes to build loyalty and grow the business. CE is an interactive, co-creative experience and occurs under a specific set of context-dependent conditions that generate different CE levels that create value for the customer in some form or other. This produces cognitive, emotional and/or behavioural dimensions that one hopes result in positive attitude responses and patron satisfaction.

The hospitality industry has a long history of developing customer loyalty through engagement because the industry focuses on developing a dialogue with the customers, finding out their needs and delivering a product that satisfies. Businesses should develop a method of measuring and evaluating the success of their engagement level that focuses on the multiple levels of customer experience: prior, initial, actual, the digital experience, the social experience and the post experience. The CE process works best when rooted in the organizational culture and should not be compartmentalized. Share the business results with your associates to help empower them in their communication with the customers. This means developing a dialogue and an understanding of what your business's key strengths are.

It is important for your associates to know why the customers like your business. Have your associates identify the 'mystique' your business uses to please the customers and build on your strengths. Utilize customer dialogue to respond to performance and behaviour comments. Focus on performance issues related to customer experiences and try to understand what judgemental issues customers are commenting on. Keep the dialogue going and know your customers. Let your customers communicate what they love about your business. To do this you need to track your customers and build a synergistic model that makes your customers as much a part of the business as any employee.

1   What is the difference between social and cognitive involvement in the business?
2   What is relationship marketing?
3   What is a difference between the prior experience and the initial experience?
4   Describe the post experience and how a business might impact it?
5   What three strategies might a small business find particularly successful to improve customer loyalty through CE?
6   What is customer tracking and what strategies could your business use to effectively track customers?

References

Advertising Research Council (ARC) (2006). 'Advertising industry turned on by new measurement model', Available from https://web.archive.org/web/20070401045631/http://www.thearf.org/about/pr/2006-03-21.html [Accessed: 4 September 2015].

Anderson, C. (2006). *The Long Tail: Why the Future of Business Is Selling Less of More*, New York, NY: Hyperion.

Baloglu, S. (2002). 'Dimensions of customer loyalty: Separating friends from well wishers', *Cornell Hotel and Restaurant Administration Quarterly*, 43(1): 47–59.

Barsky, J. (1992). 'Customer satisfaction in the hotel industry: Meaning and measurement', *Journal of Hospitality and Tourism Research*, 16(1): 51–73.

Berry, L. L. (1983). 'Relationship marketing', in L. L. Berry, G. L. Shostack and G. D. Upah (eds.), *Perspectives on Services Marketing* (pp. 25–28), Chicago, IL: American Marketing Association.

Bowen, J. and Chen, S. L. (2001). 'The relationship between customer loyalty and customer satisfaction', *International Journal of Contemporary Hospitality Management*, 13(5): 213–217.

Bowen, J. and Shoemaker, S. (1998). 'Loyalty: Strategic commitment', *Cornell Hotel and Restaurant Administration Quarterly*, 39(1): 12–25.

Brodie, R. J., Hollebeek, L. D., Ilic, A. and Juric, B. (2011). 'Customer engagement: Conceptual domain, fundamental propositions and implications for research in service marketing', *Journal of Service Research*, 14(3): 252–271.

Constant Contact (2016). Available from http://www.constantcontact.com/home [Accessed: 4 September 2015].

Denove, C. and Power, J. D. IV. (2007). *Satisfaction: How Every Company Should Listen to Their Customers*, New York, NY: Penguin.

Dick, A. S. and Basu, K. (1994). 'Customer loyalty: 'Toward an integrated conceptual framework', *Journal of the Academy of Marketing Science*, 22(2): 99–113.

Dube, L. and Renaghan, L. M. (1999). 'Building customer loyalty: Guests' perspectives on the lodging industry's functional best practices (part I)', *Cornell Hotel and Restaurant Administration Quarterly*, 40(5): 78–88.

Getty, J. M. and Thompson, K. N. (1995). 'The relationship between quality, satisfaction and recommending behaviour in lodging decisions', *Journal of Hospitality and Leisure Marketing*, 2(3): 3–22.

Hayes, B. E. (2008). 'Customer loyalty 2.0: The net promoter score debate and the meaning of customer loyalty', *Quirk's Marketing Research Review*, 23(October): 54–62, Available from http://businessoverbroadway.com/resources/articles [Accessed: 4 October 2015].

Hollebeek, L. D. (2011). 'Exploring customer brand engagement: Definition and themes', *Journal of Strategic Marketing*, 19(7): 555–573.

Kandampully, J. and Suhartanto, D. (2000). 'Customer loyalty in the hotel industry: The role of customer satisfaction and image', *International Journal of Contemporary Hospitality Management*, 12(6): 346–351.

Mattila, A. (2006). 'How affective commitment boosts guest loyalty', *Cornell Hospitality Quarterly*, 47(2): 174–181.

NBRI (2016). 'National Business Research Institute', Available from https://www.nbrii.com/ [Accessed: 8 September 2015].

Oh, H. and Parks, S. (1997). 'Customer satisfaction and service quality: A critical review of the literature and research implications for the hospitality industry', *Hospitality Research Journal*, 20(3): 35–64.

Oliver, R. L. (1997). *Satisfaction: A Behavioural Perspective on the Consumer*, New York: McGraw-Hill.

Oliver, R. L. (1999). 'Whence consumer loyalty?', *Journal of Marketing*, 63(4): 33–44.

Peoplemetrics (2010). 'Why the Ritz-Carlton is #1 in customer engagement', 27 October, Available from http://www.peoplemetrics.com/blog/why-the-ritz-carlton-is-1-in-customer-engagement [Accessed: 4 September 2015].

Pizam, A. and Ellis, T. (1999). 'Customer satisfaction and its measurement in hospitality enterprises', *International Journal of Contemporary Hospitality Management*, 11(7): 326–339.

Robison, J. (2008). 'How the Ritz Carlton manages the mystique', *Gallup Topics*, Available from http://www.gallup.com/businessjournal/112906/How-RitzCarlton-Manages-Mystique.aspx [Accessed: 15 September 2015].

Shiri, D. V., Beatty, S. E. and Morgan, R. M. (2012). 'Customer engagement: Exploring customer relationships beyond purchase', *Journal of Marketing Theory and Practice*, 20(2): 122–146.

Skogland, I. and Siguaw, J. (2004). 'Are your satisfied customers loyal?', *Cornell Hotel and Restaurant Administration Quarterly*, 45(3): 221–234.

Toporek, A. (2011). 'The definition of customer loyalty', 27 August, Available from http://customersthatstick.com/blog/customer-loyalty/the-definition-of-customer-loyalty/ [Accessed: 4 September 2015].

28

CONSUMER LOYALTY TRENDS IN THE HOTEL INDUSTRY

John Bowen

Challenges for customer loyalty

There has been considerable research on customer loyalty in general and specifically customer loyalty within the hotel industry. This study will start with a brief discussion of customer loyalty and hotel loyalty programmes. The focus of the study is on environmental factors that will affect hotel loyalty programmes. Based on previous research, propositions relating to the emerging environmental factors will be developed. It is hoped these propositions will lead to future research improving hotel loyalty programmes.

It is generally accepted that loyalty has both behavioural and attitudinal components (Day 1969). Some behavioural traits of consumers include increased frequency of purchases, increased dollar amount of purchases and the purchase of a broader variety of products. The last refers to a situation where, rather than just staying at a hotel, the guest may have meals in the hotel or plan meetings in the hotel. Baloglu (2002) claimed that the majority of loyalty programmes provide awards for only the behavioural component of loyalty. Programmes reward behaviour by giving the guest loyalty awards based on the number of nights they stay and/or the amount of money they spend. The consequences of behavioural loyalty create financial benefits for the brand.

Baloglu (2002) cited a number of studies that called for including attitudinal loyalty as part of reward programmes. When the attitudinal component of loyalty is lacking, the consumer does not have an emotional attachment to the company and may even not have a favourable view of the company. Dick and Basu (1994) developed a 2 × 2 matrix based on high and low repeat patronage and high and low relative attitude. The authors classified consumers who have high repeat patronage and low relative attitude towards the firm as having spurious loyalty. Baloglu (2002) empirically tested Dick and Basu's matrix using members of a casino's loyalty programme as the sample. He found that 56% of the respondents who exhibited high behavioural loyalty had low attitudinal loyalty. Baloglu proposed that these players are coming to the casino on a regular basis because it is convenient. However, they did not have an emotional attachment to the casino and did not have strong enough positive feelings towards the casino to recommend the casino to others. The casino was convenient. It was a place they would come to until another casino that was more convenient or just as convenient and had a better product opened. When that happened their high behavioural loyalty to the casino they were presently frequenting would quickly disappear.

Today most hospitality and travel loyalty programmes are still based on only the behavioural component. For example, the tiers of two major hotel loyalty programmes are based on the nights spent with the brand's hotels and points are earned by dollars spent with the brand's hotels. As guests move up into higher tiers, they gain more benefits, including more points per dollar spent. Lee et al. (2015) provided empirical support for the use of awards that create attitudinal loyalty. In their study participants were given either social rewards or economic rewards in their loyalty programme. Those receiving social rewards had access to the members-only hotel lounge and health club. They were recognized by name when they entered the hotel and received special treatment from the concierge but did not receive any points or economic rewards such as free rooms. Those who received economic benefits received points that could be redeemed for free rooms, room upgrades and spa treatments. They claimed that social benefits would lead to emotional attachment and commitment, thus creating attitudinal loyalty. They found that those receiving social rewards felt the hotel was devoting more effort, resources and attention to maintaining a relationship. The authors called this relationship marketing investment (RMI). The study found RMI had a positive influence on customer loyalty, providing empirical support for the need to develop attitudinal loyalty.

The consequences of attitudinal loyalty include positive word of mouth and voluntary partnerships, such as volunteering to serve on advisory boards and focus groups to help improve the operation (Bowen and Shoemaker 1998). The influence of user-generated communication (UGC) on social media and the use of social media to determine hotel choices by the guest increases the importance of the attitudinal component of loyalty.

The changing environment and the effect these changes have on hotel loyalty programmes

Through an exploration of current environmental trends this study will look at how to manage the effects of these trends to increase or maintain behavioural and attitudinal loyalty. The trends discussed in this study include the growth of social media, the emergence of Millennials as the most important travel market segment, corporate social responsibility (CSR) and the emergence of online travel agencies (OTAs) as a powerful distribution channel.

The development of social media has increased the power of the consumer. For example, Dave Carroll's 'United Breaks Guitars' has received over 15 million views on YouTube. Millennials are now the most important business travel segment, replacing the Baby Boomers. As CSR has increased in importance, research has shown a relationship between consumers' perceptions of corporate responsibility and trust, an important antecedent of customer loyalty. Online travel agencies and meta-search sites such as Kayak and Trivago have increased price transparency. OTAs have had a disruptive effect on the hotel industry, through their relatively high fees. They have also countered hotel loyalty programmes by starting their own loyalty programmes. These environmental changes have affected loyalty programmes. A review of literature on these trends resulted in the development of five propositions.

Social media

One of the guidelines for 'walking' customers when a hotel is overbooked is to make sure that upper-tier loyalty members' reservations are honoured. Often those who are walked are first-time guests, especially those booked by a third party (Shannon 2010). The common wisdom before social media was that a customer who had a bad experience would tell ten people and one who had a good experience would tell three people. Walking a guest to another hotel was not a good thing, but was viewed as an occasional consequence of revenue management.

User-generated comments on social media have expanded the reach of guest comments from a few to many. If they are negative, they can result in cancellations as travellers modify their plans. In the incident referenced earlier, Dave Carroll, an ordinary traveller on United Airlines, could not get a resolution to a guitar being damaged by baggage handlers. He wrote a song about the poor service recovery procedures he received from United and uploaded it to YouTube. To date the video has received over 15 million views on YouTube. He estimates over 100 million people have seen the video, as it is available on other sites and is often shown to groups of viewers. Social media has increased the importance of good service delivery systems as well as service recovery. Although top-tier loyalty members are still important, social media has narrowed the gap between top-tier members and non-loyalty programme members. Companies can no longer assume that an infrequent guest has little value. Any guest has the capability of creating positive or negative communications which will reach hundreds of thousands of people.

Even though a traveller does not personally know the users posting UGC, prospective guests view these reviews by past guests as being credible (Lodging Interactive 2015). Social media has now expanded the conversation, in terms of both breadth and depth. On their fact sheet, TripAdvisor (2015) mentions it has over 200 million posts and 29 million user-generated images (UGIs). Many travel products have scores of reviews on TripAdvisor, which also covers 4.5 million businesses in 147,000 destinations. In addition to commercial websites, social media networking sites, such as Facebook, provide travel information to friends and their friends. Social media sites vary in popularity among users, depending on different cultures. WeChat is one of the most popular micro-blogging sites in China, but many people in North America are unfamiliar with the site. Social media has given the consumer a powerful voice, one that can influence many other consumers.

In addition to changing how a hotel views the occasional customer, social media can also increase customer loyalty. There is evidence that social media and online communities can build customer loyalty (Laroche et al. 2013). Balakrishnan et al. (2014) found that both online communities and electronic word of mouth (eWOM) had a positive effect on brand loyalty with Millennials. McAlexander et al. (2002) conducted research on participants of Jeep brand fests. These were gatherings of Jeep owners in one geographic location. The researchers looked at how integration into the brand community was developed through these events and investigated the effect of social media generated by the events. Laroche et al. (2013) found that a brand community positively influenced the consumer's relationship with the product, the brand, the company and other customers. Each of these relationships had a positive influence on brand trust, which in turn had a positive effect on brand loyalty.

Nusair et al. (2013) studied online affective commitment, which they defined as the psychological attachment of one partner in the marketing exchange to the other. In their study they found that there was a positive relationship between trust and affective commitment with online communities. They also found a positive relationship between trust and loyalty. One consequence of loyalty is an increase in price insensitivity. Anderson (2012) states that a one-point increase in a hotel's TripAdvisor score will enable the hotel to increase the room rate by 11% and still maintain the same level of occupancy.

The implications of these studies are that hotels could serve as a catalyst for an online community related to the brand. These communities could discuss things of interest to both the business traveller and leisure traveller, with the content developed by the communities and facilitated by the hotel brand. Social media can be used to create trust either for the hotel brand or for an OTA. This effect created by social media is also consequential for customer loyalty.

Proposition 1: When a customer perceives a brand has positive social media their trust of the brand will be positive.

Proposition 2: When a customer perceives a brand has positive social media this will have an indirect positive effect on loyalty through trust.

Millennials

One way of segmenting markets is to look at cohorts who have experienced similar events during their lives, particularly during the formative early adulthood years from their teens to their early twenties (Parment 2012). Parment states there is a difference between generations and generational cohorts; generational cohorts are defined by the occurrence of events that shape their lives, while generations involve set numbers of years, typically 20 or 25. Millennials, also called Gen-Y, are people born between 1977 and the mid-1990s (Bowen and Chen-McCain 2015). Ellis (2013) states there are approximately 86 million US Millennials, which represents 27% of the American population. Their spending power is approximately $200 billion per year (Nusair et al. 2013), and in terms of travel consumption, Millennials will account for over half of all travel spending by 2020 (Walsh 2014). They are a powerful force now and their economic power will continue to increase as they continue to graduate from university and/or advance in their careers over the next four decades. In reality there are a number of different segments within the Millennial generation. For the purpose of this study we will discuss Millennials based on major traits of the overall generational segment.

Millennials rated 'ability to value me' and 'ability to understand my needs' as the most important attributes in creating loyalty (Weissenberg et al. 2013). In the same study, loyalty programmes ranked sixteenth. Millennials want to feel special from the moment they arrive at the hotel for the first time; they desire experiences that are customized for them (Mayock 2014). Hotels have invested heavily in tier-based programmes. Not surprisingly, the Baby Boomers and Gen-Xers who hold the bulk of memberships in travel programmes continue to drive the expectations in those sectors. The challenge for marketers will be to evolve the design of loyalty programmes to maintain the loyalty of Baby Boomers and Gen-Xers, while also adding features to attract Millennials.

Consumers over the age of 30 are twice as likely to participate in travel programmes and are significantly more likely to carry rewards, credit and debit cards (Weissenberg et al. 2013). Millennials now account for the highest percentage of members in retail store programmes. Many of these programmes provide instant rewards when the customer or cashier swipes the loyalty card at the checkout, and discounts are applied immediately to the cardholder's invoice. Citizen M, a hotel brand targeted at Millennials, has a one-level loyalty programme called 'citizen', and when you join, you instantly get 15% off the room rates and a more liberal cancellation policy. The biggest change for hotel loyalty programmes is the shift in the importance of generational cohorts, with Millennials trending and Baby Boomers fading.

Corporate responsibility

Marketers are re-examining their relationships with social values and responsibilities and with the very Earth that sustains us. As the worldwide consumerism and environmentalism movements mature, today's marketers are being called on to develop sustainable marketing practices. Corporate ethics and social responsibility have become important initiatives for many companies. Today's customers expect companies to deliver value in a socially and environmentally responsible way.

The social responsibility and environmental movements will place even stricter demands on companies in the future. Forward-looking companies readily accept their responsibilities to the world around them. They view sustainable marketing as an opportunity to do well by doing well. They seek ways to serve the immediate needs and the best long-run interests of their owners, customers and communities.

One group of customers that considers a brand's ethical credentials and ethical value to be important are the Millennials. A study of Millennials conducted in the UK revealed that 97% of the participants viewed corporate ethics as important, and 51% would choose a brand that acts in an ethical manner (Arnold 2013). The Millennials are shaped with civic purpose and are social cause-oriented (Foscht et al. 2009; Lazarevic 2012). Therefore, corporations must convey their mission of being socially responsible and environmentally conscious to the Millennials (Lazarevic 2012; Gurau 2012). Kotler et al. (2010) redefined the marketing concept to include contributions to the well-being of humans.

Recent research studies have shown a direct positive relationship between both CSR and loyalty and CSR and trust. In addition to the benefit of increased loyalty, CSR initiatives can positively affect consumer attitudes towards a firm and its offerings (Mandhachitara and Poolthong 2011). These researchers, using a sample of Thai retail bank customers, found a positive relationship between CSR and attitudinal loyalty, as well as a positive relationship between CSR and perceived service quality. A study of consumer perceptions of Spanish hotels (Martinez and Bosque 2013) found CSR positively influenced trust and trust positively influenced customer loyalty. Lombart and Louis (2014) conducted an experiment using French Millennial consumers, to gain their perceptions of CSR in a food retail store. They found CSR had a positive influence on customer satisfaction and customer trust. A study of consumers across a number of US firms found a positive relationship between CSR and customer trust and a positive relationship between CSR and customer loyalty (Stanaland et al. 2011). US consumers also indicated that CSR had a positive influence on trust (Kang and Hustvedt 2014). These studies using samples of consumers from around the globe and on a variety of products, including hotels, all found a positive relationship between CSR and trust and/or loyalty.

Two trends should increase the importance of CSR in the future. First, as societal issues such as air quality, global warming, scarcity of food, scarcity of water, and human rights become more critical and consumers' awareness of these issues increases, one can predict that social responsibility will be more valued. Also, as mentioned, Millennials are interested in a firm's social responsibility issues. As Millennials grow in importance, CSR will become more important.

Proposition 3: Millennial consumers will exhibit a positive relationship between CSR for a brand and loyalty for the brand.

Proposition 4: Millennials will exhibit a stronger relationship between CSR and loyalty than consumers born before 1977.

Online travel agencies

Although OTAs only produce 14% of a hotel's reservations, it is estimated that 75% of US online hospitality shoppers go on OTA sites prior to booking (Mayock 2014). They are popular booking channels for younger travellers making under $75,000 (Weissmann 2013).

Airline brands control most of their inventory. Thus, airlines are less dependent on OTAs than hotels. Southwest Airlines books 80% of its revenues through its brand.com sites (SouthwestAirlines.com 2015). Recently Lufthansa Airlines added an $18 fee for tickets purchased through an OTA to discourage travellers from using this channel (Trefis Team 2015). The hotel industry is a very fragmented industry in terms of ownership. Even though major global brands like Hilton and Marriott have thousands of hotels that carry their brand names, they do not own most of these hotels. The hotels are owned by hundreds of franchisees and developers. Control of the inventory is spread across these companies. This creates an opportunity for OTAs to provide a channel for hotel owners that are willing to pay a high price to sell their rooms rather than have them sit vacant. This in turn creates a competitive environment where other hotel owners turn to OTAs to compete.

Commissions and fees paid to OTAs can represent one third or more of the net profits of a hotel. A major discussion among hotel owners is how to reduce the dependence on and the amount paid to OTAs. Bui et al. (2015) studied the influence that online communities affiliated with an OTA have on their members. They found that a member's affective belonging to the online community had a positive influence on both intention to use and intention to purchase from the OTA, while cognitive loyalty to the OTA had a positive influence on intention to use the OTA. As OTAs affiliate with online communities they can gain a direct influence over the members. To illustrate the power and profitability of OTAs in August 2015, Priceline, an OTA, was worth $66 billion and Marriott was worth $19 billion.

Hotel brands did not give loyalty points or benefits for guests booking through OTAs, in order to encourage customers to book through their brand Internet sites. OTAs countered by developing their own loyalty programmes, allowing a traveller to stay across multiple brands and still gain rewards (Weiss 2014). Gurau (2012) mentions that Millennials seek products that match their personality and lifestyle, paying little attention to brands. This makes OTAs an attractive choice for Millennials as they can choose across hotel brands at each destination, looking for a hotel that matches their personality and lifestyle. Another study found that over 80% of Millennials did not consider themselves loyal to a hotel brand. Instead they looked for an ideal location at a good price. This study also supports the use of OTAs for Millennials. Hotels.com has one of the best loyalty programmes, giving one free night for every ten you book on their site (Zachrisson 2015). Expedia, which owns Hotels.com, has started its own tiered loyalty programme. Expedia breaks its benefits into three groups: save money, reward you and service. These benefits are a mix of financial and social rewards. Expedia credit cards allow cardholders to earn bonus points when they use the card, and gain instant gold or silver status depending on the card they pick. Agado, owned by Priceline, also offers a loyalty programme. The OTA loyalty programmes allow travellers to book across brands and still earn points. The development of OTA loyalty programmes, and the attraction to OTAs of younger travellers, make them a threat to hotel brand loyalty. OTAs are also reducing the profitability of hotels, while they have become very profitable. This means they have the financial ability to create and maintain loyalty programmes that will challenge hotel loyalty programmes.

Earlier in the study it was mentioned that online communities could create trust and price insensitivity, a consequence of loyalty. TripAdvisor has moved from a meta-search site to an OTA. As an OTA, TripAdvsior has an extensive online community through which it can build loyalty. The expertise OTAs have in developing online communities has given them the skill sets to develop customer loyalty.

Proposition 5: Millennials will favour an OTA loyalty programme over traditional tiered hotel brand loyalty programmes.

Summary

The propositions developed by the study summarize what the author believes to be the effect of these trends on customer loyalty. These propositions have management implications; some of these are as follows. Social media has increased the need for great service delivery and great service recovery. Social media amplifies the voice of the customer. Good reviews on social media can lead to trail and loyalty by persons connected with the reviewer's social media. Millennials will emerge as the most important travel segment. As a group, the consumer behaviour of Millennials is very different from that of the segment they will replace (Baby Boomers). Managers will need to understand the wants of this segment, changing their loyalty programmes so they will be more effective with Millennials. CSR is increasingly being viewed as an important corporate action. Those companies that practise CSR and communicate their CSR to the public will develop customer loyalty through their CSR. Finally, OTAs represent a significant challenge to hotels. It is important for hotel brands to develop strong customer loyalty with the brand to help offset the power of the OTAs.

The five propositions presented in the chapter can all be tested empirically. Each proposition is supported by past research. One of the desired outcomes of this chapter is that it will spawn empirical research.

References

Anderson, C. (2012). 'The impact of social media on lodging performance', *Cornell Reports*, 12(15): 6–11, Available from: http://scholarship.sha.cornell.edu/chrpubs/5/ [Accessed: 9 September 2015].

Arnold, C. (2013). 'The truth about students - five steps to help market your brand to students', *Marketing Magazine*, Available from: www.marketingmagazine.co.uk/article/1192239/truth-students—five-tips-help-market-brand-students [Accessed: 20 July 2014].

Balakrishnan, B., Dahnil, M. and Yi, W. (2014). 'The impact of social media marketing medium toward purchase intention and brand loyalty among generation Y', *Procedia – Social and Behavioral Sciences*, 148: 177–185.

Baloglu, S. (2002). 'Dimensions of customer loyalty: Separating friends from well wishers', *Cornell Hotel and Restaurant Administration Quarterly*, 43(1): 47–59.

Bowen, J. and Chen-McCain, S. (2015). 'Transitioning loyalty programs: A commentary on the relationship between customer loyalty and customer satisfaction', *International Journal of Contemporary Hospitality Management*, 27(3): 415–430.

Bowen, J. and Shoemaker, S. (1998). 'Loyalty: A strategic commitment', *Cornell Hotel and Restaurant Administration Quarterly*, 39(1): 12–25.

Bui, M., Jeng, D. and Lin, C. (2015). 'The importance of attribution: Connecting online communities with online travel agencies', *Cornell Hospitality Quarterly*, 56(3): 285–297.

Day, G. (1969). 'A two-dimensional concept of brand loyalty', *Journal of Advertising Research*, 9(3): 29–35.

Dick, A. S. and Basu, K. (1994). 'Customer loyalty: Toward an integrated conceptual framework', *Journal of the Academy of Marketing Science*, 22(2): 99–113.

Ellis, G. (2013). 'Invest in Millennials: The youth market is the future of CE', *Dealerscope*, 55(7): 28, 30, 32.

Foscht, T., Schloffer, J., Maloles III, C. and Chia, S. (2009). 'Assessing the outcomes of Generation Y customers' loyalty', *International Journal of Bank Marketing*, 27(3): 218–241.

Gurau, C. (2012). 'A life-stage analysis of consumer loyalty profile: Comparing Generation X and Millennial consumers', *Journal of Consumer Marketing*, 29(2): 103–113.

Kang, J. and Hustvedt, G. (2014). 'Building trust between consumers and corporations: The role of consumer perceptions of transparency and social responsibility', *Journal of Business Ethics*, 125(2): 253–265.

Kotler, P., Kartajaya, H. and Setiawan, I. (2010). *Marketing 3.0.*, Hoboken, NJ: John Wiley and Sons.

Laroche, M., Habibi, M. and Richard, M. (2013). 'To be or not to be in social media: How brand loyalty is affected by social media?', *International Journal of Information Management*, 33(1): 76–82.

Lazarevic, V. (2012). 'Encouraging brand loyalty in fickle Generation Y consumers', *Young Consumers*, 13(1): 45–61.

Lee, J., Tsang, N. and Pan, S. (2015). 'Examining the differential effects of social and economic rewards in a hotel loyalty program', *International Journal of Hospitality Management*, 49: 17–27.

Lodging Interactive (2015). 'Lodging interactive expands reputation management and social media marketing to restaurants', *Hospitality Net*, Available from: www.hospitalitynet.org/news/4069404.html [Accessed: 16 March 2015].

Lombart, C. and Louis, D. (2014). 'A study of the impact of corporate social responsibility and price image on retailer personality and consumer's reactions (satisfaction, trust and loyalty to the retailer)', *Journal of Retailing and Consumer Services*, 21(4): 630–642.

McAlexander, J., Schouten, J. and Koenig, H. (2002). 'Building brand community', *Journal of Marketing*, 66(1): 38–54.

Mandhachitara, R. and Poolthong, Y. (2011). 'A model of customer loyalty and corporate responsibility', *Journal of Services Marketing*, 25(2): 122–133.

Martinez, P. and Bosque, I. (2013). 'CSP and customer loyalty: The roles of trust, customer identification with the company and satisfaction', *International Journal of Hospitality Management*, 35: 89–99.

Mayock, P. (2014). 'Personalization equals loyalty for Millennials', *HotelNewsNow.com*, Available from: http://www.hotelnewsnow.com/article/13067/Personalizationequalsloyalty-for-millennials [Accessed: 10 October 2014].

Nusair, K., Bilgihan, A., Okumus, F. and Cobanoglu, C. (2013). 'Generation Y travelers' commitment to online social network websites', *Tourism Management*, 35(April): 13–22.

Parment, A. (2012). 'Generation Y vs. Baby Boomers: Shopping behavior, buyer involvement and implications for retailing', *Journal of Retailing and Consumer Services*, 20(2): 189–199.

Shannon, L. (2010). 'Travellers left stranded as hotel booking websites fail to deliver', *The Times* (London), 11 December: 71–72, Available from: http://www.thetimes.co.uk/tto/money/consumeraffairs/article2840567.ece [Accessed: 16 September 2015].

Southwestairlines.com (2015). 'Southwest corporate: Fact sheet', Available from: http://swamedia.com/channels/Corporate-Fact-Sheet/pages/corporate-fact-sheet#funfacts [Accessed: 4 August 2015].

Stanaland, A., Lwin, M. and Murphy, P. (2011). 'Consumer perceptions of the antecedents and consequences of corporate social responsibility', *Journal of Business Ethics*, 102(1): 47–55.

Trefis Team (2015). 'Airlines to thwart air ticket sales through OTAs: The possible ramifications', *Forbes.com*, 23 June, Available from: http://www.forbes.com/sites/greatspeculations/2015/06/23/airlines-to-thwart-air-ticket-sales-through-otas-the-possible-ramifications/3/ [Accessed: 4 August 2015].

TripAdvisor (2015). 'Fact Sheet', Available from: http://www.tripadvisor.com/PressCenter-c4-Fact_Sheet.html/ [Accessed: 17 March 2015].

Walsh, E. (2014). 'Looking ahead: Millennial travel trends – part 1', *Turner*, 10 March, Available from: https://www.turnerpr.com/blog/millennial-travel-trends-part-1/ [Accessed: 23 July 2014].

Weiss, L. (2014). 'The booking battle: OTAs break into the loyalty market', *USNEWS.com*, 4 August, Available from: http://travel.usnews.com/features/The-Booking-Battle-OTAs-Break-into-the-Loyalty-Market/ [Accessed: 4 August 2015].

Weissenberg, A., Katz, A. and Narula, A. (2013). 'A restoration in hotel loyalty – Developing a blueprint for reinventing loyalty programs', Available from: https://www2.deloitte.com/content/dam/Deloitte/global/Documents/Consumer-Business/dttl_cb_ConsumerLoyalty_THL_POV.pdf [Accessed: 2 September 2015].

Weissmann, A. (2013). '2014 consumer trends; Widening "advantage gap" bodes well for agents', *TravelWeekly.com*, Available from: http://www.travelweekly.com/Travel-News/Travel-Agent-Issues/2014-Consumer-Trends [Accessed: 7 September 2015].

Zachrisson, L. (2015). 'Which online booking site has the best reward program?', 4 April, Available from: https://usattravel.wordpress.com/2015/04/04/the-online-booking-site-with-the-best-reward-program/ [Accessed: 4 August 2015].

29

BRAND EXPERIENCE AND LOYALTY

Camille Erika Kapoor and Renata Fernandes Guzzo

Brand experience

As consumers search for more meaningful experiences through consumption of goods and services, the construct of brand experience has evolved new and more ways for marketers to better understand consumer behaviour regarding brands. Many studies demonstrate that creating valuable customer experiences has become crucial for developing marketing strategies (Brakus et al. 2009; Schmitt 1999). As open markets grow throughout the world and competition has increased among brands, offering unique brand experiences is fundamental in achieving customer satisfaction and brand loyalty.

Brand experience is a complex construct, related to a wide range of fields, including marketing, psychology, management and cognitive science. Experiences occur while consumers are searching, shopping and consuming products or services (Brakus et al. 2009). In an era where products and services are (or should be) produced based on customers' needs and desires, goods are being transformed into services and services into experiences (Pine and Gilmore 2011). Consequently, in order to be competitive, companies should look forward to understanding and developing unique and long-lasting experiences. Schmitt (1999) proposed a theoretical foundation for brand experience via experiential marketing. He suggested five essential concepts of experiential marketing: 'Sense', which appeals to the senses; 'Feel', which appeals to consumers' inner feelings and emotions; 'Think', which appeals to the intellect creating cognitive engagement with consumers; 'Act', which appeals to different ways of doing things; and 'Relate', which appeals to the individuals' desire for self-improvement (Schmitt 1999). One of the most comprehensive definitions of brand experience was conceptualized by Brakus et al. (2009). They defined brand experience as: 'subjective internal consumer responses (sensations, feelings, and cognitions) and behavioural responses evoked by brand-related stimuli that are part of a brand's design and identity, packaging, communications, and environments' (Brakus et al. 2009: p. 53). Moreover, Brakus et al. (2009) identified that brand experiences vary in strength and intensity, where some experiences can be stronger or more intense than others; vary in valence, such as being more positive or negative than others; and vary in spontaneity, where some brand experiences occur without much reflection and others occur more deliberately, thereby increasing the chance that it will last longer in consumers' memory. Therefore, since brand experience is a sum of different interactions between consumers and a brand, it is especially relevant to understand how those interactions happen and what will lead consumers to have memorable experiences.

Consumer reactions regarding a brand differ based on a variety of circumstances. In order to better understand how various experiences affect consumers, Brakus et al. (2009) further developed and tested Schmitt's (1999) concepts, validating four dimensions of brand experience: sensory, affective, intellectual and behavioural. Brakus et al. (2009) confirmed that brand experience does have a behavioural impact, affecting consumer satisfaction and loyalty in a direct way and brand personality in an indirect way. Walter et al. (2013) tested the same four dimensions of brand experience with the BMW brand. However, the construct was only partially confirmed, since deviations were found in the factor analysis, especially for the behavioural dimension of the scale. Moreover, no correlations between brand experience and brand personality with customer satisfaction were found. Testing how consumers experience brands can be daunting: there are several aspects that could influence these results, such as the industry type, the product type (e.g. luxury in BMW's case) and the brand size in the market. Still, studies that provide consistent results can generate insights for organizations by explaining how consumers experience brands and how those experiences can help organizations improve brand equity (Ding and Tseng 2015; Lin 2015), brand satisfaction (Brakus et al. 2009; Lin 2015; Nysveen et al. 2013) and brand loyalty (Brakus et al. 2009; Nysveen et al. 2013; Walter et al. 2013).

Brand experience does not just explain general judgements about a brand; rather this concept aggregates specific sensations and behavioural responses triggered by actually experiencing a brand. Brand experience is not about one specific experience, but rather explores how consumers perceive and behave while experiencing a brand in different moments. Brand experience also differs from motivational and affective concepts and from brand association and image (Brakus et al. 2009). In other words, brand experience can happen when consumers do not have a personal connection or are involved with the brand; brand experiences may result in emotional bonds, but emotions are just one of many outcomes that experiences can bring; and brand experiences do not necessarily need to be a surprising experience (Brakus et al. 2009). For instance, some would say that a consumer searching online for a hotel would not have any emotional connection involved in the process. However, based on the brand experience construct, if consumers are searching for products or services online (that action being much more common now than a few years ago), they will start experiencing and developing different feelings and perceptions about the brand even within that virtual environment.

Products and services have similar experience dimensions and characteristics (e.g. colours, designs, sensory experiences) created and stimulated by brands. However, since services are intangible and produced and consumed simultaneously, understanding consumer experiences in services is intrinsically related to a brand's ability to succeed. Because service experiences are actually based on a variety of different brands (e.g. a hotel room, where the shampoo's brand and the television's brand differ), consumers will experience the hotel brand based on their experiences of each individual and distinct brand, thereby placing a greater emphasis on one brand over another in their ultimate brand evaluation. Therefore, service brands need to have specific brand strategies as well as a holistic view of their components in order to avoid guest dissatisfaction or ambivalence.

Morrison and Crane (2007) suggest that strong service brands can be built by developing and managing the customer's emotional brand experience. These authors propose that emotion is 'a state of physical and mental readiness that involves valence (directional force), evaluative appraisal, a target (or object of stimulus) and behavioural tendencies'

(Morrison and Crane 2007: p. 412). The depth of emotional connection between the brand offering and the consumer is the main difference between a simple service and purchasing an experience (Pine and Gilmore 2011). Once the emotional connection is made, the probability for satisfaction and loyalty increases. Nysveen et al.'s (2013) study on service organizations found that relational experiences represent a unique dimension of brand experience, and are a predictor of customer satisfaction and loyalty. These authors found that services are characterized by intangibility, heterogeneity, perishability, service-dominant logic such as understanding that goods are appliances used to provide services, and are more consumer-based and oriented and, therefore, the relational character of services is substantiated. The dimensions of brand experience are as complex as its construct.

In a similar direction, Lee and Jeong's (2014) study empirically investigated the effects of congruity on consumer online experiences and responses within the context of the hotel industry. The principle of congruity theory, proposed by the seminal work of Osgood and Tannenbaum (1955), can be understood as 'changes in evaluation [that] are always in the direction of increased congruity with[in] the existing frame of reference' (p. 43). The main findings of Lee and Jeong's (2014) research indicated that self-image congruity influenced both consumer online brand experiences and trust towards hotels. They also found that online–offline brand image congruity also had influence over consumers' online brand experience as well as their trust towards the hotel. Self-congruity can be explained as being customers' tendencies to buy products and services congruent, or similar, to their own self-image while online–offline brand image congruity stands for a compatibility between the online images and offline images perceived by customers (Lee and Jeong 2014). Furthermore, the authors also found that trust and brand satisfaction of hotels, as outcomes of online brand experiences, were influenced by these online experiences. Congruity theory presents a different range of possibilities with which to interpret consumers' behaviours towards a brand. Lee and Jeong's (2014) study suggests that hotels should develop strategies which capture the congruity effects of online and offline channels in order to improve brand experiences for consumers.

Researchers have been making attempts to use different theories such as congruity theory and cognitive theories to help practitioners improve consumer brand experience, and as a consequence, obtain brand satisfaction and ultimately brand loyalty. Even though experiences are singular to each consumer, companies can and should make their brand analyses and decisions based on current relevant customer surveys. This chapter demonstrates how important it is for organizations to include brand experience in their marketing strategies because doing so will enable them to better comprehend and engage their market segment and verify whether the experiences that customers are having are what was planned and expected. It is crucial to perceive that brand experience can and should be analysed in different ways, while retaining the peculiarities each company has based on size, industry type and offered products and services.

Brand experience: satisfaction versus loyalty

It is important to understand that satisfaction and loyalty are not the same thing, although satisfaction is critical for developing loyalty. In the seminal work by Shoemaker and Lewis (1999), they distinguished between customer loyalty and customer satisfaction:

> Customer loyalty is not the same as customer satisfaction. Customer satisfaction
> measures how well a customer's expectations are met by a given transaction, while

customer loyalty measures how likely a customer is to repurchase and engage in partnership activities. Satisfaction is a necessary but not a sufficient condition for loyalty. In other words, we can have satisfaction without loyalty, but it is hard to have loyalty without satisfaction.

(Shoemaker and Lewis 1999: p. 353)

Bloemer and de Ruyter (1999) argued that 'service loyalty management should focus on increasing customer satisfaction, increasing the positive emotions experienced by the customers during the service providing and increasing the level of involvement of the customer with the service' (p. 326). They suggested that 'making the service important to the consumer, [and] linking it with important values of the consumer's personal situations, by accentuating personalized services and customer-oriented layout and design', can significantly contribute to the customer's level of involvement in the service experience and therefore significantly increase customer satisfaction levels (Bloemer and de Ruyter 1999: p. 326). Bowen and Shoemaker (2003) pointed out that the end result of customer loyalty is measured by 'how likely a customer is to return' and can measure 'how willing that person is to perform partner-like activities for the hotel – starting with recommendations to friends' (pp. 32–33).

Although satisfied customers are not necessarily loyal customers, Dubé and Maute (1998) suggested that, in fact, loyal customers may not necessarily be satisfied. They pointed out that 'much like satisfaction, commitment to a relationship is affected by current relationship value, with high rewards and low costs engendering greater commitment' (Dubé and Maute 1998: p. 777). The seminal figure by Oliver (1999) (see Figure 29.1) further demonstrates this point. Oliver (1999) suggested that the first five models are incorrect illustrations of the relationship between loyalty and satisfaction; rather, it is the sixth model that accurately depicts this complex relationship. Notice how in this model satisfaction with the brand actually spirals and builds into loyalty and that once this brand loyalty is achieved, it is completely separated from satisfaction, so that episodic dissatisfaction with the brand will not negatively affect brand loyalty.

Youjae and Suna (2004) confirmed this, arguing that 'episodic or transactional CS (customer satisfaction) as well as cumulative CS can influence future expectations and thus repurchase intentions' and pointing out that 'the degree of satisfaction at each transaction will affect post-purchase expectations. Adjusted expectations are updated from prior expectations on the basis of newly acquired information, and they are affected by CS, an overall evaluation of the consumption experience' (p. 355). Youjae and Suna (2004) further pointed out that:

As loyal consumers buy a particular brand more frequently and have more reliable knowledge about the brand, they must have relatively more accurate and realistic expectations about the brand. Therefore, loyal consumers may tend to ignore disconfirmation to some extent and regard it as an episodic product/service failure (or success) rather than as a lasting problem (or enhancement). In contrast, non loyals may have less knowledge of the brand and hold more inaccurate or unrealistic expectations, which will probably result in high disconfirmation between prior expectations and perceived performance. Even when the same amount of disconfirmation occurs, non loyals may regard it as an important indicator in evaluating the brand. Hence, non-loyal consumers will tend to use disconfirmation more sensitively in judging satisfaction than loyal consumers will.

(p. 355)

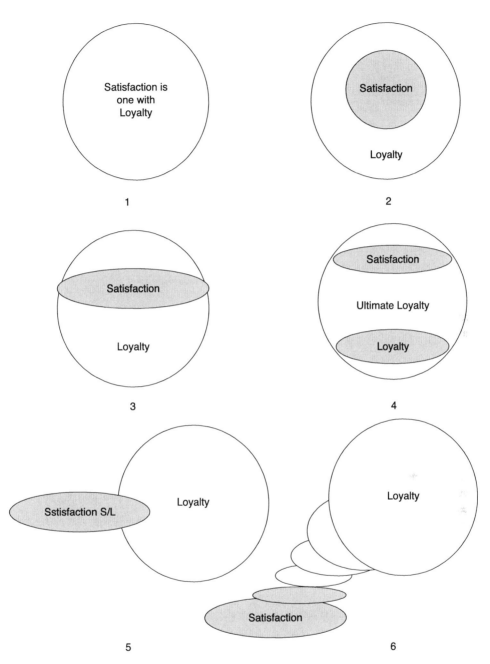

Figure 29.1 Six representations of satisfaction and loyalty

Source: Adapted from Oliver (1999: p. 34).

Youjae and Suna (2004) also found that loyal customers have higher repurchase intentions because they have lower customer satisfaction thresholds. Additionally, because customers have knowledge about the brands to which they are loyal they are more likely to stay with 'their' brand, rather than search for something new (Youjae and Suna 2004). This is especially true as time becomes more and more important to consumers.

Brand communities

One of the best manifestations of brand loyalty for companies is the formation of brand communities. Aggarwal (2004) suggested that 'people sometimes form relationships with brands in much the same way in which they form relationships with each other in a social context' (p. 87). He continued by saying that 'people sometimes form a very intimate bond with brands and, in some extreme cases, a passion that is often associated only with a close circle of friends and family' (Aggarwal 2004: p. 87). Ambler (1997) propounded this theory earlier, writing that 'brands are, in the relational paradigm, anthropomorphized to the extent that people have "relationships" with them' (p. 283). Cooper (1999) then discussed how brands themselves had changed from lifeless, malleable artefacts to living entities with their own personalities, which allows customers to form relationships with the brand and also allows the brand to change and evolve over time.

However, it is important to realize that customers do not distinguish brands from brand manufacturers (Aggarwal 2004). Aggarwal (2004) argued that 'this perception is more likely for service brands (e.g., hotels and airlines) and for brands that have a combination of products and services (e.g., many online stores)' (p. 88). Earlier, Kim et al. (2003) also found that 'in the service industry, customers generally choose or reject based on the company brand . . . That is, customers develop company brand associations rather than the brand association of product items' (p. 336). Aggarwal (2004) proposed that when 'brands behave like socialized members of a culture then they are evaluated by the rules that govern the society and have to act in accordance to these rules' (p. 88). These actions have other negative or positive evaluations, depending on whether they violate or conform to the norms of a relationship (Aggarwal 2004). It is critical for companies to recognize that while customer–brand relationships have many benefits for the brand, these relationships must be treated with respect.

Despite the 'exchange-ness' nature of brand relationships, Ambler (1997) pointed out the difficulty of measuring and financially valuing the brand–customer relationships. One way to value brands is by measuring brand equity. David Ogilvy defined brand equity as the 'consumer's idea of a product' (as found in Blackston 2000: p. 101). According to the seminal work by Ambler (1997):

> Brand equity is made up of memories of different kinds . . . Declarative memory can be cognitive (thinking-related) and affective (feeling-related). Awareness is cognitive, as is our knowledge of a brand's functional performance characteristics and price. Attitudes towards the brand are primarily affective.
>
> *(p. 284)*

Ambler (1997) explained that 'the perceived quality of the brand will be a mix of actual quality facts we may know, e.g. from consumer reports, image characteristics from advertising, packaging, word of mouth and usage experience' (p. 285). Blackston (2000) proposed that in order to directly manage and understand some of the intangible elements of brand equities, companies need to rely on their customers. Understanding the brand's attitudes and behaviours towards its customers means 'acknowledging that the individual is more than just a statistic or a client code' (Blackston 2000: p. 104). Blackston (2000) warned that if a corporate brand 'does not act as if it knows who its customers are', it 'will not earn their trust, regardless of its credibility and reliability' (p. 104). Blackston (2000) further summarized the brand–customer relationship by recognizing that first companies must understand customers' attitudes and behaviours towards the brand and then consider the brand's attitude and behaviours towards their customers.

Although customers often purchase a variety of brands, understanding how people form relationships with brands can assist companies in developing brand loyalty out of consumer brand experiences. Escalas and Bettman (2003) proposed that 'consumers use brands to meet self-needs such as self-verification or self-enhancement' (p. 339). People form connections with brands when their associations with the brands are used to construct or communicate their self-concept (Escalas and Bettman 2003). According to the formative work by McCracken (1989), when consumers form connections with brands, these connections help consumers create and build their self-identities (as found in Escalas and Bettman 2003). Therefore, people choose brands because of a need for self-consistency and in order to match themselves to prototypical users of the brand offering (Escalas and Bettman 2003).

Fournier (1998) agreed, arguing that 'meaningful relationships are qualified not along symbolic versus functional product category lines, or in terms of high versus low involvement classes, but by the perceived ego significance of the chosen brands' and proposing that 'individual consumer-brand relationships make the most sense when considered at the aggregate level of the personal brandscape' or the totality of brands that each customer utilizes and identifies with (p. 366). As she summarized, 'consumers do not choose brands, they choose lives' (Fournier 1998: p. 367).

Escalas and Bettman (2003) pointed out that brand connections are psychological manifestations of brand equity. These 'self–brand' connections may lead consumers to form attitudes about the brand that are not very susceptible to change (Escalas and Bettman 2003). In fact, they found that 'when consumers' self-concepts are linked to a brand, then the company behind the brand may be able to gain an enduring competitive advantage because this type of connection is difficult for competitors to imitate' (p. 347). Some of the aspects of this competitive advantage may include being more forgiving of marketing blunders (i.e. poor advertising campaigns) or a temporary product quality problem, being more loyal to the brand and being less likely to switch brands due to price cuts, coupons, etc. (Escalas and Bettman 2003).

Before customers can form relationships with brands, however, they must have a positive brand experience. Dunne (2004) presented the four domains inherent in brand experiences: physical, emotional, intellectual and spiritual. According to Dunne (2004), each of these domains 'can provide a company with new ways of connecting with its consumers on a much more intimate level' (p. 11). Lozito (2004) argued that the:

> restaurant emotional brand experience starts creating a bond from the minute the patron sees an ad, a name or a logo and doesn't end until the music, lights and aroma are only a recent memory. Every touch point in between is an opportunity to differentiate and reinforce the brand promise . . . what you want the consumer to think about your business.
>
> *(p. 58)*

Nevertheless, Lury (2002) cautioned that brands cannot appeal to every person all of the time but suggests that brands can be hated as long as they are also loved. As he puts it, 'a brand that appeals strongly to one group while alienating another is nearly always going to be more successful than a brand that neither inspires nor irritates anyone' (Lury 2002: p. 7).

Muniz and O'Guinn (2001) proposed the idea of brand communities, which 'may form around any brand, but are probably most likely to form around brands with a strong image, a rich and lengthy history, and threatening competition' (p. 415). According to Muniz and O'Guinn (2001):

> A brand community is a specialized, non-geographically bound community, based on a structured set of social relationships among admirers of a brand. It is specialized because at its center is a branded good or service. Like other communities, it is marked by a shared consciousness, rituals and traditions, and a sense of moral responsibility.
>
> *(p. 412)*

These communities transcend geographical boundaries because mass media transcends geographical boundaries (Muniz and O'Guinn 2001). Fortunately for the hospitality industry, they found that 'things that are publicly consumed may stand a better chance of producing communities than those consumed in private' (Muniz and O'Guinn 2001: p. 415).

Three positive aspects of brand communities are: 'first, brand communities . . . represent a form of consumer agency . . . Second, brand communities represent an important information resource for consumers . . . Third, to the extent that communal interaction generally provides wider social benefits to its members . . . brand communities likewise provide these' (Muniz and O'Guinn 2001: p. 426). Bagozzi and Dholakia (2006) pointed out that brand communities are 'venues where intense brand loyalty is expressed and fostered and emotional connections with the brand forged in customers' (p. 45). Muniz and O'Guinn (2001) not only showed that brands are social objects that are socially constructed, but they also found that brand community affects brand equity. They argued that 'developing a strong brand community could be a critical step in truly actualizing the concept of relationship marketing. A strong brand community can lead to a socially embedded and entrenched loyalty, brand commitment' (Muniz and O' Guinn 2001: p. 427). It is clear, therefore, that brand–customer relationships, whether as part of brand communities or in other contexts, are a critical step towards developing brand commitment and eventual brand loyalty.

References

Aggarwal, P. (2004). 'The effects of brand relationship norms on consumer attitudes and behaviour', *Journal of Consumer Research*, 31(1): 87–101.

Ambler, T. (1997). 'How much of brand equity is explained by trust?', *Management Decision*, 35(3/4): 283–292.

Bagozzi, R. and Dholakia, U. (2006). 'Antecedents and purchase consequences of customer participation in small group brand communities', *International Journal of Research in Marketing*, 23(1): 45–61.

Blackston, M. (2000). 'Observations: Building brand equity by managing the brand's relationships', *Journal of Advertising Research*, 40(6): 101–105.

Bloemer, J. and de Ruyter, K. (1999). 'Customer loyalty in high and low involvement service settings: The moderating impact of positive emotions', *Journal of Marketing Management*, 15(4): 315–330.

Bowen, J. and Shoemaker, S. (2003). 'Loyalty: A strategic commitment', *Cornell Hotel and Restaurant Administration Quarterly*, 44(5/6): 31–46.

Brakus, J. J., Schmitt, B. H. and Zarantonello, L. (2009). 'Brand experience: What is it? How is it measured? Does it affect loyalty?', *Journal of Marketing*, 73(3): 52–58.

Cooper, P. (1999). 'Consumer understanding, change and qualitative research', *Journal of the Market Research Society*, 41(1): 1–6.

Ding, C. G. and Tseng, T. H. (2015). 'On the relationships among brand experience, hedonic emotions, and brand equity', *European Journal of Marketing*, 49(7/8): 994–1015.

Dubé, L. and Maute, M. (1998). 'Defensive strategies for managing satisfaction and loyalty in the service industry', *Psychology and Marketing*, 15(8): 775–791.

Dunne, D. (2004). 'Branding the experience', *Marketing Magazine*, 109(38): 11.

Escalas, J. and Bettman, J. (2003). 'You are what they eat: The influence of reference groups on consumers' connections to brands', *Journal of Consumer Psychology*, 13(3): 339–348.

Fournier, S. (1998). 'Consumers and their brands: Developing relationship theory in consumer research', *Journal of Consumer Research*, 24(4): 343–373.

Kim, H., Kim, W. and An, J. (2003). 'The effect of consumer-based brand equity on firms' financial performance', *Journal of Consumer Marketing*, 20(4): 335–351.

Lee, S. and Jeong, M. (2014). 'Enhancing online brand experiences: An application of congruity theory', *International Journal of Hospitality Management*, 40: 49–58.

Lin, Y. H. (2015). 'Innovative brand experience's influence on brand equity and brand satisfaction', *Journal of Business Research*, 68(11): 2254–2259.

Lozito, W. (2004). 'Brands: More than a name', *Restaurant Hospitality*, 88(9): 56–60.

Lury, G. (2002). 'Love and loathing in the brand world', *Brand Strategy*, p. 7.

McCracken, G. (1989). 'Who is the celebrity endorser? Cultural foundations of the endorsement process', *Journal of Consumer Research*, 16(3): 310–321.

Morrison, S. and Crane, F. G. (2007). 'Building the service brand by creating and managing an emotional brand experience', *Brand Management*, 14(5): 410–421.

Muniz Jr., A. and O'Guinn, T. (2001). 'Brand community', *Journal of Consumer Research*, 27(4): 412–432.

Nysveen, H., Pedersen, P. E. and Skard, S. (2013). 'Brand experiences in service organizations: Exploring the individual effects of brand experience dimensions', *Journal of Brand Management*, 20(5): 404–423.

Oliver, R. (1999). 'Whence consumer loyalty?', *Journal of Marketing*, 63(4): 33–44.

Osgood, C. E. and Tannenbaum, P. H. (1955). 'The principle of congruity in the prediction of attitude change', *Psychological Review*, 62(1): 42–55.

Pine, B. J. II and Gilmore, J. H. (2011). *The Experience Economy*, Updated edition, Boston, MA: Harvard Business Review Press.

Schmitt, B. H. (1999). *Experiential Marketing: How to Get Customers to Sense, Feel, Think, Act, Relate to Your Company and Brands*, New York: The Free Press.

Shoemaker, S. and Lewis, R. C. (1999). 'Customer loyalty: The future of hospitality marketing', *International Journal of Hospitality Management*, 18(4): 345–370.

Walter, N., Cleff, T. and Chu, G. (2013). 'Brand experience's influence on customer satisfaction and loyalty: A mirage in marketing research?', *International Journal of Management Research and Business Strategy*, 2(1): 130–144, Available from: http://ijmrbs.com/ijmrbsadmin/upload/IJMRBS_50e 554b968e3f.pdf [Accessed: 13 January 2016].

Youjae, Y. and Suna, L. (2004). 'What influences the relationship between customer satisfaction and repurchase intention? Investigating the effects of adjusted expectations and customer loyalty', *Psychology and Marketing*, 21(5): 351–373.

30

RELATIONSHIP MARKETING ON SOCIAL SOFTWARE PLATFORMS

Sandra Maria Correia Loureiro and Eduardo Moraes Sarmento

Introduction

Relationship marketing strategies are typically designed to gather information in order to help firms to identify and retain customers or guests. Firms organize relationship marketing programmes, described as 'the ongoing process of engaging in cooperative and collaborative activities and programmes with immediate and end-user customers to create or enhance mutual economic value at reduced cost' (Parvatiyar and Sheth 2000: p. 9). Examples of programmes include: (1) loyalty card programmes, (2) company credit cards, (3) opting in for personalized offers delivered via mailing and (4) via e-mail lists, and (5) rebate offers (Noble and Phillips 2004).

With the advent of Web 2.0, we are witnessing a change in the form of communication. Web 2.0 technologies have caused three effects: (1) a shift in the locus of activity from the desktop to the Web, (2) a shift in the locus of value production from the firm to the consumer, and (3) a shift in the locus of power away from the firm to the consumer. Web 2.0 consists of a series of technological innovations whereby the creation of content and ideas is fostered inexpensively, which leads to user collaboration with brands, shifting the focus from organizations to consumers, individuals to communities, nodes to networks, publishing to participation, and intrusion to invitation (Berthon et al. 2012).

In this connection, managers are becoming aware of the ability of Web 2.0 to connect and reinforce the bond with their stakeholders, particularly with customers or guests. Therefore, this chapter is intended to give an overview of the relationship marketing paradigm, its conceptualizations, driving forces and multiple consumer–brand relationships, which can be developed face-to-face and through social software platforms.

The remainder of this chapter is organized as follows. First, the foundation and conceptualization of relationship marketing are presented. This is followed by a theoretical argument about multiple consumer–brand relationships and social software platforms. In order to better understand the phenomenon, we conduct semi-structured interviews with 15 hotel managers with an average duration of 60 minutes and we also explore how luxury hotels are using social software platforms, particularly Facebook, as an e-tool. Finally, the chapter provides a set of directions for future research, conclusions and managerial implications.

Theoretical background

Relationship marketing foundation and conceptualization

In the late 1980s a new paradigm emerged in marketing: relationship marketing (Grönroos 1990a; Sheth et al. 1988; Webster 1992). Business practice exhorts both the customer and supplier to be close and form collaborative relationships (Copulsky and Wolf 1990; Goldberg 1988). This change in focus from value exchanges to value creation relationships has led organizations to develop a more integrative approach, whereby other firms are not always competitors and rivals, but may be partners in providing value to customers.

Five main environmental and organizational forces may be considered responsible for the trend towards relationships between producers and consumers: (1) rapid technological advancements, especially in information technology; (2) companies' adoption of total quality programmes; (3) the growth of the service economy; (4) the organizational development processes leading to empowerment of individuals and teams; and (5) the increase in competitive intensity leading to concern for customer retention. These forces reduce the reliance of producers, as well as consumers, on middlemen to effect the consummation and facilitation processes of relationships.

Indeed, the growth of competitiveness, more enterprises producing similar products, but above all the development of information technology, leads producers to become more knowledgeable about their consumers through sophisticated databases that capture information about each interaction with consumers.

The Total Quality Management (TQM) movement allowed organizations to provide quality products and services to customers at the lowest possible prices. In order to do so, it became necessary to involve suppliers and customers in implementing the programme at all levels of the value chain. TQM also led organizations to establish and implement reward systems and develop processes to empower individuals and teams.

Therefore, retaining customers, influencing repeat purchases, fostering trust and facilitating future marketing have become more and more important for all organizations. At the same time, producer organizations are giving more importance to the service component of their products. Regarding organizations that essentially provide services, such as the tourism industry, particularly hotels and other lodgings, these are organizations where services and the relationship with guests become a crucial point in order to provide a favourable experience (Pizam 2010; Loureiro 2014).

Nevertheless, how can we define relationship marketing? The following three definitions, from some of the founders of this field of knowledge, give us an overall view of the meaning of relationship marketing:

> To establish, maintain, and enhance (usually but not necessarily long-term) relationships with customers and other partners, at a profit, so that the objectives of the parties involved are met. This is achieved by a mutual exchange and fulfilment of promises.
>
> *(Grönroos 1990b: p. 138)*

> Relationship marketing refers to all marketing activities directed toward establishing, developing, and maintaining successful relational exchanges.
>
> *(Morgan and Hunt 1994: p. 22)*

315

Relationship marketing is the ongoing process of engaging in cooperative and collaborative activities and programs with immediate and end-user customers to create or enhance mutual economic value at reduced cost.

(Parvatiyar and Sheth 2000: p. 9)

In sum, relationship marketing is a process of exchange and mutual cooperation that has been shown to generate strong customer relationships that enhance customer loyalty and firm profits (Abdul-Muhmin 2005; Chiu et al. 2005; Palmatier et al. 2006). Gummesson (2008) alludes to total relationship marketing, meaning the connections among the networks of suppliers and customers. Therefore several assumptions are presented:

- It is marketing based on relationships, networks and interaction.
- It recognizes that marketing is embedded in the total management of the selling organization's networks, the market and society.
- It is directed to long-term win-win relationships with individual customers.
- Value is created jointly between the parties involved (goods and services are created with the customers and other stakeholders, co-creation).
- It transcends the boundaries between specialist functions and disciplines.
- It is made tangible through the thirty market (30 types of relationships mentioned by Gummesson when regarding several stakeholders), mega (operating on the societal level and concerning relationships to authorities, the media and so on) and nano (existing on the organizational level, that is, the case of relationships between internal customers) relationships.

Multiple consumer–brand relationships

Embedded in the conceptualization of relationship marketing are the interconnections between brands and consumers. According to the American Marketing Association, a brand is a 'Name, term, design, symbol, or any other feature that identifies one seller's good or service as distinct from those of other sellers' (AMA 2007). The current definition takes both the logo and legal perspectives simultaneously. The definition provided by Kapferer and Mayring (1992: p. 11) highlights that:

> a brand is not a product, it is the product's essence, its meaning, and its direction, and it defines its identity in time and space . . . Too often brands are examined through their component parts: the brand name, its logo, design, or packaging, advertising or sponsorship, or image or name recognition, or very recently, in terms of financial brand valuation. Real brand management, however, begins much earlier, with a strategy and a consistent, integrated vision, its central concept is brand identity, not brand image.

Here intangibility emerges in the word 'essence', but also in the value system. Consumers' decisions are influenced by their cultural values. Through the brand's value system, its heritage and consumers' personal experience, consumers may or may not see a reflection of their own identity and values.

A brand is the expression of the relationship between stakeholders, particularly consumers, and a firm or product (which could be a hotel, a restaurant, a spa or other lodgings). Indeed, a strong relationship between customers and the company may help to build a successful brand

(McKenna 1991). As Loureiro (2015a: p. 419) points out, 'brands can live and interact through their managers and act or re-act to the consumers'. Brands are regarded as having a personality like a human being. In fact, following the interdependency and attraction theories, emotional attachment may be created between human beings and animals, places, lodgings, special objects, brands (Schouten and McAlexander 1995; Price et al. 2000; Ahuvia 2005; Loureiro 2015a) and even human brands or celebrities (Thomson 2006). In the field of consumer behaviour, Thomson et al. (2005) identified a higher-order emotional attachment construct consisting of three factors: affection, passion and connection. Thus, attachments reflect an emotional bond similar to love. The quality of the relationship between brands and consumers is associated with self-connection, when the consumer's inner and social self fits the identity system of a brand; the interactions leading to interdependence; trust in the brand's promises and accountability for its actions; commitment or the intention to continue the relationship; and having faith in the future of the relationship, promoting its longevity. Intimacy lies in the elaborate knowledge structures and beliefs that identify the brand as superior and irreplaceable (Wood 1982); and an overall relationship of satisfaction and strength which represents a brand's positive orientation towards the consumer (Fournier 1998).

Regarding the process behind creating and maintaining relationships, firms (such as hotels, restaurants or other lodgings) should propose the brand system value and brand identity as a form of cooperation between the different stakeholders. Communication of the brand identity can lead to an inner self and social identification with the brand by consumers or guests and to an attachment which contributes to a connection (Loureiro et al. 2012; Loureiro 2014). A guest or customer tends to form connections with a restaurant, lodging or place (a brand) that become meaningful in association with their own self and/or consistent with a reference group (which could be family, friends, a professional group, a sport, celebrities or brand communities). This connection can be justified and reinforced by the positive image, credibility and reputation of the brand, and also because consumers identify with celebrities, reference groups and other consumer groups who use and approve the brand (Baek et al. 2010; Brown et al. 2003).

Parallel to identification is the personal experience of potential guests when looking for a hotel or destination to visit (Loureiro 2015b) and also during the stay and afterwards. Having a positive experience can engage the guest in a process of activation leading to strong positive emotions such as delight (consumers will be more than satisfied) (Oliver et al. 1997; Loureiro 2010). Strong emotions can create a close link with the lodging or destination that keeps the two partners affectively committed.

A committed consumer is more likely to want to continue the relationship with the brand and will be more likely to speak favourably about it (Loureiro et al. 2012), forgive mistakes, promote the brand to others, pay a premium price and make sacrifices (Loureiro 2011). All this engagement process could be mediated and influenced by several variables such as personality traits, lifestyle, self-esteem, value system, gender, age or a country's social culture.

Nevertheless, non-identification with the hotel, destination or product supplied, dysfunctional communication (unfavourable word of mouth using social networking and blogs), breaches of ethics, and antagonistic anti-brand relations waged for reasons of politics, values or transgression (Johnson et al. 2011; Kozinets and Handelman 2004) can plague companies and have harmful effects. Negative interconnections contribute to developing bad consumer–brand relationships, or even avoiding a relationship. Previous studies have highlighted that negative emotions tend to be more valuable and remembered better than positive ones in an adaptive sense, and so avoiding danger is more critical for survival than seeking pleasure (Baumeister et al. 2001; Thomson 2006).

Social software platforms

Virtual communities are social relationship aggregations that emerge from the Internet when enough people embark on long public discussions and create webs of personal relationships in cyberspace (Rheingold 1994, 2000). Fernback and Thompson (1995) regard virtual communities as social relationships forged in cyberspace through repeated contact within a specified place with set boundaries (e.g. a conference or chat line), which is symbolically delineated by topics of interest. Virtual communities are groups of people with common interests and shared goals, who use computer-mediated communication technology as the basis of communication instead of face-to-face, that is, groups of people who engage in many-to-many online interactions (Williams and Cothrel 2000; Blanchard and Markus 2004).

Miller et al. (2009) summarize these definitions by suggesting that such communities operate in a wide range of Internet forums, including markets and auction sites, electronic bulletin boards, list servers, social networking sites (SNSs), blog hosts or sites, gaming communities and shared-interest websites (online brand community).

Boyd and Ellison (2007) state that SNSs (e.g. Facebook, LinkedIn, Hi5, Netlog, Twitter, YouTube, TripAdvisor) allow individuals to build a public or semi-public profile within a bounded system, to interact and share connections with other users on a list and to view and navigate their lists of connections and those made by others within the system. Since the creation of Facebook in 2006, a very popular SNS, social networks have quickly become a platform on which citizens feel comfortable interacting with each other. They have not only become a sociological phenomenon, but also a marketing opportunity that firms want to be part of.

Facebook can have a real impact on the four stages of purchasing decision processes that follow recognition of need: the search for information, evaluation of alternatives, purchase and subsequent evaluation. With the appropriate applications, firms can also create a system on Facebook that allows business transactions to be finalized without referring to the firm's own website or a physical store. In this sense, 'f-commerce' (Facebook commerce) or 's-commerce' (social commerce) complements e-commerce. Through such an exchange of opinions and ideas in online spaces, known as 'e-WoM' (electronic word-of-mouth), consumers and the firm co-create the brand's image together.

Although studies on consumers' online brand relationships are still scarce, previous studies started to analyse how consumers are engaging and collaborating with firms, using social software platforms. For instance, Michaelidou et al. (2011) examine how firms operating in business-to-business markets use and perceive social networks, how effective they find them, and the main barriers they encounter in this area. Muntinga et al. (2011) analyse consumers' online brand-related activities and their consequences for firms. Another study shows that social support and website quality (meaning the tourist's overall judgement of a website's excellence and superiority) positively influence the user's intention to use s-commerce and to continue using a social networking site. These effects are found to be mediated by the quality of the relationship between the user and social networking (Liang et al. 2011). In the tourism context, Loureiro (2015b) tests the mediated effect of emotions (pleasure, arousal and dominance) between website quality and attitude and intentions to visit.

Although there is no standard method of evaluating websites, and there are no standard website attributes or features that can be integrated into website evaluation in tourism and hospitality, Loureiro (2015b) reviewed the components of website quality that were identified in prior studies and published in tourism and hospitality journals. She found that the aspects of visual appeal, information (content), ease of use and interactive features (Han and Mills

2006; Park et al. 2007) are among the most consistently employed and appropriate to the context of destination websites (island website quality).

The study points out that a well-designed, uncluttered structure, appropriate multimedia features and colours, easily used navigational cues, interactive features and well-balanced information will make potential tourists feel in control and autonomous. Positive emotions felt when browsing a website contribute significantly to willingness to visit the destination and recommend it to others.

In this connection, social software platforms allow tourists greater involvement in the selection and decision-making process, as well as in co-creating products. Through online word-of-mouth, consumers become the protagonists of brand communication, not only in their role as disseminators of information but also as generators of new ideas and promoters of either fidelity to or even rejection of some of those brands.

Insights from luxury hotels

The purpose of the case study is to explore the co-creation of hospitality experiences and the use of social software platforms by luxury hotels. Thus, the aims of this exploratory study are to: (1) capture enhancers and tools used in luxury hotels to co-create hospitality experiences with guests; and (2) explore how luxury hotels use social software platforms, particularly Facebook, as an e-tool.

Methodology

Regarding the methodology employed, the first step was the hotel selection process; the second step considered contact with managers and holding the interviews; and the last step was the analysis of websites and Facebook pages. The selection of hotels starts in Booking.com. This website has about 250,000 registered hotels in 177 countries and allows a search for hotels by region and theme. For the purpose of this study, hotels in Portugal with luxury as their main concept (5-star rating) were selected.

After searching through the online platform, a list of 100 Portuguese hotels was formed. From this total, 20 located in Lisbon were randomly selected to contact and check the information appearing on the website. Each interview began by explaining the purpose of the research and the request to record, then following the semi-structured questions, according to Gubrium and Holstein (2001) and Johnson (2001). The average length of each interview was 60 minutes. The main specific questions asked were: In this hotel what are the core features of the relationship with guests to co-create a favourable hospitality experience? What tools do you employ to achieve this favourable relationship? After 15 interviews no new or relevant information emerged, that is, saturation was achieved (Saumure and Given 2008). Participants are between 35 and 50 years old and have 5–15 years of experience in their position.

Regarding data treatment, we followed McCracken's (1988) process and started with an impressionistic reading of transcriptions and identification of recurrent enhancers and tools employed. The second level of interpretation involved cross-person analysis in order to discover patterns among individuals that could help structure an understanding of the elements behind the core features of the hospitality relationship experience. Concerning the hotels' Facebook pages, we carried out content analysis for a period of one year, analysing likes, posts and comments.

Findings

Our analysis yielded five core enhancers to create an environment to arouse customers' experience in luxury five-star hotels: (1) Personalized service, (2) Brand image, (3) Service quality, (4) Contact with guests and (5) Adapted services.

(1)   Personalized service: Treat guests as unique; hotels are aware of individual needs and wishes, which should be reflected in hotels' services. Mentioned as the main enhancer of customer experience, a personalized service is a major step towards creating memorable experiences. Know the name, profile and particular tastes and interests of guests.

(2)   Brand image: To enhance customers' experiences, managers and staff are concerned with making a connection with guests even before their arrival; in this way brand image is important not only to transmit to customers the hotel's identity and individual character, but also to reach the hotel's target.

(3)   Service quality: In luxury hotels, service quality is extremely important and has to be among the core enhancers offered. Excellence, perfection and special attention to detail are characteristics that have to be presented in what the hotel offers.

(4)   Contact with guests: Personal contact with guests promotes a good environment to develop the customer experience. A close relationship with customers helps in getting quick feedback from them about the hotel experience and allows customers' wishes and complaints to be heard, which is indispensable in arousing memorable experiences.

(5)   Adapted services: It is important to adapt services to provide customers with the 'something more' factor and to surprise them. Managers and staff have to understand customers, to adapt services focusing on each hotel target, which could be a way to differentiate.

Moreover, managers also mention some tools used in luxury hotels which contribute to co-creating hospitality relationship experiences: (1) gastronomy, (2) decoration, (3) spa and wellness, (4) staff and (5) social media.

(1)   Gastronomy: Related to food and beverage services, gastronomy is the preferred tool used by hotels to engage customers through taste, smells and vision.

(2)   Decoration (atmospheric cues): An important tool in the aesthetic composition of the hotel; decoration is related to design, sophistication and hotel image.

(3)   Spa and wellness: Including spa and wellness services, massage, hairdressers and gyms, these are mentioned as important tools that hotel managers use to relax and change customers' mood.

(4)   Staff: Staff should be aligned with the hotel's identity and values and should always be ready to attend customers. A crucial point in engaging with and involving guests is a good connection between staff and guests.

(5)   Social media: Online social media (like Facebook or other more professional versions) are tools hotels are investing in. As a place to interact with customers, social media allow managers to be in touch with customers, before and after their stay; they are also a place to learn more about the client and obtain quick feedback about services.

Based on our content analysis of the hotels' Facebook pages, we can point out that:

(1) Potential guests tend to look first at the number of likes and then search for information about the hotel (such as room size, room service, decoration, photos);

(2) Hotel managers tend to post announcements, events, advertising, and links shared by other users;

(3) On the side of hotel managers, there is no coherent and consistent communication policy regarding Facebook and web pages, that is, posts and photos are not checked, renewed or revised regularly, and questions asked by guests and potential guests are not always answered.

Here, emotional ties (stimulating guests' feelings and changing their mood) and sensorial appeal (engaging guests' senses and emphasizing the aesthetic aspect) are core aspects, which together with engagement and participation in social software platforms contribute to a favourable hospitality relationship experience.

Conclusions, managerial implications and further research

Relationship marketing has been at the core of research in recent years. Although some efforts to understand relationship experiences in tourism have been made in previous research, little has been added to tourism theory considering a marketing approach, and mainly the business (hotel) perspective as part of the process of co-creating hospitality relationship experiences with guests.

Based on the findings, we may highlight that the crucial point is to build a relationship with guests to engage and connect them to the organization (managers and staff) (see Figure 30.1). The interactions between guests and hotel staff allow managers to be alert to their customers' wishes and needs and differentiate the offer, involving guests' subjective and emotional aspects. Building and maintaining online engagement, through the website SNS pages, is essential to be closer to guests and co-create experiences with them. Top managers in hotels should be aware that to engage guests five points are crucial: (1) assess guests' needs and interests; (2) develop rules of engagement online and offline, and ensure that staff understand them; (3) identify the right managers for the online and offline relationship process; (4) establish an internal and external process to promote the relationship with guests; and finally (5) train staff and deploy the process.

Particularly in the case of engagement through social software platform communities, the managers dealing with these platforms should (1) continuously read and consider the content in such platforms, that is, the ongoing narrative (stories) which inspires, informs and connects; (2) have a deep understanding of how participants within the community engage and the tools they use to do so; (3) connect members of the community in mutually beneficial ways; (4) sustain efforts over time, ensuring the community is healthy and productive; and (5) promote the collaborative efforts of participants who share and co-create the relationship experience (the hotel manager delegated to deal with these online communities should boost participation and interaction). Thus, managing social software platforms demands great effort, not only to stimulate participation, post photos and information about the hotel, but also to provide answers to questions, solve problems and be a source of knowledge in order to help other managers and staff to continuously improve the service provided to guests.

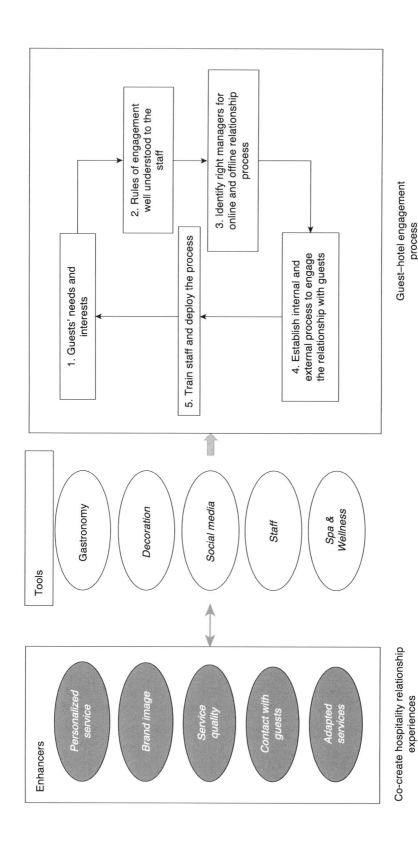

Figure 30.1 Hospitality relationship experiences as drivers of guest–hotel engagement

Source: Authors' elaboration.

Despite the rigour of the method applied in this research, we can point out some limitations regarding not only our study but also what we did not find in the literature. These can also be suggestions for future avenues of research. Firstly, the scarce literature relating to customer experience, customer engagement and the use of social software platforms in the tourism industry, and less specifically, regarding hospitality. This gap in the literature also reflects limitations in specific models to sustain guests' relationship experience and the use of social software platforms applied to the hospitality industry. Secondly, the reduced sample size could be also considered a limitation. A larger sample, including other countries and a deeper analysis, in order to consider cultural aspects, could be interesting for future research. Finally, the difficulty in getting positive feedback from managers to be part of the research and schedule meetings should also be mentioned.

Regarding future empirical research, some suggestions may be made:

(1) Investigate the drivers of anti-branding attitude; who are the initiators, leaders and organizers of the bloggers or other viral mechanisms of anti-branding movements; what are the new attitudes and behaviours?
(2) Use mixed techniques to go further towards understanding the engagement and interconnection relationship between guests and hotels, considering both personal contact and social software platforms.
(3) Future studies can explore user profiles (age, gender, income or social status, personality traits, self-esteem) to analyse how different user profiles influence offline and online experience perceptions, emotional feelings, behavioural intentions and actual use. For instance, extroversion involves characteristics like talkativeness, assertiveness and risk-taking and this type of guest could appreciate more interaction with website managers or prefer not to use the website to book hotels or other lodgings.

References

Abdul-Muhmin, G. (2005). 'Instrumental and interpersonal determinants of relationship satisfaction and commitment in industrial markets', *Journal of Business Research*, 58(5): 619–628.

Ahuvia, C. (2005). 'Beyond the extended self: Loved objects and consumers' identity narratives', *Journal of Consumer Research*, 32(1): 171–184.

AMA (2007). 'Brand', Available from https://www.ama.org/resources/pages/dictionary.aspx?dLetter=B [Accessed: 2 June 2015].

Baek, H., Kim, J. and Yu, H. (2010). 'The differential roles of brand credibility and brand prestige in consumer brand choice', *Psychology and Marketing*, 27(7): 662–678.

Baumeister, F., Bratslavsky, E., Finkenauer, C. and Vohs, D. (2001). 'Bad is stronger than good', *Review of General Psychology*, 5(4): 323–370.

Berthon, R., Pitt, F., Planger, K. and Shapiro, D. (2012). 'Marketing meets Web 2.0, social media, and creative consumers: Implications for international marketing strategy', *Business Horizons*, 55(3): 261–271.

Blanchard, L. and Markus, L. (2004). 'The experienced "sense" of a virtual community: Characteristics and processes', *The Data Base for Advanced Information Systems*, 35(1): 64–79.

Boyd, M. and Ellison, B. (2007). 'Social network sites: Definition, history, and scholarship', *Journal of Computer-Mediated Communication*, 13(1): 210–230.

Brown, S., Kozinets, V. and Sherry, F. (2003). 'Teaching old brands new tricks: Retro branding and the revival of brand meaning', *Journal of Marketing*, 6(73): 19–33.

Chiu, C., Hsieh, C., Li, C. and Lee, M. (2005). 'Relationship marketing and consumer switching behavior', *Journal of Business Research*, 58(12): 1681–1689.

Copulsky, R. and Wolf, J. (1990). 'Relationship marketing: Positioning for the future', *Journal of Business Strategy*, 11(4), 16–20.

Fernback, J. and Thompson, B. (1995). 'Virtual communities: Abort, retry, failure? Computer mediated communication and the American collectivity', Available from http://www.well.com/~hlr/texts/ VCcivil.html [Accessed: 12 February 2013].

Fournier, S. (1998). 'Consumers and their brands: Developing relationship theory in consumer research', *Journal of Consumer Research*, 24(4): 343–373.

Goldberg, B. (1988). 'Relationship marketing', *Direct Marketing*, 51(6): 103–105.

Grönroos, C. (1990a). 'Relationship approach to marketing in service contexts: The marketing and organizational behavior interface', *Journal of Business Research*, 20(1): 3–11.

Grönroos, C. (1990b). *Service Management and Marketing*, Lexington, MA: Lexington Books.

Gubrium, F. and Holstein, A. (2001). 'From the individual interview to the interview society', in J. F. Gubrium and J. A. Holstein (eds.), *Handbook of Interview Research* (pp. 3–32), Thousand Oaks, CA: Sage.

Gummesson, E. (2008). *Total Relationship Marketing: Marketing Management, Relationship Strategy, CRM, and a New Dominant Logic for the Value-creating Network Economy*, Oxford: Butterworth-Heinemann.

Han, H. and Mills, E. (2006). 'Zero acquaintance benchmarking at travel destination websites: What is the first impression that national tourism organizations try to make?', *International Journal of Tourism Research*, 8(6): 405–430.

Johnson, M. (2001). 'In-depth interviewing', in J. F. Gubrium and J. A. Holstein (eds.), *Handbook of Interview Research*, 2nd edition (pp. 103–120), Thousand Oaks, CA: Sage.

Johnson, R., Matear, M. and Thomson, M. (2011). 'A coal in the heart: Self-relevance as a post-exit predictor of consumer anti-brand actions', *Journal of Consumer Research*, 38(1): 108–125.

Kapferer, J. and Mayring, P. (1992). *Strategic Brand Management*, London: Kogan Page.

Kozinets, V. and Handelman, M. (2004). 'Adversaries of consumption: Consumer movements, activism, and ideology', *Journal of Consumer Research*, 31(3): 691–704.

Liang, T., Ho, Y., Li, W. and Turban, E. (2011). 'What drives social commerce: The role of social support and relationship quality', *International Journal of Electronic Commerce*, 16(2): 69–90.

Loureiro, S. (2010). 'Satisfying and delighting the rural tourists', *Journal of Travel and Tourism Marketing*, 27(4): 396–408.

Loureiro, S. (2011). 'Consumer's love and willingness to sacrifice for a brand', in M. MacCarthy (ed.), *Proceedings of ANZMAC conference – Marketing in the Age of Consumerism: Jekyll or Hyde?*, Perth, Australia: Monash University, Available from http://pandora.nla.gov.au/tep/25410 [Accessed: 13 November 2016].

Loureiro, S. (2014). 'The role of the rural tourism experience economy in place attachment and behavioral intentions', *International Journal of Hospitality Management*, 40: 1–9.

Loureiro, S. (2015a). 'Loving and hating brands: Multiple relationships between consumers and brands', in H.-R. Kaufmann (ed.), *Handbook of Research on Managing and Influencing Consumer Behavior* (pp. 417–438), Hershey, PA: IGI Global.

Loureiro, S. (2015b). 'The role of website quality on PAD, attitude and intentions to visit and recommend island destination', *International Journal of Tourism Research*, 17(6): 545–554.

Loureiro, S., Kaufmann, R. and Vrontis, D. (2012). 'Brand emotional connection and loyalty', *Journal of Brand Management*, 20(1): 13–27.

McCracken, G. (1988). *The Long Interview*, Newbury Park, CA: Sage.

McKenna, R. (1991). 'Marketing is everything', *Harvard Business Review*, 69(1): 65-79.

Michaelidou, N., Siamagka, N. and Christodoulides, G. (2011), 'Usage, barriers and measurement of social media marketing: An exploratory investigation of small and medium B2B brands', *Industrial Marketing Management*, 40(7): 1153–1159.

Miller, K. D., Frances, F. and Lin, S. J. (2009). 'Strategies for online communities', *Strategic Management Journal*, 30(3): 305–322.

Morgan, R. and Hunt, S. D. (1994). 'The commitment-trust theory of relationship marketing', *Journal of Marketing*, 58(3): 20–38.

Muntinga, D., Moorman, M. and Smit, E. (2011). 'Introducing COBRAs: Exploring motivations for brand-related social media use', *International Journal of Advertising*, 30(1): 13–46.

Noble, M. and Phillips, J. (2004). 'Relationship hindrance: Why would consumers not want a relationship with a retailer?', *Journal of Retailing*, 80(4): 289–303.

Oliver, L., Rust, T. and Varki, S. (1997). 'Customer delight: Foundations, findings, and managerial insight', *Journal of Retailing*, 73(3): 311–336.

Palmatier, W., Dant, P., Grewal, D. and Evans, R. (2006). 'Factors influencing the effectiveness of relationship marketing: A meta-analysis', *Journal of Marketing*, 70(4): 136–153.

Park, Y. A., Gretzel, U. and Sirakaya-Turk, E. (2007). 'Measuring website quality for online travel agencies', *Journal of Travel and Tourism Marketing*, 23(1): 15–30.

Parvatiyar, A. and Sheth, N. (2000). 'The domain and conceptual foundations of relationship market-ing', in N. Sheth and A. Parvatiyar (eds.), *Handbook of Relationship Marketing* (pp. 3–38), Thousand Oaks, CA: Sage.

Pizam, A. (2010). 'Creating memorable experiences', *International Journal of Hospitality Management*, 29(3): 343.

Price, L., Arnould, J. and Curasi, F. (2000). 'Older consumers' disposition of special possessions', *Journal of Consumer Research*, 27(2): 179–201.

Rheingold, H. (1994). 'A slice of life in my virtual community', in L. M. Harasim (ed.), *Global Networks: Computers and International Communication* (pp. 57–80), Cambridge, MA: MIT Press.

Rheingold, H. (2000). *The Virtual Community: Homesteading on the Electronic Frontier*, Cambridge, MA: MIT Press.

Saumure, K. and Given, M. (2008). 'Data saturation', in L. M. Given (ed.), *The Sage Encyclopedia of Qualitative Methods (Vol. 1)* (pp. 195–196), Thousand Oaks, CA: Sage.

Schouten, W. and McAlexander, H. (1995). 'Subcultures of consumption: An ethnography of the new bikers', *Journal of Consumer Research*, 22(1): 43–61.

Sheth, N., Gardner, M. and Garett, E. (1988). *Marketing Theory: Evolution and Evaluation*, New York: John Wiley and Sons.

Thomson, M. (2006). 'Human brands: Investigating antecedents to consumers' strong attachments to celebrities', *Journal of Marketing*, 70(3): 104–119.

Thomson, M., MacInnis, J. and Park, W. (2005). 'The ties that bind: Measuring the strength of con-sumers' emotional attachment to brands', *Journal of Consumer Psychology*, 15(1): 77–91.

Webster, F. E. Jr. (1992). 'The changing role of marketing in the corporation', *Journal of Marketing*, 6(4): 1–17.

Williams, L. and Cothrel, J. (2000). 'Four smart ways to run online communities', *Sloan Management Review*, 41(4): 81–91.

Wood, T. (1982). 'Communication and relational culture: Bases for the study of human relationships', *Communication Quarterly*, 30(2): 75–83.

31

DESTINATION BRANDING AND CUSTOMER BEHAVIOURAL INTENTIONS

The case of Istanbul as a cultural destination brand

Stella Kladou

Introduction

The importance of culture has been highlighted in a number of relevant academic works (e.g. Buhalis 2000; Richards 2002; Richards and Wilson 2004). According to Florian (2002: p. 24), 'urban renewal . . . touches upon such points as structure, programming, functions, the sort of actions and activities that characterise the image of the city, events and the chemistry of the people who operate there'. In the attempt to assess customers' behavioural intentions with regards to destination brands, researchers have built upon corporate branding studies (most commonly Aaker 1991 and Keller 1993, 2003) as they may be adjusted and put into effect in destination branding (for instance, Konecnik and Gartner 2007; Boo et al. 2009). Within these lines, a few recent studies have focused specifically on cultural destination brands (Kladou and Kehagias 2014a, 2014b), yet the rising popularity and significance of identity-based branding efforts (as recently further supported by Kavaratzis and Hatch 2013 and Kavaratzis and Ashworth 2015) call for additional investigation in what drives consumer behaviour in the case of cultural destination brands. As a result, an insight into cultural brand assets, awareness, associations, quality and loyalty emerges as necessary. The study builds upon the case of Istanbul, a developing cultural destination with arrivals that outscored those of traditionally popular destinations, such as Rome (Euromonitor International 2014). The final structural model appears beneficial for practitioners and scholars as it specifically investigates customer behavioural intentions.

Literature review

Destination brands: culture and cultural brand assets

Brands are traditionally defined as products or services 'made distinctive by their positioning relative to the competition and by their personality, which comprises a unique combination of functional attributes and symbolic values' (Hankinson and Cowking 1993: p. 10). Similarly, destination branding, according to Blain et al. (2005: p. 337), is:

> the set of marketing activities that (1) support the creation of a name, symbol, logo, word mark or other graphic that readily identifies and differentiates a destination; (2) consistently conveys the expectation of a memorable travel experience that is uniquely associated with the destination; (3) serves to consolidate and reinforce the emotional connection between the visitor and the destination; and (4) reduces consumer search costs and perceived risk.

Consistent with such definitions, the role of culture and heritage has been repeatedly emphasized in the tourism and place branding literature (Anholt 2002; Kavaratzis and Ashworth 2015).

Culture is a term with multiple meanings. Within a tourism context, cultural products become tourist products as soon as they start attracting tourists to the destination or create the motivation to extend one's stay (McKercher et al. 2004). Moreover, cultural tourist products should effectively tell a story, be accessible, qualitative, and offer a sense of authenticity and experience (McKercher et al. 2004).

From a place branding perspective, tourism and culture and heritage, next to people, export brands, governance, and investment and immigration, make up two of the six place brand dimensions (Anholt 2002). Branding a tourist destination, based on culture and heritage, just like in the case of corporate brands, may facilitate response to tourists' expectations, which, in turn, enhances overall positive experience, repeated visits and word of mouth (Bouncken et al. 2006). Besides, destination branding is defined as 'the process used to develop a unique identity and personality that is different from all competitive destinations' (Morrison and Anderson 2002: p. 17). Building upon the identity-based approach of place branding, success lies in understanding the interaction between culture, identity and image (Kavaratzis and Hatch 2013) as culture is crucial to the narrative of the place (Jensen 2007), which branding may tap into and reinforce. Three techniques are employed in various combinations in order to build successful place and destination brands through culture: 'event hallmarking', 'personality association', and the 'flagship building and signature district' (Ashworth 2009). Kavaratzis and Ashworth (2015) in their recent work review such techniques and discuss the superficial relationship created between culture and place branding given how culture is currently used for place branding purposes, while Kladou and Kehagias (2014a, 2014b) identify cultural brand assets of importance for destination brands.

Brand assets in corporate branding usually refer to brand elements (e.g. logo, slogan and tagline) and their potential financial value ('I♥NY' can be identified as an example of this approach in the case of place and destination branding). Yet, in terms of culture-based city regeneration and the economic benefit of arts and culture, interest focuses on cultural festivals and events along with industries in entertainment, arts, media and design (Dungey 2004). A great number of studies concerning, for example, heritage management, focus on museums and art galleries and other flagship projects (Orbasli 2000). In short, specific cultural representations, which may lead to increased attractiveness and competitiveness (for example, see Arzeni 2009), are considered to contribute to the destination being identified as unique; therefore, such representations of culture constitute potential brand assets. A review of cultural tourism and culture in the destination branding literature suggests specific attributes which tourists may perceive as important cultural brand assets. These attributes refer to monuments/heritage sites, cultural events, street culture, cuisine, traditions, contribution to world heritage, entertainment/nightlife options, cultural festivals, museums and art centres (Evans 2003; Richards 2007; McKercher et al. 2006; Prentice 1994; Trueman et al. 2004; van der Ark and Richards 2006; Konecnik and Gartner 2007).

From awareness to image and quality and from there to loyalty

In an attempt to investigate the impact of branding efforts using a bottom–up approach, studies on the consumer perspective still largely focus upon awareness, associations or image, quality and loyalty.

Awareness represents the strength of the brand's presence in the mind of the target audience along a continuum (Aaker 1996). Destination branding scholars often assess awareness by including items connected to the destination selection process (Boo et al. 2009; Motameni and Shahrokhi 1998; Yoo and Donthu 2001). Brand associations reflect consumers' perceptions (Keller 1993) and, in line with the aforementioned identity-based approach to place branding (Kavaratzis and Hatch 2013), they are often referred to as brand image and include visitors' perceptions of values, quality, feelings and brand personality (de Chernatony and Dall'Olmo Riley 1998; Hosany et al. 2006; Kapferer 1997; Sirgy and Su 2000; Phau and Lau 2000). Focusing particularly on culture, other associations refer to hospitality, authenticity and exoticness (Lassar et al. 1995; Boo et al. 2009; Buhalis 2000; Iversen and Hem 2008; Ambler et al. 2002; Sweeney and Soutar 2001; Dodds et al. 1991). Brand quality discusses organization, atmosphere and quality experiences (Aaker 1991; Sweeney and Soutar 2001; Boo et al. 2009; Richards 2007). Back and Parks (2003) further note that, in tourism and hospitality, loyalty has been considered as the result of multidimensional cognitive attitudes towards a specific brand. Brand loyalty has been defined as the attachment a customer has to a brand (Aaker 1991; Keller 2003), which emerges as the outcome of attitudinal and behavioural evaluation (Keller 2003; Odin et al. 2001; Yoo and Donthu 2001; Boo et al. 2009; Aaker 1991).

Awareness, association, quality and loyalty are not dimensions independent from one another. Higher levels of awareness mean that the brand is more dominant in the mind of potential travellers, thereby increasing the probability of the brand being considered (Yasin et al. 2007). A destination brand represents a potential node, to which a variety of associations are linked (Pike et al. 2010). As brand awareness relates to the ability of the consumer to recall and recognize the brand (Ferns and Walls 2012), brand assets unique to a place may also contribute to increased awareness. Furthermore, given that awareness reflects the strength of the brand node in the minds of consumers, it may be expected that greater awareness will enhance the associations linked to the destination, both those that compose the brand image (Bigné et al. 2013) and those related to quality (Pike et al. 2010). Previous literature on consumer behaviour has recognized that the evaluation judgements of a product (e.g. quality perceptions) are influenced by the image of that product (Bloemer et al. 1999). The significant role of image in the evaluation of perceived quality has also been discussed both in the services sector (Grönroos 1993) and in a hospitality context (Kotler et al. 1996).

In tourism research, the causal relationship between associations and perceived quality has been confirmed in several works focusing on tourism destinations (Bigné et al. 2005; Kladou and Kehagias 2014a, 2014b). Previous research has discussed the direct connection between unique characteristics and quality (Konecnik and Gartner 2007) or between unique image and quality (Qu et al. 2011). Moreover, according to the model proposed by Chen and Phou (2013), the impact of image on loyalty is indirect, while in other studies, quality and associations are both found to enhance loyalty (Jayanti and Ghosh 1996). More recently, some efforts to shed light on to the complete 'network' of relationships between awareness, image/associations, quality and loyalty have been noted (Boo et al. 2009). Still, there is room for studies that will investigate the causal relationships and provide a comprehensive understanding of the challenges which destinations face given their attempt to capitalize on different sets of assets and simultaneously prioritize the needs of distinct target markets.

The case of Istanbul as a cultural destination

In order to assess the dimensions of assets, awareness, associations, quality and loyalty, the investigation of a cultural destination seems appropriate. In Istanbul, most cultural activities, museums and historical attractions are located within a cultural triangle (Aksoy and Enlil 2011), which is well communicated (Alvarez and Yarcan 2010). The nomination of Istanbul as a 2010 European Capital of Culture was part of an attempt to develop a brand name that would link the modern city with its history and heritage. In the same direction of establishing a city brand, there are evident attempts to capitalize on internationally known Turkish artists. This, for instance, leads to publicity for the Nobel literature award winner Orhan Pamuk and his Museum of Innocence (a museum in Istanbul which is based on one of his novels that carries the same title). The transformation of former industrial regions further supports the cultural city brand by converting former industrial plants into cultural centres, leisure facilities and museums. Despite the significant developments of Istanbul in the cultural arena during the past decade, there are also major problems and difficulties that challenge the city's potential to become a global centre of culture (Alvarez and Yarcan 2010). Within these lines, investigating such an emerging cultural destination may further benefit practitioners.

Methodology

This study seeks to provide an insight into assets, awareness, associations and quality as they may lead to loyal visitors who will proceed to make recommendations and return visits. Unique assets, in particular, influence familiarity and thus may attract more tourists (Horng et al. 2011). Therefore, a relationship between assets and awareness is expected (this relationship in Kladou and Kehagias (2014a, 2014b) takes the form of a positive, causal one). According to the path model suggested by Boo et al. (2009), associations and quality form the alternative construct of brand experience which (1) is influenced by awareness and (2) impacts on loyalty. To reach the research goal, the role of cultural brand assets with regards to awareness, associations, quality and loyalty, as well as their in-between structural relationships, need to be further investigated and confirmed.

Respondents evaluated the level of their agreement with specific propositions. The research instrument builds upon Aaker's (1991) dimensions of assets, awareness, associations, quality and loyalty, but, like in the case of Kladou and Kehagias (2014a, 2014b), it considers cultural brand assets that may contribute to the unique selling proposition of Istanbul. Therefore the study investigates the significance of art centres (AST1) (Orbasli 2000), entertainment/nightlife (AST2) (Richards 2007; Evans 2003), cultural festivals (AST3) (Richards 2007; Evans 2003; McKercher et al. 2006), traditions (AST4) (Richards 2007) and street culture (AST5) (Evans 2003; van der Ark and Richards 2006). Focusing on the awareness dimensions, tourists may identify Istanbul as a famous cultural destination (Motameni and Shahrokhi 1998; Oh 2000; Boo et al. 2009), as a city coming to their minds immediately when thinking about culture (Kaplanidou and Vogt 2003; Boo et al. 2009) and, finally, as a city the characteristics of which come to their minds immediately (Arnett et al. 2003; Pappu and Quester 2006; Yoo and Donthu 2001; Boo et al. 2009). In terms of associations, Istanbul may be evaluated with questions adapted by Aaker (1991) that refer to the city personality (ASS1), its interesting culture (ASS2) and to fulfilling cultural experiences (ASS3), but also adapted by Buhalis (2000) and relating to the possibility of having an authentic cultural experience. Similarly, the items evaluating quality include: 'I can rely on there being a good atmosphere' (QUA1) (adapted by Aaker 1991), 'Istanbul provides quality cultural experiences' (QUA2) (adapted by Aaker 1991; Sweeney and Soutar 2001; Boo et al. 2009), and 'This experience has increased my cultural knowledge' (QUA3) (adapted by Richards 2007). Finally, evaluating loyalty is possible through tourists' assessments of four items: tourists rated how much they enjoy visiting Istanbul (LOY1) (Baloglu 2001; Back and Parks 2003; Boo et al. 2009), Istanbul being their preferred choice for a cultural holiday (LOY2) (Keller 2003; Odin et al. 2001; Yoo and Donthu 2001; Boo et al. 2009), Istanbul meeting their expectations (LOY3) (Aaker 1991), and recommending friends/relatives to visit Istanbul (LOY4) (Arnett et al. 2003; del Río et al. 2001; Boo et al. 2009).

The research addresses international tourists. Contacting tourism authorities led to a pool of tourist guides and hotels which facilitated the collection of 450 questionnaires. The final analysis included questionnaires which were at least 90% complete. Preliminary analysis included testing for normality and led to a few outliers being removed. As a result, a final sample of 377 usable questionnaires (response rate: 83.8%) was tested for reliability and validity and, upon confirmation, further analysed in SPSS and AMOS.

Study findings

In line with the actual international tourists' demographics, the majority of the respondents are Americans, Germans or British (10.1%, 10.6% and 9.5%, respectively). Additionally, 54.6% of the respondents are female tourists, with 26.9% of the sample being between 20 and 29 years old, and 25% between 30 and 39. In terms of education, 27% hold a bachelor's degree, and 28% a master's or doctorate degree. 45.7% are currently employed with 26.7% holding managerial positions. Finally, 19.1% have an annual gross household income of 40–50,000 euro, and 22% more than 60,000 euro.

Although historical and religious associations are primarily what visitors link Istanbul with prior to their visit (87.9% and 76.3%, respectively), street culture, traditions, landscapes and cuisine are also identified as quite significant pre-existing associations (identified as such by 60%, 58.5%, 58.2% and 56.7%, respectively). Furthermore, 58.1% of the sample was visiting Istanbul for the first time. Istanbul could be a preferred choice for a cultural holiday for 60.2% of the respondents and 89.9% of them would recommend it to others. The travel motives respondents recognized are depicted in Table 31.1.

Fit indices help in assessing model fit and the structural relationships. The aforementioned literature review suggests various alternative causal relationships between the investigated dimensions; yet, in the case of Istanbul, the model depicted in Figure 31.1 appears to be confirmed.

The comparative fit index (CFI), the Tucker-Lewis index (TLI) and the goodness-of-fit index (GFI) all exceed the suggested threshold of .90 (CFI = 0.926; TLI = 0.911; GFI = 0.906).

Table 31.1 Tourists' motivations[1]

	Motives	*Valid percentage*
General	Holidays	67.4
	Business	20.7
	Conference/studies	12.7
	Visiting friends/relatives	6.4
	Shopping	10.6
Cultural[2]	History of the city	70.6
	Visiting heritage sites	57.9
	Visiting museums	40.0
	Attending festivals	18.3
	Attending events	21.2
	Visiting art centres	26.8

Source: Author.

Notes: [1] More than one answer was possible for each question.
[2] The columns refer to the cumulative valid percentage of those having recognized the relevant motive 'much' and 'very much'.

Moreover, the root mean square error of approximation (RMSEA = 0.069) is less than 0.085. According to its fit indices, the model is acceptable. Except for the measure of the χ^2 statistic, where the significance level was no greater than 0.000 (i.e. $\chi^2(df) = 312.902(113)$, significant at the 99% level), all other indices reached the level needed for their acceptance (Byrne 2001).

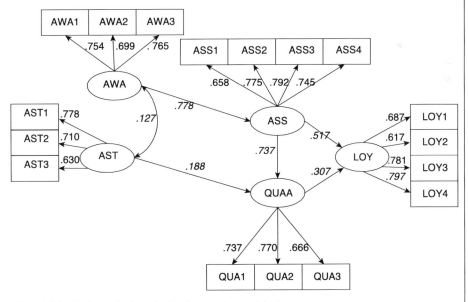

Figure 31.1 Path results (standardized regression weights)

Source: Author.

Conclusions and implications

The present study investigates a destination brand that seeks to capitalize on its cultural assets and assesses international tourists' evaluations of such branding efforts. In line with the identity-based place branding stream of research and given the significance of culture for destination branding scholars (e.g. Kavaratzis and Ashworth 2015), this study adopts a marketing perspective in order to approach the assets dimension and the causal relationships between assets, awareness, associations, quality and loyalty. The study builds upon previous literature and its findings are congruent with previous research.

In detail, in the case of Istanbul, analysis reveals that cultural brand assets and awareness are exogenous parameters in the evaluation of the cultural destination brand. Given that brand awareness relates to the ability of the consumer to recall and recognize the brand (Ferns and Walls 2012), brand assets unique to a place may also contribute to increased awareness. Thus, assets and awareness appear to be correlated. Furthermore, analysis suggests significant paths from assets and associations to quality. Kotler et al. (1996) have previously established the sequence of image and quality, and earlier studies have proven the connection between unique characteristics and quality (Konecnik and Gartner 2007), and between unique image and quality (Qu et al. 2011). Moreover, loyalty is the outcome of both image and quality (Jayanti and Ghosh 1996).

The significance of all investigated dimensions emerges and aligns with previous studies in the field (Boo et al. 2009; Kladou and Kehagias 2014a, 2014b). Such findings highlight the need of evaluating destination brands not with the use of simple quantitative tools (e.g. arrivals, length of stay), but by attempting an in-depth understanding of how actual tourists experience the brand and evaluate its cultural dimension based on their experience: it appears that through the influence of unique cultural brand assets, the strength of the brand and its characteristics in people's minds, tourists will come to experience specific aspects of the brand, appreciate their quality and proceed to make recommendations and return visits. Still, some differences appear in the final form of the structural model, thereby suggesting the uniqueness of each destination in the way it is evaluated even by the same target group (in this case cultural tourists). As a result, future studies should refer to a number of different cultural destination brands in order to suggest a model of possible applicability in more brands of the same category. Additionally, practitioners may benefit further from studies assessing the destination brand more holistically, as what may emerge is the need to choose between targeting more consumer groups simultaneously or focusing on specific growing markets that align with the destination's personality and identity.

Acknowledgements

The research in Istanbul has been supported by the Scientific and Technological Research Council of Turkey.

References

Aaker, D. A. (1991). *Managing Brand Equity*, New York: Free Press.
Aaker, D. A. (1996). *Building Strong Brands*, New York: Free Press.
Aksoy, A. and Enlil, Z. (2011). *Inventory of the Cultural Economy*, Istanbul: Istanbul Bilgi University.
Alvarez, M. D. and Yarcan, Ş. (2010). 'Istanbul as a world city: A cultural perspective', *International Journal of Culture, Tourism and Hospitality Research*, 4(3): 266–276.
Ambler, T., Bhattacharya, C. B., Edell, J., Keller, K. L., Lemon, K. L. and Mittal, V. (2002). 'Relating brand and customer perspectives on marketing management', *Journal of Service Research*, 5(1): 13–25.

Anholt, S. (2002). 'Foreword to the Special Issue on place branding', *Brand Management*, 9(4–5): 229–239.

Arnett, D. B., Laverie, D. A. and Meiers, A. (2003). 'Developing parsimonious retailer equity indices using partial least squares analysis: A method and applications', *Journal of Retailing*, 79(3): 161–170.

Arzeni, S. (2009). 'Foreword', in *The Impact of Culture on Tourism* (p. 3), Paris: OECD.

Ashworth, G. J. (2009). 'The instruments of place branding: How is it done?', *European Spatial Research and Policy*, 16(1): 9–22.

Back, K.-J. and Parks, S. C. (2003). 'A brand loyalty model involving cognitive, affective, and conative brand loyalty and customer satisfaction', *Journal of Hospitality and Tourism Research*, 27(4): 419–435.

Baloglu, S. (2001). 'Image variations of Turkey by familiarity index: Informational and experiential dimensions', *Tourism Management*, 22(2): 127–133.

Bigné, J. E., Andreu, I. and Gnoth, J. (2005). 'The theme park experience: An analysis of pleasure, arousal and satisfaction', *Tourism Management*, 26(6): 833–844.

Bigné, E., Borredá, A. and María José, M. (2013). 'The store equity and its relationship with the private brand image: The moderating effect of the knowledge of private brand being recognised as the retailer's own product', *Revista Europea de Direccion y Economia de la Empresa*, 22(1): 1–10.

Blain, C., Levy, S. E. and Ritchie, J. R. B. (2005). 'Destination branding: Insights and practices from destination management organizations', *Journal of Travel Research*, 43(4): 328–338.

Bloemer, J., de Ruyter, K. and Wetzels, M. (1999). 'Linking perceived service quality and service loyalty: A multi-dimensional perspective', *European Journal of Marketing*, 33(11/12): 1082–1106.

Boo, B., Busser, J. and Baloglu, S. (2009). 'A model of customer-based brand equity and its application to multiple destinations', *Tourism Management*, 30(2): 219–231.

Bouncken, R. B., Pick, C. and Hipp, C. (2006). 'Standardization and individualization strategies of hotel brands: Matching strategy to quality management instruments and marketing in Germany', *Journal of Hospitality Marketing and Management*, 13(3): 29–51.

Buhalis, D. (2000). 'Marketing the competitive destination of the future', *Tourism Management*, 21(1): 97–116.

Byrne, B. M. (2001). *Structural Equation Modeling with AMOS: Basic Concepts, Applications, and Programming*, Mahwah, NJ: Lawrence Erlbaum.

Chen, C.-F. and Phou, S. (2013). 'A closer look at destinations: Image, personality, relationship and loyalty', *Tourism Management*, 36: 269–278.

de Chernatony, L. and Dall'Olmo Riley, F. (1998). 'Defining a brand: Beyond the literature with experts' interpretations', *Journal of Marketing Management*, 14(5): 417–443.

del Río, B., Vázquez, R. and Iglesias, V. (2001). 'The effect of brand associations on consumer response', *Journal of Consumer Marketing*, 18(5): 410–425.

Dodds, W. B., Monroe, K. B. and Grewal, D. (1991). 'Effects of price, brand, and store information on buyers' product evaluations', *Journal of Marketing Research*, 28(3): 307–319.

Dungey, J. (2004). 'Overview: Arts, culture and the local economy', *Local Economy*, 19(4): 411–413.

Euromonitor International (2014). 'Top 100 city destinations ranking', Available from: http://blog.euromonitor.com/2014/01/euromonitor-internationals-top-city-destinations-ranking.html [Accessed: 10 May 2014].

Evans, G. (2003). 'Hard-branding the cultural city – From Prado to Prada', *International Journal of Urban and Regional Research*, 27(2): 417–440.

Ferns, B. H. and Walls, A. (2012). 'Enduring travel involvement, destination brand equity, and travelers' visit intentions: A structural model analysis', *Journal of Destination Marketing and Management*, 1(1–2): 27–35.

Florian, B. (2002). 'The city as a brand: Orchestrating a unique experience', in Hauben, T., Vermeulen, M. and Patteeuw, V. (eds.), *City Branding: Image Building and Building Images* (pp. 18–31), Rotterdam: NAI Uitgevers.

Grönroos, C. (1993). 'Quality comes to service', in Scheuing, E. E and Christopher, W. F. (eds.), *The Service Quality Handbook* (pp. 17–24), New York: American Management Association.

Hankinson, G. A. and Cowking, P. (1993). *Branding in Action*, Maidenhead: McGraw-Hill.

Horng, J.-S., Liu, C.-H., Chou, H.-Y. and Tsai, C.-Y. (2011). 'Understanding the impact of culinary brand equity and destination familiarity on travel intentions', *Tourism Management*, 33(4): 815–824.

Hosany, S., Ekinci, Y. and Uysal, M. (2006). 'Destination image and destination personality: An application of branding theories to tourism places', *Journal of Business Research*, 59(5): 638–642.

Iversen, N. M. and Hem, L. E. (2008). 'Provenance associations as core values of place umbrella brands: A framework of characteristics', *European Journal of Marketing*, 42(5/6): 603–626.

Jayanti, R. K. and Ghosh, A. K. (1996). 'A structural analysis of value, quality, and price perceptions of business and leisure travelers', *Journal of Travel Research*, 39(1): 45–51.

Jensen, O. B. (2007). 'Culture stories: Understanding cultural urban branding', *Planning Theory*, 6(3): 211–236.

Kapferer, J. N. (1997). *Strategic Brand Management: Creating and Sustaining Brand Equity Long Term*, 2nd edition, London: Kogan Page.

Kaplanidou, K. and Vogt, C. (2003). 'Destination branding: Concept and measurement', Available from: http://www.tourismcenter.msu.edu [Accessed: 1 May 2010].

Kavaratzis, M. and Ashworth, G. J. (2015). 'Hijacking culture: The disconnection between local culture and place branding', *Town Planning Review*, 86(2): 155–176.

Kavaratzis, M. and Hatch, M. J. (2013). 'The dynamics of place brands: An identity-based approach to place branding theory', *Marketing Theory*, 13(1): 69–86.

Keller, K. L. (1993). 'Conceptualizing, measuring, and managing customer-based brand equity', *Journal of Marketing*, 57(1): 1–22.

Keller, K. L. (2003). *Strategic Brand Management: Building, Measuring and Managing Brand Equity*, Upper Saddle River, NJ: Prentice-Hall.

Kladou, S. and Kehagias, J. (2014a). 'Developing a structural brand equity model for cultural destinations', *Journal of Place Management and Development*, 7(2): 112–125.

Kladou, S. and Kehagias, J. (2014b). 'Assessing destination brand equity: An integrated approach', *Journal of Destination Marketing and Management*, 3(1): 2–10.

Konecnik, M. and Gartner, W. C. (2007). 'Customer-based brand equity for a destination', *Annals of Tourism Research*, 34(2): 400–421.

Kotler, P., Bowen, J. and Makens, J. (1996). *Marketing for Hospitality and Tourism*, Upper Saddle River, NJ: Prentice-Hall.

Lassar, W., Mittal, B. and Sharma, A. (1995). 'Measuring customer-based brand equity', *Journal of Consumer Marketing*, 12(4): 11–19.

McKercher, B., Ho, P. S. Y. and Du Cros, H. (2004). 'Attributes of popular cultural attractions in Hong Kong', *Annals of Tourism Research*, 31(2): 393–407.

McKercher, B., Sze Mel, W. and Tse, T. S. M. (2006). 'Are short duration cultural festivals tourist attractions?', *Journal of Sustainable Tourism*, 14(1): 55–66.

Morrison, A. M. and Anderson, D. J. (2002). 'Destination branding', Paper presented at the Missouri Association of Convention and Visitor Bureaus Annual Meeting, 10 June, Missouri, USA.

Motameni, R. and Shahrokhi, M. (1998). 'Brand equity valuation: A global perspective', *Journal of Product and Brand Management*, 7(4): 275–290.

Odin, Y., Odin, N. and Valette-Florence, P. (2001). 'Conceptual and operational aspects of brand loyalty: An empirical investigation', *Journal of Business Research*, 53(2): 75–84.

Oh, H. (2000). 'Diners' perceptions of quality, value, and satisfaction', *Cornell Hotel and Restaurant Administration Quarterly*, 41(3): 58–66.

Orbasli, A. (2000). *Tourists in Historic Towns: Urban Conservation and Heritage Management,* London: Spon Press.

Pappu, R. and Quester, P. (2006). 'A consumer-based method for retailer equity measurement: Results of an empirical study', *Journal of Retailing and Consumer Services*, 13(5): 317–329.

Phau, I. and Lau, K. C. (2000). 'Conceptualizing brand personality: A review and research propositions', *Journal of Targeting, Measurement and Analysis for Marketing*, 9(1): 52–69.

Pike, S., Bianchi, C., Kerr, G. and Patti, C. (2010). 'Consumer-based brand equity for Australia as a long-haul tourism destination in an emerging market', *International Marketing Review*, 27(4): 434–449.

Prentice, R. (1994). 'Perceptual deterrents to visiting museums and other heritage attractions', *Museum Management and Curatorship*, 13(3): 264–279.

Qu, H., Kim, L. H. and Im, H. H. (2011). 'A model of destination branding: Integrating the concepts of the branding and destination image', *Tourism Management*, 32(3): 465–476.

Richards, G. (2002). 'Tourism attraction systems: Exploring cultural behavior', *Annals of Tourism Research*, 29(4): 1048–1064.

Richards, G. (2007). 'ATLAS cultural tourism research project questionnaire', Available from: http://www.tram-research.com/atlas/surveytools.htm [Accessed: 10 February 2010].

Richards, G. and Wilson, J. (2004). 'The impact of cultural events on city image: Rotterdam, Cultural Capital of Europe 2001', *Urban Studies*, 41(10): 1931–1951.

Sirgy, M. J. and Su, C. (2000). 'Destination image, self-congruity, and travel behavior: Toward an integrative model', *Journal of Travel Research*, 38(4): 340–352.

Sweeney, J. and Soutar, G. N. (2001). 'Consumer perceived value: The development of a multiple item scale', *Journal of Retailing*, 77(2): 203–220.

Trueman, M., Klemm, M. and Giroud, A. (2004). 'Can a city communicate? Bradford as a corporate brand', *Corporate Communications: An International Journal*, 9(4): 317–330.

van der Ark, A. and Richards, G. (2006). 'Attractiveness of cultural activities in European cities: A latent class approach', *Tourism Management*, 27(6): 1408–1413.

Yasin, N., Noor N. and Mohamad, O. (2007). 'Does image of country-of-origin matter to brand equity?', *Journal of Product and Brand Management*, 16(1): 38–48.

Yoo, B. and Donthu, N. (2001). 'Developing and validating a multidimensional consumer-based brand equity scale', *Journal of Business Research*, 52(1): 1–14.

PART V

E-consumer behaviour

The emergence of technological advances, especially the use of the Internet and social media in hospitality and tourism operations, has contributed enormous changes in the consumer environment and consumers' purchasing behaviour. Part V of the *Handbook* deals with such issues and presents seven chapters covering the pertinent issues.

Chapter 32 by Ulrike Gretzel and Kyung-Hyan Yoo looks into the contribution of social media in hospitality and tourism businesses. The chapter quotes that social media is performing an escalating role for hospitality and tourism consumers by assisting them to dream about travel, find and process information, make travel-related decisions, connect with other travellers, improve their experiences at the destination, share experiences with others, voice complaints and establish/maintain relationships with hospitality and tourism providers. The chapter provides an overview of hospitality and tourism-specific social media applications, theoretical foundations of social media-related travel consumer behaviours and implications for tourism experiences as well as the emerging trends towards increased visual content and mobile social media.

Bonita M. Kolb talks about the use and contribution of social media in creation of authentic travel experiences for tourists in chapter 33. Tourists want to interact with local people while engaging in authentic experiences and they are now using social media to purchase directly from the providers. In addition, it allows the consumption experience to be personalised to the precise needs and preferences of travellers. Travellers are continually searching for authentic experiences, verifying the quality of experiences, booking experiences and dealing directly with the service providers and documenting their travel experiences to share them with others.

Chapter 34 by Marios Sotiriadis, Anestis Fotiadis and Chris A. Vassiliadis deals with the adoption and use of Web 2.0 and user-generated content (UGC) for hospitality/tourism consumers. The first section of the chapter highlights Web 2.0 and its various tools and applications in the tourism context. Travel review websites and their uses by consumers for tourism purposes are the topic of the next sections. The chapter concludes that websites and interactive travel forums offer opportunities and challenges for tourism destinations and enterprises to formulate relevant strategies by mapping consumer behaviour.

The growth of social media and Web 2.0 have facilitated word of mouth to be shared amongst millions of potential customers; one therefore can suggest that electronic word of mouth (eWOM) has been the successor of the traditional word of mouth. eWOM includes sharing of information about products, services and brands through modern electronic communication mediums. Chapter 35 by Alana Harris and Bruce Prideaux showcases eWOM, differentiating factors of eWOM from traditional WOM besides the impact of eWOM on consumer behaviour in tourism. The chapter also summarises criteria of online information quality as a framework to explain how consumers might employ eWOM communication, besides outlining the integrated and supplementary roles of traditional WOM and eWOM in consumer behaviour.

Roberta Minazzi in chapter 36 analyses the growth and developments in travel distribution systems due to the advances in information and communication technologies (ICT). The chapter begins by reviewing the evolution of the different travel distribution systems. The chapter further marks the changes taking place in both structural and functional aspects because of the emergence of new ICT tools. This also leads to the development of different connection paths between suppliers and consumers, attributable to which are the decline of some traditional types of operators and the emergence of new players competent with using new communicative and selling tools.

Chapter 37 by Shirley Rate, Ronnie Ballantyne, Finlay Kerr and Luiz Moutinho explores the emerging trends and implications of online marketing communications in hospitality and tourism. The authors argue that the online environment has, in recent times, seen spectacular and violent transformations influencing the impact and effectiveness of communication messages. Tourism and hospitality professionals must develop a deeper understanding of this fast-evolving environment and the way their audiences are responding to it, to broaden effective communication strategies.

Melissa A. Baker in chapter 38 details electronic customer relationship management (E-CRM) and customer satisfaction and subsequent influences on consumer behaviour. The chapter further includes how to engage key customers, measure satisfaction, increase purchasing and loyalty, improve positive WOM and mitigate negative WOM. In addition to this the chapter also highlights the management of social media, online reviews and other online marketing efforts to get the maximum advantage from E-CRM in addition to encouraging customer relationships.

32

SOCIAL MEDIA IN HOSPITALITY AND TOURISM

Ulrike Gretzel and Kyung-Hyan Yoo

Introduction

Social media are websites and applications that use Web 2.0 technology to facilitate content creation, sharing and social networking. Morrison and Gretzel (2016) define social media as Web-based tools/platforms or mobile apps that make it possible for users to easily create, co-create, discuss, modify and/or share contents with a community of known or unknown others. It is important to recognize that the term social media encompasses a large array of specific types of media such as blogs, message boards, review sites, social networking sites, messaging apps, video sharing sites, etc. Safko and Brake (2009) describe the phenomenon as a social media ecosystem. This suggests that social media do not represent a uniform species of technology applications but rather a multitude of channels and platforms that are interlinked and perform different functions. In addition, it is important to note that while social media were largely used by consumers in the early days of their emergence, they now support both consumers and corporate users. This opened up opportunities for consumers to not only talk to other consumers but also engage with brands in new ways.

New opportunities moreover are emerging from the rapid evolvement of the ecosystem, with new social media types constantly emerging (e.g. Instagram and Snapchat). In its new social media map, Overdrive Interactive (2016) provides a snapshot of 25 different categories of social media, with livestreaming being a very recently identified class of social media. Another factor to consider is the rapid increase in smartphone penetration across the world, with currently over 2 billion smartphone users globally (Smsglobal 2015) and a majority of mobile users in developed countries owning smartphones.

While there are still significant national/regional differences in the availability and use of specific social media platforms, the phenomenon of social media use is global. Statista (2016) reports that as of January 2016, the top three global social media platforms based on active accounts are Facebook (1,550 million), WhatsApp (900 million) and QQ (860 million). This suggests that travellers can use social media not only at home but also when they travel and connect to other users and companies from around the world in various ways and through various platforms. There are also travel-specific platforms such as Airbnb, TripAdvisor, WAYN, Couchsurfing and Tripit (Overdrive Interactive 2016). Tilly et al. (2015) argue that social media are now the main means for travellers to plan trips and connect with others and because of the global nature of the phenomenon, the data produced by travellers on these platforms now very closely reflects consumer behaviour and can be used to estimate visitor volume at destinations.

Literature reviews by Leung et al. (2013), Zeng and Gerritsen (2014) and Schuckert et al. (2015) and contributions in the edited book by Sigala et al. (2012) summarize the status quo of what the field knows about social media in tourism. This chapter builds on this existing research to reflect on traveller behaviour with respect to social media as information sources, as striving social communities, as media that shape tourism experiences and as spaces that facilitate consumer–company interactions and relationship building.

Social media as information sources

Social media have been predominantly conceptualized as a type of information source for travellers. They are usually seen as a form of electronic word of mouth, with those planning travel being able to obtain information from like-minded others with first-hand experience of the product. With the help of social media, word of mouth becomes asynchronous and very public and persistent (Minazzi 2015). Most importantly, social media provide easy access to such personal sources beyond one's immediate social circle. Given the importance of word of mouth in tourism due to the perceived risks and intangible/experiential nature of the product (Litvin et al. 2008), it is not surprising that social media were quickly adopted.

Yoo et al. (2009) indicate that the use of social media as travel information sources is mostly due to favourable perceptions of the trustworthiness of the contents generated by other consumers. Consumer-generated content is seen as more up to date, enjoyable and reliable than information provided by tourism marketers. Zeng and Gerritsen (2014) report that research suggests such trust perceptions differ across different social media platforms and across websites on which content is posted (e.g. third-party sites vs. supplier websites vs. official tourism destination websites) and that perceived credibility determines the influence consumer-generated contents have on those making travel decisions. Parra-López et al. (2011) indicate that travel consumers are likely to ignore potential costs of social media use (e.g. privacy loss, time investment) and rather focus on such trust incentives as well as benefits of social media use when deciding to adopt them for their travel planning purposes. However, social media use can also increasingly be accidental given the exponential growth in travel-related contents on social media. Indeed, research has shown that even when not specifically looking for social media-related sources, travel planners will likely be exposed to social media-related contents as part of their travel searches (Xiang and Gretzel 2010).

Travel consumer studies indicate that the impact of social media is the greatest in the pre-trip phase, with consumers using reviews and other contents to get ideas, evaluate alternatives and narrow down their choices (Gretzel et al. 2007). Use of social media for travel planning purposes and their impacts on travel decisions in the pre-trip stage have therefore been a major focus in the literature on social media in tourism (Leung et al. 2013). However, with growing use of mobile devices in the context of travel (Wang et al. 2012), decisions are increasingly postponed and planning with the help of social media also occurs during the trip itself. Restaurant and attraction reviews, location-based social media, livestreaming and video sharing apps can feed travellers with context-relevant information for their decision-making on the go.

Social media as community

Kozinets (1999) describes the power of social media as spaces where consumers gather as consumption tribes. This argument moves the focus away from only the information that is contained in social media and centres on the opportunities for social connections and support. Sharing and participatory culture are the essence of social media. However, consumers often differ in their level of participation, with many lurking and not so many actively contributing content (Yoo and Gretzel 2011). Blogworks (2011) suggests that social media users can be classified based on their level of involvement as:

Searchers – visit profiles/pages to look for specific information
Lurkers – repeatedly visit a page or community
Casuals – respond to posts with liking/favouriting and follow others
Actives – comment and share, post content
Defenders – start threads, help manage conversations.

Social media platforms critically depend on those consumers that not only use social media as information sources but also actively contribute. Understanding what motivates social media use and especially content creation is therefore very important and has been studied extensively in the tourism context (Schuckert et al. 2015).

Tuten and Solomon (2014) suggest that consumers follow a range of social impulses that lead them to mingle and interact on social media platforms, namely affinity needs, curiosity about others, contact comfort/immediacy/psychological closeness to others, altruism and need for validation. Parra-López et al. (2011) identified deriving social benefits (staying in touch, feelings of belonging, connecting with like-minded others) as a major factor determining social media adoption for travel purposes. The importance of social motives specifically for content creation has also been confirmed in the travel context (Wang and Fesenmaier 2004; Yoo and Gretzel 2008; Munar and Jacobsen 2014), with altruistic motives of helping other consumers avoid bad travel experiences being an especially important motivation (Yoo and Gretzel 2008). Reciprocity, i.e. the feeling that one has benefited from social media and therefore should be giving back to the community, is also a strong driver of content creation behaviour (Yoo and Gretzel 2011). Minazzi (2015) further cites gaining respect and recognition from others as important to content creators and, in addition, suggests that by sharing experiences with others, travellers can restore balance from either extremely positive or extremely dissatisfactory travel experiences. What motivates content creators and what barriers non-creators perceive are often a function of their personality (Yoo and Gretzel 2011). The general likelihood of being an active social media content creator is also influenced by demographic variables such as age and race (Yoo and Gretzel 2012).

Lee and Gretzel (2014) report that social identity construction is a major focus of bloggers residing in collectivist cultures. Analysing blogs of Korean travellers, they found that directing their blog postings to a wider audience and interacting with others through the travel blog is a common activity for these collectivist bloggers. In contrast, US travel bloggers produce much more self-centred blogs that focus on experience documentation. Lo and McKercher (2015) further discuss social dimensions of social media by looking specifically at social comparison and impression management. They conclude that social media provide travellers with new opportunities to present their ideal self to others and experiment with their identities. They suggest that travellers are very much aware of others judging them on the basis of their social media posts and adjust their tourist photographic practice and social media content creation behaviours accordingly. Seeking status on social media is also a phenomenon that is widespread in the tourism context, with platforms such as TripAdvisor officially recognizing review activity with badges displayed to others via the user profile and awarding particularly active members with a 'Destination Expert' label.

Some virtual travel communities specifically emphasize the facilitation of connections among travellers. WAYN, for instance, lets people find travel companions and knowledgeable locals. Couchsurfing provides a platform for travellers to find free accommodation. Through elaborate profiles and sophisticated reputation management systems, these social media types facilitate trust building and therefore foster social connections among strangers. They have become popular ways for travellers to engage in alternative tourism and seek out more authentic, local travel experiences.

Social media as experience

Gretzel et al. (2011) report that while sharing with and helping others are the most important motivations for travellers when creating social media contents, documenting the experience and reflecting on the experience are also frequently mentioned motives. 'Tourism is not just about travel; it is an opportunity to explore ones [*sic*] own self' (Pudliner 2007: p. 49) and travellers often engage in reflexive practices like keeping a trip diary. Desforges (2000) also recognizes the important relationship between tourism and self-identity and stresses that tourists use narratives to explore various aspects of their self. Tussyadiah and Fesenmaier (2008) explain that writing about travel experience presents 'a picture of lived identities' (p. 309). Social media can take on the function of journaling, facilitating the documentation of the tourism experience as it happens as well as the process of memory construction and recollection long after the trip. Blogs and vlogs (video-based blogs) play an especially important role in this as their focus is on voicing opinions and providing chronologically ordered entries while at the same time receiving comments from others that can support the identity construction process. More recently, social media tools that support livestreaming have further pushed the boundaries of what kinds of documenting are possible and what levels of immediacy can be achieved. As such, social media have the potential to not only influence the experience before and during travel but also after a trip as a means of facilitating the re-experiencing of past travel.

Past research has shown that 'real-time' sharing during the trip is limited (Munar and Jacobsen 2014) and that most tourists upload contents after the trip (Fotis et al. 2011). This further emphasizes the role of social media in the narrative memory-work that tourists do, telling themselves and others stories of their trips to further help in constructing/reconstructing the experience. Gretzel et al. (2011) indicate that many travel consumers also derive a lot of enjoyment from creating contents and Dinhopl and Gretzel (2016) draw attention to the practice of high-profile editing, suggesting that a lot of travellers now spend considerable time editing their contents and taking pride in their creations, especially in the context of tourist videography. Social media then are not just spaces through which experiences are documented but are inherently experiences themselves. Enjoyment is not limited to content creation but extends to content consumption as consumers find the information posted on social media especially engaging (Yoo et al. 2009). Munar and Jacobsen (2014) found that there is a great emphasis on visual contents being shared on travel social media and such vivid records of travel experiences can be both inspiring and entertaining for oneself and others to watch/look at. Indeed, hedonic benefits of social media use have been discussed from the very beginning of virtual travel communities (Wang and Fesenmaier 2004) and continue to be mentioned in the literature as important in explaining social media use (Parra-López et al. 2011).

However, social media use not only brings happiness to travel consumers. The heightened opportunities for social comparison provided by social media can also lead to what researchers have coined as 'facebook envy' (Krasnova et al. 2013). Seeing other people's wonderful vacation pictures while one has to be at work on a cold winter day can significantly reduce one's life satisfaction. Further, being focused on social media rather than being immersed in the travel experience can reduce the beneficial impact of vacations on one's well-being (Pearce and Gretzel 2012).

Consumer–brand relationships on social media

Consumers not only interact with other consumers via social media but increasingly also connect and interact with travel companies and their favourite travel brands through social media platforms. Consumers' behavioural manifestations towards a brand or firm on social media are usually summarized under the umbrella term of 'customer engagement' (Van Doorn et al. 2010). While consumers mostly seek functional benefits from social media-based relationships with brands, including special offers and new product information, they also form connections on the basis of strong emotional attachment, especially in the case of travel destinations (Gretzel and Fesenmaier 2012). While achieving 'likes' or being followed by consumers was relatively easy in the early days of social media use, consumers are now being more selective in terms of which brands they associate with and also do not shy away from ending brand relationships if they no longer derive benefits from them, feel betrayed by the brand or are worried about negative brand images spilling over to their personal social media identities (Gretzel and Dinhopl 2014).

Brands are trying to exploit this general willingness of consumers to interact with them on social media and increasingly use social media channels, for example, as low-cost customer service platforms and complaint management tools. Companies also take advantage of the viral nature of social media and the 'megaphone effect' well-connected consumers can have on social media when spreading company messages (McQuarrie and Philips 2014). They specifically design promotional campaigns with highly 'spreadable' contents and incentivize consumers to share their messages with their friends. Consumers seem to derive a lot of pleasure from brand–related social media interactions and often become brand 'evangelists' on social media (Collins et al. 2015). Some even create brand-specific contents or help design advertising campaigns.

Tourism Australia takes advantage of the general willingness of its Facebook, Twitter and Instagram followers to share their best travel photographs on the destination's official social media pages. These photographs represent valuable promotional material to the destination and it therefore actively encourages visitors and residents alike to keep posting their materials. For example, the description of its official Facebook page states:

> Tourism Australia has created this page as a hub for people who are planning to visit, have visited, or simply have a great love for holidays in Australia. Here you'll find general information, tips on travelling to and/or working in Australia, as well as plenty

of images and video that help capture the Australian experience. We welcome all those who have ever gone 'walkabout' in Australia to share your comments, images and videos.

It publicly recognizes consumer contributions by publishing a photo album of the most impressive fan photos every Friday. It calls these albums 'Friday Fan Photos' and '@Australia Instagram Photos That Made Us Happy This Week'. In doing so it fosters its fans' motivations to contribute contents and at the same time is able to promote the destination through the lens of consumers whose photos have more credibility than professionally shot photographs used in traditional marketing campaigns. For instance, it commented on a recently posted fan photo of a baby wombat with information on how to find the sanctuary where the animal is being raised. Tourism Australia also actively engages with potential and past visitors by answering questions and commenting on consumer posts/comments. It often wishes those fans who express plans to visit Australia a great time and encourages those who post about their great memories of the destination to come visit again. In its posts it adopts a very casual and personal language and often includes humour in order to further engage consumers in online conversations. One of its recent responses encouraged a fan to come to Australia and not to worry too much about the spiders. Its social media strategy is often mentioned as one of the best and has made it the most successful tourism destination on social media in terms of followers/fans (Australian Marketing Institute 2013).

Conclusion

Social media use is already widespread in the tourism context and continues to grow. Travellers can take advantage of social media in many ways: to inform their decisions, to form and present travel identities, to dream about vacations, to connect with like-minded others through communities of shared interest, to vicariously share experiences with those staying at home, to help others have better experiences, to gain status, to starve boredom, to regulate psychological states (e.g. vent frustration), to seek support and validation, to express their creativity, etc. In many ways, social media support consumer behaviours that have always played an important role in tourism, such as documenting trips, telling travel stories and seeking advice from other travellers. However, they also fundamentally change these practices and make them more visible to other consumers as well as marketers. They create new opportunities for connections, interactions and transactions that were not possible, or at least not at this scale, without the technological support social media platforms provide.

While recent literature reviews on social media in tourism indicate that there is already a substantial body of knowledge related to the topic, they also outline many areas in which more research is needed, example regarding ethical issues in relation to social media use (Zeng and Gerritsen 2014) and in terms of social media use across all phases of the travel experience (Leung et al. 2013). Social media is changing so rapidly that studies conducted even a few years ago are in many ways already outdated. For instance, the rise of mobile technology and ever greater availability of free Wi-Fi at destinations encourages more and more real-time sharing of contents and challenges the assumptions of social media as predominantly pre-trip information sources and post-trip sharing platforms. Some new technological developments like livestreaming tools, snapchat, etc. have not been studied at all. In addition, most of the literature has researched the topic in Western contexts, which limits our understanding of culture-based differences and culturally embedded social media practices.

References

Australian Marketing Institute (2013). 'How Tourism Australia became the world's biggest social media team', Available from: http://www.ami.org.au/imis15/AMI/Information_Folder/How_Tourism_Australia_became_the_world_s_biggest_social_media_team.aspx [Accessed 1 February 2016].

Blogworks (2011). 'Can social media engagement be meaningfully measured?', Available from: http://www.blogworks.in/post/can-social-media-engagement-be-meaningfully-measured/ [Accessed 20 February 2016].

Collins, N., Glabe, H., Mizerski, D. and Murphy, J. (2015). 'Identifying customer evangelists', *Review of Marketing Research*, 12: 175–206.

Desforges, L. (2000). 'Traveling the world: Identity and travel biography', *Annals of Tourism Research*, 27(4): 926–945.

Dinhopl, A. and Gretzel, U. (2016). 'Conceptualizing tourist videography', *Information Technology and Tourism*, 15(4): 395–410.

Fotis, J., Buhalis, D. and Rossides, N. (2011). 'Social media impact on holiday travel planning: The case of the Russian and the FSU markets', *International Journal of Online Marketing*, 1(4): 1–19.

Gretzel, U. and Dinhopl, A. (2014). 'Breaking up is hard to do: Why do travellers unlike travel-related organizations?', in Z. Xiang and I. Tussyadiah (eds.), *Information and Communication Technologies in Tourism* (pp. 267–280), Berlin: Springer.

Gretzel, U. and Fesenmaier, D. R. (2012). 'Customer relations 2.0 – Implications for destination marketing', Paper presented at the TTRA Annual International Conference, 17–19 June 2012, Virginia Beach, VA.

Gretzel, U., Fesenmaier, D. R., Lee, Y.-J. and Tussyadiah, I. (2011). 'Narrating travel experiences: The role of new media', in R. Sharpley and P. Stone (eds.), *Tourist Experiences: Contemporary Perspectives* (pp. 171–182), New York: Routledge.

Gretzel, U., Yoo, K.-Y. and Purifoy, M. (2007). 'Online travel reviews study: Role and impact of online travel reviews', Available from: http://www.tripadvisor.com.au/pdfs/OnlineTravelReviewReport.pdf [Accessed 4 February 2016].

Kozinets, R. V. (1999). 'E-tribalized marketing?: The strategic implications of virtual communities of consumption', *European Management Journal*, 17(3): 252–264.

Krasnova, H., Wenninger, H., Widjaja, T. and Buxmann, P. (2013). 'Envy on Facebook: A hidden threat to users' life satisfaction?', *Wirtschaftsinformatik*, 92: 1–16.

Lee, Y. J. and Gretzel, U. (2014). 'Cross-cultural differences in social identity formation through travel blogging', *Journal of Travel and Tourism Marketing*, 31(1): 37–54.

Leung, D., Law, R., Van Hoof, H. and Buhalis, D. (2013). 'Social media in tourism and hospitality: A literature review', *Journal of Travel and Tourism Marketing*, 30(1–2): 3–22.

Litvin, S. W., Goldsmith, R. E. and Pan, B. (2008). 'Electronic word-of-mouth in hospitality and tourism management', *Tourism Management*, 29(3): 458–468.

Lo, I. S. and McKercher, B. (2015). 'Ideal image in process: Online tourist photography and impression management', *Annals of Tourism Research*, 52: 104–116.

McQuarrie, E. F. and Philips, B. J. (2014). 'The megaphone effect in social media: How ordinary consumers become style leaders', *GfK Marketing Intelligence Review*, 6(2): 16–20.

Minazzi, R. (2015). *Social Media Marketing in Tourism and Hospitality*, Cham: Springer.

Morrison, A. and Gretzel, U. (in press). *Tourism Marketing in the Age of the Consumer*, Routledge, forthcoming.

Munar, A. M. and Jacobsen, J. K. S. (2014). 'Motivations for sharing tourism experiences through social media', *Tourism Management*, 43: 46–54.

Overdrive Interactive (2016). '2016 social media map', Available from: http://www.ovrdrv.com/social-media-map/ [Accessed 1 March 2016].

Parra-López, E., Bulchand-Gidumal, J., Gutiérrez-Taño, D. and Díaz-Armas, R. (2011). 'Intentions to use social media in organizing and taking vacation trips', *Computers in Human Behavior*, 27(2): 640–654.

Pearce, P. L. and Gretzel, U. (2012). 'Tourism in technology dead zones: Documenting experiential dimensions', *International Journal of Tourism Sciences*, 12(2): 1–20.

Pudliner, B. A. (2007). 'Alternative literature and tourist experience: Travel and tourist weblogs', *Journal of Tourism and Cultural Change*, 5(1): 46–59.

Safko, L. and Brake, D. K. (2009). *The Social Media Bible: Tactics, Tools and Strategies for Business Success*, Hoboken, NJ: John Wiley and Sons.

Schuckert, M., Liu, X. and Law, R. (2015). 'Hospitality and tourism online reviews: Recent trends and future directions', *Journal of Travel and Tourism Marketing*, 32(5): 608–621.

Sigala, M., Christou, E. and Gretzel, U. (eds.) (2012). *Social Media in Travel, Tourism and Hospitality: Theory, Practice and Cases*, Ashford: Ashgate.

Smsglobal (2015). 'Smartphone ownership, usage, and penetration by country', 13 October, Available from: http://www.smsglobal.com/thehub/smartphone-ownership-usage-and-penetration/ [Accessed 18 February 2016].

Statista (2016). 'Global social networks ranked by number of users 2016', Available from: http://www.statista.com/statistics/272014/global-social-networks-ranked-by-number-of-users/ [Accessed 15 February 2016].

Tilly, R., Fischbach, K. and Schoder, D. (2015). 'Mineable or messy? Assessing the quality of macro-level tourism information derived from social media', *Electronic Markets*, 25(3): 227–241.

Tussyadiah, I. P. and Fesenmaier, D. R. (2008). 'Marketing places through first-person stories – An analysis of Pennsylvania Roadtripper Blog', *Journal of Travel and Tourism Marketing*, 25(3–4): 299–311.

Tuten, T. L. and Solomon, M. R. (2014). *Social Media Marketing*, Thousand Oaks, CA: Sage.

Van Doorn, J., Lemon, K. N., Mittal, V., Nass, S., Pick, D., Pirner, P. and Verhoef, P. C. (2010). 'Customer engagement behavior: Theoretical foundations and research directions', *Journal of Service Research*, 13(3): 253–266.

Wang, D., Park, S. and Fesenmaier, D. R. (2012). 'The role of smartphones in mediating the touristic experience', *Journal of Travel Research*, 51(4): 371–387.

Wang, Y. and Fesenmaier, D. R. (2004). 'Towards understanding members' general participation in and active contribution to an online travel community', *Tourism Management*, 25(6): 709–722.

Xiang, Z. and Gretzel, U. (2010). 'Role of social media in online travel information search', *Tourism Management*, 31(2): 179–188.

Yoo, K. H. and Gretzel, U. (2008). 'What motivates consumers to write online travel reviews?', *Information Technology and Tourism*, 10(4): 283–295.

Yoo, K. H. and Gretzel, U. (2011). 'Influence of personality on travel-related consumer-generated media creation', *Computers in Human Behavior*, 27(2): 609–621.

Yoo, K. H. and Gretzel, U. (2012). 'Use and creation of social media by travelers', in M. Sigala, E. Christou and U. Gretzel (eds.), *Social Media in Travel, Tourism and Hospitality* (pp. 189–206), Brookfield, VT: Ashgate.

Yoo, K. H., Lee, Y., Gretzel, U. and Fesenmaier, D. R. (2009). 'Trust in travel-related consumer generated media', in W. Höpken, U. Gretzel and R. Law (eds.), *Information and Communication Technologies in Tourism* (pp. 49–59), Vienna: Springer.

Zeng, B. and Gerritsen, R. (2014). 'What do we know about social media in tourism? A review', *Tourism Management Perspectives*, 10: 27–36.

33

SOCIAL MEDIA AND THE DESIRE FOR AUTHENTIC TRAVEL EXPERIENCES

Bonita M. Kolb

Introduction

Tourists have relied on tourism intermediaries due to the risk of purchasing an unknown tourist experience as a wrong choice might result in a ruined vacation (Kozak and Baloglu 2011). This was understandable consumer behaviour when tourists did not have access to information on the benefits and quality of tourism destinations except through intermediaries.

However, tourism consumer behaviour is now changing because of access to information. Because they are familiar with destinations before arrival, travellers want to experience the unique activities that they discovered online (Beeton 2006). Rather than be passive consumers of tourism products, the desire to engage in an activity is a motivation shared by most travellers (Pesonen 2015). Because they want to interact with local people while engaging in authentic experiences they are now using social media to research tourism products that they will purchase directly from the provider (Parra-López 2012).

Because social media allows the ability to verify experiences via consumer reviews along with the ability to communicate with local community members, travellers can use direct booking websites to create their own travel experience (O'Brien 2015). These travellers are continually searching for authentic experiences, verifying the quality of experiences, booking experiences directly with the provider and then documenting what they experienced. All of this activity is being done online simultaneously before, during and after the trip.

To build personalized itineraries travellers are embracing the use of direct booking websites, such as Airbnb, to find unique places to spend the night (Clarke 2015). Other websites, such as vayable.com, allow direct booking of tours by connecting with locals who will provide experiences authentic to the community (Zax 2014). While these sites still rely on a company that maintains the website and handles payments for a fee, the connection is between the individual buyer and seller. While the smaller role played by the intermediary can save costs, travellers are not just using these sites to save money (Why 2014). They are using them because these services connect the traveller with locals in a way that cannot be achieved using a tourism intermediary. In addition it allows the tourism experience to be personalized to the exact needs and preferences of travellers.

Tourists and tourism motivation

Before examining how tourism consumer behaviour has changed, it is useful to consider the difference between a traveller and a tourist. In addition the motivation for travel can help understand why some travellers are no longer using tourism intermediaries to provide the type of trip desired. However, the use of social media has now resulted in tourism consumer behaviour that is similar no matter how the traveller is defined or the motivation for the trip.

Traveller vs. tourist

The old definition of traveller versus tourist was based on an elitist view of life (Stavans and Ellison 2015). A traveller had the occupation and income that provided the free time and money needed to experience new places. In addition they had the education to appreciate the cultural heritage of the destination they were visiting. In contrast, tourists were seen as lacking in time, money and education. As a result they wanted to book inexpensive pre-planned trips through travel intermediaries that provided experiences that already conform-ed to their preconceptions of the place they were to visit. Today, more people have the money to travel and, because of technology, an understanding and appreciation of places they are visiting (Beeton 2006). As a result this distinction between traveller and tourist is no longer as valid, as more people are planning and booking their own trip.

Escapism- vs. experience-motivated travellers

There are several methods of categorizing tourists that are common (Swarbrooke and Horner 2007). These methods, based on the motivation for the trip, can be useful when considering which tourists will be most affected by the desire for an authentic personalized experience and the ability to directly book services that can make this desire a reality (O'Regan 2014).

One of the early attempts to capture the varying and often simultaneous motivations for travel is relevant when discussing the relationship between tourists and their use of social media. Tourists may be divided into people whose travel is motivated by a desire for escapism and those who are motivated by a desire to seek experiences (Iso-Ahola 1980). Although the motivations may overlap, the two groups of tourists differ in what they seek. Escape travellers want fewer stimuli from their travel, not more. The tourist motivated by a desire to escape doesn't want to take a trip that is challenging, as they want to get away from stress and simply enjoy themselves.

On the other hand experience travellers seek new stimuli. They travel because of a desire to experience a new culture or engage in an activity. As a result they want new and unique experiences that they will document and then share online. These travellers are more likely to make use of new technology including trip planning and review sites to both plan and document travel (Parra-López et al. 2012). They will use these sites to find tourism activities that fit their individual interests while providing them with the opportunity to interact with local community members as they desire an authentic, personalized experience.

The use of social media to plan a personalized trip has become so widespread that it is now considered part of the travel experience. In fact 64% of travellers categorized themselves as excited during the planning process while only 40% of travellers categorized them-selves as excited during the trip. This does not mean they were disappointed with their journey as 79% of these travellers state they will start planning their next trip upon their return (TripAdvisor 2014). The online research before the trip has now become a pleasurable part of the travel experience.

Desire for authenticity and personalization

Because technology allows people to purchase online, consumers have a large number of available competing products from which to choose. As a result, a change in how products were marketed occurred. In order to differentiate a tangible product from its competitors, the experience of the consumption of the product was now marketed as part of the value (Hartl and Gram 2008). In addition, because of the desire of consumers for products that are both authentic and personalized, these product attributes started to be marketed to differentiate a product from its competitors (Gilmore and Pine 2007).

Desire for authenticity

Authenticity can have a variety of meanings depending on the context in which the word is used (Knudsen and Waade 2010). When considering tourism it can mean that a destination is both credible and reliable in how the reality is represented. In this context Disneyland is authentically Disney in that it provides the experience that the tourist expects when visiting. Authenticity can also mean that something exists and is not imaginary. While people can read a book or view a video about a country and culture this is not considered to be as authentic an experience as would be visiting personally. Lastly, authenticity can mean that a place is the original and not a copy. The intensity of an experience is increased and an emotional relationship is created when encountering an original place or culture. The most authentic tourism experiences can be said to be a credible encounter with the original place that generates a feeling of relationship. In the context of tourism the search for authenticity can be defined as a desire to experience life as it is really lived somewhere else (Hirschorn and Hefferon 2013).

Another issue that relates to the current change in tourism consumer behaviour is the type of experience desired. Earlier studies of tourism were built on the idea that tourists wanted to have an experience different from daily life (MacCannell 1976). While they knew that there was an 'everyday' life happening behind the scenes while they consumed a tourist product, they were not interested in that part of the experience. Now what travellers want is to be part of a local experience that fits their individual interests (Stavans and Ellison 2015).

In the past some travellers may have been in search of an experience that was different to what they could obtain at home, but lacking both the knowledge of the destination and the ability to access tourism providers directly, they relied on travel intermediaries to book their trip. However, to please the most travellers, these intermediaries tended to homogenize the travel experience (Godfrey and Clarke 2000). Now people are no longer satisfied with this homogenized approach to tourism. Because they are globally aware through reading about and viewing destinations online, they want to do more than simply see a place. As a result the travellers' expectations of what constitutes authentic travel experience have changed. They want to experience the local culture in a way that technology can't provide (Beeton 2006).

Desire for personalization

Travellers seeking authentic experiences are savvy consumers who have a resistance to packaged products and generalized marketing messages. The packaging and marketing done by tourism intermediaries are seen as making travel just another commodified product rather than a personalized experience (Yeoman et al. 2007). Because most travellers will have researched a destination online, they will have very specific desires as to what they wish to experience, including its sites, culture, activities and people.

As a result travellers will take advantage of current technology to personalize their trip by finding the exact type of lodging and activities they prefer. If they are interested in music, photography or sports at home, they will want to experience the local cultural expression of the same. While they are looking for cultural difference, they want experiences that mirror their already existing interests and lifestyles (Bosangit 2014).

New technology changes consumer behaviour

Because social media allows almost instantaneous customer feedback, the consumer purchase process has changed (Downes and Nunes 2014). First, the introduction of the Internet allowed the purchase of products that could not be found locally. Second, social media allowed direct consumer-to-consumer communication about the benefits and quality of products. Finally, direct booking sites offered the opportunity for direct and easy business transactions between an individual seller and buyer.

Travellers are now using social media and direct booking to bypass the tourism intermediary. Instead they are purchasing directly from individual tourist service providers who are members of the community they will be visiting as the travellers see them as more knowledgeable (Almeida et al. 2012). This allows the travel experience to be both more authentic and more personalized.

Changing purchase expectations

The easy access to products because of technology has changed consumers' expectations of the purchase process (Gilmore and Pine 2007). First, they now expect the product to be readily available, the cost to be appropriate and the quality to be high. In addition they want the product to be authentic as the consumer's self-image depends on this factor (Coolsen and Kumashiro 2009). Because the product must enhance their sense of identity, purchasing a product that is not as it was represented in marketing information is not only a purchasing mistake; it affects the consumers' sense of who they are.

It is the issues of quality and authenticity that most affect consumer purchase behaviour when buying tourism products. Quality is critical when purchasing tourism products as it is difficult to ascertain before purchase. In addition, authenticity is the deciding factor when purchasing experiences such as travel (Rickly-Boyd 2013). The problem for the consumer was how to obtain the desired high-quality authentic travel experience.

Social media and review sites

The problem with purchasing experiences such as tourism has always been how to verify the quality and authenticity of what is offered. Social media now offers the tourism consumer the solution to this problem. When social media first appeared, its use was restricted to simple information searches to find tourism products (Kang and Schuett 2013). As social networking sites developed and participation grew, information posting became common as a way to document the trip. This resulted in review sites becoming a critical factor in the tourism purchase decision process. In addition, because social media allows online communication with the tourism product provider, tourists can personally co-produce the travel experience to meet their exact personal specifications (Decrop 2014).

Sharing information on travel has become part of the travel experience. This has given rise to a new term, social travel, which is used to describe the traveller's desire for shareable experiences (Narayanan 2015). This behaviour starts even before the trip as can be seen by the fact that 50% of travellers download phone apps for the location they will be visiting when researching a potential travel destination (Živković et al. 2014). Because they know so much about a destination before visiting, upon arrival, just seeing is not enough. The visitor is no longer interested in just having the standard tourist experience; instead they want a local experience that is personalized to their interests (Narayanan 2015).

Direct booking between individuals

The development of websites that would handle financial transactions for the buying and selling of products between individuals has affected how tourism products are purchased. There are now direct booking sites that provide means for the sharing of information as previous users of the services can post reviews. These websites also provide the ability to directly purchase a tourism product from a provider. These direct booking websites such as Airbnb and vayable.com allow individuals who have lodging or local knowledge to sell their spare rooms or tour services without having to worry about handling the financial transaction. This direct booking model has been successful as it meets the needs of the tourism consumer by providing access to individuals offering tourism products so that the experience is both authentic and personalized to the exact needs of the traveller.

Consumer behaviour model

Consumer behaviour is the process of both why and how the decision to purchase a specific product is made. As the motivations for travel can vary widely from one traveller to another, the marketing of tourism has always been challenging. Now a new challenge has arisen as consumers are moving away from using the usual tourism intermediaries as a source of information.

There have been a number of models that have attempted to explain how consumers make the decision to purchase a product. The most accepted model of need recognition, search for information, evaluating alternatives, purchase and post-purchase led marketing professionals to focus on the role of promotional information in motivating a purchase decision. A model more focused on the travel consumer describes a process of pre-trip, during-trip and post-trip consumer behaviour (Minazzi 2015). However, even this model is no longer as relevant as social media have changed how travellers purchase the tourism product (Xiang et al. 2014).

In fact the use of social media has changed every step of the consumer behaviour purchase process. During the first step of need recognition, the desire for travel might not be based on information from a travel intermediary that then prompts a search for information. Instead consumers might be online updating their Facebook page or perusing information on a video or photo sharing site when they might notice that someone has posted videos of their trip along with information on what they found enjoyable. This might inspire consumers to develop a need to travel to engage in a specific activity that was not prompted by any promotional material produced by an intermediary. The evaluation of alternatives stage has also changed. Rather than request information from tourism intermediaries, the travel consumer is much more likely to use consumer review sites such as TripAdvisor to compare the benefits of different tourism products. As a result consumers no longer rely on professional travel intermediaries to provide access to information. Instead the average traveller now uses 22 websites before booking travel (Rudnansky 2015).

Once the decision was made and the trip purchased it was thought that the search for information and evaluation of alternatives were completed. However, social media have also changed this step in the tourism consumer behaviour process as travellers continue to search for information and evaluate alternatives during the trip. In fact the traveller becomes a co-creator of tourism content by continually customizing their travel experience (Rihova et al. 2015).

Another change resulting from social media is that the post-purchase evaluation now starts during the trip. While in the past a common motivation ascribed to travel was a desire to get away from everyday life, now the tourist stays in contact with home while away. In fact almost as many of the conversations with people at home about a trip now take place during the trip via social media as when the trip has been concluded (Davies 2015). Even the most adventurous of backpackers takes at least a smartphone if not a tablet with them. They do so as part of travel is now sharing the experience online (Molz 2012). While social media are used to enrich the trip by sharing information with those back home, they are also used to communicate with local residents. After the trip social media are used to critique the trip by writing reviews and share the trip by posting photos. While it may have been the technologically sophisticated trendsetters who first used online sites to directly access tourism products and social media to share experiences, this change in consumer behaviour has spread rapidly (Jaconi 2014).

The response of Marriott Hotels

Social media communication has reshaped tourists' consumer purchase behaviour. Tourists are now using direct booking and social media to skip the intermediary and purchase directly with individual tourist service providers. This makes the travel experience both more authentic and more personalized. This behaviour has become widespread very rapidly which can be seen by the fact that from 2008 to 2014 over 11 million nights of lodging were booked using Airbnb. It is safe to assume that at least a portion of these travellers would have booked rooms in a hotel if Airbnb had not existed. People have confidence in the reviews provided by Airbnb users, which can be seen by the fact that 64% of users are booking a room in another country which presumably entails the most purchase risk (Kurtz 2014).

The reaction of some hotels is to fight the threat by asking the government to enact restrictive regulations (O'Neill 2014; Weed 2015). A more viable option may be to join the movement. This approach can be seen in the way that Marriott is reacting to the success of Airbnb. While saying that traditional hotel bookings are not in jeopardy, hotels, including Marriott, understand that there is a market segment that wants something different (Barton 2014). Marriott, which owns brands as diverse as Courtyard and Ritz-Carlton that vary as to price and the level of service that is offered, has started its own boutique hotel line. The new Autograph hotels are specifically designed to attract travellers bored with brands. Marriott is using the Autograph hotels to try to reach the same segment of travellers that want authentic local experiences and are currently using Airbnb. The hotels are designed to reflect the communities in which they exist rather than the Marriott brand (Oates 2014b).

Each Autograph hotel is in an existing building that reflects the history of the community. In addition the interior design in the rooms and lobby along with the menus in the restaurants are also created to reflect local tastes. The reason for doing so is that Marriott understands that by 2020, a third of all business travel hotel nights will be booked by those aged 20–40 (Barnes 2014). This is the group that is also booking rooms at Airbnb because they are looking for an authentic travel experience.

Marriott recognizes that some travellers can still be persuaded to use their other branded hotels if the experience is personalized. Therefore Marriott started the 'Travel Brilliantly' campaign. This campaign used crowd sourcing to solicit ideas so that travellers could co-create at least some aspects of the hotel experience (Oates 2014a). Since it was launched, the programme has received over 700 ideas from hotel guests for improvements to the travel experience. They included requests that the hotel guest be able to personalize the toiletries they will find in the bathroom and the food that will be stocked in the mini-fridge. In addition the travellers want to not only choose their own room but also pre-set the temperature using their phone. Other ideas have been the ability to upload photos on to digital photo frames to make the room more like home.

One question that will need to be researched is whether direct booking of tourism products will replace business done with intermediaries or supplement it. It cannot be expected that consumer behaviour will return to almost exclusive use of intermediaries. Hotel brands such as Marriott have responded by developing their own hotels authentic to the community, and providing personalized services at their existing hotel brands. It has been suggested that the next step might be that the large hospitality companies may emulate Airbnb by building homes that they will then rent out as hotel rooms (Mangla 2015).

References

Almeida, N., Silva, J., Mendes, J. and Oom do Valle, P. (2012). 'The effects of marketing communication on the tourist's hotel reservation process', *Anatolia: An International Journal of Tourism and Hospitality Research*, 23(2): 234–250.

Barnes, B. (2014). 'But it doesn't look like a Marriott', *New York Times*, 4 January, Available from: http://www.nytimes.com/2014/01/05/business/marriott-international-aims-to-draw-a-younger-crowd.html [Accessed 29 September 2015].

Barton, C. (2014). 'Why Hilton, Marriott, and Choice are buying up boutique hotels', 7 June, *The Motley Fool*, Available from: http://www.fool.com/investing/general/2014/06/07/why-hilton-marriott-and-choice-are-buying-up-bouti.aspx [Accessed 29 September 2015].

Beeton, S. (2006). *Community Development through Tourism*, Collingwood, VIC: Land Links.

Bosangit, C. (2014). 'Virtual communities: Online blogs as a marketing tool', in S. McCabe (ed.), *The Routledge Handbook of Tourism Marketing* (pp. 268–280), London: Routledge.

Clarke, P. (2015). 'Airbnb's business travel program growing in popularity', *Travel Pulse*, 26 August, Available from: http://www.travelpulse.com/news/business-travel/airbnbs-business-travel-program-growing-in-popularity.html [Accessed 20 September 2015].

Coolsen, M. and Kumashiro, M. (2009). 'Self-image congruence models conceptualized as a product affirmation process', *Advances in Consumer Research*, 36: 980–981.

Davies, P. (2015). 'Travel conversations peak when people return home', *Travel Weekly* (UK), 2269: 19.

Decrop, A. (2014). 'Theorizing tourist behavior', in S. McCabe (ed.), *The Routledge Handbook of Tourism Marketing* (pp. 179–192), London: Routledge.

Downes, L. and Nunes, P. (2014). *Big Bang Disruption: Strategy in the Age of Devastating Innovation*, New York: Portfolio.

Gilmore, J. and Pine, B. (2007). *Authenticity: What Consumers Really Want*, Boston, MA: Harvard Business School Press.

Godfrey, K. and Clarke, J. (2000). *The Tourism Development Handbook: A Practical Approach to Planning and Marketing*, London: Cassell.

Hartl, A. and Gram, M. (2008). 'Experience production by family tourism providers', in J. Sandbo and P. Darmer (eds.), *Creating Experiences in the Experience Economy* (pp. 232–252), Cheltenham, UK: Edward Elgar.

Hirschorn, S. and Hefferon, K. (2013). 'Leaving it all behind to travel: Venturing uncertainty as a means to personal growth and authenticity', *Journal of Humanistic Psychology*, 53(3): 283–306.

Iso-Ahola, S. (1980). *The Social Psychology of Leisure and Recreation*, Dubuque, IA: W. C. Brown.

Jaconi, M. (2014). 'The "on-demand economy" is revolutionizing consumer behaviour – Here's how', *Business Insider*, 13 July, Available from: http://www.businessinsider.com/the-on-demand-economy-2014-7 [Accessed 20 September 2015].

Kang, M. and Schuett, M. (2013). 'Determinants of sharing travel experiences in social media', *Journal of Travel and Tourism Marketing*, 30(1/2): 93–107.

Knudsen, B. and Waade, A. (2010). 'Performative authenticity in tourism and spatial experience: Rethinking the relations between travel, place and emotion', in B. T. Knudsen and A. M. Waade (eds.), *Re-investing Authenticity: Tourism, Place and Emotions* (pp. 1–19), Bristol, UK: Channel View Publications.

Kozak, M. and Baloglu, S. (2011). *Managing and Marketing Tourist Destinations: Strategies to Gain a Competitive Edge*, New York: Routledge.

Kurtz, M. (2014). 'In focus: Airbnb's inroads into the hotel industry', *HVS Global Hospitality Report*, 12 June, Available from: https://www.hvs.com/article/6952/in-focus-airbnbs-inroads-into-the-hotel-industry/ [Accessed 14 November 2016].

MacCannell, D. (1976). *The Tourist: A New Theory of the Leisure Class*, New York: Schocken Books.

Mangla, I. (2015). 'Major hotel brands compete for space in the boutique hotel trend', *International Business Times*, 23 January, Available from: http://www.ibtimes.com/major-hotel-brands-compete-space-boutique-hotel-trend-1793168 [Accessed 27 September 2015].

Minazzi, R. (2015). *Social Media Marketing in Tourism and Hospitality*, Cham: Springer International.

Molz, J. (2012). *Travel Connections: Tourism, Technology, and Togetherness in a Mobile World*, London: Routledge.

Narayanan, C. (2015). 'The rise and rise of social travel', *Business Today*, 24(11): 28–29.

Oates, G. (2014a). 'Interview: Marriott's Travel Brilliantly campaign looks to the wisdom of the crowds', *Skift*, 15 April, Available from: http://skift.com/2014/04/15/interview-marriotts-travel-brilliantly-campaign-looks-to-the-wisdom-of-the-crowds/ [Accessed 29 September 2015].

Oates, G. (2014b). 'Why every major hotel brand wants in on the boutique business', *Skift*, 17 December, Available from: http://skift.com/2014/12/17/why-every-major-hotel-brand-wants-in-on-the-boutique-business/ [Accessed 27 September 2015].

O'Brien, S. (2015). '8 start ups that will make your travel experience so much better', *CNN Money*, 2 July, Available from: http://money.cnn.com/gallery/technology/2015/07/02/best-travel-startups/5.html [Accessed 26 September 2015].

O'Neill, S. (2014). 'American hotel association to fight Airbnb and short-term rentals', *Tnooz.com*, 30 April, Available from: http://www.tnooz.com/article/american-hotel-association-launches-fightback-airbnb-short-term-rentals/ [Accessed 5 August 2015].

O'Regan, M. (2014). 'Niche tourists', in S. McCabe (ed.), *The Routledge Handbook of Tourism Marketing* (pp. 268–280), London: Routledge.

Parra-López, E., Gutiérrez-Tano, D., Díaz-Armas, R. J. and Bulchand-Gidumal, J. (2012). 'Travellers 2.0: Motivation, opportunity and ability to use social media', in M. Sigala, E. Christou and U. Gretzel (eds.), *Social Media in Travel, Tourism and Hospitality: Theory, Practice and Cases* (pp. 196–213), Farnham, UK; Burlington, VT: Ashgate.

Pesonen, J. (2015). 'Targeting rural tourists in the Internet: Comparing travel motivation and activity-based segments', *Journal of Travel and Tourism Marketing*, 32(3): 211–226.

Rickly-Boyd, J. (2013). 'Existential authenticity: Place matters', *Tourism Geographies*, 15(4): 680–686.

Rihova, I., Buhalis, D., Moital, M. and Gouthro, M. (2015). 'Conceptualizing customer-to-customer value co-creation in tourism', *International Journal of Tourism Research*, 17(4): 356–363.

Rudnansky, R. (2015). 'Why are more hotels heavily promoting direct booking today?', *TravelPulse*, 2 September, Available from: http://www.travelpulse.com/news/hotels-and-resorts/why-are-more-hotels-heavily-promoting-direct-booking-today.html [Accessed 28 September 2015].

Stavans, I. and Ellison, J. (2015). *Reclaiming Travel*, Durham, NC: Duke University Press.

Swarbrooke, J. and Horner, S. (2007). *Consumer Behaviour in Tourism*, Amsterdam: Butterworth-Heinemann.

TripAdvisor. (2014). 'New experiences and bonding with loved ones top vacation motivations for US travelers', *TripAdvisor.com*, 24 September, Available from: http://ir.tripadvisor.com/releasedetail.cfm?releaseid=872318 [Accessed 24 September 2015].

Weed, J. (2015). 'Hotels view Airbnb as hardly a threat, for now', *New York Times*, 12 May.

Xiang, Z., Choe, Y. and Fesenmaier, D. (2014). 'Searching the travel network', in S. McCabe (ed.), *The Routledge Handbook of Tourism Marketing* (pp. 281–298), London: Routledge.

Yeoman, I., Brass, D. and McMahon-Beattie, U. (2007). 'Current issue in tourism: The authentic tourist', *Tourism Management*, 28(4): 1128–1138.

Zax, D. (2014). 'With Vayable's new travel app, everyone's a local', *Fast Company*, Available from: http://www.fastcompany.com/3032816/most-creative-people/with-vayables-new-travel-app-everyones-a-local [Accessed 27 September 2015].

Živković, R., Gajić, J. and Brdar, I. (2014). 'The impact of social media on tourism', *Singidunum Journal of Applied Sciences*, 758–761.

34

TRAVEL REVIEW WEBSITES AND INTERACTIVE TRAVEL FORUMS

Marios Sotiriadis, Anestis Fotiadis and Chris A. Vassiliadis

Introduction

One of the fields and industries that have been considerably influenced by the information and communication technologies (ICT) revolution is travel and tourism. The introduction of the Internet especially has affected how consumers search for information about destinations and plan and book travel trips. Further, the Internet has spawned a new breed of intermediaries, online travel agencies (Morrison 2013). Table 34.1 depicts in more detail the influence of technology on various tourism-related industries.

The widespread adoption of the Internet has resulted in changes in the way consumers search for and book holidays that have profound implications for tourism businesses and destinations. From being an additional channel of distribution, the website has now become the centre of the marketing communications mix and an interactive dialogue and communication.

Social media (SM) have opened up a new world of dialogue among people, including conversations about travel and tourism services. Tourism destinations and businesses have joined these conversations by building their own websites. Blogging has also become very popular among consumers. Mobile phones and smartphones have become numerous around the world and their use has had a significant effect on the travel and tourism industry. Euromonitor International (2014) points out that mobile technology is currently transforming

Table 34.1 Tourism technology: world key performance indicators 2013–2015

Internet value % growth (US$)	2013	2014	2015
Car rental	7.2	7.0	7.1
Air transport	8.4	7.5	7.7
Other transportation	7.9	6.7	6.6
Hotels	10.1	9.3	8.0
Travel retail	7.8	7.9	7.8

Source: Adapted from Euromonitor International (2014).

the travel and tourism landscape in terms of bookings, customer service and consumer behaviour. All these technological developments offer benefits for both tourists and destinations, provide opportunities and raise challenges as well.

This chapter aims at analysing the adoption and use of Web 2.0 and user-generated content (UGC) by consumers for tourism purposes. Hence, the chapter is structured as follows. The first section deals with Web 2.0 and various tools and applications. The issues of travel review websites and their uses by consumers for tourism purposes are the subjects of the next sections. These travel review websites and interactive forums create opportunities and challenges for tourism providers. The case of the well-known review website TripAdvisor.com is used to illustrate this topic.

Web 2.0: social media and UGC

This section outlines the impact of the ICT revolution on consumer attitudes and behaviour and the related academic research.

Web 2.0 and related tools

A second generation of web-based applications has appeared over the past decade, applications which O'Reilly (2005) christened Web 2.0. It is enabling consumers to communicate with each other (consumer-to-consumer; C2C) more easily. This has led to commercial websites based on UGC, that is, material provided by consumers (i.e. reviews, photographs, music or information). O'Reilly calls this 'harnessing collective intelligence'.

Let us briefly present these networking platforms of UGC. Blogs appear on the Internet and have a variety of different types of authors (Morrison 2013). Many ordinary tourists write blogs about the places they have visited. Any tourist can get free web space to start his or her own online travel diary, known as a weblog or blog. Most of the blogging activity around the world is C2C. Blogging is continuously attracting more writers and readers of these online materials. Blogs have the advantage of allowing people who would not otherwise have the opportunity to exchange information (Schmallegger and Carson 2008). Travel blogs are part of another phenomenon of the Internet, online communities, groups of people who come together because of a special interest in a particular product or activity. The development of blogs, forums and social networking sites all encourage the formation of 'communities of consumption', drawn together by shared interest.

The literature suggests that one of the main challenges in the digital environment and globalized tourism markets is the rise of SM that allow tourists to interact and share their views and experiences with potentially unrestricted virtual communities (Sigala et al. 2012; Xiang and Tussyadiah 2014). Indeed, SM introduce substantial and pervasive changes to communication between organizations, communities and individuals, and their utilization is believed to be a driving force in defining the current time period as the Age of Exposure (Munar 2010). This social phenomenon has revolutionized communications and consequently tourism marketing.

These developments in ICTs are having a considerable impact, as part of tourism management and marketing strategy, on all aspects of the tourism industry. The reason for this is simultaneously simple and serious: they play a significant role in many aspects of tourism, especially in information search and decision-making behaviours (Sigala et al. 2012; Sotiriadis and Van Zyl 2015). Furthermore, leveraging of SM and UGC to promote tourism services has proved to be an excellent strategy (Xiang and Tussyadiah 2014). The growing role of SM in the tourism field has attracted the attention of researchers and scholars (Zeng and Gerritsen 2014). This is the topic of the following subsection.

Literature review

Literature on SM in tourism suggests that SM are increasingly relevant as part of tourism practices affecting destinations and businesses, as they are changing the many ways in which information about tourism experiences is disseminated (see, for instance, Munar and Jacobsen 2014). SM platforms permit tourists to digitize and share online knowledge and experiences (Sigala et al. 2012). Moreover, web-based platforms allow for recording and sharing tourism experiences. There are four main issues that researchers have examined in the field of SM in tourism, which are briefly presented next. The first is the implications of UGC. Some studies have examined the effect of UGC in tourism (e.g. Xiang and Gretzel 2010; Jacobsen and Munar 2012; Wilson et al. 2012). Second, some studies explored the factors motivating tourists' involvement in SM (e.g. Bronner and de Hoog 2011; Yoo and Gretzel 2011; Munar and Jacobsen 2014).

The third issue is the influence/impact of SM on tourists' behaviour (e.g. Parra-López et al. 2011; Sotiriadis and van Zyl 2013). These studies examined the factors influencing tourists' behaviour, and the benefits and costs of the use of SM in vacations. The fourth main topic is the impact of SM in the field of destination management and marketing. Obviously, the aforementioned issues in general, and the changes in tourists' behaviour in particular, have an impact on the approaches and tools that tourism providers have to adopt and use in managing and marketing their services and offerings in the digital environment. As argued by Sigala et al. (2012), SM are challenging existing customer services, marketing activities and promotional processes in the tourism field. Although SM are not a panacea, they are an effective marketing channel that can be wisely used in integrated communications and marketing of tourism services (Sotiriadis and van Zyl 2013).

Marketing implications

The growth of websites dependent on UGC has significant marketing implications. As stated earlier, the ICT revolution has considerably influenced consumer behaviour. The marketing effects of ICTs result in an increase of the consumers' power. The consumer is now the dominant partner in the marketing exchange and companies have to tailor their products, prices and communications to meet individual needs (Middleton et al. 2009). Additionally, information technology enables global connectivity and digital platforms that mirror reality: ICTs and particularly the Internet have completely removed the barrier of distance and offer consumers instant and continuous information about tourism services and destinations.

The challenges and opportunities for tourism-related industries that arise from the digital environment are obvious in everyday business practice. ICTs and their applications have caused profound changes to the whole business environment for tourism organizations and restructured the approach to marketing. All these developments have transformed the way tourism businesses operate and Web 2.0 has become part of the shift from company-centric towards consumer-centric approaches to modern marketing. The crucial point is, therefore, how businesses and destinations can make effective use of ICTs and SM (Ayeh et al. 2013; Morrison 2013).

These tools are above all means of communication, and both parties (businesses and consumers) involved are using them according to their needs and requirements: tourists for inspiration and information purposes and tourism providers as complementary sources and tools for feedback, marketing intelligence and innovation purposes (Sotiriadis and van Zyl 2015). The crucial point is to adopt the appropriate approach and to use SM properly in order to tap the full potential of these tools. Therefore, it is imperative for tourism destinations and businesses to consider how SM are adopted and used by tourist consumers, the ways that SM are shaping B2C (business-to-consumer) marketing communications and how businesses may tap into their full potential (Sotiriadis and van Zyl 2013, 2015).

The trend in tourism websites is for 'aggregated content', i.e. text, pictures, video clips and sounds, provided by consumers themselves through Web 2.0 channels. It is useful to consider in more detail the travel review websites and interactive travel forums.

Travel review websites and interactive travel forums

Tourist consumers are looking for suggestions and tips when they plan or during their trip. The first source of information might be the destination's website. An alternative source of reassurance can be found in reading the comments there or asking the advice of other tourists. Today, many prospective tourists will compare the information on the official websites with the views and experiences of other visitors on websites using blogs and message boards, such as TripAdvisor (Ayeh et al. 2013).

As already mentioned, any tourist can get free web space to start his or her own online blog (Schmallegger and Carson 2008). Most of the travel blogging activity around the world is C2C. There are now hundreds of specialized tourism blogs on the Internet to which consumers share their travel experiences. Some of the most popular of these include TravelPod. com, Blog.Realtravel.com, Travelblog.org, IgoUgo.com and Travellerspoint.com.

One of the Web 2.0 applications is the concept of traveller review websites dedicated to review and feedback; in other words, websites that allow users to post, read reviews, discuss, and share experiences and opinions on myriad topics. These websites include assessments by consumers who have visited destinations, hotels, attractions, restaurants or used other tourism services and facilities (Morrison 2013). The main appeal of these websites is the perceived 'objectivity' of the reviews, for consumers who are considering going to a destination or using a particular tourism business (O'Connor 2010; Ayeh et al. 2013).

TripAdvisor.com is the most used among these websites. Virtual Tourist is another popular traveller review website. Other traveller reviews are found on a variety of different sites including the sites of traditional travel guidebook publishing companies. For example, Lonely Planet has the Thorn Tree travel forum which is an online discussion group for travellers. This forum is in several parts including the 'departure lounge' (discussions by geographic region) and the 'lobby' (discussions by specific interest and topic). Travel guidebooks are trusted for their objectivity and lack of commercial ties to destinations and tourism businesses, and this extends to their online forums and discussion groups. Recent surveys of traveller review sites indicate that a majority of consumers find the reviews to be credible and useful (Morrison 2013).

Adoption and uses by tourists

All types of online platforms have become much more than an information source for tourists. Travel websites are now used for obtaining information, planning travel, final booking and online transactions. This section examines the uses of SM platforms and travel review websites by tourists.

SM platforms for tourism purposes

Consumers visit tourism-related websites and SM platforms for multiple reasons and purposes, the main being: (1) dreaming, enthusing and informing about potential destinations and choices; (2) planning, selecting and booking a destination and/or tourism providers; (3) travelling, visiting and enjoying places of interest; (4) repeating, recommending and recollecting; and (5) reading travel reviews, opinions and suggestions.

Consumers are already making significant use of UGC in gathering travel information and making trip decisions. A survey conducted in the USA in early 2012 found that 46.9% of respondents reviewed UGC when planning their leisure travel trips, and overall, 55.9% used UGC or SM. This compared with 31.1% using print or online DMO (destination marketing organization) sources (Morrison 2013). As for the motivations for online reviews and experience sharing, a recent study (Munar and Jacobsen 2014) explored the motivations of summer holidaymakers for making SM contributions and their willingness to share content through various SM. This study indicates that: (1) there is a dominance of visual content; (2) the altruistic and community-related motivations are most relevant for information sharing; (3) SM allowing audience control are most popular for online sharing; and (4) motivational factors differ depending on type of content and type of SM.

Uses of travel review websites

The literature suggests that UGC is not believed as much as traditional word-of-mouth, but is more credible than commercial sources of information. Web 2.0 applications have already established themselves as key sources of information for tourists before, during and after their trips (IPK International 2013). Table 34.2 depicts the answers per region to the question: 'Do you use special travel blogs, travel forums or review websites with regard to your travel and holiday planning?' The Chinese (95%) and the Brazilians (84%) are the heaviest users but two-thirds of Europeans and Americans check out online reviews as well.

These estimations are confirmed by the findings of the Tripbarometer survey conducted among TripAdvisor users, hoteliers and other users to understand the global travel trends, change in consumer spend, travel patterns and booking habits of tourists. These are the key findings relating to online reviews (TripAdvisor 2014):

• Online tourist reviews are third (after 'Visiting a place I have never been before' and 'Flight fares') in terms of impact on decisions to travel to a particular destination. Flight fares are the second most important factor, while price has the biggest impact on accommodation bookings.

• Both price and online reviews are perceived as having a significant impact on booking decisions by tourists (demand perspective) and businesses (offer perspective).

Table 34.2 The use of review websites and blogs for travel planning

Frequency of use	China %	Brazil %	USA %	Europe %	Japan %
Yes	33	24	17	16	18
Yes, sometimes	62	60	48	45	34
No	5	16	35	39	48

Source: Adapted from IPK International (2013: p. 26).

- Sources of information and inspiration: online and offline sources coexist, though online dominates; online sources are most commonly used, with TripAdvisor topping the list; word-of-mouth is still an important source of ideas for consumers and consequently 90% of travellers use offline sources.
- Tourists are booking online, but mobile is emerging; two-thirds (66%) of tourists booked their last trip online, with web-based travel agencies (27%) emerging as the most popular channel.
- Tourists/travel preferences: 52% of 'Millennials' (18 to 34 years old) are highly influenced by travel blogs, and 47% are influenced by travel-related pictures on SM.
- As for the reviews, it seems that customer feedback plays a key role in the travel cycle: 89% of global tourists say reviews are influential when choosing where to book. What impacts global tourists' decision for where to travel? 65% say online travel reviews, and 48% personal recommendations. 96% of global hoteliers say reviews are influential in generating bookings.

Hence, practitioners are confirming the findings from other studies (academic research and business reports). All these online platforms and consumers' activity present both opportunities and threats for tourism marketing (Sotiriadis and van Zyl 2015). One of the biggest online travel review websites is TripAdvisor.com (O'Connor 2010; Ayeh et al. 2013). This constitutes the topic of the following case study.

Case study: TripAdvisor.com

TripAdvisor website services are free to users, who provide most of the content, and the website is supported by an advertising business model. This section outlines its profile, content, key features and business model, aiming at pointing out how this interactive travel website influences (sometimes in a determining way) tourist consumers' behaviour (O'Connor 2010).

Profile

TripAdvisor is an American travel website company providing reviews of travel-related content. It also includes interactive travel forums. It was founded in February 2010 as an unbiased resource to research and plan all aspects of travel (O'Connor 2010; Lee et al. 2011). TripAdvisor, featuring real advice from real travellers, helps people decide where to go, where to stay, how to get there and what to do when they arrive.

TripAdvisor, Inc. manages and operates websites under 24 other travel media brands: AirfareWatchdog, BookingBuddy, CruiseCritic, EveryTrail, Family Vacation Critic, FlipKey, The Fork, GateGuru, Holiday Lettings, Holiday Watchdog, Independent Traveler, Jetsetter, Niumba, Onetime, Oyster, SeatGuru, SmarterTravel, Tingo, TravelPod, Tripbod, VacationHomeRentals, Viator, VirtualTourist and Kuxun. The company employs more than 2,900 people as of March 2015.

It operates websites in 45 countries, among others the USA, the UK, France, Germany, Spain, India, Japan, Brazil, Canada, China, Russia and Indonesia. It also includes TripAdvisor for Business. The website's motto is 'Reviews and advice on hotels, resorts, flights, holiday rentals, travel packages, and more so you can plan and book your perfect trip!' (TripAdvisor 2015).

Content and audience/members

TripAdvisor claims to be the largest travel review website in the world, with more than 60 million members, reviews and information on over 400,000 locations and over 225 million reviews and opinions covering more than 4.9 million hotels, restaurants, attractions and other travel-related businesses (www.tripadvisor.com). It offers advice from millions of tourists and a wide variety of travel choices and planning features. TripAdvisor branded sites make up the largest travel community in the world, reaching 340 million unique monthly visitors (Google Analytics 2015).

Table 34.3 Users' reviews on TripAdvisor.com

User reviews about	Worldwide
Destinations	134,000+
Hotels	950,000+
Holiday rentals	700,000+
Attractions	530,000+
Restaurants	2,700,000+
Candid traveller photos	17,000,000+

Source: TripAdvisor (2015).

As mentioned earlier, TripAdvisor includes more than 225 million reviews and opinions from tourists around the world, and more than 4.9 million businesses and properties. On TripAdvisor, there are 139 new contributions made every minute; on average, nearly 2,600 new topics are posted every day to the TripAdvisor forums. As for TripAdvisor Mobile, nearly 190 million tourists have downloaded the various TripAdvisor apps (as of Q1 2015) and nearly 50% of users visited TripAdvisor via tablet and phone. Its website provides easy access worldwide to leading online travel agencies including Expedia, Orbitz, Travelocity, hotels.com, Priceline and Booking.com.

These figures evidence the very significant role of TripAdvisor as a source of information, interaction and suggestions exchange and the related impact on tourists' behaviour (O'Connor 2010). Its key features include: instant booking, 'Just for You' personalization, hotel price comparison, candid traveller photos, tours features, TripAdvisor flights, vacation rentals, maps, tripwatch and forums. The last enable members to ask for and share their opinions and advice (www.tripadvisor.com). Based on these figures and features, TripAdvisor reasonably claims to be the world's largest travel website and online travel guide. Therefore, its influence on tourist consumers' behaviour is considerably important.

Business model – advertising opportunities

While it is free for tourists to use and for companies to be listed on the website, TripAdvisor Media Network offers tourism providers graphical advertising opportunities and cost-per-click marketing platforms. After reading the reviews, tourists can click through to make bookings through an affiliate network of leading online travel agencies, tour operators, airlines and hotel groups.

TripAdvisor claims to be the only place to reach 50 million informed, educated and connected tourists who are actively researching and planning a trip. It draws a diverse international audience with one interest in common: they plan to travel, and are dedicated to and enthusiastic about travel. The audience returns to TripAdvisor to share their experiences with other travellers by giving real user reviews, opinions and advice, making TripAdvisor the world's most trusted place for travel advice.

Uses by tourists

TripAdvisor taps into tourists' collective knowledge and enables their connection to share their experiences and provide advice. In doing so, the website remains transparent; its content is not edited or filtered. Its members' contributions provide current and relevant information, resulting in the best possible consumer experience (Lee et al. 2011; Ayeh et al. 2013). It offers trusted advice from real travellers and a wide variety for travel choices and planning features. Its members like to share their thoughts with other tourists and together have contributed more than 125 million reviews and opinions. TripAdvisor is also a lively discussion platform with more than 2,800 new topics posted in its forums each day. It is the world's largest travel site with 83.4 million monthly unique users (TripAdvisor 2015).

TripAdvisor announced on June 2015 the launch of the TripAdvisor application (app) for Android Wear smart watches (Travel and Tour World 2015). The free app, which is currently available on Google Play, helps tourists find nearby things to do with access to TripAdvisor traveller reviews and ratings of hotels, restaurants and attractions.

The reviews, online ratings and certificate of excellence granted by TripAdvisor have a significant influence on tourists' planning choices.

Conclusion: suggestions for tourism destinations and businesses

The Internet has become the consumer's first-choice place to search for information on destinations and tourism operations. Many ICTs empower consumers and greatly enhance their power in the marketplace. As analysed in this chapter, the tools of Web 2.0 in general, and the travel review websites and interactive forums in particular, provide opportunities and challenges for tourism destinations and providers to better listen to and understand their current and potential consumers.

This chapter attempted to provide insights into the emergent field of Web 2.0 applications. The issue has been approached from a tourist consumer perspective aiming at formulating suggestions for tourism destinations and providers. The main challenge is that they have to adopt adequate approaches in order to address the challenges and take full advantage of the opportunities. As for the DMOs, they have to move more from 'pushing' (or promoting) their destinations to potential tourists, towards 'pulling' (or attracting) people to destinations. According to Pollock (2009), the '5 Ps' have to change into the '5 Cs': customer, connections, conversations, content and community. The last C involves DMOs building online communities and then engaging others (residents, suppliers, tourists, etc.) to have conversations about their destinations. This suggestion is advocated by practitioners (IPK International 2013).

The crucial issue is, therefore, to listen to and communicate properly with tourists and to adopt and implement an integrated marketing communications (IMC) approach that aims at stimulating interactive and mutually beneficial dialogue. Within this rationale, tourism destinations and businesses, when planning the design of websites, need to be sure to provide for all potential consumer uses and purposes. Content alone is not enough to meet all of their needs and requirements; websites must be supplemented with pages on popular SM channels that allow different types of interactions with tourists. Effective websites of tourism providers and destinations must have the following elements/characteristics: (1) be a part of IMC; (2) use SM channels and generate user content, i.e. encourage users to provide their own texts, photos or videos; and then use some of these materials in business/destination promotions and share them with other potential tourists; (3) be attractive, networked, dynamic and integrated; and (4) have smartphone applications available. Therefore, in other words, a website is no longer just a website for a tourism organization, but rather an online location to interconnect with different audiences using an integrated set of ICTs.

Additionally, to take the fullest advantage of ICTs, tourism destinations and providers need to (1) continuously track comments about the destination and operations on traveller review sites, and provide feedback and comments when required; (2) continuously track travel blogs, and provide feedback and comments when required; (3) use blogging to provide ongoing information and stories; and (4) keep updated on the introduction of new ICTs in tourism and related fields.

References

Ayeh, J. K., Au, N. and Law, R. (2013). 'Do we believe in TripAdvisor? Examining credibility perceptions and online travelers' attitude toward using user-generated content', *Journal of Travel Research*, 52(4): 437–452.

Bronner, F. and de Hoog, R. (2011). 'Vacationers and eWOM: Who posts, and why, where and what?', *Journal of Travel Research*, 50(1): 15–26.

Euromonitor International (2014). *The World Travel Market Global Trends Report 2014*, London: World Travel Market (WTM) and Euromonitor International.

Google (2015). 'Google analytics', Available from: http://www.google.com [Accessed: 30 August 2015].

IPK International (2013). *ITB World Travel Trends Report*, Berlin: Messe Berlin GmbH.

Jacobsen, J. K. S. and Munar, A. M. (2012). 'Tourism information search and destination choice in a digital age', *Tourism Management Perspectives*, 1(1): 39-47.

Lee, H. A., Law, R. and Murphy, J. (2011). 'Helpful reviewers in Tripadvisor, an online travel community', *Journal of Travel and Tourism Marketing*, 28(7): 675–688.

Middleton, V. T. C., Fyall, A. and Morgan, M. with Ranchhod, A. (2009). *Marketing in Travel and Tourism*, 4th edition, Oxford, UK: Butterworth-Heinemann.

Morrison, A. M. (2013). *Marketing and Managing Tourism Destinations*, New York: Routledge.

Munar, A. M. (2010). 'Digital exhibitionism: The age of exposure', *Culture Unbound: Journal of Current Cultural Research*, 2(2): 401–422.

Munar, A. M. and Jacobsen, J. K. S. (2014). 'Motivations for sharing tourism experiences through social media', *Tourism Management*, 43(1): 46–54.

O'Connor, P. (2010). 'Managing a hotel's image on TripAdvisor', *Journal of Hospitality Marketing and Management*, 19(7): 754–772.

O'Reilly, T. (2005). 'What is Web2.0: Design patterns and business models for the next generation of software', Available from: http://www.oreilly.com/pub/a/oreilly [Accessed: 25 May 2013].

Parra-López, E., Bulchand-Gidumal, J., Gutiérrez-Taño, D. and Díaz-Armas, R. (2011). 'Intentions to use social media in organizing and making vacation trips', *Computers in Human Behavior*, 27(2): 640–654.

Pollock, A. (2009). *The Future of Destination Marketing: Why All Marketing is Social Marketing*, Presentation to BIT Reiseliv, Oslo, Norway.

Schmallegger, D. and Carson, D. (2008). 'Blogs in tourism: Changing approaches to information exchange', *Journal of Vacation Marketing*, 14(2): 99–110.

Sigala, M., Christou, E. and Gretzel, U. (eds.) (2012). *Social Media in Travel, Tourism and Hospitality: Theory, Practice and Cases*, London: Ashgate.

Sotiriadis, M. and Van Zyl, C. (2013). 'Electronic word-of-mouth and online reviews in tourism services: The use of Twitter by tourists', *Electronic Commerce Research Journal*, 13(1): 103–124.

Sotiriadis, M. and Van Zyl, C. (2015). 'Tourism services, micro-blogging and customer feedback: A tourism provider perspective', in J. N. Burkhalter and N. Wood (eds.), *Maximizing Commerce and Marketing Strategies through Micro-Blogging* (pp. 157–176), Philadelphia, PA: IGI Global.

Travel and Tour World (2015). 'TripAdvisor announces Android wear app', Available from: https://www.travelandtourworld.com/news [Accessed 2 June 2015].

TripAdvisor (2014). 'Research TripBarometer April 2014: Global edition', Available from: http://www.tripadvisor.com/TripAdvisorInsights/n2200/ [Accessed 30 April 2014].

TripAdvisor (2015). Official website, Available from: https://www.tripadvisor.com [Accessed 8 June 2015].

Wilson, A., Murphy, H. and Cambra Fierro, J. (2012). 'Hospitality and travel: The nature and implications of user-generated content', *Cornell Hospitality Quarterly*, 53(3): 220–228.

Xiang, Z. and Gretzel, U. (2010). 'Role of social media in online travel information search', *Tourism Management*, 31(2): 179–188.

Xiang, Z. and Tussyadiah, I. (eds.) (2014). *Information and Communication Technologies in Tourism 2014*, New York/Vienna: Springer.

Yoo, K. H. and Gretzel, U. (2011). 'Influence of personality on travel-related consumer-generated media creation', *Computers in Human Behavior*, 27(2): 609–621.

Zeng, B. and Gerritsen, R. (2014). 'What do we know about social media in tourism? A review', *Tourism Management Perspectives*, 10: 27–36.

35

THE POTENTIAL FOR eWOM TO AFFECT CONSUMER BEHAVIOUR IN TOURISM

Alana Harris and Bruce Prideaux

Word of mouth (WOM) is a socially constructed communication phenomenon (Harris and Prideaux 2011) where information is directly exchanged between two or more people either face-to-face or online (Sotiriadis and van Zyl 2013). The capacity of WOM to both inform and influence has been of interest to academics and industry for a considerable time. This interest has grown exponentially as the volume of WOM has skyrocketed via electronic channels, known as eWOM.

In the past 20 years there has been a proliferation of electronic communications and eWOM studies covering areas such as blogs (Carson 2008), models of online communication networks, online reviews and information-seeking behaviour. More recently the focus has expanded to recommendation websites including TripAdvisor and social media, Twitter and Facebook. While information, opinion and perceived expertise offered online appear to mirror many of the characteristics of face-to-face WOM, the degree to which these relationships, reference groups and communication channels and network dynamics influence decisions or contribute to knowledge acquisition remains unclear.

This chapter examines eWOM, how it differs from traditional WOM and how those aspects specific to eWOM impact on consumer behaviour in the tourism context. The chapter will apply Tate and Alexander's (1999) criteria of online information quality as a framework to explain how consumers might consider eWOM communication, then conclude by outlining the integrated and supplementary roles of traditional WOM and eWOM in consumer behaviour.

According to Litvin et al. (2008: p. 461), eWOM can be defined as 'all informal communications directed at consumers through Internet-based technology related to the usage or characteristics of particular goods and services, or their sellers'. Bronner and de Hoog (2011: p. 15) posited that eWOM 'involves consumers' comments about products and services posted on the Internet'. Development of the Internet has flourished in terms of channels and devices through which eWOM can take place.

Background

Academic and practitioner interest in eWOM has been driven by a number of factors, most notable being worldwide device adoption and increased Internet connectivity. Both have grown rapidly in the past decade with continued significant growth forecast in the immediate future. According to www.internetworldstats.com global Internet use has grown by 826.9% from 361 million users in 2000 to 3.3 billion users in 2015. In addition, there were 7.1 billion global SIM connections and 243 million 'machine-to-machine' connections by the end of 2014 (GSMA Intelligence 2015). The World Bank also reported a global growth in mobile telephone subscriptions (per 100 people) from 33.9 in 2005 to 96.3 in 2014. Given these numbers it is unsurprising that a large volume of research has been undertaken into the eWOM phenomenon and its implications for consumer behaviour in the tourism context.

Global tourism is also growing with international arrivals reaching a record 1.14 billion in 2014 (Crotti and Mishrahi 2015). From a tourism perspective, eWOM appears to be the panacea that couples economic efficiencies with maximum reach. eWOM offers a cost-effective means of communicating with potential travellers in an increasingly competitive environment (Crotti and Mishrahi 2015). In terms of spread or diffusion, recent studies show that forms of networked communication such as WOM and eWOM are more effective than advertising (Goldenberg et al. 2001). The networked reach of eWOM has the potential to yield a substantial return and the opportunity to cut through marketing 'noise', particularly in a climate where travellers are becoming sceptical of organisations and advertising (Bronner and de Hoog 2011). Moreover, eWOM offers destination marketers the potential to navigate the complexity of the destination experience when delivery lies outside their control.

The interest is not limited to practitioners and there is a growing volume of academic research into eWOM. While a thorough review is beyond the scope available in this chapter, Table 35.1 provides a selection of recent review articles which detail the development directions of research to date. It is worth noting that these review articles reflect the currency of the literature in this area.

Aspects of eWOM

WOM and eWOM share a number of underpinning attributes such as trust, expertise and credibility. Both are flexible, multi-purpose and effortlessly woven into the communication exchange. WOM, and by extension eWOM, is still considered to be the most frequently and highly regarded source of information for tourist decision making (Ring et al. 2016; Tham et al. 2013), and Gretzel and Yoo (2008) contended that influence continues after decisions have been made.

The model illustrated in Figure 35.1 shows how brand, detail and opinion based on experience may feature, either independently or in a combination, in the same encounter. Discussion of brand in the tourism consumer context might include multinational tourism products including hotel chains such as Hyatt and Hilton, or theme parks such as Disneyland. Informative elements might include information such as pricing, opening hours, parking, food availability, directions, weather, access and other details. Finally, the evaluative element provides opinions based on experience.

The notion that eWOM is all about influence flowing from one party to another, or others, is a narrow view. This model suggests that it is the confluence of information that makes the message. Arguably, the power of the influence stems from the consumer having access to the information they require on the terms that suit them. The nature of the content of eWOM, regardless of channel, is that the content is flexible, context driven and unique.

There are, however, other aspects that distinguish the traditional form of WOM and eWOM including timing aspects, proximity, content and presentation of content, which influence consumers in different ways.

Table 35.1 Review articles on eWOM

Author	Title	Summary
Bronner and de Hoog (2016)	Travel websites: Changing visits, evaluations and posts	Comparison of two samples sharing an equal sample structure and identical questions from 2007 and 2014
Schuckert et al. (2015)	Hospitality and tourism online reviews: Recent trends and future directions	2004–2013, 50 articles categorised into 5 topics: online reviews & buying, satisfaction & management, opinion mining, motivation, role of reviews
Cantallops and Salvi (2014)	New consumer behavior: A review of research on eWOM and hotels	2007–2011, 28 articles from 6 journals categorised as generating factors and impacts of eWOM
Law et al. (2014)	Progress on information and communication technologies in hospitality and tourism	2009–2013, 107 articles were grouped by consumer and supplier and found ICT used across units for different applications
Zeng and Gerritsen (2014)	What do we know about social media in tourism? A review	2007–2013, 207 articles identified what is known of social media, sets an agenda and observes that social media is still in its infancy
Leung et al. (2013)	Social media in tourism and hospitality: A literature review	2007–2011, 44 journal articles found strategic importance of social media to tourism competitiveness

Source: Authors.

Time

Three aspects of timing are specific to eWOM: eWOM can unfold in real time; it can also be archival; and it can be expressed both synchronously and asynchronously. The aspect of real time circumvents a significant challenge for consumers in ensuring that they have current, up-to-date and relevant information. The 24-hour nature of eWOM along channels that are always open means that information can be communicated about a tourism experience as it is occurring. The benefits for consumers are obvious, particularly in terms of minimising the risks associated with tourism consumption. Currency of information is critical in tourism decision making where consumers often only have one chance at the experience.

While a strength of eWOM is its real-time nature, paradoxically, so too is its archival properties. As early as 1998, Buttle noted that eWOM leaves threads – traces that can be stored, searched and developed. This idea of a 'persistent public record' was more recently highlighted by Bronner and de Hoog (2016). Thus eWOM can offer the consumer historic

Figure 35.1   Framework for eWOM/WOM content

Source: Authors.

information and context which differs from the traditional face-to-face WOM which dissipates as soon as uttered. These dual features of real time and archival allow consumers to check, cross reference, gain insights and use points of comparison in a way that is limited in WOM. eWOM uses synchronous and asynchronous means of communication, which ties directly to the real time/archival element previously discussed. Litvin et al. (2008) showed the level of eWOM interactivity in a framework that included blogs, emails, instant messaging (IM), chat rooms, websites and review sites against a scope ranging from 'one-to-one' through to 'one-to-many'.

Proximity

Proximity or propinquity has a long association with the volume and frequency of communication exchange. Libai et al. (2010) observed that the geographic, temporal and social distance may be much more important than customer characteristics in WOM. From a consumer behaviour perspective, the relationships between travellers, proximity and interaction have been explored in a number of different settings including a cruise environment, wineries and campgrounds where travellers are spatially confined. Close proximity tends to be a hotbed of chit-chat where discussion of touristic experiences can lead to decision making. This interaction stems from a variety of factors including similarity, social niceties, a desire to belong to a social group of particular travellers and the need for information among other things.

The discussion of eWOM often makes reference to electronic proximity while traditional WOM refers to physical proximity and it is in regard to this view of proximity that the literature diverges. Brown et al. (2007) argued that offline theory is inappropriate to describe eWOM and its influence due to the absence of close proximity and the social and environmental cues physical proximity brings with it. It has also been noted that:

> the physical world has several properties that do not translate into the context of an electronic referral, such as repeated exposures (electronic referrals are usually one-time communications) or joint consumption settings (the distance and electronic nature of the communication make that unlikely).
>
> *(De Bruyn and Lilien 2008: p. 162)*

More recently Tsiotsou et al. (2012) and Tham et al. (2013) identified this difference and separately addressed the online and offline social interactions between travellers.

A separate treatment of eWOM makes sense as the social networks from which an individual can draw information and ideas (in a traditional sense) have expanded from finite ones where all members are known to the traveller, to almost infinite ones where proportionately very few may be known personally. eWOM provides access to information and detail beyond immediate social boundaries (Gretzel and Yoo 2008) and the cultural norms associated with them.

This is important because it is the relationships between individuals, rather than the channel, that are central to the WOM phenomenon. Conversely, information provided in the eWOM context could be characterised as coming from individuals who are largely anonymous. As such there is an absence of existing relationships so constructs such as trust and familiarity do not exist; instead the relationship can lie between the individual and the channel (Bronner and de Hoog 2011). For example, a consumer might trust one form of eWOM over another because that consumer trusts TripAdvisor rather than the consumer who is communicating via that particular channel (Schuckert et al. 2015).

Content

Given that the volume of information online via eWOM is far greater than traditional WOM (Burgess et al. 2011), the presentation of the content is different. While eWOM was initially a series of written threads there have been significant shifts in the content with Web 2.0 and beyond. A criticism levelled at early eWOM was the lack of nuance and its asynchronous nature. This meant that earlier forms of eWOM (such as fora) did not enjoy the 'natural flow' of a conversation where one comment could effortlessly lead into another with consumers using tone, intonation and body language as cues to continue the momentum. However, this has since changed with personality, opinion and imagery all moulding the eWOM message.

For example, emotions have been incorporated into the eWOM message with an ever-growing selection of emojis to accompany comments and provide a clear sense of emotion tied to a comment or remark. Emojis are often a substitute for a comment or remark as the emotion portrayed speaks for itself, giving them an emotive flavour that has been lacking in past eWOM.

eWOM can be visual (Ring et al. 2016) with the inclusion of images with comments providing support or evidence of statements, opinions or assertions made. The increase in image exchange has grown rapidly. The adage that 'a picture tells a thousand words' is poignantly relevant here. The imagery contributes to the message and brings with it a degree of tone and perspective and, at the same time, adds to the volume being communicated.

Arguably, the integration of imagery in eWOM probably facilitates a level of nuance that could never be equalled by traditional WOM. The consumer can make observations as outlined in Figure 35.1 about brands, for example, or make judgements about information such as site crowdedness or cleanliness and apply their own judgement.

The increasing use of ratings (Bronner and de Hoog 2011) to accompany comments provides a scale by which consumers can judge and provides a level of objectivity. It provides a definitive opinion, even if that opinion is not ultimately shared by the consumer. It quantifies an array of opinions about a site or experience to contribute to an overall assessment. In doing so, ratings can represent an overview of opinion and this can act as a means by which the large volume of eWOM information and opinion can be consolidated.

The coupling of comments with emotional representation (emojis, stickers, etc.), images and ratings provides a sense of opinion and emotion which has seen the presentation of eWOM content evolve. Where once WOM offered trusted advice and opinion between individuals known to each other, usually based on an established relationship, now the consumer has a relationship with the channel and online advisors (Bronner and de Hoog 2011; Burgess et al. 2011; Tan and Tang 2013). However, the anonymous relationships established in the virtual world coupled with the growing complexity of the communication can be just as influential on decision making and certainly contribute to knowledge acquisition.

Even with the abundance of opinion and perceived expertise offered online, the degree to which eWOM influences decisions or contributes to knowledge acquisition remains unclear. Some suggest that eWOM is perceived as less trustworthy than WOM because the source is unknown (Leung et al. 2013). Bronner and de Hoog (2016: p. 94) noted that 'posting behaviour is rare and still limited to a small segment'. In essence, eWOM differs from traditional WOM in terms of the delivery channel (multiple online), timing (real time and historic), presentation (may be written or verbal) and reach (the capacity to tap into a network where most relationships are anonymous).

It is important to acknowledge that eWOM is both integrated and plays a supplementary role to face-to-face WOM although the extent of this is not evident from the literature. De Bruyn and Lilien (2008) noted the precision with which real-time data can be collected in the eWOM context. It is useful in the context of a review of the studies in this field to note that data obtained through hits, clicks, messages, online ratings, comments and the like can provide plentiful and objective data within strict measurement parameters for the purpose of testing hypotheses in real time.

Framework for quality of eWOM

This following section outlines a framework based on Tate and Alexander (1999) to conceptualise the quality of eWOM content. This framework can be used to extend the thinking of eWOM beyond the volume and ease of monitoring to offer insights into identifying eWOM quality and how it might be valued from the perspective of those who are participating in electronic exchanges.

Accuracy

Is it factually correct and is it expressed in a way that clearly represents the information so that its intended meaning and interpretation align? If value is to be attached to the message, there needs to be faith in the content. In terms of eWOM there is significant variance with respect to accuracy. Accusations of operators falsely espousing positive features whilst posing as a visitor have highlighted the susceptibility to inaccuracy of information online. Yet consumers have mechanisms through various online sources and content to make a determination of accuracy.

Authority

The expertise of the sender of the message speaks to its credibility. In the absence of knowing the source personally, trust lies with the channel (website, forum, social media platform, etc.) rather than the individual themselves. This provides a level of authority via proxy and has generated much debate about the legitimacy of reviews on sites such as TripAdvisor.

Currency

The immediacy of information and the real-time nature of eWOM enable it to provide the most up-to-date information. This is coupled with the frequent use of time or date stamps attached to postings. Yet this is linked to the premise that all information is current. However, like traditional WOM, there may not always be time markers in the content to provide the receiver with a sense of currency. While there are indicators which may point to currency (such as a comment attached to an image taken at a festival or one-off event), it would be incorrect to assume that the capacity for eWOM to deliver real-time information means that this is always the case.

Objectivity

One of the challenges of eWOM is anonymity, which has the capacity to mask the motivations of the individuals expressing information, reflecting on experiences or providing opinions. The credibility of WOM is often attributed to its capacity to persuade and inform (Cantallops and Salvi 2014). The sense that information is provided on the grounds of goodwill rather than commercial interest is critical. In the absence of physical cues where judgements can be made (rightly or wrongly), eWOM is dependent on other markers of objectivity such as the use of rankings.

Coverage

The ease with which communication can be undertaken simultaneously via numerous channels allows for much broader coverage. A Facebook 'like' or a Twitter 'retweet' or an Instagram 'share' are almost effortless means of propagating messages. The sharing of information in this way generates communication that can be non-specific but can still hold sway by the sheer weight and volume of messages. Coverage has not drawn the same level of attention in the realm of traditional WOM due to the limitations of the social network with which a consumer associates. The impact of volume as well as valence (positive or negative aspects of the message) remains under-researched. It raises the question: is less actually more? In the eWOM space messages across multiple platforms could suggest messages getting lost or there could be some stickiness based on repeated exposure.

Face-to-face or face-to-screen among travellers

In many respects the application of Tate and Alexander's (1999) framework for eWOM closely reflects the aspects recognised as critical to the success of its face-to-face counterpart. A recent study into the at-destination WOM behaviours of caravan (C/V) and backpacker (B/P) travellers to Far North Queensland, Australia explored the use of different channels, devices and use of communication with fellow travellers. The results suggested a relationship between device use and channels of communication. Using Litvin et al. (2008), communication was divided into synchronous and asynchronous.

Table 35.2 Communication channels used during travel

	Respondents (%)						Test statistic	
Channels used to communicate with other travellers	Daily or more		Sometimes		Not at all		Chi square	Sig.
Synchronous								
	B/P	C/V	B/P	C/V	B/P	C/V		
Face-to-face communication	80.8	47.1	15.6	51.7	3.6	1.2	111.124	.000
Mobile phone – calls	14.8	11.1	39.4	36.2	45.7	52.7	3.837	.147
Asynchronous								
	B/P	C/V	B/P	C/V	B/P	C/V		
Facebook	43.7	8.0	30.2	19.2	26.0	72.8	153.950	.000
Mobile phone – text/SMS	19.2	10.5	37.6	27.7	43.2	61.8	23.361	.000
Email	12.6	7.2	28.8	33.1	58.6	59.7	5.327	.070
Personal blog/ Twitter	14.7	4.4	25.2	11.9	59.9	83.7	42.260	.000
Social networking – other	12.9	2.0	23.5	12.4	63.6	85.6	41.210	.000
Internet – other blog	11.4	4.0	16.4	8.7	72.2	87.4	21.389	.000
Notice boards	6.4	6.6	14.5	28.5	79.1	64.8	19.726	.000
TripAdvisor/ similar sites	5.1	4.3	18.8	16.3	76.0	79.5	1.064	.587

Source: Authors.

Table 35.3 Communication devices used during travel

Device use for communicating with other travellers	Caravanner %	Backpacker %	N	Chi square	Sig.
		Case		*Test statistic*	
Mobile phone	46.4	25.2	260	106.343	.000
Smartphone or iPhone	14.2	40.7	214		
Laptop	8.0	14.5	86		
Tablet or iPad	3.3	14.0	68		
Notebook	0.9	1.2	8		
Other	10.7	4.4	54		

Source: Authors.

Table 35.2 shows that the backpackers in the study used face-to-face communications significantly more than the caravanners, even though the highest percentage from each case reported using this at least once a day as a means of communicating with other travellers. The other synchronous communication was 'mobile phone calls' where there was no significant difference reported between frequency of usage. Table 35.2 shows no significant difference between groups' frequency of email use; most reported using it less than daily (backpackers 28.8% and caravanners 33.1%). Likewise, neither group reported using TripAdvisor frequently with 76% of backpackers and 79.5% of caravanners reporting that they did not use it at all. With the exception of email, and TripAdvisor, there was a significant difference in the frequency of use of communication channels between the groups. This lends support to the notion that the increased use of smartphones by backpackers facilitates the synchronous and asynchronous communication with other travellers at the destination. Table 35.3 shows the reported device usage during travel for communicating with fellow travellers.

There was a significant association between the cases and the type of device they had most used to communicate with other travellers during their visit, $\chi^2 = 106.343$ ($p = .000$). The most popular device used for communications in both cases was the 'mobile phone' or 'smartphone'. These devices allow for synchronous communication and, in the case of 'smartphones', all of the asynchronous options (aside from 'notice boards') as well.

This case study suggests that the increase in smart device usage and connectivity will see a more seamless integration of eWOM with traditional WOM. In the cases presented here, these are groups that traditionally share close physical proximity, volumes of interpersonal communication, common traits and expertise. Even in this setting, the lines between traditional and electronic are blurring.

A convergence of eWOM and WOM

Online advisors are, more frequently, anonymous. The contact may be indirect or asynchronous and without context. WOM from such sources may contribute more to a 'knowledge bank', foster fantasy or address very specific questions, but is less likely to have the rich, nuanced detail (embedded in storytelling) or opportunistic happenstance that can influence an immediate decision. The sought expertise usually relies on the trust of the channel, rather than the individual behind the message (De Bruyn and Lilien 2008). Gretzel and Yoo (2008) and more recently Harris (2015) found that eWOM was more likely to be used to inform decision making such as about accommodation but was not used as much during travel itself. Cantallops and Salvi (2014: p. 41) noted that eWOM 'has gained importance with the emergence of new technology tools' and, given the rapid rate of technology adoption and greater online access, eWOM is likely to be used more frequently during travel as time goes on.

Conclusion

In reality, multiple sources are used for WOM at varying times, in different forms and for different purposes by consumers. In many ways eWOM reveals much about modern tourist consumer behaviour. It offers real-time and archival information and opinion and it highlights the growing importance and value in electronic proximity despite geographical and social distance. eWOM reflects the adoption of and changes to technology through the presentation of the message as written word, spoken word (Skype), image, rating, emotional expression (emoji) or combinations of all of these. What eWOM does offer is a means for consumers to use their own filters at their convenience to determine both the specific information they want along with the broader information they need to assist in their decision making. While this may take place either as a supplement to or in conjunction with other sources, such as advertising or traditional WOM, the role of eWOM is growing in importance. This chapter acknowledges this importance in consumer behaviour, identifies the features of eWOM and offers a framework within which eWOM can be considered in this quickly evolving space.

References

Bronner, F. and de Hoog, R. (2011). 'Vacationers and eWOM: Who posts, and why, where, and what?', *Journal of Travel Research*, 50(1): 15–26.

Bronner, F. and de Hoog, R. (2016). 'Travel websites: Changing visits, evaluations and posts', *Annals of Tourism Research*, 57: 94–112.

Brown, J., Broderick, A. J. and Lee, N. (2007). 'Word of mouth communication within online communities: Conceptualizing the online social network', *Journal of Interactive Marketing*, 21(3): 2–19.

Burgess, S., Sellitto, C., Cox, C. and Buultjens, J. (2011). 'Trust perceptions of online travel information by different content creators: Some social and legal implications', *Information Systems Frontiers*, 13(2): 221–235.

Buttle, F. A. (1998). 'Word of mouth: Understanding and managing referral marketing', *Journal of Strategic Marketing*, 6(3): 241–254.

Cantallops, A. S. and Salvi, F. (2014). 'New consumer behavior: A review of research on eWOM and hotels', *International Journal of Hospitality Management*, 36(January): 41–51.

Carson, D. (2008). 'The "blogosphere" as a market research tool for tourism destinations: A case study of Australia's Northern Territory', *Journal of Vacation Marketing*, 14(2): 111–119.

Crotti, R. and Mishrahi, T. (eds.) (2015). *The Travel and Tourism Competitiveness Report 2015*, Geneva: World Economic Forum.

De Bruyn, A. and Lilien, G. L. (2008). 'A multi-stage model of word-of-mouth influence through viral marketing', *International Journal of Research in Marketing*, 25(3): 151–163.

Goldenberg, J., Libai, B. and Muller, E. (2001). 'Talk of the network: A complex systems look at the underlying process of word-of-mouth', *Marketing Letters*, 12(3): 211–223.

Gretzel, U. and Yoo, K. H. (2008). 'Use and impact of online travel reviews', in P. O'Connor, W. Höpken and U. Gretzel (eds.), *Information and Communication Technologies in Tourism* (pp. 35–46), New York: Springer.

GSMA Intelligence (2015). *The Mobile Economy 2015*, London: GSMA.

Harris, A. (2015). 'Word of Mouth Communication in Destination Marketing: A Comparative Study of the Caravan and Backpacker Markets in Cairns', PhD thesis, James Cook University, Cairns.

Harris, A. and Prideaux, B. (2011). 'Towards a conceptual framework of visitor-to-visitor word-of-mouth', Paper presented at the World Research Summit for Tourism and Hospitality, 10–13 December, Hong Kong.

Law, R., Buhalis, D. and Cobanoglu, C. (2014). 'Progress on information and communication technologies in hospitality and tourism', *International Journal of Contemporary Hospitality Management*, 26(5): 727–750.

Leung, D., Law, R., Van Hoof, H. and Buhalis, D. (2013). 'Social media in tourism and hospitality: A literature review', *Journal of Travel and Tourism Marketing*, 30(1–2): 3–22.

Libai, B., Bolton, R., Bügel, M. S., De Ruyter, K., Götz, O., Risselada, H. and Stephen, A. T. (2010). 'Customer-to-customer interactions: Broadening the scope of word of mouth research', *Journal of Service Research*, 13(3): 267–282.

Litvin, S. W., Goldsmith, R. E. and Pan, B. (2008). 'Electronic word-of-mouth in hospitality and tourism management', *Tourism Management*, 29(3): 458–468.

Ring, A., Tkaczynski, A. and Dolnicar, S. (2016). 'Word-of-mouth segments: Online, offline, visual or verbal?', *Journal of Travel Research*, 5(4): 481–492.

Schuckert, M., Liu, X. and Law, R. (2015). 'Hospitality and tourism online reviews: Recent trends and future directions', *Journal of Travel and Tourism Marketing*, 32(5): 608–621.

Sotiriadis, M. D. and van Zyl, C. (2013). 'Electronic word-of-mouth and online reviews in tourism services: The use of Twitter by tourists', *Electronic Commerce Research*, 13(1): 103–124.

Tan, W.-K. and Tang, C.-Y. (2013). 'Does personality predict tourism information search and feedback behaviour?', *Current Issues in Tourism*, 16(4): 388–406.

Tate, M. A. and Alexander, J. E. (1999). *Web Wisdom: How to Evaluate and Create Information Quality on the Web*, Mahwah, NJ: Lawrence Erlbaum Associates.

Tham, A., Croy, G. and Mair, J. (2013). 'Social media in destination choice: Distinctive electronic word-of-mouth dimensions', *Journal of Travel and Tourism Marketing*, 30(1–2): 144–155.

Tsiotsou, R. H., Mild, A. and Sudharshan, D. (2012). 'Social interactions as basis for segmenting the tourism market', in R. H. Tsiotsou and R. E. Goldsmith (eds.), *Strategic Marketing in Tourism Services* (pp. 35–48), Bingley: Emerald.

Zeng, B. and Gerritsen, R. (2014). 'What do we know about social media in tourism? A review', *Tourism Management Perspectives*, 10: 27–36.

36

THE TRAVEL DISTRIBUTION SYSTEM AND INFORMATION AND COMMUNICATION TECHNOLOGIES (ICT)

Roberta Minazzi

The evolution of the travel distribution system

The evolution of information technology over the past few years has affected the travel distribution system. New dynamics have characterized an increasingly complex sector: some traditional types of operator have disappeared to make way for new players, and new communication and selling tools generate new connection lines between suppliers and consumers.

We can trace various stages of development of the digital travel distribution system. Figure 36.1 shows a possible current configuration of the travel distribution structure. The first step entailed the birth of Global Distribution Systems (GDS) during the 1960s that linked the Central Reservation Systems (CRS) of each travel supplier (airlines, hotels, etc.). GDS are travel reservation systems that provide information about travel services' (hotels/flights) prices and availability in return for fees, and make them available for travel agents to make bookings and sales. At this stage, intermediaries like travel agents and GDS expanded rapidly and power shifted from travel suppliers to distribution channels (Thakran and Verma 2013).

The second step was caused by the development of the Internet in the 1990s which enabled travel companies of all sizes (both large and small/medium-size firms) to create their own websites and then build a direct connection with travellers (customers and prospects), overcoming tourism intermediaries (GDS and travel agents). This initiated the so-called process of disintermediation (Kracht and Wang 2010; Thakran and Verma 2013); as a consequence, some travel suppliers, especially airlines and major hotel chains, started to invest in their websites and reservation systems in order to offer information about prices and availability and sell their services directly. In the hospitality industry mainly large multi-branding groups are investing in Customer Relationship Management (CRM) actions and are developing their own reservation systems to reach customers and prospects directly. Starwood, for example, has an integrated loyalty scheme for all the brands of the group (the 'Starwood Preferred Guest') and rewards customers with the lowest available rate only for direct bookings made on the group website. In 2012 Choice Hotels, Hilton, Hyatt, InterContinental, Marriott and Wyndham developed the booking engine Room Key.

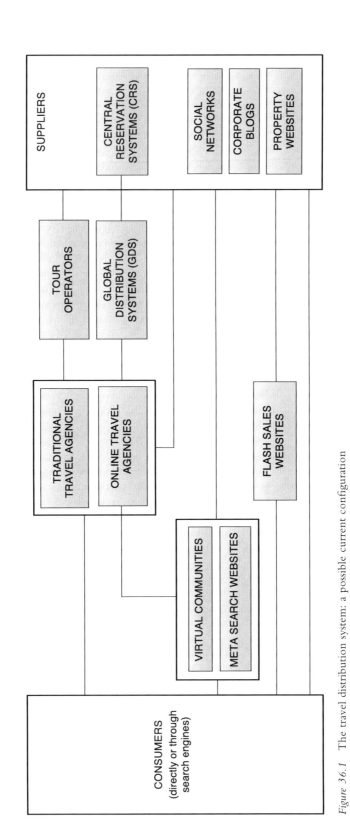

Figure 36.1 The travel distribution system: a possible current configuration

Source: Minazzi (2015: p. 78).

Various loyalty schemes have been integrated in order to allow travellers to redeem points from all the hotel members of the Room Key partnership but reward points are earned only in the case of direct bookings on the Room Key website. However, other operators, especially small chains and single-unit hotels, do not fully exploit the opportunities offered by the new tool. This may depend on the fact that hotel managers often consider IT and social media as only instruments to reach customers rather than a crucial part of the entire business strategy (Law and Jogaratnam 2005; Law et al. 2008). In order to develop a direct connection with consumers by means of corporate websites, travel suppliers should also be aware of the increasing propensity of travellers to use search engines (e.g. Google, Yahoo, Bing) to look for and compare tourism services (Kracht and Wang 2010). Therefore, Search Engine Optimization (SEO) strategies have become a crucial element to turn search engines into distribution channels (Paraskevas et al. 2011).

The combination of these factors, the popularity of the Internet, the spread of booking engines (e.g. Google, Yahoo), as well as the slow reaction of some tourism operators, created a parallel process of reintermediation that produced a proliferation of new distribution channels (Toh et al. 2011; Mauri 2014). In particular, the development of online travel agencies (OTAs) (e.g. Expedia, Booking.com, etc.) was quick and very successful. As aggregators of travel services, these operators allow consumers to compare prices across multiple suppliers (Venkateshwara Rao and Smith 2006), to evaluate alternatives and to book via the Internet. Travellers can compose their own tourism package and, at the same time, they can also purchase bundles of different services (e.g. flight, accommodation, car rental and attractions) (Toh et al. 2011). In the same way, some existing intermediaries like GDS were able to adopt and to exploit the opportunities offered by the Internet through the creation of their own OTAs. For example, until 2014 Sabre controlled Travelocity and Lastminute.com, while Travelport managed Orbitz. In 2015 some GDS sold this part of their businesses to the main OTAs. In particular Expedia acquired Travelocity and Orbitz and Bravofly Rumbo Group acquired Lastminute.com. On the contrary, offline travel agents suffered with the spread of new competitors and had to reconsider their role by focusing more on specialization and differentiation rather than on mere retail.

Owing to high commissions to be paid to OTAs, and an increase of price competition, the increase in the use of OTAs by travellers resulted for some companies in a positive effect on brand awareness but a negative effect on price margins. The recent development of new intermediaries contributed to enhance this phenomenon. In particular, flash sales (or social couponing) are website promotions generally used by travel suppliers to promote unsold inventory at large discounts for a restricted period of time with a deadline. These new intermediaries are very appealing because they attract new customers, increase sales, boost brand recognition and encourage repeat business (Dev 2012). However, travel suppliers have to sell their products at very convenient rates and have to pay high commissions to be selected for promotions on flash sales (from 20% to 50%) (Dev et al. 2011). Hence there is a great deal of concern in the sector about the use of flash sales operators. Anyway, the selling model attracted other intermediaries like OTAs which started to add 'deals of the day' to their offer. For example, Hotels.com provides a specific section called 'deals of the day' offering discounted hotel rooms (up to 50%) in some selected cities; Orbitz provides 'weekly deals' for hotels, flights, cruises and car rentals.

More recently, the spread of social media further affected the evolution of travel distribution due to a change in travellers' behaviour, in particular the style of communication with travel suppliers and with other consumers. The widespread connectedness and the proliferation of mobile devices, along with a more intense use of social media, have profoundly affected customers' habits, behaviours and decisions (Minazzi and Mauri 2015). A great corpus of research demonstrated that online travel reviews are important indicators of corporate reputation and key sources of information which influence various steps of the consumer decision-making process and purchasing intentions (Gretzel and Yoo 2008; Mauri and Minazzi 2013; Xie et al. 2014; Viglia et al. 2014; Ladhari and Michaud 2015). This new step (the third) of the evolution of the travel distribution structure is characterized by customers' increasing connectedness to the Internet and to a multitude of devices, real-time booking, personal clouds, ubiquitous communication and peer-to-peer marketplaces. Thakran and Verma (2013) analyse this stage as composed by: the SoLoMo Era (2000–2012) and the Hybrid Era (from 2013), the latter being characterized by increasing online searches on multiple devices by travellers and the spread of innovative tools.

While the Internet evolution had reduced to some extent the profit of companies owing to the commissions to be paid to new intermediaries (Thakran and Verma 2013), Web 2.0 now offers travel suppliers the opportunity to interact directly with consumers. Social media like Facebook, Twitter, YouTube, corporate blogs, etc. may give excellent tools for better travel planning, generate relationships among travellers and between travellers and companies, and stimulate direct sales (Pan et al. 2007; Jansen et al. 2009; Tussyadiah and Fesenmaier 2009; Xiang and Gretzel 2010). Indeed, the decision by travel companies to improve direct relationships with consumers by means of corporate websites and social media is likely to produce an increase in direct bookings.

Moreover, thanks to social media new players like virtual communities and meta-search websites have entered the travel distribution system. They may be defined 'mediators' because they intervene in the travel distribution process, directing consumers' choices towards travel suppliers or intermediaries. Therefore, they do not sell the products but generally the transaction is perfected on another website (of the travel supplier or of intermediaries) or offline (Minazzi 2015). Travel 'mediators' give travellers the opportunity to get more information about tourism services: compare prices, read recommendations of other customers, consult the rating and the ranking, learn more about the product, etc. This adds value for customers as it helps them to compare alternatives and to find the right service. Furthermore, even though 'mediators' are connected with the main OTAs, they provide additional opportunities to create a direct connection with travellers because they have the power to drive the customer to a specific corporate website (Christodoulidou et al. 2010). For example, TripAdvisor has recently launched new services (Business listings and TripConnect) that allow hotel companies that invest in marketing strategies to sell directly to TripAdvisor users, thus competing with OTAs. Travel reviews websites (e.g. TripAdvisor) and virtual communities (Lonely Planet) are specific categories of 'mediators' that enable travellers to share user-generated content and compare rankings and ratings about a travel company or a destination. Other categories of 'mediators' include meta-search websites (e.g. Skyscanner, Trivago, Kayak) that allow web surfers to look for and compare various tourism services (Kracht and Wang 2010) such as flights, hotels, car rentals, etc. provided by both online travel agencies and travel suppliers (airlines, hotels). Considering the large amount of data available on the Internet, they are very helpful for travellers because they reduce the number of alternatives in order to reach final decisions.

Social media and travel distribution

The foregoing analysis of the evolution of the travel distribution system shows an increasingly crowded and competitive context. In the light of recent developments, a hot topic in management is how to use the most innovative Internet applications and devices in order to communicate directly with customers, attract prospects and improve sales. In fact, customer engagement improves customers' participation, satisfaction and loyalty which in turn stimulate positive word-of-mouth activity and increase sales. Therefore, social media are not only mediators of travellers' choices: if properly connected to the corporate website, they may function as actual distribution channels. For example, hotels and airlines can upgrade their Facebook pages with a specific plug-in that allows users to check availability and prices directly on Facebook.

Social media offer travel suppliers and intermediaries various opportunities to manage relationships with customers in a more engaging environment than the corporate website. Concerning travel suppliers, for example, in the hospitality industry large multi-branding groups are investing in Social Media Customer Care (SMCC) and customer engagement on social media (Minazzi 2015). SMCC consists in providing customer care by means of social media (e.g. Hyatt concierge on Twitter), while possible actions to create customer engagement could be to set up a social network page, to post emotional content, to participate in travel blogs and to reply to online reviews. All these activities can be successful if they are properly managed and integrated in the business strategy. Considering the effects on intermediaries, social media constitute also an opportunity to engage travellers especially for OTAs and flash sales operators. Flash sales widely use social media to make deals visually appealing and to encourage conversations among members by means of viral marketing strategies. For this reason sharing functions and incentives are used mainly by these operators. On the contrary, generally speaking, OTAs are adopting social media practices more slowly. Social media could help OTAs improve their ability in relation to value-creation and personalization: CRM practices could be useful to create long-term relationships with customers and stimulate sales. The ability to create engagement with customers could help OTAs to compete with new online intermediaries and to avoid being bypassed by travel suppliers that are increasingly aware of social media opportunities. A few examples are Expedia and Hotels.com (brands of Expedia, Inc.) which have loyalty programmes to reward customers ('Expedia Rewards' and 'Welcome rewards'). Moreover, Expedia is very active also in developing online customer relationships and customer care by means of multiple channels of customer support which include a toll-free number, an email service, an online chat and, finally, the opportunity to receive a call at a number provided by the customer.

Future possible developments of the travel distribution system

Information technology has deeply affected travel distribution by generating the processes of disintermediation and reintermediation. The new structure of the market is characterized by a mix of 'old' and 'new' intermediaries which are managed by travel suppliers according to the type of customers. In this context, the study of consumers' choices with respect to their travel behaviour is crucial for the development of the most appropriate channel mix in the perspective of multichannel distribution (Mauri 2012, 2014).

The role of intermediaries is becoming even more complex in such a context. In the future, existing actors and newcomers will probably consolidate their positions (Christodoulidou et al. 2010). However, the new configuration of the system along with the development of 'social commerce' has resulted in opportunities and threats to be considered and managed by both suppliers and intermediaries. On the one hand, as mentioned before, these phenomena could be an opportunity for travel suppliers to create a direct connection with travellers, increasing direct sales and reducing the commissions to be paid to the intermediaries. Nevertheless, the ability and possibility to catch this opportunity depend heavily on the features of different travel businesses and suppliers. For example, large international hotel chains and groups are already working on the development of direct connections with travellers by means of new digital applications. On the contrary, in some countries the hotel sector is mainly composed of small to medium-sized companies which, because of their limited financial dimensions, cannot invest in digital solutions and are just starting to adopt new technologies. Regarding threats, on the other hand, OTAs could face a risk of commoditization (Carroll and Siguaw 2003). The mere activity of aggregating travel services might not be enough for the future in light of the entrance of new intermediaries into the market. Social media and Customer Relationship Management (CRM) could offer chances to move the focus of the strategy from just selling the best fare or rate to providing the best travel experience (Minazzi 2015). Some leading OTAs are already aware of this trend and are investing in the creation of large groups composed of the different businesses of travel distribution by means of acquisitions and alliances. In particular, some business operations show the interest of OTAs in meta-search business. For example, in 2012 Expedia Inc. acquired Trivago, the meta-search website specializing in hotel search, and in 2013 Priceline group acquired Kayak. Moreover, to face the competition from flash sales operators, OTAs are improving discounted deals of the day and working on opaque pricing (e.g. Lastminute. com, Priceline, Hotwire). 'Expedia coupon club' is an example: it is a service launched by Expedia in 2012 that allows all registered customers to the usual newsletter to access special discounts in specific periods.

A new trend of the travel distribution system that should be considered is the development of peer-to-peer markets, generally known as 'the sharing economy' (Belk 2014; Botsman and Rogers 2010). They are platforms that 'enable individuals to make use of under-utilized inventory via fee-based sharing' (Zervas, et al. 2013: p. 2). Sharing economy suppliers who enter the travel market may create concern for existing suppliers. An example of a peer-to-peer operator that is influencing the travel distribution system is Airbnb, a marketplace where people can rent the goods and services they need from others using technology-based networks. The main operating principle is the creation of a community of hosts and guests (travellers) who share services, information and experiences by means of social media (Yannopoulou et al. 2013). While one strong reason to choose Airbnb is to pay lower rates compared with those of hotels, social factors increasingly gain importance during the experience (Ikkala and Lampinen 2015).

With the rapid development of the sharing economy, the level of attention on legal issues has grown. In particular, travel suppliers require further controls on the activities of hosts who are expected to conform to local regulations.

But can Airbnb be considered an intermediary of travel services? For sure it is a competitor for OTAs that offer house rental (e.g. Home Away on Expedia, 'Home and Apartments' on Booking.com). However, the possible competition between operators like Airbnb and hotels is a topic at the core of discussion among academics and practitioners. A recent study by Zervas et al. (2013) analysed the impact of Airbnb on the hotel industry in the USA and identified an influence of the peer-to-peer platform on some specific types of hotels, especially the economy and middle-range operators whose target is not business travellers. Apparently the threat should be in particular for independent hotels rather than for hotel chains, but we have to consider that the main large multi-branding groups have invested over the years in real estate and all-suites businesses (e.g. Home2 by Hilton, Townplace Suites by Marriott, Residence Inn by Marriott). Moreover, the increasing improvement of Airbnb services offered to hosts and guests to enrich the travel experience could, in the future, have a further impact on middle-scale/economy independent hotels or on bed-and-breakfasts. Actually, a possible scenario might be the use of Airbnb as a distribution channel by these operators, a sort of partnership considering also that the commissions to be paid to Airbnb are definitely lower than those of OTAs.

Flash sales business in the travel sector

Flash sales started in the early 2000s during the step characterized by the development of social media. This business is considered particularly attractive by some travel operators, mainly hotels, restaurants and resorts, that over the past few years have started to incorporate the new channel in their distribution strategy. The core concept is to offer customers various promotions of short duration (deals-of-the-day) providing a substantial discount (generally 40–60%) on the official price (Byers et al. 2012). However, different operators and variations to the original business models are emerging.

Concerning tourism, at first the selling model of flash sales was based on 'generalist' websites that offered a variety of goods and services, including tourism. The leading operator in this business is the well-known Groupon which contributed to the popularity of the model. While travel and tourism account only for 3% of the total number of deals, they represent the third largest category and in 2011 they produced 11% of overall daily deal industry revenues (Piccoli and Dev 2012). As a consequence flash sales operators, in the present study called 'generalists', have decided to invest more in travel services (e.g. 'Gateways' of Groupon in partnership with Expedia for North America or the 'Escapes' section created by Living Social) and new operators specializing in tourism and hospitality have entered the market (e.g. Jetsetter, Vacationist, SniqueAway).

We can classify two different categories of flash sales operators in the travel sector: daily-deal websites (e.g. Groupon, LivingSocial) and private sales websites (e.g. Vacationist, VoyagePrivé).

Daily deals websites offer deals that cover a variety of goods and services such as restaurants, salons, fitness centres, electronic devices, etc. (Park and Chung 2012). They are based on the model of group-buying, that is, a minimum number of buyers is necessary to activate a specific promotion/deal (Groupon call it the 'tipping point'). Sellers may set a maximum threshold size to limit the number of coupons that can be purchased (Ye et al. 2012). People can subscribe by specifying one or more cities in order to receive a specific daily newsletter containing the deals of the day. This can be an advantage for local operators (such as restaurants, wellness centres, beauty services, housekeeping, medical services, etc.) and for companies that want to differentiate their strategies according to a macro-area (North America, Germany, France, Italy, etc.) and on the basis of the location indicated by the subscriber (micro-area). Only when the tipping point is reached is the customer's credit card charged and the electronic voucher (coupon) sent to the purchaser. At the same time, the travel supplier will receive the agreed revenue and will redeem the vouchers according to the terms of the deal.

The private sales business model is mainly based on a subscription, whether on invitation or free, after which users start receiving periodic emails about discounted time-limited offers. The discount usually starts from 30% and the range of time is generally one week. We can describe some differences between the two models. First, there is generally no minimum activation level for the deals of private sales websites. Second, in the past the subscription policy of private sales operators required some form of membership or invitation. This difference has progressively decreased over the years for a wider opportunity for users to register for free on the website (e.g. VoyagePrivè and Vacationist). Unsurprisingly, this had an impact also on operators who in the past have preferred to use private sales rather than daily-deal websites to avoid exposing their brands to the mass market (Piccoli and Dev 2012; Dev 2012). Third, private sales business also involves specialized travel operators. Generally speaking, private sales include retail-oriented sites, travel-only sites and online travel agent sites (Piccoli and Dev 2012). In the first case, travel is only a category among others; in the second, operators specialize in travel (i.e. hotels, resorts, etc.); and in the third, OTAs launch their own flash sales on the official website.

Travel suppliers generally use flash sales websites to reach a higher number of customers, increasing occupancy, revenue and profit, as well as to enhance customer awareness (Kimes and Dholakia 2011). A study by Piccoli and Dev (2012) found that branding and customer acquisition, profits and revenue optimization are the main reasons to use flash sales as a distribution channel in tourism. On the other hand, the reasons for not using flash sales operators are costs (high commissions), negative brand effects, misalignment with target segments and ignorance about how they work. Other studies on the case of Groupon report some other critiques about the effectiveness of daily-deal websites such as unprofitability, unsure customer loyalty and attractiveness for actual target markets (Dholakia 2010; Edelman et al. 2011).

The debate on the opportunity to use flash sales operators as a new channel of distribution for travel suppliers is particularly heated. Despite criticism, they are increasingly valued by travel suppliers who sell their products through them, especially to increase occupancy, brand awareness and to allocate unsold inventory. In particular, the ability of flash sales to activate sharing and viral marketing by means of social media is undoubtedly useful especially when the objective is brand awareness. Moreover, the proliferation of new flash sales websites and business models gives tourism operators the opportunity to differentiate the deals they offer. Obviously they are a possible additional channel of the mix that provides the opportunity to reach specific target markets, and are an alternative to OTAs even though commissions are particularly high. What the travel supplier should have clear in their mind is the kind of offer (features, price, etc.), the quantity of rooms (hotel)/seats (restaurant)/tickets (museum, amusement park, etc.), and the time window (a few days, a week, etc.). The offer should be unique in order to protect the company from cannibalization of existing customers. Although a recent study shows positive signs for the daily-deals industry (Dholakia 2012), the medium-term effect of the recurring use of these tools might be examined by ad hoc further research.

References

Belk, R. (2014). 'You are what you can access: Sharing and collaborative consumption online', *Journal of Business Research*, 67(8): 1595–1600.

Botsman, R. and Rogers, R. (2010). *What's Mine is Yours*, London: Collins.

Byers, J. W., Mitzenmacher, M. and Zervas, G. (2012). 'Daily deals: Prediction, social diffusion, and reputational ramifications', in *Proceedings of the Fifth ACM International Conference on Web Search and Data Mining* (pp. 543–552), ACM, Chicago, IL, 23–27 October.

Carroll, B. and Siguaw, J. (2003). 'The evolution of electronic distribution: Effects on hotels and intermediaries', *Cornell Hotel and Restaurant Administration Quarterly*, 44(4): 38–50.

Christodoulidou, N., Connolly, D. J. and Brewer, P. (2010). 'An examination of the transactional relationship between online travel agencies, travel meta sites, and suppliers', *International Journal of Contemporary Hospitality Management*, 22(7): 1048–1062.

Dev, C. S. (2012). *Hospitality Branding*, New York: Cornell University Press.

Dev, C. S., Falk, L. W. and Stroock, L. M. (2011). 'To Groupon or not to Groupon: A tour operator's dilemma', *Cornell Hospitality Report*, 11(19): 4–18.

Dholakia, U. M. (2010). 'How effective are Groupon promotions for businesses?', Available from SSRN: http://papers.ssrn.com/sol3/papers.cfm?abstract_id=1696327 [Accessed December 2013].

Dholakia, U. M. (2012). 'How businesses fare with daily deals as they gain experience: A multi-time period study of daily deal performance', Available from SSRN: http://papers.ssrn.com/sol3/papers. cfm?abstract_id=2091655 [Accessed January 2016].

Edelman, B., Jaffe, S. and Kominers, S. D. (2011). 'To Groupon or not to Groupon: The profitability of deep discounts', *Harvard Business School*, Working Paper 11-063: 1–13.

Gretzel, U. and Yoo, K. H. (2008). 'Use and impact of online travel reviews', in U. Gretzel and K. H. Yoo (eds.), *Information and Communication Technologies in Tourism* (pp. 35–46), Vienna: Springer-Verlag.

Ikkala, T. and Lampinen, A. (2015). 'Monetizing network hospitality: Hospitality and sociability in the context of AirBnB', in *Proceedings of the 18th ACM Conference on Computer Supported Cooperative Work and Social Computing* (pp. 1033–1044), ACM, Vancouver, BC, Canada, 14–18 March.

Jansen, B. J., Zhang, M., Sobel, K. and Chowdury, A. (2009). 'Twitter power: Tweets as electronic word of mouth', *Journal of the American Society for Information Science and Technology*, 60(11): 2169–2188.

Kimes, S. E. and Dholakia, U. M. (2011). 'Customer response to restaurant daily deals', Available from SSRN: http://ssrn.com/abstract=1925932 [Accessed December 2013].

Kracht, J. and Wang, Y. (2010). 'Examining the tourism distribution channel: Evolution and transformation', *International Journal of Contemporary Hospitality Management*, 22(5): 736–757.

Ladhari, R. and Michaud, M. (2015). 'eWOM effects on hotel booking intentions, attitudes, trust, and website perceptions', *International Journal of Hospitality Management*, 46(1): 36–45.

Law, R. and Jogaratnam, G. (2005). 'A study of hotel information technology applications', *International Journal of Contemporary Hospitality Management*, 17(2): 170–180.

Law, R., Leung, R. and Buhalis, D. (2008). 'Information technology applications in hospitality and tourism: A review of publications from 2005 to 2007', *Journal of Travel and Tourism Marketing*, 26(5): 599–623.

Mauri, A. G. (2012). *Hotel Revenue Management Principles and Practices*, Milan: Pearson.

Mauri, A. G. (2014). 'Foreword: Marketing and pricing in the digital environment', in G. Viglia (ed.), *Behavioral Pricing, Online Marketing Behavior, and Analytics* (pp. vii–xii), New York: Palgrave Macmillan.

Mauri, A. G. and Minazzi, R. (2013). 'Web reviews influence on expectations and purchasing intentions of hotel potential customers', *International Journal of Hospitality Management*, 34: 99–107.

Minazzi, R. (2015). *Social Media Marketing in Tourism and Hospitality*, Cham: Springer International.

Minazzi, R. and Mauri, A. G. (2015). 'Mobile technologies effects on travel behaviours and experiences: A preliminary analysis', in A. Inversini and I. Tussydiah (eds.), *Information and Communication Technologies in Tourism* (pp. 507–521), Cham: Springer International.

Pan, B., MacLaurin, T. and Crotts, J. C. (2007). 'Travel blogs and the implications for destination marketing', *Journal of Travel Research*, 46(1): 35–45.

Paraskevas, A., Katsogridakis, I., Law, R. and Buhalis, D. (2011). 'Search engine marketing: Transforming search engines into hotel distribution channels', *Cornell Hospitality Quarterly*, 52(2): 200–208.

Park, J. Y. and Chung, C. W. (2012). 'When daily deal services meet Twitter: Understanding Twitter as a daily deal marketing platform', Paper presented at WebSci2012, 22–24 June, Evanston, IL.

Piccoli, G. and Dev, C. S. (2012). 'Emerging marketing channels in hospitality: A global study of internet-enabled flash sales and private sales', *Cornell Hospitality Report*, 12(5): 4–18.

Thakran, K. and Verma, R. (2013). 'The emergence of hybrid online distribution channels in travel, tourism and hospitality', *Cornell Hospitality Quarterly*, 54(3): 240–247.

Toh, R. S., Raven, P. and DeKay, F. (2011). 'Selling rooms: Hotels vs. third-party websites', *Cornell Hospitality Quarterly*, 52(2): 181–189.

Tussyadiah, I. P. and Fesenmaier D. R. (2009). 'Mediating tourist experiences: Access to places via shared videos', *Annals of Tourism Research*, 36(1): 24–40.

Venkateshwara Rao, B. and Smith, B. C. (2006). 'Decision support in online travel retailing', *Journal of Revenue and Pricing Management*, 5(1): 72–80.

Viglia, G., Furlan, R. and Ladrón-de-Guevara, A. (2014). 'Please, talk about it! When hotel popularity boosts preferences', *International Journal of Hospitality Management*, 42: 155–164.

Xiang, Z. and Gretzel, U. (2010). 'Role of social media in online travel information search', *Tourism Management*, 31(2): 179–188.

Xie, K. L., Zhang, Z. and Zhang, Z. (2014). 'The business value of online consumer reviews and management response to hotel performance', *International Journal of Hospitality Management*, 43: 1–12.

Yannopoulou, N., Moufahim, M. and Bian, X. (2013). 'User-generated brands and social media: Couchsurfing and AirBnb', *Contemporary Management Research*, 9(1): 85–90.

Ye, M., Sandholm, T., Wang, C., Aperjis, C. and Huberman, B. A. (2012). 'Collective attention and the dynamics of group deals', in *Proceedings of the 21st International Conference on World Wide Web* (pp. 1205–1212), ACM, Lyon, France, 16–20 April.

Zervas, G., Proserpio, D. and Byers, J. (2013). 'The rise of the sharing economy: Estimating the impact of Airbnb on the hotel industry', *Boston U. School of Management Research Paper* (2013–16).

37

MARKETING COMMUNICATIONS IN TOURISM AND HOSPITALITY

Trends and implications of an online environment

Shirley Rate, Ronnie Ballantyne, Finlay Kerr and Luiz Moutinho

The changing face of the tourism and hospitality sector

Tourism and hospitality represents one of the most valuable economic sectors in the world. The World Travel and Tourism Council (2015) indicate that in 2014, the total contribution to GDP was 9.8%, to employment 9.4%, to exports 5.7% and to investment 4.3%. Throughout a global recession and slowing economic growth, the sector has seen volatile change in individual industries, tourist behaviours and spending, yet has weathered storms considerably more robustly than others and is set to grow significantly to 2025 (World Travel and Tourism Council 2015). Tourists and travellers continue to place holidays as an important aspect of annual expenditure which bodes well for the sector. Between 2008 and 2014 international arrivals have increased by over 23% (Mintel 2014) and in the UK in 2014 £21.8 billion was generated from overseas visitors.

Arguably, tourism marketing, communications and advertising have played a major part in weathering the recessional storms. A dynamic sector by nature, it is flexible and responsive to change. Fesenmaier and Xiang (2014) suggest that the sector has demonstrated an ability to respond to change by adopting a new paradigm of marketing. Global recession is not the underpinning driver to this, but other forces in the environment which have presented much more difficult challenges. Dramatic demographic shifts, climate change, political instability, conflict and terrorism among a plethora of other influencers have resulted in rapid change, the emergence and disappearance of markets and shifts in the perceptions and behaviours of consumers. For tourism and hospitality marketers, however, these forces are shadowed by the developments in and consumer responses to new technologies.

Projects like *Tourism 2023* led by Forum for the Future (2009) focus on horizon scanning, considering distant trends which will influence tourist behaviours such as new travel and fuel technologies and virtual reality simulation technologies. Yet more immediately, communication technologies are proving to be a major disruptive force which is fundamentally changing the way tourism and hospitality consumers are behaving. Reaching unprecedented levels of hypersociability, consumer expectations of technology according to a report by Visit Scotland (2014) have reached dependence levels with increasing demands on organizations to facilitate the use of personal technological devices at all points of the travel experience alongside increased demand for immediacy and personalization of service. Tourism marketers are realizing digital opportunities in areas such as information search and online booking, virtual communities and online reviews, maximizing the use of big data and analytics in tailoring and customizing services and developing brand relationships with consumers which have strength and endurance (Moutinho et al. 2013), and optimizing demand as well as fare and rate forecasting (Vinod 2013).

However, it is the dramatic evolutions in media and communication technologies, as well as the hyper-connectedness and information seeking and sharing behaviours of tourists, which are having most impact on traditional models of marketing. The propensity towards interactivity presents advertisers with opportunities to create meaningful and prolonged brand interactions with their consumers. McCabe (2009) argues that integrating communications into strategic marketing planning allows organizations to capitalize on this by building strong brand image. Yet repeatedly, academic researchers have been accused of being slow to respond. Indeed, even in the area of general advertising: 'there has been almost no related academic or empirical research, especially on the effectiveness of destination advertisements to attract tourists' (Byun and Jang 2015: p. 31). Furthermore, a study of travel executives (Peterson and Marshall 2015) found most lack a cohesive plan for the social communication aspects of their digital communications strategy. The aim of this chapter then is to consider the wider online marketing environment for communications and advertising in tourism and hospitality, to review current theory and practice on digital and online communications and to outline the future challenges facing tourism and hospitality executives in this dynamic aspect of marketing.

The digital marketing environment

Digital environmental forces have required marketers to dramatically alter their approaches to strategic decision making and in particular focus has been placed on the philosophical foundations of marketing and consumer behaviour.

The philosophy of marketing

Over the past two decades, the philosophy of marketing, the underpinning driver to marketing communications and advertising decision making, has fundamentally changed. The environmental shifts which businesses have been faced with have put traditional philosophies and models of practice under intolerable pressure. Increasing levels of competition have caused the focus to move towards continuous innovation as a means of differentiation. The interaction between new media technologies and formats and consumer responses to these has presented tourism and hospitality marketers with a new and challenging set of opportunities. Mass marketing and linear communication, which have long been the foundation of marketing practice, are an irrelevance in the context of a consumer with access to vast amounts of information about brands and organizations, the ability to create and share information about them and the hunger to interact with organizations.

The sector has had to alter its direction and purpose, realizing that markets must be wooed digitally and that harnessing the immense opportunities to build lasting relationships will provide a competitive advantage which cannot be imitated. Bonds can now be created and maintained with large customer bases at a fraction of the cost and labour-intensity. Therefore, the survival of marketing relies on the fundamental shift from a mass focus to a consumer-centric one. Underlying this concept is the notion that the future of marketing relies on marketers embracing the philosophies of relationship marketing, in other words, securing enough information about consumers to attract, maintain and enhance relationships with them (Berry and Parasuraman 1991). Advances in the accessibility and analytics of data have taken this concept to new levels such that organizations are able to meet needs, shape experiences and drive development of targeted and refined products and services (Gordon and Perrey 2015).

The impact on marketing communications and advertising is profound. The distinctions between advertising and marketing have blurred, as new forms of communication combine the ROI-characteristics of direct marketing with the brand characteristics of traditional advertising. The paradigm of communication has shifted towards integrated marketing communication focusing on business that drives cross-platform integration and conveyance of a consistent message. To adapt and succeed, tourism operators have had to build a new set of capabilities: cross-platform innovation, greater insights, open collaboration and digital processes (Berman et al. 2009). With digital consumers increasingly in control of their media experience, advertisers must focus on relationship communication which supports the consumer-centric approach. The role of communications has changed from information provider and persuader to relationship builder and differentiator (Hughes and Fill 2007). Becoming consumer-centric requires a combination of strategic focus on targeting the right consumers while measuring the results across integrated platforms.

Consumer behaviour

In the context of the 3.2 billion people worldwide who had access to and used the Internet in 2015, up from 400 million in 2000, the pace of growth of this global medium outstrips that of any other. The UK Online Measurement's findings indicate that UK consumers spend almost three hours per day online, over half of which is on a mobile or tablet device, and that seven out of ten people online have a social media presence. Advertisers have had to seriously reconsider their approaches to defining and targeting audiences. According to Tim Eklington, Chief Strategy Officer at the Internet Advertising Bureau (IAB) UK: '"Force-fit" advertising is a thing of the past. As today's consumers spend more of their lives online – it's time they, and we, need to spend wisely.'

With the proliferation of new and emerging communication formats and technologies, those marketers who have not shifted away from the mass approach to communication and distribution are being left behind by their consumers. Consumer expectations of market- ing practice are the biggest challenge facing practitioners. With access to a vast array of information, tourism and hospitality consumers are becoming more sophisticated and refined: 'the new sophisticated traveler has emerged as a result of experience. Tourists from the major generating regions of the world have become frequent travelers, are linguistically and technologically skilled and can function in multicultural and demanding environments overseas' (Buhalis and Law 2008: p. 610).

As such, travel consumers have completely changed the way they shop. Prior to the concept of the Internet, the purchase cycle was linear, decisions were influenced by marketers and access to and selection of products were limited. Evolutions in technologies and the level of sophistication of their use have led to a better-informed and more empowered consumer: 'Consumer empowerment is characterized by the shift from passive to active consumers driven by their search for more meaningful experiences' (Neuhofer and Buhalis 2014: p. 130). But according to Jacobsen and Munar (2012), empowerment is also driven by risk reduction tendencies. As a high-risk purchase, consumers are increasingly seeking more information about travel, engaging in more interaction and sharing more experiences online. Many tourism brands have responded to the shift in behaviours and companies like Qatar Airways, Airbnb and Visit Britain have invested heavily in content development and social media marketing to take advantage of these risk reducing behaviours, with the reward being millions of followers (Mintel 2016).

Empowerment originates from access to information, ability to share information, the proliferation of product choice, online travel content and travel comparison sites which allow consumers to be more discerning in their choice behaviour and as a result they have become more price sensitive. According to a report on travel consumption behaviours by Deloitte (2015), marketers must focus on brand relationships as a means of reducing the criticality of price as a criterion and the commoditization of travel as a product. Yet audience empowerment also relates to power over content. While advertising is being seen as the resolution to marketing challenges through building relationships, audiences have the choice as to whether and how they want to receive commercial content. Increasingly overwhelmed with information and with ad blocking technologies which allow them to avoid content altogether, audiences are now more difficult to engage. For tourism and hospitality advertisers, the application of big data analytics is critical to better understand the audience and develop creative methods of engaging them for longer periods of loyal-type behaviours.

Online marketing communications in tourism and hospitality

According to McCabe (2009: p. 265), online communications can be directed towards: 'the provision of information, raising awareness of the brand, shaping or changing attitudes, or; a call to action such as making a purchase or requesting further information, or; developing customer retention and loyalty, reminding customers'. Hence, the underlying aims of communications in a digital environment are the same as those in traditional media such as broadcast and print. However, Mulhern (2009) argues that there are a number of fundamental premises upon which traditional communications are based which have largely been disrupted by the online environment. These include: assuming homogeneous response profiles of large audiences, interrupting the delivery of media content, expecting high tolerance of this interruption based on cost and/or quality of media content, assuming a response process of awareness, preference and buying behaviour, and messaging that can span media platforms and satisfy reach and frequency requirements. These assumptions have had to be revisited because of a number of core characteristics of the online environment. These are challenging traditional thinking about message design and implementation and leading academics to consider new paradigms of online communications.

Hyper-interconnectedness

The traditional paradigm of marketing communications, based on a model of mass communication, assumes a linear process where the message sender is active, the receiver is passive and in a single step, the message is processed resulting in a behavioural response. While this cornerstone of communications theory has been largely abandoned in the wake of multidimensional models of communications that assume audiences are active participants, a new theory has dominated marketing communications for the past two decades: integrated marketing communication (IMC). Kitchen and Burgmann (2015) argue that fundamental shifts in the communications environment including technological advances, proliferation and fragmentation of media alongside power shifts towards customers, retailers and intermediaries, led marketers to alter their practices towards more integrated approaches to communication. These approaches were much more consumer-centric and were founded on the belief that to create a competitive brand, coordination between multiple channels of communication was critical (Shultz and Shultz 1998).

The adoption of IMC reflected the growing complexity of the communications environment and the recognition that 'it is important to employ a "mix" of different communication options, each playing a specific role in creating the desired communication effects or brand knowledge structures' (Keller 2001: p. 841). Since the advent of IMC, this concept of integration has continued to develop as the technological environment evolves. Peterson and Marshall (2015) argue that for the travel industry, the maturation of social media, data analytics and adoption of mobile technologies are motivating the transition from an individual-centred to an 'everyone-to-everyone economy'. They posit that integration should now be defined as consumers and organizations working together to create value through co-design, co-creation, co-production, co-marketing, co-distribution and co-funding. Kitchen and Proctor (2015) argue that the digital environment has not invented consumer interaction, a fundamental human driver, but delivers hyper-connectedness which has laid the foundation for interactive behaviours the likes of which have never before been witnessed.

For tourism practitioners, the implications are wide-ranging but underpinning them is the need to reconsider how the organization interacts with its consumers. Traditional approaches to advertising, often replicated online using banners, suffer the same challenges as offline advertising in their restrictive one-way model of transmission. Increasingly, advertisers are finding it difficult to engage consumers in contexts which are cluttered with persuasion-driven messages. Therefore, as a means of capitalizing on this drive for interaction, some tourism operators are asking their consumers to join them in co-creating advertising content. The concept of user-generated content (UGC) is relatively new and offers potentially a cost-effective, creative and novel form of messaging which creates PR around the brand and drives social engagement through discussion, collaboration and viral distribution.

Tourism Queensland

In conjunction with the advertising agency Cummins Nitro Brisbane in 2009, Tourism Queensland decided to apply their relatively small $1.2 million budget to achieve a truly global marketing campaign. They did this, not by focusing messaging on promoting travel to the Great Barrier Reef, but instead by releasing a classified ad seeking applicants for 'The Best Job in the World', an island caretaker position that required applicants to snorkel, feed fish and blog for a salary of $73,000. The response to the campaign was overwhelming. Tourism Queensland received 35,000 applications from candidates across 200 countries who uploaded video applications explaining why they should get the job. The general public was invited to vote and they narrowed the applications down to 50 and, from these, 16 were flown to Queensland for final selection.

The campaign was an excellent case study in integrating UGC with traditional advertising campaigns. The bonus was the level of PR generated around the campaign. Tourism Queensland claims that the campaign generated more than $80 million of equivalent advertising space. The campaign was covered by major outlets like the BBC and CNN, receiving an estimated $368 million in media coverage and reaching a global audience of 3 billion. Tourism Queensland received more than 8.4 million website visits and 55 million page views. The campaign was awarded three top awards at the Cannes International Advertising Festival. Most importantly, the campaign engaged a global audience in discussing, sharing and disseminating aspirational content about the islands of the Great Barrier Reef, which was the original objective of the campaign (Baumgaren 2012).

The media landscape

The media landscape has changed dramatically, largely due to technology and its constant and uncompromising evolution. In particular, the growth of social media, online video, mobile, gaming and branded entertainment alongside the diffusion of mobile device ownership has fundamentally altered audience behaviour. Consumers are adopting digital content services faster than previously anticipated, with varying levels of media engagement (Berman et al. 2009). The use of multiple devices and multiple screens reflects the prevailing simultaneous consumption of media. Cross-platform communications are now a critical path to meeting strategic objectives around reach and frequency. Success relies on marketers knowing where consumers are spending their time and on developing integrated messaging that seamlessly crosses platforms.

Furthermore, the consumption of multiple platforms of digital media is increasing empowerment, meaning consumers have more control over which content to consume and whether and how to distribute it. Increasingly, consumers are demanding interactivity with brands, opening opportunities for tourism organizations to build relationships. Consumers are willing to provide more information and make themselves more accessible if it allows a meaningful dialogue in which they perceive real benefit. These shifts in behaviours have clear implications for not just media planning, but the fundamental approach to communication and message strategy has to reflect this entirely new environment.

With such fundamental shifts in media type, fragmentation in audiences and increasing audience empowerment, trends in media spending have dramatically changed. In particular, there have been significant shifts in expenditure from broadcast and print to newer digital platforms. According to Zenith Optimedia, online advertising is the fastest-growing advertising medium in history. Global spend on digital advertising has increased from 4% in 2004 to 24% of total spend in 2014 and is expected to reach 32% by 2017. According to the IAB, in the UK this figure is already at 39% which means online advertising expenditure at £7.2 billion has overtaken all other traditional forms of media spending.

With the dramatic pace of adoption of the Internet by consumers and equally rapid engagement with social media, it is unsurprising that as these drivers continue to grow, models of media planning are evolving and more of the budget is being shifted online to follow consumers. For tourism practitioners then, the challenge has been and continues to be the question of how to apply long-practised models of advertising to this new environment. After many attempts to do just that, most academic research on online campaign development has centred around shifting perspectives of practitioners:

Of all the differences between traditional advertising and media and the emerging world of digital communications, none is greater than the fundamental difference between the idea of communications being about the delivery of messages through media channels versus communications being about an electronic world of networks, algorithms and automated systems for managing the connections between information and people.

(Mulhern 2009: pp. 85–86)

Power shifts

Arguably, one of the greatest influences of technology on marketing communications is the structure of the industry itself. As IMC theorists in the 1990s and 2000s highlighted, the power in the advertising value chain was tangibly shifting due to the proliferation of media outlets and the increasing control consumers gained from new technologies. As these new technologies evolve, the value chain continues to reshape itself in light of the opportunities delivered to the players within it. Berman et al. (2007) suggest that new platform players are offering advertisers the ability to purchase ads across aggregated networks, a trend that demonstrates the need for advertisers to capture the movement of consumers across an increasingly fragmented medium. Furthermore, as content owners and media distributors proliferate, they are working directly with advertisers, bypassing agencies, as development tools for content creation become more accessible.

Some brands have taken this a step further by developing their own channels of transmission. Thomas Cook TV has been on Sky since the early 2000s and in doing so it has successfully brought the brand into editorial content in an online environment, allowing it to have one-to-one relationships with its consumers. More recently, it has partnered with ITN productions to launch Club 18–30 TV where combinations of branded and user-generated content are distributed at consistent and regular touchpoints. Content centres on the fear of 'missing out' with holiday rep-led real-time formats and ideas and user-generated footage. Central to the strategy is the integration of YouTube, Facebook, Instagram and Twitter which ensure maximum leverage of content. This concept of branded entertainment has completely altered the roles in a traditionally over-structured sector.

With the increasing challenge of gaining and retaining the attention of audiences in cluttered environments, more advertisers are shifting focus from the traditional persuasive, benefit-driven message strategies to the development of relevant and entertaining content which can be distributed across multiple platforms. Online video advertising, according to the IAB, is one of the fastest growing advertising formats, worth £442 million in 2014, a rise of 43% from the previous year. This growth has been driven by the increase in online video viewership. Ferber (2015) argues that half of all mobile data traffic comes from video. For tourism and hospitality, online video is becoming a critical information source for decision making and YouTube has been heavily used to deliver the content (Mintel 2016). Airbnb, as a natural disrupter, relies heavily on video content to engage consumers. It utilizes crowd sourcing to generate content from its users, most recently creating a short film named 'Hollywood and Vines'. These opportunities for organizations to take full control of the distribution network of their messages reflect a new era which challenges the boundaries of creativity.

Conclusion

The tourism and hospitality sector has experienced unprecedented change with multiple forces impacting on organizations. Practitioners have had to rethink the concepts of marketing, consumer insight and communications. Traditional and linear communications are becoming less effective in a world where consumers control content and distribution. Mass messaging is not engaging enough to grasp or retain attention nor does it build long-term or meaningful relationships, the secret of marketing success. Thus, marketers are shifting focus, effort and budget to online communications. The most successful are those who invest in data collection and analytics, who spend to understand, who refine and target, who personalize when they communicate. There are success stories but equally there are many campaigns that have failed. The pace of change in the environment makes it difficult to keep up and marketers need more guidance. The challenge therefore remains the development of models of research which produce multiple channels of rapid results and which are timely and have immediacy for the sector.

References

Baumgaren, C. (2012). '3 user-generated campaigns that got it right', *Mashable*, 26 June.

Berman, S. J., Battino, B. and Feldman, K. (2009). *Beyond Advertising: Choosing a Strategic Path to the Digital Consumer*, Somers, NY: IBM Institute for BusinessValue.

Berman, S. J., Battino, B., Shipnuck, L. and Neus, A. (2007). *The End of Advertising as We Know It*, Somers, NY: IBM Institute for Business Value.

Berry, L. L. and Parasuraman, A. (1991). *Marketing Services*, New York: The Free Press.

Buhalis, D. and Law, R. (2008). 'Progress in information technology and tourism management: 20 years on and 10 years after the Internet – the state of eTourism research', *Tourism Management*, 29(4): 609–623.

Byun, J. and Jang, S. (2015). 'Effective destination advertising: Matching effect between advertising language and destination type', *Tourism Management*, 50: 31–40.

Deloitte (2015). *Travel Consumer 2015: Engaging the Empowered Holidaymaker*, London: Deloitte LLP.

Ferber, S. (2015). 'Video ad content is now pervasive and powerful', *Guardian*, 7 June.

Fesenmaier, D. R. and Xiang, Z. (2014). 'Tourism marketing from 1990–2010: Two decades and a new paradigm', in S. McCabe (ed.), *The Routledge Handbook of Tourism Marketing* (pp. 549–560), London: Routledge.

Forum for the Future (2009). *Tourism 2023: Four Scenarios, a Vision and a Strategy for UK Outbound Travel and Tourism*, London: Forum for the Future.

Gordon, J. and Perrey, J. (2015). 'The dawn of marketing's new golden age', *McKinsey Quarterly*, February.

Hughes, G. and Fill, C. (2007). 'Redefining the nature and format of the marketing communications mix', *The Marketing Review*, 7(1): 45–57.

Jacobsen, J. K. S. and Munar, A. M. (2012). 'Tourist information search and destination choice in a digital age', *Tourism Management Perspectives*, 1: 39–47.

Keller, K. L. (2001). 'Mastering the marketing communications mix: Micro and macro perspectives on integrated marketing communication programs', *Journal of Marketing Management*, 17(7–8): 819–847.

Kitchen, P. J. and Burgmann, I. (2015). 'Integrated marketing communication: Making it work at a strategic level', *Journal of Business Strategy*, 36(4): 34–39.

Kitchen, P. J. and Proctor, T. (2015). 'Marketing communications in a post-modern world', *Journal of Business Strategy*, 36(5): 34–42.

McCabe, S. (2009). *Marketing Communications in Tourism and Hospitality: Concepts, Strategies and Cases*, Oxford: Butterworth-Heinemann.

Mintel (2014). *The Changing Face of Technology in Travel and Tourism*, London: Mintel.

Mintel (2016). *Social Media in Tourism*, London: Mintel.

Moutinho, L., Rate, S. and Ballantyne, R. (2013). 'Futurecast: An exploration of key emerging mega-trends in the tourism arena', in C. Costa, E. Panyik and D. Buhalis (eds.), *Trends in European Tourism Planning and Organization* (pp. 313–325), Bristol, UK: Channel View Publications.

Mulhern, F. (2009). 'Integrated marketing communications: From media channels to digital connectivity', *Journal of Marketing Communications*, 15(2–3): 85–101.

Neuhofer, B. and Buhalis, D. (2014). 'Experience, co-creation and technology: Issues, challenges and trends for technology enhanced tourism experiences', in S. McCabe (ed.), *The Routledge Handbook of Tourism Marketing* (pp. 124–139), London: Routledge.

Peterson, S. and Marshall, A. (2015). *The Digital Reinvention of Travel: Following Travelers into a Radically Different Tomorrow*, Somers, NY: IBM Institute of Brand Value.

Shultz, D. E. and Shultz, H. F. (1998). 'Transitioning marketing communication into the twenty-first century', *Journal of Marketing Communications*, 4(1): 9–26.

Vinod, B. (2013). 'Leveraging BIG DATA for competitive advantage in travel', *Journal of Revenue and Pricing Management*, 12(1): 96–100.

Visit Scotland (2014). *Trends for 2015*, Edinburgh, UK: Insight Department, Visit Scotland.

World Travel and Tourism Council (2015). *Travel and Tourism Economic Impact 2015*, London: World Travel and Tourism Council.

38

ELECTRONIC CUSTOMER RELATIONSHIP MANAGEMENT AND CUSTOMER SATISFACTION

Melissa A. Baker

Customer relationship management

Customer relationship management (CRM) is designed to manage customer relationships and achieve long-term profits and value from the lifetime of the customer. While relationship marketing and CRM are often used interchangeably (Parvatiyar and Sheth 2001), CRM is most commonly used to describe information–enabled relationship marketing (Ryals and Payne 2001). Traditionally, CRM refers to the management strategy in the creation of value, the intelligent use of data and technology, the acquisition of customer knowledge and the development of long-term relationships with customers (Boulding et al. 2005). From a strategic standpoint, CRM is not simply an IT solution that is used to acquire and grow a customer base (Payne and Frow 2005); it involves strategic vision and the planning, implementation and control functions to manage the strategic vision. Previously, CRM technologies referred to the degree to which firms use supporting information technology to manage customer relationships (Chang et al. 2010). What is missing from this definition is the role played by new technologies and the online environment that facilitate the three-way interactions between customers, other customers and the firm.

Increasingly, companies are expanding traditional CRM to include electronic CRM (E-CRM). Eighty per cent of business executives use social media to better understand their markets (Deloitte University Press 2013), over 46% of online users use social media when making purchasing decisions (Nielsen Company 2012) and companies are anticipated to spend over $5 billion in 2016 (VanBoskirk et al. 2011) on social media expenditures. Social media and online review sites place the customer in control of driving the content and con-versation with experiences and management. The availability of online information and multiple platforms provide greater access to customer information directly through firm–customer interactions and through customer-to-customer interactions (Agnihotri et al. 2012).

The proliferation of social networking sites, third-party review sites and electronic commerce are changing the landscape of E-CRM in terms of the customer experience. In other words, these sites provide views on experiences and are increasingly important sources of marketing information about the customer experience (Baker 2016). The customer experience is seen as a journey where the service encounters are viewed as interactions embedded in a series of exchanges that may extend over a long period of time, with a variety of providers contributing to the experience (Tax et al. 2013). Throughout the customer's experience, competitive advantage is attained through engaging customers in co-production and co-creation (Baker 2016). With this shift it is critical for firms to develop new strategies that effectively manage the electronic customer relationships and enhance experience and firm value.

E-CRM and satisfaction

Service companies have shifted the emphasis from customer acquisition to creating customer engagement and participation (Prahalad and Ramaswamy 2004). One way to achieve this is through increased customer satisfaction. Customer satisfaction has significant implications for the economic performance of firms (Bolton et al. 2004). A satisfied customer buys more, is more committed to a company and is more profitable over the lifetime (Anton 1996). In other words, customer satisfaction can increase customer loyalty, decrease complaints and increase firm value. Furthermore, CRM initiatives are directly associated with customer satisfaction (Mithas et al. 2005). Furthermore, attracting, conversing, engaging and bonding with customers is part of the pathway to creating brand advocates and emotionally loyal customers (Kandampully et al. 2015). The strategic focus, beyond satisfaction and loyalty, is to achieve active engagement of customers as co-owners and co-creators of value (Kandampully et al. 2015).

The interactive and relational properties of online platforms and social media make them perfectly suited to CRM and its underlying relationship marketing principles (Hennig-Thurau et al. 2010). As such, social CRM is defined as the philosophy and business strategy, supported by a system and technology that is designed to engage the customer in a collaborative interaction, that provides mutually beneficial value in a trusted and transparent business environment (Greenberg 2010). This definition is in line with traditional CRM but expands upon it by focuses on customer engagement with two-way, interactive relationships with customers where they are encouraged to co-create marketing efforts and product offerings (Rodriguez et al. 2012). The emergence of the electronic social customer is challenging practitioners and researchers to rethink how we manage online customer relationships in order to achieve engagement, satisfaction and loyalty. This is because social media has revolutionized the way businesses interact with customers (Kim et al. 2015). With the emerging Internet environment, consumers are increasingly active participants in interactive processes comprising multiple feedback loops and communication (Prahalad and Ramaswamy 2004). Stated differently, with the advent of social media and increased online exchanges, organizations and customers now engage in two-way dialogues as opposed to one-way conversations (Goldenberg 2015). It can further be argued that the interaction is three-way, involving customers, other customers and the firm. It is therefore important to understand how to manage the electronic relationships not only between the firm and the focal customer, but between the firm and other customers, and between the customers themselves. This creates a dynamic and challenging landscape for managing consumer behaviour in hospitality and tourism.

One important element of satisfaction to manage with electronic exchanges is how reading about the product changes expectations. Traditionally, for experimental services, such as those that fall under hospitality and tourism, the quality of the service is often unknown prior to consumption (Xie et al. 2014). However, now customers can view and read about the experiences of other customers, which can affect their expectations. Satisfaction is often viewed as a customer's evaluation of the pre- and post-purchase experience of their expectations (Oliver 1997) and satisfaction is a key motivating factor for purchase behaviour. Satisfaction is higher when the actual experience exceeds the expectation and customers are dissatisfied when the expectations are not met. The breadth and depth of information available electronically on the Internet can now greatly shape customer expectations before and after purchasing. As such, this adds an additional layer to effective CRM strategies. Electronic customer experiences feature interactivity, customer-to-customer online recommendations, online word-of-mouth (WOM) and user-generated content (Rose et al. 2012). Hennig-Thurau et al. (2004) report eight specific factors which motivate consumers to make contributions to (i.e. engage with) online communities, including (1) venting negative feelings, (2) concern for other consumers, (3) self-enhancement, (4) advice-seeking, (5) social benefits, (6) economic benefits (e.g. cost savings), (7) platform assistance and (8) helping the company. All of these factors can influence the satisfaction of the focal customer and other customers before and after the trip. Consider, for example, if a customer books a reservation at a restaurant and reads online comments about how outstanding the food is. The customer may then have such high expectations that the actual experience, while good, does not meet the expectations, resulting in a disappointing experience. These multiple feedback loops for E-CRM are critical to consider in how firms manage online reviews and social media in their E-CRM strategies.

Managing online reviews

Customers search for opinions and experiences of peer consumers before purchasing a product (Xie et al. 2014). Customers often write reviews to indicate their level of satisfaction with services and products (Liu et al. 2013) and inform other customers of their experiences (Park and Allen 2013). These customer-provided reviews, WOM, online or offline, positive or negative, are closely reviewed by prospective customers. This makes it a powerful marketing tool (Khare et al. 2011). For online reviews, the most important factors are the valence of the review (the average ratings), the volume of the reviews and the variation of reviews. To enhance the readability of review information, many leading review sites, such as TripAdvisor, present not only valence and volume of reviews, but also the distribution of the rating variance (Jang et al. 2012). According to one study, 68% of customers read at least four reviews, 22% always read customer reviews, and 43% read reviews most of the time before making a purchase (Kee 2008). Another study finds that 53% of travellers would not commit to a hotel reservation until they read reviews and 77% usually or always read reviews before choosing a hotel (TripAdvisor 2013).

One of the most important roles is to diffuse information from electronic WOM. As such, companies should make serious efforts to understand the impact of online reviews and prepare better marketing strategies to address them (Kim et al. 2015). Electronic WOM is generally measured with regards to valence (positive and negative), intensity (quantity of comments), speed (number of contacts in a certain period of time), persistency (length of time), importance (role of comments in the customer decision-making process) and credibility (in terms of assurance and confidence of the source of the message) (Mauri and Minazzi 2013). Given the critical influence of electronic WOM in the hospitality industry (Cantallops and Salvi 2014), managing online reviews is a key component of hospitality management (Leung et al. 2013). Because of the simultaneous engagement of consumers and managers, consumers' purchasing decisions are often influenced by both the user-generated reviews and management responses (Levy et al. 2013).

Online reviews are a very clear indicator of customer satisfaction or dissatisfaction. Customers can use online platforms to complain more directly, conveniently, and perhaps more effectively (Balaji et al. 2015). Accordingly, hospitality companies can react to customers' satisfaction or dissatisfaction through responses to reviews. Managerial responses make two-way communication possible (Gu and Ye 2014) for both positive and negative feedback. Online management responses are a new form of CRM (Gu and Ye 2014). Many third-party websites feature manager accounts and allow firms to interact with reviewers by responding to reviews (Kim et al. 2011). Management responses to online customer complaints can address issues and recover from service failures (Xie et al. 2014).

As such, online reputation management suggests that businesses require a unique skill set to effectively manage online reviews, signifying the importance to hotels of monitoring the online conversation and engaging with customers (Pattison 2009). Although customers who post online reviews may not expect direct online responses, how the hotel responds (or does not respond) is likely to affect how others perceive the brand and may influence their willingness to book a reservation. It is important to note that responses to online reviews are not only an integral part of the experience of the customer(s) who posted the review, but also part of the experience of those individuals who are reading the review (Baker 2016).

Management responses to a positive consumer review demonstrate the firm is listening, expressing appreciation and reinforcing positive reviews (Xie et al. 2014). Management responses to negative reviews allow for service failure recovery and can increase customer satisfaction by influencing customers' perceptions of justice and fairness (McColl-Kennedy and Sparks 2003). Effective management responses to negative reviews from unsatisfied customers who give low ratings can improve the satisfaction level of these customers and consequently increase future purchase intention (Xie et al. 2014). Many firms tend to respond more frequently to negative reviews as opposed to positive reviews (Park and Allen 2013). Responding to positive reviews can establish rapport and build goodwill with customers (Xie et al. 2014). Immediate managerial responses indicate that the firm monitors guest perceptions with a proactive management style (Xie et al. 2014). Oftentimes, if customers do not receive a quick response, the complaint can be moved to a public domain, causing major problems for the service provider (Grégoire et al. 2014).

The reaction to customer reviews can often be more telling than the review itself. Management responses to customers' online reviews can be publicly seen by other customers because of the transparency of the Internet (Xie et al. 2014). Customers are likely to interpret management responses as appreciation for their customers and as part of the CRM strategies (Wei et al. 2013). The way in which a company responds to reviews has a critical influence on customer satisfaction (Homburg and Furst 2007).

A group of women gathered at an upscale restaurant to celebrate a bachelorette/hen party. Following the experience, one of the diners posted online feedback regarding their negative experience. Immediately following, the restaurant posted their rebuttal. The diners changed their reservation from 10 people to 18 people which made it difficult to accommodate them in a timely fashion. Figure 38.1 gives an excerpt from the online exchange.

Case study questions:

1   Were the guests to blame, or partially to blame for the poor experience because they showed up an hour late and increased the party size from 10 to 18 without notifying the restaurant?

Customer Comment:	We booked a reservation for a Bachelorette Party. When we arrived, we waited a long time before being shown to our 'tables' as the restaurant thought it was acceptable to put us at one table of eight and another of ten, which was never outlined to us before our arrival. They said there was no way to put us all at one table. Very disappointing
Restaurant Response:	You turned up over an hour late, booked for 10, then 18 showed up. Group was loud, rude, and the bottom of the barrel of society!
Customer Feedback:	Appalling customer service. Such an unprofessional response to customer feedback on social media.
Restaurant Response:	Peasants never having seen fine dining in their lives, wanting something off the bill as usual

Figure 38.1   Social media case study

Source: Adapted from the original Facebook posts by the author.

2   Even if the guests were partially to blame, how could the restaurant have handled this situation?

3   What opinions might customers form based solely on the responses posted by the restaurant?

4   How did the restaurant effectively or ineffectively influence their CRM?

5   What additional negative repercussions do you think came after this online exchange? What were the benefits to posting this response versus the negative repercussions that came after?

Managing social media

The use of online social networks such as Facebook, Twitter and Instagram is continuously increasing and more travellers tap into these networks for a variety of purposes (Litvin et al. 2008). Businesses are now tasked with merging existing CRM systems with online applications such as review sites, blogs and social media to develop new capabilities that foster stronger relationships with customers (Trainor et al. 2014). Social media has changed the dynamics of communication between service providers and customers, transforming the way customers communicate with companies (Balaji et al. 2015). Customers use social media to nurture and sustain their relationships with others (Joo et al. 2011), including businesses. Consumer-generated websites and emerging media channels such as Facebook, Twitter and Instagram aim to facilitate and enrich online purchases, enabling the customers to share information and experiences with other customers (Mauri and Minazzi 2013). As such, online social networks are emerging as innovative relationship-building tools (Kwon and Wen 2010). Customers are adopting social media applications to connect with peers and also increasingly expect the same level of interactivity with their business counterparts (Berthon et al. 2012).

Social CRM is a new paradigm that is defined as a philosophy and business strategy, supported by a technology platform, business rules, processes and social characteristics, that is designed to engage the customer in a collaborative conversation in order to provide mutually beneficial value in a trusted environment (Greenberg 2010). Hospitality managers are increasingly aware of the need to actively communicate with consumers on social media platforms (O'Connor 2010). Many hospitality and tourism firms have Facebook fan pages with applications that enable guests to make reservations, post comments and meet other guests (Sinha 2011). Consumers make their opinions easily accessible to others through message boards and likes. Central to these communities should be branding. Brand communities should engage the participant because of the nature of the participants' specific wants and desires towards the brand (Brodie et al. 2013). It is suggested that hospitality firms should allocate financial resources and designate staff members to regularly respond to customers' negative online comments on social media and other travel websites in order to meet customers' needs and increase customer satisfaction (Kim et al. 2015). Social media plays an increasingly important role in affecting hotel guests' satisfaction and service process enhancement (Anderson 2012).

Conclusion

Hospitality businesses, practitioners and academics recognize there is still much to be gleaned from E-CRM. Like many other strategic business initiatives, firms need a strategy for handling electronic CRM data. This includes how to engage key customers, measure satisfaction, increase purchasing and loyalty, improve positive WOM and mitigate negative WOM. While firms have dedicated significant efforts to better understanding and managing E-CRM, there is still progress to be made in terms of understanding the implications of online feedback, social media, and the online interactions between firms, management, employees and customers.

References

Agnihotri, R., Kothandaraman, P., Kashyap, R. and Singh, R. (2012). 'Bringing "social" into sales: The impact of salespeople's social media use on service behaviors and value creation', *Journal of Personal Selling and Sales Management*, 32(3): 333–348.

Anderson, C. K. (2012). 'The impact of social media on lodging performance', *Cornell Hospitality Report*, 12(15): 4–12.

Anton, J. (1996). *Customer Relationship Management: Making Hard Decisions with Soft Numbers*, Englewood Cliffs, NJ: Prentice-Hall.

Baker, M. A. (2016). 'Managing customer experiences in hotel chains', in S. Ivanov, M. Ivanova and V. P. Magnini (eds.), *Handbook of Hotel Chain Management* (pp. 240–250), Abingdon: Routledge.

Balaji, M. S., Jha, S. and Royne, M. B. (2015). 'Customer e-complaining behaviours using social media', *The Service Industries Journal*, 35(11–12): 633–654.

Berthon, P. R., Pitt, L. F., Plangger, K. and Shapiro, D. (2012). 'Marketing meets Web 2.0, social media, and creative consumers: Implications for international marketing strategy', *Business Horizons*, 55(3): 261–271.

Bolton, R. N., Lemon, K. and Verhoef, P. C. (2004). 'The theoretical underpinnings of customer asset management: A framework and propositions for future research', *Journal of the Academy of Marketing Science*, 32(3): 271–292.

Boulding, W., Staelin, R., Ehret, M. and Johnston, W. J. (2005). 'A customer relationship management roadmap: What is known, potential pitfalls, and where to go', *Journal of Marketing*, 69(4): 155–166.

Brodie, R. J., Ilic, A., Juric, B. and Hollebeek, L. (2013). 'Consumer engagement in a virtual brand community: An exploratory analysis', *Journal of Business Research*, 66(1): 105–114.

Cantallops, A. S. and Salvi, F. (2014). 'New consumer behavior: A review of research on eWOM and hotels', *International Journal of Hospitality Management*, 36: 41–51.

Chang, W., Park, J. E. and Chaiy, S. (2010). 'How does CRM technology transform into organizational performance? A mediating role of marketing capability', *Journal of Business Research*, 63(8): 849–855.

Deloitte University Press (2013). 'Social business study: Shifting out of first gear', Available from: http://dupress.com/articles/social-business-study/ [Accessed: 6 August 2014].

Goldenberg, B. (2015). *The Definitive Guide to Social CRM: Maximizing Customer Relationships with Social Media to Gain Market Insights, Customers, and Profits*, Upper Saddle River, NJ: Pearson Education.

Greenberg, P. (2010). 'The impact of CRM 2.0 on customer insight', *Journal of Business and Industrial Marketing*, 25(6): 410–419.

Grégoire, Y., Salle, A. and Tripp, T. M. (2014). 'Managing social media crises with your customers: The good, the bad, and the ugly', *Business Horizons*, 58(2): 173–182.

Gu, B. and Ye, Q. (2014). 'First step in social media: Measuring the influence of online management responses on customer satisfaction', *Production Operations Management*, 23(4): 570–582.

Hennig-Thurau, T., Gwinner, K. P., Walsh, G. and Gremler, D. D. (2004). 'Electronic word-of-mouth via consumer opinion platforms: What motivates consumers to articulate themselves on the Internet?', *Journal of Interactive Marketing*, 18(1): 38–52.

Hennig-Thurau, T., Malthouse, E. C., Friege, C., Gensler, S., Lobschat, L., Rangaswamy, A. and Skiera, B. (2010). 'The impact of new media on customer relationships', *Journal of Service Research*, 13(3): 311–330.

Homburg, C. and Furst, A. (2007). 'See no evil, hear no evil, speak no evil: A study of defensive organizational behavior towards customer complaints', *Journal of the Academy of Marketing Science*, 35(4): 523–536.

Jang, S., Prasad, A. and Ratchford, B. T. (2012). 'How consumers use product reviews in the purchase decision process', *Marketing Letters*, 23(3): 825–838.

Joo, Y. H., Kim, Y. and Yang, S. J. (2011). 'Valuing customers for social network services', *Journal of Business Research*, 64(11): 1239–1244.

Kandampully, J., Zhang, T. and Bilgihan, A. (2015). 'Customer loyalty: A review and future directions with a special focus on the hospitality industry', *International Journal of Contemporary Hospitality Management*, 27(3): 379–414.

Kee, T. (2008). 'Majority of online shoppers check at least four reviews before buying', *Online Media Daily*, 19 February, Available from: http://www.mediapost.com/publications/article/76727/majority-of-online-shoppers-check-at-least-four-re.html?edition= [Accessed: February 2016].

Khare, A., Labrecque, L. I. and Asare, A. K. (2011). 'The assimilative and contrastive effects of word-of-mouth volume: An experimental examination of online consumer ratings', *Journal of Retailing*, 87(1): 111–126.

Kim, E. E. K., Mattila, A. S. and Baloglu, S. (2011). 'Effects of gender and expertise on consumers' motivation to read online hotel reviews', *Cornell Hospitality Quarterly*, 52(4): 399–406.

Kim, W. G., Lim, H. and Brymer, R. A. (2015). 'The effectiveness of managing social media on hotel performance', *International Journal of Hospitality Management*, 44: 165–171.

Kwon, O. and Wen, Y. (2010). 'An empirical study of the factors affecting social network service use', *Computers in Human Behavior*, 26(2): 254–263.

Leung, D., Law, R., van Hoof, H. and Buhalis, D. (2013). 'Social media in tourism and hospitality: A literature review', *Journal of Travel and Tourism Marketing*, 30(1–2): 3–22.

Levy, S. E., Duan, W. and Boo, S. (2013). 'An analysis of one-star online reviews and responses in the Washington, DC lodging market', *Cornell Hospitality Quarterly*, 54(1): 49–63.

Litvin, S. W., Goldsmith, R. E. and Pan, B. (2008). 'Electronic word-of-mouth in hospitality and tourism management', *Tourism Management*, 29(3): 458–468.

Liu, S., Law, R., Rong, J., Li, G. and Hall, J. (2013). 'Analyzing changes in hotel customers' expectations by trip mode', *International Journal of Hospitality Management*, 34: 359–371.

McColl-Kennedy, J. R. and Sparks, B. A. (2003). 'Application of fairness theory to service failures and service recovery', *Journal of Service Research*, 5(3): 251–266.

Mauri, A. G. and Minazzi, R. (2013). 'Web reviews influence on expectations and purchasing intentions of hotel potential customers', *International Journal of Hospitality Management*, 34: 99–107.

Mithas, S., Krishnan, M. S. and Fornell, C. (2005). 'Why do customer relationship management applications affect customer satisfaction?', *Journal of Marketing*, 69(4): 201–209.

Nielsen Company (2012). 'How digital influences how we shop around the world', Available from: http://www.nielsen.com/us/en/insights/reports/2012/how-digital-influences-how-we-shop-around-the-world.html [Accessed: 6 August 2014].

O'Connor, P. (2010). 'Managing a hotel's image on TripAdvisor', *Journal of Hospitality Marketing Management*, 19(7): 754–772.

Oliver, R. L. (1997). *Satisfaction: A Behavioral Perspective on the Customer*, New York: McGraw-Hill.

Park, S. Y. and Allen, J. P. (2013). 'Responding to online reviews: Problem solving and engagement in hotels', *Cornell Hospitality Quarterly*, 54(1): 64–73.

Parvatiyar, A. and. Sheth, J. N. (2001). 'Conceptual framework of customer relationship management', in N. Jagdish, J. N. Sheth and A. Shainesh (eds.), *Customer Relationship Management: Emerging Concepts, Tools and Applications* (pp. 3–25), Delhi, India: Tata/McGraw-Hill.

Pattison, K. (2009). 'Managing an online reputation', *New York Times*, 29 July, Available from: http://www.nytimes.com/2009/07/30/business/smallbusiness/30reputation.html?pagewanted=alland_r=0 [Accessed: 6 September 2015].

Payne, A. and Frow, P. (2005). 'A strategic framework for customer relationship management', *Journal of Marketing*, 69(4): 167–176.

Prahalad, C. K. and Ramaswamy, V. (2004). 'Co-creation experiences: The next practice in value creation', *Journal of Interactive Marketing*, 18(3): 5–14.

Rodriguez, M., Peterson, R. M. and Krishnan, V. (2012). 'Social media's influence on business-to-business sales performance', *Journal of Personal Selling and Sales Management*, 32(3): 365–378.

Rose, S., Clark, M., Samouel, P. and Hair, N. (2012). 'Online customer experience in e-retailing: An empirical model of antecedents and outcomes', *Journal of Retailing*, 88(2): 308–322.

Ryals, L. and Payne, A. F. T. (2001). 'Customer relationship management in financial services: Towards information enabled relationship marketing', *Journal of Strategic Marketing*, 9(1): 3–27.

Sinha, S. (2011). 'Global travel goes trendy with social media, mobile phones in tow', *International Business Times*, 23 January.

Tax, S. S., McCutcheon, D. and Wilkinson, I. F. (2013). 'The service delivery network (SDN): A customer-centric perspective of the customer journey', *Journal of Service Research*, 16(4): 454–470.

Trainor, K. J., Andzulis, J. M., Rapp, A. and Agnihotri, R. (2014). 'Social media technology usage and customer relationship performance: A capabilities-based examination of social CRM', *Journal of Business Research*, 67(6): 1201–1208.

TripAdvisor (2013). '24 insights to shape your TripAdvisor strategy', Available from: http://www.tripadvisor.co.uk/TripAdvisorInsights/n2120/24-insights-shape-your-tripadvisor-strategy [Accessed: 6 August 2014].

VanBoskirk, S., Overby, C. S. and Takvorian, S. (2011). *US Interactive Marketing Forecast, 2011 to 2016*, Cambridge, MA: Forrester Research.

Wei, W., Miao, L. and Huang, Z. (2013). 'Customer engagement behaviors and hotel responses', *International Journal of Hospitality Management*, 33: 316–330.

Xie, K. L., Zhang, Z. and Zhang, Z. (2014). 'The business value of online consumer reviews and management response to hotel performance', *International Journal of Hospitality Management*, 43: 1–12.

PART VI

Emerging dimensions of consumer behaviour

Marketers face active challenges as they react to the changing world of consumers, and adapt to the forces that steer such changes. Part VI of the *Handbook* deals with the innovative and promising topics of consumer behaviour that are not dealt with in other parts. This part is divided into eight chapters.

Improving service efficiency at a nominal cost by utilising the latest technology will bring a competitive advantage over competitors. Hospitality and tourism organisations are incorporating assistive technologies in order to improve the guest experience. The technological developments of the past show that future technology will bring more flexibility, new experiences and more variability in products or services. Chapter 39 authored by Ali Bavik, Henrique Fátima Boyol Ngan and Erdogan Ekiz presents the current state of technology in the tourism and hospitality industry within a framework that encompasses pre-purchase, purchase and post-purchase stages. This chapter also highlights how techno-logical advancement is shaping consumer behaviour and future trends of technological advancements.

Chapter 40 by Samuel Adeyinka-Ojo and Catheryn Khoo-Lattimore explores consumer motivations and experiences at slow food festivals (SFFs) in rural tourism destinations. The authors point out that the understanding of tourists and their decision making regarding food and beverage consumption enables marketers to gain a better understanding of when they need to intervene in their decision-making process. In this regard, the prime objective of the chapter is to bridge the existing gap between consumer behaviour studies, food research and tourism studies. The authors have concluded through their case study that there is a need to enrich the consumers' experience during the SFF with varieties of local activities such as traditional games, cultural dances and native hospitality.

Smartphones appear to be a foremost preference for hospitality and tourism businesses as the travellers are on the move. The mobile, interactive technology offers tourism busines-ses the opportunity to enhance the guest experience and offer engaging, personalised content in real time. Chapter 41 authored by Sarah Gardiner, Joan Carlini and Noel Scott studies how smartphone technology is changing consumer behaviour and its impacts on future tourism experience design. The chapter also highlights the latest developments in smartphone technology in tourism and includes a case study on the design of a tourist attraction app.

Augmented Reality (AR) is considered to be one of the most innovative technological advancements happening in the hospitality and tourism industry. In chapter 42, Azizul Hassan and Neda Shabani critically discuss the usability of AR for tourism destination image formation. The authors conclude that having features such as innovativeness, uniqueness and playfulness, AR can be defined as a true technological improvement. AR can further fascinate tourists to motivate them to discover assorted features of a destination, leading to positive image formation.

Chapter 43 authored by Richard Tresidder investigates how servicescapes in terms of design, décor, music, the uniforms of staff, their behaviour and the type of service, etc. influence, shape and direct consumers' experiences and behaviour. The chapter further outlines that servicescapes in the tourism and hospitality industries are also explicitly linked to the senses through the gaze, touch or smell and this has led to the development of sophisticated multi-sensual environments that challenge and surround consumers' experiences. The chapter also explores the assorted facets that contribute to the creation of servicescapes.

Tourism and hospitality signify segments that have a decisive task to play in adjusting the course of our society to a more sustainable one. In chapter 44, Frans Melissen reviews some of the socially responsible and sustainable practices that tourism and hospitality organisations could or even should engage in. The role of tourists and guests in successfully implementing these practices is also outlined in the chapter. By highlighting some of the latest theoretical insights related to sustainable consumer behaviour, this chapter suggests specific challenges and opportunities for tourism and hospitality policymakers and service providers to stimulate tourists' and guests' appreciation and engagement with sustainable development of tourism and hospitality.

In chapter 45, Adam Weaver studies residents' perception regarding Chinese tourists visiting New Zealand using Doxey's Irridex frameworks. Though there are numerous efforts to understand the behaviour of Chinese tourists, there have only been a few attempts to study the way in which players within the tourism industry perceive them and make adjustments to face such challenges. The present chapter examines evolving industry perspectives in New Zealand that relate to the Chinese outbound travel market and the adaptations these perspectives have prompted. The chapter concludes that conceptually, a series of 's' words – scepticism, segmentation, shortcomings and sophistication – capture the way in which industry perspectives have changed.

Luke R. Potwarka and Kai Jiang in chapter 46 provide a synthesis of consumer behaviour research that has been conducted in the context of the Olympic Games. Consumer behaviour relating to Olympic media and sponsorship consumption is the focus of the chapter. Particular emphasis is placed on highlighting salient decision-making processes and motivational factors involved in sponsorship patronage, media consumption, volunteerism, travel, and sport/physical activity-related behavioural domains. The deliberation integrates key theoretical approaches that have been used in the study of consumer behaviour relating to the Olympic Games.

39

TECHNOLOGICAL ADVANCEMENTS SHAPING CONSUMER BEHAVIOUR

Ali Bavik, Henrique Fátima Boyol Ngan and Erdogan Ekiz

Introduction

Undoubtedly, different types of technology have been playing an important role in tourism and hospitality consumer behaviour. Nonetheless, in the past century perhaps the transportation technologies and information technology (IT), particularly the Internet, have had the greatest impact on consumer behaviour. During the Industrial Revolution, technological developments in transportation particularly in the early 1900s, greatly increased people's ability to travel (Goeldner et al. 2009). First roads were built and improved, canals were constructed, the railway was established, and eventually in the early 1950s, long-haul flights had started. These technological changes had an impact upon tourism activities as well as the purchasing behaviour of the tourists. The development of transportation facilities shortened travel times over longer distances and enabled people to travel to new destinations (Ekiz et al. 2009). With the development of technology, vehicles have tended to become larger and faster, and more affordable. This allowed low-income level tourists to experience different destinations. It not only made different destinations attractive, but also turned travelling into a consumer product. Originally, the purpose of travelling was to reach the desired destination (Bavik 2008). The general motives would be business or leisure. However, the technological developments in transportation have changed choosing the mode of travel. Tourists had alternatives to choose their mode of travel based on their main motives. For example, some tourists prefer cruises to have entertainment during their travel while some tourists choose buses or trains to experience beautiful scenery en route to their destination.

In the early 1990s, improvements such as the personal computer, instant communication and the Internet greatly increased people's ability to access information regarding tourism destinations and hospitality. Many accommodation establishments and travel agents made their greatest efforts to develop their own websites to remain competitive, promote their services, market their products and provide for online transactions (Yeung and Law 2004). Since the Internet works in cyberspace, it brings the opportunity of being free from geographical and national borders (Anckar and Walden 2001). Therefore, the Internet increased the marketing and communication opportunities especially for far-away destinations (Vich-i-Martorell 2004). From the consumer perspective, the Internet not only increased the awareness of the destinations, but also allowed people to make bookings directly with the tourism and hospitality companies. Since websites are available 24 hours a day and 365 days a year, the Internet provides several advantages to tourists such as convenience, low-price offers and greater speed. Traditionally, tourism and hospitality consisted of a bundle of tangibles and intangibles in a significant service component (Chen and Gursoy 2001). However, the development of the Internet reduced the service interaction between the service provider and the guest. This allowed guests to purchase their transportation and accommodation online, rather than at a physical travel agency (Bai et al. 2008).

Technological advancement and consumer behaviour

The introduction of technology and subsequent advancements have drastically changed how individuals shop, what they shop for and when they shop. Amongst the bewildering array of technological advancements over the past few decades, the most influential on consumer behaviour is perhaps the digital revolution. Although the digital revolution covers a wide range of technological aspects that each influence consumers' behaviour in their own way, the interplay of the Internet, mobile devices and social media has a pivotal role in the consumer's daily life. In fact, when looking at the evolution of these three technological advances, consumers' behaviour too has evolved, changed and adapted correspondingly.

The influence of the Internet on consumers' behaviour (1990s)

The development of the Internet dates back to the late 1980s and early 1990s, but it only became popularized in the mass market during the late 1990s. An overwhelming amount of information was made freely available over the Internet, which enables the user to enjoy relative ease of access.

It is known that prior to consumption, consumers make their decisions based on the information and brand of the product or service (Solomon et al. 2014). Prior to the existence of the Internet, consumers' decisions were mainly driven by a limited number of media channels (e.g. TV, radio, magazines and posters), in which product or service-related information was exposed. In that sense, the consumer (end user of the product or service) has no control over the product information that they are being exposed to. The emergence of the Internet allowed a greater degree of choice, and provided an enhanced knowledge of products and services to the consumer. Companies no longer dictate the information that is made available. However, while it seems to be of great convenience, it raises other issues. Not only does the consumer have to deal with an overwhelming amount of information, the media channel also needs to be decided based on which product or service-related information is acquired and purchased (online vs. offline). Considering that, consumers' behaviour has shifted from being passive receivers of information, to actively engaging in information search.

Thus, customers decide through which channel they acquire product or service-related information that is most suitable to them. As a result, consumers no longer compare products with competing brands, but with a settled benchmark of 'what should be a good product/service' and this is often generalized across different products and brands. More than ever, consumers are less tolerant and more demanding, expecting ease of service and good quality of the product being purchased. In that sense, product/services branding is becoming less influential over customers' loyalty, as they are able to switch provider more easily than ever.

While the introduction of the Internet has made a significant impact on consumers' behaviour, it is only when coupled with the second stream of the digital revolution that it has notoriously changed consumers' behaviour.

The influence of mobile devices and technology on consumers' behaviour (2000s)

Despite handheld mobile devices (smartphones, personal digital assistants (PDAs), tablets) and their corresponding technologies (3G, 4G, wireless) being made publicly available in the early 1990s, they were only widely adopted by the mass market early in the new millennium. This was mainly because when handheld mobile devices were first released, they offered nothing much more than regular mobile communication. However, when 3G, 4G and public wireless were made available, access to the Internet was possible any-where, anytime at a relatively low cost. In that sense, the mobile technology allowed consumers to access virtually any information on a real-time basis without any geo-graphical or logistical constraints. In many cases, guest interaction with front-line personnel of product and service providers is greatly reduced, as there is less dependency on them to acquire product or service-related information. As another case, where traditional maps would have enabled the user to navigate through a new environment, these are now rarely or never needed due to GPS tracking/Google Maps or mobile apps. These may even dictate where the consumer goes or what to buy based on their online behaviour.

While Internet access through mobile handheld devices and technology may have changed how consumers approach or acquire products and related information at the individual level, social media has brought major changes at the group level.

The influence of social media on consumers' behaviour (2000s)

Recently, the new addition of social media shifted consumers' behaviour from the predominantly individual level to more of a group level orientation. In that sense, consumption is no longer determined by individual decision making, or perception, but now occurs at a group level. What makes social media stand out as a consumers' platform is the fact that it facilitated and increased customer-to-customer dialogue. In that sense, consumers are led further away from organizations' marketing and branding strategies, and led by other consumers' opinions. These may be within their circle of friends, or outside their network such as on consumer/community forums. In some instances, consumption may even be driven by a single key opinion leader found on blogs or review websites (e.g. TripAdvisor).

Despite the novelty of these platforms that enable consumers to take a different approach to interaction with the products and services they are interested in, the underlying phenomenon has always been the same: social influence. Prior to social media, one of the many forms of social influence would be evidenced through word of mouth (WOM). Currently, it is known as e-WOM as it has transitioned to the virtual space. Given that restriction on geographical location and time constraints are no longer tied to e-WOM, social influence is assuming a pivotal role in consumers' decisions.

Technological advancement and current trends in hospitality

According to the three-stage model of service consumption, consumers go through three major stages when they consume services: the pre-purchase stage, the service encounter stage and the post-encounter stage (Lovelock et al. 2011). This section is designed to cover all the technological advances of the tourism and hospitality industry in these three stages.

Pre-purchase

Pre-purchase refers to the stage where consumers make decisions based on the available information they have (Solomon et al. 2014). Therefore at this stage, tourists search for information about the desired product or service. Before the Internet was publicly available, tourists would choose the airline tickets, travel agency or hotel accommodation that yielded the highest reliability or best reputation (Lang 2000). In other cases, they might go for the brand that they had been exposed to or had had past experience with. However, these determinants that were once deemed influential on consumers' decisions no longer exert the same amount of effect on travellers' choice.

Rather, tourists pay much more attention to online communities and other forms of social media that allow a great deal of sharing and exchanging of information. It has been shown that tourists are more motivated to process product or service-related information when it is generated by consumer reviews rather than a corporate webpage (Chen and Xie 2008). In addition to information processing, it is more likely that purchase intentions will be determined by user-generated reviews (Chevalier and Mayzlin 2006). The real-time interactive nature of social media platforms allows customers to actively engage with other customers and mutually influence purchase decisions, in a fashion of social conformity. In addition, it indirectly reinforces the customer's product involvement (Wang et al. 2012).

Service providers have not only been increasing the product involvement but also have been looking for innovative ways to enhance guest experience by using both natural and man-made attractions. Servicescape is one of the tools that have been commonly used in order to enhance guest experience. According to Bitner (1992), a servicescape is defined as *a man-made environment, not a natural or social environment*. A servicescape stimulates five senses combining tangibles (physical environment) and intangibles (ambient conditions) (Bavik et al. 2014).

Technological advancements through the development of virtual reality (VR) advance the guest experience one step forward by replacing the physical environment with simulation. In the past three decades, virtual reality has been used in different contexts, including entertainment, gaming, architecture, design and simulation training (Mennecke et al. 2011). Virtual reality has become increasingly popular in the tourism and hospitality industry as well. Virtual reality can be defined as 'the use of a computer-generated 3D environment – called a "virtual environment" that one can navigate and possibly interact with, resulting in real-time simulation of one or more of the user's five senses' (Guttentag 2010: p. 639). Currently, virtual reality has been commonly used in the pre-purchase phase in the tourism and hospitality industry. Particularly, simulations enable guests to experience the general atmosphere before they physically visit a place. For example, http://www.youvisit.com/ simulation provides information about restaurants, travel destinations and accommodation establishments. Virtual reality provides guests with some prior ideas about the product and/ or destination, reducing the gap between service expectation and perception.

Service encounter

Unlike tangible goods or pure services, hospitality-related products or services require amalgamation of various goods and services such as food and beverage, entertainment, recreation and gaming facilities (Hemmington 2007). Therefore, service encounter in the hospitality industry is not a snap-shot practice, it is a longitudinal experience. Service encounter refers to 'the person to person interaction between the service provider and the guest' (Ford et al. 2012: p. 40). The developments in technology have also shown influences on consumer behaviour in the hospitality industry during service interactions.

An example is airline companies fostering self-check in instead of standing in a line to wait for a counter check. Customers are able to check in without human interactions. With the invention of tablets, restaurants can provide an electronic menu. Customers are able to choose and order items without service personnel. It is clear that inventions of service machines not only save time but also allow customers to choose their own seats. It also allows freedom and flexibility. However, technology is changing customer behaviour. Particularly, it has been reducing the service interaction between host and guest. With the replacement of humans by machines, customers have started to go through service processes individually.

Post-encounter

According to Lovelock et al. (2011), the post-encounter stage refers to 'the consumers' behavioural and attitudinal responses to the service experience' (p. 69). Based on their experiences consumers may share positive or negative WOM. WOM refers to 'transmitting the service experience to other individuals' (Solomon et al. 2014: p. 96). Apart from friends and relatives, social media became a popular area in which to share service experience. Previous studies (Chevalier and Mayzlin 2006) also show that consumer reviews are determinants of consumer purchase decisions and product sales. For example, TripAdvisor, a travel website company, provides reviews of travel-related content. It also provides interactive travel forums. This technology allows customers to provide accounts of positive and negative service experiences to the service provider. Reviews and comments not only allow customers to provide feedback to the service providers but can also provide some information to customers who are in the pre-purchase stage. Potential customers exposed to online consumer reviews also show more interest in the product than those who see only the corporate webpage. Moreover, behavioural economics suggests positive relationships between user-generated content and product sales (Duan et al. 2008).

Offline communities are shifting to online communities through social networks (Fournier and Lee 2009). Customers share their unique experiences on various social networks such as Facebook, YouTube and Instagram. This allows customers to share their service experience not only in their own circle but also with the entire world. Since the millennium, social media has not only become a reliable source of information but also serves as a promotional tool.

Future trends affecting consumer behaviour

The growth of technologies in the past 100 years, such as in transportation, has been astounding and it seems that developments in transportation technology will continue to significantly change the hospitality industry and consumer behaviour. Virgin Galactic Airways is one of the pioneer companies that took the initial step towards space tourism (Hudson 2008). Despite the fact that space tourism is in the initial stage and expensive, it is expected to become affordable in the next 20 years (Goeldner et al. 2009). Space tourism may not directly change consumer behaviour; however, the mysterious attraction of space travel is a strong pull factor that is expected to change the mode of travel in the future.

In such a short amount of time, the Internet has altered the way of service in the hospitality industry. There is no doubt that the Internet is dictating and changing consumers' behaviour. Nowadays, it allows customers limitless possibilities for accessing information about products and services. In addition to that, with the exponential growth of users of social media, millions of people have been signing up to different social platforms. Considering the amount of time spent and dependency on these platforms parallel with the speed of technology, it is expected to take up more space in consumers' lives. Services and products will also be tailored and customized based on consumers' expressions over these social media platforms.

Not only have the functions of the Internet been changing consumers' behaviour, the speed of the Internet is expected to grow and change consumer behaviour in the future. For example, Li-Fi technology refers to 'transmission of data through illumination by taking the fibre out of fibre optics by sending data through a LED light bulb that varies in intensity faster than the human eye can follow' (Rani et al. 2012: p. 703). It is basically considered as a fast and cheap wireless-communication system, the optical version of Wi-Fi. As mentioned before among the advantages of the Internet, the speed of the Internet may also influence consumers' behaviour. The new technology will allow users to have connection speeds 100 times faster. Therefore, consumers in the future will be able to access, upload and download information faster as well as being able to exchange big data.

Some of these technologies are already available and commonly used in the hospitality industry, or will be in the not-too-distant future; customers will be interacting with their mobile in many ways. Mobile technology has the potential to make many things in the future's hospitality industry drastically different. Some mobile developers and credit card companies have already created a mobile wallet allowing customers to pay for products and services. The mobile wallet refers to 'the newest form of mobile payment that enables users to share content and access services as well as conduct payments and ticketing transactions' (Shin 2009: p. 1344). In the future, there will be no need to carry a separate wallet or cash. Hotel room keys are other examples of mobile technology in the hospitality industry. This technology already exists and guests use their smartphones as a room key by having a coded signal sent to the guest's smartphone that is unique to each user. In the future, this technology is expected to give more control over tangible and intangible elements of hospitality products and/or services.

Despite the fact that virtual reality is still primitive, it is expected to change consumer behaviour in the tourism and hospitality industry in the future. Virtual reality tours are expected to eliminate destination accessibility problems. Therefore, it will allow more tourists to experience different tourism destinations as well as imaginary destinations. It will also remove the barriers that constrain tourists with physical disabilities, or elderly people, from experiencing travelling. Since time and money are important factors in destination selection, virtual reality may also attract low-income level tourists and people who have no or limited time for holidays. In addition, virtual reality tours may promote destinations by providing tourists with advanced understanding about their features and tourism destinations.

Summary

This chapter presents some of the technological developments and how these developments influence consumer behaviour in tourism and hospitality. Undoubtedly, technological developments have been closely followed and adapted in tourism and hospitality, especially in the past century. As mentioned earlier, service consumption has three stages including the pre-purchase stage, the service encounter stage and the post-encounter stage. Each stage requires different expectations and necessities. Within the tourism and hospitality industry, the aforementioned technological advancements present a pivotal role in dictating consumers' behaviour. In that sense, it may be reasonable to assert that each stage of the consumption behaviour is influenced by different aspects of the technological advancement. To that end, prior to consumption (pre-purchase), the Internet and social media exert the greatest influence on consumer, whereas during the service encounter, handheld mobile devices and service machines and technology may have the greatest impact, and social media in the post-encounter experience.

Conclusion

The technological developments in the past show that the future technology will bring more flexibilities, new experiences and more variability in products or services. It also shows that customer experience will be more customized and will be more tailored to individual experience. Human interaction may reduce, especially in the service encounter phase. Nonetheless, the interaction between the organization and the customer will not in any way be diminished; it will keep shifting from tangible to intangible platforms.

References

Anckar, B. and Walden, P. (2001). 'Introducing web technology in a small peripheral hospitality organization', *International Journal of Contemporary Hospitality Management*, 13(5): 241–250.

Bai, B., Law, R. and Wen, I. (2008). 'The impact of website quality on customer satisfaction and purchase intentions: Evidence from Chinese online visitors', *International Journal of Hospitality Management*, 27(3): 391–402.

Bavik, A. (2008). 'Online purchasing actions of international tourists in North Cyprus', *International Journal of Management Perspectives*, 1(2): 32–49.

Bavik, A., Bavik, L. Y. and Ekiz, E. H. (2014). 'Where I dine does matter: Testing the impact of servicescape on perceived service quality', Paper presented at the Global Tourism & Hospitality Conference and Asia Tourism Forum, 18–20 May, Hong Kong Polytechnic University, Hong Kong.

Bitner, M. J. (1992). 'Servicescapes: The impact of physical surroundings on customers and employees', *The Journal of Marketing*, 56(2): 57–71.

Chen, J. S. and Gursoy, D. (2001). 'An investigation of tourists' destination loyalty and preferences', *International Journal of Contemporary Hospitality Management*, 13(2): 79–85.

Chen, Y. and Xie, J. (2008). 'Online consumer review: Word-of-mouth as a new element of marketing communication mix', *Management Science*, 54(3): 477–491.

Chevalier, J. A. and Mayzlin, D. (2006). 'The effect of word of mouth on sales: Online book reviews', *Journal of Marketing Research*, 43(3): 345–354.

Duan, W., Gu, B. and Whinston, A. (2008). 'The dynamics of online word-of-mouth and product sales – An empirical investigation of the movie industry', *Journal of Retailing*, 84(2): 233–242.

Ekiz, E. H., Bavik, A. and Arasli, H. (2009). 'RENTQUAL: A new measurement scale for car rental services', *Turizam: znanstveno-stručni časopis*, 57(2): 135–153.

Ford, R. C., Sturman, M. C. and Heaton, C. P. (2012). *Managing Quality Service in Hospitality*, International edition, London: Cengage.

Fournier, S. and Lee, L. (2009). 'Getting brand communities right', *Harvard Business Review*, 87(4): 105–111.

Goeldner, C. R., Ritchie, J. B. and McIntosh, R. (2009). *Tourism: Principles, Practices, Philosophies*, Hoboken, NJ: Wiley.

Guttentag, D. A. (2010). 'Virtual reality: Applications and implications for tourism', *Tourism Management*, 31(5): 637–651.

Hemmington, N. (2007). 'From service to experience: Understanding and defining the hospitality business', *The Service Industries Journal*, 27(6): 747–755.

Hudson, S. (2008). *Tourism and Hospitality Marketing: A Global Perspective*, London: Sage.

Lang, T. C. (2000). 'The effect of the Internet on travel consumer purchasing behaviour and implications for travel agencies', *Journal of Vacation Marketing*, 6(4): 368–385.

Lovelock, C., Wirtz, J. and Hemzo, M. A. (2011). *Marketing de serviços: pessoas, tecnologia e estratégia*, São Paulo: Pearson Prentice-Hall.

Mennecke, B. E., Triplett, J. L., Hassall, L. M., Conde, Z. J. and Heer, R. (2011). 'An examination of a theory of embodied social presence in virtual worlds', *Decision Sciences*, 42(2): 413–450.

Rani, J., Chauhan, P. and Tripathi, R. (2012). 'Li–Fi (light fidelity): The future technology in wireless communication', *International Journal of Applied Engineering Research*, 7(11).

Shin, D.-H. (2009). 'Towards an understanding of the consumer acceptance of mobile wallet', *Computers in Human Behavior*, 25(6): 1343–1354.

Solomon, M. R., Dahl, D. W., White, K., Zaichkowsky, J. L. and Polegato, R. (2014). *Consumer Behavior: Buying, Having, and Being*, Upper Saddle River, NJ: Prentice Hall.

Vich-i-Martorell, G. À. (2004). 'The Internet and tourism principals in the Balearic Islands', *Tourism and Hospitality Research*, 5(1): 25–44.

Wang, X., Yu, C. and Wei, Y. (2012). 'Social media peer communication and impacts on purchase intentions: A consumer socialization framework', *Journal of Interactive Marketing*, 26(4): 198–208.

Yeung, T. A. and Law, R. (2004). 'Extending the modified heuristic usability evaluation technique to chain and independent hotel websites', *International Journal of Hospitality Management*, 23(3): 307–313.

40

EXPLORING CONSUMER BEHAVIOUR AT SLOW FOOD FESTIVALS IN RURAL DESTINATIONS

Samuel Adeyinka-Ojo and Catheryn Khoo-Lattimore

Introduction

Despite extant consumer behaviour research that deals with the 'whys' and 'hows' of consumer decision making, studies on food and tourism are largely limited to food safety and hygiene issues (MacLaurin 2001; MacLaurin et al. 2000 cited in Mitchell and Hall 2003). Food and tourism studies that have been focused on tourist and visitor behaviour at food events are limited, mainly because research on food- and beverage-related festivals is at its formation stage (Kim et al. 2010) and studies that research consumers' attitudes and behaviours towards food festivals in tourism destinations are at an embryonic level (Sparks 2007; Kim et al. 2009). This is surprising considering the emergence of food festivals in many tourism destinations as a means of promoting locally sourced food consumption (Organ et al. 2015). To this end, consumer behaviour research is important to food tourism stakeholders in the hospitality and tourism industry such as restaurant and café owners, cookery school providers, festival organisers, hotel and resort managers, bed and breakfast operators, food producers as well as destination marketers (Mitchell and Hall 2003). By understanding how tourists make their decisions to consume food-related products, we will be able to gain a better understanding of when we need to intervene in their decision-making process. In this regard, the aim of this chapter is to bridge the existing gap between consumer behaviour studies, food research and tourism studies. In particular, the following questions guided this study: (1) What are the motives for visiting slow food festivals (SFFs) in rural destinations; and (2) How are these motives conceptualised into post–consumption experiences such as satisfaction and intention to revisit?

Literature review

SFFs and rural tourism destinations

'Slow food is a term used to describe food with methods of production, distribution and consumption similar to that of fast food. . . but uses a variety of approaches to disguise these methods in order to associate itself with slow food' (Donati 2005: p. 210). Relatedly, festivals that celebrate slow food are a noble attempt to preserve our cultural beliefs and food identity from being homogenised by a worldwide food culture devoid of pleasure and diversity (Donati 2005). In other words, an SFF is regarded as 'a means of promoting and protecting locally produced food from the small scale food producers from being lost' to the global fast food culture (Frost and Laing 2013: p. 68; Tam 2008). The staging of SFFs is crucial for the growth of tourism (Nilsson et al. 2011; Tam 2008; Donati 2005), and these festivals have been used as a source of destination identity (Stille 2001) and to promote a particular tourism destination (Hall and Mitchell 2005; Hall 2012).

In developed countries, SFFs are a growing phenomenon. A review of the literature shows that Italy, Australia and New Zealand are the three main countries that have embraced slow food events (Frost and Laing 2013: p. 67). For example, SFFs have been held in Mildura, Victoria in Australia (Donati 2005; Frost and Laing 2013); Barossa Valley, South Australia (Frost and Laing 2013); and Nelson in New Zealand (Frost and Laing 2013). Likewise, 'Salone del Gusto' (The Taste Fair) in Turin and 'Terra Madre SFFs' are two events in Italy (Frost and Laing 2013) that are recognised as leading destinations developed for regional food (Schneider 2008). SFFs have been staged successfully in Italian towns such as Bra, Abbiategrasso and Levanto and other rural destinations (Nilsson et al. 2011). Different tourism events where local food is emphasised and slow food restaurants are part of the promotional activities aimed at the visitors and other consumers in these three towns and surrounding rural destinations (Nilsson et al. 2011).

There has recently been a focus on the employment of SFFs as a high-yield strategy for rural tourism destinations (Adeyinka-Ojo and Khoo-Lattimore 2013), which is sensible as the concept of 'slow' is in accord with the unhurried image of rural destinations. This view is corroborated by Tam (2008), who argues that the promotion of slow food is to act as an antidote to a modern fast-paced lifestyle that is increasingly unhealthy. The 'slow' vision emphasises the promotion of economic activities in order to market various types of activities involving fishing, agriculture and recreational forest as rural destination attractors (Yamaguchi Prefecture 2010). This is essential in order to achieve the concept of 'slow' in rural destinations by creating attractive tourism resources and evolve tourist-oriented attractions such as the SFF as a new tourism business (Murayama and Parker 2012: p. 171). Moreover, the hosting of SFFs in rural tourism destinations could attract high-end tourist arrivals who are willing not only to pay more but also to extend their length of stay (Adeyinka-Ojo and Khoo-Lattimore 2013).

Post-consumption experience and motivation as determinants of intention to revisit

The staging of food festivals presents consumers with an authentic lifestyle experience in a tourism destination (Getz 2000). In hospitality and tourism-related research, consumers' involvement in food tourism may be more inclined towards new food experiences in tourism destinations (Cohen and Avieli 2004). Consumer behaviour is a key concept underpinning marketing activities that develop, promote and sell tourism destinations and their products (Swarbrooke and Horner 1999). In this regard, the knowledge of consumer behaviour in terms of where they visit and what informed their decision to revisit the destination is crucial in tourism destination planning and marketing (Choibamroong 2006). Several studies have shown that there is a positive correlation between consumer satisfaction and loyalty (Kim et al. 2010). A consumer's intention to revisit the same tourism destination in the future is associated with the consumer's overall satisfaction during the previous visit (Hui et al. 2007), and further amplified by word-of-mouth (WOM) communication. This highlights the importance of recommendations as important determinants of consumer intention to revisit a tourism destination (Lee et al. 2006), and as a crucial source for influencing consumers' choice of tourism destination to visit (Weaver and Lawton 2002). However, a review of the literature showed that the majority of the studies in the context of SFFs were conducted predominantly with a focus on economic benefits, communication persuasive strategy, destination identity, perceived authenticity, and preservation of local and regional food production. It appears that empirical studies on consumer motivations and experiences as determinants of a repeat visit at SFFs in rural tourism destinations are lacking in the literature (Li and Petrick 2006). Within tourism, the study of motivation forms the foundation of any attempt to obtain information on travel behaviour (Li et al. 2016) and motivation has been highlighted as a missing link in understanding tourist revisit intention (Li et al. 2010).

Methodology

This study has adopted qualitative research methodology because the researchers are interested in multiple interpretations, rather than one specific answer. The purpose is to elicit rich, detailed data that can be used in the data analysis (Lofland and Lofland 1995).

Data collection involved in-depth interviews and participant observation of the SFFs held at Bario, a remote village in Sarawak in east Malaysia. It is situated between 3,200 and 6,000 feet or at an altitude of about 1,100 m above sea level (Jiwan et al. 2006), with a population of about 1,200 people (Malaysian Government 2011). The village is accessible via an 18-seater Otter aircraft twice a day depending on the weather conditions. Alternatively, it takes 12–14 hours in a four-wheel drive vehicle on a logging road in and out of Bario to the major towns and cities (Jiwan et al. 2006) as the quality of the roads is poor. Bario is predominantly a rice farming community without amenities such as good roads, water, electricity, hotels and modern houses. In an attempt to attract tourists to this village, the first Bario Slow Food and Cultural Festival (Pesta Nukenen) was held in 2006 and ever since, it has become an annual event (Adeyinka-Ojo and Khoo-Lattimore 2013), marking the 10th time held in July 2015.

For three consecutive years between 2012 and 2014, we undertook visits to Bario's Pesta Nukenen. In total, we conducted a total of 9 days of participant observation during the 3 events which generated 16 pages of field notes. In-depth interviews were conducted with consumers at the SFFs until the point of data saturation was reached when the inclusion of additional data yielded no new dimensions to the common ideas (Jennings 2010; Strauss and Corbin 2008). A semi-structured interview protocol was developed that focuses on why visitors attended the SFFs in Bario; their experiences at the festival; if they were willing to recommend the festival to other consumers (friends, relatives and potential visitors); and if they were likely to attend the SFF in future. The in-depth interview sessions lasted an average of 60 minutes and were digitally recorded (Rasmussen et al. 2006). Transcription was undertaken immediately after the conclusion of each interview (Gubrium and Holstein 2001), so that the data collected from the participants would still be fresh in the researcher's mind (Prayag and Ryan 2011).

Thematic analysis was adopted, so data was systematically read and reread several times (Fereday and Muir-Cochrane 2006). The analysis procedures refer to the six stages of thematic analysis recommended by Braun and Clarke (2006) which allows the researcher to become acquainted with the data, develop the initial or open codes, search for relevant themes, review themes that have emerged, define, label and name the codes, and finally produce a report of the findings. This analytic method specifically identified codes and themes that provide answers to our two research questions. The field notes from the participant observation were content analysed for triangulation purposes.

Findings and discussion

The tourists

In this study, 30 respondents were interviewed during the SFFs (Pesta Nukenen) in Bario over a period of 3 years. Table 40.1 presents the tourists' profiles which indicate their age, country of origin, gender, respondents code number (RCN), number of visits and year of attending an SFF in Bario.

Respondents' profile

Table 40.1 Summary of tourists interviewed

No.	RCN	Age	Gender	Country	Respondent 2012	Respondent 2013	Respondent 2014	No. of visits to Bario
Local tourists								
1	RCN01	53	Male	Malaysia	❖			4
2	RCN02	47	Female	Malaysia	❖			1
3	RCN03	60	Male	Malaysia	❖			1
4	RCN04	27	Female	Malaysia	❖			2
5	RCN05	34	Female	Malaysia	❖			5
6	RCN06	42	Male	Malaysia		❖		2
7	RCN07	25	Male	Malaysia		❖		1
8	RCN08	39	Male	Malaysia		❖		2
9	RCN09	66	Male	Malaysia			❖	3
10	RCN10	48	Female	Malaysia			❖	4
International tourists								
11	RCN11	45	Male	United Kingdom	❖			1
12	RCN12	47	Female	United Kingdom	❖			1
13	RCN13	58	Male	United States	❖			1
14	RCN14	55	Male	United States	❖			1
15	RCN15	28	Female	Japan	❖			4
16	RCN16	34	Male	Spain	❖			1

No.	RCN	Age	Gender	Country	Respondent 2012	Respondent 2013	Respondent 2014	No. of visits to Bario
17	RCN17	37	Male	Austria	❖			1
18	RCN18	53	Male	Germany	❖			1
19	RCN19	45	Male	Brunei	❖			1
20	RCN20	54	Female	United States	❖			1
21	RCN21	72	Male	Australia		❖		2
22	RCN22	46	Male	Slovakia		❖		1
23	RCN23	51	Male	Australia		❖		2
24	RCN24	27	Male	Norway		❖		1
25	RCN25	33	Male	France		❖		1
26	RCN26	48	Male	Canada			❖	1
27	RCN27	65	Male	New Zealand			❖	1
28	RCN28	28	Female	United Kingdom			❖	3
29	RCN29	24	Female	Netherlands			❖	2
30	RCN30	30	Male	Poland			❖	4
Total No. of Respondents					15	8	7	N = 30

Source: Authors.

Note: Local tourists (N = 10), international tourists (N = 20).

The ten local tourists from Malaysia consisted of six male and four female participants. Similarly, there were 15 male and 5 female international tourists. Overall, these participants came from 16 different countries. In addition, these tourists ranged between 24 and 72 years old. Most of the tourists were visiting Bario for the first time. However, six of the international tourists and seven of the local tourists have visited Bario more than once. Notably, most of these international tourists had stayed between four and six nights in Bario at the time of their interviews, and a few of them still had more days to spend after the SFFs.

Consumer motives for attending SFFs

Table 40.2 provides some illustrative comments from the respondents in this study on their motives for attending the SFFs in Bario.

Findings indicate three primary consumer motives for attending the slow food events: (1) desire to taste authentic local food from local producers; (2) desire to experience the diverse cultures and lifestyles of the host community; and (3) desire to meet new people and establish networks of relationship with the local people and other consumers. The motivation to attend SFFs is dependent on the availability of varieties of authentic local food. The first two findings are to a large extent consistent with Hall et al.'s (2003) study that travel behaviour of tourists to participate in any food festival should be primarily motivated by the desire to have a different

Table 40.2 Consumer motives for attending slow food festivals

Motives	Respondent comments
Taste authentic local food Experience diverse cultures and lifestyles	(RCN30) – I love food so to say, I decided to attend the slow food festival to experience something authentic and different. I mean the reason for attending this event is to taste varieties of local food and to meet new people from the village and to learn their culture and lifestyles.
Establish networks of relationship	(RCN26) – I'm here to see the people, make new friends, and establish networks of relationship, to see diverse cultures, their lifestyles, tasting the authentic local food and to experience something interesting and new.

Source: Authors.

experience. Besides that, studies have shown that food events and festivals are part of food tourism which can play important roles in motivating consumers to participate in food festivals for a unique and different experience during their holiday seasons in tourism destinations (Getz 2000; Yuan et al. 2005). However, the third motive from these findings appears to be a new discovery in the literature on consumer motives for attending tourism events and in particular SFFs in rural destinations.

Consumers' post-consumption experiences and determinants of revisit intention

In describing tourists' post-consumption experiences and satisfaction at the SFFs in Bario, and in particular their intention to revisit for future events, sample tourists' responses are presented in Table 40.3.

The findings show that the consumers' overall experience and satisfaction at this event are enriched by the varieties of the local food, participation of young people and the number of attendees. These factors for satisfaction are underpinned by the three motives identified in this study for attending SFFs. Consumers' participation at the food festivals allowed them to meet with the local food producers and learn about the food display at the event in a holistic manner. Food tasting and consumption for the consumers became a hedonistic experience (Mason and Paggiaro 2012).

In this study findings revealed that hospitality, happiness and friendliness of the host community also contribute to satisfaction with the experience, which in turn encourages consumer intention to revisit future SFFs at the same destination. The findings also reveal that the consumers at the SFFs in Bario were willing to attend future events and inform friends, relatives and other potential consumers due to their positive overall satisfaction. These findings lend support to previous studies that visitors' satisfaction in attending a festival is an important predictor of future repeat intentions (Baker and Crompton 2000; Organ et al. 2015) and answer the call by Moore et al. (2015) to move beyond consumer satisfaction to loyalty at the nature-based (rural tourism) destination. These findings are also consistent with Qu et al. (2011) in that the

Table 40.3 Consumers' post-consumption experiences as determinants of revisit intention

Post-consumption experiences	Respondent comments
Varieties of local food, youth involvement and outdoor activities	(RCN02) – This slow food event for me is a very good experience, I'm happy to see a good number of people attended this festival, different programmes for the children, local games for the adult, varieties of local food are on display and everybody is involved in the food tasting and cultural dances.
Consumer's overall experience and satisfaction	(RCN29) – Intriguing, exciting, tasty and fulfilling; that is the best way I could describe my overall experience and satisfaction at this slow food festival currently ongoing in Bario. I was excited to see the participation of the children. As a visitor this event lives up to its expectation in terms of food, dancing and tasting quite a range of foods and drinks produced locally… it has been fun, partying and fulfilment.
Determinants of revisit intention	*Respondent comments*
Positive WOM communication and recommendation Hospitality, happiness and friendliness of the host community	(RCN27) – Yes I would mainly attend the next coming slow food festival because the food produced in Bario is great. I'll tell my friends to attend the food event because I enjoy the food and the people here are hospitable, so it would be interesting to see and participate in different kinds of culture, local games again and varieties of local food.
Participation in cultural activities	(RCN9) – Definitely I will come again with my family to enjoy the local food produced in Bario. The friendliness and happiness here I want my children to visit this place and also experience the food culture, visit the paddy rice fields (Bario rice) and participate in the traditional cultural dance during the food event.

Source: Authors.

consumer intentions to make a repeat visit to the tourism destination and to interest potential consumers in the place through WOM are dependent on fulfilled expectation and satisfaction, which are imperative for behavioural consequences in tourism destination post-buying behaviour of consumers. Our field notes on participant observation also confirmed findings from the in-depth interviews that tourists were involved in food tasting, making friends and outdoor engagements such as cultural dance and traditional games.

Implications and conclusion

This study has found that consumers are driven to a SFF at a rural destination despite its difficult access, by three main motives: their desire to (1) experience and taste authentic local food, (2) experience local lifestyle and culture and (3) establish networks of relationship with the locals and other attendees. It should be noted that consumers' motives to attend SFFs at a rural destination are based on the individual desire to have a new experience during the event. The fulfilment of this experience through positive satisfaction at the SFF could lead to positive WOM, recommendations to potential visitors and intentions to revisit by the consumer for future SFFs.

Post-consumer experience constructs at SFFs in rural destinations are interrelated and influence each other. These factors include: (1) varieties of local food and activities such as cultural dance, youth engagement, local games and other outdoor activities; (2) hospitality and friendliness of the local community; (3) consumer's overall satisfaction; (4) positive WOM and recommendation to other visitors; and (5) consumer's revisit intention. These post-consumer experiences are crucial in determining consumers' repeat visit at SFFs. In other words, positive WOM is influenced by the consumer's satisfying experience at the SFFs, which is an important determinant to trigger the intention to revisit for future events. Importantly, these findings are conceptualised to develop a framework presented in Figure 40.1.

Findings suggest that rural tourism destination managers, entrepreneurs, SFF organisers and the host community should ensure that the consumer motives for attending the SFFs are clearly identified, managed and maintained throughout the organisation of such events. Likewise,

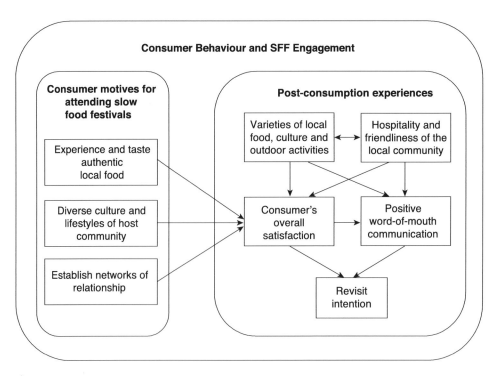

Figure 40.1 Framework for consumer behaviour at slow food festivals in rural tourism destinations
Source: Authors.

there is a need to enrich the consumers' experience during the SFF with varieties of local activities such as traditional games, cultural dances and native hospitality. These activities are imperative in order to encourage positive WOM and repeat visits at SFFs. In conclusion, it is acknowledged that the number of respondents in this study is limited in its ability to generalise the findings to other rural destinations organising SFFs. Therefore, future studies should consider surveying a large sample to test the framework resulting from this study.

Acknowledgements

The funding for this project was made possible through a research grant obtained from the Malaysian Ministry of Education Long Term Research Grant Scheme (LRGS) Programme [Reference No.: JPT.S (BPKI)2000/09/01/015Jld.4(67)].

References

Adeyinka-Ojo, S. F. and Khoo-Lattimore, C. (2013). 'Slow food events as a high yield strategy for rural tourism destinations: The case of Bario, Sarawak', *Worldwide Hospitality and Tourism Themes*, 5(4): 353–364.

Baker, D. and Crompton, J. (2000). 'Quality, satisfaction and behavioral intentions', *Annals of Tourism Research*, 27(3): 785–804.

Braun, V. and Clarke, V. (2006). 'Using thematic analysis in psychology', *Qualitative Research in Psychology*, 3(2): 77–101.

Choibamroong, T. (2006). 'Knowledge of tourists' behaviour: A key success factor for managers in tourism business', Available from: http://www.bu.ac.th/knowledgecenter/paper [Accessed: 30 September 2015].

Cohen, E. and Avieli, N. (2004). 'Food in tourism: Attraction and impediment', *Annals of Tourism Research*, 31(4): 755–778.

Donati, K. (2005). 'The pleasure of diversity in slow food's ethics of taste', *Food Culture and Society*, 8(2): 207–218.

Fereday, J. and Muir-Cochrane, E. (2006). 'Demonstrating rigor using thematic analysis: A hybrid approach of inductive and deductive coding and theme development', *International Journal of Qualitative Methods*, 5(1): 1–11.

Frost, W. and Laing, J. (2013). 'Communicating persuasive messages through slow food festivals', *Journal of Vacation Marketing*, 19(1): 67–74.

Getz, D. (2000). *Explore Wine Tourism: Management, Development and Destinations*, New York: Cognizant Communication Corporation.

Gubrium, J. A. and Holstein, J. A. (2001). *Handbook of Interview Research: Context and Method*, Thousand Oaks, CA: Sage.

Hall, C. M. (2012). 'The contradictions and paradoxes of slow food: Environmental change, sustainability and the conservation of taste', in S. Fullagar, K. Markwell and E. Wilson (eds.), *Slow Tourism: Experiences and Mobilities* (pp. 53–68), Bristol: Channel View Publications.

Hall, C. M. and Mitchell, R. (2005). 'Gastronomic tourism – Comparing food wine experiences', in B. Novelli (ed.), *Niche Tourism: Contemporary Issues, Trends and Cases* (pp. 73–89), Oxford: Elsevier Butterworth-Heinemann.

Hall, C. M., Sharples, E. and Smith, A. (2003). 'The experience of consumption or the consumption of experiences?: Challenges and issues in food tourism', in C. M. Hall, E. Sharples, R. Mitchell, B. Cambourne and N. Macionis (eds.), *Food Tourism around the World: Development, Management and Markets* (pp. 314–336), Oxford: Butterworth-Heinemann.

Hui, T., Wan, D. and Ho, A. (2007). 'Tourists' satisfaction, recommendation and revisiting Singapore', *Tourism Management*, 28(4): 261–267.

Jennings, G. (2010). *Tourism Research*, 2nd edition, Milton, Australia: Wiley and Sons.

Jiwan, D., Paul Chai, P. K., Teo, G. K. and Jiwan, M. (2006). 'Integrated highland development in Bario, Sarawak, Malaysia: An overview', Paper presented at the International Symposium towards Sustainable Livelihoods and Ecosystems in Mountainous Regions, 7–9 March, Chiang Mai, Thailand.

Kim, Y. G., Eves, A. and Scarles, C. (2009). 'Building a model of local food consumption on trips and holidays: A grounded theory approach', *International Journal of Hospitality Management*, 28(3): 423–431.

Kim, Y. G., Suh, B. O. and Eves, A. (2010). 'The relationships between food-related personality traits, satisfaction, and loyalty among visitors attending food events and festivals', *International Journal of Hospitality Management*, 29: 216–226.

Lee, S., Kim, W. and Kim, H. (2006). 'The impact of co-branding on post-purchase behaviours in family restaurants', *International Journal of Hospitality Management*, 25(2): 245–261.

Li, M., Cai, L. A., Lehto, X. Y. and Huang, J. Z. (2010). 'A missing link in understanding revisit intention – The role of motivation and image', *Journal of Travel and Tourism Marketing*, 27(4): 335–348.

Li, M., Zhang, H. and Cai, L. A. (2016). 'A subcultural analysis of tourism motivations', *Journal of Hospitality and Tourism Research*, 40(1): 85–113.

Li, X. and Petrick, J. F. (2006). 'A review of festival and event motivation studies', *Event Management*, 9(4): 239–245.

Lofland, J. and Lofland, L. H. (1995). *Analysing Social Settings: A Guide to Qualitative Observation and Analysis*, 3rd edition, Belmont, CA: Wadsworth.

Malaysian Government (2011). *Population and Housing Census of Malaysia: Preliminary Count Report 2010*, Putrajaya, Malaysia: Department of Statistics, Available from: https://www.statistics.gov.my [Accessed: 30 September 2015].

Mason, M. C. and Paggiaro, A. (2012). 'Investigating the role of festivalscape in culinary tourism: The case of food and wine events', *Tourism Management*, 33(6): 1329–1336.

Mitchell, R. D. and Hall, C. M. (2003). 'Consuming tourists: Food tourism consumer behaviour', in C. M. Hall, E. Sharples, R. Mitchell, B. Cambourne and N. Macionis (eds.), *Food Tourism around the World: Development, Management and Markets* (pp. 60–80), Oxford: Butterworth-Heinemann.

Moore, S. A., Rodger, K. and Taplin, R. (2015). 'Moving beyond visitor satisfaction to loyalty in nature-based tourism: A review and research agenda', *Current Issues in Tourism*, 18(7): 667–683.

Murayama, M. and Parker, G. (2012). 'Fast Japan, slow Japan: Shifting to slow tourism as a rural regeneration tool in Japan', in S. Fullagar, K. Markwell and E. Wilson (eds.), *Slow Tourism Experiences and Mobilities* (pp. 170–184), London: Channel View Publications.

Nilsson, J. H., Svard, A.-C., Widarsson, Å. and Wirell, T. (2011). 'Cittaslow' eco-gastronomic heritage as a tool for destination development', *Current Issues in Tourism*, 14(4): 373–386.

Organ, K., Koenig-Lewis, N., Palmer, A. and Probert, J. (2015). 'Festivals as agents for behaviour change: A study of food festival engagement and subsequent food choices', *Tourism Management*, 48: 84–99.

Prayag, G. and Ryan, C. (2011). 'The relationship between the "push" and "pull" factors of a tourist destination: The role of nationality – an analytical qualitative research approach', *Current Issues in Tourism*, 14(2): 121–143.

Qu, H., Kim, L. H. and Im, H. H. (2011). 'A model of destination branding: Integrating the concepts of the branding and destination image', *Tourism Management*, 32(3): 465–476.

Rasmussen, E. S., Ostergaard, P. and Beckmann, C. S. (2006). *Essentials of Social Science Research Methodology*, Odense: University Press of Southern Denmark.

Schneider, S. (2008). 'Good, clean, fair: The rhetoric of the slow food movement', *College English*, 70(4): 384–420.

Sparks, B. (2007). 'Planning a wine tourism vacation?: Factors that help to predict tourist behavioural intentions', *Tourism Management*, 28(5): 1180–1192.

Stille, A. (2001). 'Slow food: An Italian answer to globalisation', *The Nation*, 20–27 August, Available from: https://www.thenation.com/article/slow-food/ [Accessed: 10 November 2016].

Strauss, A. L. and Corbin, J. M. (2008). *Basics of Qualitative Research: Techniques and Procedures for Developing Grounded Theory*, London: Sage.

Swarbrooke, J. and Horner, S. (1999). *Consumer Behavior in Tourism*, Oxford: Butterworth-Heinemann.

Tam, D. (2008). 'Slow journeys: What does it mean to go slow?', *Food Culture and Society: An International Journal of Multidisciplinary Research*, 11(2): 207–218.

Weaver, D. B. and Lawton, L. J. (2002). *Tourism Management*, Milton, Australia: John Wiley and Sons.

Yamaguchi Prefecture (2010). 'Yamaguchi slow tourism', Available from: http://www.yamaguchi-slow.jp/ [Accessed: 30 September 2015].

Yuan, J., Cai, L., Morrison, A. M. and Litnon, S. (2005). 'An analysis of wine festival attendees' motivations', *Journal of Vacation Marketing*, 11(1): 41–58.

41

SMARTPHONE TECHNOLOGICAL ADVANCEMENT AND CONSUMERS

Sarah Gardiner, Joan Carlini and Noel Scott

Introduction

Consumers around the world are increasingly reaching for their smartphone to research and book travel (Lu et al. 2016; Murphy et al. 2016). This technology can also be used to enhance the travel experience and share that experience with others. For some consumers, smartphones have become an essential travel companion and guide, assisting them to make travel more enjoyable, increasing their confidence and reducing anxiety associated with experiencing an unfamiliar place (Tussyadiah and Wang 2016). Consumers are using the functionalities of smartphones when travelling to manage and organize their trip, for direction and navigation and social networking, to receive push recommendations and to search for online reviews, deals and discounts (Tussyadiah 2016).

The introduction of smartphones almost two decades ago has transformed communication. Users are no longer limited to talk and text, but can access camera and video capabilities, specialist mobile software applications (known as 'apps') and connect with others through Internet access. Thus, smartphones have become a mini portable computer in consumers' pockets offering interactive, immediate, measurable, actionable and fun experiences (Krum 2010 in Bruck and Rao 2013). The functionality of smartphones in everyday life and travel (Wang et al. 2016), combined with the portability of this technology, has resulted in dramatic increases in worldwide smartphone ownership. Over 1 billion smartphones have been sold around the world since Apple launched the iPhone in 2007 (Statista 2015). Of particular note is the growth in smartphone ownership in the world's top two outbound travel markets (by spend), China and the United States (United Nations World Tourism Organization 2015). In 2013, 436 million Chinese owned smartphones and this number is expected to increase to 687 million by 2019. Similarly, 62 million Americans owned a smartphone in 2010 with ownership projected to increase to 220 million by 2015. Over 1.6 million Android apps and 1.5 million Apple apps are now available. Travel apps are the seventh most popular type in Apple's App Store, representing 4.32% of those available (Statista 2015). This technology now plays an important role in travel consumption, providing greater convenience, personalization and empowerment.

This chapter examines the state-of-play for smartphone technology adoption in tourism, highlighting the various uses of this technology to aid consumer decision-making and enhance the customer experience. It begins by highlighting the functionalities of smartphones and discusses their application during travel. The importance of tourism businesses offering consumers a mobile-friendly version of their website is discussed and the role and types of apps in tourism examined. A case study involving market research to inform the design of a tourist attraction app is presented, offering insights into the design process and management challenges faced in embracing this technology. Accordingly, leading views on smartphone technology are given and implications for integrating this technology in consumer travel behaviour presented.

Smartphone technology's influence on how we travel

Wang et al. (2016) argue that ubiquitous use of smartphones in people's everyday life has created new patterns in how people communicate and consume entertainment and information. This change affects how they interact, consume content and use their time when travelling. The everyday use of smartphone technology blurs the distinction between home and travel. The dependence of people on the everyday use of smartphones to connect, have fun, be entertained, and be more productive, innovative and informed leads naturally to their use during the travel experience. It enables travellers to feel connected to family and friends, secure and confident, and informed during their travel. Travellers can also use smartphones for entertainment and fun. They can help with information acquisition and trip planning en route as well as sharing of experiences during the trip, ultimately leading to a more mobile population that travels more frequently.

One of the most advantageous features of smartphone technology for travel is the use of sensors that are context aware. Contextual design is user-centred, aggregating data from the users' real-world behaviour and patterns, making it easier for people to 'move through space, to move from place to place or to go on a journey' (Dickinson et al. 2014: p. 86). One common application of smartphone technology to travel is to assist way-finding and provide a mapping function. Geographic Information Systems (GIS) accessed through smartphones integrate 'place' and 'time' to provide consumers with real-time Geographic Positioning System (GPS) geographic and spatial intelligence to assist navigation (Chu et al. 2012). Because context sensors can determine a consumer's location dynamically, they can influence how a person's personal and social experience of travel is constructed. Consumers are therefore not limited to static, isolated experiences; smartphones enable them to interact with physical and social elements of the environment, and, as a result, construct an experience that is tailored, open and dynamic. This also facilitates reciprocal information sharing and on-the-go, spontaneous decision-making (Lamsfus et al. 2015). As a result, consumers can make better location-based decisions, enhancing the ease and convenience of travel, and make it possible to tailor content to the smartphone users based on their location (Tussyadiah and Wang 2016). Live traffic and weather updates, offers based on user proximity to businesses, and transport services advice established by user vicinity assist consumer decision-making and improve the consumer experience (Dickinson et al. 2014).

Internet and software innovations accessed through smartphones have made them a social device (Tuten and Solomon 2014), providing users with connectivity and content sharing capabilities not possible before. In this manner, 'travelers are constantly sending signals and generating new information' (Lamsfus et al. 2015: p. 697). Consumer-to-consumer engagements using social Internet platforms can inform their consumer choice. This technology has given consumers more power and, accordingly, they are increasingly relying on reviews and feedback from other consumers to inform their purchase decisions. In addition it is possible to push information to consumers based on their characteristics, allowing 'in the moment' customization. For example, a business can alert customers within a geographical area to a special offer through a push notification and consequently generate sales from passers-by (Tussyadiah and Wang 2016).

Smartphones are also being increasingly used to book travel. It is estimated that one-third of e-commerce transactions in the United States (40% globally) are through mobile phones, with travel representing over 25% of e-commerce transactions in the United States (Criteo 2015). The world's largest online review website, TripAdvisor, in a survey of 40,000 consumers and hoteliers worldwide, found 8% of travellers booked accommodation via their smartphone and 45% of connected travellers (i.e. consumers who use their smartphone to plan and book travel) book travel activities pre-trip (TripAdvisor 2015). In short, smartphones are overtaking personal computers as the device of choice to access Internet content and purchase online.

Mobile-friendly websites and apps in tourism

The adoption of new technology is underpinned by its perceived usefulness (Rivera et al. 2015) and ease of use (Lu et al. 2016). Accordingly, given the widespread use of smartphone technology in everyday life and travel (Wang et al. 2016), an ever-increasing number of tourism operators have upgraded their website to a more responsive design (Warner 2013), ensuring their website is mobile enabled. These websites are described as 'mobile friendly' and offer enhancements that ensure that the website loads quickly and displays content correctly on a mobile device, improving the user experience (Google 2015a). Research by the Internet search engine Google suggests that 74% of mobile users are more likely to return to a website that is mobile friendly. Design elements, like having large buttons, limited scrolling and pinching (the ability to directly phone the business with one click and link to the business's social media) are considered important (Miller 2012). Offering a mobile-friendly option has been further promoted by Google, as, from April 2015, the mobile-friendliness of websites was also added as a criterion to determine Google's search rankings (Google 2015b).

Another way tourism businesses are interacting with consumers using smartphones and other mobile devices, such as tablets, is through software applications specifically designed for a mobile device, commonly referred to as apps. The two main smartphone operating systems for apps are iOS (for Apple devices) and Android. As with mobile-friendly websites, apps must be simple, intuitive and easy to navigate to enhance their perceived usefulness among consumers. There are four primary benefits of having an app. Firstly, once downloaded, apps can be used with or without an Internet connection. For example, travellers can download TripAdvisor reviews, photos and city maps before they leave home and access this information while travelling through the TripAdvisor app on their smartphone. This function is also widely used for language translation apps. Secondly, consumers can also create and store personalized information in an app. For example, the Qantas airline app allows users to manage their bookings, check-in and access flight information and entertainment through their app. The TripIt app allows users to build and manage their personalized master travel itinerary through collating all hotel, transport and other confirmations and bookings together. Thirdly, apps can also help improve the travel experience. For instance, the SeatGuru app assists consumers to find the best seat on a plane. Finally, apps can offer gaming and entertainment functions: for example, a wildlife attraction at Phillip Island, Australia, has an app, *Penguins*, that has an interactive quiz and children's game about penguins catching fish, as well as interpretative content about penguins and the history and management of the site.

These examples indicate that smartphones offer an opportunity to make travel easier, convenient and pleasurable. Accordingly, consumers are increasingly reaching for their smartphone when travelling, and the tourism industry has begun to embrace this technology as a means to enhance customer service and business performance. It is therefore timely that we explore how tourism businesses can design apps to augment the visitor experience. This chapter provides a case study of a wildlife attraction that is planning to create a new park app. In doing so, the case provides in-depth insights into the consumer research and management considerations that inform app design, and on the use of smartphones in tourism to influence consumer behaviour.

Method

The case study concerns research on the consumer preferences of Chinese international students as a subgroup of the Chinese youth independent travel market. There are approximately 120,000 Chinese international students studying in Australia (Australian Government 2015) and these students represent a new generation of Chinese independent travellers (King and Gardiner 2015). The first phase of the study concentrated on Chinese international students studying in South East Queensland. This target population was selected because they are international visitors living for an extended period in close proximity to the research site, Currumbin Wildlife Sanctuary (CWS), and therefore, they are more likely to be familiar with tourism experiences in the region and able to visit the site and participate in the study. The first phase of the study involved eight off-site focus groups of approximately 45-minute duration including seven sessions with Chinese international students and one mixed-nationality focus group. Each session had four to eight participants. At the end of each session, participants were invited to participate in a site visit to experience the attraction. Snowball sampling was also employed to recruit additional site visit participants. Approximately 3 hours into the site visit, a 30-minute focus group interview was undertaken with participants. Interviews were recorded and transcribed verbatim. The researchers also met with the site managers to discuss the interim findings and implications for the app design and technology implementation at the attraction upon the conclusion of each phase of data collection. Field notes were also taken during the manager interviews and site visits to inform the findings.

Designing a wildlife attraction smartphone app

Currumbin Wildlife Sanctuary (CWS) is an Australian wildlife zoological park located on the Gold Coast, Australia. CWS is a not-for-profit organization operated by the National Trust of Australia (Queensland) (Currumbin Wildlife Sanctuary 2015). The attraction offers visitors the opportunity to see Australian wildlife through exhibits and animal encounters (including hand-feeding kangaroos and lorikeets), and provides shows such as the free flight bird show and keepers feeding various Australian animals. Visitors can also view CWS's state-of-the-art veterinary and rehabilitation hospital. CWS attracts over 440,000 visitors annually. Approximately half of these visitors are from overseas countries. CWS has a well-established business model for servicing the Chinese group tour market, attracting about 70,000 Chinese visitors annually. However, the Chinese independent travel market was seen as a new and potentially lucrative opportunity to expand their Chinese visitation. Accordingly, consumer research was undertaken to explore the potential to develop a smartphone app to augment the in-park visitor experience.

Key consumer considerations in the design of the app

Study participants considered one of the most useful functions for a park app is to provide information about how to get to the attraction and navigate around it. This would use the geographic contexts sensors of the smartphone. Several participants used public transport to get to the attraction and mentioned they used the Google maps app to find their way. Participants also suggested that way-finding within CWS is particularly difficult because the attraction is located in a valley with dense tree coverage, therefore, physical landmarks to aid navigation are absent. Furthermore, on-site visitors also found it difficult to read the park's hard-copy map, as they were more familiar with using electronic technology. Therefore trying to locate the coordinates of the show on the map proved challenging. The natural landscaping of the park made it difficult to find free-ranging animals, with participants suggesting that an app could assist them by providing them with the location of animals they wanted to look at.

Independent visitors experience CWS as a self-guided experience. Therefore, in addition to the navigation tools, participants thought that having a smartphone app that could provide a guiding function would enhance identification and interpretation of the animal exhibits and shows. This tool was particularly important to the Chinese students as they were familiar with guided experiences when visiting national parks in China.

Interviews with CWS managers suggested that an app could also provide behind-the-scenes content, such as real-time camera footage of the surgical theatre in the animal hospital. Furthermore, since many Australian native animals are nocturnal, video content of the animal in the burrow during the day or when it was more active during the night provided through the app could augment the experience. Participants felt this 'backstage pass' content would enhance the value of the app and improve the visitor experience.

Both focus group and on-site research participants were asked if they were interested in playing a game as a feature in the smartphone app. An example of a treasure hunt trail game was provided where users had to answer questions about their surroundings based on clues provided in order to win a prize. There was limited interest in this feature as many of them were unfamiliar with this type of game and those participants interested indicated they would expect a decent reward for the time and effort required to complete the trail.

Although all focus group participants could speak English as a second language, most participants still wanted interpretative information and show narration translated into Chinese. Even university-level participants expressed a preference for Chinese translation, in part because descriptions would often use words that are not commonly part of the everyday vocabulary. One respondent noted: 'If you don't transfer completely from English to Chinese, you may lose some information. I don't want to miss out.' Participants also wanted less text and more imagery – both still images and video content – in the app. For instance, one participant commented, 'I like information with pictures, I don't really like reading.' This sentiment is not surprising given that tourist experiences are visiting to have fun. In terms of content in the app, participants mostly wanted to learn about mothers and their babies, what they eat and where they live. The animal 'cuteness' factor was viewed as important, for example, seeing and touching iconic wildlife, such as the koala and kangaroo, and taking photographs to send home through social media. Thus, the app's ability to facilitate this content sharing was viewed as essential. Given these findings, the potential to take branded photographs (i.e. photos that displayed the CWS logo) and to purchase photography (e.g. the iconic photo of a visitor cuddling a koala) through the app was also considered an important part of the app design.

Key management considerations in designing and implementing a smartphone app

Interviews with the CWS management team highlighted four main issues to consider in the design and implementation of a smartphone app and associated technology. The first consideration was determining the value of investing in designing an app versus designing a mobile-friendly website. Thus, CWS needed to consider a business model to see a return-on-investment (ROI) for creating the app. An important part of the park's business model was 'visitor time on-site' as increased time is related to increased on-site spend per visitor. Thus, the design of the app had as an objective to retain people at CWS. Offering upselling and e-commerce functions through the app and push notifications while on-site were identified as possible ways to create an ROI in the development of an app.

Another consideration of park managers was whether to use iOS or Android as a platform. In making this decision, managers should take into account where their consumers are from, as each country has different penetration rates of mobile phones. As such, an analysis of mobile phone ownership in the target country should be undertaken (Cabral and Vieira 2015). Also, due to the standardized costs of Apple iPhones, consumers tend to be wealthier, whereas, Android is a platform used by many manufacturers of phones at diverse price points (Taylor and Levin 2014), allowing ownership by a more diverse group of consumers and thus giving organizations access to a wider target market. However, determining which platform to use should also take into consideration the analysis of the organization's own data to establish the type of device and/or operating system currently landing on their website.

Although CWS recognized that development of an app would further enhance their digital readiness, they were also conscious that they did not want visitors continuing looking at content on their mobile phones and as a result not engaging in the real-world, hands-on activities that are central to the CWS experience. Research by Tussyadiah (2016) supports this notion, finding that 'participants fear that being too reliant on smartphones to make on-site decisions would deter them from having a meaningful tourism experience' (p. 815). Thus, consideration of the compatibility of technology and nature settings during app design is important (Lu et al. 2016).

Upon commencement of this project, Currumbin Wildlife Sanctuary did not offer Wi-Fi connectivity to visitors. However, since conclusion of the research, CWS have upgraded their website so that it is now mobile-friendly and installed two Wi-Fi hotspots within the attraction to enable visitors to connect to the Internet and download the proposed app on-site at no charge. Complete Wi-Fi coverage across the site would be preferred (particularly to facilitate content sharing); however, the cost of installing and maintaining this infrastructure may be prohibitive.

Conclusion

Smartphones have infiltrated everyday life around the world and this technology has changed the way consumers research, book and experience travel. The emerging body of research on the influence of smartphone technology on travel behaviour (e.g. Lamsfus et al. 2015; Wang et al. 2012) and the development of smartphone apps by tourism operators suggest this is an expanding area of interest for both academics and practitioners. This chapter has discussed some of these advances. Context-based sensors and the adoption of e-commerce functions in smartphone apps have made tourism consumption easier and more convenient, instant, entertaining, personalized and social through sharing of travel stories, images, video and other content through the Internet functionalities of these devices.

The chapter also discusses how tourism businesses are responding to this technology change through the development of mobile-friendly websites and apps. Key design features of apps are explored through a case study involving consumer (demand side) and manager (supply side) interviews to inform the design and development of an app for a tourist attraction. The study confirms consumer demand for an app and using this technology. In fact, the findings suggest that, given the pervasiveness of smartphone technology in everyday life, the absence of an app may detract from the visitor experience. This finding is particularly evident in the navigation realm as study participants were so accustomed to using digital mapping technology that reverting back to reading a physical map was difficult. The case study also highlights visitor expectations relating to guiding, interpretative content and language translation capabilities in the app. Study participants reported that they wanted a self-guiding feature in the app and expected a variety of content in the app that included more images and video content and less text, as well as additional content that acts as a 'backstage pass' to experiences and content that were not available without app access.

Furthermore, interest in gamification of the experience through the app was also examined; however, study participants questioned the value of this experience and, therefore, did not view this feature as overly useful. However, the technology adoption model would suggest that more experience with using a gaming function in a tourism app to augment the experience may alter this perception. Other tourism research on Chinese students found being entertained through mobile games is of interest (Pan et al. 2013), suggesting potential to develop this feature of apps. The emergence of more interactive games through augmented reality could also promote participation in games as part of the tourism app experience. The case study also highlights the tourism manager's perspective when seeking to develop a smartphone app. Developing a business model for the app that delivers an ROI, as well as infrastructure to enable Internet connectivity, notably offering free Wi-Fi access to visitors, were identified as key business considerations.

In summary, this chapter reviewed the state-of-play of smartphone technology in tourism and case study research, in an attempt to advance understanding of smartphone technology in tourism and how it can be applied to attraction app design. Given smartphone proliferation and penetration into everyday life and consumption worldwide, consumers have high expectations of employing this technology when engaging in travel experiences. It is therefore important that the tourism industry continue to consider innovative ways to be at the forefront of embracing smartphone technology in order to meet evolving consumer expectations.

References

Australian Government (2015). 'International students in Australia up to 2014', Available from: https://internationaleducation.gov.au/research/Research-Snapshots/Documents/Total%20student%20counts%20to%202014.pdf [Accessed: 7 October 2015].

Bruck, P. and Rao, M. (eds.) (2013). *Global Mobile: Applications and Innovations for the Worldwide Mobile Ecosystem*, Medford, NJ: Information Today.

Cabral, F. and Vieira, G. (2015). 'Impact of mobile app user acquisition on managerial decisions: Evidence from empirical experiment', Available from: http://hdl.handle.net/10362/15602 [Accessed: 25 October 2015].

Chu, T.-H., Lin, M.-L. and Chang, C.-H. (2012). 'mGuiding (mobile guiding) – Using a mobile GIS app for guiding', *Scandinavian Journal of Hospitality and Tourism*, 12(3): 269–283.

Criteo (2015). 'State of mobile commerce Q1 2015', Available from: http://www.criteo.com/resources/mobile-commerce-q1-2015/ [Accessed: 21 October 2015].

Currumbin Wildlife Sanctuary (2015). 'Alex Griffiths and our history', Available from: http://www.cws.org.au/alex-griffiths-and-our-history/ [Accessed: 7 October 2015].

Dickinson, J., Ghali, K., Cherrett, T., Speed, C., Davies, N. and Norgate, S. (2014). 'Tourism and the smartphone app: Capabilities, emerging practice and scope in the travel domain', *Current Issues in Tourism*, 17(1): 84–101.

Google (2015a). 'Make your site mobile friendly', Available from: https://support.google.com/webmasters/answer/6001177?hl=en [Accessed: 7 October 2015].

Google (2015b) 'Mobilegeddon? We're going for Mobiletopia', http://google-au.blogspot.com.au/2015/04/mobilegeddon-were-going-for-mobiletopia.html [Accessed: 7 October 2015].

King, B. and Gardiner, S. (2015). 'Chinese international students: An avant-garde of independent travellers?', *International Journal of Tourism Research*, 17(2): 130–139.

Lamsfus, C., Wang, D., Alzua-Sorzabal, A. and Xiang, Z. (2015). 'Going mobile: Defining context for on-the-go travelers', *Journal of Travel Research*, 54(6): 691–701.

Lu, J., Mao, Z., Wang, M. and Hu, L. (2016). 'Goodbye maps, hello apps? Exploring the influential determinants of travel app adoption', *Current Issues in Tourism*, 18(11): 1059–1079.

Miller, M. (2012). '72% of consumers want mobile-friendly sites: Google research', Available from: http://searchenginewatch.com/sew/study/2208496/72-of-consumers-want-mobilefriendly-sites-google-research [Accessed: 21 October 2015].

Murphy, C., Chen, M. and Cossutta, M. (2016). 'An investigation of multiple devices and information sources used in the hotel booking process', *Tourism Management*, 52: 44–51.

Pan, D., Chen, N. and Rau, P. (2013). 'The acceptance and adoption of smartphone use among Chinese college students', in P. Rau (ed.), *Cross-Cultural Design, Methods, Practice, and Case Studies* (pp. 450–458), Berlin/Heidelberg: Springer.

Rivera, M. A., Gregory, A. and Cobos, L. (2015). 'Mobile application for the timeshare industry: The influence of technology experience, usefulness, and attitude on behavioural intentions', *Journal of Hospitality and Tourism Technology*, 6(3): 242–257.

Statista. (2015). Available from: http://www.statista.com/ [Accessed: 7 October 2015].

Taylor, D. and Levin, M. (2014). 'Predicting mobile app usage for purchasing and information-sharing', *International Journal of Retail and Distribution Management*, 42(8): 759–774.

TripAdvisor (2015). 'Are you reaching the lucrative connected traveller?', Available from: https://www.tripadvisor.com.au/TripAdvisorInsights/n2642/are-you-reaching-lucrative-connected-traveller [Accessed: 21 October 2015].

Tussyadiah, I. P. (2016). 'The influence of innovativeness on on-site smartphone use among American travelers: Implications for context-based push marketing', *Journal of Travel and Tourism Marketing*, 33(6): 806–823.

Tussyadiah, I. and Wang, D. (2016). 'Tourists' attitudes toward proactive smartphone systems', *Journal of Travel Research*, 55(4): 493–508.

Tuten, T. L. and Solomon, M. R. (2014). *Social Media Marketing*, Upper Saddle River, NJ: Prentice-Hall.

United Nations World Tourism Organization (2015). *UNWTO Tourism Highlights: 2015 Edition*, Available from: http://www.e-unwto.org/doi/pdf/10.18111/9789284416899. [Accessed 25 October 2015].

Wang, D., Park, S. and Fesenmaier, D. R. (2012). 'The role of smartphones in mediating the touristic experience', *Journal of Travel Research*, 51(4): 371–387.

Wang, D., Xiang, Z. and Fesenmaier, D. R. (2016). 'Smartphone use in everyday life and travel', *Journal of Travel Research*, 55(1): 52–63.

Warner, J. (2013). 'Mobile web design strategies', in P. Bruck and M. Rao (eds.), *Global Mobile: Applications and Innovations for the Worldwide Mobile Ecosystem* (pp. 139–158), Medford, NJ: Information Today.

42

USABILITY ANALYSIS OF AUGMENTED REALITY FOR TOURISM DESTINATION IMAGE PROMOTION

Azizul Hassan and Neda Shabani

Introduction

Augmented Reality is very often considered as one of the key innovative technologies of the future. This technology is seen as contributing towards tourist destination image formation. In tourism destination image formation, the entire consumption experience can be encompassed by imagery (MacInnis and Price 1987). Explicit consumption can take place via imagery even before making an actual purchase. Imagery can inject value and increase satisfaction during consumption. After consumption, imagery can play a reconstructive role where an individual revives the experience through vacation souvenirs and memories. Difference persists between non-visitors and visitors about a particular destination that can be invaluable. Such dissimilarities enable prominent attributes of the naive image and re-evaluated image to be integrated into tourism market planning (Selby and Morgan 1996). Still, image assessment by itself cannot guarantee the success of a tourism destination in a new market when other variables such as price, distance or access can become more important in tourists' general decision-making process (Ahmed 1991). A huge amount of literature deals with tourist demand and destination decision-making (Pizam et al. 1978; Van Raaij and Francken 1984; Woodside and Lysonski 1989); however, this conceptual study limits the discussion within technological applications in tourism destination image and discusses from the perspective of theoretical analysis.

Tourist destination image formation

Each individual as a potential tourist has an image about a particular destination that can be unique, attaching to it his or her own memories, alliances and imaginations (Jenkins and McArthur 1996). According to Stabler (1988), a consumer's destination image formulation is divided into two broad factor groups: demand and supply. The demand factors generally match with Gunn's organic image formation where the supply factors tend to correspond to induce image formation. Regarding the definition of tourist destination image, researchers emphasise the necessity of a tourist destination image (Mayo 1973;

Crompton 1979; Chon 1992). These researchers argue that tourist destination image necessarily has to influence decision-making mechanisms of prospective tourists followed by their degree of satisfaction as related to real tourist experience. On the other side, researchers like MacInnis and Price (1987) believe that marketers need to place added attention on destination image for its capacities to the affect purchase decisions of tourism consumers. These two researchers have established three stages of the consumption experience: (i) *prior purchase* – through imagery, substitutive consumption can be experienced; (ii) *during consumption* – such imagery can lead to increased value and enhanced satisfaction; (iii) *after consumption* – imagery plays a crucial role in re-experiencing the destination by recalling memories or remembrances.

For instance, according to Hunt (1975) and Scott et al. (1978), destination image formation is settled partly by the destination's distance. One of the common reasons for this is that people are more willing to visit destinations close to their home when they are exposed to information about those destinations by media or friends and family members. Thus, it was concluded that individuals are likely to get tougher and more pragmatic images of a destination when the location remains near to their home. Gunn (1972), as one of the lead researchers in tourist destinations, differentiates two tourist types. The first type has already visited a tourist destination while the second type has not managed to have experiences related to destination image formation. Thus, in terms of information gathering about a specific destination, the first tourist type recalls their personal experiences while the other type tends to be benefited by external sources such as the Internet, advertisements, media, travel magazines, books, etc.

The seven-stage theory of destination image (Gunn 1972)

The theoretical framework of the tourism destination image formation process still remains unclear even after some notable research (Phelps 1986; Stabler 1988; Chon 1990, 1992; Echtner and Brent Ritchie 1991; Botterill and Crompton 1996; Selby and Morgan 1996). Gunn's (1972) seven-stage theory becomes relevant at this stage. This theory envisages a gradual building and revision of images consisting of naive or organic non-tourist information about a destination (e.g. books, school stories, friends' experience stories and television documentaries), promoted or induced information (e.g. advertisements, publicity and travel brochures) and modified induced images resulting from individual experiences of the destination. The stage theory finds particular relevance in this perspective: that potential visitors, non-visitors, hold images and returned visitors tend to differ (Gunn 1972). Pearce (1982) and Chon (1990, 1992) support this theory in their studies by showing that images held by returned visitors are more likely to be complex, realistic and diverse.

However, as criticism, Phelps (1986) and Narayana (1976) explored that a destination's image reverts or fades over time when dominant visitors visit other similar destinations.

In relation to conventional forms of destination image formation, researchers find that until today the conventional approach has relied more on advertising to develop a destination's pleasant attributes (Matos et al. 2015); however, this trend is gradually changing over the years, meaning that marketers are relying more on introducing new approaches for influencing consumer beliefs and attitudes towards a product or service offer to meet their demands and expectations. Recently, researchers and marketers have been changing this situation with the introduction of new approaches that consider tourists' attitudes and beliefs towards the products destinations offer, as well as their expectations and desires. AR can become a good option in this context.

Organic Image:	1. Accumulation of mental images of a place through life
Induced Image:	2. Modification of images through research before travelling
	3. Decision to travel based on image efficiency but kept within time, money and other constraints
	4. Travel to attraction may condition the image (for example road-signs, landscapes, guides)
Modified-Induced Image:	5. Participation or experience at the destination (activities and services that influence image)
	6. Return travel allows reflection and evaluation
	7. New accumulation occurs after the visit (circular process)

Figure 42.1   The seven-stage theory of destination image

Source: Adapted from Gunn (1972) as cited in Cano (2011).

Augmented Reality (AR) – definitions and features

AR is thought of as the next stage of Virtual Reality (VR). The relevance of AR has expanded across the tourism industry (e.g. museums, heritage, hospitality, shopping, gastronomy, gaming or even entertainment, etc.). AR as an innovative technology is a live vision of a real-world, physical environment when its components are augmented by computer-simulated sensory input in forms of video, graphics, sound and even the Global Positioning System (GPS). It is evident that the use of AR influences tourist destination image formation. The application of a sophisticated technology such as AR can hardly be generalised due to its operational complexities and limited accessibility for tourism destination image formation. Still, as far as perceptions are attached to destination image formation, AR also remains a valid facilitator.

AR is seen as a technological innovation that combines visuals with computer-simulated imageries in a real-life environment (Hassan and Ramkissoon in press). A number of definitions of AR are offered outlining essential features of this technology; however, in its simplest meaning, AR is referred to as the enhancement of the real environment with the support of computer-generated contents (Hassan and Jung 2016). Computer-generated content in this perspective is meant as graphical overlays. By co-existing with the actual world, AR as a visual system expands the surroundings of a user with virtual information as registered in 3D space (Azuma 1997). The recent trend of AR access on wearable computing devices and smartphones has initiated an unprecedented acceleration of AR application; however, the internal development of AR has witnessed not less than a decade's contributions. In the past decade, AR has been incorporated with the GPS navigation technology, offering more provisions for localisation and navigating to specific points of information of interest (Yovcheva et al. 2012). Relevant literature shows that the inclusion of image recognition acted as a triggering feature for AR creating more awareness about the use of QR codes; even though this started out as a gimmick, it very soon proved competent for purposeful use.

AR is seen as a mixed reality combining the real and computer-simulated imageries. This feature has allowed AR to be applied in diverse industries with dissimilar back-grounds including medical, gaming or advertising (Reinhart and Patron 2003). Still, AR is seen as having high application values for the tourism industry mainly for its better abilities to enhance the immediate surroundings (Fritz et al. 2005). This is one of the basic reasons why tourism researchers are exploring the diverse features of AR to be applied for destination image formation in tourism by using the immediate surroundings (Olsson et al. 2012).

AR and some challenges

Respecting users' personal data and information is challenging (Hyman 2013). Technology invasion is becoming common in the present day, while another concern is the uncontrolled amount of virtual spam and advertising (Zacharias 2010). These are unauthorised on open source networks where AR operates. Tour operators are expected to capitalise the full potentials of AR technology application, meaning that the potentials of AR for destination image formation become immense (Hassan 2014a). The application of AR can hardly be limited to tourism only and in particular destination image formation of tourism destinations. One of the key reasons for this trend is the wearable devices or smartphones for both on-trip use and destination marketing (Azim and Hassan 2013). Search engines and Google AdSense can also play pivotal roles in the formation of destination images by AR applications (Hassan and Dadwal 2016; Hassan and Donatella 2016).

Still, it is argued that information layer design is crucial for preventing information overload, because faulty information layering can lead to poor performance and distraction (Wang and Dunston 2004). An innovative technology such as AR can possibly impact everyday life of the user; however, the practical aspects of an innovative technology need to be focused on gradual improvements relating to its initial design and implementation.

AR in tourism – some potentials

According to Business Wire (2013), the revenue generation capacities of AR can possibly reach up to US$ 600 billion by 2016. AR can reinforce a strong shift to replace a valid technology. An example is the wearable devices and smartphones where people interact with updated contents and technologies. Research by Semico (2016) shows that more than 864 million cell phones and 100 million vehicles are going to be AR-enabled in their equipment. Again, it is predicted that the number of AR users as the outcome of increased market penetration by smartphones will exceed 1 billion by 2020. Spreading smartphone and wearable mobile applications mainly increases the penetration of AR among the general public. According to Juniper Research (2016), such a trend is desired to continue, resulting in 2.6 billion AR app downloads by 2017. The trend persists, while developers are investing significantly in AR technology application for serving diverse consumer needs. AR development and research have already witnessed investment of more than US$ 670 million, increasing to US$ 2.5 billion over the next five years (Breeze 2012). The combination with a cloud-based database for granting information access in any part of the world offers increasing potential for investments in AR. AR technology is seemingly applied for destination image formation, branding or increasing social capital. Industry analysis suggests that businesses engaging with AR are expanding their capacities. This happens by repeated investments that enable consumers to undertake AR technology-induced decision making. The development and advancements of both software and hardware supported wearable computing devices are triggering the wider application of AR technology. The Google Glass project, smartphones or smartwatches are examples (Daily Mail 2012).

Factors of AR application for destination image formation

AR tends to play crucial roles in supporting destination image formation. The benefits of AR in this purpose can be widespread, affecting a tourism destination more positively. AR symmetrically helps to support both the end-user and marketer in destination image formation followed by electronic word-of-mouth (Hassan 2015). Increasing use of the Internet helps in AR technology expansion and fruitful tourism business initiatives. Tourism products or services offerings have grown more competitive. Technology has empowered tourists in making contacts with tourist destinations prior to their actual visits. The interaction between tourists and a destination prior to making an actual visit very often is seen as influenced by destination image. In earlier times, tourists enjoyed very limited freedom for destination selection, while innovative technologies such as AR have widely expanded the opportunities for interaction. The appearance and introduction of AR applications in tourism help in creating interactions between the tourists, tourism product or service offers and the destination itself (Lu and Smith 2008).

AR technology is relying more on the Internet. AR application in tourism destinations is linked with tourism product or service offer updates such as the use of the GPS system. This in an actual sense helps in pinpointing an exact tourism destination by providing relevant information about its surroundings (Höllerer and Feiner 2004).

AR is an interactive technology meaning that both prospects and challenges lie ahead to adopt this technology. A meaningful implementation of AR relies on critical information presentation and management for meeting a consumer's need. AR technology provides standard information adjusted to each user's demand (Comerford and Johnson 2007). Research by Grubert et al. (2011) showed that by using AR, male users achieved more productivity compared with female users to complete a work successfully. Thus, it is evidenced that AR application can enhance users' experiences in given environments. Such use also offers a path for directing and interacting for immediate information.

AR and destination image around the world

This is evidenced from mobile applications such as 'Paris, Then and Now', where tourists can go back as far as 100 years ago, experiencing at least 200 different locations in Paris (Hutchings 2013). On the other side, can incorporate entertainment-based tourist destinations, making them widely popular. In many cases, tourist destinations are very often presented in AR technology-led gaming. By using personalised contents, an ordinary place can obviously become popular as a tourist destination in the world. For this purpose, AR is acknowledging interests within end-users and tourism business operators for visitor attractions (Hassan 2014b, in press a, in press b). AR has already managed to affect users' shopping behaviour. This becomes evident from businesses such as TryLive, which allows the users to use virtual glasses. These users can then test the look using a particular website without physically going to a shop (Total Immersion 2016).

The effective role of companies such as Layar and HP's Aurasma has been to remain the pioneers in introducing AR application for interactive overlay (Kan et al. 2009). It has been evident that the limitations and availability of hardware have slowed down AR application for the public; however, developers are consistently working towards improving and developing hardware issues that include battery life expansion or image tracking (Gazzard 2011).

By introducing interactive marketing and AR games such as TryLive, destination marketing companies attempt to implement digital marketing campaigns, but this helps in exploring market segments by allowing closer customer interactions with a particular destination or brand (Total Immersion 2016). AR evidently offers the ability to replace physically demanding activities such as purchasing or fitting. AR tends to offer information to influence consumer purchase decisions. AR supports the revenue generation and sales of tourism destination marketing while exploring more opportunities.

AR application for destination image formation expects to not only attract people's attention in general but also replace the ways a person interacts with contents and technologies. Contribution of this research can expand the knowledge of technology application for destination image formation. The study summarises that destinations are constantly embracing innovative technologies. The study focuses on exploring diverse aspects of AR application in destination image formation relying on consumer experience enhancement and generation. This study identifies AR as an innovative technology gradually contributing to the development of tourism destination image formation. This technology has moved from the gimmick stage into purposeful implementations in diverse industries including tourism. The study explores that even though termed as a relatively new concept, AR begets familiarity within diverse consumer groups, making it rapidly popular. The study establishes that the application of AR for tourist destination image formation is a subject of required facilities.

Tourist destination image formation in the Australian context is relevant to this research. According to Pearce (1988), Ross (1993) and QTTC (1995), tourist destination image has already been given considerable importance. The Australian Tourist Commission (ATC) as the National Tourist Organisation (NTO) of Australia tracks the images held by prospective visitors in a global marketplace. Promotional activity designing then relies on the results of such tracks and market segmentation analysis. This outlines that Australia has a leading and positive position in terms of travel desire compared with other destinations in the world. Based on theoretical underpinning as offered by Gunn (1972) in the seven-stage theory of destination image, AR has certain roles to play to form tourist destination images.

Conclusion

To sum up, people's every impression, belief and idea attached to a destination are also characterised as elements of destination image formation. On the contrary, tourist destination image development is seen as relying on consumers' emotionality and rationality. These establish tourists' prior perceptions as essentially attached to destination image formation. Marketers apply imagery for increasing remembered satisfaction and for encouraging repeated holiday purchases. Tourism marketers are commonly interested in tourist destination image, because it connects tourist products or services sales with decision-making. This study outlines the usability analysis of AR for tourism destination image formation. From the theoretical perspective, the usability of AR is promising as outlined in the seven-stage theory of destination image (Gunn 1972). The usability of AR for tourist destination image formation is evidenced both theoretically and empirically. The adoption of AR is dominant for the second tourist type as outlined by Mayo (1973): those who rely on the Internet. This is evidenced from examples across the world demonstrating that tourist destinations are adopting AR for destination image formation. The cases of Paris or Australia come across as examples that certainly reveal that AR can be applied for tourist destination image formation in meaningful ways. This research thus supports that AR can be applied for tourist destination image formation, because this has capacities to enhance tourist experience. Such experience expansions can lead to a successful purchase decision by tourism consumers, making AR a valid tool for marketing. This conceptual chapter could possibly be buttressed by empirical evidence. Thus, a basic limitation of this research is the lack of adequate empirical evidences. Future research needs to focus on empirical data-led arguments rather than being purely conceptual.

References

Ahmed, Z. (1991). 'The influence of the components of a state's tourist image on product positioning strategy', *Tourism Management*, 12(4): 331–340.

Azim, R. and Hassan, A. (2013). 'Impact analysis of wireless and mobile technology on business management strategies', *Journal of Information and Knowledge Management*, 2(2): 141–150.

Azuma, R. T. (1997). 'A survey of augmented reality', *Presence*, 6(4): 355–385.

Botterill, T. D. and Crompton, J. L. (1996). 'Two case studies exploring the nature of the tourist's experience', *Journal of Leisure Research*, 28(1): 57–82.

Breeze, M. (2012). 'How augmented reality will change the way we live', Available from: http://thenextweb.com/insider/2012/08/25/how-augmented-reality-will-change-way-live/ [Accessed: 6 March 2016].

Business Wire (2013). 'Revenues for augmented reality in consumer electronics industry to approach $600 billion by 2016, says Semico research', Available from: http://bit.ly/1LGVWcE [Accessed: 6 March 2016].

Cano, R. H. (2011). 'Investigating Cuba destination image using P.E.I.', Available from: http://bit.ly/1Ts6xQ4 [Accessed: 6 March 2016].

Chon, K. S. (1990). 'The role of destination image in tourism: A review and discussion', *Tourist Review*, 45(2): 2–9.

Chon, K. S. (1992). 'The role of destination image in tourism: An extension', *The Tourist Review*, 2(2): 2–7.

Comerford, D. and Johnson, W. W. (2007). 'Potential capabilities in a future, augmented cockpit', *Ergonomics in Design: The Quarterly of Human Factors Applications*, 15(1): 8–13.

Crompton, J. L. (1979). 'An assessment of the image of Mexico as a vacation destination and the influence of geographical location upon that image', *Journal of Travel Research*, 17(4): 18–23.

Daily Mail (2012). 'Google Glasses on sale for $1,500: Firm launches prototype augmented reality eyewear with spectacular skydiving demo', Available from: http://dailym.ai/1KvjaBC [Accessed: 6 March 2016].

Echtner, C. M. and Brent Ritchie, J. R. (1991). *The Measurement of Tourism Destination Image*, Calgary: University of Calgary.

Fritz, F., Susperregui, A. and Linaza, M. T. (2005). 'Enhancing cultural tourism experiences with augmented reality technologies', Available from: http://bit.ly/1OJe1Mo. [Accessed: 19 March 2016].

Gazzard, A. (2011). 'Location, location, location: Collecting space and place in mobile media', *Convergence: The International Journal of Research into New Media Technologies*, 17(4): 405–417.

Grubert, J., Langlotz, T. and Grasset, R. (2011). *Augmented Reality Browser Survey*, Graz: Graz University of Technology.

Gunn, C. A. (1972). *Vacationscape: Designing Tourist Regions*, Austin, TX: University of Texas.

Hassan, A. (2014a). 'Tour on an imagined heritage trail set in the Mosque City of Bagerhat, Bangladesh: Cogitation for market potentials', in S. P. Bansal, S. Walia and S. A. Rizwan (eds.), *Tourism: Present and Future Perspective* (pp. 30–44), New Delhi: Kanishka Publishers.

Hassan, A. (2014b). 'Revising the "five-fold framework" in human resource management practices – Insights from a small scale travel agent', *Tourism Analysis*, 19(6): 799–805.

Hassan, A. (2015). 'The customization of electronic word of mouth: An industry tailored application for tourism promotion', in S. Rathore and A. Panwar (eds.), *Capturing, Analyzing and Managing Word-of-Mouth in the Digital Marketplace* (pp. 61–75), Hershey, PA: IGI Global.

Hassan, A. (in press a). 'Destination image formation: The function analysis of augmented reality application', in Khosrow-Pour, M. (ed.), *The Encyclopaedia of Information Science and Technology*, Hershey, PA: IGI Global.

Hassan, A. (in press b). 'Visitor accounts of the Museum of London Docklands', *e-Review of Tourism Research (eRTR)*.

Hassan, A. and Dadwal, S. (2016). 'Search engine marketing – An outlining of conceptualization and strategic application', in W. Ozuem and G. Bowen (eds.), *Competitive Social Media Marketing Strategies* (pp. 219–234), Hershey, PA: IGI Global.

Hassan, A. and Donatella, P. S. (2016). 'Google AdSense as a mobile technology in education', in J. L. Holland (ed.), *Handbook of Research on Wearable and Mobile Technologies in Education* (pp. 200–223), Hershey, PA: IGI Global.

Hassan, A. and Jung, T. (2016). 'Augmented reality as an emerging application in tourism education', in D. H. Choi, A. Dailey-Hebert and J. S. Estes (eds.), *Emerging Tools and Applications of Virtual Reality in Education* (pp. 168–185), Hershey, PA: IGI Global.

Hassan, A. and Ramkissoon, H. (in press). 'Augmented reality for visitor experiences', in J. N. Albrecht (ed.), *Visitor Management*, Wallingford: CABI.

Höllerer, T. H. and Feiner, S. K. (2004). 'Mobile augmented reality', in H. Karimi and A. Hammad (eds.), *Telegeoinformatics: Location-based Computing and Services* (pp. 221–260), New York: CRC Press.

Hunt, J. D. (1975). 'Image as a factor in tourism development', *Journal of Travel Research*, 13(3): 1–7.

Hutchings, E. (2013). 'Time travel through Paris with augmented reality app', Available from: http://bit.ly/1PhcgnV [Accessed: 6 March 2016].

Hyman, P. (2013). 'Augmented-reality glasses bring cloud security into sharp focus', *Communications of the ACM*, 56(6): 18–20.

Jenkins, O. H. and McArthur, S. (1996). 'Marketing protected areas', *Australian Parks and Recreation*, 32(4): 10–15.

Juniper Research (2016). 'Mobile augmented reality IFx1 2013-2018', Available from: http://bit.ly/1kIublK [Accessed: 6 March 2016].

Kan, T. W., Teng, C. H. and Chou, W. S. (2009). 'Applying QR code in augmented reality applications', in S. N. Spencer (ed.), *Proceedings of the 8th International Conference on Virtual Reality Continuum and its Applications in Industry* (pp. 253–257), New York: ACM.

Lu, Y. and Smith, S. (2008). 'Augmented reality e-commerce: How the technology benefits people's lives', Available from: http://bit.ly/1Wca8C1 [Accessed: 6 March 2016].

MacInnis, D. J. and Price, L. L. (1987). 'The role of imagery in information processing: Review and extension', *Journal of Consumer Research*, 13(4): 473–491.

Matos, N., Mendes, J. and Pinto, P. (2015). 'The role of imagery and experiences in the construction of a tourism destination image', *Journal of Spatial and Organizational Dynamics*, 3(2): 65–84.

Mayo, E. J. (1973). 'Regional images and regional travel behavior', in *The Fourth Annual Conference Proceedings of the Travel Research Association, Research for Changing Travel Patterns: Interpretation and Utilization* (pp. 211–217), Saltlake: Travel Research Association.

Narayana, C. L. (1976). 'The stability of perceptions', *Journal of Advertising Research*, 16(2): 45–49.

Olsson, T., Kärkkäinen, T., Lagerstam, E. and Ventä-Olkkonen, L. (2012). 'User evaluation of mobile augmented reality scenarios', *Journal of Ambient Intelligence and Smart Environments*, 4(1): 29–47.

Pearce, P. L. (1982). 'Perceived changes in holiday destinations', *Annals of Tourism Research*, 9(2): 145–164.

Pearce, P. L. (1988). *The Ulysses Factor: Evaluating Visitors in Tourist Settings*, New York: Springer Verlag.

Phelps, A. (1986). 'Holiday destination image: The problem of assessment', *Tourism Management*, 7(3): 168–180.

Pizam, A., Neumann, Y. and Reichel, A. (1978). 'Dimensions of tourist satisfaction with a destination area', *Annals of Tourism Research*, 5(3): 314–322.

Queensland Tourist and Travel Corporation (QTTC) (1995). *Sunshine Coast Holiday Destination Survey*, Brisbane: QTTC.

Reinhart, G. and Patron, C. (2003). 'Integrating augmented reality in the assembly domain: Fundamentals, benefits and applications', *CIRP Annals-Manufacturing Technology*, 52(1): 5–8.

Ross, G. F. (1993). 'Ideal and actual images of backpacker visitors to northern Australia', *Journal of Travel Research*, 21(3): 54–57.

Scott, D. R., Schewe, C. and Frederick, D. (1978). 'A multi-brand/multi-attribute model of tourist state choice', *Journal of Travel Research*, 17(3): 23–29.

Selby, M. and Morgan, N. J. (1996). 'Reconstruing place image: A case-study of its role on destination market research', *Tourism Management*, 17(4): 287–294.

Semico (2016). 'Augmented reality: Envision a more intelligent world', Available from: http://www.semico.com/content/augmented-reality-envision-more-intelligent-world [Accessed: 6 March 2016].

Stabler, M. J. (1988). 'The image of destination regions: Theoretical and empirical aspects', in B. Goodall and G. Ashworth (eds.), *Marketing in the Tourism Industry: The Promotion of Destination*

Total Immersion (2016). 'The future of augmented reality', Available from: http://www.t-immersion.com/augmented-reality/future-vision [Accessed: 6 March 2016].

Van Raaij, W. F. and Francken, D. A. (1984). 'Vacation decisions, activities and satisfaction', *Annals of Tourism Research*, 11(1): 101–112.

Wang, X. and Dunston, P. S. (2004). 'Compatibility in augmented reality prototypes for assembly', *Proceedings of the Human Factors and Ergonomics Society Annual Meeting*, 48(23): 2637–2641.

Woodside, A. G. and Lysonski, S. (1989). 'A general model of traveler destination choice', *Journal of Travel Research*, 27(4): 8–14.

Yovcheva, Z., Buhalis, D. and Gatzidis, C. (2012). 'Overview of smartphone augmented reality applications for tourism', *e-Review of Tourism Research (eRTR)*, 10(2): 63–66.

Zacharias, N. (2010). '5 real problems in an augmented world', Available from: http://digitallynumb.com/post/399172973/augmented-reality/ [Accessed: 6 March 2016].

43

SERVICESCAPES FOR HOSPITALITY AND TOURISM CONSUMERS

Richard Tresidder

Introduction

This chapter explores the role of tourism and hospitality servicescapes in shaping and directing the experiences and subsequent behaviour of consumers. In simplistic terms, servicescapes are the material representations of the tourism or hospitality product; this includes: the design of the hotel, restaurant or tourist attraction, its décor, music, art; the clothing of staff and their behaviour; the level of formality of service; and the link to particular cultures, times or societies. What is also important to recognize is that servicescapes are also the material representations of a company's or destination's brand image and their values, etc. As such there is a direct link between product, consumer behaviour and brand; consequently, if the servicescape does not match these, then it may have a direct impact upon the brand equity of organizations, levels of customer satisfaction and loyalty. This chapter now explores the various aspects that contribute to the construction of servicescapes utilizing Heston Blumenthal's Fat Duck in Melbourne, Australia as a case study.

It is clear that there exists a direct correlation between the design of retail spaces such as restaurants and the impact of the design upon consumers' behaviour (Bitner 1992). As far back as 1973, Kotler defined this phenomenon, the intentional control and structuring of environmental cues, as atmospherics, and even small changes in the environment can impact upon customers' perception of the space and their behaviour (Turley and Milliman 2000; Turley and Chebat 2002). Kotler explored these atmospheric cues in terms of the senses (i.e. visuals, smells, sight and touch); however, Bitner (1992) in her seminal work on the environmental dimensions of retail atmospherics suggested that this consists of three elements, namely ambient conditions (lighting, temperature, etc.), space (its layout, design, flow, etc.) and function (what is its use or, it can be argued also, what was the building use prior to being adopted by the tourism or hospitality industries?). However, much of the foundational work undertaken in the area of understanding the relationship between buildings, décor and design has been undertaken in areas other than tourism and hospitality. It may be argued that the nature of the central concept of service and the creation of experiences in the hospitality and tourism industries means that, rather than thinking of them in terms of retail atmospherics, it may be better to think about these in terms of the idea of servicescapes.

Servicescapes

In attempting to understand the concept of servicescapes, it is possible to think of a servicescape as a commercially staged experience (Chronis et al. 2012) that adds to or supplements the experience or consumption of the tourism or hospitality product, often elevating it to the level of the extraordinary. Servicescapes are important as consumers find meaning 'in the world' (McCracken 1989) through their relationship to certain places, times, practices, colours, music, people, etc. In some cases the servicescape actually is the product; a good example of this is the concept of the Irish Bar. No matter where you go in the world there is always an Irish Bar. At the basic level, like any bar, it will provide food and drink. However, the consumption experience is mediated by the servicescape, which generally consists of Irish music being played, the themed interior dominated by the colour green, the use of symbols such as shamrocks, harps and leprechauns, staff with Irish accents (often learnt for the role), the provision of beverages that are often dominated by the global Irish brands of Guinness, Bushmills, Jameson, etc. and food that is broadly associated with the country such as soda bread and salmon. In this context, the servicescape elevates the experience of eating and drinking to the level of the extraordinary; it allows consumers to immerse themselves in a reconstructed and hyper-real ideal of Ireland, to consume a piece of it without leaving the country. Additionally, for expats and those with Irish ancestry it provides them with the ability to evoke past traditions and cultural memories (Chronis et al. 2012). Consequently, servicescapes create a space in which experience is generated by owners or managers and then negotiated or mediated (Aurier et al. 2005) and influenced by the customers themselves in the form of joint cultural production (see Peñaloza 2000; Kozinets et al. 2004). However, as highlighted by authors such as Thompson and Haytko (1997) or Arnould and Thompson (2005), like other aspects of marketing, servicescapes have marketplace meanings that are negotiated by consumers and will be understood according to the consumer resources each of them possesses. Thus servicescapes will not have the same meaning for every consumer as they may be seen as 'polysemic symbolic resources that allow for significant variation in consumer interpretation and use' (Holt 1997: p. 334).

Servicescapes in tourism and hospitality are formed through the adoption of a set of images (primary element), sounds (secondary element) and sometimes even smells (see the foregoing example of the Irish Bar) that consumers recognize; these elements or senses form a servicescape language that is used to define a country or culture. This language can be seen to consist of:

Geographical signposts: This is where servicescapes are attempting to utilize or reinforce the experience of a place or destination, for example pictures of Rome, murals of the Grand Canal in Venice, or the Italian Opera all reinforce the idea of Italian culture, food, etc. The result of this is that the servicescape creates notions of 'Frenchness', 'Indianness', 'Americanness', etc.

Variations in time and space: Servicescapes also often adopt and explore the differentiation of time and space as a convention, for example the 'Ye Olde' café or bar offers a servicescape that is embedded in a traditional non-specific time. This manipulation of time and space can be seen to operate at a number of levels, whether that be in terms of offering empty spaces in which consumers can find joy or pleasure, or offering a refuge of authenticity from an inauthentic world. However, what links all of these conventions together is that the representations and messages contained within servicescapes provide a representation of the bar, restaurant, attraction, etc. as not being ordinary, as not being part of everyday life.

Design and product conventions: This is where the design of the product and service encounter identifies the various rules and conventions that define experiences. For example, the décor, dress rules, design of the service encounter (this covers areas such as the formal setting of a table, etc.) all intimate to the consumer the way they should behave and what type of experience they are to expect. Often we will see phrases like 'a relaxing informal environment' or 'splendid grandeur of the setting'; all of these inform the way that, as consumers, we behave.

Forms of service encounter: This is the way the servicescape is presented to us by staff. Often, staff members take on an important role as a geographical signpost (staff sourced from the actual country of experience or through adoption of a geographical accent), guide or mediator to forms of service (often they will guide consumers into ways of behaviour that are appropriate for that servicescape). Thus the formality of the relationship between service staff and customer, the language used, the style of dress worn, etc. all become an integral part of the experience.

The consumers' understanding of these four aspects has been informed by their own social and cultural understandings that have been fashioned historically, through representations of place, people, food, wine or attractions within the media and from the consumer's own past experiences and their social cultural backgrounds.

It is possible to think of the design of servicescapes as a form of communicative staging (see Arnould et al. 1998 for discussion), that is, the servicescape directly informs and directs how the consumer should behave in and interact with the space. Communicative staging includes all communicative items that help constitute a servicescape and includes items such as menu boards, interpretation boards, images and signs and significantly includes the staff or host as well. In terms of personal interactions between the host and the guest, communicative staging can range from a highly scripted and commercial performance to a more flexible and authentic dialogue. In their study of wilderness servicescapes such as white water rafting, Arnould et al. (1998) demonstrate how the natural environment is commercially adopted for the enjoyment and consumption of adventure tourists, and that the experience was elevated through the scripts and role performances of the raft guides. Not only do service delivery personnel bring the experience and the environment to life for participants through narrative framing and storytelling, they also act to make it safe and magical (Arnould and Price 1993). In a similar manner, tourism reps from companies such as Club Med and Club 18–30 holidays are central to the communicative staging of hedonistic experiences and extreme play in holiday resorts and destinations across Europe. As such, it is possible to explore how the promise of experiences is offered in hospitality and tourism marketing and is ultimately communicated and presented to consumers within the servicescape. Building on the work of Kotler (1973) and Kim et al. (2009) in identifying the significance of the senses in the retail environment, it is possible to argue that the tourism and hospitality industry has created a multi-sensual language that is used in the marketing and development of hospitality and tourism experiences, that is understood by consumers (Tresidder 2011, 2015), and that this language directly underpins the construction of servicescapes. As such, it is conceivable to think about not just how servicescapes are defined by their décor, design or theme, but also how they impact upon the consumer's senses and how meaning is constructed for them and communicated to them.

Servicescapes as sensescapes

As stated in the previous section, servicescapes often provide a multi-sensual experience. As such, when the consumer is immersed within a servicescape, whether that be a historical tourist attraction such as the Jorvik Viking Centre in the UK (http://jorvik-viking-centre.co.uk) or the world-famous Noma Restaurant in Denmark (http://noma.dk), their multi-sensual 'sensescapes' contribute significantly to the success of servicescapes, and as such play a significant role in the consumption process as it reflects embodied and imaginary experiences of the consumer (Trauer and Ryan 2005). For example, many stores and restaurants will pump the smell of fresh coffee or newly baked bread into the commercial area, thus stimulating taste buds and bringing about memories of home comforts and cooking. As Chronis et al. (2012: p. 263) comment:

> human perception privileges sensations felt through the body, they conceive imagination too as steeped in embodied perception. For them, perception is a synthetic experience. Consumers grasp the world directly through their multiple senses and by imaginary modes of embodiment.

The significance of senses in contributing to the tourism experience is well charted (Pan and Ryan 2009; Low 2005; Law 2001). As Dann and Jacobsen (2003: p. 19), recognizing the significance of recognizing other senses apart from the gaze within the tourism experience, state:

> the successful tourist destination, which otherwise could be regarded as something of a hybrid and living anachronism, blending ancient with post-modern, now can be the winning formula, precisely because it does not rely on sight alone.

The servicescapes of tourism and hospitality often offer unique sensual experiences in which all of the senses are engaged during the experience. In exploring the complexity of the relationship between senses and servicescapes and linking the consumer's experiences to touch, smell, feel, etc., it is clear that servicescapes are largely multi-sensual. In trying to understand the significance of this it is worth considering Sutton's (2010: p. 217) concept of 'synaesthesia'. Synaesthesia encompasses the idea that senses do not operate in isolation, but rather that they operate in relation with all of the other senses. This is important when attempting to define and comprehend the multi-sensual experience offered in the servicescapes of tourism and hospitality. For instance, Pan and Ryan (2009) identify the multi-sensory nature of tourism and its significance to the contemporary tourist. Senses have always been an important part of tourism; we can chart this beginning with Baudelaire's (1863) notion of the 'flâneur' and the idea of exploring the city through a heightened sensual awareness of the environment. According to Biehl-Missal (2012), we need to consider the impact senses have on our understanding of the world and how they influence our behaviour. She states that we gather 'aesthetic experiences through our five senses[. These] create an embodied, tacit knowing that . . . can influence behaviour' (2012: p. 5). However, as a result of their New Zealand research, Pan and Ryan (2009) have found that although tourists utilized all of their senses, taste was privileged as the most significant sense experience within all of the sites investigated in New Zealand. As we have seen, the role and construction of servicescapes and the accompanying sensescapes are key to engaging guests, influencing their behaviour and providing extraordinary experiences. One of the most successful exponents of this has been the award-winning chef Heston Blumenthal; the Fat Duck in Bray, UK has been voted the best restaurant in the world on a number of occasions and is renowned for its multi-sensual dining experience. The following case study explores how this experience has been temporarily transplanted to Melbourne, Australia.

The Fat Duck

In February 2015 Heston Blumenthal moved the Fat Duck restaurant halfway around the world for a six-month residency at the Crown Towers in Melbourne, Australia. 250,000 people applied for only 15,500 seats and the Fat Duck was fully sold out for the entire six months (Thomsen 2014). The menu consisted of many of Heston Blumenthal's signature dishes such as 'Snail Porridge' and 'Sound of Sea', which requires diners to put on a pair of headphones that plays a soundtrack of the sea while eating the complicated oyster, clam, urchin and seaweed dish. This approach in linking both atmospherics and servicescapes is an example of Sutton's (2010) concept of synaesthesia. Although it was billed as a 'pop up' restaurant, no expense or thought was spared in creating a servicescape that was designed to complement the famous multi-sensual dining experience. The challenge was to create the Fat Duck experience in Melbourne in a modern hotel without duplicating the servicescape of the Fat Duck in Bray.

In order to achieve this, the design company, Seymour Powell, were employed not only to design the space in terms of its flow and logic, but more importantly to create the experience that defines the dining experience. They took a cue from Heston Blumenthal's food, where not everything is as it seems; often there is an incongruity to his food, for example the ideas of 'savoury lollies' or 'hot and iced tea', breakfast for dessert, etc. offer an alternative view of how food should be presented or constructed. For the designers, the experience begins even before entering the restaurant. To enter the restaurant guests are required to walk down a long corridor; however, using the trick of 'forced perspective' whereby the corridor tapers as you move down it, the perceptions of the guest are challenged as the corridor is only 20 yards long, but it appears to be 100 yards. The designers feel that it creates an 'other worldly' feel, that challenges time and space and prepares the guest for the dining experience they are about to engage in. On reaching at the end of the corridor you arrive at a little door which slams, leaving a large one which automatically opens, inviting you into the restaurant.

The design of the restaurant is largely formulated according to the established design conventions ascribed to a contemporary fine dining restaurant: white tablecloths and napkins, white leather seats and black paintwork. Yet throughout the restaurant there are cues to the Fat Duck at Bray that include glass display cloches with artefacts within them. However, the two major elements are 'The Melbourne Clock' which was especially built for the restaurant in the form of a giant fob watch reminiscent of the one worn by Lewis Carroll's Mad Hatter character in Alice in Wonderland; and the famous 'Mad Hatter's Tea Party: Mock turtle soup, pocket watch and toast sandwich' course. The clock shows both the time in Bray and Melbourne and counts down the six months until the restaurant closes and returns to Bray. The longest uninterrupted wall at the Fat Duck is adorned with a massive 19,000-piece jigsaw puzzle with an image of Heston Blumenthal at its centre; each of the 15,500 guests will add a jigsaw piece until the last diner completes it. The jigsaw piece forms part of 'The not-so-full English breakfast' course and is hidden within the cereal box element of the dish.

Conclusion

The relationship between the servicescapes of tourism and hospitality and the behaviour and perception of the experience by guests cannot be underestimated. It is possible to think of servicescapes not only as a design exercise but also a psychological one that stimulates all of the senses and perceptions of the place of space. Servicescapes are constructed through a mixture of employees playing a particular role in the communicative staging of experience by mediating and guiding guests in their consumption of a meal or attraction, and the 'atmospherics' of the place in which this occurs. Atmospherics are also key to creating mood and supporting the multi-sensual sensescapes of the tourism and hospitality industry. The Fat Duck in Melbourne is an exemplar of how all of these elements come together to create an innovative and stimulating servicescape that not only engages and enhances the dining experience, but also challenges perceptions and creates extraordinary experiences and memories.

References

Arnould, E. J. and Price, L. L. (1993). 'River magic: Extraordinary experience and the extended service encounter', *Journal of Consumer Research*, 20(1): 24–45.

Arnould, E. J., Price, L. L. and Tierney, P. (1998). 'Communicative staging of the wilderness service-scape', *The Service Industries Journal*, 18(3): 90–115.

Arnould, E. J. and Thompson, C. J. (2005). 'Consumer culture theory (CCT): Twenty years of research', *Journal of Consumer Research*, 31(4): 868–882.

Aurier, P., Fort, F. and Sirieix, L. (2005). 'Exploring terroir product meanings for the consumer', *Anthropology of Food*, 4 May.

Baudelaire, C. (1863). *The Painter of Modern Life*, New York: Da Capo Press (1964), Orig. published in *Le Figaro*.

Biehl-Missal, B. (2012). 'The atmosphere of the image: An aesthetic concept for visual analysis', *Consumption Markets and Culture*, 16(4): 1–12.

Bitner, M. (1992). 'Servicescapes: The impact of physical surroundings on customers and employees', *Journal of Marketing*, 56(2): 57–71.

Chronis, A., Arnould, E. J. and Hampton, R. D. (2012). 'Gettysburg re-imagined: The role of narrative imagination in consumption experience', *Consumption Markets and Culture*, 15(3): 261–286.

Dann, G. and Jacobsen, J. K. S. (2003). 'Tourism smellscapes', *Tourism Geographies*, 5(1): 3–25.

Holt, D. (1997). 'Poststructuralist lifestyle analysis: Conceptualizing the social patterning of consumption in postmodernity', *Journal of Consumer Research*, 23(4): 326–350.

Kim, H., Knight, D. K. and Crutsinger, C. (2009). 'Generation Y employees' retail work experience: The mediating effect of job characteristics', *Journal of Business Research*, 62(5): 548–556.

Kotler, P. (1973). 'Atmospherics as a marketing tool', *Journal of Retailing*, 49(4): 48–64.

Kozinets, R., Sherry, J., Storm, D., Duhachek, A., Nuttavuthisit, K. and Benet, D. (2004). 'Ludic agency and retail space', *Journal of Consumer Research*, 31(3): 658–672.

Law, L. (2001). 'Home cooking: Filipino women and geographies of the senses in Hong Kong', *Ecumene*, 8(3): 264–283.

Low, K. (2005). 'Ruminations on smell as a sociocultural phenomenon', *Current Sociology*, 53(4): 397–417.

McCracken, G. (1989). 'Who is the celebrity endorser? Cultural foundations of the endorsement process', *Journal of Consumer Research*, 16(3): 310–321.

Pan, S. and Ryan, C. (2009). 'Tourism sense-making: The role of the senses and travel journalism', *Journal of Travel and Tourism Marketing*, 26(7): 625–639.

Peñaloza, L. (2000). 'The commodification of the American West: Marketers' production of cultural meanings at the trade show', *Journal of Marketing*, 64(4): 82–109.

Sutton, D. (2010). 'Food and the senses', *Annual Review of Anthropology*, 39: 209–223.

Thompson, C. and Haytko, D. (1997). 'Speaking of fashion: Consumers' uses of fashion discourses and the appropriation of countervailing cultural meanings', *Journal of Consumer Research*, 24(1): 15–42.

Thomsen. S. (2014). 'Heston Blumenthal's world famous restaurant, the Fat Duck, is coming to Melbourne next year', *Business Insider Australia*, 31 March, Available from: http://www.businessinsider.com.au/heston-blumenthals-world-famous-restaurant-the-fat-duck-is-coming-to-melbourne-next-year-2014-3 [Accessed 15 November 2016].

Trauer, B. and Ryan, C. (2005). 'Destination image, romance and place experience – An application of intimacy theory in tourism', *Tourism Management*, 26(4): 481–491.

Tresidder, R. (2011). 'Reading hospitality: The semiotics of Le Manoir aux Quat' Saison', *Hospitality and Society*, 1(1): 28, 67–84.

Tresidder, R. (2015). 'Eating ants: Understanding the terroir restaurant as a form of destination tourism', *Journal of Tourism and Cultural Change*, 13(4): 344–360.

Turley, L. and Chebat, J. C. (2002). 'Atmospheric design and shopping behaviour', *Journal of Marketing Management*, 18(1–2): 125–144.

Turley, L. and Milliman, R. (2000). 'Atmospheric effects on shopping behaviour: A review of the experimental evidence', *Journal of Business Research*, 49(2): 193–211.

44

SOCIALLY RESPONSIBLE AND SUSTAINABLE PRACTICES

How to involve tourists and guests

Frans Melissen

Introduction

Global climate change and its consequences, such as rising sea levels and extreme weather conditions, in turn resulting in flooding and droughts, pose a serious and ever-increasing threat to our health and economies, and water and food supplies for billions of people (IPCC 2014). Global climate change is caused by greenhouse gas (GHG) emissions – CO_2 being the best-known GHG. However, these emissions also cause other problems, such as acidification of our soil and oceans, which in turn further damage the functioning of ecosystems. Together with, for instance, other types of emissions (of hazardous substances) and deforestation this can lead to habitat loss and thus biodiversity loss, but also to erosion and, ultimately, further increases in GHG emissions. If you combine these and many more environmental problems facing us now and in the (near) future with the unequal division of wealth across our globe and our apparent limited ability, and oftentimes even inability, as a society to tackle these problems, it is not difficult to see how all this could result not only in the collapse of specific ecosystems, but also in the disruption and even collapse of our social systems. It is now also widely acknowledged that 'it is not human technology so much as patterns of human activity that are challenging the sustainability of human development' (Parrish 2007: p. 846). Consequently, we, as humanity, are faced with the urgent challenge of moving beyond discussions on the concept of sustainability and focusing our attention on development and implementation of actual socially responsible and sustainable practices – practices that consider social values and notions such as equity and fairness, while accounting for the systemic dimensions of sustainable development, including the limitations of our environment to (continue to) support our development (see e.g. Destatte 2010; Solecki et al. 2015; UNWCED 1987). Given that many of the patterns of human behaviour mentioned earlier relate to the behaviour of (people working in and consuming products and services from) businesses, it goes without saying that striving for sustainable development not only requires effective (governmental and intergovernmental) policies but also a significant contribution from the corporate sector (Moon 2007). Tourism and hospitality are no exception to that rule.

Sustainable development of tourism and hospitality

As indicated by Solecki et al. (2015), socially responsible and sustainable practices are part of a process towards a specific goal – this goal is called sustainable development. The most widely accepted and influential definition of sustainable development is: development that meets the needs of current generations without harming the possibilities of future generations to meet their needs (UNWCED 1987). It is important to note that the term 'generations' refers to all people and not just those fortunate enough to live in Western countries or those from wealthy families and privileged to have an education or job. What is more, the relation between current and future generations relates to the fact that overexploiting resources or damaging current and future socio-environmental systems would make it impossible to meet the needs of our children and our grandchildren. Consequently, sustainable development encompasses a lot more than developing and implementing practices based on simply balancing People, Planet and Profit – the well-known three pillars of sustainability. It also encompasses a systemic – related to both space and time – and ethical dimension. Given the complexities involved with accounting for all relevant social-environmental-economic interactions in deciding on appropriate courses of action, striving for sustainable development cannot but be based on an adaptive approach that involves all relevant stakeholders in decision-making – an approach that could best be described as a collaborative learning process.

Tourism and hospitality represent sectors that have a crucial role to play in adjusting the course of our society to a more sustainable one. The reason for this is twofold. Tourism and hospitality are currently responsible for a significant portion of global resource use – including substantial fossil fuel consumption linked to (air) travel and accommodation, global GHG emissions and pollution, but also (fresh) water, land and food use – and this (negative) impact is predicted to increase quite ominously over the next few decades (De Grosbois and Fennell 2011; Gössling and Peeters 2015). Simultaneously, it is important to note that tourism and hospitality businesses range from globally operating powerful multinationals to locally operating (often independent) businesses that are intertwined with local communities (Melissen 2013). Consequently, these sectors not only impact a lot of people and ecosystems as a result of their absolute size, spread and environmental and economic impact. A lot of people in local communities are also dependent on these companies – as inhabitant, neighbour, supplier and employee – for both their livelihood and the livability of the local socio-environmental system. In turn, tourism and hospitality businesses are heavily reliant upon local labour markets and the attractiveness of local socio-environmental systems for tourists and guests for their (long-term) success and survival. Based on these characteristics, tourism and hospitality are not just important sectors to address from a 'mitigation of negative impacts' perspective; through their people-oriented nature and their interrelationships with all levels of our global socio-environmental system these sectors could also play the crucial role of catalysts for the kind of collaborative learning processes needed for sustainable development of our society.

Unfortunately, progress towards sustainable tourism and hospitality, so far, is limited at best (Bramwell and Lane 2013; Gössling and Peeters 2015) and policymakers, practitioners and researchers still seem preoccupied with discussing concepts, constraints and scenarios rather than developing and implementing actual socially responsible and sustainable practices as part of, and the result of, a collaborative learning process. The immense scale of the problem and a lack of knowledge combined with vested interests of parties involved – tourism and hospitality businesses and their shareholders, policymakers and researchers alike – most certainly explain a portion of this lack of progress (Melissen and Koens 2016).

However, another portion is explained, as indicated by Bramwell and Lane (2013), by the way these practices are (not) appreciated and favoured by one of the key stakeholders: consumers. Tourism and hospitality, like any other sector, will only be successful in providing sustainable products and services if consumers are willing to buy them and even prefer those products and services to unsustainable ones. Simultaneously, the actual consumption process within tourism and hospitality is oftentimes based on direct interaction between the provider and consumer. This characteristic implies that socially responsible and sustainable practices will have to be shaped and executed as part of a co-creation process that involves – and thus is also dependent on – both provider *and* consumer. Ultimately, any significant reduction in the negative impact of these sectors would for instance require tourists to choose alternative ways of travelling, such as train instead of air travel, or alternative destinations, such as those not requiring (long-haul) air travel and not located in vulnerable ecosystems. Simultaneously, it would require guests to accept a hospitality concept that for instance incorporates water-efficient showerheads; reuse of towels and linen; no air-conditioning; vegetarian and seasonal food and drink; and a different type of staff working in the hotel as a result of the hotel participating in a municipal programme aimed at reducing long-term and youth unemployment. Obviously, these are just a few examples of the types of practices that tourists and guests would have to be willing to accept and co-create. Regardless of the specific practices that are developed and implemented, however, it is evident that sustainable development of tourism and hospitality requires an in-depth understanding of the behavioural responses of tourists and guests – an in-depth understanding of consumer behaviour in relation to sustainable development.

Sustainable development and consumer behaviour

As indicated by Stern (2000: p. 525), 'some believe that to preserve the environment, people's values and attitudes need to change'. As Higham et al. (2013) explain, this belief is very much linked to the dominant role of Ajzen's (1991) theory of planned behaviour, and subsequent modifications and complementing theories focusing on the role of values, in research dedicated to (predicting and influencing) pro-environmental and sustainable (consumer) behaviour. The basic premise of these theories is that displayed behaviour of individuals is the combined outcome of one's attitudes (and/or values and/or beliefs), social norms and perceived behavioural control. In other words, behaviours that harm sustainable development are the result of anti-sustainable values and attitudes. However, real-life (consumer) behaviour seems to be much more complex. Actual behaviour appears to be much more situationally determined (Stern 2000). Over the years, many surveys have indicated that while consumers are often reluctant to buy or favour sustainable products and services, these same consumers do actually value the environment and support the idea of sustainable development (see e.g. Vringer et al. 2015). This contrast between values and attitudes on the one hand and actual behaviour on the other is usually referred to as the attitude–behaviour or intention–behaviour gap (see e.g. Carrington et al. 2014). Habits and various so-called lock-in effects of (current and dominant) social and cultural practices are often mentioned to explain (part of) this gap. Higham et al. (2013) highlight many of these within the specific context of sustainable tourism mobility. Others refer to a so-called social dilemma being at play here (Vringer et al. 2015): everyone would be better off, especially in the long term, if we all displayed sustainable behaviour, but the immediate benefits linked to unsustainable behaviour, often combined with not trusting others to go for the sustainable alternative, stimulate people to choose the unsustainable behaviour (see e.g. Dawes 1980).

The foregoing presents some of the complexities and uncertainties involved with predicting and influencing sustainable (consumer) behaviour. Not surprisingly, therefore, this topic has received 'quite some' attention in literature: the number and variety of papers devoted to specific factors, and their interrelationships, hypothesized to impact real-life sustainable (consumer) behaviour are overwhelming. Combined with the oftentimes conflicting outcomes, this makes both providing a full overview and arriving at (a set of) unambiguous practical guidelines for policymakers and businesses aiming to introduce socially responsible and sustainable practices quite a challenge, if not impossible. Simultaneously, reviewing some of the latest publications in this field can certainly reveal some important lessons. Therefore, the remainder of this section discusses (the key outcomes of) some of these most recent studies, before the next section returns to tourism and hospitality as important sectors to address within this context.

Carrington et al. (2014) have studied the intention–behaviour gap in more detail and list four interrelated factors explaining this gap: (1) prioritization of ethical concerns, (2) formation of plans/habits, (3) willingness to commit and sacrifice, and (4) modes of (shopping) behaviour. Their study clearly highlights the relevance of habitual behaviour in decision making by consumers and explains how consumers rank specific ethical concerns. The latter needs to be taken into account if and when policymakers and providers of sustainable products and services want to stimulate changes in unsustainable habits. In practice, this means that not all consumers can and will be persuaded by the same topics and arguments; one needs to take into account that not all individual consumers will value the same sustainability aspects in the same way. Consequently, one and the same (sustainability) message for all will not work!

The work by de Vries et al. (2015) further substantiates the importance of the (content of the) message sent by businesses to consumers in relation to their sustainability efforts. Communication about one's socially responsible and sustainable practices should be based on honesty. In other words, if a business is investing in specific practices because these practices also lead to financial benefits, this should be part of the message. Framing your efforts as 'green' or 'environmentally conscious' without acknowledging apparent financial motives will only lead to being accused of 'greenwashing' and will certainly not be appreciated by consumers. Simultaneously, Cho (2015) shows that sustainability claims need to be backed up by detailed information on actual impacts of provided products and services. In fact, consumers who value sustainability the highest – usually also the most knowledgeable consumers – clearly prefer detailed impact assessments to generic sustainability claims. Once again, not backing up your claims with actual data at a product/service or even personal – individual consumer – level could seriously damage credibility and willingness to buy and co-create. As indicated by Collins (2015), the latter sometimes even requires accounting for different priorities between different types of consumers at the household/family level. Especially for sectors such as tourism and hospitality, which oftentimes provide products and services for complete households/families, this is a further complicating factor, but also one that businesses cannot afford to ignore.

A number of other authors have focused on aspects such as social pressure, self-esteem, identity and even mindfulness as crucial factors to address in promoting sustainable consumer behaviour (Cowan and Kinley 2014; Ericson et al. 2014; Johnstone and Tan 2015; Naderi and Strutton 2015). Lessons to be learned from research in this field can be summarized as follows: promoting sustainable consumer behaviour requires more than 'smart' and honest marketing messages. In the long term, consumers will only prefer sustainable products and services to unsustainable ones if not only the marketing message promoting them but also the actual products and services support them in feeling good about themselves. This links to more than just altruism as a possible source of 'feeling good'. Somehow, businesses need to create sustainable products and services that link up with consumers' identity and self-esteem, and with the identity and norms of the group to which those consumers (want to) belong. Naderi and Strutton (2015: p. 80) describe this as 'developing socially-oriented motives and programs that successfully promote sustainability as a mega-trend' in order to have 'a substantial portion of the populace' embrace them. Consequently, the challenge for policymakers and businesses is to somehow turn sustainable products and services into products and services that live up to what today's consumer appreciates and wants. For some (groups of consumers) this might mean that the approach used to do so needs to 'lighten up' (Johnstone and Tan 2015: p. 818), whereas for others this might require assisting them in avoiding the 'hedonic treadmill' (Ericson et al. 2014: p. 73) of today's consumerism.

Ultimately, regardless of whether one refers to this as the attitude–behaviour gap or the social dilemma, sustainable behaviour often relates to conflicts between the various goals that people aim at in life. Steg et al. (2014) explain that the conflicting goals at work are hedonic and gain goals on the one hand and normative goals on the other. Hedonic goals lead people to focus on improving their (immediate) feelings in a specific situation through, for instance, avoiding effort and seeking pleasure and excitement. Gain goals relate to costs and benefits in relation to personal resources, such as the time and money needed to engage in specific behaviour. In contrast, normative goals refer to what one considers as representing appropriate behaviour. Obviously, the latter directly links to values and attitudes towards sustainable development, but also to knowledge about what would be the appropriate course of action within a given situation. Consequently, promoting sustainable behaviour needs to account for this conflict by either making all goals compatible or strengthening normative goals to the extent that they 'override' the hedonic and gain goals. An example of the first approach would be to make sustainable products and services more exciting, more enjoyable and less expensive. However, solely promoting hedonic and gain goals as a way to stimulate sustainable behaviour is a dangerous route, because this results in strengthening them and would 'make these goals more influential in decision-making, thereby weakening normative goals to engage in other [socially responsible and] pro-environmental actions' (Steg et al. 2014: p. 106). Therefore, policymakers and businesses aiming to introduce socially responsible and sustainable practices should also, and preferably especially, target normative goals and try to strengthen them. One way to do so would be to change the context for sustainable behaviour and make sure that this context encompasses cues that support this type of behaviour, such as clear signals that 'others' have engaged in this behaviour as well. Simultaneously, one needs to make sure that the context does not encompass cues linked to competing goals, such as signals that others 'could not be bothered' as the result of high costs involved with sustainable behaviour.

Obviously, this bird's-eye overview of recent literature is far from complete. However, it does portray a clear and consistent picture. Predicting and influencing the behavioural responses of consumers to socially responsible and sustainable practices need to account for current knowledge levels, motivations and contextual factors (Steg et al. 2015). It is also evident that these knowledge levels and motivations may vary quite significantly among different (groups of) consumers and may relate to multiple – and very different – goals. Purposively influencing them while improving and controlling the contextual factors therefore represents the challenging assignment for any policymaker or business that wants to make a meaningful contribution to sustainable development.

Sustainable consumer behaviour in tourism and hospitality

As noted earlier, progress towards sustainable tourism and hospitality, so far, is limited at best (Bramwell and Lane 2013; Melissen 2013; Melissen and Koens 2016). There are many and oftentimes interrelated reasons that explain this status quo. One of those is, without doubt, the fact that it can be extremely difficult to 'convince' tourists and guests to 'accept' socially responsible and sustainable practices. The previous section has explained why trying to predict and influence consumer behaviour can be quite a challenge. There is no reason to assume that this would be easier in tourism and hospitality than in any other sector. However, some actually claim that tourists and guests are less likely to prefer sustainable products and services when on holiday than at home (Becken 2007). Others seriously question whether they are willing and open to be educated (Mody et al. 2014). If this were true that would mean that stimulating tourists and guests to engage in sustainable behaviour could be even more difficult than for other types of consumers. This perception of tourists and guests representing a 'special' kind of consumer is not just present in academic circles but also among practitioners, as is illustrated by the following case study.

In a special issue of the *Journal of Vacation Marketing*, focusing on the future of hotels, Melissen et al. (2016) recently reported on 12 in-depth interviews with hoteliers in leading positions in sizable hotels in the Netherlands. The following excerpts provide a telling example of the hoteliers' perception of guests:

. . . please consider the following statements by one of the hoteliers:

In my private life, I have [repeatedly] visited a hotel in [. . .], where a lot of eco-efficiency measures have been integrated into daily operations [. . .] very visible [. . .]. In the rooms you find explanations of how these measures are used and why [. . .] and it is all based on creating a situation that resembles a homely situation, so that guests can easily apply and rely on their own values in what is still a strange environment.

A little later, the interviewee continues by stating the following:

I don't want to sound too 'black or white', but this is never going to be a hit. Sustainability will only be instigated by employers [read: hoteliers]. A user or guest will never instigate sustainability, because they already get annoyed when an energy-saving lamp takes five seconds to start [lighting the room].

These statements reveal something peculiar emerging from almost all interviews. Hoteliers seem to feel that guests will never ask for or demand sustainability. In fact, they [feel that they] – hoteliers – will have to take the lead and will have to do so in a way that does not significantly change – that is, negatively influence – guest experiences. Interestingly, almost all hoteliers that were interviewed [indicated that they] are willing to do so, to take the lead. (Melissen et al. 2016: p. 234)

> This highlights a rather interesting contrast. On the one hand, hoteliers are convinced of the need for and benefits linked to pursuing sustainable development. On the other hand, however, they are also convinced that their own hotels' guests are not interested and do not want to be bothered . . . It seems as if hoteliers assume their own values, norms and beliefs . . . to be significantly different from those of their guests. (Melissen et al. 2016: p. 235)

The key question that needs answering here is whether there is any truth in this kind of assumptions. Are tourists and guests really different from other types of consumers? None of the studies reported on in the previous section include statements or findings that would suggest this is the case. What is more, even though being a hotelier can be a challenging occupation that requires specific qualities and personality traits to be successful, when a hotelier visits another hotel as a guest – as reported on in the case study – he or she is simply one of many guests visiting that hotel. All of these guests have their own qualities and personality traits. If the hotelier can be 'convinced' to appreciate socially responsible and sustainable practices of the hotel he or she visits, why would that be any different or even impossible for those other guests?

The answer is that it is far more likely that observations related to reluctance of consumers to engage in sustainable behaviour within tourism and hospitality contexts are actually the direct result of those contexts. As explained by Hall (2013), if the systems of provision within tourism and hospitality have not significantly changed, it is not at all surprising to observe that tourists and guests have also not significantly changed their behaviour. As indicated earlier, ultimately, the behaviour of all consumers, including tourists and guests, is influenced by their knowledge levels, their motivations *and* contextual factors (Steg et al. 2015). Thus, a much more credible explanation for unsustainable behaviour of tourists and guests – than the assumption that they represent a 'special type' of consumers – is that tourism's and hospitality's 'socio-technical systems constrain choice . . . and can therefore "lock-in" consumers to particular social practices of behaving and consuming' (Hall 2013: p. 1100). Consequently, promoting sustainable behaviour of tourists and guests requires addressing their knowledge levels, their motivation *and* the context for this behaviour. The latter implies addressing *and* changing 'the organization of systems of consumption and provision [in tourism and hospitality]' (Hall 2013: p. 1099).

Conclusion

This chapter has shown that sustainable development of tourism and hospitality requires an in-depth understanding of the behavioural responses of tourists and guests. It has also shown that tourism and hospitality now need to move on from discussing concepts, constraints and scenarios to actually developing and implementing socially responsible and sustainable practices within the context of a collaborative learning process that involves policymakers, practitioners, researchers *and* tourists and guests. Stimulating tourists and guests to accept or even prefer socially responsible and sustainable practices requires a combination of (1) a utilitarian approach – aimed at providing information and education, (2) a social/psychological approach – for instance applying nudging and social marketing to influence tourists' and guests' choices, and (3) a systems of provision approach – aimed at changing the context for tourists' and guests' behaviour (Hall 2013). Through reviewing some recent publications from the field of sustainable consumer behaviour, important lessons for doing so have been highlighted, such as the need to make hedonic, gain and normative goals more compatible and/or strengthen normative goals (Steg et al. 2014) as well as accounting for differences in (groups of) individual consumers and the need to be honest and transparent. Only through accepting these reference points, taking these lessons on board and rejecting some of the myths that have dominated tourism and hospitality practice and theory (McKercher and Prideaux 2014) can these sectors take a meaningful step in the direction of sustainable development. This will require no longer accepting that the contexts of tourism and hospitality are a 'given' but rather focusing on collectively reformulating *and* reshaping the social construct – including its institutions, rules, norms, structures and infrastructures (Hall 2013) – entitled tourism and hospitality (Bramwell and Lane 2014).

References

Ajzen, I. (1991). 'The theory of planned behavior', *Organizational Behavior and Human Decision Processes*, 50(2): 179–211.

Becken, S. (2007). 'Tourists' perception of international air travel's impact on the global climate and potential climate change policies', *Journal of Sustainable Tourism*, 15(4): 351–368.

Bramwell, B. and Lane, B. (2013). 'Getting from here to there: Systems change, behavioural change and sustainable tourism', *Journal of Sustainable Tourism*, 21(1): 1–4.

Bramwell, B. and Lane, B. (2014). 'The "critical turn" and its implications for sustainable tourism research', *Journal of Sustainable Tourism*, 22(1): 1–8.

Carrington, M. J., Neville, B. A. and Whitwell, G. J. (2014). 'Lost in translation: Exploring the ethical consumer intention-behavior gap', *Journal of Business Research*, 67(1): 2759–2767.

Cho, Y.-N. (2015). 'Different shades of green consciousness: The interplay of sustainability labeling and environmental impact on product evaluations', *Journal of Business Ethics*, 128(1): 73–82.

Collins, R. (2015). 'Keeping it in the family? Re-focusing household sustainability', *Geoforum*, 60: 22–32.

Cowan, K. and Kinley, T. (2014). 'Green spirit: Consumer empathies for green apparel', *International Journal of Consumer Studies*, 38(5): 493–499.

Dawes, R. M. (1980). 'Social dilemmas', *Annual Review of Psychology*, 31: 169–193.

De Grosbois, D. and Fennell, D. (2011). 'Carbon footprint of the global hotel companies: Comparison of methodologies and results', *Tourism Recreation Research*, 36(3): 231–245.

Destatte, P. (2010). 'Foresight: A major tool in tackling sustainable development', *Technological Forecasting and Social Change*, 77(9): 1575–1587.

Ericson, T., Kjønstad, B. G. and Barstad, A. (2014). 'Mindfulness and sustainability', *Ecological Economics*, 104: 73–79.

Gössling, S. and Peeters, P. (2015). 'Assessing tourism's global environmental impact 1900–2050', *Journal of Sustainable Tourism*, 23(5): 639–659.

Hall, M. C. (2013). 'Framing behavioural approaches to understanding and governing sustainable tourism consumption: Beyond neoliberalism, "nudging" and green growth?', *Journal of Sustainable Tourism*, 21(7): 1091–1109.

Higham, J., Cohen, S. A., Peeters, P. and Gössling, S. (2013). 'Psychological and behavioural approaches to understanding and governing mobility', *Journal of Sustainable Tourism*, 21(7): 949–967.

IPCC (2014). 'Climate change 2014: Synthesis report', in R. K. Pachauri and L. A. Meyer (eds.), *Contribution of Working Groups I, II and III to the Fifth Assessment Report of the Intergovernmental Panel on Climate Change*, Geneva: IPCC.

Johnstone, M.-L. and Tan, L. P. (2015). 'An exploration of environmentally-conscious consumers and the reasons why they do not buy green products', *Marketing Intelligence and Planning*, 33(5): 804–825.

McKercher, B. and Prideaux, B. (2014). 'Academic myths of tourism', *Annals of Tourism Research*, 46: 16–28.

Melissen, F. (2013). 'Sustainable hospitality: A meaningful notion?', *Journal of Sustainable Tourism*, 21(6): 810–824.

Melissen, F., Cavagnaro, E., Damen, M. and Düweke, A. (2016). 'Is the hotel industry prepared to face the challenge of sustainable development?', *Journal of Vacation Marketing*, 22(3): 227–238.

Melissen, F. and Koens, K. (2016). 'Adding researchers' behaviour to the research agenda: Bridging the science–policy gap in sustainable tourism mobility', *Journal of Sustainable Tourism*, 24(3): 335–349.

Mody, M., Day, J., Sydnor, S., Jaffe, W. and Lehto, X. (2014). 'The different shades of responsibility: Examining domestic and international travelers' motivations for responsible tourism in India', *Tourism Management Perspectives*, 12: 113–124.

Moon, J. (2007). 'The contribution of corporate social responsibility to sustainable development', *Sustainable Development*, 15(5): 296–306.

Naderi, I. and Strutton, D. (2015). 'I support sustainability but only when doing so reflects fabulously on me: Can green narcissists be cultivated?', *Journal of Macromarketing*, 35(1): 70–83.

Parrish, B. D. (2007). 'Designing the sustainable enterprise', *Futures*, 39(7): 846–860.

Solecki, W., Brondizio, E. S. and Leemans, R. (2015). 'Editorial overview: Open issue: Sustainability – from concept to practice', *Current Opinion in Environmental Sustainability*, 14: v–vii.

Steg, L., Bolderdijk, J. W., Keizer, K. and Perlaviciute, G. (2014). 'An integrated framework for encouraging pro-environmental behaviour: The role of values, situational factors and goals', *Journal of Environmental Psychology*, 38: 104–115.

Steg, L., Perlaviciute, G. and van der Werff, E. (2015). 'Understanding the human dimensions of a sustainable energy transition', *Frontiers in Psychology*, 6: 805.

Stern, P. C. (2000). 'Psychology and the science of human-environment interactions', *American Psychologist*, 55(5): 523–530.

United Nations' World Commission on Environment and Development (UNWCED) (1987). *Our Common Future ('The Brundtland Report')*, Oxford: Oxford University Press.

de Vries, G., Terwel, B. W., Ellemers, N. and Daamen, D. D. L. (2015). 'Sustainability or profitability? How communicated motives for environmental policy affect public perceptions of corporate green-washing', *Corporate Social Responsibility and Environmental Management*, 22(3): 142–154.

Vringer, K., Vollebergh, H. R., van Soest, D., van der Heijden, E. and Dietz, F. (2015). 'Sustainable consumption dilemmas', *OECD Environmental Working Papers*, 84, Paris: OECD Publishing.

45

TOURISM INDUSTRY ADAPTATION TO A CHANGING CONSUMER MARKET

A case study of New Zealand

Adam Weaver

Introduction

Mainland China has become increasingly integrated into the global economy. Reforms spearheaded by the Chinese government have prompted increased marketization. The affluence and mobility acquired by the Chinese middle class are a stark counter-image to the austere, immobile nature of Chinese society in the past. Commentators have noted that consumption behaviour in China should be seen in the context of change (Gerth 2010; Yu 2014). Rising aspirations have accompanied the improvement of material conditions, thus stimulating the growing popularity of pleasure travel. Tourism has become an emblem of personal identity and a symbol of cosmopolitanism.

In New Zealand, the growing significance of the Chinese market to the tourism industry has been noted. Predictions have been made regarding the expanding number of consumers who can afford to travel. In 2014, nearly 300,000 travellers from mainland China came to New Zealand (Anthony 2015), roughly 10% of the total number of international visitors received by the country. It is anticipated that the number of Chinese travellers could increase to nearly 900,000 by 2025 (Martin 2014a). Chinese tourists have become objects of intensified analytical attention; there are attempts to become better acquainted with their behaviour.

Various people affiliated within New Zealand's tourism industry have been quoted in the print media regarding the Chinese market. Exploring the perspectives expressed through the quotations may prove useful to (prospective) practitioners around the world. To some extent, the perspectives of industry figures reflect social and economic developments in China. They also, however, signal significant changes within New Zealand's tourism industry. The tourism industry's competitive nature requires adaptation, including revised approaches to marketing and product provision. Perspectives that are articulated by industry figures often make reference to proposed or concrete actions. This chapter is situated at the intersection between a changing consumer market and industry practice.

Tourism is an important industry in New Zealand and a national concern. The overall performance of the tourism industry as well as issues related to specific sectors are the subject of media reports. Prominent industry figures in New Zealand are sometimes asked by journalists to share their thoughts about matters related to the Chinese market. Although scholarly articles in the field of tourism management often include a section devoted to managerial implications and frequently suggest ways in which the research may have applications for practitioners, it is unfortunate that tourism research does not more often feature the perspectives of practitioners. The industry's role with respect to interpreting the characteristics of the Chinese market can be seen as a form of 'market sensemaking' (Theoharakis and Wong 2002: p. 400), a version of Karl Weick's approach to meaning construction within organizations. Behaviour is observed, patterns are documented, and then strategies are developed.

This chapter is divided into five sections. The introduction, the first section, is followed by the literature review and methods sections (the second and third sections, respectively). A fourth section contains findings. It is argued that three 's' words (scepticism, segmentation and shortcomings) summarize the way in which industry perspectives have changed over the past five years in New Zealand. The final section of the chapter is the conclusion.

Literature review

The impacts of tourism at a destination have been measured in terms of the perceptions of residents. One framework that has been used to assess residents' attitudes towards tourism development is the 'index of irritation' created by G. V. Doxey. The index has four phases: euphoria, apathy, annoyance and antagonism (Page and Connell 2006). Doxey's framework demonstrates that tourism can be potentially disruptive for resident communities. Instead of exploring the views of many different people within the resident community, this chapter examines the perceptions of a particular group: prominent industry figures. Practitioners have sometimes been very enthusiastic about the Chinese market and its potential, almost euphoric to use Doxey's terminology, but concerns (or 'irritations') have also been expressed.

Chinese outbound tourism has become a major area of enquiry within tourism studies. Tourism scholars have tried to determine the size of the Chinese market (Li et al. 2010) as well as understand aspects of the behaviour of Chinese tourists: their motivations (Lu 2011), their expectations (Li et al. 2011), their preferences when visiting certain destinations (Agrusa et al. 2011) and their attitudes towards nature and culture-based attractions (Fountain et al. 2011). Researchers have also explored the segmentation of the Chinese market (Prayag et al. 2015). This broad range of demand-side scholarship has advanced the study of the Chinese market. However, industry perspectives regarding this market have not been thoroughly explored.

The benefits of market segmentation are widely accepted. Previously accepted categories of consumers are subdivided into heterogeneous market segments, each with its own defining features (Turow 1997). Different perspectives with respect to a market may circulate at different times, and the notion that a market consists of identifiable segments is one perception that could emerge at a particular moment. The evolution of the market for a number of products in the United States and the related rise of a consumer society have been examined by Blaszczyk (2009). Various phases of consumer product marketing are interwoven with the evolution that has occurred (Tedlow 1996).

Tedlow (1996) proposes a three-phase schema of marketing history that summarizes the development of the US market for consumer goods. Certain perceptions of the market during each phase prompted particular responses. The initial phase (market fragmentation) existed prior to the 1880s. Small producers were dominant; national brands were, for the most part, non-existent due to the nature of the country's communication and transportation infrastructure. Many enterprises were only in a position to understand and reach nearby markets. Market unification (1880s to 1950s) followed fragmentation as industries exploited improved infrastructure and could benefit from economies of scale. The entire nation, the USA, was treated as one market. A final phase, market segmentation (1950s to the 1990s), emerged as it became profitable to identify certain groups of consumers and produce specialized outputs. Segmentation is an important theme in the study of tourism marketing (Hsu et al. 2008). Tedlow's structured periodization has appeal but the most recent phase, market segmentation, does not capture the smaller shifts that have characterized the evolution of the Chinese travel market in New Zealand over the past few years.

Understanding phenomena, such as tourism markets, involves interpreting occurrences, seeking patterns and making sense of the situations in which one finds oneself. This notion of sensemaking has been used to examine the structure and behaviour of organizations (Weick 1995) but there have been fewer attempts to apply it to the study of markets (but see Theoharakis and Wong 2002). Sensemaking can describe the efforts made by industry figures to come to terms with the distinguishing and changing features of the Chinese market. It is interpretative as well as action oriented.

Methods

Newspaper content has been analysed by tourism scholars (Bremner 2013). One valuable attribute of newspaper articles as a source of data is the quoted remarks they feature, especially those made by prominent or noteworthy individuals. These people may occupy positions of authority; they may manage a sizeable commercial enterprise or represent an industry body. Their points of view are deemed to be significant because their interpretations of certain events have implications for practice. Planned or current actions with respect to a market may be mentioned.

Quoted remarks featured within newspaper articles are typically quite short, not more than a few sentences, and they cannot be compared with face-to-face interviews when one considers variables such as richness of detail and depth of explanation. However, across a number of newspaper articles, there are telling comments made by a range of industry figures. Quotations extracted from newspaper articles enable one to capture the perspectives of recognized industry representatives and offer some insight regarding their interests and concerns. Past newspaper articles are available as an archive of viewpoints. They can be used to develop a historical narrative about critical events.

The inclusion of quoted statements made by industry figures may be seen as adding credibility to the newspaper articles. There is a risk, though, that only certain perspectives will be disseminated if it is simply senior industry figures who are consulted. The quoted respondents may not be representative of the entire population of industry stakeholders. Through selection, journalists only publish certain statements and frame historical events and experiences in a particular manner.

A source of data that mainly features 'official' perspectives, and a restricted range at that, still has considerable value. For those seeking to understand dominant, established voices within the tourism industry, newspaper articles are an accessible source of information. Quotations incorporated into newspaper articles may be the product of a selection process undertaken by journalists or editors but they still offer access, even if only partially, to the mindsets of industry decision makers. Capturing the perspectives of industry actors can expose their thinking.

The articles that were part of the sample were obtained through a key word search of Newztext Newspapers, a searchable database of New Zealand newspapers. Two sets of two search terms were used in association with each other: 'China' and 'Chinese' were combined with 'tourist' and 'visitor' in order to extract relevant articles. A decision was made to examine articles within a five-year time frame, from August 2010 until August 2015, in order to see if patterns, either differences or similarities, were apparent. Fifty-seven newspaper articles from several daily newspapers (for example, *The Dominion Post* and *The New Zealand Herald*), a weekly newspaper (*The Sunday Star Times*) and a weekly business-focused newspaper (*The National Business Review*) were identified.

Statements made by industry figures in the newspaper articles were inserted into a Microsoft Word document. A short note was often made about the content and context of each quotation. Fifty-six quotations were extracted. Eight newspaper articles had multiple quotations; 23 had none. Using an iterative process, the statements made by the industry figures were read several times and an effort was made to identify patterns (Long 2007). There was a concerted effort made to remain open to unexpected themes. A simultaneous, back and forth juggling of the study's focus (the perspectives of industry figures in New Zealand with respect to the Chinese market) and quotations in newspaper articles underpins the method of inquiry. The quotations were read repeatedly and annotated; differences as well as similarities were noted. Concise quotations that expressed a clear perspective were selected for inclusion.

This study is the product of one researcher's interpretation of written texts. The potential exists for relevant ideas to remain unexamined as the analysis of the data is unavoidably selective. One means of making the author's argument convincing is to intersperse relevant quotations (the data) with interpretative commentary. Verbatim statements from industry actors are used, a practice consistent with Patton's suggestion that 'sufficient description and direct quotations should be included to allow the reader to enter into the situation and thoughts of the people represented in the report' (2002: p. 503). The quoted industry figures are professionally engaged in activities associated with understanding and coming to terms with the attributes of the Chinese market.

Findings

The openness to both differences and similarities in the analysis came to define the interpretation of the data. Differences are reflected by the three-phase account of the relationship between practitioners and the Chinese travellers they target. These phases have been named in order to differentiate them: scepticism, segmentation and shortcomings. The differences noted are, in one sense, evident but the phases identified are by no means disconnected.

There are points at which the phases intersect. Scepticism about the value of Chinese package tour travel characterized the comments made by industry figures between August 2010 and the end of 2013. This scepticism then prompted efforts to target specific market segments. Remarks made about the benefits of market segmentation (that is, targeting certain groups of Chinese travellers) defined the content of newspaper articles in 2014. During the first eight months of 2015, the shortcomings of the Chinese market with respect to road safety came to the fore. These shortcomings emerged as New Zealand increasingly targeted segments of the market that undertook independent travel and rented vehicles. Each of the three phases (scepticism, segmentation and shortcomings) is discussed.

Scepticism

For some industry figures, Chinese travellers had not quite arrived as a commercial force prior to 2014. The chief executive (CE) of the Tourism Industry Association New Zealand (TIANZ) between 2012 and the middle of 2014, Martin Snedden, has indicated that 'some Kiwi tour operators are sceptical that the Chinese numbers are increasing so quickly' (Wood 2013: p. C7). Snedden made some additional remarks about this scepticism:

> It is almost like there's quite a lot of people that have been a bit suspicious about the China potential and have not really been prepared to totally accept and believe it is happening, and that it's going to grow.
>
> *(Wood 2013: p. C7)*

Doubts, then, have been expressed about the possibility that high-value Chinese tourists will materialize in significant numbers. Snedden's predecessor as the CE of the TIANZ, Tim Cossar, expressed a similar view when he observed, in 2011, that some operators within the tourism industry 'may not feel immediate benefits from increasing Chinese numbers' (Rutherford 2011a: p. B5). Perceptions of the Chinese market have been shaped by the prevalence of package tours that typically attract 'low value visitor[s]', a term used by Kevin Bowler, the CE of Tourism New Zealand (TNZ), the organization that promotes New Zealand as a travel destination internationally (Rutherford 2011b: p. C1). According to Snedden, 'value from [these tours]', many of which are shopping focused, 'is not retained in New Zealand' (Weir 2012: p. C21). Sensemaking underpinned these critical appraisals of the Chinese market; the market was assessed by influential observers and was seen as having deficiencies.

That New Zealand is targeting the Chinese market more aggressively has been seen as a problem by large companies such as Tourism Holdings Limited (THL). The Chinese market is perceived as a problem in that it does not have the same consumption patterns as more established European markets. Grant Webster, the CE of THL, did not believe that the Chinese market possessed characteristics that suited one of the main products offered by his firm: self-drive campervans. Chinese tourists do not, in Webster's view, 'grasp the concept of what [campervan travel] is and what that type of travel is. They want to be led, certainly at the moment' (Rutherford 2011a: p. B5). There was a sense, then, that the Chinese market had an inbuilt preference for structured tours.

This preference provoked a response. Fergus Brown, the CE of the Holiday Parks Association New Zealand (HPANZ), observed that 'China is mobile. If you go to China and expect to see bicycles you are going to be sadly mistaken. There are cars in huge numbers' (Wood 2013: p. C7). As a result, efforts were made to make Chinese tourists more adept at using campervans. A short instructional video produced by HPANZ is available via YouKu, the Chinese equivalent to YouTube (Wood 2013). The strategy, in this instance, was to create the market for campervan travel amongst Chinese consumers by trying to condition them to see certain tasks, such as the emptying of septic tanks, as easy to perform and to promote the pleasures of self-drive travel.

Segmentation

Initial scepticism about the value of the Chinese market as a singular entity prompted certain organizations to pursue specific market segments. Quoted statements made by prominent industry figures in 2014 emphasized the importance of targeting certain types of travellers. Auckland, New Zealand's largest city, has implemented a tourism strategy oriented around golf, horse racing, sailing and fishing. The tourism manager, Jason Hill, at Auckland Tourism, Events and Economic Development (ATEED), an organization operated by the city's municipal government, has described the implementation of a 'golfing, equine and marine (GEM) strategy' that 'targets the activities favored by wealthy Chinese' (Martin 2014a: p. B4). Adrian Littlewood, the CE at Auckland International Airport, noted that 'the [tourism] industry needed to see China as a series of market niches that were large enough to boost New Zealand revenues' (Martin 2014b: p. B5). This CE also made a remark about the size of such niches by stating that: 'In a market of one billion, a niche can be several million people strong.' As a result, Auckland International Airport 'has encouraged a marketing push into the Shanghai wedding market' (Martin 2014b: p. B5).

The Chinese wine tourism market has also been targeted by Auckland International Airport. Jason Delamere, the airport's manager of marketing and communications, stated that a food and wine tourism initiative developed by the airport represented 'an immediate and significant opportunity to increase the number of high value visitors from China' (Gibson 2014: p. 21). Promotion for the initiative 'will start in the Guangdong region, which has a direct link to Auckland operated by China Southern Airlines from its Guangzhou hub'. Food and wine are described by Delamere as 'one of the most important triggers for Chinese travelers' (Gibson 2014: p. 21).

The Chinese market is a varied collection of consumers who are different in terms of, for example, their spending power. In the tourism industry's search for more profit, a segment-based focus has emerged that is oriented around value (attracting specific groups of affluent tourists) as opposed to volume (simply attracting a greater number of tourists). The sensemaking undertaken by the industry with respect to the Chinese market involves endeavours that name, describe and target different types of tourists. Trying to comprehend a flow of events related to a still-evolving overseas market, and responding to the preferences observed, is a manifestation of the adaptability of commercial activity to social and economic transformation.

In addition to market segments that are seen to be associated with certain activities (for example, golf or wine tours), there is a desire to attract more independent travellers from China. The former CE of the TIANZ, Martin Snedden, stated that 'independent Chinese travelers stayed longer, traveled more widely and spend more than their tour bus counterparts' (Martin 2014b: p. B5). That these independent travellers are growing in number reflects the emergence of an expanding number of Chinese consumers who are using their disposable income to customize their travel itineraries. Moreover, various activity-based segments no doubt possess an independent orientation. Rental vehicles, including campervans, are an attractive option for a segment of visitors seeking independence. A rented automobile or campervan enables Chinese travellers to shift from being a passenger, as part of a package tour, to being in charge of their own vehicle and schedule.

Shortcomings

The shortcomings associated with the Chinese market are related to rental vehicles. A series of widely publicized accidents, in early 2015, involving international tourists who were driving rental vehicles prompted discussion within the tourism industry about independent Chinese travellers. Hazards have historically been connected to the freedom and excitement of automobile use (Eastman 1984). The flexibility and independence offered by rental vehicles were seen as having unintended consequences.

Greg Wensley, owner of the vehicle rental company Wai Hire Queenstown, acknowledged the driving-related problems associated with the Chinese market: 'Just like the public has become more aware of it. . ., the operators are also more aware of it' (Barclay 2015: p. A12). An editorial that appeared in the *New Zealand Herald* in 2015, written by the current CE of TIANZ, noted that 'The Christmas New Year road toll was the worst for 17 years, prompting soul searching among the authorities' (Roberts 2015: p. A33). The feasibility of testing overseas drivers before they receive their rental vehicle is, however, questioned by Roberts. Vehicle accidents involving international drivers, many of whom are identified as Chinese by newspaper articles, presented problems for some senior industry figures who were under pressure to develop an appropriate response. Stricter regulations, including requiring international visitors to pass driving tests, were proposed by some safety advocates outside of the tourism industry.

Those affiliated with the tourism industry who are quoted by the print media preferred to address the situation through education. Providing clearer information to Chinese visitors that would help them drive safely was recommended by Kevin Bowler, the CE of TNZ, as it was in the interests of 'prospective visitors to consider how weather conditions, fatigue and unfamiliarity with [New Zealand's] roads will impact on their journey' (Barclay 2015: p. A12). The CE of Christchurch Airport, Malcolm Johns, suggested that 'foreign drivers do some practical driving around the Christchurch Airport campus, before they headed out on the open road' (Wood 2015: p. A8). Barry Kidd, the CE of the Rental Vehicle Association of New Zealand, recognized that the sector 'needed to take more action', including inter-firm information sharing when a driver's contract is cancelled. Sensemaking and industry adaptation are ongoing endeavours; they reflect the opportunities that emerge as well as the problems that present themselves.

As noted by Roberts (2015: p. A33) in his editorial, there are parts of New Zealand where there are 'challenging roads and road conditions'. He reminds the reader that 'New Zealand's economy relies strongly on the tourism industry', a signal that the perceived shortcomings of the Chinese market with respect to road safety have to be considered in relation to a potential dilemma. Chinese travellers may choose to visit other countries should the rules associated with driving in New Zealand be viewed as too restrictive. A market that is growing accustomed to freedom and independence within the realm of tourism may not react well to safety reform initiatives that inconvenience them.

From package tourists to tourist drivers

The emergence of independent Chinese travellers has created a mobility management conundrum in New Zealand. A series of vehicle accidents involving international travellers were the subject of numerous media reports in 2015. Particular concern was expressed about Chinese drivers as they were, in some cases, simply victims of road accidents and, in others, the at-fault individuals. Many of the accidents, including a disproportionate number of fatalities, occurred in the South Island of New Zealand (Tait 2015). The incidents provoked a response from the Consul General of the People's Republic of China in Christchurch, Jin Zhijian, who stated that he endorsed the implementation of measures that would 'make the Chinese drivers fully prepared before they are on the road' (Wood 2015: p. A8). Problems associated with tourist drivers do not appear to have been anticipated by industry decision makers in New Zealand, who had been eager to promote the availability of rental vehicles.

Consumption-related decisions, such as renting an automobile or campervan, may involve personal choice but the consequence of such decisions may present serious risks to other road users. A more independently oriented Chinese market was suddenly seen as a threat; the belief that Chinese travellers posed serious problems for New Zealand drivers eclipsed the notion that they were, at times, the victims of the automobile accidents as well. The 'dangerous' tourist driver came to define discussions about international travellers and rental vehicles. A dilemma arose regarding a travel market that was becoming more accustomed to independence of mobility and that, simultaneously, needed to be managed with respect to its freedom of mobility.

One of the accidents that received considerable media attention involved a Chinese student who crashed into, and killed, two New Zealand motorcyclists. The student was a relatively inexperienced driver and had only been in the country for a short time. A young child of one of the victims initiated a petition to have international drivers complete a mandatory driving test (Moir 2015). This petition received over 30,000 signatures.

Many stakeholders within the tourism industry are not in favour of compulsory driving tests. Such tests would contravene certain international conventions and potentially discourage independent Chinese travellers from visiting New Zealand. The TIANZ and the Rental Vehicle Association of New Zealand asked rental vehicle companies to comply with a code of practice by October of 2015 that would ensure the provision of better information about the rules of the road to international drivers. Jim Harland, a senior manager affiliated with the organization responsible for matters such as vehicle registration and road infrastructure, the New Zealand Transport Agency, indicated that the code of practice could create 'better driving outcomes' but that it does not have 'statutory teeth' (Barclay 2015). There is a widespread sense that an intervention of some description must take place in order to moderate the problems created by these drivers. However, the absence of 'statutory teeth' with regards to the code of practice and the reluctance of government to implement mandatory driving tests for international travellers renting automobiles or campervans are still concerns for many safety advocates and private citizens.

Conclusion

There have been, to date, numerous efforts to understand the behaviour of Chinese tourists but few attempts to study the way in which actors within the tourism industry perceive them and adapt to the challenges they present. Research that explores tourist behaviour typically concludes with some recommendations for practitioners. However, what about the views of actual practitioners with respect to a market? This chapter has established that perspectives regarding the mainland Chinese market, far from being static, can change. The industry has progressed from scepticism about the value of the Chinese market, to enthusiasm regarding its rising affluence and potential for segmentation, to the identification of shortcomings.

Tourism providers and industry representatives engage in interpretative behaviours which could be described as 'market sensemaking' (Theoharakis and Wong 2002: p. 400) whereby they seek to understand the nature of the market (or markets) they wish to serve more thoroughly. Sensemaking is a means of making aspects of the commercial world, such as (prospective) markets, comprehensible (Weick 1995). It can be compared to navigation whereby conditions have a tendency to change from time to time. Navigators respond to weather conditions; analogously, marketers and product development managers must adapt to evolving conditions in international markets. These changing conditions, a reflection of the dynamism of commerce, prompt shifting conceptions of Chinese tourists. Change offers economic opportunities (the potential to target market segments that are seen to be emerging) as well as challenges (the shortcomings associated with the rising number of Chinese visitors wishing to drive within an unfamiliar environment).

This chapter has used a different approach to capture the perspectives of prominent industry figures within the tourism industry. A more frequently used way to obtain such perspectives is to conduct face-to-face interviews. Interviews have certain advantages vis-à-vis using quoted remarks extracted from newspaper articles; the interviewer can ask questions that invite in-depth explanation. However, one can obtain ready access to industry perspectives from media sources. Prominent industry figures are often quoted, some of whom may be difficult to interview due to their busy schedules. Even recent newspaper articles feature the views of executives or officials who have, since the publication of the articles, vacated a senior position. They may be reluctant to be interviewed about the opinions they shared with the media in their previous role out of courtesy for their successor(s).

In this chapter, one has heard the voices of practitioners rather than those of Chinese travellers. The accounts of Chinese visitors to New Zealand are, unfortunately, absent from newspaper articles. To understand the perspectives of Chinese travellers who have visited or wish to visit New Zealand, evidence obtained from other sources would be needed. Social media offers a repository of past and current comments and observations that could be analysed (Sun et al. 2015). The way in which New Zealand is perceived by Chinese travellers has, potentially, passed through a series of identifiable phases that could be named and studied.

References

Agrusa, J., Kim, S. and Wang, K.-C. (2011). 'Mainland Chinese tourists to Hawaii: Their characteristics and preferences', *Journal of Travel and Tourism Marketing*, 28(3): 261–278.

Anthony, J. (2015). 'Heyday for hotel trade', *Sunday Star-Times*, 17 May, D6.

Barclay, C. (2015). '"Lax" rental code for foreign drivers', *The Press*, 15 August, A12.

Blaszczyk, R. L. (2009). *American Consumer Society, 1865–2005: From Hearth to HDTV*, Wheeling, IL: Harlan Davidson.

Bremner, H. (2013). 'Tourism development in the Hot Lakes District c. 1900', *International Journal of Contemporary Hospitality Management*, 25(2): 282–298.

Eastman, J. (1984). *Styling vs. Safety: The American Automobile Industry and the Development of Automobile Safety, 1900-1966*, Lanham, MD: University Press of America.

Fountain, J., Espiner, S. and Xie, X. (2011). 'A cultural framing of nature: Chinese tourists' motivations for, expectations of, and satisfaction with, their New Zealand tourist experience', *Tourism Review International*, 14(2/3): 71–83.

Gerth, K. (2010). *As China Goes, So Goes the World: How Chinese Consumers Are Transforming Everything*, New York: Hill and Wang.

Gibson, N. (2014). 'Ministry backs wine tourism for China', *The National Business Review*, 23 May, 21.

Hsu, C., Killion, L., Brown, G., Gross, M. and Huang, S. (2008). *Tourism Marketing: An Asia-Pacific Perspective*, Milton, QLD: Wiley.

Li, X., Harrill, R., Uysal, M., Burnett, T. and Zhan, X. (2010). 'Estimating the size of the Chinese outbound travel market: A demand-side approach', *Tourism Management*, 31(2): 250–259.

Li, X., Lai, C., Harrill, R., Kline, S. and Wang, L. (2011). 'When East meets West: An exploratory study on Chinese outbound tourists' travel expectations', *Tourism Management*, 32(4): 741–749.

Long, J. (2007). *Researching Leisure, Sport and Tourism: The Essential Guide*, London: Sage.

Lu, Z. (2011). 'The study of Chinese tourists' motivations to Canada', *Journal of China Tourism Research*, 7(4): 345–354.

Martin, J. (2014a). 'Auckland woos rich Chinese', *The Dominion Post*, 3 June, B4.

Martin, J. (2014b). 'High-value Chinese tourists key to growth plan', *The Dominion Post*, 25 March, B5.

Moir, J. (2015). 'Dad's death spurs road campaign', *The Dominion Post*, 20 March, A3.

Page, S. and Connell, J. (2006). *Tourism: A Modern Synthesis*, 2nd edition, London: Thomson Learning.

Patton, M. Q. (2002). *Qualitative Research and Evaluation Methods*, 3rd edition, London: Sage.

Prayag, G., Cohen, S. and Yan, H. (2015). 'Potential Chinese travelers to Western Europe: Segmenting motivations and service expectations', *Current Issues of Tourism*, 18(8): 725–743.

Roberts, C. (2015). 'We can make roads safer without creating tests for foreign drivers', *The New Zealand Herald*, 26 February, A33.

Rutherford, H. (2011a). 'The changing face of tourism', *The Dominion Post*, 19 February, B5.

Rutherford, H. (2011b). 'Tourism chief: Wealthy Chinese a neglected opportunity', *The Dominion Post*, 24 May, C1.

Sun, M., Ryan, C. and Pan, S. (2015). 'Using Chinese travel blogs to examine perceived destination image: The case of New Zealand', *Journal of Travel Research*, 54(4): 543–555.

Tait, M. (2015). 'Tourists' driving skill just below Kiwis', *The New Zealand Herald*, 4 April, A6.

Tedlow, R. (1996). *New and Improved: The Story of Mass Marketing in America*, Boston, MA: Harvard Business School Press.

Theoharakis, V. and Wong, V. (2002). 'Marking high-technology market evolution through the foci of market stories: The case of local area networks', *Journal of Product Innovation Management*, 19(6): 400–411.

Turow, J. (1997). *Breaking Up America: Advertisers and the New Media World*, Chicago, IL: University of Chicago Press.

Weick, K. (1995). *Sensemaking in Organizations*, Thousand Oaks, CA: Sage.

Weir, J. (2012). 'Chinese tourists' shopping restricted', *The Press*, 22 December, C21.

Wood, A. (2013). 'Building the Chinese connection', *The Dominion Post*, 27 April, C7.

Wood, A. (2015). 'China aware of NZ crashes', *The Press*, 3 March, A8.

Yu, L. (2014). *Consumption in China: How China's New Consumer Ideology is Shaping the Nation*, Cambridge: Polity Press.

46

CONSUMER BEHAVIOUR AND THE OLYMPIC GAMES

Luke R. Potwarka and Kai Jiang

International mega-sport events such as the Olympic Games are thought to have positive social and economic impacts on host regions, as well as attract global television audiences and corporate sponsorships (Getz 1997; Majid et al. 2007). Indeed, the Olympic Games garner considerable monetary and in-kind investment from both public and private sector organizations. In exchange for their substantial investment of tax dollars, governments hope that hosting such events will improve the local economy via tourism and urban development (Crompton and Lee 2000). Further, governments often feel their financial support can result in increased social cohesion, community pride, volunteerism and health among citizens (Potwarka and Snelgrove 2013).

Mass media conglomerates are also key stakeholders in the delivery of the Olympic Games. In particular, television networks pay considerable amounts of money for exclusive rights to cover these events. As Table 46.1 illustrates, Canadian and US networks have paid increasing amounts of money to televise the Summer and Winter Olympic Games. In return for the purchase of exclusive rights to cover the Olympics, media companies hope to generate heightened ratings of their television broadcasts and, thus, make substantial profits from the sale of advertising during telecasts (Coakley and Donnelly 2009). Networks also use mega-sport events to promote their prime-time television shows.

Similarly, the amount of money corporations spend to sponsor the Olympic Games has increased dramatically over the past three decades. In 1984, the cost to sponsor the Olympic Games was $4 million, up from $250,000 for the previous Games. For the 2008 Beijing Games, the 12 Worldwide Olympic Sponsors provided an estimated $866 million, which was divided among the IOC, national Olympic committees and international sports federations. Unlike philanthropy and donations, Olympic sponsors seek to fulfil commercial objectives in exchange for their support (McCarville and Copeland 1994). For example, numerous companies have cited reasons such as increased brand awareness and sales for their association with mega-sport events (Cornwell and Maignan 1998). Now, more than ever, sponsors demand evidence of a commercial return for their investment of cash or non-cash resources (Crompton 2004).

The extent to which the Olympic Games deliver the social and economic objectives established by funding stakeholders (i.e. government, media and corporate sponsors) depends, at least in part, on the event's ability to make people take action in the marketplace.

Table 46.1 Escalating media rights fees for the Olympics (in US$ millions)

Summer Olympics	Canadian network	US network
1976 Montreal	1.8	25.0
1980 Moscow	1.044	87.0
1984 Los Angeles	3.0	225.0
1988 Seoul	4.17	300.0
1992 Barcelona	16.5	401.0
1996 Atlanta	22.0	456.0
2000 Sydney	28.0	705.0
2004 Athens	37.0	793.0
2008 Beijing	45.0	894.0
2012 London	63.0	1,002.0

Winter Olympics	Canadian network	US network
1976 Innsbruck	0.36	10.0
1980 Lake Placid	0.907	15.5
1984 Sarajevo	1.8	91.5
1988 Calgary	3.4	309.0
1992 Albertville	10.1	243.0
1994 Lillehammer	12.0	300.0
1998 Nagano	17.0	375.0
2002 Salt Lake City	22.0	545.0
2006 Turin	28.0	613.0
2010 Vancouver	90.0	998.0
2014 Sochi	n/a	n/a

Source: Adapted from Coakley and Donnelly (2009: p. 393).

Therefore, it is important for sport researchers to develop a better understanding of what motivates people to perform a given behaviour that might ultimately lead to the attainment of an event stakeholder's objective. As Pons et al. (2006) noted, 'a growing concern shared by researchers and sport marketers is to understand the various motivations that bring individuals to consume sporting events and related goods and services' (p. 276). Behavioural responses of particular interest to Olympic stakeholders will be explored in more detail in the following sections.

Behaviours of interest to Olympic stakeholders

Researchers (e.g. Stewart et al. 2003) have suggested that there are likely several behavioural responses to the Olympic Games of potential importance to event stakeholders. Some of these behaviours include, but are certainly not limited to, increasing sport/physical activity levels, watching Olympic events on television, travelling to a host city during or after the event, purchasing products/services from corporate sponsors and/or becoming an event volunteer. Each of these behaviours is discussed below.

Sport/physical activity participation

Public sector investment in hosting the Olympic Games is often justified in terms of 'trickle-down effects'. Such effects refer to the event's capacity to increase sport and/or physical activity (PA) levels within host populations (Murphy and Bauman 2007; Potwarka and Leatherdale 2016). For instance, in an address to the House of Commons, the UK's Olympic Minister suggested that hosting the 2012 Summer Games would be 'the catalyst that inspires people of all ages and all talents to lead more active lives' (Jowell 2003). London 2012's official Olympic bid document went on to predict that 'grassroots participation would be boosted. An already sports-mad nation would get fitter and healthier' (Vigor and Tinline 2005).

To date, however, the existence of trickle-down effects remains largely anecdotal. Indeed, the few studies examining this phenomenon suggest that the effects of the Olympic Games on host populations' activity levels appear only marginal at best (Weed et al. 2012). Not to mention, it is still not clear whether such an event will have its greatest influence on increasing participation in Olympic sporting activities or physical activity more generally (Potwarka and McCarville 2010). The relative lack of understanding of the dynamics surrounding the trickle-down effect emerges from both practical and conceptual challenges. In practical terms, there has been only limited coordination among public health organizations in capitalizing on the sport-related excitement created by the Olympic Games. As a result, the potential of the Games is perhaps being squandered and opportunities to induce changes in citizens' physical activity levels are being lost (Murphy and Bauman 2007; Soteriades et al. 2006). In conceptual terms, existing research on the trickle-down effect is not underpinned by any explanatory theory or model of health behaviour change (Boardley 2012). Therefore, the application of more theory-driven approaches to behaviour change might better demonstrate the Games' capacity to alter activity levels among host residents (Potwarka 2015; Potwarka and McCarville 2010).

Recently, for example, Potwarka (2015) applied Ajzen's theory of planned behaviour (TPB) to understand motivational factors associated with individuals' intention to become more active in response to the Vancouver Olympics. Ajzen's (1991) TPB suggests that much human behaviour can be understood in terms of three factors: the valued consequences people associate with a particular behaviour (i.e. attitudes towards the behaviour); the normative pressure people perceive from others to perform the action (i.e. subjective norms); and the extent to which the individual perceives the behaviour as being difficult or easy to perform (i.e. perceived behavioural control). Potwarka (2015) found that attitude towards the behaviour (i.e. perceived valuable consequences in the form of becoming fitter and healthier), past behaviour and descriptive norms (i.e. people's perceptions about the degree to which other people were going to become more active as a result of the Olympic Winter Games) emerged as significant predictors of intention to become more active in response to the event. Findings from TPB-based studies can be used to inform the development of promotional efforts, which sport and recreation organizations can deploy in conjunction with Olympic Games (Potwarka 2015). This activity will be the focus of the case study that appears next. Moreover, the TPB has recently been employed to explain a variety of Olympic-related consumer behaviours including media consumption (Potwarka et al. 2014b) and sponsorship patronage (Potwarka et al. 2014a). Consumer behaviour related to Olympic media and sponsorship consumption will be the focus of subsequent sections of the chapter.

Leveraging the Olympic Games to increase sport participation impacts

Suggested readings

Ajzen, I. (1991). 'The theory of planned behavior', *Organizational Behavior and Human Decision Processes*, 50(2): 179–211. This article provides the theoretical foundation for the design of the flyer/poster which will be created in the case study.

Potwarka, L. R. (2015). 'Exploring physical activity intention as a response to the Vancouver Olympics: An application and extension of the theory of planned behavior', *Event Management*, 19(1): 73–92. This article provides a contextually relevant application of the TPB. The findings from this study may offer insights into key messages that could be used in the development of the flyer/poster.

Sport participation impacts of the Olympics must be leveraged if the event is to have an impact on participation (Weed et al. 2012). In other words, participation impacts or 'trickle - down effects' described previously in this chapter may not automatically result from hosting the Olympics, but they should be planned for and funded (i.e. leveraged) in the same way as the mega-sport event (Mahtani et al. 2013). In this way, leveraging efforts have become one avenue to compensate for the lack of any 'inherent' sport participation impacts (Weed et al. 2012). Leveraging is based on the premise that increased participation levels are more likely to result from the combined influence of staging an event and the implementation of interventions/marketing efforts designed to promote sport opportunities (Coalter 2004).

With this in mind, imagine you are an employee of your university's athletic department's marketing team. Your team's goal is to increase physical activity levels among students at your institution and in conjunction with the upcoming Summer Olympic Games. The idea with this promotional campaign is to capitalize on the 'buzz' and 'excitement' about participation created by the Olympics to promote increased enrolment in sport or physical activity-related programmes.

Your task is to design a flyer/poster which encourages students to become more active in response to the upcoming Olympics. These flyers/posters would be distributed across campus. Consistent with Ajzen's (1991) TPB and previous research (e.g. Potwarka 2015), your flyer/poster should attempt to influence students' attitudes towards the behaviour. In other words, it should include messages that convey valued consequences that might result from becoming more active in response to the Games. Moreover, your flyer/poster might contain messages that address social norms (i.e. that people important to them approve of them participating) and perceived behavioural control (i.e. factors that make it easy to participate) elements of the theory.

Media consumption/spectatorship

Watching televised sport events is one of the most popular forms of leisure among North American adults (Mason 1999). Not surprisingly then, television networks attempt to include the Olympic Games in their programming because they believe the event will increase their profits from the sale of advertising (Coakley and Donnelly 2009). In fact, the Olympic Games have become one of the biggest world television events in human history (Coakley and Donnelly 2009). It was reported that in August 2008, over 24 million Canadian viewers watched as the four networks of the Canadian Broadcasting Corporation (CBC) offered a record 2,400 hours of Summer Olympics coverage from Beijing. This CBC survey revealed that 77% of Canadians watched at least some portion of the Beijing Summer Olympic Games on television, with the average person taking in 13.76 hours from the opening to closing ceremonies. According to a poll conducted by Harris Interactive, television coverage of the Turin 2006 Olympic Winter Games was most popular among middle-aged adults in the USA. The survey found that middle-aged (those aged 35–64) and older adults (those aged 55 and over) were more likely than younger adults (those aged 18–34) to say they intended to watch televised coverage of the 2006 Winter Olympics.

Majid et al. (2007) noted that there appears to be increased global appeal of the Winter Olympic Games. According to the authors, there is now heavy television viewership of this event in non-traditional markets (e.g. Mexico, Brazil and South Africa). Majid et al. identified three factors that might help explain this trend. First, the authors argued that the values underpinning the Olympic Games such as equality and togetherness create strong brand associations among global audiences. Second, they explained that certain experiential aspects associated with the event (e.g. seeing the unknown or witnessing an unexpected outcome) might help to draw faithful viewers. Third, the authors suggested that the Winter Olympics provide global television audiences with inspiring heroes (i.e. athletes) who triumph over adversity. Moreover, networks that operate in hosting nations are likely equally as concerned with attracting a solid base of domestic viewership.

In addition to television audiences, Olympic stakeholders hope the event will attract millions of dollars in foreign and domestic ticket sales. For instance, 6.8 million tickets ranging in price from $12 to $653 were sold for the Beijing Olympics ('Going, going, gone' 2008). These figures are especially important for government officials who believe that the influx of foreign and domestic spectators into the host region will have positive implications for the local economy (Crompton and Lee 2000). Despite claims that the Olympics will increase a television network's profits or improve a host city's economy, relatively few studies have examined factors that might actually compel an individual to skip work to watch the event, or travel thousands of miles to witness it in person. According to Pons et al. (2006), 'unraveling the motivations that bring individuals in front of their TV or to stadiums is vital to the industry and represents a growing concern for both researchers and practitioners' (p. 277).

Potwarka et al. (2014b) applied the TPB to understand viewership motivations associated with the Vancouver 2010 Winter Olympic Games. The authors reported that watching the Games on television was associated with: (1) a belief that important others would perform the behaviour (i.e. descriptive norms); (2) previous viewing of the Games' televised coverage (i.e. past behaviour); (3) a favourable evaluation of performing the behaviour (i.e. attitude towards the behaviour); and (4) a perceived ease of performing the behaviour (i.e. perceived behavioural control). The authors concluded that watching the Olympics on television was:

> determined (in part) by the extent to which respondents believed performing the action would have valuable consequences for them in the form of: (a) feeling a sense of national pride, (b) cheering on athletes without having to travel to the event, and (c) improving conversations with peers by staying up to date with current events.
>
> *(Potwarka et al. 2014b: p. 554)*

Post-event tourism

As mentioned, the commitment of public money to host the Olympics is often justified by the assumption that such an event will improve the local economy via increased tourism

(Crompton and Lee 2000). Consequently, politicians and researchers are concerned with the degree to which staging a mega-sport event can enhance the destination image of a host region, and subsequently, stimulate post-event domestic and international travel behaviour (Chalip et al. 2003; Gibson et al. 2008). As Gibson et al. (2008) stated:

> The debate over the benefits of hosting mega sports events continues to evolve with many beginning to doubt the long-term economic and tourism benefits touted by politicians and organizing committees. What we do know is that destination image is linked to intent to travel and so, with the strategic leveraging of images that are shown to the world in conjunction with the event (pre, during, and after), the level of awareness of a particular city and/or country can be raised, which may in turn provide the impetus to visit at some point in the future, or at the very least be used to educate the world about a particular locale.
>
> *(p. 446)*

In addition to destination image, other variables might also affect people's decisions/intentions to visit a region after it has played host to a mega-sport event. For example, Kaplanidou and Gibson (2010) found that attitude towards event participation (i.e. the degree to which respondents perceived the event to be pleasant, worthwhile and entertaining) mediated the impact of satisfaction with the event and destination image on respondents' intention to return to a subsequent Senior Games event. Moreover, the authors speculated that past behaviour (i.e. participation in a previous Senior Games event) would play a role in predicting intention to attend the following year's event. However, this construct did not emerge as a significant predictor of intention in this regard.

Sponsorship patronage

For many corporations, the ultimate goal of sponsoring the Olympic Games is to increase sales (Cornwell and Maignan 1998). However, researchers have tended to rely on more distal (i.e. intermediate) measures of patronage when attempting to evaluate sponsorship effectiveness in the context of athletic events (Crompton 2004). Specifically, Walliser (2003) noted that the vast majority of sponsorship valuation research has relied on measures of brand awareness (i.e. brand name recall and recognition tests), with a limited number looking at image constructs, and only a few exploring actual purchase intentions.

The use of intermediate measures of sponsorship effectiveness (e.g. attitudes, awareness and image constructs) may be due to the challenges researchers encounter when trying to isolate, and determine, the direct influence of the sponsorship on consumers' actual purchase behaviour. Recently, O'Reilly et al. (2008) argued that 'the true long-term impact of a sponsorship on sales, or intent to purchase, however, is difficult to evaluate, and thus, often questioned' (p. 393). For example, a person's decision to purchase a product/service from a corporate sponsor may be unrelated to the company's association with a mega-sport event, but instead may result from some other simultaneous or previously used communication effort. Nevertheless, researchers (Crompton 2004; O'Reilly et al. 2008) have called for models of sponsorship patronage that focus on more proximal determinants of behaviour (i.e. measures of behavioural intention, actual purchase behaviour).

For instance, Potwarka et al. (2014a) used the TPB to predict people's decision to purchase from sponsors of the Olympic Games. The authors found that attitude towards the behaviour, subjective norms, descriptive norms and past behaviour emerged as significant predictors of purchase intention. Intention, in turn, predicted self-reported purchase behaviour. According to the authors, favourable intentions and subsequent purchase behaviours were strongly associated with beliefs that performing the action would have valuable consequences for them in the form of: (1) helping financially support Canadian athletes; (2) allowing the individual to express their feelings of national pride/patriotism; (3) not having adverse economic impacts for smaller (i.e. local) companies that were unable to sponsor the event; and (4) allowing the individual to consume products/services that are of better quality than those available from competing organizations that did not sponsor the event.

Event volunteerism

Many elected officials believe that staging the Olympics can improve social cohesion/capital among host residents via increased volunteer opportunities (Misener and Mason 2006). Baum and Lockstone (2007) noted that:

> within the context of mega-sporting events, the issue of employment creation is an important motivator for host cities and features high on the political justification agenda for bids to host events. At the same time, the most significant working contribution to major events in sports, as in other areas, is provided by the very large numbers of volunteers who undertake tasks across the range of opportunities afforded by such events.
>
> *(p. 29)*

According to Baum and Lockstone (2007), organizing committees have reported between 40,000 and 60,000 volunteers for Olympic events but they added that, despite these substantial numbers, relatively little is known about what motivates these thousands of people to volunteer at such events. Tables 46.2 and Table 46.3 present the numbers of volunteers for recent Summer and Winter Olympic Games.

Motivations of Olympic volunteers are intriguingly multifaceted (Clary and Snyder 1999). Notably, the first established survey instrument for assessing sports events volunteer motivation – the Volunteer Functions Inventory (VFI) – is multidimensional (Clary and Snyder 1999), including 30 volunteer motive items organized into 6 categories: (1) values (related to altruism and humanitarian concerns); (2) understanding (about knowledge, skills and abilities necessary for the volunteer role); (3) social (relationships with others); (4) career (career-related benefits gained from volunteer participation); (5) protective (escape from negative feelings); and (6) enhancement (personal growth and development). Recently, using the context of the 2010 Vancouver Olympic and Paralympic Winter Games, Dickson et al. (2013: p. 88) identified six multi-motivational dimensions of Olympic and Paralympic volunteers: (1) altruistic (giving back to society and community); (2) transactional (gained experience, job contacts and skills); (3) variety (broadened horizons, new knowledge of different cultures and languages); (4) passion for and interest in the Games; (5) application (chances to use skills); and (6) availability (having free time).

As noted by Baum and Lockstone (2007), 'without the personal investment of the volunteers, mega-events could simply not have been arranged' (p. 30). Satisfaction with the volunteer experience may be an important predictor of future volunteer participation intention. Indeed, the priority of Olympic volunteer managers should be to fulfil the range of volunteer motivations, and enhance volunteer satisfaction through improved strategies for volunteer recruitment. Such strategies should address appropriate personnel allocation, training and rewards.

Table 46.2 Number of volunteers for Summer Olympic Games

Year	Hosting city	Number of volunteers
1984	Los Angeles	28,742
1988	Seoul	27,221
1992	Barcelona	34,548
1996	Atlanta	60,422
2000	Sydney	47,000
2004	Athens	60,000
2008	Beijing	100,000
2012	London	70,000

Sources: Athens Greece Guide (2004); Independent (2012); International Olympic Committee (IOC) (2010); Moreno et al. (1999).

Table 46.3 Number of volunteers for Winter Olympic Games

Year	Hosting city	Number of volunteers
1980	Lake Placid	6,703
1984	Sarajevo	10,450
1988	Calgary	9,498
1992	Albertville	60,422
1994	Lillehammer	9,054
1998	Nagano	32,579
2002	Salt Lake City	24,000
2006	Torino	18,000
2010	Vancouver	18,500
2014	Sochi	25,000

Sources: Anderson (2013); IOC (2006); Moreno et al. (1999); Roche (2012).

Conclusion

This chapter presented a synthesis of consumer behaviour research that has been conducted in the context of the Olympic Games. Particular emphases were placed on highlighting salient decision-making processes and motivational factors involved in sponsorship patronage, media consumption, volunteerism, travel and sport/physical activity-related behavioural domains. The discussion integrated key theoretical approaches and constructs that have been used in the study of consumer behaviour related to the Olympics. Readers had an opportunity to apply the knowledge gleaned in this chapter by completing a case study. This case study explored how marketers might better leverage the potential of the Olympics to increase sport participation impacts.

References

Ajzen, I. (1991). 'The theory of planned behavior', *Organizational Behavior and Human Decision Processes*, 50(2): 179–211.

Anderson, B. G. (2013). 'Sochi 2014 announces 25,000 volunteers for Winter Olympic and Paralympic Games', *Inside the Games*, 5 December, Available from: http://www.insidethegames.biz/articles/1017313/sochi-2014-announces-25-000-volunteers-for-winter-olympic-and-paralympic-games [Accessed 10 December 2015].

Athens Greece Guide (2004). 'The unforgettable dream games', Available from: http://www.athensguide.org/athens2004.html [Accessed 10 December 2015].

Baum, T. and Lockstone, L. (2007). 'Volunteers and mega sporting events: Developing a research framework', *International Journal of Event Management Research*, 3(1): 29–41.

Boardley, I. D. (2012). 'Can viewing London 2012 influence sport participation? – a viewpoint based on relevant theory', *International Journal of Sport Policy and Politics*, 5(2): 245–256.

Chalip, L., Green, B. C. and Hill, B. (2003). 'Effects of sport event media on destination image and intention to visit', *Journal of Sport Management*, 17(3): 214–234.

Clary, E. G. and Snyder, M. (1999). 'The motivations to volunteer: Theoretical and practical considerations', *Current Directions in Psychological Science*, 8(5): 156–159.

Coakley, J. and Donnelly, P. (2009). *Sports in Society: Issues and Controversies*, 2nd Canadian edition, Toronto: McGraw-Hill Ryerson.

Coalter, F. (2004). 'Stuck in the blocks? A sustainable sporting legacy?', in A. Vigor, M. Mean and C. Tims (eds.), *After the Goldrush: A Sustainable Olympics for London* (pp. 93–108), London: The London Olympics Institute for Public Policy Research/DEMOS.

Cornwell, T. B. and Maignan, I. (1998). 'Research on sponsorship: International review and appraisal', *Journal of Advertising*, 27(2): 1–21.

Crompton, J. L. (2004). 'Conceptualization and alternate operationalizations of the measurement of sponsorship effectiveness in sport', *Leisure Studies*, 23(3): 267–281.

Crompton, J. L. and Lee, S. (2000). 'The economic impact of 30 sports tournaments, festivals, and spectator events in seven U.S. cities', *Journal of Park and Recreation Administration*, 18(2): 107–126.

Dickson, T. J., Benson, A. M., Blackman, D. A. and Terwiel, A. F. (2013). 'It's all about the games! 2010 Vancouver Olympic and Paralympic Winter Games volunteers', *Event Management*, 17(1): 77–92.

Getz, D. (1997). *Event Management and Event Tourism*, New York: Cognizant Communications Corporation.

Gibson, H. J., Qi, C. X. and Zhang, J. J. (2008). 'Destination image and intent to visit China and the 2008 Beijing Olympic Games', *Journal of Sport Management*, 22(4): 427–450.

Going, going, gone! Beijing tickets sold out. (2008). *Associated Press*, 28 July, http://www.nbcolympics.com/destinationbeijing/news/newsid=156713.html.

Independent (2012). 'London 2012: Olympics success down to 70,000 volunteers', 10 August, Available from: http://www.independent.co.uk/sport/olympics/news/london-2012-olympics-success-down-to-70000-volunteers-8030867.html [Accessed 12 December 2015].

International Olympic Committee (IOC) (2010). 'Beijing enjoying multiple post-games legacies', 19 July, Available from: http://www.olympic.org/news/beijing-enjoying-multiple-post-games-legacies/168501 [Accessed 18 December 2015].

IOC (2006). 'IOC marketing report: Torino 2006', Chapter 5, Available from: http://www.olympic.org/Documents/Reports/EN/en_report_1144.pdf [Accessed 15 November 2015].

Jowell, T. (2003). 'Full text of Tessa Jowell's statement to the Commons on the government's backing for London's Olympic bid', Available from: http://www.theguardian.com/uk/2003/may/15/olympicgames.london [Accessed 15 November 2016].

Kaplanidou, K. and Gibson, H. (2010). 'Predicting behavioral intentions of active event sport tourists: The case of a small-scale recurring sports event', *Journal of Sport and Tourism*, 15(2): 163–179.

McCarville, R. E. and Copeland, R. P. (1994). 'Understanding sport sponsorship through exchange theory', *Journal of Sport Management*, 8(2): 102–114.

Mahtani, K. R., Protheroe, J., Slight, S. P., PivaDemarzo, M. M., Blakeman, T., Barton, C. A., Brijnath, B. and Roberts, N. (2013). 'Can the London 2012 Olympics "inspire a generation" to do more physical or sporting activities? An overview of systematic reviews', *British Medical Journal*, 3(1): 1–8.

Majid, K., Chandra, R. and Joy, A. (2007). 'Exploring the growing interest in the Olympic Winter Games', *Sport Marketing Quarterly*, 16(1): 25–35.

Mason, D. S. (1999). 'What is the sport product and who buys it? The marketing of professional sports leagues', *European Journal of Marketing*, 33(3/4): 402–418.

Misener, L. and Mason, D. S. (2006). 'Creating community networks: Can sporting events offer meaningful sources of social capital?', *Managing Leisure*, 11(1): 39–56.

Moreno, A. B., Moragas, M. and Paniagua, R. (1999). 'The evolution of volunteers at the Olympic Games', Available from: http://olympicstudies.uab.es/volunteers/moreno.html [Accessed 6 February 2016].

Murphy, N. M. and Bauman, A. (2007). 'Mass sporting and physical activity events – are they "bread and circuses" or public health interventions to increase population levels of physical activity?', *Journal of Physical Activity and Health*, 4(2): 193–202.

O'Reilly, N., Lyberger, M., McCarthy, L., Séguin, B. and Nadeau, J. (2008). 'Mega-special-event promotions and intent to purchase: A longitudinal analysis of the Super Bowl', *Journal of Sport Management*, 22(4): 392–409.

Pons, F., Mourali, M. and Nyeck, S. (2006). 'Consumer orientation toward sporting events: Scale development and validation', *Journal of Service Research*, 8(3): 276–287.

Potwarka, L. R. (2015). 'Exploring physical activity intention as a response to the Vancouver Olympics: An application and extension of the theory of planned behaviour', *Event Management: An International Journal*, 19(1): 73–92.

Potwarka, L. R. and Leatherdale, S. (2016). 'The Vancouver 2010 Olympics and leisure-time physical activity rates among youth in Canada: Any evidence of a trickle-down effect?', *Leisure Studies*, 35(2): 241–257.

Potwarka, L. and McCarville, R. (2010). 'Exploring the trickle-down effect of the Olympics on activity levels within host nations: Suggestions for research and practice', in C. Anagnostopoulos (ed.), *International Sport: A Research Synthesis* (pp. 179–190), Athens: Athens Institute for Education and Research.

Potwarka, L. R., McCarville, R. E. and Kaplanidou, K. (2014a). 'Predicting decisions to purchase from sponsors of the Vancouver 2010 Olympics', *International Journal of Sport Management and Marketing*, 15(5–6): 238–260.

Potwarka, L. R., McCarville, R. E. and Nunkoo, R. (2014b). 'Understanding television viewership of a mega event: The case of the 2010 Winter Olympics', *Journal of Hospitality Marketing and Management*, 23(5): 536–563.

Potwarka, L. R. and Snelgrove, R. (2013). 'Leveraging sport events to achieve health and economic benefits', in R. E. McCarville and K. J. MacKay (eds.), *Leisure for Canadians*, 2nd edition (pp. 43–48), State College, PA: Venture Publishing.

Roche, L. R. (2012). 'As 10th anniversary of 2002 Winter Games nears, governor weighing another Olympic bid', *Deseret News*, Available from: http://www.deseretnews.com/article/700222089/As-10th-anniversary-of-2002-Winter-Games-nears-governor-weighing-another-Olympic-bid.html?pg=all [Accessed 21 December 2015].

Soteriades, E. S., Haddjichristodoulou, C., Kremastinou, J., Chelvatzoglou, F. C., Minogiannis, P. S. and Falagas, N. E. (2006). 'Health promotion programs related to the Athens 2004 Olympic and Para Olympic Games', *BMC Public Health*, 6(1): 47.

Stewart, B., Smith, A. C. T. and Nicholson, M. (2003). 'Sport consumer typologies: A critical review', *Sport Marketing Quarterly*, 12(4): 206–216.

Vigor, A. and Tinline, D. (2005). 'Going for gold', *Progress*, 25 August, Available from: http://www.progressonline.org.uk/2005/08/25/going-for-gold/ [Accessed 15 November 2016].

Walliser, B. (2003). 'An international review of sponsorship research: Extension and update', *International Journal of Advertising*, 22(1): 5–40.

Weed, M., Coren, E., Fiore, J., Wellard, I., Mansfield, L., Chatziefstathiou, D. and Dowse, S. (2012). 'Developing a physical activity legacy from the London 2012 Olympic and Paralympic Games: A policy-led systematic review', *Perspectives in Public Health*, 132(2): 75–80.

INDEX

For Product Safety Concerns and Information please contact our EU
representative GPSR@taylorandfrancis.com Taylor & Francis Verlag GmbH,
Kaufingerstraße 24, 80331 München, Germany

Printed and bound by CPI Group (UK) Ltd, Croydon, CR0 4YY
12/05/2025
01867489-0001